MODERN BANKING LAW

76 -> 112

MODERN BANKING LAW

E. P. Ellinger

CLARENDON PRESS · OXFORD

Oxford University Press, Walton Street, Oxford OX2 6DP
Oxford New York Toronto
Delhi Bombay Calcutta Madras Karachi
Petaling Jaya Singapore Hong Kong Tokyo
Nairobi Dar es Salaam Cape Town
Melbourne Auckland
and associated companies in
Berlin Ibadan

Oxford is a trade mark of Oxford University Press

First published 1987
Reprinted 1989

British Library Cataloguing in Publication Data
Ellinger, E. P.
Modern banking law.
1. Banking law—Great Britain
I. Title
344.106'82   KD1715
ISBN 0–19–876156–2
ISBN 0–19–876157–0 (Pbk)

Library of Congress Cataloging in Publication Data
Ellinger, E. P. (Eliahu Peter), 1933–
Modern banking law.
Includes index.
1. Banking law—Great Britain. I. Title.
KD1715.E45 1987   346.41'082   87–12407
ISBN 0–19–876156–2   344.10682
ISBN 0–19–876157–0 (Pbk)

Printed in Great Britain
by Biddles Ltd.,
Guildford and King's Lynn

To my wife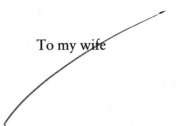

Preface

The last two decades have seen some major changes in the English banking world and in its practices. Mergers of certain clearing banks during the late sixties and early seventies led to the emergence of giants with extensive networks of branches in England and Wales. During the same period, there has been a steady influx of foreign banks into the City, in which about six hundred banks now operate. The structure of banking in England and Wales has effectively undergone a metamorphosis. Practice has had to adapt itself and some new legal regimes were required. The introduction of the statutory regulation of the acceptance by banks of deposits from the public is but one example.

A further major impact on banking practice was occasioned by the contemporary advances in communications, in electronics and in computer technology. The clearing of cheques has become a largely automated process and new, fully automated, systems such as BACS, CHAPS, and SWIFT were developed for the handling of periodic payments and of international money transfers. Other important developments include the abolition of exchange control at the end of 1979 and the beginning of the drive for the de-regulation of the banking system. By and large, the changes in the patterns of banking during the last twenty years have overshadowed the developments that had taken place during the preceding sixty years.

In this work I have sought to re-examine the principles of banking law in the light of the developments of these last, definitive, two decades. I hope that the book will be of use to all persons interested in English banking law. But my main aim has been to provide a new text suitable for students. Whilst the book is meant primarily for the English market, I have discussed many cases decided by courts in Commonwealth countries which have a similar system of banking and of banking law. It is, therefore, anticipated that the book will be useful also in countries such as Australia, New Zealand, and Singapore.

The present volume deals with domestic banking law. It is divided into three parts, examining respectively the structure of banking and the regulation of banking law in the United Kingdom, the bank's position as its customer's paying and collecting agent and the bank's position as a credit provider. A second volume, dealing with international banking and banking law, is in preparation.

All three parts of the present volume discuss banking law in the light of modern banking practice. Thus, the chapters discussing the banks as monetary agencies with a central role in the settlement of payments in England

and Wales include a detailed description of the clearing systems currently in use. The third part, concerning the banks' role as credit providers, deals with overdrafts and loans and discusses the security devices used in modern practice. The provisions of regulatory legislation, such as the Consumer Credit Act 1974, are considered in detail where relevant. Generally, I have sought to discuss the applicable legal concepts in the context of their economic background.

The division of the work into two volumes, to be published separately, gave rise to problems respecting the discussion of topics which are relevant to both domestic and international banking. Thus, bills of exchange and other negotiable instruments, which are used extensively in international sales, are also utilized in certain inland transactions. My solution was to include in the present volume a general discussion of bills of exchange and other negotiable instruments with a view to covering specific aspects, relevant mainly to international transactions, in the second volume. In the case of guarantees, which are another facility used extensively in both inland and international transactions, I decided, after some hesitation, to incorporate the relevant chapter in the second volume with the object of bringing together the analysis of ordinary guarantees and indemnities and of the modern types of performance bond and first demand guarantee.

Another problem which I encountered was how much space to devote to subjects which, though pertinent to banking law, fall mainly within the scope of some other legal domain. Thus, the problems respecting floating charges are of importance to banks but, in effect, are a facet of the general principles of company law rather than of banking law. Similarly, the common clauses found in bankers' lending agreements are also used in standard forms of other financial institutions. My solution has been to highlight in the discussion of such topics the aspects which are of specific relevance to banks. For instance, I decided to cover overdrafts—the typical bankers' lending facility—in detail, but to leave out a discussion of all the standard clauses used in lending agreements. A specific problem of this type arose in respect of land mortgages. A detailed discussion of this subject would, of course, be out of place in a book on banking law. However, for the sake of overseas readers who may not wish to consult comprehensive works on English land law, I have included a section on land mortgages and a basic review of English land law.

It is a mark of the volatile nature of banking law in recent years, that my manuscript had to be revised thoroughly twice as a result of reforms introduced at the time the work was nearing completion. Initially, the text had to be updated in order to take into account the relevant provisions of the Companies Act 1985 and the Insolvency Act 1985. When this task was completed I had to revise the manuscript again upon the passing of the Insolvency Act 1986 and of some less cardinal, but all the same important,

Acts, such as the Building Societies Act 1986. Unfortunately, I have been unable to give a full account of the Banking Act 1987, which has repealed and replaced the Banking Act 1979. But chapter 2, which deals with bank supervision, includes references to the relevant White Paper and to the Banking Bill. I propose to prepare in due course a supplement, so as to give a full account of the 1987 Act and of new and important judgments delivered since going to press. At present, the law is generally stated as it was on 1 September 1986, although, wherever possible, I have included references to later authorities and statutes.

My thanks are due to the many bankers who provided me with information on banking practice generally and on the clearing systems in particular, to colleagues who have helped me greatly with their comments, to research assistants both at Monash University and at the National University of Singapore who assisted me in checking sources and references, to administrative personnel who converted an illegible manuscript into a neat typescript and to the Press and its staff. I am indebted to all of them and in particular like to express my gratitude to Mr M. N. Karmel of the CLSB, to Messrs Martyn Yorke and Bill Dale of the Royal Bank of Scotland, to Mr J. W. Bullock of Lloyds Bank, to Mr J. D. Davies of St Catherine's College Oxford, for his immense help with the section on land mortgages, and last but not least to Professor A. G. Guest, Q.C., of King's College London, who had encouraged me to write this book and who assisted me throughout with all matters concerning the Consumer Credit Act. My thanks are also due to the Royal Bank of Scotland for permitting me to reproduce some of their standard banking forms in the Appendix and to Mr D. A. Greenwood who had actually selected the forms and prepared them for publication. Naturally, all mistakes in the text are my sole responsibility.

The National University of Singapore   E. P. Ellinger
Kent Ridge
31 July 1987

Contents

Table of Cases

Table of Statutes

PART I. Banks and Banking Business

1. The Structure of the British Banking World   3
   1. The problem in context   3
   2. The clearing banks   5
   3. The 'functional' clearing banks   11
   4. The merchant banks   14
   5. The discount houses   17
   6. Overseas and foreign banks   17
   7. The British Bankers' Association   21
   8. Comparison with building societies   21
   9. Other financial institutions   23
   10. Review of the system   24

2. The Control of Banking Activities in the United Kingdom   25
   1. The need for controls   25
   2. The Bank of England   27
   3. The Banking Act 1979   31
   4. Monetary controls   47

3. Legal Definition and Privileges of Banks   51
   1. Banks at common law   51
   2. Defences conferred on banks by statutes utilizing other definitions   58
   3. The meaning of 'bank' where the term is undefined   61
   4. The Consumer Credit Act   62
   5. Assessment of the statutory treatment of banking   74

4. The Bank and its Customers   76
   1. The legal nature of the problem   76
   2. Who is a customer?   76
   3. The nature of the relationship between banker and customer   81
   4. The bank's duty of care and position as fiduciary   84
   5. The confidential nature of the contract   96
   6. Termination of relationship   112

PART II. The Bank as a Monetary Agency in Domestic Transactions

5. The Bank's Role as a Depository   117
   1. Economic function and legal concept   117

Contents

2. Practical implications of the economic and legal concept 120
3. The bank as a depository of its customer's funds and as paymaster
of his accounts 121
4. The bank as its customer's agent for collection 124
5. Conclusion 126

6. The Current Account 127
1. Special nature of the current account 127
2. The statement of account 130
3. Combination of accounts 139
4. Third party claims 161

7. Special Types of Account 167
1. Type of problem 167
2. Joint accounts 168
3. Partnership accounts 175
4. Executors' accounts 179
5. Trust accounts 181
6. Solicitors' accounts 186
7. Estate agents' accounts 188
8. Local authorities' accounts 189
9. Companies' accounts 191
10. Unincorporated associations' accounts 197
11. Married women's accounts 199
12. Minors' accounts 200
13. Mentally incapacitated persons' accounts 205

8. Interest-bearing Accounts 208
1. Classification and comparison with current accounts 208
2. Legal nature of the arrangement 210
3. Dispositions over balance 214
4. Deposit receipts and pass-books 219
5. Assessment 224

9. The Bank's Role as Paying Agent: Cheques 226
1. Cheques and their background 226
2. The clearing process 230
3. The cheque as negotiable instrument 238
4. Crossed cheques 252
5. The holder's duties in respect of cheques 258
6. Implications of the Consumer Credit Act 1974 262
7. Travellers' cheques 262

10. The Paying Bank 264
1. The bank's duty to pay cheques 264
2. The bank's liability for wrongful payment: nature of the problem 285
3. The paying bank's defences for wrongful payment at common law
and in equity 290

4. The paying bank's defences for wrongful payment: statutory protections   302
5. The customer's remedies for wrongful dishonour of his cheques   310

11. Recovery of Money Paid by Mistake   315
1. The problem in practice and the basic principle   315
2. Recovery where the mistake is known to the payee   317
3. Recovery in cases of payments not involving negotiable instruments   319
4. Action against a collecting bank   329
5. Recovery problems in cases of negotiable instruments   334
6. Tracing orders   341

12. The Giro System and Electronic Transfers of Funds   343
1. Introduction and basic concepts   343
2. Domestic giro forms and their comparison with cheques   347
3. The clearence of giro transfers   351
4. International money transfers   357
5. The legal nature of money transfer orders   363
6. Time of payment and countermand   375
7. Confidentiality of information   387

13. Credit Tokens   389
1. Available tokens reviewed and classified   389
2. Tripartite credit tokens   391
3. T & E cards   393
4. Cheque cards   395
5. Cashpoint cards   399
6. The provisions of the Consumer Credit Act 1974   401
7. Criminal proceedings for misuse of token by holder   410

14. The Bank's Role in Collecting Cheques   412
1. The bank's role in the transaction   412
2. The true owner's cause of action   412
3. Collection and discount distinguished   418
4. The collecting bank's protection   421
5. The defence of contributory negligence   437
6. The discounting bank's protection   439
7. The processing bank's position   442
8. The collecting bank which is also the paying bank   444
9. The collecting bank's duty to its own customer   449

15. Incidental Services Performed by Banks   453
1. The common thread   453
2. Bankers' references   454
3. Giving advice on financial investments   463
4. The banker as bailee and custodian   466

PART III. The Bank as Financier and Lender in Domestic Transactions

16. Current Account Financing and Loans   475
     1. Overdrafts and loans compared   475
     2. Overdrafts   476
     3. Bank loans   488

17. Acceptance Credits and Bills of Exchange   494
     1. The nature of acceptance credits   494
     2. Basic principles of bills of exchange   495
     3. Special problems of bills drawn under acceptance credits   522
     4. Negotiable instruments and the Consumer Credit Act 1974   527

18. Securities for Bankers' Advances: The General Part   530
     1. The object served by and the classification of securities   530
     2. The effect of valid security in insolvency   532
     3. The right of redemption   534
     4. Effect of the Consumer Credit Act 1974   536

19. Proprietary Securities   541
     1. Scope   541
     2. Mortgages over land   542
     3. Proprietary securities over goods   550
     4. Securities granted by companies   555

20. Possessory Securities   568
     1. The pledge   568
     2. The banker's lien   576

21. Choses in Action as Securities   580
     1. Basic problems and scope of security   580
     2. Security over book debts   582
     3. Bank balances as security   590
     4. Life policies as securities   599

Appendix   602

Index   607

Table of Cases

A-G v. De Winton [1906] 2 Ch. 106 185
A-G v. National Provincial Bank Ltd. (1928) 44 TLR 701 102
A/S Awilco of Oslo v. Fulvia SPA di Navigazione of Cagliari ('The Chikuma')
   [1981] 1 WLR 314 385
Abbott v. Bank of Toronto [1934] 3 DLR 256...134, 138
Admiral Shipping v. Portlink Ferries Ltd. [1984] 2 Lloyd's Rep. 166 278
Admiralty Commissioners v. National Provincial and Union Bank of England
   (1922) 127 LT 452...332, 333, 413
Agra and Masterman's Bank Ltd. v. Leighton (1866) LR 2 Ex. 56............508, 509
Aiken v. Short (1856) 25 LJ Ex. 321 ....320, 328
Akbar Khan v. Attar Singh [1936] 2 All ER 545 ....210, 220
Akrokerri (Atlantic) Mines Ltd. v. Economic Bank [1904] 2 KB 465 254,
   257, 578
Alan (W.J.) & Co. Ltd. v. El Nasr Export and Import Co. [1972] 2 QB
   189...392, 526
Alcom Ltd. v. Republic of Columbia [1984] AC 580 ....272, 597, 598
Alexander v. Burchfield (1842) 7 Man. & G 1061 260
Alexander Stewart & Son of Dundee Ltd. v. Westminster Bank Ltd. [1926] WN
   126 195
Alicia Hosiery Ltd. v. Brown, Shipley & Co. Ltd. [1970] 1 QB 195 ....569, 574
All Trades Distributors Ltd. v. Agencies Kaufman Ltd. (1969) 113 SJ
   995...507, 509
Alliance Bank v. Kearsley (1871) LR 6 CP 433 176
Aluminium Industrie Vaassen BV v. Romalpa Aluminium Ltd. [1976] 1 WLR
   676 589
Anderson (W.B.) & Sons Ltd. v. Rhodes (Liverpool) Ltd. [1967] 2 All ER
   850..458, 461
Anning v. Anning (1907) 4 CLR 1049 ....216, 221
Arab Bank Ltd. v. Barclays Bank (DCO) [1954] AC 495 ....129, 270
Arab Bank Ltd. v. Ross [1952] 2 QB 216................................... 306, 440, 505, 513
Archer v. Bamford (1822) 3 Stark. 175 509
Ardern v. Bank of New South Wales [1956] VLR 569 ....169, 170
Aries Tanker Corporation v. Total Transport Ltd. [1977] 1 All ER 398 591
Armagh Shoes Ltd., Re [1984] BCLC 405 583
Arnott v. Hayes (1887) 36 Ch. D 731 101
Arrow Transfer Co. Ltd. v. Royal Bank of Canada [1971] 3 WWR 241, affd.
   [1972] 4 WWR 60.. 133, 135, 413, 415
Arthur Anderson & Co. v. Finesilver 546 F 2d 338 (1976) 108
Aschkenasy v. Midland Bank Ltd. (1934) 50 TLR 209; affd. 51 TLR 34 78
Asien-Pazifik Merchant Finance Ltd. v. Shanghai Commercial Bank Ltd. [1982]
   HKLR 273 136

Associated Midland Corporation *v.* Bank of New South Wales [1980] 1 NSWLR 533 301

Astro Amo Compania Naviera SA *v.* Elf Union SA ('The Zographia M') [1976] 2 Lloyd's Rep. 382 385

Asylum for Idiots *v.* Handysides [1906] 22 TLR 573 102

Atkinson *v.* Bradford Third Equitable Benefit Building Society (1890) 25 QBD 377 .... 218, 221, 222

Attenborough *v.* Solomon [1913] AC 76 .... 180, 568

Auchteroni & Co. *v.* Midland Bank Ltd. [1928] 2 KB 294 305

Australia and New Zealand Bank Ltd. *v.* Ateliers de Constructions Electriques de Charleroi [1967] AC 86 431

Australia and New Zealand Bank Ltd. *v.* Ryan [1968] 3 NSWLR 118 102

Australia and New Zealand Savings Bank Ltd., Re, Mellas *v.* Evriniadis [1972] VR 690 .... 213, 221, 272

Australian Independent Distributors Ltd. *v.* Winter (1964) 112 CLR 443 ...... 52, 53

Australian Mutual Provident Society *v.* Derham (1979) 39 FLR 165 306

Automobile Finance of Australia Ltd. *v.* Henderson (1928) 23 Tas. LR 9 506

Ayers *v.* South Australian Banking Co. (1871) LR 3 PC 548 569

B & G Construction Co. Ltd. *v.* Bank of Montreal [1954] 2 DLR 753 135

Babcock *v.* Lawson (1880) 5 QBD 284 568

Bache & Co. (London) Ltd. *v.* Banque Vernes et Commerciale de Paris SA [1973] 2 Lloyd's Rep. 473 .... 136, 400

Backhouse *v.* Charlton (1878) 8 Ch. D 444 .... 93, 177

Bad Boy Appliances and Furniture Ltd. *v.* Toronto Dominion Bank (1972) 25 DLR (3d) 257 135

Baden, Delvaux & Lecuit *v.* Société Général [1983] BCLC 325 .... 93, 95

Bagley *v.* Winsome and National Provincial Bank Ltd. [1952] 2 QB 236 ... 211, 272

Bailey *v.* Barnes [1894] 1 Ch. 25 561

Bailey *v.* Bodenham (1864) 16 CB (NS) 288 237

Bailey *v.* Finch (1871) LR 7 QB 34 153

Baines *v.* National Provincial Bank Ltd. (1927) 32 Com. Cas. 216 ..... 129, 270, 305

Baker *v.* Australia and New Zealand Bank [1958] NZLR 907 .... 313, 314

Baker *v.* Barclays Bank Ltd. [1955] 1 WLR 822 .... 169, 254, 432, 505

Banbury *v.* Bank of Montreal [1918] AC 626 .... 52, 453, 458, 463

Banca Populare di Novara *v.* John Livanos & Sons Ltd. [1965] 2 Lloyd's Rep. 149 506

Banco di Roma SpA *v.* Orru [1973] 2 Lloyd's Rep. 505 505

Bank of Australasia *v.* Breillat (1847) 6 Moore PC 152 176

Bank of Baroda Ltd. *v.* Punjab National Bank [1944] AC 176 .... 251, 265

Bank of Bengal *v.* Fagan (1849) 7 Moore PC 61 195

Bank of British North America *v.* Haslip (1914) 30 OLR 299, affd. 31 OLR 442 237

Bank of Chettinad Ltd. *v.* Commissioners of Income Tax, Colombo [1948] AC 378 52

Bank of Cyprus (London) Ltd. *v.* Jones (1984) 134 NLJ 522 505

Bank of England *v.* Anderson (1837) 3 Bing NC 589 28

Bank of England *v.* Vagliano Bros. [1891] AC 107 .... 137, *244*, 305, 327, 334, 504, 512

Bank of Montreal *v.* Dezcam Industries Ltd. (1983) 5 WWR 83 497

Bank of Montreal *v.* Young (1966) 60 DLR (2d) 220 463

Bank of New South Wales *v.* Deri (1963) 80 WN (NSW) 1499 .... 319, 323, 335

Bank of New South Wales *v.* Goulburn Valley Butter Co. Pty. Ltd. [1902] AC 543 ....93, 152, 159, 160, 183

Bank of New South Wales *v.* Laing [1954] AC 135............................ 128, 266, 267

Bank of New South Wales *v.* Milvain (1884) 10 VLR 3 ....*311*, 313

Bank of New South Wales *v.* Murphet [1983] 1 VR 489.................... *324*, 335, 340

Bank of New South Wales *v.* Ross, Stuckley and Morawa [1974] 2 Lloyd's Rep. 110 577

Bank of New South Wales *v.* Vale Corporation (Management) Ltd. (in Liq.) [1978] 1 WLR 798 .... *94*

Bank of New South Wales Ltd. *v.* Barlex Investments Pty. Ltd. (1964) 64 SR (NSW) 274 273

Bank of New South Wales Savings Bank *v.* Freemantle Auto Centre Pty. Ltd. [1973] WAR 161 272

Bank of Scotland *v.* Dominion Bank [1891] AC 592 518

Bankers Trust Co. *v.* Shapira [1980] 1 WLR 1274 .... *100*

Banque Belge Pour L'Etranger *v.* Hambrouck [1921] 1 KB 321 .... 163, *165*

Barber *v.* Richards (1851) 6 Ex. 63 509

Barclay & Co. Ltd. *v.* Malcolm & Co. (1925) 133 LT 512 ....*322*, 335

Barclays Bank Ltd. *v.* Aschaffenburger Zellstoffwerke AG [1967] 1 Lloyd's Rep. 387..*507*, 510

Barclays Bank Ltd. *v.* Astley Industrial Trust Ltd. [1970] 2 QB 527.. 419, 421, 506, 508

Barclays Bank Ltd. *v.* Bird [1954] Ch. 274 545

Barclays Bank Ltd. *v.* Commissioners of Customs and Excise [1963] 1 Lloyd's Rep. 81 572

Barclays Bank Ltd. *v.* Okenarhe [1966] 2 Lloyd's Rep. 87 209

Barclays Bank Ltd. *v.* Quistclose Investments Ltd. [1970] AC 567, affg. [1968] Ch. 540 151

Barclays Bank Ltd. *v.* Simms (W.J.) Son & Cooke (Southern) Ltd. [1980] QB 677.. 323, *324*, 327, 328, 335, 337, 338, 340

Barclays Bank plc *v.* Bank of England [1985] 1 All ER 385 237

Barker *v.* Wilson [1980] 1 WLR 884 .... *102*

Barnes *v.* Addy (1874) LR 9 Ch. App. 244 89

Barrow *v.* Bank of New South Wales [1931] VLR 323 464

Batten (L.G.) Pty. Ltd., Re [1962] QWN 2 102

Bavins Jnr. & Sims *v.* London and South Western Bank [1900] 1 QB 270..241, 289, 413, *415*, 434

Baxter Equipment Ltd. *v.* Canadian Imperial Bank of Commerce (1981) 46 NSR (2d) 590 (Can.) *95*

Bayer AG *v.* Winter [1986] 1 All ER 733 276

Beaulieu *v.* National Bank of Canada (1983) 124 APR 220 (Can.) 89

Beaumont, Re, Beaumont *v.* Ewbank [1902] 1 Ch. 889 279

Beavan, Re, Davies, Banks & Co. *v.* Beavan [1912] 1 Ch. 196 206
Bechuanaland Exploration Co. *v.* London Trading Bank Ltd. [1898] 2 QB
   658 221
Belfast Banking Co. *v.* Doherty (1879) 4 Ir. LR 124 202
Belfast Banking Co. *v.* Stanley (1867) 15 WR 989 495
Bellamy *v.* Majoribanks (1852) 7 Exch. 389 .... 251, 253, 265
Belmont Finance Ltd. *v.* Williams Furniture Ltd. [1979] Ch. 250 93
Beresford *v.* Royal Insurance Co. Ltd. [1938] AC 586 600
Bernstein *v.* Northwestern National Bank of Philadelphia, 41 A 2d 440
   (1985) 469
Berry *v.* Gibbons (1873) LR 8 Ch. App. 747 ....180, *181*
Bevan *v.* National Bank Ltd. (1906) 23 TLR 65 433
Bickerdike *v.* Bollman (1786) 1 TR 405 452
Biggerstaff *v.* Rowatt's Wharf Ltd. [1896] 2 Ch. 93 194
Birch *v.* Treasury Solicitor [1951] 1 Ch. 298 ....220, 224
Birckhead and Carlisle *v.* Brown 5 Hill (NY) 634 (1843), affd. 2 Den. (NY) 375
   (1845) 396
Bird & Co. *v.* Thomas Cook & Son Ltd. [1937] 2 All ER 227 ....308, 513
Birkbeck Permanent Benefit Building Society, Re [1912] 2 Ch. 183 ....53, 56
Bishop decd., Re, National Provincial Bank Ltd. v. Bishop [1965] Ch.
   450 ....170, 172
Bissell & Co. *v.* Fox Bros. & Co. (1884) 51 LT 663 .... 424, 434, 446, 448
Blackburn Building Society *v.* Cunliffe, Brooks and Co. (1882) 22 Ch. D 61,
   affd. sub. nom. Brooks & Co. *v.* Blackburn and District Benefit Building
   Society (1884) 9 App. Cas. 857 .... *137*
Blackhan *v.* Doren (1810) 2 Camp. 503 452
Boardman *v.* Phipps [1967] 2 AC 46 96
Bobbett *v.* Pinkett (1876) 1 Ex. D 368 ....255, 413
Bodenham *v.* Hoskyns (1852) 2 De G M & G 903 163
Bolivinter Oil SA *v.* Chase Manhatten Bank [1984] 1 Lloyd's Rep. 251 136
Bolognesi's Case (1870) LR 5 Ch. App. 567 283
Bolton *v.* Dugdale (1833) 4 B & Ad. 619 497
Bond Worth Ltd., Re [1980] Ch. 228 589
Booth Fisheries Canadian Co. Ltd. *v.* Banque Provinciale du Canada (1972) 7
   NBR (2d) 138 135
Bottomsgate Industrial Co-operative Society, Re (1891) 65 LT 712 .... *56*
Bourne, Re [1906] 2 Ch. 427 .... *178*
Bovill *v.* Endle [1896] 1 Ch. 648 535
Bower *v.* Foreign and Colonial Gas Co. Ltd. (1874) 22 WR 740..............144, 591
Bowes, Re (1886) 33 Ch. D 586 577
Box *v.* Midland Bank Ltd. [1979] 2 Lloyd's Rep. 391 465
Boyd *v.* Emmerson (1834) 2 Ad. & El. 184 450
Bradford Old Bank Ltd. *v.* Sutcliffe [1918] 2 KB 833..........................82, 148, *149*
Bradler *v.* Craig, 79 Cal. Reptr. 401 (1969) 395
Bradley *v.* Copley (1845) 1 CB 685 470
Bradley Egg Farm Ltd. *v.* Clifford [1943] 2 All ER 378 198
Brandao *v.* Barnett (1846) 12 Cl. & F 787..576, 579

Brandt *v.* Liverpool, Brazil and River Plate Steam Navigation Co. Ltd. [1924] 1 KB 575 571

Brewer *v.* Westminster Bank Ltd. [1952] 2 All ER 650 .... 133, 169

Brice *v.* Bannister (1878) 3 QBD 569 584

Brien *v.* Dwyer (1979) 22 ALR 485 249

Brighton Empire and Eden Syndicate *v.* London and County Banking Co. Ltd.; The Times, 24 March 1904 305

Bristol and West of England Bank *v.* Midland Ry. Co. [1891] 2 QB 653 ...569, 572

British and North European Bank Ltd. *v.* Zalzstein [1927] 2 KB 92 132

British Bank of the Middle East *v.* Sun Life Assurance Co. of Canada [1983] 2 Lloyd's Rep. 9 .... 195, 196

British Eagle International Air Lines Ltd. *v.* Compagnie Nationale Air France [1975] 1 WLR 758 596

British Guiana Bank *v.* OR (1911) 104 LT 754 (JC, Guiana) 147, 154

British Thomson-Houston Co. Ltd. *v.* Federated European Bank Ltd. [1932] 2 KB 176 194

Broad *v.* Commissioner of Stamp Duties [1980] 2 NSWLR 40 598

Brocklebank, Re (1877) 6 Ch. D 358 202

Brook *v.* Hook (1871) LR 6 Ex. 89.. 291, 292, 298

Brown, Re, Brown *v.* Brown [1893] 2 Ch. 300 495

Brown *v.* IRC [1965] AC 244 188

Brown *v.* Westminster Bank Ltd. [1964] 2 Lloyd's Rep. 187...................... 138, 291

Brown, Shipley & Co. Ltd. *v.* Alicia Hosiery Ltd. [1966] 1 Lloyd's Rep. 668 507

Buckingham Co. *v.* London and Midland Bank 154, 478

Bucknell *v.* Bucknell [1969] 1 WLR 1204 98

Building and Civil Engineering Holidays Scheme Management Ltd. *v.* Post Office [1964] 2 QB 430 415

Buller *v.* Crips (1703) 6 Mod. 29 227

Buller *v.* Harrison (1777) 2 Cowp. 565... 329, 332

Bumpus, Re, ex p. White [1908] 2 KB 330 280

Bunyard, Re, ex p. Newton (1880) 16 Ch. D 330 510

Burchfield *v.* Moore (1854) 23 LJQB 261 516

Burdick *v.* Sewell (1883) 10 QBD 363, affd. (1884) 10 App. Cas. 74 568

Burnett *v.* Westminster Bank Ltd. [1966] 1 QB 742...................... 120, 136, 264

Business Computers Ltd. *v.* Anglo-African Leasing Ltd. [1977] 1 WLR 578...144, 564, 585, 591, 594

Bute (Marquess of) *v.* Barclays Bank Ltd. [1955] 1 KB 202...................... 413, 416, 417, 430, 431

Byfield, Re, ex p. Hill Samuel & Co. Ltd. *v.* Trustee of the Property of a Bankrupt [1982] Ch. 267 342

Byrne *v.* Nickel [1950] QSR 57 464

Calico Printers' Association Ltd. *v.* Barclays Bank Ltd. (1931) 36 Com. Cas. 71, affd. do. 197.. 370, 371

Calland *v.* Loyd (1840) 6 M & W 26 202

Cameron, Re (1967) 62 DLR (2d) 389.. 170, 172

Campanari *v.* Woodburn (1854) 15 CB 400 278

Canada Trust Co. *v*. The Queen [1982] 2 FC 722 512
Candler *v*. Crane, Christmas & Co. [1951] 2 KB 164 79
Cando Trust Co. *v*. The Queen [1982] 2 FC 722 (Can.) 245
Capital and Counties Bank Ltd. *v*. Gordon [1903] AC 240 129,
                      243, 268, 418, 421, 424, 439, 440, 446
Capital Finance Co. Ltd. *v*. Stokes [1969] 1 Ch. 261 586
Carl Zeiss Stiftung *v*. Herbert Smith & Co. [1969] 2 Ch. 276 93
Carlisle and Cumberland Banking Co. *v*. Bragg [1911] 1 KB 489 306
Carlon *v*. Ireland (1856) 23 LJQB 113 253
Carpenters' Co. *v*. British Mutual Banking Co. Ltd. [1938] 1 KB 511 304,
                      466, 448, 450
Carron *v*. Newpark Cinemas Ltd. [1951] 1 All ER 295 274
Carter *v*. Wake (1877) 4 Ch. D 605 ....568, 575
Castell and Brown Ltd., Re, Roper *v*. Castell and Brown Ltd. [1898] 1 Ch.
  315 562
Catlin *v*. Cyprus Finance Corporation (London) Ltd. [1983] QB 759 169
Cebora SNC *v*. SIP (Industrial Products) Ltd. [1976] 1 Lloyd's Rep. 271 507
Chamberlain *v*. Young and Tower [1893] 2 QB 206 244
Chambers *v*. Miller (1862) 13 CB (NS) 125 336
Channon *v*. English Scottish and Australian Bank (1918) 18 SR (NSW) 30 417
Charge Card Services Ltd., Re [1986] 3 All ER 289 ....392, 593, 598
Charles *v*. Blackwell (1877) 2 CPD 151 288
Chase Manhattan Bank, Application of, 297 F 2d 611 (1962) 107
Chase Manhattan Bank NA *v*. Israel–British Bank (London) Ltd. [1981] 1 Ch.
  105 342
Chatterton *v*. London and County Bank—Unreported, The Times, 21 Jan.
  1891 137
Choice Investments Ltd. *v*. Jeromnimon (Midland Bank Garnishee) [1981] QB
  149...271, 579
Chow Yoong Hong *v*. Choong Fah Rubber Manufactory [1962] AC 209 581
Christonette International Ltd., Re [1982] 1 WLR 1245 564
City and County Property Bank, Re (1895) 21 VLR 405 480
City Equitable Fire Insurance Co. Ltd., Re [1930] 2 Ch. 293 156
Clarke *v*. London and County Banking Co. [1897] 1 QB 552 78
Clayton *v*. Le Roy [1911] 2 KB 1031 468
Clayton's Case (see Devaynes *v*. Noble) *131, 164*, 178, 332, 483, 485, 548
Cleadon Trust Ltd., Re [1939] Ch. 286 301
Clerke *v*. Martin (1702) 2 Ld Raym. 757 227
Clifton Place Garage Ltd., Re [1970] Ch. 477 284
Clutton *v*. Attenborough & Son [1897] AC 90 ....*245, 512*
Cocks *v*. Masterman (1829) 9 B & C 902.. 334, *338*, 339
Coleman *v*. Bucks and Oxon Union Bank [1897] 2 Ch. 243 .... 93, *163*, 185
Collins, Re [1925] Ch. *556* 557
Collins *v*. Dominion Bank (1915) 8 OWN 432 132
Colonial Bank *v*. Exchange Bank of Yarmouth, Nova Scotia (1885) 11 App.
  Cas. 84 .... *322*
Colonial Bank of Australasia Ltd. *v*. Marshall [1906] AC 559 293

Colonial Trusts Corporation, Re (1879) 15 Ch. D 465 564
Columbia Graphaphone Co. *v.* Union Bank of Canada (1916) 34 DLR 743 ...... *134*
Columbian Fireproofing Co. Ltd., Re [1910] 2 Ch. 120 563
Commercial Bank of Australia Ltd. *v.* Amadio (1983) 46 ALR 402 (Aust.) 86
Commercial Bank of Australia Ltd. *v.* Younis [1979] 1 NSWR 444 ... 315, 324, 335
Commercial Bank of Scotland *v.* Rhind (1860) 3 Macq. HL 643 132
Commercial Bank of South Australia, Re (1887) 36 Ch. D 522 243
Commercial Banking Co. Ltd. *v.* Hartigan (1952) 86 Ir. LTR 109 .... 52, 53
Commercial Banking Co. of Sydney Ltd. *v.* Brown (R.H.) & Co. [1972] 2
   Lloyd's Rep. 360 .... 457, 460, *461*
Commercial Banking Co. of Sydney Ltd. *v.* Mann [1961] AC 1 .... 243, 417, 423
Commissioners of the State Savings Bank of Victoria *v.* Permewan, Wright &
   Co. Ltd. (1914) 19 CLR 457 .... 52, *53, 119*
Commissioners of Taxation *v.* Australia and New Zealand Banking Group Ltd.
   (1979) 53 ALJR 336 470
Commissioners of Taxation *v.* English, Scottish and Australian Bank Ltd.
   [1920] AC 683 .... 77, 423, 425, 428, 440
Commonwealth Trading Bank *v.* Reno Auto Sales Pty. Ltd. [1967] VR
   790 .... 320, 323, *335*
Cossill *v.* Strangman (1962) 80 WN (NSW) 628 274
Coutts & Co. *v.* Brown-Lecky [1947] KB 104 203
Coutts & Co. *v.* Irish Exhibition in London (1891) 7 TLR 313 .... *198*
Crears *v.* Hunter (1887) 19 QBD 341 508
Creative Press Ltd. *v.* Harman [1973] IR 313 496
Cretanor Maritime Co. Ltd. *v.* Irish Marine Management Ltd. (The "Cretan
   Harmony") [1978] 1 WLR 966 278
Cripps (Pharmaceuticals) Ltd. *v.* Wickenden [1973] 2 All ER 606 564
Cripps (R.A.) & Sons Ltd. *v.* Wickenden [1973] 1 WLR 944 478
Cromwell Property Investment Co. Ltd. *v.* Western & Toovey [1934]
   Ch. 322 .... 534, 535
Crouch *v.* Crédit Foncier of England Ltd. (1873) LR 8 QB 374 .... 221, 521
Crumplin *v.* London Joint Bank Ltd. (1913) 19 Com. Cas. 69 .... 426, 433
Cuckmere Brick Co. Ltd. *v.* Mutual Finance Ltd. [1971] Ch. 949 545
Cunliffe, Brooks & Co. *v.* Blackburn and Distict Benefit Building Society (1884)
   9 App. Cas. 857 299
Curtice *v.* London City and Midland Bank Ltd. [1908] 1 KB 293 91
Customs and Excise Commissioners *v.* Guy Butler (International) Ltd. [1977]
   QB 377 522
Cuthbert *v.* Roberts Lubbock & Co. [1909] 2 Ch. 226 .... 477, 577, 579

Dagger *v.* Shepherd [1946] 1 All ER 133 521
Daily Telegraph Newspaper Co. Ltd. *v.* McLaughlin [1904] AC 776 .... 206, 280
Daintrey, Re [1900] 1 QB 546 592
Dalgety Ltd. *v.* John J. Hilton Pty. Ltd. [1981] 2 NSWLR 169 497
Dalton, Re, ex p. Harrington and Carmichael [1963] Ch. 336 281
Daniels *v.* Imperial Bank of Canada (1914) 19 DLR 166 .... *152*
Daun and Vallentin *v.* Sherwood (1895) 11 TLR 211 244

Davey & Co. *v.* Williamson & Sons Ltd. [1898] 2 QB 194 565
David Allester Ltd., Re [1922] 2 Ch. 211 .... *553, 569, 572, 573*
Davidson *v.* Barclays Bank Ltd. [1940] 1 All ER 316 .... 312, 313
Davies *v.* Kennedy (1869) IR 3 Eq. 668 52
Dawson *v.* Isle [1906] 1 Ch. 633 .... 582, 586
Day *v.* Bank of New South Wales (1978) 19 ALR 32 .... 432, 436
Day and Dent Constuction Pty. Ltd. *v.* North Australian Properties Pty. Ltd.
    (1981) 34 ALR 595, affd. (1982) 40 ALR 399 592
De la Bere *v.* Pearson Ltd. [1907] 1 KB 483 .... 464, 467
De la Chaumette *v.* Bank of England (1829) 9 B & C 208 510
Dearle *v.* Hall (1828) 3 Russ. 1 .... 588, 589
Debtor, Re a [1956] 1 WLR 1226 .... 592, 593
Deeley *v.* Lloyds Bank Ltd. [1912] AC 756, reversing [1910] 1 Ch. 648 483,
                                                                                          548
Delbrueck *v.* Barclays Bank International Ltd. [1976] 2 Lloyd's Rep. 341 378
Delbrueck *v.* Manufacturers Hanover Trust Co. (1979) 609 F 2d 1047, affg.
    (1979) 464 F Supp. 989 .... *366, 379*
Denmark Productions Ltd. *v.* Boscobe Productions Ltd. (1967) 111 So J. 715 ... 202
Derry *v.* Peek (1889) 14 App. Cas. 337 462
Deutsche Bank (London Agency) *v.* Benro & Co. (1895) 1 Com. Cas. 255 315
Deutsche Bank und Disconto Gesellschaft *v.* Banque des Marchands de Moscou
    (1931) 4 LDAB 293 .... *480*
Devaynes *v.* Noble (Clayton's Case) (1816) 1 Mer. 529 .... *131, 164,*
                                                                178, 332, 483, 485, 548
Devitt *v.* Kearney (1883) 13 Ir. LR 45 180
Devonald *v.* Rosser & Sons [1906] 2 KB 728 221
Dey *v.* Pullinger Engineering Co. [1921] 1 KB 77 .... 194, 195
Diamond *v.* Bank of London and Montreal Ltd. [1979] QB 333 459
Diamond *v.* Graham [1968] 1 WLR 1061 508
Dillon, Re, Duffin *v.* Duffin (1890) 44 Ch. D 76 .... 221, 222, *223*
Dilworth, Re, ex p. Armistead (1828) 2 Gl. & J 371 578
Dimond (H.H.) (Roturua 1966) Ltd. *v.* Australia and New Zealand Banking
    Group Ltd. [1979] 2 NZLR 739 237
Diplock, Re [1948] Ch. 465 .... *165*, 483
Direct Acceptance Corporation *v.* Bank of New South Wales (1968) 88 WN
    (NSW) (Pt. 1) 498 .... *147, 148*
Dixon *v.* Bank of New South Wales (1896) 17 LR (NSW) Eq. 355 .... 93, 208
Doe d. Thomas *v.* Roberts (1847) 16 M & W 778 202
Dominion Bank *v.* Jacobs [1951] 3 DLR 233 335
Dominion Bank *v.* Union Bank of Canada (1908) 40 SCR 366 331
Donald *v.* Suckling (1866) LR 1 QB 585 .... 568, 570
Douglass *v.* Lloyds Bank Ltd. (1924) 34 Com. Cas. 263 .... 83, 99
Dowse *v.* Gorton [1891] AC 190 182
Drew *v.* Nunn (1879) 4 QBD 661 .... 206, 280, 376
Dublin City Distillery Ltd. *v.* Doherty [1914] AC 823 555
Dudley and District Benefit Building Society *v.* Emerson [1949] 1 Ch. 707 549
Duffin *v.* Duffin (1890) 44 Ch. D 76 .... 221, 222, 223

Duke *v.* Robson [1973] 1 WLR 267 534
Duncan, Fox & Co. *v.* North and South Wales Bank (1880) 6 App. Cas. 1 500,
517, 526
Dungarvin Trust (Pty.) Ltd. *v.* Import Refrigeration Co. (Pty.) Ltd. [1971] 4
SALR 300...256, 433
Durham Bros. *v.* Robertson [1898] 1 QB 765 .... 367, 583, 597

Earle (G. & T.) (1925) Ltd. *v.* Hemsworth RDC (1928) 140 LT 69 584
Eckman *v.* Midland Bank Ltd. [1973] QB 519 98
Edelstein *v.* Schuler & Co. [1902] 2 KB 144 221
Edmunds *v.* Edmunds [1904] P 362 273
Edward Nelson & Co. Ltd. *v.* Faber & Co. [1903] 2 KB 367 564
Edward Owen Engineering Ltd. *v.* Barclays Bank International Ltd. [1978] QB
159...136, 397
Edwards *v.* Grace (1826) 2 M & W 190 180
Edwards *v.* Walters [1896] 2 Ch. 157 517
Elijah Murphy Estate, Re (1930) 74 Sol. J 321 182
Elliott *v.* Director General of Fair Trading [1980] 1 WLR 977.................... 402, 407
Elliott *v.* Elliott (1899) 15 WN (NSW) 186...215, 216
Ellis & Co's Trustees *v.* Dixon-Johnson [1925] AC 489 571
Ellow Co. Ltd. *v.* Lloyds Bank Ltd. (1934) 4 LDAB 455 312
Elsey *v.* Federal Commissioner of Taxation (1969) 121 CLR 99 102
Emmott *v.* Star Newspaper Co. (1892) 62 LJQB 77 100
Empresa Cubana de Fletes *v.* Lagonisi Shipping Co. Ltd. ('The Georgios C')
[1971] 1 QB 488 385
English and Scottish Mercantile Investment Co. Ltd. *v.* Brunton [1892] 2 QB
700..560, 562
Equitable Trust Co. of New York *v.* Dawson Partners Ltd. (1927) 27 Ll. LR
49 369
Esso Petroleum Co. Ltd. *v.* Mardon [1976] QB 801....................................460, 464
Etablissement Esefka International Anstalt *v.* Central Bank of Nigeria [1979] 1
Lloyd's Rep. 445 276
European Asian Bank AG *v.* Punjab and Sind Bank (No. 2) [1983] 1 WLR
642 .... 285, 300,
368
European Bank, Agra Bank Claims, Re (1872) LR 8 Ch. App. 41.............*141*, 147
Evans *v.* London and Provincial Bank; "The Times", 1 March 1917 311
Evans *v.* National Provincial Bank of England (1897) 13 TLR 429 .... *212*
Evans *v.* Rival Granite Quarries Ltd. [1901] 2 KB 979..............................558, 564
Evans, Coleman & Evans Ltd. *v.* Nelson (R.A.) Construction Ltd. (1958) 16
DLR 123 ....582, 595
Evans (D.B.) (Bilston) Ltd. *v.* Barclays Bank Ltd. (1961) 7 LDAB 283 284
Evansville National Bank *v.* Kaufman (1883) 93 NY 273 396
Evra Corporation *v.* Swiss Bank Corporation 522 F Supp. 820 (1981).......*372*, 374
Ewer *v.* Jones (1846) 9 QB 623 202
Ewing *v.* Dominion Bank (1904) 35 SCR 133 (Can.) 134, 138, 291
Ex p. Coe (1861) 3 De GF & J 335 55

FDC Co. *v.* Chase Manhattan Bank—Unreported; nos. 65 and 131 (Civil) of 1984; judgement of 17 Oct. 1984 .... *109*

FIDC *v.* European American Bank and Trust Co. (1983) 576 F Supp. 950..368, 375

Fairclough *v.* Swan Brewery Co. Ltd. [1912] AC 565 534

Fairline Shipping Corporation *v.* Adamson [1975] QB 180 471

Farhall *v.* Farhall (1871) LR 7 Ch. App. 123 180

Farrow's Bank Ltd., Re [1923] 1 Ch. 41 ....*418*, 440

Feaver *v.* Feaver [1977] 5 WWR 271 170

Federal Savings Credit Union Ltd. *v.* Hessian (1979) 98 DLR (3d) 488 464

Fenton, Re, ex p. Fenton Textile Association Ltd. [1956] 1 Ch. 85 592

Fenwicke *v.* Clarke (1862) 4 De GF & J 240 59

Fergusson *v.* Fyffe (1840) 8 Cl. & F 121 481

Feuer Leather Corporation *v.* Frank Johnstone & Sons [1981] Com. LR 251, affd. [1983] Com. LR 12 560

Fibrosa Spolka Akcyjna *v.* Fairbairn Lawson Combe Barbour Ltd. [1943] AC 32 289

Fielding and Platt Ltd. *v.* Najjar [1969] 1 WLR 357 509

Figgis, decd., Re, Roberts *v.* McLaren [1969] 1 Ch. 123 172

Fine Art Society Ltd. *v.* Union Bank of London Ltd. (1866) 17 QBD 705 413

First National City Bank of New York *v.* IRS 271 F 2d 616 (1959), cert. den 361 US 948 (1960) 107

Fitzgerald's Trustee *v.* Mellersh [1892] 1 Ch. 385 535

Flach *v.* London and South Western Bank Ltd. (1915) 31 TLR 334 313

Fleming *v.* Bank of New Zealand [1900] AC 577................................128, 266, 477

Fleming *v.* Hector (1836) 2 M & W 172 198

Florence Land and Rubber Works Co., Re, ex p. Moor (1878) 10 Ch. D 530 563

Flower and Metropolitan Board of Works, Re (1884) 27 Ch. D 592 181

Fok Cheong Shing Investments Co. Ltd. *v.* Bank of Nova Scotia (1981) 32 OR (2d) 705 ....246, 512

Foley *v.* Hill (1848) 2 HLC 28 ....*81*, 121, 127, 533

Fontaine-Besson *v.* Parr's Banking Co. (1895) 12 TLR 121 166

Footman Bower & Co. Ltd., Re [1961] Ch. 443 83

Forestal Mimosa Ltd. *v.* Oriental Credit Ltd. [1986] 1 WLR 631 507

Forman *v.* Bank of England (1902) 18 TLR 339 449

Forman *v.* Wright (1851) 11 CB 481 ....507, 508, 509

Forster *v.* Baker [1910] 2 KB 636 583

Forster *v.* Bank of London (1862) 3 F & F 214 268

Forster *v.* Mackreth (1867) LR 2 Ex. 163 .... *176*

Forster, Hight & Co. *v.* Ward (1883) 1 Cab. & E 168 517

Foster *v.* Driscoll [1929] 1 KB 470 518

Foxton *v.* Manchester and Liverpool District Banking Co. (1881) 44 LT 406 .... *184*

France *v.* Clark (1883) 22 Ch. D 830 570

Freeman and Lockyer *v.* Buckhurst Park Properties (Mangal) Ltd. [1964] 2 QB 480 196

Frost *v.* London Joint Stock Bank Ltd. (1906) 22 TLR 760 313

Fuglsang *v.* English Scottish and Australian Bank Ltd. [1959] Tas. SR 155 185

Gaden *v* Newfoundland Savings Bank [1899] AC 281 251
Gage *v*. King [1961] 1 QB 188 171
Galaxia Maritime SA *v*. Mineralimportexport [1982] 1 WLR 539 277
Garnett *v*. M'Kewan (1872) LR 8 Ex. 10 ....141, *144*, *146*, *154*, *159*
Garret *v*. Noble (1834) 6 Sim. 504 180
Gaunt *v*. Taylor (1843) 2 Hare 413 179
Geary *v*. Physic (1826) 5 B & C 234 242
General Auction Estate and Monetary Co. *v*. Smith [1891] 3 Ch. 432 192
General Horticultural Co., Re, ex p. Whitehouse (1886) 32 Ch. D 512 595
General Produce Co. *v*. United Bank Ltd. [1979] 2 Lloyd's Rep. 255 576
George Parker (Transport) Ltd. *v*. Eynon [1973] 1 WLR 1461 158
George Thompson (Aust.) Pty. Ltd. *v*. Vittadello [1978] VR 199 513
Gibbons *v*. Westminster Bank Ltd. [1939] 2 KB 882 311
Giblin *v*. McMullen (1868) LR 2 PC 317..466, 467
Gibson *v*. Minet (1824) 2 Bing. 7 252
Glasscock *v*. Balls (1889) 24 QBD 13 516
Glenie *v*. Smith [1908] 1 KB 263 502
Glyn, Mills, Currie & Co. *v*. East and West India Dock Co. (1880) 6 QBD 475,
    affd. (1882) 7 App. Cas. 591 468
Gooch, Re [1921] 2 KB 593 ....ᵜ.. 502
Goodman *v*. J. Eban Ltd. [1954] 1 QB 550 242
Goodwin *v*. Robarts (1875) LR 10 Ex. 337, affd. (1876) 1 App. Cas.
    476..221, 250
Gorden *v*. Harper (1796) 7 Term Rep. 9 470
Gordon *v*. London City and Midland Bank Ltd. [1902] 1 KB 242 446
Government of Newfoundland *v*. Newfoundland Ry. Co. (1888) 13 App. Cas.
    199 585
Governments Stock and Other Securities Investment Co. *v*. Manila Ry. Co. Ltd.
    [1897] AC 81 ....562, 563, 565
Gowers *v*. Lloyds and National Provincial Foreign Bank Ltd. [1938] 1 All ER
    766... 166, *329*, 413
Grand Junction Canal Co. *v*. Bates [1954] 2 QB 160 543
Gray *v*. Johnston (1868) LR 3 HL 1............................93, 127, *163*, 185, 186
Gray *v*. Lewis (1869) LR 8 Eq. 526 93
Gray's Inn Construction Co. Ltd., Re [1980] 1 WLR 711 283
Great Western Railway Co. *v*. London and County Banking Co. Ltd. [1901] AC
    414...77, *255*, 423, 433, 440
Green *v*. Whitehead [1930] 1 Ch. 38 181
Greenhalgh (W.P.) & Sons *v*. Union Bank of Manchester [1924] 2 KB 153 .... *150*
Greenwood *v*. Martins Bank Ltd. [1933] AC 51 ....138, *291*,
    295, 296
Greenwood Teale *v*. William, Williams, Brown & Co. (1894) 11 TLR
    56...*145*, 147, 150, 151, 152, 184
Gregory Love & Co. Ltd., Re [1916] 1 Ch. 203 556
Griffin, Re, Griffin *v*. Griffin [1899] 1 Ch. 408.................................*215*, 221, 223
Griffiths *v*. Dalton [1940] 2 KB 264 129
Gross, Re, Ex p. Kingston (1871) LR 6 Ch. App. 632.................. 59, 149, *183*, 184

Guaranty Trust Co. of New York v. Hannay & Co. [1918] 2 KB 623 496,
506, 513, 572
Guaranty Trust Co. of New York v. Lyon (1953) 124 NYS 2d 680 378
Guertin v. Royal Bank of Canada (1983) 43 OR (2d) 363 ....98, 103
Guildford Trust Ltd. v. Goss (1927) 136 LT 725 177
Gulf Refining Co. v. Williams Roofing Co., 186 SW 2d 790 (1945)...........394, 395
Gurney v. Womersley (1854) 4 E & B 133 513

Halesowen Presswork and Assemblies Ltd. v. National Westminster Bank Ltd.
  [1971] 1 QB 25, affd. sub. nom. National Westminster Bank Ltd. v.
  Halesowen Presswork and Assemblies Ltd. [1972] AC 785 .... 128, 142, 159
Hall v. Heward (1886) 32 Ch. D 430 535
Hallett's Estate, Re, Knachball v. Hallett (1879) 13 Ch. D 696..................164, 485
Halliday v. Holgate (1868) LR 3 Ex. 299..568, 570
Hambro v. Burnand [1904] 2 KB 10...194, 195
Hamilton v. Spottiswoode (1849) 4 Exch. 200 240
Hamilton v. Vaughan Sherrin Electrical Engineering Co. [1894] 3 Ch. 589 201
Hamilton Finance Co. Ltd. v. Coverley, Westray, Walbaum and Tosetti Ltd.
  [1969] 1 Lloyd's Rep. 53 449
Hamilton Young & Co., Re [1905] 2 KB 722....................552, 553, 554, 572, 573
Hamilton's Windsor Ironworks, Re, ex p. Pitman and Edwards (1879) 12 Ch.
  D 707 562
Hammond, Re (1903) 3 SR (NSW) 270 180
Hampstead Guardians v. Barclays Bank Ltd. (1923) 39 TLR 229 428
Hanak v. Green [1958] 2 QB 9 591
Hannan's Lake View Central Ltd. v. Armstrong (1900) 5 Com. Cas. 188 424
Harbottle (R.D.) (Mercantile) Ltd. v. National Westminster Bank Ltd. [1948]
  QB 146 ....136, 397
Harding v. Williams (1880) 14 Ch. D 197 99
Harding Carpets Ltd. v. Royal Bank of Canada [1908] 4 WWR 149 ....588, 590
Hare v. Henty (1861) 10 CB (NS) 65 ....237, 260
Harmer v. Steele (1849) 4 Exch. 1...516, 517
Harris (Oscar) Son & Co. v. Vallerman & Co. [1940] 1 All ER 185 509
Harrison, Re (1920) 90 LJ Ch. 186 172
Harrold v. Plenty [1901] 2 Ch. 314 575
Hart, Re, ex p. Caldicott (1884) 25 Ch. D 716 598
Hart v. Barnes (1982) 13 ATR 694 583
Hart v. Frontino and Bolivia South American Gold Mining Co. Ltd. (1870) LR
  5 Ex. 623 335
Hart v. Sangster [1957] 1 Ch. 329 210
Hassan v. Willson [1977] 1 Lloyd's Rep. 431 508
Haughton v. Haughton [1965] 1 OR 481 98
Haythorpe v. Rae [1972] VR 633 224
Head, Re, Head v. Head (No. 2) [1894] 2 Ch. 236 209
Heald v. O'Conner [1971] 1 WLR 497 203
Hedley, Byrne & Co. Ltd. v. Heller and Partners Ltd. [1964] AC
  465 .... 79, 252, 371, 456, 459, 461, 462, 464

Helby *v.* Matthews [1895] AC 471 530
Heller Factors Pty. Ltd. *v.* Toy Corporation Pty. Ltd. [1984] 1 NSWLR 121 518
Helson *v.* McKenzies (Cuba Street) Ltd. [1950] NZLR 878 438
Helstan Securities Ltd. *v.* Hertfordshire County Council [1978] 3 All ER 262 ... *584*
Hely-Hutchinson *v.* Brayhead Ltd. [1968] 1 QB 549 196
Heppenstall *v.* Jackson (Barclays Bank, Garnishee) [1939] 1 KB 585 273
Heywood *v.* Pickering (1874) LR 9 QB 428 449
Hibernian Bank Ltd. *v.* Gysin and Hanson [1939] 1 KB 483, affg. [1938] 2 KB
    384 247
Hill *v.* Bank of Hochelaga [1921] 3 WWR 430 .... *152*
Hilton *v.* Tucker (1888) 39 Ch. D 669..*569, 574*
Hiort *v.* London and North Western Railway Co. (1879) 4 Ex. D 188 468
Hirst *v.* West Riding Union Banking Co. Ltd. [1901] 2 KB 560 458
Hitchcock *v.* Edwards (1889) 60 LT 636 249
Hockley *v.* Goldstein (1922) 90 LJKB 111 366
Holland *v.* Manchester and Liverpool District Banking Co. (1909) 14 Com.
    Cas. 241 .... *131*
Holland *v.* Russell (1861) 30 LJ (NS) QB 308, affd. (1863) 4 B & S 14.....331, *333*
Hollins *v.* Fowler (1875) LR 7 HL 757 421
Holmes *v.* Walton [1961] WAR 96...*464, 465*
Holroyd *v.* Marshall (1862) 10 HLC 191 .... *556*
Holt *v.* Ely (1853) 1 El & Bl. 795 .... *318*
Holt *v.* Heatherfield Trust Co. Ltd. [1942] 2 KB 1 583
Holt *v.* Markham [1923] 1 KB 504...131, 328
Hone, Re, ex p. The Trustee *v.* Kensington Borough Council [1951] Ch. 85 477
Hong Kong and Shanghai Banking Corporation *v.* Lo [1928] AC 181 .... *518*
Hopkins *v.* Abbott (1875) LR 19 Eq. 222 .... 208, 210, 220, 221
Hopkins *v.* Ware (1869) LR 4 Ex. 268 261
Hopkinson *v.* Forster (1874) LR 19 Eq. 74 265
Hornby *v.* McLauren (1908) 24 TLR 494 523
Horne & Hellard, Re (1885) 29 Ch. D 736 565
Houben *v.* Bank of Nova Scotia (1970) 3 NBR (2d) 366 159
Houghland *v.* Low (R.R.) (Luxury Coaches) Ltd. [1962] 1 QB 694 467
Houghton & Co. *v.* Nothard, Lowe & Wills Ltd. [1927] 1 KB 246 195
House Property Co. of London Ltd. *v.* London County and Westminster Bank
    (1915) 84 LJKB 1846... 257, 432, 433
Howard *v.* Beall (1889) 23 QBD 1 101
Howard Marine and Dredging Co. Ltd. *v.* Ogden (A.) & Son (Excavations) Ltd.
    [1978] QB 574 464
Howe Richardson Scale Co. Ltd. *v.* Polimex-Cekop [1978] 1 Lloyd's Rep.
    161 136
Hudson *v.* Royal Bank of Canada (1920) 19 OWN 93 132
Hughes *v.* Pump House Hotel Co. Ltd. [1902] 2 KB 190 597
Husband *v.* Davies (1851) 10 CB 645 ....172, *214*
Hutley *v.* Peacock (1913) 30 TLR 42 202

Illingworth *v.* Houldsworth [1904] AC 355, affg. [1903] 2 Ch. 284 ....*557, 565*

Imperial Bank *v.* Kean (1916) 10 OWN 80 132
Imperial Bank of Canada *v.* Bank of Hamilton [1903] AC 49 .... 320, *321*, 334, 339
Imperial Bank of Canada *v.* Begley [1936] 2 All ER 367 298
Imperial Bank of India *v.* Abeyesinghe (1927) 29 NLR 257 334
Imperial Loan Co. *v.* Stone [1892] 1 QB 599 .... *205*
Importers Co. Ltd. *v.* Westminster Bank Ltd. [1927] 1 KB 869, affd. [1927] 2
    KB 297 .... *78*, 242, 434
Independent Automatic Sales Ltd. *v.* Knowles & Foster [1962] 1 WLR
    974 .... 582, 584, 586
Ingham *v.* Primrose (1859) 7 CB (NS) 82 518
Inglis *v.* Commonwealth Trading Bank of Australia (1973) 47 ALJR 234 266
Ings *v.* Ferguson 282 F Supp. 149 (1960) 107
Innes *v.* Stephenson (1831) 1 M & Rob. 145 .... *213*
International Factors Ltd. *v.* Rodriguez [1979] QB 351 .... *414*, 416
Introductions Ltd., Re [1970] Ch. 199 191
Iraqi Ministry of Defence *v.* Arcepey Shipping Co. SA [1981] QB 65 278
Ireland *v.* Livingston (1872) LR 5 HL 395 .... 285, 299
Ironmonger & Co. *v.* Dyne (1928) 44 TLR 579 .... 100, 101
Irwin *v.* Bank of Montreal (1876) 38 UCQB 375 154
Isaacs *v.* Barclays Bank Ltd. [1943] 2 All ER 682 470

Jackson *v.* Hudson (1810) 2 Camp. 447 503
Jackson *v.* White and Midland Bank Ltd. [1967] 2 Lloyd's Rep. 68 .... *169*, 301
Jackson & Bassford Ltd., Re [1906] 2 Ch. 467 556
Jacobs *v.* Morris [1902] 1 Ch. 816 139
Jade International Steel Stahl und Eisen GmbH & Co. KG *v.* Robert Nicholas
    (Steels) Ltd. [1978] QB 917 .... 503, 507, *515*
James *v.* ANZ Banking Group Ltd. (1986) 64 ALR 347 (Aust.) 88
James Kirkwood & Sons *v.* Clydesdale Bank Ltd. (1908) SC 20 .... 141, 146, 157
James Lamont & Co. Ltd. *v.* Hyland Ltd. [1950] 1 KB 585 507
Jauncey, Re, Bird *v.* Arnold [1926] Ch. 471 480
Jayson *v.* Midland Bank Ltd. [1968] 1 Lloyd's Rep. 409 .... 311, 313, 314
Jeffreyes *v.* Agra and Masterman's Bank (1866) LR 2 Eq. 674 .... 144, *216*,
                                                                                       220, 577, 579, 591
Jenkins *v.* Jenkins [1928] 2 KB 501 517
Jenkins & Son *v.* Coomber [1898] 2 QB 168 502
Joachimson *v.* Swiss Bank Corporation [1921] 3 KB 110 ...... 82, 218, 266, 270, 271
John *v.* Dodwell & Co. Ltd. [1918] AC 563 .... *185*, 318
John Burrows Ltd. *v.* Subsurface Surveys Ltd. [1968] SCR 607 .... 496, 521
John Shaw (Rayner's Lane) Ltd. *v.* Lloyds Bank Ltd. (1945) 5 LDAB 396 127
Johnson *v.* Roberts (1875) LR 10 Ch. App. 505 578
Johnson & Co. Ltd., Re [1902] 1 IR 439 149
Jon Beauforte (London) Ltd., Re [1953] Ch. 131 192
Jones *v.* Gordon (1877) 2 App. Cas. 616 505
Jones *v.* Humphreys [1902] 1 KB 10 .... 583, 597
Jones *v.* Maynard [1951] 1 Ch. 572 .... 170, 171
Jones *v.* Peppercorne (1858) John. 430 576

Jones & Co. *v.* Coventry [1909] 2 KB 1029 273

Jones (R.E.) Ltd. *v.* Waring and Gillow Ltd. [1926] AC 670, rev'ng [1925] 2 KB
   612 .... *320, 322, 323, 324, 326, 327, 341, 506*

Judd *v.* Citibank, 435 NYS 2d 210 (1980) *400*

Kahler *v.* Midland Bank Ltd. [1948] 1 All ER 811; affd. [1950] AC 24 78,
   466, 470

Karak Rubber Co. Ltd. *v.* Burden [1972] 1 WLR 602 94

Kauter *v.* Hilton (1953) 90 CLR 86 .... *221, 224*

Kayford Ltd., Re [1975] 1 WLR 279 .... *163*

Keelan *v.* Norray Distributing Ltd. (1967) 62 DLR (2d) 466 506

Keenan Bros. Ltd. (in Liq.), Re [1958] ILRM 254 582

Keever (a bankrupt), Re [1967] Ch. 182 .... 142, 158, 577, 578

Kelly *v.* Solari (1841) 9 M & W 54 .... 319, 324

Kendal *v.* Wood (1871) LR 6 Ex. 243 .... *318*

Kendall *v.* Hamilton (1879) 4 App. Cas. 504 521

Kent and Sussex Sawmills Ltd., Re [1947] 1 Ch. 177 .... *586*

Kepitigalla Rubber Estates Ltd. *v.* National Bank of India Ltd. [1909] 2 KB
   1010 .... 133, *137*, 295

Kerrigan, Re [1916] VLR 516 180

Kerrison *v.* Glyn, Mills, Currie & Co. (1911) 17 Com. Cas. 41 .... *320, 324, 328*

Keyes *v.* Royal Bank of Canada [1947] 3 DLR 161 .... 249, 252

Kilsby *v.* Williams (1822) 5 B & Ald. 815 452

Kinlan *v.* Ulster Bank Ltd. [1928] IR 171 313

Kirkman *v.* Booth (1848) 11 Beav. 273 180

Kitchen Trustee *v.* Madders [1949] 2 All ER 54 593

Kleinwort, Sons & Co. *v.* Dunlop Rubber Co. (1907) 97 LT 263 ...... 323, 327, 332

Knight & Searle *v.* Dove [1964] 2 QB 631 12

Knightsbridge Estates Trust Ltd. *v.* Byrne [1939] Ch. 441 535

Koch *v.* Dicks [1933] 1 KB 307 518

Korea Exchange Bank *v.* Debenhams (Central Buying) Ltd. [1979] 1 Lloyd's
   Rep. 100 496

Koster's Premier Pottery Pty. Ltd. *v.* Bank of Adelaide (1981) 28 SASR
   335 .... 413, 415

Kreditbank Cassel GmbH *v.* Schenkers Ltd. [1927] 1 KB 826 .... 194, *298*

Krelinger *v.* New Patagonia Meat and Cold Storage Co. Ltd. [1914] AC 25 534

Kum *v.* Wah Tat Bank Ltd. [1971] 1 Lloyd's Rep. 439 572

L'Amie *v.* Wilson [1907] 2 IR 130 101

Lacave & Co. *v.* Crédit Lyonnais [1897] 1 QB 148 .... 77, 417, 504

Ladbroke & Co. *v.* Todd (1914) 30 TLR 433 .... 77, 78, 417, 427

Ladenburg *v.* Goodwin Ferreira & Co. Ltd. [1912] 3 KB 275 .... 554, 573

Ladup *v.* Shaik [1983] QB 225 508

Lam *v.* Hang Lung Bank Ltd. [1982] HKLR 215 136

Land Credit Co. of Ireland, Re, ex p. Overend, Gurney & Co. (1896) LR 4
   Ch. App. 460 194

Langton *v.* Waite (1868) LR 6 Eq. 165 570

Larner *v.* London County Council [1949] 2 KB 683 319

Laurence Henderson, Sons & Co. Ltd. *v.* Wallace and Pennell (1902) 40 SLR
  70 244

Lawrie *v.* Commonwealth Trading Bank of Australia [1970] Qd. R 373 424

Laws *v.* Rand (1857) 3 CB (NS) 442 176

Lawson *v.* Commercial Bank of South Australia (1888) 22 SALR 74 (Aust.) 93

Lazarus *v.* Cowie (1843) 3 QB 459 524

Lazarus Estates Ltd. *v.* Beasley [1956] 1 QB 702 242

Leach *v.* Buchanan (1802) 4 Esp. 226 .... 138, 291

Ledward *v.* Hansells (1856) 2 K & J 370 202

Leslie (R.) Ltd. *v.* Sheill [1914] 3 KB 607 .... *201*

Levene *v.* Brougham (1909) 25 TLR 265 202

Lever *v.* Maguire [1928] VLR 262 102

Levy *v.* Sewill (1887) 31Ch. D 90 534

Lewes Sanitary Steam Laundry Co. Ltd. *v.* Barclay & Co. Ltd. (1906) 95 LT
  444 .... 133, 295

Lewis *v.* Alleyne (1888) 4 TLR 560 201

Lickbarrow *v.* Mason (1787) 2 TR 63, revd. (1790) 1 H Bl. 357, restored
  (1793) 2 H Bl. 211 571

Ligget (B.) (Liverpool) Ltd. *v.* Barclays Bank Ltd. [1928] 1 KB 48............. 170, 195,
                                                                                207, *300*, 328

Lilly *v.* Doubleday (1881) 7 QBD 510 468

Lind, Re [1915] 2 Ch. 345 .... 556, 557

Little *v.* Slackford (1828) 1 M & M 171 240

Lloyd *v.* Banks (1868) LR 3 Ch. App. 488 586

Lloyd *v.* Grace, Smith & Co. [1912] AC 716 296

Lloyds & Scottish Finance Ltd. *v.* Cyril Lord Carpet Sales Ltd. (1979) 129 NLJ
  366 581

Lloyds Bank Ltd. *v.* Bank of America National Trust and Savings Association
  [1938] 2 KB 147... 553, 569, 573

Lloyds Bank Ltd. *v.* Brooks (1950) 6 LDAB 161....................................... 131, 133

Lloyds Bank Ltd. *v.* Bundy [1975] QB 326 .... *85*, 96

Lloyds Bank Ltd. *v.* Chartered Bank of India, Australia and China [1929] 1 KB
  40.. 301, 413, 429, 431, 432, 436

Lloyds Bank Ltd. *v.* Cooke [1907] 1 KB 794 292

Lloyds Bank Ltd. *v.* Savory & Co. [1933] AC 201 .... 199, 413,
                                                                      424, 425, 426, 428, 430,
                                                                                     436, 442

Loescher *v.* Dean [1950] Ch. 491.. 187, 188

Lofts *v.* MacDonald (1974) 3 ALR 404 485

Lombard Banking Ltd. *v.* Central Garage & Engineering Co. Ltd. [1963] 1 QB
  220 502

London and County Banking Co. *v.* Groome (1881) 8 QBD 288 240

London and Globe Finance Corporation, Re [1902] 2 Ch. 416.................... 576, 577

London and Mediterranean Bank, Re (1870) LR 5 Ch. App. 567 283

London and Montrose Shipbuilding and Repairing Co. Ltd. *v.* Barclays Bank
  Ltd. (1925) 31 Com. Cas. 67 432

London and River Plate Bank Ltd. *v.* Bank of Liverpool Ltd. [1896] 1 QB 7 ....335, 339

London and Westminster Bank *v.* Button (1907) 51 Sol. J 466 485

London Association for Protection of Trade *v.* Greenland Ltd. [1916] 2 AC 15 455

London Bank of Australia Ltd. *v.* Kendall (1920) 28 CLR 401 417

London Borough of Bromley *v.* Ellis [1971] 1 Lloyd's Rep. 97 371

London Intercontinental Trust Ltd. *v.* Barclays Bank Ltd. [1980] 1 Lloyd's Rep. 241 297

London Joint Stock Bank *v.* Macmillan [1918] AC 777 .... 83, 139, 195, 221, 229, 285, 292, *293*, 299, 430

London Joint Stock Bank *v.* Simmons [1892] AC 201 195

Longman *v.* Bath Electric Tramway Ltd. [1905] 1 Ch. 646 575

Lovegrove, Re [1953] Ch. 464 587

Lovell and Christmas *v.* Beauchamp [1894] AC 607 205

Lubbock *v.* Tribe (1838) 3 M & W 607 451

Lumsden & Co. *v.* London Trustee Savings Bank [1971] 1 Lloyd's Rep. 114.. 427, 428, 429, 438

MacKenzie *v.* Imperial Bank [1938] 2 DLR 764 134

MacKinnon *v.* Donaldson Lufkin & Jenrette Securities Corporation [1986] 1 All ER 653 .... *111*

McCall Bros. Ltd. *v.* Hargreaves [1932] 2 KB 423 502

McDonald (Gerald) & Co. *v.* Nash & Co. [1922] WN 272 .... 307, 502, 511

McEvoy *v.* Belfast Banking Co. [1935] AC 24.................................. *173*, 203, 223

McInerny *v.* Lloyds Bank Ltd. [1974] 1 Lloyd's Rep. 246 461

McIntosh (D.W.) Ltd. *v.* Royal Bank of Canada [1940] 3 DLR 782 157

McKenzie *v.* British Linen Co. (1881) 6 App. Cas. 82................................291, 298

McLean *v.* Clydesdale Banking Corporation (1883) 9 App. Cas. 95..........419, 508

McLean *v.* Vessey [1935] 4 DLR 170 172

McMahon *v.* Brewer (1897) 18 LR (NSW) Eq. 88 93

Macbeth *v.* North and South Wales Bank [1908] 1 KB 13, affd. [1908] AC 137 413

Mackersy *v.* Ramsays, Bonars & Co. (1843) 9 Cl. & F 818 369

Macleod Savings and Credit Union Ltd. *v.* Perrett [1978] 6 WWR 178 497

Magill *v.* Bank of North Queensland (1985) 6 QLJ 262 249

Magnolia Petroleum Co. *v.* McMillan 168 SW 2d 881 (1943) 394

Mahoney *v.* East Holyford Mining Co. (in Liq.) (1875) LR 7 HL 869 192

Mal Bower's Macquarie Electrical Centre Pty. Ltd., Re [1974] 1 NSWLR 254 283

Man (E.D. & F.) Ltd. *v.* Nigerian Sweets and Confectionery Co. Ltd. [1977] 2 Lloyd's Rep. 50 526

Manchester Trust *v.* Furness [1895] 2 QB 539 560

Mander *v.* Evans & Rose (1888) 5 TLR 75 502

Manurewa Transport Ltd., Re [1971] NZLR 909.....................................*565*, 566

Maran Road Saw Mill *v.* Austin Taylor & Co. Ltd. [1975] 1 Lloyd's Rep. 156..*392*, 526

Mardorf Peach & Co. Ltd. *v.* Attica Sea Carriers Corporation of Liberia ('The Laconia') [1977] AC 850 .... *385*

Mareva Compania Naviera SA *v.* International Bulk Carriers SA ('The Mareva') [1975] 2 Lloyd's Rep. 509 276

Marfani & Co. Ltd. *v.* Midland Bank Ltd. [1968] 1 WLR 956 ....79, *425*, 426, 428, 444

Marines (T.C.) Ltd., Re [1973] 34 DLR (3d) 489 157

Marshall *v.* Broadhurst (1831) 1 C & J 403 180

Marshall *v.* Crutwell (1875) LR 20 Eq. 328 .... *172*

Martin *v.* Morgan (1819) 1 Broad & B. 290 318

Martin *v.* Reid (1862) 11 CB (NS) 730 ....*569*, 570

Marzetti *v.* Williams (1830) 1 B & Ad. 415 .... 128, *267*, 311

Mason *v.* Savings Bank of South Australia [1925] SASR 198 52

Mather *v.* Maidstone (1856) 18 CB 273 338

Mathew and Cousins *v.* Sherwell (1810) 2 Taunt. 439 415

Matthews *v.* Williams, Brown & Co. (1894) 10 TLR 386....................................77, *423*

Matthiessen *v.* London and County Bank (1879) 5 CPD 7 421

Maxform SpA *v.* Mariani and Goodville Ltd. [1979] 2 Lloyd's Rep. 385 193

May *v.* Chapman (1834) 16 M & W 355 507

Mecca, The [1897] AC 286 485

Merchanisations (Eaglescliffe) Ltd., Re [1966] Ch. 20 561

Melbourne Corporation *v.* Commonwealth of Australia (1974) 74 CLR 31 52

Mellas *v.* Evriniadis [1972] VR 690 ....*213*, 272

Mercantile Bank of India Ltd. *v.* Central Bank of India Ltd. [1938] AC 287..*553*, 573

Merchant Banking Co. of London *v.* Phoenix Bessemer Steel Co. (1877) 5 Ch. D 205 572

Metropolitan Police Commissioner *v.* Charles [1977] AC 177 .... 392, *397*, 410

Meyappan *v.* Manchanayake (1961) 62 NLR 529 242

Mid-Kent Fruit Factory Ltd., Re [1896] 1 Ch. 567 156

Middleton *v.* Pollock (1875) LR 20 Eq. 515 591

Midland Bank Ltd. *v.* Harris (R.V.) Ltd. [1963] 1 WLR 1021 .... *441*

Midland Bank Ltd. *v.* Reckitt [1933] AC 1 430

Midland Bank Ltd. *v.* Seymour [1955] 2 Lloyd's Rep. 147................. *285*, 368, 457

Miles *v.* Commercial Banking Co. of Sydney (1904) 1 CLR 470 313

Miller *v.* Race (1758) 1 Burr. 452 ....119, 163

Miller *v.* Associates (Australia) Pty. Ltd. *v.* Bennington Pty. Ltd. (1975) 7 ALR 144..243, 256, 508, 512, 513

Mills *v.* Barber (1836) 1 M & W 425 509

Milnes *v.* Dawson (1850) 5 Exch. 948 507

Ministry of Health *v.* Simpson [1951] AC 251 165

Minter *v.* Priest [1930] AC 558 96

Misa *v.* Currie (1876) 1 App. Cas. 554 .... 510, 577, 578

Momm *v.* Barclays Bank International Ltd. [1977] QB 790 378

Monolithic Building Co., Re, Tacon *v.* Monolithic Building Co. [1915] 1 Ch. 463 560

Montague, Re, ex p. Ward (1897) 76 LT 203 199

Montebianco Industrie Tessili SpA *v.* Carlyle Mills (London) Ltd. [1981] 1
Lloyd's Rep. 509 509
Montecchi *v.* Shimco (UK) Ltd. [1979] 1 WLR 1180 509
Moore *v.* Ulster Banking Co. (1877) 11 IR CL 512............................ 215, 220, 224
Morel (E.J.) Ltd., Re [1962] Ch. 21 .... 142, *148*
Morgan *v.* Ashcroft [1938] 1 KB 49 320
Morgan *v.* Jeffreys [1910] 1 Ch. 620 535
Morison *v.* London County and Westminster Bank Ltd. [1914] 3 KB
356 .... 138, 257, 288, 299, *339*, 413, 417, 424, 430,
433, 437
Morley *v.* Culverwell (1840) 7 M & W 174 249
Morrell *v.* Wooten (1852) 16 Beav. 197 367
Morris *v.* Martin (C.W.) & Sons Ltd. [1966] 1 QB 716 467
Morris (K.D.) & Sons Pty. Ltd. (in Liqu.) *v.* Bank of Queensland Ltd. (1980) 54
ALJR 424 525
Morritt, Re, ex p. Official Receiver (1886) 18 QBD 222 .... 568, 570
Moser *v.* Commercial Banking Co. of Sydney Ltd. (1974) 22 FLR 123 430
Moss, Re (1887) 31 Ch. D 90 534
Moss *v.* Hancock [1899] 2 QB 111 163
Motor Traders Guarantee Corporation Ltd. *v.* Midland Bank Ltd. [1937] 4 All
ER 90..432, 436
Muir *v.* Muir (1912) 1 SLT 304 521
Music Makers Pty. Ltd. *v.* Minelle (1968) Qd. R 326 272
Mutual Life and Citizens' Assurance Co. Ltd. *v.* Evatt [1971] AC 793 460,
461, 463, 464
Mutual Mortgage Corporation Ltd, *v.* Bank of Montreal (1965) 55 DLR (2d)
164 291
Mutual Provident Society *v.* Derham (1979) 39 FLR 165 304
Mutton *v.* Peat [1900] 2 Ch. 79 .... 150, *160*

Natal Bank Ltd. *v.* Roorda (1903) TH 298 335
Nathan *v.* Ogdens Ltd. [1905] 93 LT 553, affd. (1905) 94 LT 126 .... *241*
National Bank *v.* Silke [1891] 1 QB 435.. 247, 256
National Bank of Australasia *v.* United Hand-in-Hand and Bank of Hope Co.
(1879) 4 App. Cas. 391 480
National Bank of Australasia Ltd. *v.* Scottish Union and National Insurance Co.
(1951) 84 CLR 177 220
National Bank of New Zealand Ltd. *v.* Walpole and Patterson Ltd. [1975] 2
NZLR 7 ....292, 296
National Bank of South Africa Ltd. *v.* Paterson [1909] 2 LDAB 214 305
National Permanent Benefit Building Society, Re (1869) LR 5 Ch. App. 309 201
National Provincial Bank and Union Bank of England *v.* Charnley [1924] 1 KB
431 561
National Provincial Bank and Union Bank of England *v.* Lindsell [1922] 1 KB
21 553
National Provincial Bank Ltd. *v.* Bishop [1965] Ch. 450.............................. 170, 172
National Sales Corporation Ltd. *v.* Bernardi [1931] 2 KB 188 502

National Westminster Bank Ltd. *v*. Barclays Bank International Ltd. [1975] QB
654..*326*, 334, 335, 338, 340
National Westminster Bank Ltd. *v*. Halesowen Presswork and Assemblies Ltd.
[1972] AC 785 ....*142*, 146, *148*, *155*, *156*, 592
National Westminster Bank plc *v*. Morgan [1985] AC 686 reversing [1983] 3
All ER 85 ....*86*, *95*, *96*
Newall *v*. Tomlinson (1871) LR 6 CP 405 331
Niles *v*. Lake [1947] SCR 291 172
Ninemia Maritime Corp. *v*. Trave Schiffahrtsgesellschaft (The Niedersachsen)
[1984] 1 All ER 398 276
Ningchow, The [1916] P 221 570
Nippon Yusen Kaisha *v*. Karageorgis [1975] 1 WLR 1093 276
Noakes & Co. Ltd. *v*. Rice [1902] AC 24 535
Nocton *v*. Ashburton [1914] AC 932 459
Norman *v*. Federal Commissioner of Taxation (1963) 109 CLR 9 584
North and South Wales Bank Ltd. *v*. Macbeth [1908] AC 137 ....246, 512
North Western Bank Ltd. *v*. John Poynter, Son and Macdonalds [1895] AC
56..*569*, *572*, *573*
Northumberland County Bank *v*. Eyer (1868) 58 Pa. St. 97 396
Nottingham Permanent Benefit Building Society *v*. Thurstan [1903] AC 6 .... *203*
Nova (Jersey) Knit Ltd. *v*. Kammgarn Spinnerei GmbH [1977] 1 WLR
713..*508*, *510*
Nu-Stilo Footwear Ltd. *v*. Lloyds Bank Ltd. (1956) 7 LDAB 121..............429, 436
Number 10 Management Ltd. *v*. Royal Bank of Canada (1977) 69 DLR (3d)
99 415
Nye (C.L.) Ltd., Re [1971] Ch. 442 560

O'Hara *v*. Allied Irish Banks Ltd. [1985] BCLC 52 88
O'Reilly *v*. Richardson (1865) 7 ICLR 74 307
O'Reilly *v*. State Bank of Victoria (1938) 57 ALJR 342 102
O'Rourke *v*. Darbishire [1920] AC 581 96
Oceania Castelana Armadora SA *v*. Mineralimportexport (The Theotokos)
[1983] 2 All ER 65 278
Odessa, The [1916] 1 AC 154..*568*, *571*
Official Assignee of Madras *v*. Mercantile Bank of India Ltd. [1935] AC
53..*552*, *569*, *571*, *574*
Ognibene *v*. Citibank NA (1981) 446 NYS (2d) 845 .... *402*
Olds Discount Ltd. *v*. John Playfair Ltd. [1938] 3 All ER 275 ....**581**
Oliver *v*. Davis [1949] 2 KB 727 ....**508**
Oliver *v*. Woodroffe (1839) 4 M & W 650 ....**202**
Ontario Woodsworth Memorial Foundation *v*. Grozbord (1964) **48 DLR (2d)**
385 291
Operator Control Cabs Ltd., Re [1970] 3 All ER 657 ....**284**
Orbit Mining and Trading Co. *v*. Westminster Bank Ltd. [1963] 1 QB
794..258, 413, 415, 422, **425**, **428**, **4**36, 442
Oriental Financial Corporation *v*. Overend, Gurney & Co. (1871) **LR 7** Ch.
App. 142 524

Orr *v.* Maginnis (1806) 7 East. 359 452
Orwell Steel (Erection and Fabrication) Ltd. *v.* Asphalt and Tarmac (UK) Ltd.
  [1985] 3 All ER 747 276
Österreichische Länderbank *v.* S'Elite Ltd. [1980] 2 All ER 651 506

Palmer *v.* Carey [1926] AC 703 597
Palmer *v.* Pratt (1824) 2 Bing. 185 496
Panama, New Zealand and Australia Royal Mail Co., Re (1870) LR 5 Ch. App.
  318...557, 564
Parry Jones *v.* Law Society [1969] 1 Ch. 1 97
Parsons *v.* Barclay & Co. Ltd. (1910) 103 LT 196 461
Partridge *v.* Bank of England (1846) 9 QB 396 215
Paton *v.* IRC [1938] AC 341 480
Patrick and Lyon Ltd., Re [1933] Ch. 786 563
Paul *v.* Western Canada Lottery Foundation (1981) 127 DLR (3d) 502.....246, 512
Paul and Frank Ltd. *v.* Discount Bank (Overseas) Ltd. [1967] 1 Ch. 348 584
Pearce *v.* Brain [1929] 2 KB 310 ....201, 202
Pearce *v.* Creswick (1843) 2 Hare 286 ....220, 222
Pearce *v.* Morris (1869) LR 5 Ch. App. 227 535
Penmount Estates Ltd. *v.* National Provincial Bank Ltd. (1945) 173 LT
  344..186, 436
Pennington and Owen Ltd., Re [1925] Ch. 825 591
Performing Right Society Ltd. *v.* London Theatre of Varieties Ltd. [1924] AC
  1 583
Perpetoire Opera Co. Ltd., Re (1895) 39 Sol. Jo. 505 284
Photo Production Ltd. *v.* Securicor Transport Ltd. [1980] AC 827 479
Picker *v.* London and County Banking Co. Ltd. (1887) 18 QBD 515 221
Pigot *v.* Cubley (1864) 15 CB (NS) 701 570
Pinto Leite, Re, ex p. Olivaes [1929] 1 Ch. 221..................................216, 217, 585
Planning Associates (Australia) Pty. Ltd. *v.* Commissioner of Stamp Duties
  (1984) 16 ATR 862 598
Plater *v.* Brealey [1938] 4 DLR 765, affd. (no opinion) [1939] 2 DLR 767n 171
Plunkett *v.* Barclays Bank Ltd. [1936] 2 KB 107 ....187, 272, 313
Polak *v.* Everett (1876) 1 QBD 699..261, 571
Pollard Re [1903] 2 KB 41 282
Pollard *v.* Bank of England (1871) LR 6 QB 623 336
Pollitt, Re [1893] 1 QB 455 156
Pollock *v.* Bank of New Zealand [1902] 20 NZLR 174 249
Pollock *v.* Garle [1898] 1 Ch. 1 101
Pollway Ltd. *v.* Abdullah [1974] 1 WLR 493..498, 508
Pool *v.* Pool (1889) 58 LJP 67 376
Port Swettenham Authority *v.* Wu (T.W.) & Co. (M.) Sdn. Bhd. [1979] AC
  580 466
Porter *v.* Latec Finance (Qld.) Pty. Ltd. (1964) 111 CLR 177 ....323, 324
Pott *v.* Clegg (1847) 16 M & W 321 82
Potter, Re (1926) 39 OWN 327 172
Potter *v.* Pearson (1702) 2 Ld Raym. 759 227

Power Curber International Ltd. *v.* National Bank of Kuwait [1981] 1 WLR 1233 445
Price *v.* Neal (1762) 3 Burr. 1354 .... 334, 338, 339, 341
Prideaux *v.* Criddle (1869) LR 4 QB 455 .... 237, 449, 450
Prince *v.* Oriental Bank Corp. (1878) 3 App. Cas. 325 .... 237, 336
Project Development Co. Ltd. *v.* KMK Securities Ltd. [1982] 1 WLR 1470 277
Prosperity Ltd. *v.* Lloyds Bank Ltd. (1923) 39 TLR 372 .... *112*
Pyke *v.* Hibernian Bank Ltd. [1950] IR 195 .... 266, 313, 314

Quistclose Investments Ltd. *v.* Rolls Razor Ltd. [1970] AC 567 93

R. *v.* Bevan, The Times, 24 Oct. 1986 411
R. *v.* Bono (1913) 29 TLR 635 100
R. *v.* Consolidated Churchill Copper Corporation Ltd. [1978] 5 WWR 652 ...... *565*
R. *v.* Duru [1974] 1 WLR 2 498
R. *v.* Gilmartin [1983] 1 All ER 829 411
R. *v.* Grossman (1981) 73 Cr. App. Rep. 302 111
R. *v.* Inhabitants of Longnor (1833) 4 B & Ad. 647 202
R. *v.* Kinghorn [1908] 2 KB 949 101
R. *v.* Kohn [1979] Crim. LR 675 498
R. *v.* Lambie [1982] AC 449 .... *411*
R. *v.* Lovitt [1912] AC 212 211
R. *v.* Marlborough St. Metropolitan Stipendiary Magistrate, ex p. Simpson [1980] Crim. LR 305 .... *100*, 101
R. *v.* Page [1971] 2 QB 330 411
R. *v.* Randall (1811) Russ & Ry. 195 244
R. *v.* Thompson [1984] 3 All ER 565 411
R. *v.* Townshend (1884) 15 Cox CC 466 554
Rahman (Prince Abdul) *v.* Abu-Taha [1980] 1 WLR 1268 276
Rama Corporation Ltd. *v.* Proved Tin and General Investment Ltd. [1952] 2 QB 147 195
Rand Investments Ltd. *v.* Bertrand (1966) 58 DLR (2d) 372 506
Rasu Maritima SA *v.* Perusahaan Pertambangan Minyak dan Gas Bumi Negara (Pertamina) [1978] QB 644 276
Rawley *v.* Rawley (1876) 1 QBD 460 201
Reckitt *v.* Barnett, Pembroke and Slater Ltd. [1929] AC 176 318
Reddie *v.* Williamson (1863) 1 Macph. 228 480
Reeve *v.* Lisle [1902] AC 461 535
Reeves *v.* Capper (1838) 5 Bing. NC 136 569
Regal (Hastings) Ltd. *v.* Gulliver [1942] 1 All ER 378 96
Rehden *v.* Wesley (1861) 29 Beav. 213 59
Reid, Re (1921) 50 Ont. LR 595 172
Reis, Re [1904] 2 KB 769 557
Rekstin *v.* Severo Sibirsko Gosudarstvennoe Akcionernoe Obschestvo Komseverputj [1933] 1 KB 47 .... 274, 377
Rhostar (Pvt.) Ltd. *v.* Netherland Bank of Rhodesia Ltd. [1972] 2 SALR 703 .... 246, 256, 433, 512

Richards *v.* Kidderminster Overseers [1896] 2 Ch. 212 556
Richardson *v.* Commercial Banking Co. of Sydney Ltd. (1952) 85 CLR 110 158
Richardson *v.* Richardson [1927] P 228 272
Richdale, ex. p (1882) 19 Ch. D 409 508
Rickford *v.* Ridge (1810) 2 Camp. 537 449
Riedell *v.* Commercial Bank of Australia Ltd. [1931] VLR 382 237
Rimalt *v.* Wartwright (1924) 40 TLR 803 517
Robarts *v.* Tucker (1851) 16 QB 560 516
Robbie (N.W.) & Co. Ltd. *v.* Witney Warehouses Co. Ltd. [1963] 3 All ER
    613 ....563, 585, 591
Roberts *v.* McLaren, Figgis, decd., Re [1969] 1 Ch. 123 172
Roberts & Co. *v.* Marsh [1915] 1 KB 42 264
Robinson *v.* National Bank of Scotland (1916) SC (HL) 154 459
Robshaw *v.* Smith (1878) 38 LT 423 ....455, 463
Robson *v.* Bennett (1810) 2 Taunt. 388 ....250, 251
Roe's Legal Charge, Re [1982] 2 Lloyd's Rep. 370 ....55, 56
Rogers *v.* Challis (1859) 27 Beav. 175 555
Rogers *v.* Whitley [1892] AC 118 273
Rogerson *v.* Ladbroke (1822) 1 Bing. 94 279
Rolin *v.* Steward (1854) 14 CB 595 ....268, *311*
Rolls Razor Ltd. *v.* Cox [1967] 1 QB 552 593
Rosenberg *v.* International Banking Corporation (1923) 14 L1. LR 344 ....571, 576
Rosenhain *v.* Commonwealth Bank of Australia (1922) 31 CLR 46 497
Ross *v.* London County Westminster and Parr's Bank Ltd. [1919] 1 KB
    678 .... 425, 432, 433, 442
Ross *v.* Royal Bank of Canada (1965) 52 DLR (2d) 578 158
Rother Iron Works Ltd. *v.* Canterbury Precision Engineers Ltd. [1974] QB 1 597
Rouquette *v.* Overmann (1875) LR 10 QB 525 500
Rouse *v.* Bradford Banking Co. [1894] AC 586 478
Rouxel *v.* Royal Bank of Canada [1918] 2 WWR 791 .... *144*
Row Dal Construction Pty. Ltd., Re [1966] VR 249 587
Rowlandson *v.* National Westminster Bank Ltd. [1978] 1 WLR 798 ...... *80*, 94, 95,
                                                                           96, *185*, 202
Roxburgh & Co. *v.* Cox (1881) 17 Ch. D 520 585
Royal Bank *v.* Mack [1932] 1 DLR 753 463
Royal Bank of Canada, Re (1979) 94 DLR (3d) 692 587
Royal Bank of Canada *v.* Bank of Montreal (1976) 67 DLR (3d) 755 484
Royal Bank of Canada *v.* Boyce (1966) 57 DLR (2d) 683 335
Royal Bank of Canada *v.* Concrete Column Clamps (1961) Ltd. (1976) 74 DLR
    (3d) 26 246
Royal Bank of Canada *v.* Hinds (1978) 88 DLR (3d) 428 85
Royal Bank of Canada *v.* Nowosad [1972] 6 WWR 705 463
Royal Bank of Canada *v.* Poisson (1977) 103 DLR (3d) 735 ....*88*, 95
Royal Bank of Canada *v.* R. [1931] 2 DLR 685 335
Royal Bank of Canada *v.* Savage (1983) 126 APR 117 (Can.) 88
Royal Bank of Ireland *v.* O'Rourke [1962] Ir. R 159 .... *237*
Royal Bank of Scotland *v.* Tottenham [1894] 2 QB 715 ....249, 508

Royal British Bank *v.* Turquand (1856) 6 E & B 327 192
Royal Products Ltd. *v.* Midland Bank Ltd. [1981] 2 Lloyd's Rep. 194 368
370, 371, *381*
Royal Trust Co. *v.* Molsons Bank (1912) 8 DLR 478 142
Russell *v.* Scott (1936) 55 CLR 440 .... *171, 173*
Russian Commercial and Industrial Bank, Re [1955] 1 Ch. 148....................83, 113
Rust *v.* Abbey Life Insurance Co. Ltd. [1978] 2 Lloyd's Rep 386..............461, 465
Rutherford *v.* Royal Bank of Canada [1932] 2 DLR 332 134

SCF Finance Co. Ltd. *v.* Marsi [1985] 2 All ER 747 277
SEC *v.* Banca della Svizzera Italiana 92 FRD 111 (1981) 108
Saffron *v.* Société Minière Cafrika (1958) 100 CLR 231 526
Saga of Bond Street Ltd. *v.* Avalon Promotions Ltd. [1972] 2 QB 325 507
Sale Continuation Ltd. *v.* Austin Taylor & Co. Ltd. [1968] 2 QB 849 ....392, 526
Salot *v.* Naidoo [1981] 3 SA LR 959...*496, 521*
Salt *v.* Marquess of Northampton [1892] AC 1 535
Salton *v.* New Beeston Cycle Co. [1900] 1 Ch. 43 376
Samuel *v.* Jarrah Timber and Wood Paving Corporation [1904] AC 323 535
Sanders Bros *v.* Maclean & Co. (1883) 11 QBD 327 ....*529, 571*
Sapelberg *v.* Barclays Bank (DCO) 3 SALR 120 305
Saskatchewan and Western Elevator *v.* Bank of Hamilton (1914) 18 DLR
   411 132
Saunders *v.* Anglia Building Society (Gallie *v.* Lee) [1971] AC 1004 306
Savory & Co. *v.* Lloyds Bank Ltd. [1932] 2 KB 122, affd. [1933] AC 201 424,
437
Sawyer *v.* Thomas (1890) 18 OAR 129 261
Scarth *v.* National Provincial Bank Ltd. (1930) 4 LDAB 241 207
Schioler *v.* Westminster Bank Ltd. [1970] 2 QB 719 95
Scholefield Goodman & Co. Ltd. *v.* Zyngier [1985] 3 All ER 105..............500, 526
Sholfield *v.* Earl of Londesborough [1896] AC 514....................................*292, 518*
Schroeder *v.* Central Bank of London Ltd. (1876) 34 LT 735 265
Schroeder (A.) Music Publishing Co. Ltd. *v.* Macaulay [1974] 1 WLR 1308 490
Scott *v.* Lifford (1808) 1 Camp. 246 508
Scottish Loan and Finance Co. Ltd. *v.* Payne (1935) 52 WN (NSW) 175 506
Searose Ltd. *v.* Seatrain (UK) Ltd. [1981] 1 All ER 806..............................276, 277
Securitibank Ltd., Re [1978] 1 NZLR 97...*524, 526*
Securities Fund Services Inc. *v.* American National Bank and Trust Co. 542 F
   Supp. 323 (1982)...*372, 374*
Selangor United Rubber Estates Ltd. *v.* Cradock (No. 3) [1968] 2 Lloyd's
   Rep. 289...*89, 95, 96, 161, 196*
Sethia (S.L.) Liners Ltd. *v.* State Trading Corporation of India Ltd. [1985] 1
   WLR 1398 307
Sewell *v.* Burdick (1884) 10 App. Cas. 74....................................*569, 571, 572*
Sewell *v.* Corp (1824) 1 Car. & P 392 221
Seymour *v.* Pickett [1905] 1 KB 715 485
Shaddock (L.) & Associates Pty. Ltd. *v.* Council of the City of Parramatta
   (1981) 150 CLR 225 461

Shand *v.* Du Buisson (1874) LR 18 Eq. 283 265
Shephard, Re, Shephard *v.* Cartwright [1953] Ch. 728 202
Sherlec *v.* Wells Fargo Bank 96 Cal. Reptr. 434 (1971) 395
Sherry, Re, London and County Banking Co. *v.* Terry (1883) 25 Ch. D 692 484
Shields' Estate, Re [1901] 1 Ir. R 173 ....52, 53
Shiloh Spinners *v.* Harding [1973] AC 697 490
Shipley *v.* Marshall (1863) 14 CB (NS) 566 582
Siebe Gorman & Co. Ltd. *v.* Barclays Bank Ltd. [1979] 2 Lloyd's Rep.
    142 .... 484, 498, 558, 560, 577, 579, 582,
                                             583, 589
Silverstein *v.* Chartered Bank 392 NYS (2d) 296 (1977) 372
Simm *v.* Anglo-American Telegraph Co. (1879) 5 QBD 188 335
Simmonds *v.* Taylor (1857) 27 LJCP 248 253
Simos *v.* National Bank of Australasia Ltd. (1976) 10 ACTR 4 169
Simson *v.* Ingham (1823) 2 B & C 65 485
Sinclair *v.* Brougham [1914] AC 398 .... *165*
Singer *v.* Yokohama Specie Bank (1944) 47 NYS (2d) 881, affd. (1944) 48 NYS
    (2d) 799, revd. (1946) 58 NE (2d) 726, see further proceedings in (1949) 85
    NE (2d) 894 .... *377*
Singer Manufacturing Co. *v.* Clark (1879) 5 Ex. D 37 568
Skyring *v.* Greenwood and Cox (1825) 4 B & C 281 ....*131*, 328
Slee, Re, ex p. North Western Bank (1872) LR 5 Eq. 69 ....*552*, 553
Slingsby *v.* District Bank Ltd. [1931] 2 KB 588, affd. [1932] 1 KB 544......*307*, 430
Smith *v.* Commercial Banking Co. of Sydney Ltd. (1910) 11 CLR 667 ......305, 310
Smith *v.* Green (1844) 1 Coll. 555 535
Smith *v.* Mercer (1815) 6 Taunt. 76 334
Smith *v.* Nightingale (1818) 2 Stark. 375 497
Smith *v.* Prosser [1907] 2 KB 735 292
Smith *v.* Union Bank of London (1875) LR 10 QB 291, affd. (1875) 1 QBD
    31 ....253, 287, 417
Smith and Baldwin *v.* Barclays Bank Ltd. (1944) 5 LDAB 370 ....433, 436
Smorgon *v.* Australia and New Zealand Banking Group Ltd. (1976) 134 CLR
    475 470
Snyder's Ltd. *v.* Furniture Finance Corporation Ltd. [1931] 1 DLR 398 587
Société Internationale pour Participation Industrielles et Commerciales SA *v.*
    Rogers (1958) 357 US 197 107
Solicitor, A, Re [1952] Ch. 328 ....187, 188
Solomon *v.* Davis (1883) 1 Cab. & E 83 524
Soltykoff, Re, ex p. Margrett [1891] 1 QB 413 ....201, 202
Sommers *v.* Sturdy (1957) 10 DLR (2d) 269 100
Souchette *v.* London County Westminster and Parr's Bank Ltd. (1920) 36 TLR
    195 430
Souhrada *v.* Bank of New South Wales [1976] 2 Lloyd's Rep. 444 .... 176, 257, 434
South Australian Cold Stores Ltd. *v.* Electricity Trust of South Australia (1957)
    98 CLR 65 320
South Staffordshire Tramways Co. *v.* Ebbsmith [1895] 2 QB 669 ....100, 101
Southend-on-Sea Corporation *v.* Hodgson (Hickford) Ltd. [1962] 1 QB 416 190

Southland Savings Bank *v.* Anderson [1974] 1 NZLR 118 ....251, 252, 317, 319, 323, 335
Southwell *v.* Martin (1901) 1 SR (NSW) Eq. 32 180
Sovereign Bank of Canada *v.* Bellhouse, Dillon Co. Ltd. (1911) 23 Que. KB 413 397
Spellman *v.* Spellman [1961] 2 All ER 498 584
Spencer *v.* Clarke (1878) 9 Ch. D 137 600
Stafford *v.* Henry (1850) 12 Ir. Eq. R 400 55
Standard Bank of South Africa Ltd. *v.* Sham Magazine Centre [1977] 1 SALR 484 ....256, 433
Standard Insurance Co. Ltd., Re [1970] 1 NSWLR 392 526
Standard Manufacturing Co., Re [1891] 1 Ch. 627 556
Standish *v.* Ross (1849) 3 Exch. 527 326
Stanton (F. & D.) Ltd., Re [1929] 1 Ch. 180 563
Staunton *v.* Counihan (1957) 92 ILT 32 101
Steane's (Bournmouth) Ltd., Re [1950] 1 All ER 21 284
Steel Wing Co. Ltd., Re [1921] 1 Ch. 349 583
Steele *v.* M'Kinlay (1880) 5 App. Cas. 754 ....502, 503
Stein *v.* Ritherdon (1868) 37 LJ Ch. 369 ....208, 211
Stein *v.* Saywell [1969] ALR 481 ....564, 565
Stenning *v.* Radio and Domestic Finance Ltd. [1961] 1 NZLR 7 506
Stephenson *v.* Hart (1828) 4 Bing. 476 468
Stevens, Re, Stevens *v.* Keily [1888] WN 110 582
Stocks *v.* Dobson (1853) 4 De G M & G 11 586
Stoney Stanton Supplies (Coventry) Ltd. *v.* Midland Bank Ltd. [1966] 2 Lloyd's Rep. 373 ....79, 298, 413, 415
Sully *v.* Frean (1854) 10 Exch. 535 508
Sunderland *v.* Barclays Bank Ltd. (1938) 5 LDAB 163 .... *103*
Sutcliffe & Sons Ltd., Re, ex p. Royal Bank [1933] 1 DLR 562 .... 141, 142, 158
Sutters *v.* Briggs [1922] 1 AC 1 ....254, 578
Swan *v.* Bank of Scotland (1836) 10 Bligh NS 627 203
Swift *v.* Jewsbury (1874) LR 9 QB 301 .... *458*
Swiss Bank Corporation *v.* Lloyds Bank Ltd. [1982] AC 584 ....596, 597, 598
Sydney Wide Stores Pty. Ltd. *v.* Commonwealth Trading Bank (1981) 55 ALJR 574 .... *293*
Syndicat des Camionneurs Artisans du Quebec Metropolitain *v.* Banque Provinciale du Canada (1969) 11 DLR (3d) 610 135
Sze Hai Tong Bank Ltd. *v.* Rambler Cycle Co. Ltd. [1959] AC 576 572
Szek *v.* Lloyd's Bank (1908) 2 LDAB 159 ....312, 313, 314

TDK Tape Distributor (UK) Ltd. *v.* Videochoice Ltd. [1985] 3 All ER 345 277
Taff Vale Railway Co. *v.* Amalgamated Society of Railway Servants [1901] AC 426 197
Tai Hing Cotton Mill Ltd. *v.* Liu Chong Hing Bank Ltd. [1986] AC 80, [1985] 2 Lloyd's Rep. 313, affg. [1984] 1 Lloyd's Rep. 555 ....*136*, 292, 295
Tailby *v.* Official Receiver (1888) 13 App. Cas. 523 ....556, 584
Tancred *v.* Delagoa Bay & East Africa Ry. Co. (1889) 23 QBD 239 ....583, 597

Tankexpress A/S *v.* Compagnie Financière Belge de Pétroles SA [1949] AC
76 385
Tapp *v.* Jones (1875) LR 10 QB 591 .... 274, 592, 595
Tappenden *v.* Artus [1964] 2 QB 185 144
Tarn *v.* Turner (1888) 39 Ch. D 456 535
Tassell *v.* Cooper (1850) 9 CB 509 166
Tate *v.* Wilts and Dorset Bank (1899) 1 LDAB 286; 20 JIB 376 77
Tatton *v.* Wade (1856) 18 CB 371 458
Taylor *v.* Russell [1892] AC 244 561
Teevan *v.* Smith (1882) 20 Ch. D 724 535
Temple Terrace Assets Co. Inc. *v.* Whynot [1934] 1 DLR 124 497
Tenax Steamship Co. Ltd. *v.* Brimnes (Owners of) ('The Brimnes') [1975] QB
929 384
Texaco Inc. *v.* Goldstein (1962) 229 NYS (2d) 51, (1963) affd. 241 NYS (2d)
495 394
Thairwall *v.* Great Northern Ry. Co. [1910] 2 KB 509 241
Thomas *v.* Central Charge Services Inc. (1965) 212 A (2d) 533 394
Thomas *v.* Houston Corbett & Co. [1969] NZLR 151 331
Thomson *v.* Clydesdale Bank Ltd. [1893] AC 282 .... 93, 127, 163, 183, *184*, 432
Thomson *v.* Federal Commissioner of Taxation (1949) 80 CLR
344 .... 173, 223, 224
Thoni GmbH & Co. KG *v.* RPT Equipment Ltd. [1979] 2 Lloyd's Rep.
282 .... 508, 509
Thornett *v.* Barclays Bank (France) Ltd. [1939] 1 KB 675 463
Thornton *v.* Maynard (1875) LR 10 CP 695 510
Tidd, Re Tidd *v.* Overell, [1893] 3 Ch. 154 .... 82, 221
Tina Motors Pty. Ltd *v.* Australia and New Zealand Banking Group Ltd.
[1977] VR 205 .... 138, 291, 438
Tom Shaw & Co. *v.* Moss Empires Ltd. and Bastow (1908) 25 TLR 190 584
Torkington *v.* Magee [1902] 2 KB 427 599
Tournier *v.* National Provincial and Union Bank of England [1924] 1 KB
461 .... 98, 103, 104, 107, 456
Trade Development Bank *v.* Continental Insurance Co. 469 F 2d 35 (1972) 108
Transvaal and Delagoa Bay Investment Co. Ltd. *v.* Atkinson [1944] 1 All ER
579 .... 165, 166, 326, 330, 331
Travis *v.* Milne (1851) 9 Hare 141 180
Tropic Plastic and Packaging Industry *v.* Standard Bank of South Africa Ltd.
[1969] 4 SA LR 108 497
Tucker *v.* Linger (1883) 8 App. Cas. 508 221
Turcan, Re (1889) 40 Ch. D 5 584
Turner *v.* London and Provincial Bank Ltd. (1903) 2 LDAB 33 .... 427, 433
Twibell *v.* London Suburban Bank [1869] WN 127 .... 169, 170

Underwood (A.L.) Ltd. *v.* Bank of Liverpool and Martins [1924] 1 KB
775 .... 195, 268, 413, 419, 425, 426, 428, 430, 440
Union Bank of Australia *v.* Murray–Aynsley [1898] AC 693 .... *151*, 183
Union Oil Co. of California *v.* Lull (1960) 349 P 2d 243 394

United Australia Ltd. *v.* Barclays Bank Ltd. [1941] AC 1 .... 288, 413, 431
United Dominions Trust *v.* Kirkwood [1966] 2 QB 431.............................37, *53*
United Overseas Bank *v.* Jiwani [1976] 1 WLR 964 .... *132*
United Service Co., Re (1871) LR 6 Ch. App. 212 .... 467, *577*, 578
United States *v.* Bank of Nova Scotia (1976) 691 F 2d 1384 108
United States *v.* Field (1976) 532 F 2d 404 ....*107*, 108
United States *v.* First National City Bank (1968), 396 F 2d 897 affd. 285 F
    Supp. 845 (1968) sub nom. Re First National City Bank *107*
United States of America and Republic of France *v.* Dollfuss Mieg et Cie SA and
    Bank of England [1952] AC 582 469
Universal Guarantee Pty. Ltd. *v.* Derefink [1958] VR 51 273
Universal Guarantee Pty. Ltd. *v.* National Bank of Australasia Ltd. [1965] 1
    Lloyd's Rep. 525 ....256, 257
Universal Permanent Building Society *v.* Cooke [1952] Ch. 95 549

Vagliano Bros. *v.* Bank of England (1889) 23 QBD 243 137
Valentini *v.* Canali (1890) 24 QBD 166..201, 202
Vance *v.* Lowther (1876) 1 Ex. D 176 240
Varker *v.* Commercial Banking Co. of Sydney Ltd. [1972] 2 NSWLR 967 438
Victoria Steamboats Ltd., Re [1897] 1 Ch. 158 564
Vinden *v.* Hughes [1905] 1 KB 795...246, 512

Walker *v.* Bradford Old Bank Ltd. (1884) 12 QBD 511 367
Walker *v.* Manchester and Liverpool District Banking Co. Ltd. (1913) 108 LT
    728 133
Wall, Re (1885) 1 TLR 522 183
Wallinder *v.* Imperial Bank of Canada [1925] 4 DLR 390 154
Wallis, Re, ex p. Jenks [1902] 1 KB 719 601
Wallyn Industries Pty. Ltd., Re (1983) 7 ACLR 661 583
Walter and Sullivan Ltd. *v.* Murphy & Sons Ltd. [1955] 2 QB 584 367
Walters *v* Neary (1904) 21 TLR 146 513
Walton *v.* Mascall (1844) 13 M & W 452 82
Ward, Re Ward *v.* Warwick [1946] 2 All ER 206 223
Warner Bros. Records Inc. *v.* Rollgreen Ltd. [1976] QB 430 586
Warren Metals Ltd. *v.* Colonial Catering Co. Ltd. [1975] 1 NZLR 273 79
Warwick *v.* Nairn (1855) 10 Exch. 762 508
Waters *v.* Widdows [1984] VR 503 583
Watson *v.* Duff Morgan & Vermont (Holdings) Ltd. [1974] 1 WLR 450 562
Watson *v.* Parapara Coal Co. Ltd. (1951) 17 GLR 791 582
Watson *v.* Russell (1864) 5 B & S 968...504, 510
Watts *v.* Christie (1849) 11 Beav. 546...153, *179*
Watts *v.* Public Trustee (1949) 50 SR (NSW) 130 224
Wauthier *v.* Wilson (1912) 28 TLR 239, affg. (1927) 27 TLR 582 ....*204*, 522
Webb *v.* Stenton (1883) 11 QBD 518 272
Webb (Genny) Transport *v.* Brenner [1985] 5 CL 19 273
Welch *v.* Bank of England [1955] Ch. 508 169
Weld Blundell *v.* Stephens [1920] AC 956 103

Weniger's Policy, Re [1910] 2 Ch. 291 600
West *v.* Commercial Bank of Australia Ltd. (1935) 55 CLR 315 298
West Bay Sales Ltd., Re (1979) 30 CBR (NS) 274 157
Westinghouse Uranium Contract, Re [1978] AC 547................................*105*, 108
Westminster Bank Ltd. *v.* Arlington Overseas Trading Co. [1952] 1 Lloyd's
  Rep. 211 319
Westminster Bank Ltd. *v.* Hilton (1926) 43 TLR 124 .... 91, 285, 299
Westminster Bank Ltd. *v.* Zang [1966] AC 182 .... 268, 419, 435, 441
Whistler *v.* Forster (1863) 14 CB (NS) 248 ....*509*, 513
White *v.* City of London Brewery Co. (1889) 42 Ch. D 237 545
Whitehouse & Co., Re (1878) 9 Ch. D 959 591
Wigzell, Re, ex p. Hart [1921] 2 KB 835 281
Wilkinson *v.* Johnson (1823) 3 B & C 428 339
Wilkinson *v.* London and County Banking Co. (1884) 1 TLR 63 577
William Bean & Son *v.* Flaxton Rural District Council [1929] 1 KB
  450...190, 198
William Brand's Sons & Co. *v.* Dunlop Rubber Co. Ltd. [1905] AC
  454...323, 366
Williams *v.* Atlantic Assurance Co. Ltd. [1933] 1 KB 81............................367, 583
Williams *v.* Ayers (1877) 3 App. Cas. 133 243
Williams *v.* Bayley (1866) LR 1 HL 200 298
Williams *v.* Burlington Investments Ltd. (1977) 12 SJ 424 556
Williams *v.* Curzon Syndicate Ltd. (1919) 35 TLR 475 467
Williams *v.* Davies (1864) 3 Sw. & Tr. 437 172
Williams *v.* Everett (1811) 14 East. 582 367
Williams *v.* Mason (1873) 28 LT 232 458
Williams *v.* Morgan [1906] 1 Ch. 804 535
Williams *v.* Summerfield [1972] 2 QB 512 .... *100*
Williams *v.* Williams (1693) Carth. 269 227
Williams *v.* Williams (1980) SLT 25 506
Williams and Glyn's Bank *v.* Barnes [1980] Com. LR 205 ....479, *481*
Williams and Glyn's Bank *v.* Belckin Packaging Ltd. (1981) 123 DLR (3d)
  612 506
Williams and Glyn's Bank Ltd. *v.* Boland [1979] Ch. 312 200
Williams Deacon & Co. *v.* Shadbolt (1885) 1 TLR 417 515
Williams Porter & Co. Ltd., Re [1937] 2 All ER 361 265
Williamson *v.* Rider [1963] 1 QB 89..496, 521
Willis *v.* Association of Universities of the British Commonwealth [1964] 2 All
  ER 39 197
Willis, Percival & Co. Ltd., Re, ex p. Morier (1879) 12 Ch. D 491 153
Wilson, Re, ex p. Salaman [1926] 1 Ch. 21 281
Wilson *v.* Kearse (1800) Peake Add. Cas. 196 202
Wilson *v.* Kelland [1910] 2 Ch. 306 560
Wilson *v.* United Counties Bank Ltd. [1920] AC 102................................312, 466
Wilson and Meeron *v.* Pickering [1946] KB 422 292
Wilton *v.* Commonwealth Trading Bank of Australia [1973] 2 NSWLR 644 438
Windsor Refrigerator Co. Ltd. *v.* Branch Nominees Ltd. [1961] Ch. 375 564

Wise *v.* Perpetual Trustee Co. Ltd. [1903] AC 139 198
Wood *v.* Clydesdale Bank Ltd. (1914) SC 397 .... 212, 222
Woodhams *v.* Anglo-Australian and Universal Family Assurance Co. (1861) 3 Giff. 234 .... 215, 220
Woodland *v.* Fear (1857) 7 El. & Bl. 519 .... 129, 270, 336, 447
Woods *v.* Martins Bank Ltd. [1959] 1 QB 55 .... *52, 78, 85, 89, 96,*
453, 463, 464, 465, 466
Woollatt *v.* Stanley (1928) 138 LT 620 518
Wrightson *v.* McArthur and Hutchinsons (1919) Ltd. [1921] 2 KB 807 ..... 569, 574
Wylde *v.* Radford (1863) 33 LJ Ch. 51 577

X AG *v.* A Bank [1983] 2 All ER 464 .... *108,* 110

Yates, ex p. (1857) 2 De G & J 191 503
Yeoman Credit Ltd. *v.* Gregory [1963] 1 WLR 343 .... 451, 502
Yeoman Credit Ltd. *v.* Latter [1961] 1 WLR 828 .... *203*
Yglesias, Re, ex p. Gomez (1875) LR 10 Ch. App. 619 524
Yianni *v.* Edwin Evans & Sons [1982] QB 438 460
Yonge *v.* Toynbee [1910] 1 KB 215 .... 206, 280
Yorkshire Woolcombers Association Ltd., Re [1903] 2 Ch. 284 .... 557, 558
Young *v.* Glover (1857) 3 Jur. (NS) 627 503
Young *v.* Grote (1827) 4 Bing. 253 .... 229, 292
Young *v.* Kitchin (1878) 3 Ex. D 127 585
Young *v.* Lambert (1870) LR 3 PC 142 .... 569, 574
Young *v.* Sealey [1949] Ch. 278 172
Yourell *v.* Hibernian Bank Ltd. [1918] AC 372 480

Z Ltd. *v.* A–Z [1982] QB 558 .... 276, 278
Zephyr, The [1984] 1 Lloyd's Rep. 58, revd. [1985] 2 Lloyd's Rep. 529 371
Zivnostenska Banka National Corporation *v.* Frankman [1950] AC 57 470

Table of Statutes

ENGLAND

1694	Bank of England Act (5 & 6 Will. & Mar., c. 20)	27
1696	Bank of England Act (8 & 9 Will. 3, c.20)	28
1704	Bills of Exchange Act (3 & 4 Anne, c. 9)	227
1716	Bank of England Act (3 Geo.1, c. 8)	25
1774	Life Assurance Act (14 Geo. 3, c. 48)	
	s. 1	601
1800	Bank of England Act (39 & 40 Geo. 3, c. 28)	28
1815	Stamp Act (55 Geo. 5, c. 184)	
	s. 12	318
1826	Bank Notes Act (7 Geo. 4, c. 6)	29
1828	Statute of Frauds Amendment Act (9 Geo. 4, c. 14)	
	s. 6 ....458, 459	
1836	Benefit Building Societies Act (6 & 7 Will. 4, c. 32)	21
1840	Loan Societies Act (3 & 4 Vict., c. 110)	45
1844	Bank Charter Act (7 & 8 Vict., c. 32)	
	s. 1	29
	s. 11 ....29, 251	
1853	Stamp Act (16 & 17 Vict., c. 32)	
	s. 19 ....57, 227, 253, 305, 306, 448	
1856	Crossed Cheques Act (19 & 20 Vict., c. 25)	253
	Foreign Tribunal Tribunals Evidence Act (19 & 20 Vict., c. 113)	105
1858	Crossed Cheques Act (21 & 22 Vict., c. 79)	253
1861	Forgery Act (24 & 25 Vict., c. 98)	
	s. 22	299
1862	Companies Act (25 & 26 Vict., c. 89)	
	s. 47	193
1863	Trustee Savings Banks Act (26 & 27 Vict., c. 87)	11
1867	Policies of Assurance Act (30 & 31 Vict., c. 144)	
	s. 1	600
	s. 2	600
	s. 3	600
	s. 5	600
	s. 6	600
1873	Judicature Act (36 & 37 Vict., c. 66)	
	s. 25(6)	588
1874	Building Societies Act (37 & 38 Vict., c. 42)	21
	Infants' Relief Act (37 & 38 Vict., c. 62)	
	s. 1 ....200, 203	
	s. 1(1)	201

1874	Infants' Relief Act—*cont.*	
	s. 1(2)	200
1876	Crossed Cheque Act (39 & 40 Vict., c. 81)	253
	s. 4	421
	s. 9	306
	s. 12	421
1878	Bills of Sale Act (41 & 42 Vict., c. 31)	
	s. 4	553, 554, 556, 587
	s. 8	551
	s. 10	551
1879	Bankers' Books Evidence Act (42 & 43 Vict., c. 11)	60, 99
	s. 3	99
	s. 4	99
	s. 5	99
	s. 6	99
	s. 7	99, 102, 111
	s. 9	61
	s. 10	*101*
1882	Bills of Exchange Act (45 & 46 Vict., c. 61)	45, 56, 61, 74, 75
	s. 2	*51*, 228, 242, *503*, *504*
	s. 3	227, *364*, *365*, 422
	s. 3(1)	*239*, 496
	s. 3(2)	496
	s. 3(3)	*240*, 496
	s. 4(1)	262
	s. 4(2)	262
	s. 5	496
	s. 6(2)	496
	s. 7(1)	244
	s. 7(2)	496
	s. 7(3)	244, 246, 512
	s. 8(1)	246, 247, 514
	s. 8(3)	*243*, 512
	s. 8(4)	*243*, 247, *365*, 512, 514
	s. 8(5)	*243*, 512
	s. 10(1)	239
	s. 10(1)(a)	365
	s. 10(1)(b)	*249*, 365
	s. 11	497
	s. 11(2)	496
	s. 12	507
	s. 13	318
	s. 13(2)	249
	s. 16(1)	511
	s. 16(2)	511
	s. 17(1)	500
	s. 17(2)(a)	500

s. 18 251
s. 18(1) 501
s. 18(2) 501
s. 19 ....304, 500
s. 19(2)(c) 503
s. 20(1) 292
s. 20(2) 507
s. 21 512
s. 21(1) 515
s. 21(2) 507, 515
s. 21(3) 515
s. 22 .... *201*
s. 22(1) 202
s. 22(2) 202
s. 24 ....298, 334, 415
s. 26 459
s. 27 158
s. 27(1) 326, 508
s. 27(2) 508, 509
s. 27(3) 420, 509, 578
s. 28(1) *523, 525*
s. 28(2) 523
s. 29 ....228, 440, 505, 506
s. 29(2) 505, 509
s. 29(3) 507
s. 30(1) 506
s. 30(2) 505, 506
s. 31(1) 511
s. 31(2) 228, 302, 512
s. 31(3) 228, 359, 513
s. 31(4) 513
s. 32 513
s. 32(5) 513
s. 34(1) 512
s. 34(2) 512
s. 34(3) 514
s. 34(4) *243*
s. 35(1) 514
s. 35(2) 514
s. 35(3) 514
s. 36(3) 240, 505
s. 37 ....*193*, 503, 515
s. 38(1) 228, 239, 507, 509
s. 38(2) 506, 507, 509
s. 39 510
s. 39(1) 501
s. 39(2) 501, 511

1882 Bills of Exchange Act—*cont.*
   s. 39(3) 501
   s. 40 510
   s. 40(1) 510
   s. 40(2) 511
   s. 41 510
   s. 41(2) 510
   s. 43(2) 511
   s. 44 500
   s. 45 .... 260, 510, 511
   s. 45(2) 259, 449
   s. 45(4)(a) 503
   s. 46(1) 511
   s. 46(2)(a) 511
   s. 46(2)(c) 511, 523
   s. 46(2)(d) 511, 523
   s. 46(2)(e) 511
   s. 47(2) 511
   s. 48 .... 261, 452, 519
   s. 49 .... 261, 452
   s. 49(b) 261
   s. 49(5) 519
   s. 49(6) 519
   s. 49(12) 519
   s. 49(13) 235, 261, 452
   s. 49(14) 519
   s. 50 519
   s. 50(1) 340
   s. 50(2) 452
   s. 50(2)(c) 261, 340
   s. 51(1) 520
   s. 51(2) 262, 520
   s. 51(9) 523
   s. 51(2)(c) 523
   s. 51(2)(d) 523
   s. 51(3) 520
   s. 51(4) 520
   s. 51(5) 520
   s. 51(6) 520
   s. 51(7) 520
   s. 51(8) 520
   s. 51(9) 520
   s. 52(1) 519
   s. 52(2) 519
   s. 52(2)(c) 502
   s. 52(3) 519
   s. 52(4) 519

s. 53 500
s. 53(1) 229, 239, 265, 289, 500
s. 53(2) 265
s. 54...245, 495
s. 54(1) 501
s. 54(2) 507
s. 55(1)(a) 500
s. 55(2) 240, 248, 501, 507
s. 56...501, 502
s. 58(1) 513
s. 58(2) 513
s. 58(3) 513
s. 59... 287, 302, 515, 516
s. 59(1) 516
s. 59(2) 517
s. 59(3) 524
s. 60...57, 227, 304, 309, 310, 445, 446, 447, 448, 515
s. 61...515, 516, 517
s. 61(1) 517
s. 62...515, 516
s. 62(2) 517
s. 63...515, 516
s. 63(1) 517
s. 63(2) 517
s. 63(3) 518
s. 64...286, 290, 334, 415, 515, 516
s. 64(1) 240, 255, 518
s. 64(2) 240, 507, 518
s. 69 359
s. 70 359
s. 73...57, 193, 227, 239, 249
s. 74 449
s. 74(1) 259, 260, 451
s. 74(2) 259
s. 74(3) 260
s. 75 397
s. 75(1) 229
s. 75(2) 278, 279, 280
s. 76 254
s. 76(1) 253
s. 76(2) 253
s. 77...253, 254
s. 78...253, 255
s. 79...230, 253
s. 79(1) 255
s. 79(2) 255, 287, 416
s. 80...253, 255, 306, 309, 416, 445, 498

1882   Bills of Exchange Act—*cont.*
      s. 81...253, 254, 255
      s. 82.............................76, 253, 421, 423, 424, 439, 447
      s. 83...227, 520
      s. 84 521
      s. 86 521
      s. 87(1) 521
      s. 87(2) 521
      s. 89(1) 521
      s. 89(2) 521
      s. 89(3) 521
      s. 89(4) 521
      s. 90 505
      s. 93 520
      s. 94 520
      s. 95 258
    Bills of Sale Act (1878) Amendment Act (45 & 46 Vict., c. 43)
      s. 5 552
      s. 7A 540
      s. 8 551
      s. 9...551, 556
      s. 17 556
    Married Women's Property Act (45 & 46 Vict., c. 75)
      s. 7 199
1889   Factors Act (52 & 53 Vict., c. 45)
      s. 1(4) 571
      s. 2 573
1890   Partnership Act (53 & 54 Vict., c. 39)
      s. 5...176, 482
      s. 6 176
      s. 33 179
      s. 36(3) 482
      s. 37 482
      s. 38 179
1891   Bills of Sale Act (54 & 55 Vict., c. 34)
      s. 1 555
1892   Betting and Loans (Infants) Act (55 & 56 Vict., c. 4) 201
1900   Money-lenders Act (63 & 64 Vict., c. 51) 63
      s. 6(d) 54
1906   Bills of Exchange (Crossed Cheques) Act (6 Edw. 7, c. 17) 418
      s. 1 439
      s. 1(b) 440
1913   Forgery Act (3 & 4 Geo. 5, c. 27)
      s. 1(1) 298
1914   Bankrupcty Act (4 & 5 Geo. 5, c. 59)
      s. 7(2) 533
      s. 18 532

s. 30(3) 592
s. 31.. 143, 156, 157, 592
s. 33 532
s. 37 280
s. 38(c) 572
s. 43(1) 587
s. 44 158
s. 45 .... 158, 281, 477
s. 46 281
s. 62(1) 533
s. 126 572
Schedule 2, para. 10 533

1925 Administration of Estates Act (15 & 16 Geo. 5, c. 23)
s. 39 180
s. 40 180
s. 49 180

Land Registration Act (15 & 16 Geo. 5, c. 21)
s. 25(1) 543
s. 27(1) 543
s. 48 546
s. 49 546

Law of Property Act (15 & 16 Geo. 5, c. 20)
s. 1 542
s. 40(1) 544
s. 49(3) 548
s. 50 546
s. 86(1) 543
s. 87(1) 543
s. 88(2) 545
s. 89(1) 545
s. 90(1) 545
s. 91(2) 545
s. 94(1) 546, 547
s. 94(2) 547
s. 99 549
s. 99(13) 549
s. 99(19) 545
s. 101(1) 544, 545, 546
s. 101(4) 544, 546
s. 103 600
s. 107 601
s. 109(1) 545
s. 109(3) 545
s. 136...215, 366, 581, 583, 597
s. 136(a) 583
s. 136(1) 274
s. 198(1) 547

1925	Law of Property Act—*cont.*	
	s. 205(1)	552
	Trustee Act (15 & 16 Geo. 5, c. 19)	61
	s. 11	182
	s. 16	182
	s. 17	182
	s. 18	182
	s. 21	180
	s. 23	181
	s. 25	181
	s. 28	182
1926	Bankruptcy (Amendment) Act (16 & 17 Geo. 5, c. 7)	
	s. 4	282
1927	Landlord and Tenant Act (17 & 18 Geo. 5, c. 36)	
	s. 19	543
1928	Agricultural Credits Act (18 & 19 Geo. 5, c. 13)	
	s. 5	59
	Currency and Bank Notes Act (18 & 19 Geo. 5, c. 13)	29
1932	Solicitors Act (22 & 23 Geo. 5, c. 37)	
	s. 65(2)	242
1935	Law Reform (Married Women and Tortfeasers) Act (25 & 26 Geo. 5, c. 30)	291
1936	Income Tax Assessment Act (26 Geo. 5 & 1 Edw. 8, c. 34)	
	s. 264	471
1945	Law Reform (Contributory Negligence) Act (8 & 9 Geo. 6, c. 28)	
	s. 1	438
1946	Bank of England Act (9 & 10 Geo. 6, c. 27)	
	s. 1	30
	s. 4	48
	s. 4(1)	30
	s. 4(2)	30
	s. 4(3)	*31*
	s. 4(4)	31
	s. 4(6)	74
	s. 26	27
	s. 27	27
1947	Exchange Control Act (10 & 11 Geo. 6, c. 14)	27, 357
	s. 42	75
1948	Companies Act (11 & 12 Geo. 6, c. 38)	
	s. 33	193
	s. 95(1)(e)	586
	s. 108(4)	193
	s. 227	283
	s. 229	283
	s. 302	596
	s. 317	156, 533, 592
	s. 320	158

Table A, art. 79 192
1954 Currency and Bank Notes Act (2 & 3 Eliz. 2, c. 12)
s. 2 29
Trustee Savings Banks Act (2 & 3 Eliz. 2, c. 63) 11
1956 Administration of Justice Act (4 & 5 Eliz. 2, c. 46)
s. 38 .... 211, 218, 272
Restrictive Trade Practices Act (4 & 5 Eliz. 2, c. 68) 346
Sexual Offences Act (4 & 5 Eliz. 2, c. 69)
s. 30 100
1957 Cheques Act (5 & 6 Eliz. 2, c. 36) 56, 76, 286
s. 1 .... 306, 445
s. 1(1) 309
s. 1(2) 309
s. 2 441
s. 3 .... 134, 234
s. 4 .... 76, 253, 257, 330, 405, 438, 439, 440, 445, 447
s. 4(1) 422, 444
s. 4(1)(b) 418, 444
s. 4(2) 422
s. 4(2)(b) 258
s. 4(2)(c) 258
s. 4(2)(d) 258
s. 4(3) 435
s. 5 258
1958 Prevention of Fraud (Investments) Act (6 & 7 Eliz. 2, c. 45)
s. 16 60
1960 Building Societies Act (8 & 9 Eliz. 2, c. 64) 21
Payment of Wages Act (8 & 9 Eliz. 2, c. 37)
s. 1 59
s. 7 59
1961 Finance Act (9 & 10 Eliz. 2, c. 36) 249
Suicide Act (9 & 10 Eliz. 2, c. 60)
s. 1 601
1962 Building Societies Act (10 & 11 Eliz. 2, c. 37) 21, 44
s. 2 22
s. 3 22
1963 Protection of Depositors Act (c. 16) 31, 59, 60
1964 Married Women's Property Act (c. 19) 199
1965 Administration of Estates (Small Payments) Act (c. 32) 12
1967 Companies Act (c. 81) 54
1968 Port of London Act (c. xxxii)
s. 164 571
Theft Act (c. 60)
s. 16 410
1969 Post Office Act (c. 48) 13
s. 7(1)(b) 13
Trustee Savings Banks Act (c. 50) 11

1970 Finance Act (c. 24)
    s. 32 249
    Income and Corporation Taxes Act (c. 10)
    s. 19 491
    s. 54 58
    s. 54(2) 58
    s. 481 102
    s. 518(3) 102
    Taxes Management Act (c. 9)
    s. 24 102
1971 Banking and Financial Dealings Act (c. 80) 61
    Finance Act (c. 68)
    s. 64 581
    s. 69 581
    Powers of Attorney Act (c. 27)
    s. 4(1) 545
    s. 9(4) 181
1972 European Communities Act (c. 68)
    s. 9(1) *191*, 195, 196
    Land Charges Act (c. 61)
    s. 2(4) 546
    s. 3(7) 559
    s. 3(8) 559
    s. 17(1) 559
    Local Government Act (c. 70)
    s. 172 189
    Schedule 13 189
        para. 1 189
        para. 2 190
        para. 10(1) 189
        para. 20 .... *190*
1974 Consumer Credit Act (c. 39) 47, 62, 262, 391, 392, 393, 476, 488
    s. 4 405
    s. 8 ....64, 485
    s. 8(1) 404
    s. 8(2) 62
    s. 8(3) 63, 403, 404
    s. 9 ....63, 485
    s. 10 65
    s. 10(1) 485
    s. 10(1)(b) 64
    s. 10(2) 486
    s. 10(3) 65
    s. 11 394
    s. 12 73
    s. 12(b) 409
    s. 12(c) 409

s. 13(c) 404
s. 14 .... 402, 403, 405
s. 14(1) 401
s. 14(1)(b) 402
s. 14(2) 403, 405
s. 14(3) 402, 409
s. 14(4) 403
s. 15 64
s. 15(2) 63
s. 16 .... 64, 404, 549
s. 18(2) 486
s. 19 73
s. 19(1)(b) 410
s. 19(3) 73
s. 20 .... 66, 486
s. 21 65
s. 23(3) 70
s. 25 65
s. 31 65
s. 32 65
s. 33 65
s. 39 65
s. 40 65
s. 41 65
s. 43 69
s. 44 69
s. 46 69
s. 48 70
s. 49 .... 70, 487
s. 49(3) 70, 487
s. 51(1) 407
s. 51(2) 407
s. 51(3) 407
s. 52 .... 71, 486
s. 56 486
s. 57 550
s. 57(1) 73, 410
s. 57(4) 550
s. 58 .... 67, 550
s. 58(1) 490
s. 58(2) 67, 492
s. 60 .... 66, 487, 490
s. 61 66
s. 61(b) 491
s. 61(2) 67
s. 62 .... 66, 492
s. 63 .... 66, 492

1974 Consumer Credit Act—*cont.*

s. 63(2) 408
s. 63(4) 408
s. 63(5) 408
s. 64 66
s. 64(1) 408
s. 64(1)(b) 492
s. 64(2) 408
s. 65 66
s. 66 406
s. 66(2) 406
s. 67 .... 67, 490, 549
s. 67(a) 550
s. 68 67
s. 69(1) 73, 410
s. 70 73
s. 70(3) 408
s. 70(5) 408
s. 74(1)(b) 63, 404, 486
s. 74(3) 63, 486
s. 74(3)(a) 63, 486
s. 75 409
s. 75(1) 73, 409
s. 75(2) 409
s. 75(3) 73, 409
s. 76(1) 487, 493, 539
s. 76(2) 487
s. 77 .... 67, 492
s. 78 67
s. 78(4) 487
s. 81 .... 69, 484
s. 82 67
s. 82(2) 486, 492
s. 83 406
s. 83(1) 405
s. 83(2) 405
s. 84 .... 405, 406
s. 84(1) 405
s. 84(2) 405
s. 84(3) 405
s. 84(4) 405
s. 84(5) 406
s. 84(6) 406
s. 84(7) 405
s. 84(8) 406
s. 85(1) 408
s. 85(2) 408

s. 87 .... 68, 487, 493
s. 88 .... 68, 493
s. 88(3) 68
s. 93 68
s. 94 68
s. 95 68
s. 96 68
s. 97 68
s. 98 .... 69, 493
s. 105 .... 536, 539
s. 105(1) 537
s. 105(2) 537, 538
s. 105(3) 538
s. 105(4) 538
s. 105(5) 538
s. 105(6) 537
s. 105(7) 537, 539
s. 105(9) 538
s. 106 .... 536, 537, 538, 539
s. 107 539
s. 107(1)(c) 539
s. 107(4) 539
s. 108 539
s. 108(1)(c) 539
s. 108(4) 539
s. 109 539
s. 109(1)(c) 539
s. 109(4) 539
s. 110 539
s. 111(1) 539
s. 111(2) 539
s. 112 .... 537, 540
s. 113 540
s. 113(1) 537, 540
s. 113(2) 538, 540
s. 113(3) 538, 540
s. 113(3)(c) 540
s. 113(4) 538
s. 113(5) 538
s. 113(6) 536
s. 113(7) 538
s. 114(1) 576
s. 114(3)(a) 575
s. 116(1) 576
s. 116(2) 576
s. 116(3) 576
s. 117 576

1974 Consumer Credit Act—*cont.*
    s. 119(1) 576
    s. 120 576
    s. 121 576
    s. 121(3) 576
    s. 121(6) 576
    s. 123 228
    s. 123(1) 527
    s. 123(2) 262, 527
    s. 123(3) 262, 527
    s. 123(4) 527
    s. 123(5) 527
    s. 125(1) 527
    s. 126 550
    s. 127(3) 491
    s. 137 64
    s. 138 64
    s. 139 64
    s. 140 64
    s. 145..65, 71
    s. 145(5) 72
    s. 145(6) 72
    s. 145(8) 72
    s. 147..65, 71, 72
    s. 157 72
    s. 158 72
    s. 159 72
    s. 170(1) 407, 550
    s. 170(3) 550
    s. 171(1) 65
    s. 173(2) 550
    s. 177 539
    s. 177(2) 550
    s. 177(4)(a) 406
    s. 185(2) 487
    s. 188(2) 404
    s. 189(1) 62, 63, 64, 403, 407, 536, 537
    s. 189(4) 538
    s. 192(4) 54
    s. 193(2) 575
    Schedule 2 485
            para. 2..403, 404
            para. 7(3) 70
    Schedule 4, para. 1 540
    Schedule 5..54, 575
  Friendly Societies Act (c. 46) 21
  Solicitors Act (c. 47) 58

s. 32...58, 186
s. 85 186
s. 85(b) 187
s. 85(2) 151
s. 87...59, 186
1975   Evidence (Proceedings in Other Jurisdictions) Act (c. 34)
s. 1 .... *105*
Finance Act (c. 45)
s. 22 223
1976   Finance Act (c. 40)
Schedule 4 491
Local Government (Miscellaneous Provisions) Act (c. 57) 189
Post Office (Banking Services) Act (c.10) 343
Race Relations Act (c. 74)
s. 20...10, 61
Trustee Savings Banks Act (c. 4) 11
1977   Insurance Brokers (Registration) Act (c. 46)
s. 11(2) 59
Torts (Interference with Goods) Act (c. 32)
s. 2(1) 468
s. 11(1) 438
s. 11(2) 468
Unfair Contract Terms Act (c. 50) 370
s. 2(2) 462, 468
s. 3 462
s. 3(2) 394, 401
s. 11...401, 462, 468
1978   Home Purchase Assistance and Housing Corporation Guarantee Act
(c. 27)
s. 1 60
State Immunity Act (c. 33)
s. 13(2)(b) 597
1979   Banking Act (c. 37) 3, 17, 22, 27, *31*, 47, 48, 51, 56, 58, 60, 61, 62, 120
s. 1...32, 42
s. 1(3) 12
s. 2 32
s. 2(1) 44
s. 2(2)(a) 45
s. 2(2)(b) 45
s. 3...36, 45
s. 3(1) 38
s. 3(4) 35, 36
s. 3(5) 35, 36, 37
s. 3(6) 37
s. 3(7) 38
s. 4 35
s. 5(1) 38

1979 Banking Act—*cont.*

s. 5(2) 38
s. 5(4) 38
s. 5(5) 38
s. 5(6) 38
s. 6 38
s. 7(1) 39
s. 7(2) 39
s. 7(3) 39
s. 7(4) 40
s. 10 39
s. 11(1) 40, 41
s. 11(2) 40
s. 11(3) 41
s. 11(4) 40
s. 12(1) 41
s. 12(2) 41
s. 13(1) 41
s. 13(2) 41
s. 13(3) 41
s. 14 43
s. 15(1) 43
s. 16.. 42, 50
s. 17 42
s. 18 43
s. 19 43
s. 20 43
s. 20(1)(a) 102
s. 21.. 43, 44
s. 22 43
s. 23.. 43, 44
s. 24.. 43, 44
s. 25.. 43, 44
s. 26.. 43, 44
s. 27.. 43, 44
s. 28 43
s. 29 43
s. 30 43
s. 31 43
s. 32 43
s. 33 43
s. 34 42
s. 35 42
s. 36(1) 34, 42
s. 36(2) 34, 42, 45
s. 36(3) 35
s. 36(4) 35, 42

s. 36(5) 35
s. 36(8) 35, 42
s. 36(9) 42
s. 38(1) 63, 486
s. 38(2) 575
s. 38(3) 488
s. 47..438, 468
s. 48 44
s. 49 34
s. 51(2) 34
Schedule 1.. 3, 12, 21, 32, 42, 44, 45, 74
     para. 6 22
     para. 7 60
Schedule 2 46
     para. 1 36
     para. 2(1) 36
     para. 2(2) 36
     para. 2(3) 36
     para. 2(5) 37
     para. 3 36
     para. 4 36
     para. 7 35
     para. 8 35
     para. 9 35
     para. 10 35
Schedule 4, para. 1..39, 40
     para. 2 40
     para. 3 40
     para. 4 40
     para. 5(1) 40
     para. 5(3) 40
     para. 7 13
Schedule 5, para. 4(5) 44
Schedule 6..58, 99
     para. 1(1) 61
     para. 2 59
     para. 3 59
     para. 4 60
     para. 5 60
     para. 9 59
     para. 10 59
     para. 12 60
Credit Unions Act (c. 34) 45
Estate Agents Act (c. 38)
s. 12 188
s. 13 188
s. 14(1) 188

1979   Sale of Goods Act (c. 54)
         s. 3 201
         s. 61(1) 571
1980   Limitation Act (c. 58)
         s. 5 .... 84, 218
         s. 6 .... 84, 219
1981   British Telecommunications Act (c. 38)
         s. 58(1) 13, 343
         Forgery and Counterfeiting Act (c. 45)
         s. 9(1)(d) 298
         Supreme Court Act (c. 54)
         s. 37 276
         Trustee Savings Banks Act (c. 65)
         s. 1 11
         s. 2 11
         s. 7 12
         s. 10 12
         s. 18(1) 12
         s. 21 12
         Schedule 4 12
1982   Finance Act (c. 39)
         s. 26 58
1983   Mental Health Act (c. 20)
         s. 95 205
         s. 96 205
         s. 96(1)(h) 205
         s. 99(1) 205
         s. 99(2) 205
1984   Data Protection Act (c. 35)
         s. 1(2) 388
         s. 1(3) 388
         s. 1(5) 388
         s. 1(6) 388
         s. 5(2) 388
         s. 15 388
         s. 42(1) 388
         s. 43(5) 388
         s. 43(6) 388
         Finance Act (c. 43)
         s. 27(1) 58
1985   Companies Act (c. 6)
         s. 35 196
         s. 37 .... *193*, 308
         s. 193 535
         s. 380 563
         s. 394(4) 308
         s. 395 .... 484, 498, 556, 559, 561, 573

s. 396 ....559, 599
s. 396(1) 559
s. 396(1)(c) 555
s. 396(1)(d) 559
s. 396(1)(e) 586
s. 396(2) 559, 586
s. 396(4) 586
s. 401(1) 560
s. 401(2) 560
s. 434(2) 102
s. 435 102
s. 452(1)(b) 102
s. 597 596
s. 612 ....156, 533, 592
s. 615 158
s. 716(1) 51

1985   Insolvency Act (c. 65)
       s. 219 43
       Local Government Act (c. 51) 189
       Trustee Savings Bank (c. 58) 61
       s. 3 11

1986   Building Societies Act (c. 53) 21, 22
       s. 34 23
       Schedule 8, para. 1 23
                     para. 3 23
       Financial Services Act (c. 60) 60
       Insolvency Act (c. 45) 477
       s. 40 ....563, 564
       s. 86 592
       s. 107 596
       s. 123 563
       s. 127 ....283, 557
       s. 129 ....283, 592
       s. 143 596
       s. 168(4) 533
       s. 175 ....532, 564
       s. 175(1) 127
       s. 175(2) 563
       s. 239 158
       s. 239(6) 158
       s. 245 557
       s. 245(4) 563
       s. 269 533
       s. 278 ....281, 592
       s. 283 280
       s. 283(3)(a) 188
       s. 284(1) 281

1986   Insolvency Act—*cont.*
            s. 284(2) 281
            s. 284(3) 281
            s. 284(4) 281, 284
            s. 284(5) 282, 284
            s. 306...280, 532
            s. 306(1) 188
            s. 307(1) 280
            s. 312(4) 280
            s. 322(3) 592
            s. 323.. 143, 156, 592, 596
            s. 323(2) 157
            s. 324 533
            s. 328 532
            s. 328(3) 533
            s. 340 158
            s. 340(4) 158
            s. 344...587, 598
            s. 344(1) 587
            s. 344(3)(b) 587, 595
            s. 344(4) 587
            s. 386 532
            s. 396(1)(e) 596
            s. 411...156, 592
            s. 438...156, 592, 596
            Schedule 6 532
                        para. 9 127
                        para. 10 127
                        para. 11 127
                        para. 12 127
            Schedule 8, para. 12...156, 592
                        para. 14..156, 592

NORTHERN IRELAND

1940   Prevention of Fraud (Investments) Act (Northern Ireland)
            s. 12 60
1967   Building Societies Act (Northern Ireland) 22, 44
1970   Industrial and Provident Societies Act (Northern Ireland) 45

SCOTLAND

1929   Agricultural Credits (Scotland) Act 59

CANADA

1952   Bankruptcy Act, RCS
            s. 64 158

NEW ZEALAND

1924 Chattels Transfer Act
       s. 4 565
1971 Bill of Exchange (Amendment) Act
       s. 2 279

UNITED STATES

1978 Electronic Fund Transfer Act (15 USCA)
       s. 1693a 364

PART I

BANKS AND BANKING BUSINESS

CHAPTER 1

The Structure of the British Banking World

1. THE PROBLEM IN CONTEXT[1]

The public tends to regard banks as comprising a single group. More frequently than not, banks are contrasted with rival institutions such as the building societies. In truth, the banks themselves can be divided into a number of groups on the basis of different criteria. From a geographical point of view, the banks in the United Kingdom comprise the banks of England and Wales, the banks of Scotland, and the banks of Northern Ireland. From the viewpoint of the Bank of England, which supervises the soliciting of deposits from the public, finance houses can be classified into recognized banks, licensed deposit-takers, and 'Schedule 1 Bodies'.[2] The most important classification of banking institutions is based on their business activities. However, to a person who is unfamiliar with the City, the fine distinctions that will be shown to exist are likely to appear unnecessarily complex.

It should not be presumed that in other Western countries the banks constitute a monolithic group. Thus, German and Swiss banks can be divided into large branch banks and private banks. American banks comprise state banks, national banks, and international banks. The difficulty in finding a sound conceptual criterion for the classification of the British banks on the basis of their business is due to the considerable overlap in the activities of the separate groups. In reality, their division into groups is largely explainable by historical reasons and on the basis of orientation.

A factor that removes some of the hurdles of the classification involved is that each group within the banking world has its own organization or organizations. The members of each organization follow a defined general pattern in their business activities. But naturally there are certain variations of business practices even among members of any given group.

Subject to these observations, it is realistic to divide the British banks into nine groups. First and foremost is the group comprising the seven full members and three functional members of the Committee of London and

---

[1] My thanks are due to bankers and to their organizations for assisting me with this descriptive chapter. All mistakes are, of course, mine. The position is described as at August 1986.

[2] This is the classification of the Banking Act 1979; see Ch. 2, esp. pp. 32 et seq.

Scottish Bankers. This new organization, which has replaced the Committee of London Clearing Banks, was formed in the wake of the complete amalgamation of Williams & Glyn's Bank with the Royal Bank of Scotland. There still remains in existence a separate organization comprising the Scottish Clearing Banks, some of whose members have also joined the CLSB. The Irish clearing banks, too, have their own organization. Practically, though, all clearing banks of the United Kingdom perform the same functions and offer to the public full branch banking services; it is therefore correct to regard them as constituting a single group.[3]

The second group is that of the merchant banks, which comprise the accepting houses and the issuing houses. The accepting houses constitute a small but powerful group of banks which do not maintain branch networks. Their organization—the London Accepting Houses Committee—is closely connected with the association of the issuing houses. The business of the issuing houses is more restricted than that of the accepting houses. As suggested by their name, the issuing houses are predominantly concerned with the issuing of marketable securities.

The third group comprises the discount houses. The main business of these houses is the discount of commercial and negotiable paper and the placing of short-term deposits, such as surplus funds available to a bank on its daily balance. Their activities are thus confined to the short-term money market.

Whilst members of the above three groups and their associations are predominantly British or British-controlled,[4] the fourth group comprises banks active in Commonwealth countries and in former British protectorates. Their organization is known as the British Overseas and Commonwealth Banks Association. Its membership includes the Standard Chartered Bank, most Australian banks and a substantial number of South East Asian banks. Another group of foreign banks—the fifth group—is known as the Foreign Banks Association. It has more than one hundred members, including banks from all over the world. The sixth and seventh groups are, respectively, the American banks, whose organization is the American Banks Association in London and the Japanese banks.

The eighth group, the newcomer in the City, is the Organization of Consortium Banks. It comprises banks that wish to have a presence in London although they choose not to open an office of their own.[5]

In addition to the eight specific groups of banks, there is a more broadly based organization known as the British Bankers' Association. Many of the banks which are members of any of the first eight groups are also members

---

[3] These banks are colloquially described as 'the clearers'.
[4] But note that this is not so in the case of the issuing houses.
[5] Note that the Consortium Banks are actually incorporated in the United Kingdom, and that London is usually their main place of business.

of this additional association, which provides a general forum for bankers with a presence in Britain. At the same time, there are a number of banks that have decided to remain altogether apart. Thus, the well-established house of C. Hoare & Co. continues to be a private bank that does not belong to any association. It is believed that other banks are going the same way. Furthermore, there are certain ill-matched affiliations within some of the defined groups. Thus, the trustee savings banks are currently functional members of the clearing house. But they continue to have features that distinguish them from the ordinary clearing banks. Another two members of the clearing house which require separate treatment are the Co-operative Bank and the National Girobank maintained by the Post Office.[6]

A discussion of the different types of banks operating in the United Kingdom is of considerable importance. It should clear the way for the analysis of the general principles of law governing the activities of the banking world. The supervision of the banks in the United Kingdom by the Bank of England, and the nature of this central bank, is the subject of Chapter 2.

2. THE CLEARING BANKS[7]

(i) The London scene

The clearing banks, which are the institutions regarded by the public as 'the banks', are the successors of the joint stock banks. The development of these bodies can be traced back to the late eighteenth century: but they flourished during the nineteenth century. They acquired their original name because their capital was subscribed by public issues. Their influence and financial strength became paramount during the last three decades of the nineteenth century. This was also the time when they became known as the 'clearing banks'.

The four major clearing banks of England and Wales—Barclays, Lloyds, Midland, and National Westminster—are members of the Committee of London and Scottish Bankers. The remaining members are the Bank of Scotland, the Royal Bank of Scotland (which is now fully amalgamated with Williams & Glyn's Bank), and the Standard Chartered Bank. There is also a

---

[6] The distinction applies mainly in respect of involvements in business dealings. See pp. 13–14 below.

[7] For the most comprehensive information available see The London Clearing Banks—*evidence submitted by the Committee of London Clearing Bankers to the Committee to Review the Functioning of Financial Institutions*, Nov. 1970. Changes occurring since then are taken into account in the text.

commitment to admit the Trustee Savings Banks Groups to full membership
when they have become quoted companies. The Clydesdale Bank, which is a
fully owned subsidiary of Midland, and Coutts, which is owned by National
Westminster, are represented on the CLSB by their respective parent
company.

The number of the original clearing banks had decreased as a result of
amalgamations that took place in the late 1960s and early 1970s. Before
that time banks were dissuaded from attempts to merge by the report of the
Colwyn Committee on Bank Amalgamations which expressed concern in
1918 about the concentration of banking in the hands of a limited number
of powerful houses. It had been accepted since that time that mergers of
banks were subject to the approval of the Bank of England in consultation
with the Treasury. It was one of the many cases in which the City observed a
norm that had not been made the subject of legislation.

The assumption was that mergers would be approved only if the banks
concerned were not in direct competition with each other. Thus, the first significant merger, that of the National Provincial Bank with the District Bank,
was proposed because the District Bank had its main network of branches in
the North West of England, where National Provincial was relatively
inactive.

The scene was cleared for other mergers in 1967, when the report on
banks' charges, prepared by the National Board for Prices and Incomes,
advised that:[8]

the Bank of England and the Treasury have made it plain to us that they would not
obstruct some further amalgamations if the banks were willing to contemplate such
a development.

This policy statement initiated the amalgamations of Barclays Bank with
Martins Bank; of the National Provincial Bank (which was then already
amalgamated with District Bank) with Westminster Bank; and of Williams
Deacon & Co. with Glyn Mills & Co. and with the National Bank. A
merger of Barclays Bank with Lloyds Bank was opposed by the Monopolies
Commission, which was concerned about the effect that such a development
was bound to have on competitiveness in the banking world.

The clearing banks used to be the only active participants in the clearing
house's activities. But this is no longer the case. Three additional banks are now
functional members of the clearing house although they do not have seats on
the CLSB. They are the Trustee Savings Bank England and Wales, the Co-
operative Bank, and the National Girobank. The three banks concerned are

[8] Ibid., 20 et seq.

discussed subsequently. It is, however, important to consider at this stage the significance of the distinction between the membership of the clearing house and that of the CLSB.

Like its predecessor (the CLCB), the CLSB is basically a policy-making body. In recent years it has laid down the policy on such central issues as the automation of the clearing house and the development of electronic transfers, and on many issues relevant to international banking. It is also the principal body that represents the clearing banks in their dealings with the Bank of England and with the Government. it maintains the Inter-bank Research Organization (IBRO), which is run on autonomous lines.

One of the CLSB's main concerns is the system of rules of the clearing house. These have to be amended from time to time in the light of changes in modern technology and business practice.[9] The CLSB is also the body that considers applications for membership of the clearing house.

Up to 1985 a number of clearing systems operated in harmony but independently of each other. Thus, the clearing house itself—known as the Bankers' Clearing House Ltd.—was owned by a company the shareholders of which were the English clearing banks and the three other participating banks. Since the beginning of the nineteenth century the clearing house has been maintained at 10 Lombard Street. These are the premises at which the exchange of cheques takes place daily between the participants of the clearing house. Two processes are in operation: the general clearing, which involves the exchange of the bulk of cheques drawn on bank branches in England and Wales (including London); and the town clearing, which is used solely for the clearance of effects of not less than £10,000, which are drawn on one branch within the boundaries of the City of London and collected by another. The general clearing is at present largely automated, whilst the town clearing continues to be effected on a purely manual basis. Both systems are discussed in Chapter 9.

Two other money transfer systems remain under the effective control of the CLSB. One is run by the Bankers' Automated Clearing Services (BACS), which used to be a private company owned by the major clearing banks. It effects bank giro transfers, which include all types of periodic payments and direct debiting arrangement. The other, Clearing House Automated Payment System (CHAPS), effects the electronic transfer of specific payments of substantial amounts (£10,000 and above). At some future date it might possibly replace the town clearing system. At present, however, it is still at an early operational stage. Accordingly, the manual and the automated 'same

---

[9] The legal implications of the clearing system are discussed in Chs. 9 and 12. Note that the original rules of the clearing house were promulgated at the very beginning of the nineteenth century.

day' clearing are being run concurrently.[10] One advantage of CHAPS is that, unlike the manual town clearing system, its operation is not confined to the City. Branches can be linked to it from all over the United Kingdom, as indeed can substantial customers sponsored for this purpose by one of the clearing banks.

A formal restructuring was undertaken in 1985. The existing clearing systems were placed under the control of three operating companies governed by an 'umbrella' body named the Association for Payment Clearing Systems. The three companies controlled by this Association are in charge respectively of the paper bulk clearing, of the high value clearing (covering the town clearing and CHAPS), and of the electronic bulk clearings of BACS. The main object of this new structure is to harmonize the operations of the different clearing systems. Practically, the new structure has not led to any significant changes in the day to day operations of the various clearing systems.

The importance of the function of the clearing banks in the settlement of payments in England and in Wales cannot be overstated. The number of items cleared through the various clearing systems is approximately 3.3 billion each year. Furthermore, it is estimated that over 75 per cent of the adult population of the United Kingdom maintains current accounts with banks. Whilst the number of items cleared through CHAPS and the town clearing is small in comparison with the vast number of cheques processed by the general clearing, the amounts cleared by the town clearing and by CHAPS are of considerable magnitude. In effect, the different clearing processes are complementary. To retain the existing system, the clearing banks have to maintain their widely spread network of branches, although the decrease in amounts kept by customers in their current accounts has rendered many branches unprofitable.

To participate in the clearing house activities, a bank requires a clearing department of its own. This is the centre to which all cheques payable to the banks' customers are sent by the branches charged with their collection. These are largely processed at the centre. Thereafter, each bank delivers to the clearing house all cheques drawn on other banks and picks up the cheques drawn on itself.

The processing at the clearing centres involves an automated procedure and is costly. Any bank which applies for membership of the clearing house has to undertake to maintain a clearing department of its own. This has been done by the Central Trustee Savings Bank (whose presence in the clearing house has now been taken over by the Trustee Savings Bank England and Wales), by the Co-operative Bank, and more recently by the National Girobank.

---

[10] Discussed in Ch. 12.

Many banks in England and Wales consider it unprofitable to maintain a clearing department of their own. The foreign banks, most of which are situated in London, and the Yorkshire Bank, operative mainly in the North, are only two examples in point. The merchant banks, too, have decided not to apply for membership of the clearing house. But all these banks have customers who maintain current accounts. This means that cheques drawn by customers of these banks, as well as cheques payable to them, have to be cleared.

Up to the end of the Second World War, cheques drawn on, or payable to, customers of the majority of non-clearing banks were presented for payments by a procedure known as the 'walks'. It involved the dispatch of the cheques by messengers several times each day and was, of course, inefficient and time-consuming. Although some isolated houses have retained this practice, it has been largely replaced by the system of 'agency banks'.[11]

Under the new system, a non-clearing bank uses one of the clearing banks as its agent for clearing purposes. This entails that each cheque payable to a customer of the respective non-clearing bank is sent to the clearing department of the agent for collection. Cheques drawn on an account maintained with the non-clearing bank are delivered by the collecting bank to the agent bank at the clearing house. The process is facilitated by a simple device: the non-clearing bank is given a sorting number,[12] which is printed on each form in cheque books issued by it and is encoded on cheques to be collected for its customers. The non-participant bank is thus treated, for clearing purposes, as if it were a branch of the agency bank.

The network established by the use of the agency banks' system is formidable. It covers many banks of considerable size. The Yorkshire Bank, which uses the Royal Bank of Scotland as its agent, is a good example.

The maintenance of current accounts, which has remained one of the major fields of activity of the clearing banks, means that they control substantial amounts of money repayable on demand. These have traditionally been made available to customers on the basis of overdrafts, which are by their nature advances repayable on demand. Interest on this type of accommodation has always been at a rate more favourable than that applicable to term loans. In recent years, however, customers became increasingly aware of the earning capacity of money, and have therefore tended to pay their savings to the credit of interest-bearing accounts, such as fixed deposits.

---

[11] The practice of using a clearing bank as an agent developed earlier than that; but the system was used by very few banks.

[12] A sorting number is either a printed or an imprinted message readable by the computer. A sorting number indicates the bank and its branch. Where a non-clearing bank uses a clearer as agent, it is given a sorting number that facilitates the delivery of cheques drawn by its customers to the agent's clearing department.

This has enabled the clearing banks to lend more money to customers on the basis of medium- and even long-term loans, which are available at a higher rate.

Apart from their typical branch banking activities, the clearing banks engage in all other types of banking business. Each clearing bank has an overseas department or division—such as Barclays Bank International. Furthermore, in the case of most clearers, each major branch is in a position to engage in international banking activities. These cover the financing of exports and imports, dealings in foreign currency and in gold, and the furnishing of guarantees, performance bonds and letters of credit.

In addition, the clearing banks underwrite new issues of commercial paper and, like the merchant banks, provide lines of credit to their customers. From about the end of the Second World War, the clearing banks have been willing to advise customers on their financial affairs and, indeed, to provide portfolio investment services for them. These services are quite separate from the furnishing of bank references, which has been a traditional activity of the clearing banks.[13]

The clearing banks are thus engaged in a wide range of banking business. They are, further, liberal in accepting members of the public as customers. Their approach is sanctioned by law. There is a specific prohibition of any racial discrimination in the furnishing of banking services.[14] Moreover, the clearing banks are just as willing to accept individual customers as corporate customers. Legal considerations, though, require the clearing banks to request every new customer to furnish a reference.[15]

(ii) The Scottish and Northern Irish clearing banks

The procedures used by the clearing banks in London are also used by the clearing banks of Scotland and of Northern Ireland. The Scottish Clearing Banks—the Bank of Scotland, the Clydesdale Bank, and the Royal Bank of Scotland—maintain clearing centres in Glasgow and in Edinburgh. The banks of Northern Ireland—which include the Northern Bank and the Ulster Bank—maintain a clearing house in Belfast. The practices used are those of the general clearing system of London. There are no town clearing centres outside the City.[16] However, even at this early stage of operations,

---

[13] The bank's liability in respect of such transactions and also as regards the furnishing of references is discussed in Ch. 15.

[14] Race Relations Act 1976, s. 20.

[15] The reasons for the insistence on a referee's report are related to the bank's liability where cheques are converted. See pp. 412 et seq. below.

[16] For a description of the town clearing, see pp. 236–7 below.

some Scottish banks have direct access to CHAPS and BACS. The business of the Scottish and Northern Irish clearing banks is comparable with that of the London clearers.

3. THE 'FUNCTIONAL' CLEARING BANKS

(i) The trustee savings banks[17]

The trustee savings banks used to constitute a network of local banks, operative in all parts of the United Kingdom. In recent years they have participated in the clearing house through the Central Trustee Savings Bank, which functioned as their clearing department.

The establishment of the trustee savings banks was sanctioned in the nineteenth century by a series of Acts commencing with that of 1817.[18] Their initial object was to provide facilities for the savings of the working classes, who were for a long time unable to open accounts with the trading banks. The most recent development is the restructuring of the network of the trustee savings banks under the Trustee Savings Banks Act 1985. The Act provides for the reorganization of these banks as a group of companies under the umbrella of a holding company. In view of the increasing diversification of the activities carried on by trustee savings banks, the corporate structure appears the most appropriate form for their business operations. The end result of the reorganization is the establishment of the Trustee Savings Bank of England and Wales and the similar banks of Scotland and of Ireland. At the time of going to press, the restructuring is virtually complete and the Trustee Savings Bank England and Wales has taken over the Central Trustee Savings Bank's seat in the clearing house..

Under the old regime, a new trustee savings bank could be established only if the Registrar of Friendly Societies confirmed that its proposed rules were in conformity with the applicable statute, the last of which was the Trustee Savings Banks Act 1981.[19] The banks were supervised by an independent authority, known as the Trustee Savings Banks Central Board.[20] Under section 3 of the 1985 Act, the rights and liabilities of the Central Board are being taken over by the new holding company. The Board itself will cease to exist on a date to be appointed.

---

[17] See generally Halsbury, *Laws of England*, 4th edn., vol. 3, paras. 17 et seq.
[18] There has been a great deal of legislation in point. The most important statutes were the Trustee Savings Banks Acts 1863, 1954, 1969, and 1976; the statute now in force, which is the Trustee Savings Banks Act 1981, will be repealed when the reorganization sanctioned by the Trustee Savings Bank 1985 has been completed.
[19] Ss. 1, 2 (originating from the 1976 Act).
[20] Established under the Trustee Savings Banks Act 1976; now s. 7 of the 1981 Act.

The powers of the Central Board were extremely wide.[21] To avoid dupli-
cation of controls, the trustee savings banks were therefore included in
Schedule 1 of the Banking Act 1979.[22] This meant that they could solicit
deposits from the public without the sanction of a Bank of England's
licence. But under the new regime, the trustee savings banks have ceased to
be Schedule 1 bodies.

The traditional business of the trustee savings banks was the acceptance
of money on deposit.[23] But under section 18(1) of the 1981 Act, they were
empowered to engage in banking business generally. The phrase was not
defined in the Act and was, presumably, to be understood in terms of the
common law definition. In modern practice, trustee savings banks open for
their customers current accounts operable by cheques. They also collect
cheques payable to their customers and participate in the network of money
transfers known as the giro system.[24] Their customers have remained predominantly individuals; but some small unincorporated business firms have
started to use the trustee savings banks. One of the effects of the reorganization is likely to be that corporations, too, will be encouraged to open
accounts with the trustee savings banks.[25]

One of the attractions of maintaining an account with a trustee savings
bank was that the customer used to be able to nominate the person to be
entitled to the balance upon his demise. This nominations system—which
served the same function as a will—was discontinued under the Trustee Savings Banks (Amendment) Regulations 1979.[26]

One conceptual point has been settled in the course of the current reorganization. Traditionally, it was questionable whether trustee savings banks had
a separate legal personality, although it was accepted that they could sue
and be sued in their own name.[27] The new companies, such as the Trustee
Savings Bank England and Wales, have a separate legal entity by reason of
their incorporation.[28] It is noteworthy that, even before the passing of the
1985 Act, there were very few restrictions on the manner in which a trustee
savings bank could invest its funds.[29] Under Schedule 4 of the 1981 Act, it

---

[21] Trustee Savings Banks Act 1981, ss. 7, 10.

[22] And see pp. 44–45 below.

[23] Ibid., s. 1(3).

[24] See pp. 343 et seq. below.

[25] Up to 1973 most trustee savings banks had rules sanctioning personal accounts only.
This is no longer the case. Cf. J. R. Paget, *Law of Banking*, 9th edn., London, 1982, pp. 9–10.

[26] The nominations, though, were subjected to restrictions of maxima, set under the Administration of Estates (Small Payments) Act 1965.

[27] *Knight and Searle* v. *Dove* [1964] 2 QB 631; and see Paget, *Law of Banking*, 9th edn.,
p. 9.

[28] For a lucid short discussion, see K. Puttick, 'Trustee Savings Bank Bill', (1985) 135 *New
LJ* 59.

[29] But see the 1981 Act, s. 21.

could deposit funds with 'other banks', which, presumably, included licensed deposit-takers approved under the Banking Act 1979.

(ii) The Co-operative Bank

The Co-operative Bank maintains branches throughout the United Kingdom. Most of them are located in department stores of its owners, the Co-operative Wholesale Society. As a result, most of the bank's customers are regular clients of the stores. This affects the type of business carried on by the Co-operative Bank, as its operations are geared to the needs of individuals. There is, however, no policy which precludes the acceptance of business enterprises, incorporated or unincorporated, as customers. Indeed, the bank has a Corporate Business Department.

The Co-operative Bank provides the usual facilities of payment and of collection available from the ordinary clearers. It does not engage in international banking business.

(iii) The National Girobank

This bank is in effect a body of the Post Office. Its establishment was sanctioned by the Post Office Act 1969.[30] The Act authorized the Post Office to provide such banking services as it thought fit, and deemed it 'for all practical purposes to be a banker and to be carrying on the business of banking'[31] in the exercise of these powers. From a practical point of view, this means that the National Girobank has the defences conferred on other bankers in respect of the payment and the collection of cheques.[32] The National Girobank is not under the regime of the Banking Act 1979.[33]

The National Girobank maintains its branches in post offices. Initially, it offered its customers mainly the use of money transfers, known as giro operations. As the ordinary clearing banks introduced their own money transfer system, the National Girobank broadened its own activities. At present, it offers regular current account facilities, overdrafts, personal loans and a credit card. It also accepts interest-bearing deposits from its customers. A

---

[30] Section 7(1)(*b*), replaced by s. 58 (1) of the British Telecommunications Act 1981.

[31] The Post Office Act 1969, as amended by para. 7 of Sched. 4 of the Banking Act 1979.

[32] See pp. 421 et seq. below.

[33] The National Girobank is one of the Schedule 1 banks, under the Banking Act 1979, which means that it is not under the control of the Bank of England pertaining to the acceptance of deposits from the public. It is so excluded as it is under the control of the Post Office. See pp. 44–45 below.

particularly useful service is the postcheque, against which customers can obtain cash in many post offices overseas. Money can also be transferred to the credit of overseas giro accounts in Western European countries.

The vehicle for the corporate business of the National Girobank is Girobank plc, founded in September 1985.

(iv) Comparison with ordinary clearers

The main differences between the ordinary clearers and the three new, functional ones are in the scope of their respective business activities and in size. Whilst the ordinary clearers are currently marked by the comprehensive services provided to customers, the newcomers have remained, primarily, banks which cater for the needs of individual customers and of small businesses. Large firms and corporations generally continue to use the services of the ordinary clearers or of accepting houses.

The demarcation in respect of size is quite startling. In 1984 the smallest of the ordinary clearers—Williams & Glyn's Bank—had a share of 6 per cent of the market; each of the new, functional, members had approximately 1 per cent.[34]

4. THE MERCHANT BANKS[35]

(i) Accepting houses and issuing houses

In contrast with the clearing banks, the merchant banks do not maintain chains of branches. Many of them operate from a single office in the City, although some have up to three or four branches or offices in the City or in major industrial towns. Further, the merchant banks cater mainly for the needs of business firms, such as corporations and large unincorporated enterprises, and do not seek out the individual customer. The merchant banks are not members of the clearing house. However, most of them provide current account facilities to their customers, using one of the clearing banks as an agent for the operations involved.

The merchant banks comprise the accepting houses and the issuing houses. The former group includes only seven banks, which are members of

[34] But note that their sizes compare with that of Coutts which, however, is a fully owned subsidiary of the National Westminster Bank.

[35] For an excellent account of merchant banking, see J. J. Clay and B. S. Wheble, *Modern Merchant Banking*, 2nd edn., London, 1983.

the Accepting Houses Committee. Their influence in the City is demonstrated by the fact that most of them are also members of the governing body of the Issuing Houses Association.

(ii) The accepting houses[36]

The accepting houses originated in the late eighteenth and nineteenth centuries. They include well-known houses such as Brown, Shipley & Co., Baring Bros. and N. M. Rothschild & Sons. Although most of them have now incorporated themselves, they usually commenced their operations either as individual merchants or as partnerships. At the early stages, they were merchants in the true sense of the word. They traded on their own capital, primarily in the import and export of goods. Some of them had their own fleets of ships. Later on, their ships were also used by other merchants engaged in current transactions; and, in due course, the merchant banks began to finance such smaller traders.

The facility used by the merchant banks in the nineteenth century to finance other traders was the acceptance credit.[37] Such a facility provided for bills of exchange to be drawn by the trader on the merchant bank. The acceptance of the bills by the merchant bank facilitated their discount.[38] The merchant bank was reimbursed for the amounts paid out on its acceptances out of the proceeds of the mercantile transaction involved. It was paid an acceptance fee, which constituted its direct profit from the transaction.

The accepting houses were thus predominantly active in the export trade. They played an important role in the development of such commercial facilities as the c.i.f. and f.o.b. contract and the documentary letter of credit.[39] At present, their activities are of a considerably wider scope. In addition to their traditional business, they are engaged in foreign exchange dealings, in all aspects of money management dealings (including portfolio investments for customers), in the financing of current and capital transactions by means of short-term, medium-term and even long-term loans, and in capital ventures.

All the accepting houses are involved in capital issues. They underwrite share and bond issues of clients. Some of them also perform the services

[36] Some accepting houses have published their stories; see, e.g., V. Cowles, *The Rothschilds: A Family of Fortune*, London, 1973; J. Ellis, *Heir to Adventure: The Story of Brown Shipley & Co.*, London, 1960.
[37] As to the nature of acceptance credits, see pp. 494–5 below.
[38] It may not appear surprising that accepting houses frequently discounted each other's acceptances.
[39] As regards the history of documentary credits, see E. P. Ellinger, *Documentary Letters of Credit—A Comparative Study*, Singapore, 1970, ch. 2.

usually provided by stockbrokers.[40] In addition, most of the houses engage in bullion transactions.

As a rule, the accepting houses do not engage in the factoring of accounts, which involves the purchase of a merchant's book debts by the financier.[41] Transactions of this type are at present the province of specialized firms. Some merchant banks engage, however, in another specialized type of business, namely the acquisition of equipment leased by them to customers.

It is clear that the accepting houses constitute a financial group of considerable importance in the City. Apart from substantial corporations, their customers include some government departments and local authorities. It is clear that only the most distinguished merchant banks are members of the group and of its committee. One contributing factor to this state of affairs is that membership is restricted to merchant banks which are under British control.

(iii) The issuing houses

As indicated by their name, the issuing houses' main business is in the field of capital issues. Their activities thus overlap with those of the accepting houses. They are, however, less involved with current transactions than the accepting houses. Indeed, some issuing houses do not carry on this type of business.

Another difference is that a bank may qualify for membership of the Issuing Houses Association although it is not under British control.[42]

(iv) Assessment

There are firms in the City which engage in activities similar to those of the accepting and issuing houses but which are not members of either one of the organizations involved. This is not surprising, as an institution need not qualify under any Act if it wishes to engage in the activities of a merchant bank.

The only type of business which requires authorization is the soliciting of deposits from the public. Merchant banks do, therefore, usually hold the

---

[40] The merchant banks had launched in ARIEL: the Automated Real-Time Investment Exchange Ltd., which, as indicated by its name, constituted an automated dealing mechanism for securities.

[41] Factoring of accounts may be either with or without recourse. On the subject generally, see P. M. Biscoe, *Law and Practice of Credit Factoring*, London, 1975.

[42] Some of the clearing banks maintain substantial shareholdings in, and occasionally even control, an issuing house. See, e.g., Barclays Merchant Bank Ltd. As an issuing house need not be under British control, there have been cases of accepting houses which, on changing hands, left their original organization and joined the Issuing Houses Association.

required licence of the Bank of England under the Banking Act 1979. If they also wish to use the word 'bank' in their name, or seek to advertise that they provide banking services, they have to acquire the status of a recognized bank under this Act.[43]

5. THE DISCOUNT HOUSES

The function of the discount houses is described by their name. Originally, they were discounters of bills of exchange drawn under acceptance credits issued by banks.[44] They have expanded their business by arranging to discount other obligations, such as Treasury bills, and further specialized in the placing of money on the short-term market. To this end, the discount houses accept deposits from the banks and from other financial institutions and invest the money in marketable securities and in bonds issued by government departments, by local authorities, and by business firms.

The discount houses are distinguishable from discount brokers. A discount house borrows money, or discounts securities, in its own name. A broker places money or discountable securities of his principal with suitable third parties.

The thirteen discount houses operating in the City at the present time are members of the London Discount Market Association. The largest house is the Union Discount Co. of London. Another well known firm is Gillett Bros. Discount Co. Conceptually, the discount houses are to be regarded as banks that provide a specialized type of service for their clients. This fact is appreciated by the Bank of England. It would appear that all the discount houses have been granted the status of recognized banks under the Banking Act 1979.[45]

6. OVERSEAS AND FOREIGN BANKS

(i) Overview

London is one of the major centres of international banking. It is therefore not surprising that most major banks in the Western world have a presence

---

[43] All the accepting houses and quite a number of the thirty or so issuing houses are recognized banks under the Act. The others hold licences issued thereunder.

[44] The dealings of the discount houses in bills are lucidly explained in *The Bill on London*, 1976, published by the House of Gillett Bros.

[45] Note that a body may be recognized as a bank under the Banking Act 1979 even if it provides a specialized banking service rather than banking services generally; see pp. 36–7 below.

in the City. There are five organizations of such banks: the Foreign Banks Association; the British Overseas and Commonwealth Banks Association; the Association of Consortium Banks; the American Bankers Association of London; and the Japanese Banks' Association.[46]

(ii) The Foreign Banks Association

Approximately 130 banks are affiliated to this organization, which thus has the largest membership of banks in the City. All its members are banks incorporated in countries other than the United Kingdom. They may not be members of any other organization of banks in the United Kingdom, except the British Bankers' Association, discussed subsequently. Obviously, banks belonging to one of the other organizations of foreign banks, such as the Japanese Banks Association, cannot be members of the instant group. Foreign banks which operate in their own name in the United Kingdom, and have an office in it, are entitled to full membership. This is so even if the Bank of England treats them as licensed deposit-takers and refuses to recognized them as banks.[47] Foreign banks which do not carry on business in the United Kingdom in their own name but which have a representative are entitled to an associate membership.

The association has three regional committees: the EEC Committee, the Europe Committee (concerned with banks of European countries outside the EEC), and a World Committee (covering the banks in the remaining countries of the world). The three committees are subordinate to the Central Committee, whose function it is to protect the interests of all the members of the association in the United Kingdom.

The business activities of the members of a group as diverse in its membership as the banks organized under the umbrella of this Association is bound to vary a great deal. It is natural that each bank in the group has a special interest in customers from its home country, and in the promotion of the business links of firms in its country with correspondents in the United Kingdom. Primarily, the banks involved effect financial transactions between merchants in the United Kingdom and in the respective banks' home countries, although in many cases their business activities are much wider than that.

It is understood that some banks which are members of the group provide current accounts to their customers. Most of them furnish the usual travel

---

[46] For interesting information see H. McRae and F. Cairncross, *Capital City: London as a Financial Centre*, London, 1974.

[47] In such a case, the institution may still use the word 'bank' as part of its name, provided it adds to its designation the fact that it is a licence holder and not a recognized bank; see p. 35 below.

facilities and, generally, deal in foreign currencies and in securities. In addition, most of them are involved in Eurodollar transactions.

(iii) The British Overseas and Commonwealth Banks Association

The BOCBA is an organization which, on the face of it, appears to comprise British banks. Membership is open to any bank in the United Kingdom. Historically, though, the Association's members are British banks whose main business is in former British colonies and protectorates or in present Commonwealth countries. In the East, its members are the Standard Chartered Bank, the Hongkong and Shanghai Bank, and the leading local banks in Singapore, Hongkong, Malaysia and India. In the Antipodes, they include the established banks of Australia and of New Zealand. In the Middle East and in Africa, the members are a number of established banks in territories formerly under British influence. In North America, they encompass a significant number of the Canadian banks. It is noteworthy that the Moscow Narodny Bank Ltd., established in the wake of Anglo-Russian co-operation before the revolution, belongs to this group.[48]

Despite their British affiliation and background, the members of the BOCBA group resemble the foreign banks. The BOCBA banks draw clients, both corporate and individual, from their own countries. They provide current account facilities for them in London and often act on their behalf and back them in business transactions. Furthermore, all BOCBA members deal in foreign currencies and in securities. Not a single one of them maintains a nation-wide network of branches in the United Kingdom, although the Standard Chartered Bank is now a member of the CLSB.[49]

(iv) The consortium banks

The most exciting development in the City during the last fifteen years has been the establishment of the consortium banks. All members of the Association are banks incorporated in the United Kingdom. They were founded by foreign banks which felt that there was no justification for their opening individual offices in the City, but which at the same time wished to have a presence in London. They compromised by founding London-based banks, in which a number of them were shareholders, and which, though distinct

---

[48] For a fascinating account of these banks, see R. Mackenzie, *Realms of Silver*, London, 1982; J. A. Henry and H. A. Siepman, *The First Hundred Years of the Standard Bank*, London, 1982; R. Fry, *Bankers in West Africa*, London, 1982.

[49] The financial success of some of the banks in this group can be attested by the fact that the Hongkong and Shanghai Banking Co. made a take-over bid for the Royal Bank of Scotland during the last few years.

from the parent companies, basically looked after their affairs. However, consortium banks are not necessarily fully owned by foreign banks. British banks are among the shareholders of some of them. Thus, the Midland Bank is a shareholder of the Scandinavian Bank. Some of the consortium banks are so successful in their business that they have outgrown their founders.

As may be expected, many consortium banks come from a given geographical region. This is revealed by such names as the Scandinavian Bank, the European Arab Bank and the Atlantic International Bank. Some members, though, are consortia of banks in a single country. The United Bank of Kuwait and the Saudi International Bank furnish examples in point. Some consortium banks are, further, devoted to a specific task. An example is the International Energy Bank.

It is clear that there is lack of uniformity in the business of the consortium banks. Many of them resemble the foreign banks in that they are concerned with the interests of the region to which they owe allegiance. By and large all of them are engaged in foreign currency transactions, and some furnish current account facilities to customers, predominantly from the representative region. As regards lending activities, many banks specialize in medium-term transactions.

All the regional and single-country-orientated consortia see their vocation as the promotion of business between their respective home countries or country and the United Kingdom. Thus, they finance both export and import transactions. They also engage, on their own or in co-operation with an issuing house, in floating bonds and shares issued for the purposes of the countries to which they are affiliated.

The rate of growth of the consortium banks has been the fastest in the City in the course of the last decade. There is no doubt that the repeal of the exchange control legislation of the United Kingdom gave impetus to their drive.[50]

(iv) The American and Japanese banks

The American and the Japanese banks have established a presence of such significance in the City that it was reasonable for them to found their own respective organizations in London. As can be expected, each of the two respective organizations is concerned solely with the interests of its members.

---

[50] As regards the repeal of exchange control in the United Kingdom, see p. 75 n. 133 below.

7. THE BRITISH BANKERS' ASSOCIATION

The existence in the banking world of so many groups of banks and of associations representing them resulted in the need for an additional organization that might be regarded as a co-ordinator. This function is performed by the British Bankers' Association, which is located in the same building as the CLSB.

The Association has two types of membership: full and associate. Banks are entitled to full membership only if they are established under English law, have their head offices in the United Kingdom and are under British control. An exception to this principle is that full membership is available to a UK branch or subsidiary of a bank with a head office in another EEC country. The latter type of bank must, however, be either a recognized bank under the Banking Act 1979 or a 'Schedule 1' institution. Fundamentally, all other banks recognized under the Act are entitled to associate membership.

The main objects of the Association are to provide facilities for the discussion of matters of interest to the British banks and to make representations on their behalf. These interests, however, coincide on many occasions with those of the London banking community as a whole.

8. COMPARISON WITH BUILDING SOCIETIES[51]

During the last decade there has been a narrowing of the gap between the banks and the building societies. The most recent development has been the passing of the Building Societies Act 1986, which at the time of going to press is only partly in force. The building societies are accordingly still under the regime of the Building Societies Act 1962,[52] although the new Act is likely to come into full effect in 1987. It is inevitable that some substantial changes in the nature and in the business of building societies will take place in the next few years. It is believed that many building societies will decide to transfer their entire business to a commercial company, in accordance with sections 97–102.[53] It remains to be seen whether in the end building societies will become, for all practical purposes, a specialized type of bank.

---

[51] The standard work is J. Mills, *Building Society Law*, London, 14th edn., 1976; see also C. E. I. Thornton and J. P. McBrien, *Building Society Law*, London, 1975.

[52] There used to be two types of building society: the incorporated and the unincorporated varieties. The incorporated building society became predominant. At present it is governed by the Building Societies Act 1962, which consolidated the Acts passed between 1874 and 1960. Unincorporated societies were governed by the Benefit Building Societies Act 1836 none remains in existence. The incorporated building society may be either terminating, which means that its existence ends at a given date or on the happening of a given event, or—as is the norm—permanent.

[53] Building societies originated in the early nineteenth century, as friendly societies.

Even under the existing regime, there is an overlap between some of the activities of the building societies and some of those of the clearing banks. Both types of institution accept deposits from the public for the purpose of reinvesting the funds obtained. Furthermore, both the building societies and the banks operate through branches, although the networks of such giants as National Westminster and Barclays Bank are far more extensive than those of building societies. At present, an important distinction between the institutions is that whilst the banks are subject to the controls exercised by the Bank of England under the Banking Act 1979, the building societies are excluded.[54] They have been subject to a separate regime introduced by the Building Societies Act 1962.[55] Furthermore, up to 1986, their incorporation has been subject to the approval of the Registrar of Friendly Societies.[56] The 1986 Act has introduced far-reaching changes. It has sanctioned the establishment of a new Commission, which will be in charge of, and supervise, the building societies.[57] The building societies will, further, be brought under the regime of the Banking Act 1979.[58]

Traditionally, there is rivalry for the custom of the public between the clearers and the building societies. The main argument in support of the building societies is that they pay their customers a higher rate of interest than the banks. The banks assert that they provide a wider range of services and furnish a superior access to available facilities.

There can be no doubt that the broader spectrum of services is offered to customers by the banks. Whilst the clearers have traditionally been providers of credit facilities for general purposes, the building societies' lending has remained predominantly related to transactions involving the acquisition of land. Another fundamental limitation of the services offered by them up to now was due to the fact that, under the old regime, a building society could not issue to its customers cheque-books in which the society figured as drawee. In addition, the building societies did not have direct access to the clearing house. Some building societies tried to overcome this obstacle by making arrangements for the payment of their customers' accounts by issuing their own cheques. A novel scheme, introduced in collaboration with some of the clearers, enabled the customer to draw cheques, bearing the name of the building society, on the bank which supported the scheme. In cheques of this type the building society figured as the drawer

[54] The Banking Act 1979 exonerates building societies from the controls imposed by it: Sched. 1, para. 6.
[55] Or the Building Societies Act (Northern Ireland) 1967.
[56] Building Societies Act 1962, ss. 2, 3.
[57] Building Societies Act 1986, ss. 36–45. For details, see A. Coles, 'The Building Societies Bill and New Financial Services', (1986) 136 *New LJ* 270; C. D. French, 'Building Societies Bill—New Requirements', (1986) 136 *New LJ* 378; R. G. Armstrong, 'Building Societies—Constitutional Aspects', (1986) 136 *New LJ* 427.
[58] Annual Report by the Bank of England 1985/86, p. 16.

and the bank as the drawee. The customer, the details of whose account were set out in the magnetic ink line of the instrument, completed it by appending his signature and by inserting the required details, i.e. the amount, the name of the payee, and the date. These cheques were customized so that they could be cleared through the respective bank by means of a debit entry made directly in the customer's account. Conceptually, the customer drew the cheque on the bank under the building society's authority.

The 1986 Act renders this arrangement obsolete. The building societies are now authorized to provide money transmission services and are entitled to make and to receive payments as agents.[59] These powers are wide enough to enable the building societies to become directly involved in the operations associated with current accounts, including the provision of clearing facilities for cheques and for giro payments. To protect the building societies in respect of this type of business, the 1986 Act confers on them the defences available to banks in respect of the payment and the collection of cheques.[60]

But despite the growing similarity between the activities of the banks and those of the building societies, there will, at least for the time being, remain two important differences. First, the vast majority of the building societies' customers will continue to be individuals. Secondly, the building societies will continue to transact a very substantial part of their business with members. Theoretically at least, banks are prepared to borrow from, and to lend to, the public. It is believed that considerable expansion of the building societies is to be expected in the next few years.

9. OTHER FINANCIAL INSTITUTIONS

The banks and building societies are the major financial institutions in the United Kingdom. There are, in addition, some houses with a specialized type of business that do not fall under either umbrella. Thus, the finance companies—the best-known of which is United Dominions Trust—specialize in what used to be the hire purchase business, but which has now become the general provision of consumer finance. Many of these finance companies engage, in addition, in the leasing of equipment to business firms.

The finance houses have grown rapidly since the end of the Second World War, and are at present providing finance not only to consumers but also to industry and commerce. Quite a number of banks have substantial shareholdings in finance houses.

There are some other bodies which carry on borrowing and lending

[59] Building Societies Act 1986, s. 34 and Sched. 8, Pt. I, paras. 1, 3.
[60] Ibid., Sched. 8, Pt. IV, para. 3.

activities but which are not involved in full-scale banking. These include the Crown Agents, the credit unions and the National Savings Banks.

10. REVIEW OF THE SYSTEM

The banking world of the City of London is split into a number of groups which have frequently developed on historical rather than on functional lines. Some organizations are regional in character, such as BOCBA (encompassing banks from within the British influence zone). Others comprise institutions which have similar interests. The accepting houses and their organization are a case in point.

It is clear that there are overlaps between the different groups. Accordingly, where the rules of an organization do not prohibit this, a given house may belong to two associations. Thus, the Scandinavian Bank is a member both of the Consortium Banks Association and of the Issuing Houses Association. Some bankers, though, have maintained their splendid isolation.

From a functional point of view, it is best to classify both the banks and their organizations into specialists and general providers of banking services. The clearers (including the three new functional members of the clearing house) constitute the generalists. All other organizations represent specialized banks. Thus, the BOCBA banks may offer all the required services to their group of customers. But, in realistic terms, they do not expect the general public to open accounts with them. The BOCBA banks have neither the personnel nor the clearing facilities required to deal with such a volume. It is typical that, when one member of this group—the Hongkong and Shanghai Bank—wished to establish a presence in the United Kingdom, it offered to take over the Royal Bank of Scotland.

From the viewpoint of the public, the clearing banks tend to be regarded as 'the banks'. This is a realistic approach, as only the clearers from amongst the banks[61] cater for all the needs of the public. They can accommodate the individual, the small business, and the multinational corporation. It is realistic to regard them as the major force in the City.

---

[61] The same will be true in respect of the trustee savings banks, which are in any event functional clearers, when they become more deeply involved with corporations.

CHAPTER 2

The Control of Banking Activities in the United Kingdom

1. THE NEED FOR CONTROLS

The business of banking is fraught with dangers, arising principally from instability in the world economy and from human error or misjudgment. Like any other enterprise, a bank may be overtaken by events or may be governed unwisely. Bank failures are, therefore, no novelty. It is interesting that the Bank of England itself faced serious financial problems within two years of its foundation in 1694.[1] Modern examples are not hard to find. The best-known one is the upheaval in the financial world during the Depression between the two World Wars,[2] which led to the collapse of numerous banks.

The most recent period of difficulties in the United Kingdom occurred in 1973–6, as a result of the sharp fall in property prices. This development triggered off the secondary bank crisis, which led to the failure of a number of fringe houses in the City, and exercised a great deal of pressure on some medium-sized and even substantial banks. To prevent a general loss of trust in financial institutions, the Bank of England launched the 'lifeboat operation', joining fronts with the sound banks in order to bail out the endangered bodies. Similar operations were undertaken during the same period in Germany (in respect of Bankhaus Herstatt).[3]

Banks face many pitfalls in their daily operations. The better-known examples are unwise investments in questionable industrial projects, hazardous dealings in foreign currencies, and the investment of money received on short deposits in long-term transactions.[4] This last dangerous practice has achieved notoriety. When, contrary to expectations, short-term deposits

---

[1] Sir John Clapham, *The Bank of England—A History*, Cambridge, 1944, pp. 30–1. A shortage of funds resulted—just two decades later—in the widening of the Bank's borrowing powers: Bank of England Act 1716.

[2] Particularly the crash of 1929–33.

[3] For a vivid description of the crisis and lifeboat operation, see 'The Secondary Banking Crisis and the Bank of England's Support Operation', *Bank of England Quarterly Bulletin* (hereinafter BEQB) of June 1978, pp. 230 et seq. See also the Ernest Sykes Memorial Lecture of 26 Apr. 1983 delivered by P. W. Cooke. For a detailed treatment, see M. Reid, *The Secondary Banking Crisis 1973–75*, London, 1983.

[4] This unwise practice was one of the factors that triggered off the secondary banking crisis: 'The Secondary Banking Crisis', BEQB, n. 5.

are not renewed, a bank that has lent the funds involved on a long-term basis faces a liquidity crisis.

Turbulence in the banking system has an unfavourable effect on the economy. To start with, banks operate largely by investing funds deposited with them by the public. The collapse of a bank has a disastrous effect on the position of its customers, be they individual account-holders or business enterprises. In addition, the collapse of a medium-sized bank or even of a small one—to say nothing of a major bank—can induce a financial panic. A run on any bank by its customers sends ripples throughout the banking system generally. Thus, the collapse of the fringe London and County Securities Ltd. in November 1973 started the secondary bank crisis. The calamity that could have ensued is succinctly described in an authoritative publication:[5]

The Bank [of England] thus found themselves confronted with the imminent collapse of several deposit-taking institutions, and with the clear danger of a rapidly escalating crisis of confidence. This threatened other deposit-taking institutions and, if left unchecked, would have quickly passed into parts of the banking system proper.

The same source explains:[6]

As a result of their experience with the Overend Gurney crash of 1866, the Baring crisis of 1890 and the prolonged international crisis of 1929–33, the Bank—and the world at large—had come to regard the taking of prompt and decisive action to prevent a spreading of a loss of confidence as one of the essential roles of a central bank.

These two passages highlight the dangers of a panic resulting from a loss of confidence in the world of finance. But even if such a panic is obviated, the collapse of a substantial bank spells out serious repercussions for international trade. The banking systems of the Western world are at present inter-linked and have to function harmoniously. Money transfers require to be effected promptly. Bankers' drafts and travellers' cheques have to be cashed when presented. Letters of credit need to be issued and confirmed forthwith in every trading country in the world on the instruction of foreign correspondents. In all these cases there is no time to verify the creditworthiness of the issuing or transmitting bank. In reality, international banking operates on the basis of trust and confidence. When this is shaken, the system loses its versatility and viability.

Two matters have to be constantly watched in order to avoid disruption to the system. The first may be loosely described as the general standing of institutions carrying on banking business. One way of achieving this object is to enact laws that regulate banking transactions. The other is to impose restrictions on the free entry of firms into the main line of banking business.

[5] Ibid., para. 25.
[6] Ibid.

English law has chosen the latter course; some countries in Western Europe, such as Germany, have adopted the former.

The second matter that needs to be regulated is the stability of individual banks. This involves the introduction of measures to ensure that banks are able to meet their liabilities. Experience shows that, in practice, the drawings of customers of banks follow a predictable pattern. A bank that maintains 'adequate margins', i.e. funds available to meet current demands, has the required liquidity. It can be regarded as a basically sound institution.

English law seeks to safeguard the stability of the banking system by imposing certain controls affecting the two aspects just discussed. Entry into the banking scene is controlled by the restrictions imposed by the Banking Act 1979 on the acceptance of deposits from the public. To engage in this type of business, an institution must be licensed by the Bank of England as a deposit-taking institution or be recognized as a bank. The maintenance of adequate capital liquidity, and other matters of banking prudence, are covered in regular informal discussions between financial institutions and the Bank of England. In addition, the Bank of England used to administer the exchange control system of the United Kingdom. But exchange control was practically abolished in 1980.[7]

2. THE BANK OF ENGLAND

The supervision of banking in the United Kingdom is in the hands of the Bank of England. A brief discussion of the Bank's history will throw light on its role. The Bank of England Act 1694[8] authorized the incorporation of the Bank by means of public subscription. Originally, the object of the Bank was to raise the money required for the war with Louis XIV. The Bank was to transact its business under the style of the Governor and Company of the Bank of England.[9] It was invested with a perpetual succession and granted a common seal. In modern terminology, this meant that it was invested with a legal personality. The Bank was prohibited from engaging in general trade,[10] but was authorized to deal in bills of exchange and in the then equivalent of promissory notes. It was, further, allowed to trade in gold coins, bullion, and silver.[11]

---

[7] The Exchange Control Act 1947 is still in effect. The subordinate legislation made under it was, however, repealed and replaced by a general licence. See p. 75, n. 133 below.

[8] 5 & 6 Will. & Mar., c. 20 (originally known as the Ways and Means Act).

[9] The Bank of England was, in addition, granted the Bank of England Charter 1694, which was augmented and modified by the Bank of England Charter 1890, which, in turn, was repealed and replaced by the Bank of England Charter 1946 (Cmnd. 6752).

[10] Bank of England Act 1946, s. 26.

[11] Ibid., s. 27.

The Bank of England Act 1696[12] granted the Bank a virtual monopoly as regards the carrying on of fully-fledged banking business by a corporation. It thus prohibited the 'erection' of another bank. Obviously, the idea of opening competing banks had been mooted.[13] Although the Act in question did not specifically grant the Bank of England the status of an issuing bank, engaged in printing and in circulating banknotes constituting legal tender, there is evidence that the Bank carried on this activity from the beginning.[14]

It is interesting to note that, in its first years, the Bank dealt in three types of instrument. The first was a note payable to bearer, which had to be indorsed. The second was in the form of a book or sheets in which accounts were kept. These might have been forerunners of the pass-book and of the monthly statement. The third was the 'accomptable note' issued in respect of money deposited. This, undoubtedly, was a primitive type of deposit receipt. It was possible to draw 'notes'—the functional forerunners of cheques—against the last two types of instrument, but not in respect of the first.[15]

Right from its inception, and for many generations to follow, the Bank of England was a joint stock corporation. Apart from its dealings in bills of exchange and in the issuing of banknotes, the Bank further effected remittances of money to Flanders for the purposes of the war with France. The resultant engagement in foreign currency dealings remained one of its activities for a long period afterwards. The Bank also started to maintain accounts opened by private bankers–goldsmiths of the period.

The maintenance of the bankers–goldsmiths' accounts can, possibly, be regarded as the origin of another function of the Bank of England, namely its role in the settlement of the daily accrued balances between individual banks. Where two banks maintained accounts with the Bank of England, it was natural for one bank to pay a balance due to the other by effecting a direct transfer of funds. This function became firmly entrenched with the development of the clearing house in the eighteenth century.[16]

The Bank of England's three main functions—that of an issuing bank, of a central bank and of a settlement bank—became well established in the nineteenth century. The first attempt to give the Bank a substantial monopoly of

---

[12] 8 & 9 Will. 3, c. 20.

[13] Clapham, *The Bank of England*, pp. 1–3.

[14] Ibid., pp. 20–1. And see the historical assessment in *Bank of England* v. *Anderson* (1837) 3 Bing. NC 589, 653. Note also that the preamble of the 1696 Act refers to frequent counterfeiting of Bank of England notes. The monopoly over banking business, first granted to the Bank in the 1696 Act, was removed and reintroduced from time to time. It was instituted for the last time by the Bank of England Act 1800, but did not last.

[15] Clapham, *The Bank of England*, p. 25.

[16] R. M. Holland, 'The London Bankers' Clearing House' and 'The English Banking System', *US Monetary Commission*, 1910, pp. 269, 280. And see Clapham, *The Bank of England*, vol. 3, p. 222, vol. 2, pp. 250–1.

issuing banknotes was made in the Bank Notes Act 1826, under which other banks were precluded from issuing notes for less than £5. After several changes, the Bank Charter Act 1844 established, by section 1, an issue department within the Bank. This role of the Bank has been further entrenched by the Currency and Bank Notes Acts of 1928 and 1954. For all practical purposes, only notes issued by the Bank of England are legal tender in England and in Wales and, in addition, notes for less than £5 constitute legal tender in Scotland and in Northern Ireland.[17] Under section 2 of the 1954 Act, the Bank, in consultation with the Treasury, can issue notes up to the value of its gold reserves and for an additional amount, determined from time to time. Such issues are known as 'fiduciary notes issues'.

The Bank's supervisory function—its role as a central bank—developed at a late date. The idea of conferring some supervisory powers on the Bank was first mooted during the second half of the nineteenth century. Before then, the Bank's indirect control of the banking system was based on its ability to influence interest rates by applying them to the accounts maintained with it. In 1873, Bagehot[18] emphasized the Bank's duties in its role as lender of last resort, and asserted that the Bank therefore required suitable supervisory powers. Although the Bank Charter Act 1844 imposed no such duty and, accordingly, did not confer the proposed rights, the Bank nevertheless acted promptly in the Baring failure. Joining forces with some sixteen banking institutions, the Bank guaranteed Baring's debts.[19]

The emergence of powerful joint stock banks during the last two decades of the nineteenth century prevented the Bank of England from effectively exercising the de facto control it had been able to impose on the banking network earlier. The Bank, though, continued its tradition of attempting to regulate the system by manipulating interest rates. It lent its funds to ordinary customers at a competitive commercial rate. This applied to all four groups of the Bank's customers: to the government departments; to the joint stock banks, the merchant banks and the foreign banks; to the discount houses; and to a small number of individual customers. But when the Bank was called upon to act as a lender of last resort, usually to one of the banks, it accommodated at the 'official rate'. This rate was considerably higher than the market rate, and was determined by the Bank on the basis of fiscal considerations. The main object of these activities was to control the gold standard of the pound sterling.[20]

---

[17] Under the Bank Charter Act 1844, s. 11, banks were allowed to continue issuing notes if they were authorized to do so under their charter or under a licence granted by the Bank. In England and Wales there are no banks that continue to enjoy the privilege. Some Scottish banks continue to have the power to issue notes. For certain restrictions, see the Currency and Bank Notes Act 1928, s. 13.

[18] W. Bagehot, *Lombard Street*, London, 1873.

[19] H. S. Sayers, *The Bank of England 1891–1944*, Cambridge, 1976, vol. 1, pp. 1–3.

[20] Ibid., p. 63.

The next development in the Bank's role as a central bank occurred during 1913–14. The need to confer on the Bank the power to determine the margins to be maintained by it with the banks was one of the main topics of the general debate on the regulation of the banking system in the United Kingdom. The maintenance of substantial margins by the banking institutions of the country had the object of providing the funds required by the Bank of England in order to maintain and even increase its gold reserves, which, of course, were essential in an age in which the currency was tied to the gold standard.[21] However, the decisive step in the direction of developing the Bank's function as a central bank took place after the end of the First World War.

The Bank's role as the venue for the settlement of the daily balances between the trading banks became entrenched during the nineteenth century. Although the clearing house remained at 10 Lombard Street, settlement was effected by the transfer of the daily global balance due from the account of the paying bank to that of the recipient bank. Both accounts were invariably kept in the Bank of England.

A new function was conferred on the Bank of England during the First World War and, subsequently, from the beginning of the Second World War. This was the monitoring and administration of exchange control in the United Kingdom. This function, though, ceased to be operative in 1980.[22]

In terms of structure, the Bank remained largely unchanged until 1946. Under the Bank of England Act of that year, the Bank's stock was transferred from the then owners to the Treasury Solicitor. The previous stockholders were, of course, compensated. The Bank is now a government institution. Under section 1, it is headed by a Governor, appointed for a five year period. It has a Deputy Governor, appointed for a similar period, and sixteen directors, each of whom is appointed for a period of four years. These officers form the governing body of the Bank: the Court. All appointments to this body are renewable. To ensure the Bank's independence, it is provided that a person cannot at one and the same time hold office as a Minister of State or as a civil servant and be an officer of the Bank.[23]

The acquisition of the Bank by the government did not affect its legal personality.[24] Theoretically the Bank is subordinate to the Treasury, which can give it directions after consultation with the Governor. Generally, the Court has to administer the Bank in accordance with the provisions of the

---

[21] Ibid. Further useful sources on the history of the Bank of England are W. M. Acres, *The Bank of England from Within*, Oxford, 1931; J. Giuseppi, *The Bank of England*, London, 1966.

[22] See p. 75 n 133 below.

[23] Bank of England Act 1946, s. 4(1).

[24] See note 9 to this chapter. Note reference to Charter in s. 4(2) of the Act.

Bank of England Charter 1946, which replaced the earlier charters in point. In practice, the Treasury and the Bank work in harmony and on a basis of effective equality.

Section 4(3) of the Bank of England Act 1946 spells out the powers exercisable by the Bank over the trading banks. This provision reads:

The Bank, if they think it necessary in the public interest, may request from and make recommendations to bankers, and may, if so authorised by the Treasury, issue directions to any banker for the purpose of securing that effect is given to any such request or recommendation:

Provided that:–

(a) no such request or recommendation shall be made with respect to the affairs of any particular customer of the banker; and

(b) before authorising the issue of any such directions the Treasury shall give the banker concerned, or such person as appears to them to represent him, an opportunity of making representations with respect thereto.

Under section 4(4), a direction can, where necessary, be made by means of a secret document.

It is clear that in the present era the roles of the Bank of England as an issuing bank, as a supervisory central bank, and as a settlement bank are well established. The Bank's supervisory powers require a closer look.

3. THE BANKING ACT 1979[25]

(i) Background

Two main factors led to the passing of the Act. The first was the secondary bank crisis, discussed above.[26] It was realized that one risk of a system of free banking was the ease with which deposits could be solicited from the public. The Protection of Depositors Act 1963, which was then in effect, had proved an inadequate measure.[27]

The second factor that prompted the passing of the Act was the issuing by the Council of the European Communities of its Directive no. 77/780 of 12 December 1977.[28] The main objects of this directive were to facilitate

---

[25] For a detailed treatment, see I. Morison, P. Tillett, and J. Welch, *The Banking Act 1979*, London, 1979; F. R. Ryder, *The Banking Act 1979*, London, 1979.

[26] And see the White Paper prepared before the enactment of the 1979 Act: *The Licensing and Supervision of Deposit Taking Institutions*, 1976, Cmnd. 6584.

[27] Repealed under s. 51(2) of the Banking Act 1979 and the Banking Act (Commencement No. 3) Order 1985, SI 797. The 1963 Act affected mainly advertisements for deposits, and concerned returns to be made periodically. These measures were demonstrated to be inadequate by the secondary banking crisis.

[28] *Official Journal of the European Communities*, 17 Dec. 1977, vol. 20, no. L 322/30, augmented by Directive no. 7363 of 6 June 1983.

harmony in controls, and to avoid any discrimination in the granting of authorizations to credit institutions wishing to establish themselves in member countries. A credit institution is defined in article 1 as an undertaking 'whose business is to receive deposits or other repayable funds from the public and to grant credits for its own account'. Under article 3, clause 1, members are instructed to 'require credit institutions subject to [the] Directive to obtain authorization before commencing their activities'. It is known that the Treasury and the Bank of England were advocates of the Directive. The Banking Act 1979 provides, in the spirit of the Directive, for the required 'authorizing' of credit institutions in the United Kingdom.

The Act does not apply a uniform criterion for the authorization of all the institutions covered by it. Instead, it divides deposit-taking institutions into four groups and, in addition, makes provision for the exemption of given transactions from the requirements of the Act. The four groups are: (*a*) the Bank of England; (*b*) recognized banks; (*c*) licensed institutions, which are usually described as 'licensed deposit-takers'; and (*d*) institutions listed in Schedule 1 of the Act. The last group includes, inter alia, the central banks of the EEC and building societies. Schedule 1 institutions are exempt from the provisions of section 1 of the Act. So are the transactions prescribed by the Treasury in regulations made under section 2 of the Act. The transactions involved include the acceptance of certain deposits by charities, by industrial and provident societies, by solicitors, by estate agents, and by certain public undertakings, such as the BBC.[29]

Any enterprise encompassed by one of the four groups is entitled to accept deposits from the public. The Bank of England, which is the only body listed in the first group, and the enterprises of the fourth group—the Schedule 1 institutions—do not require a specific authorization. Bodies of the Second group (the 'deposit-takers') have to be 'licensed' by the Bank of England. Bodies of the third group (the banks) have to be 'recognized' by the Bank.

The bodies listed in these four groups are entitled to solicit deposits generally. The position differs in respect of the special category of 'exempt transactions'. These are covered by the applicable regulations only if they fall within the scope of the definition of the transaction involved. Thus, a deposit made with a solicitor is covered by the exemption only if it is accepted in the ordinary course of his business as a professional man.

(ii) Meaning of deposit

The key to the Act is to be found in section 1. Under subsection (1), only the four groups of institutions mentioned above are allowed to engage in a

---

[29] The Banking Act (Exempt Transactions) Regulations 1983, SI 1865, as amended by SI 396 of 1984.

regular 'deposit-taking business'. However, in the case of 'exempt transactions', the Act specifically sanctions the taking of deposits in the course of
the prescribed types of business. In general, the Act does not preclude the
taking of an isolated deposit by enterprises other than those falling within
one of the four groups; the prohibition applies the moment such a body acts
as a deposit-taking business.[30]

According to subsection (2) an enterprise engages in a deposit-taking
business if its activities fall within one of two headings. The first is the
receipt of money on deposit for the purpose of re-lending. The other
category covers the financing of a business, wholly or to any material extent,
'out of the capital or the interest of money received on deposit'. Subsection
(3) makes an important saving. An enterprise is excluded from the ambit of
the definition if, in the normal course of its business, it is not being held out
as one that accepts deposits on a day-to-day basis, and provided it accepts
deposits on 'particular occasions' only.

The elaborate definition of the apparently simple concept of a 'deposit-
taking business' aims at drawing a distinction between the regular acceptance of loans from the public for re-lending or investment purposes and the
occasional taking up of a loan by a firm other than a bank or the other prescribed financial institutions. The functional word 'deposit' is defined in
subsection (4) as a sum of money paid on the basis that it will be repaid with
or without interest or premium either on demand or 'at a time or in circumstances agreed by or on behalf of the person making the payment and the
person receiving it'. In itself, this phrase covers any loan of money made for
either personal or business purposes.

The Act, however, restricts the generality of the definition. In the first
place, under subsection (4)(*b*), as augmented by subsection (6), a 'deposit'
does not include an arrangement for the payment of money on terms which
are 'referable to the provision of property or services or to the giving of
security'. This phrase is defined as meaning arrangements under which
money is paid as an advance on a price due under a sale or a similar transaction, or as a security in respect of a payment pertaining to the provision of
property or services or as a security thereof. In practical terms, this involves
the exclusion of advances made on account of sales or as security for the
furnishing of goods, the conveyance of real property, and the supply of
services.[31]

Secondly, subsection (5) excludes from the definition of a 'deposit' any

---

[30] The Act intentionally refrains from using the legal term 'loan' for describing deposits.
That a sum of money deposited by a customer with a bank constitutes a loan, see pp. 81 et seq.
below.
[31] It is, however, important to bear in mind that, whenever a concept involves fine distinctions of this type, there are bound to be borderline cases that are hard to place.

loans made by the four groups of institutions discussed earlier, as well as loans made in the course of a money-lending business. Loans made by one company to another company within the same group (holding company, subsidiary and sister company) and loans made to a company by a director, controller, or manager[32] are also excluded. Thus, in practice, the Act prohibits the acceptance by an institution, other than those authorized by the Act, of deposits made by the public for investment purposes. The Act refrains from regulating the making of business loans and the movement of money within a group of companies.

(iii) Licensed deposit-takers

The standards imposed by the Act for admitting an institution to the status of a licensed deposit-taker are not quite as stringent as those laid down for the recognition of an institution as a bank. But it would be wrong to assume that licensed deposit-takers are to be regarded as second-class banks. The list of licensed deposit-takers includes some highly influential institutions, such as the Manchester Exchange Trust and United Dominions Trust. Moreover, some leading banks have subsidiaries which are licensed deposit-takers. Midland Bank Trust Co. Ltd., a member of the Midland Bank group, is one of them. It is noteworthy that at the end of February 1983 the official list of institutions, published by the Bank of England, contained 295 licensed deposit-takers and the very same number of recognized banks. Although in February 1986 the number had changed to 304 licensed deposit-takers and 291 recognized banks, the numerical disparity in the number of institutions in the two respective groups has remained marginal.[33]

From a practical point of view, the Act does not confer substantive rights on a bank that are not equally enjoyed by a licensed deposit-taker. The distinction is that, in general, the latter type of institution cannot use the word 'bank' or any derivation thereof in its name, and is precluded from holding itself out as being engaged in banking business.[34] The prohibition, though, is formal. Nothing in the Act is meant to affect the determination of any question as to whether a given licensed deposit-taker is a bank for purposes other than those of the Act itself.[35] Neither does the Act preclude a licensed institution from effectively carrying on banking business, provided it does

---

[32] As defined in s. 49 of the 1979 Act.

[33] Annual Report by the Bank of England 1982–3, para. 2; and Annual Report for 1985–6, para. 5.

[34] S. 36(1). The prohibition does not apply to the Bank of England; to the Central Banks of EEC member states; to trustee savings banks; or to the National Girobank.

[35] S. 36(2).

not hold itself out as doing so. Furthermore, there are two instances in which an institution can refer to itself as a bank. One is where it wishes to comply with or take advantage of 'any relevant provision of law or custom' and needs to use the expression in order to assert its right to do so.[36] The other is that a foreign institution may use the word 'bank', where it is part of its ordinary name, provided it specifically describes itself as a licensed deposit-taker.[37]

In reality, the Act does not interfere with the business activities of licensed deposit-takers. They may engage in some facets of banking business and are even allowed to refer to this fact, provided they do not hold themselves out as being banks.[38] The only advantage gained by a licensed deposit-taker from being recognized as a bank is the increase in its prestige.

The criteria for the grant to an institution of a deposit-taker's licence are to be found in Schedule 2, Pt. 2, of the Act. First, every manager, director, or controller of the institution must be a person fit to hold office.[39] Secondly, the business must be directed by at least two individuals.[40] Thirdly, an institution other than a body corporate cannot be granted a licence if all the assets available to it are owned by a single person.[41] Fourthly, the business has to be conducted in a prudent manner. Particular elements emphasized in this regard are: (a) the need to maintain net assets and other financial resources at an amount adequate to safeguard the interests of depositors; (b) the maintenance of adequate liquidity; and (c) the making of provision for bad debts and for obligations of a contingent nature.[42] The last criterion is that the net assets of the firm must be of a value of at least £250,000; but the amount specified may be increased from time to time by the Treasury.[43] The criteria are modified in respect of institutions whose principal place of business is abroad.[44]

The annual reports of the Bank of England, presented to Parliament under section 4 of the Act,[45] indicate that there has been no change regarding the construction and application of the applicable criteria. The number

[36] Ibid. And see subs. (3) as regards the meaning of 'relevant provision of law or custom'.
[37] S. 36(8).
[38] S. 36(4). And see subs. (5) as to when the word is deemed to be part of the institution's name or description.
[39] Sched. 2, Pt. 2, para. 7.
[40] Ibid., cl. 8.
[41] Banking Act 1979, s. 3(4).
[42] Sched. 2, Pt. 2, para. 10.
[43] Ibid., cl. 9.
[44] Banking Act 1979, s. 3(5).
[45] Annual Reports by the Bank of England 1979–80 and 1981–2. The interpretation and application of the statutory criteria for authorization to carry on a deposit-taking business are discussed in detail in the first report; the second report mentions that these have remained unchanged. And see Annual Report for 1983–4, pp. 7–8; Annual Report for 1985–6, pp. 14–15.

of licensed deposit-takers has been quite steady since the promulgation of the Act.[46]

(iv) Recognized banks

The Act provides stringent criteria for the recognition of an institution as a bank.[47] The effect is that only the finest financial institutions qualify. As in the case of licensed deposit-takers, the criteria for the recognition of a bank are modified in respect of institutions whose principal place of business is abroad.[48]

To be recognized as a bank, an institution must, by and large, satisfy the criteria discussed in respect of licensed deposit-takers,[49] and has to meet the following standard. First, the institution must have enjoyed for a reasonable time a high reputation and standing in the financial community.[50] In the case of a house which has not been previously engaged in obtaining money on deposit for any length of time, it must be under the control of a recognized bank or some other institution of impeccable repute.[51] Secondly, the institution must provide in the United Kingdom either a wide range of banking services or a specific, highly specialized, banking service.[52] Obviously, a clearing bank will be considered on the basis of its general banking services, whilst a discount house is assessed on the basis of the quality of the specialized service rendered by it.

'Banking services' are defined as (a) the maintenance of current or deposit accounts in sterling or in foreign currency; (b) the provision of finance in the form of overdraft facilities or loans, or of the lending in the wholesale money market; (c) the provision of foreign exchange services; (d) the provision of finance by means of bills of exchange and promissory notes, and of ancillary services related to the documentation prevailing in foreign trade; and (e) the furnishing of financial advice or investment management services.[53] An institution may, however, be regarded as providing a wide range of banking services even if it does not carry on two of the last three mentioned services.

The third criterion pertinent to the recognition of a bank concerns the

---

[46] 187 on 23 July 1980; 297 on 28 Feb. 1981 (sharp increase was partly due to the Bank catching up with its backlog of the initial year); 300 on 28 Feb. 1982; back to 295 on 28 Feb. 1983; but up to 308 on 28 Feb. 1984, and 315 on Feb. 1985 but down to 304 on 28 Feb. 1986. And see n. 59 below as regards the number of recognized banks.
[47] Banking Act 1979, s. 3, and Sched. 2, Pt. 1.
[48] S. 3(5).
[49] This is achieved by cls. 3 and 4; and see s. 3(4) of the Act.
[50] Sched. 2, Pt. 1, cl. 1(1)–(3).
[51] Ibid., cl. 2(1).
[52] Ibid., cl. 2(2).
[53] Ibid., cl. 2(3).

institution's net assets. Currently, the relevant minimum figure is £5 million in the case of an institution providing a wide range of banking services, and £250,000 in the case of an institution providing a highly specialized banking service.[54]

The criteria emphasized by the Act are more flexible than those proposed in *United Dominions Trust* v. *Kirkwood*[55] for the common law test. Thus, whilst the importance of 'reputation' is reflected in the Act, an institution need not establish that it is considered by the City to be a 'bank'. Further, the Act expects an institution to establish that it opens accounts for its customers. But these need not be current accounts operable by cheques. They may be savings or fixed deposit accounts. There is an additional element in which the Act is more in accord with practice than the *Kirkwood* test. Usually, the Act expects a bank to engage in at least two banking services other than the maintenance of accounts. However, an institution may be 'recognized' even if it engages in only one highly skilled banking service. Under the *Kirkwood* test it would not be regarded as engaged in banking services.

As pointed out above, the criteria provided by the Act for the recognition of an institution whose principal business is in the United Kingdom are modified in respect of institutions whose main operations are abroad. The Bank of England need not satisfy itself of the financial soundness and the quality of the management of such a body. The Bank can act on an assurance given to it by the 'supervisory authority' in the country of the institution concerned.[56] Usually, such a supervisory authority is a central bank.[57]

Since the coming into force of the Act, there has been no change in the construction given by the Bank of England to the criteria set out for the recognition of an institution as a bank.[58] As in the case of licensed deposit-takers, the number of recognized banks has remained steady.[59] A perusal of the list of recognized banks, published annually, suggests that initially institutions tend to apply to be licensed as deposit-takers. United Kingdom-based institutions are frequently satisfied with this status. Major overseas institutions are inclined to seek recognition as a bank once they are established in the United Kingdom as licensed deposit-takers.

---

[54] Ibid., cl. 2(5).
[55] [1966] 2 QB 431, discussed on pp. 54 et seq. below.
[56] Banking Act 1979, s. 3(5).
[57] Ibid., s. 3(6), which requires the supervisory authority to be a body comparable with the Bank.
[58] See authorities cited in note 45 to this chapter.
[59] 277 on 23 July 1980; 283 on 28 Feb. 1981; 293 on 28 Feb. 1982; 290 on 28 Feb. 1984 and 1985; and 291 on 28 Feb. 1986. The composite number of banks and licensed institutions was 464 on 23 July 1980; 580 on 28 Feb. 1981; 593 on 28 Feb. 1982; 590 on 28 Feb. 1983; 598 on 28 Feb. 1984; 605 on 28 Feb. 1985; but only 595 on 28 Feb. 1986. The slight drops in 1983 and in 1986 were partly occasioned by the revocation of some authorizations.

(v) Application procedure; revocations; appeals

Applications by institutions for a deposit-taker's licence or for recognition as a bank are considered by the Bank of England.[60] The Bank has the power to prescribe the manner in which an application is to be made and is entitled to demand reasonable information in its support.[61] If the Bank proposes to reject the application, it has to give the institution notice of its intention and the chance to make submissions in writing.[62] If, thereafter, the Bank's resolution remains unchanged, it has to 'give notice in writing to the applicant of its decision and the reasons for it before the expiry of six months beginning with the date on which the application was received by the Bank'.[63]

The provisions of the Act, discussed up to this point, lay down general principles concerning applications for licences or for recognition. A detailed procedure has been prescribed by the Bank of England and is outlined in its first annual report under the Act. The report also mentions that the Bank has devised a common form for all applications, be they for recognition as a bank or for a deposit-taking licence. The form indicates that, if recognition is applied for and is denied, the application will be treated as one for a licence. To assist it in reaching a decision, the Bank usually asks for information about those responsible for the running of the business and demands statistics concerning the institution's affairs. Where the application is for recognition as a bank, the Bank of England further demands information establishing that the institution's record meets with the stringent requirements concerning reputation, the range and extent of banking services, the institution's business standards, and its management.[64]

The recognition of a bank and the licence of a deposit-taker are, by their nature, subject to cancellation. They can either be surrendered by the institution or revoked by the Bank in accordance with the procedure prescribed by the Act.[65] The question of revocation arises in a number of situations listed in section 6. First, there is room for revocation if a bank or a licensed deposit-taker ceases to meet the prudential criteria prescribed for institutions of its type. The second case is where the institution concerned fails to carry on any deposit-taking business in the twelve months following its authorization, or has ceased to carry on such services for six months. Third is the case in which the institution becomes insolvent. Fourthly, there is room for revocation where a foreign-based institution's authorization is

---

[60] Banking Act 1979, s. 3(1).
[61] Ibid., s. 5(1). Under subs. (2), the Bank has the power to request additional information.
[62] Ibid., s. 5(4).
[63] Ibid., s. 5(5). Under s. 5(6) this period can be extended up to a maximum of twelve months from the date of the application if any information has been formally requested by the Bank.
[64] Annual Report by the Bank of England 1979–80, pp. 1–2.
[65] Banking Act 1979, s. 3(7).

withdrawn from its home office. Finally, there is the general type of case in which the Bank considers that the body in question has conducted its affairs in a manner that threatens its depositors' interests. The Bank has made the following statement concerning the policy guiding it in cases in which the question of revocation arises:[66]

> In deciding whether to use its powers to revoke the authorization of a particular institution, the Bank has to consider the degree to which the interests of the existing and future depositors are seriously threatened and whether the problems that the Bank has identified are capable of remedy.
>
> The circumstances that are taken into account in considering revocation include evidence that the capital invested in the business has become inadequate to absorb actual and future losses; that liquidity has become insufficient to meet obligations likely to fall due; that provisions set aside to cover bad and doubtful debts are deficient; or that there is other evidence of imprudence or of impropriety on the part of those directing an institution's affairs. The Bank expects creditors, managers and controllers to carry out their individual and collective responsibilities with integrity and professional skill. Instances of lack of judgment, recklessness, provision of false information to the Bank, failure to keep proper books and records or undue reliance on a single person in the direction of the business call into question the prudent conduct of the business and the fitness of those responsible to hold their positions.

It is clear that the Bank places emphasis on the adequacy of an institution's management. Thus, in one case, a deposit-taker's licence was revoked as the business ceased to be conducted by two persons of adequate standing.[67]

Where one of the unfavourable events specified in the Act takes place in respect of a given institution, the Bank of England may revoke its respective licence or recognition altogether, or may grant it a conditional licence.[68] Further, if the institution is a recognized bank, the Bank of England may withdraw recognition and grant either an unconditional or a conditional licence.[69]

The Act prescribes two procedures for the revocation of a licence or the withdrawal of a recognition. One applies in the majority of cases; the other is employed in cases in which the licence or recognition is to be replaced by a temporary licence and, in the Bank's opinion, the matter is one of urgency.

Under the ordinary procedure, the institution involved has to be given both notice specifying why the Bank intends to intervene and an opportunity to make representations.[70] The Bank's decision has to be conveyed to

---

[66] Annual Report by the Bank of England 1982–3, p. 6.

[67] See Treasury Press Notice 204/83 of 14 November 1983.

[68] Banking Act 1979, s. 7(1). And see s. 10 as regards conditional licences. These are to be issued only in the context of revocation proceedings.

[69] Ibid., s. 7(2). And see explanation of policy in Annual Report by the Bank of England 1983–4, p. 10; Annual Report 1985–6, pp. 14–15.

[70] Banking Act 1979, s. 7(3). And see Sched. 4, Pt. 1, para. 1.

the institution within twenty-eight days of the initial notice.[71] In the case of the urgent, or emergency, procedure, the Bank has to give the institution notice of its decision concerning the revocation of the licence or the withdrawal of the recognition and the grant of the conditional licence.[72] The institution has fourteen days for making representations. If it avails itself of this right, the Bank is under a duty to review its decision in the light of the submission made to it.[73] Notice of the Bank's ultimate decision has to be served on the institution within twenty-eight days from the date on which the 'immediate revocation notice' was served.[74] If the Bank resolves to rescind its original decision, the respective authorization is deemed 'never to have been revoked'.[75]

The Bank's power to withdraw recognition from, or to cancel a licence of, an institution provides an ultimate weapon. Its existence means that neither a bank nor a deposit-taker can afford to relax its standards after it has obtained its authorization. It has to be mindful of the Bank's vigilant eye. Throughout its working life under the regime, an institution has to observe the stringent standards that it had to meet at the stage of its initial application to enter the deposit-taking market.

It is clear that the Bank exercises its supervisory powers severely. Thus, in the year ending 28 February 1984, the Bank revoked one recognition, two full licences and one conditional licence. In the previous year, it revoked seven licences. Conditional licences were granted in only some of these cases. Further revocations of licences and of recognitions took place in 1985 and in 1986. In each year a number of institutions surrendered their authorizations. Presumably, some elected to adopt this course in order to avoid the humiliation of revocation proceedings.[76]

An institution aggrieved by a decision of the Bank has the right to appeal to the Chancellor of the Exchequer. The decision contested may be from the Bank's refusal to grant the institution the type of authorization applied for. Equally, an institution has the right to appeal from revocation proceedings in which it has not been fully vindicated. It could thus appeal from the Bank's decision to convert its full licence into a conditional one.[77]

The Act prescribes the basic procedure for appeals,[78] and confers on the Treasury the power to make regulations in consultation with the Council on

---

[71]   Ibid., Sched. 4, Pt. 1, para. 2.

[72]   Ibid., s. 7(4); and see Sched. 4, Pt. 2, paras. 1–3.

[73]   Ibid., Sched. 4, Pt. 2, para. 4.

[74]   Ibid., Sched. 4, Pt. 2, para. 5(1).

[75]   Ibid., Sched. 4, Pt. 2, para. 5(3).

[76]   The Bank has the power to give directions affecting the business of a bank or a deposit-taker whose authority has been revoked under s. 8 of the Act; under s. 9, such a direction basically remains in effect for 28 days.

[77]   Banking Act 1979, s. 11(1)–(2).

[78]   Ibid., s. 11(4).

Tribunals.[79] Such regulations, which are subject to annulment by Parliament,[80] have been made.[81] The appeals in question are not heard by the Chancellor of the Exchequer in person but by 'appointed persons',[82] two of whom are legally qualified persons of standing and the third an accountant or a financial expert.[83] The Chancellor of the Exchequer, acting on the advice of these persons, has wide-ranging powers in giving his final decision. Basically, he can issue any directive that could have been given by the Bank.[84]

The decision of the Chancellor is final as regards points of fact. There is an appeal on points of law to the High Court at the instance of either the institution concerned or the Bank.[85] If the Court is satisfied that the decision appealed from is erroneous in law, it has to remit the matter to the Chancellor for re-hearing and determination.[86] The Act provides that an appeal from the High Court's decision is subject to the grant of leave by the judge or by the Court of Appeal.[87]

To date there have been a number of appeals to the Chancellor of the Exchequer from decisions of the Bank.[88] There is no reported decision of an appeal on a point of law.

(vi) Protective measures and powers of the Bank of England

The Act introduces certain measures for the protection of depositors, and in addition imposes certain duties on licensed deposit-takers and on recognized banks. The object is to maintain the high standard of institutions accepting deposits from the public. The Bank of England is given the powers needed to enable it to exercise control. The protective provisions of the Act are technical. A general discussion is all that can be here included.

The most important principle—which may be described as the cornerstone of the Act—is that deposits from the public may be accepted only by the four groups of financial institutions mentioned at the outset: the Bank of

[79] Ibid., s. 12(1).
[80] Ibid., s. 12(2).
[81] The Banking Act 1979 (Appeals) Regulations 1980, SI 353, and the Banking Act 1979 (Scottish Appeals) Regulations 1980, SI 348.
[82] Banking Act 1979, s. 11(1).
[83] The Banking Act 1979 (Appeals) Regulations 1980, SI 353, reg. 7(3).
[84] Banking Act 1979, s. 11(3).
[85] Ibid., s. 13(1)–(2).
[86] Ibid., s. 13(1).
[87] Ibid., s. 13(3). And note specific provision concerning Northern Ireland and Scotland.
[88] The nature of such a hearing emerges from Treasury Press Release 11/81 of 21 July 1981, where an institution appealed against the Bank's decision to refuse to 'recognize' it. And see Annual Report by the Bank of England 1983–4, pp. 10–11.

England; the recognized banks; the licensed deposit-takers; and Schedule 1 institutions.[89] As between the four groups, the Act does not draw any distinction concerning the engagement in this type of business. In addition, it will be recalled that other prescribed enterprises may accept deposits that fall within the ambit of an 'exempt transaction'.

As a complementary measure, the Act has empowered the Treasury to make regulations controlling the contents of advertisements issued to solicit deposits from the public.[90] Regulations were made in 1985.[91]

Another measure introducing fairness in information prohibits the use of the word 'bank' or 'banker' in the title of any institution which is not a recognized bank,[92] or one of the institutions designated for this purpose from among those listed in Schedule 1.[93] Other institutions may not even describe themselves as conducting the business of banking or as providing banking services.[94] The main exception to this provision applies where a licensed institution, other than one entitled to use the word 'bank' in its name, carries on at least two types of 'banking services'.[95] It may then describe these services as such, provided that, in doing so, it does not create the impression that the reference to 'banking' forms part of its name. Furthermore, the institution may not refer to its banking services in any notice to the public.

To enable the Bank of England to exercise its control effectively, the Act confers on it four powers. First, the Bank may demand information from licensed institutions as regards the conduct of their business and its nature.[96] In practice, banks—including recognized banks—furnish this information voluntarily. Secondly, the Bank has the power to require a licensed institution to produce documents and books.[97] Thirdly, the Bank has the power to appoint persons charged with the investigation of both recognized banks and licensed deposit-takers.[98] Fourthly, where the Bank is

[89] Banking Act 1979, s. 1; as regards Schedule 1 institutions, see pp. 44–45 below.

[90] Ibid., s. 34. As regards the Bank's powers where a licensed institution publishes a misleading advertisement, see s. 35.

[91] Banking Act 1979(Advertisement) Regulations 1985, SI 220.

[92] But note that the Act does not preclude the institution from furnishing banking services provided they are not being advertised.

[93] Banking Act 1979, s. 36(1). The institutions included are the Bank of England; the central banks of EEC member states; the trustee savings banks and the Central Trustee Savings Bank; and the Post Office (viz. the National Girobank). For exceptions see s. 36(2), discussed on pp. 34–35 above. And see subs. (4) as regards 'banking services'. A licensed deposit-taker whose main business is abroad can use the word 'bank' in his name, provided it is immediately followed by prominently displayed words denoting that, in the United Kingdom, it is a deposit-taker: s. 36(8)–(9).

[94] Banking Act 1979, s. 36(1).

[95] Ibid., s. 36(4).

[96] Ibid., s. 16.

[97] Ibid., s. 16.

[98] Ibid., s. 17.

dissatisfied with the institution's solvency or liquidity, it has the power to present a petition for its winding-up.[99]

It is clear that the powers conferred on the Bank of England are extremely wide. To protect the interests of the institutions governed by the Act, it is provided that information received by the Bank is confidential. However, this principle applies subject to certain exceptions, applicable mainly where the Bank considers it in the public interest to publish the information.

The powers conferred on the Bank do not, in themselves, provide the means to alert it to imminent dangers arising in the case of any given institution. One important measure that is bound to put the Bank on notice is that licensed institutions have the duty to notify it of any changes of directors.[100] The public, too, is given the opportunity to investigate. Under section 15(1) of the Act:

At each place within the United Kingdom at which it holds itself out to accept deposits, a licensed institution shall keep a copy of its most recent audited accounts; and during normal business hours that copy shall be made available for inspection by any person on request.

Without doubting the spirit of this provision, it may be asked how many members of the public have either the initiative or the ability to conduct such an inspection meaningfully before depositing their money with the institution concerned. It is noteworthy that neither this provision, nor the duty to inform the Bank of changes in an institution's directorate, applies to recognized banks. Presumably, the last provision is considered unnecessary in their case. The information mentioned in the former provision is supplied by the banks voluntarily.

A more positive measure, which is bound to be of importance to depositors where the applicable controls fail to avert the collapse of a bank or of a licensed institution, is the introduction of a deposit protection scheme.[101] Basically, the Act has made provision for the establishment of a fund which, in the event of the failure of a licensed institution or a recognized bank, is required to pay depositors an amount equal to 75 per cent of any sterling deposit or deposits not exceeding £10,000 and made with a branch or office in the United Kingdom.[102] Upon each such payment, the fund is subrogated to the depositor's rights against the defaulting institution.[103] Contributions to the fund are made by all institutions governed by the Act, unless they have been

---

[99] Ibid., s. 18, as amended by s. 219 of the Insolvency Act 1985. And see ss. 19 and 20 as to information received by the Bank from indirect sources.

[100] Ibid., s. 14.

[101] Ibid., ss. 21–33. The scheme came into effect on 19 Feb. 1982: Banking Act 1979 (Commencement no. 2) Order 1982, SI 188.

[102] Ibid., ss. 28, 29.

[103] Ibid., s. 31.

specifically excluded.[104] The scheme does not cover Schedule 1 institutions. The Fund is known as the Deposit Protection Fund, and is managed by an independent body, the Deposit Protection Board.[105]

(vii) Schedule 1 bodies

Institutions listed in Schedule 1 are exempt from the prohibition of taking deposits without the Bank's authorization.[106] In effect, these institutions are altogether outside the regime of the Act. The reasons for this wide exemption emerge from a consideration of the nature of the institutions involved. For this purpose, Schedule 1 institutions can be divided into four groups.

The first group includes the central banks of EEC states. These institutions can be deemed to be solvent and well managed. In any event, they had to be excluded from the ambit of the 1979 Act to ensure compliance with the EEC directive in point.[107]

The second group encompasses bodies which are affiliated either to the Government or to local authorities. They may be regarded as being supervised effectively by bodies other than the Bank. The institutions of this group include: (a) the National Savings Bank, which is a body of the Department of Trade and Savings, and thus answerable to Parliament; (b) the Post Office, which effectively means the National Girobank; (c) municipal banks, which are bodies corporate transacting aspects of banking business in conjunction with a local authority;[108] (d) local authorities; and (e) any other body which has the power to issue a precept to a local authority in England or Wales or to issue a requisition to a local authority in Scotland.

The third group includes enterprises supervised or controlled under other enactments. They are (a) trustee savings banks (although these banks will cease to be Schedule 1 bodies and will be brought under the regime of the Act when their reorganization as bodies corporate is complete); (b) building societies;[109] (c) friendly societies; (d) insurance companies; (e) loan societies

---

[104] Ibid., ss. 23–7. For such exclusions see the Deposit Protection Fund (Excluded Institutions) Orders 1982, 1983, and 1984, SI 1808 of 1982, 1100 of 1983, and 897 and 1990 of 1984. Bodies are so excluded if the Treasury is satisfied that their depositors are adequately protected under another scheme which, in the case of a foreign bank, may be maintained through its home office.

[105] Ibid., s. 21. And see generally the annual reports of the Deposit Protection Board, submitted in accordance with para. 4(5) of Sched. 5 of the Banking Act 1979 on 28 Feb. 1983 and 1984 respectively.

[106] Ibid., s. 2(1). And as regards exempt transactions, see p. 32 above.

[107] See note 28 to this chapter.

[108] Banking Act 1979, s. 48.

[109] Within the meaning of the Building Societies Act 1962 or the Building Societies Act (Northern Ireland) 1967; such bodies are supervised by the Chief Registrar of Friendly Societies; but see p. 22 below.

controlled under the Loan Societies Act 1840; (*f*) credit unions;[110] and (*g*) school banks certified for this purpose by a trustee savings bank.

The fourth group includes stockbrokers and stockjobbers; these fall within the scope of Schedule 1 only in respect of transactions made in the course of their business.

The Treasury has exercised its power to add institutions to the list set out in Schedule 1.[111] Subject to the approval of Parliament, the Treasury can also exclude institutions from the list.[112] The effect of such an action is, of course, to bring the institution concerned within the ambit of the Act.

(viii) Assessment of the Act

The measures introduced by the Act are relevant mainly for the carrying on of one type of banking business—the acceptance of deposits from the public—in the United Kingdom. The importance of the Act as regards the traditional domain of banking law—the relationship of banker and customer—is to be found in the criteria set out for the recognition of banks under the Act. The criteria defining the nature of banking business are bound to influence a court which is asked to determine whether or not a given institution carries on 'banking business' within the common law definition. The reason for this is that the Act must be taken to reflect the nature of activities currently carried on by banks.

It is true that section 36(2) provides that nothing in the Act is meant to affect the determination of whether or not a given institution is a bank within the meaning of some other enactment. On this basis, the Act ought not to affect the common law definition of a 'bank', which is employed in statutes such as the Bills of Exchange Act 1882. But the common law definition makes a reference to the 'business of banking'.[113] The criteria employed by the Bank of England to determine the meaning of this phrase for the purposes of the 1979 Act cannot, realistically, be brushed aside.

Is the Act likely to be successful in obviating a crisis such as that of 1973–6? It is forgivable to entertain some doubts on this point. The economic climate in the present era is so volatile and the network of international banking is so closely interwoven that a major setback in one part of

---

[110] Presently governed by the Industrial and Provident Societies Act (Northern Ireland) 1970 and the Credit Unions Act 1979.

[111] Banking Act 1979, s. 2(2)(*a*). For such additions, see the Banking Act 1979 (Excepted Persons) Orders 1980 and 1982, SI 347 of 1980 and 1681 of 1982. The bodies involved are organs of the EEC and development banks and other governmental or international institutions.

[112] Ibid., ss. 2(2)(*b*) and 3.

[113] See pp. 51 et seq. below.

the world is bound to trigger off reactions elsewhere.[114] The control measures introduced by the Act ought to prevent the collapse of isolated banks or, at the very least, may forestall the chain reaction that can follow without the existence of a protective scheme. But a wide loss of confidence, occasioned by international factors and leading to a general run on banks and other financial institutions, cannot be avoided by domestic legislation.

Indeed, dissatisfaction with the existing regime has been voiced by the Government in the wake of the collapse of Johnson Matthey Bankers in October 1984. Proposals for a reform have been made in a White Paper entitled Bank Supervision, presented to Parliament by the Chancellor of the Exchequer in December 1985.[115] These proposals are reflected in the Banking Bill, tabled in November 1986. The principal measures involved can be summarized as follows.

First and foremost is the recommendation for the formation of a new Bank of England Board of Banking Supervision. Its members are to be the three senior officers of the Bank and five experienced members of the business community. The function of the Board will be to give advice on issues arising in the context of the supervisory powers of the Bank. It is believed that, although the Bill is still pending, a Board has been constituted by the Governor of the Bank of England on an informal basis.

The second measure recommended in the White Paper is the strengthening of the Banking Supervision Division. It is understood that steps are being taken to increase the number of experienced accountants and bankers seconded to the Division.

The third and most interesting recommendation affects the very structure of the regime introduced by the Banking Act 1979. The two-tier system, involving the distinction between licensed deposit-takers and recognized banks, is to be abolished. When the new Act is passed, the two groups will be amalgamated. Bodies authorized under the Act to accept deposits from the public will then be known as authorized institutions. Entities exempt from the need of seeking authorization will be listed in Schedule 2.

It is noteworthy that restrictions on the use of the word 'bank' (or any derivation thereof) in the name of a firm will be retained. By and large, an institution will be able to use it if it has either a paid-up share capital or undistributable reserves of £5m. Special provisions are made in the Bill as regards the use of the word 'bank' by foreign financial institutions.

Fourthly, although the Government has rejected the idea of establishing a formal bank inspectorate conducted on lines familiar on the Continent, it proposes to intensify and increase the number of inspection visits to banks,

---

[114] See the prominence given to the international debt position in the Annual Report by the Bank of England 1983–4, pp. 3–4.

[115] Cmnd. 9695. And see Bank of England Notice BSD/1986/3 of Mar. 1986, concerning 'Consolidated Supervision' of financial institutions.

and of interviews conducted by personnel of the Bank of England. Although the Bill does not include any express provisions defining the change, the new policy is reflected in the spelling out of the investigatory powers of the Bank, and in the definition of the information that is to be made available to it by authorized institutions. These provisions of the Bill are considerably more detailed than those of the 1979 Act.

There are, of course, numerous consequential and supplementary amendments to be introduced as part and parcel of the proposed reform. Of considerable importance is clause 84, under which consumer credit agreements, entered into by authorized institutions to enable borrowers to acquire land or to erect a dwelling, could be exempted from the provisions of the Consumer Credit Act 1974. However, a detailed discussion of all the proposed changes is premature because, at the time of going to press, it is impossible to be certain that the Bill will be enacted in its present form.

The enactment of a new Banking Act will be a development of major importance. It is expected that a new Act, which will repeal and replace the Banking Act 1979, will be passed in 1987.

4. MONETARY CONTROLS

The supervision exercised by the Bank of England under the Banking Act 1979 does not involve a direct monetary control of the activities of financial institutions. Traditionally, two measures have been employed for this purpose. The first may be described as the manipulation of short-term interest rates. The second is the provision for minimum amounts that have to be utilized by financial institutions in a manner prescribed by the Bank. This measure, which is known as the maintenance of margins, has the object of ensuring liquidity by controlling the use of funds deposited by the public with financial institutions.

The manipulation of interest rates used to be achieved by the determination of the 'minimum lending rate' (MLR). This is the minimum rate at which the Bank places funds with the discount houses to enable them to cover any deficiency arising by the close of working hours from loans made to banks and other financial institutions during the day. Naturally, the determination of such a rate is bound to affect the entire structure of interest rates in the United Kingdom, as it has a direct bearing on the rate at which banks and other financial institutions can lend money profitably. The rate at which money is made available by the banks has, in turn, a major influence on the economy at large. Interest rates constitute a crucial factor in the demand for loans. As the rate decreases, demand tends to improve; as the rate increases, demand slackens and, eventually, comes to a halt. Thus, the MLR is expected either to stimulate or reduce the pace of economic activity.

The control of the use of funds deposited with banking institutions can be achieved by means of direct margins placed by them either with the Bank or in specified securities.[116] The system is traditionally based on voluntary arrangements between the Bank and the financial institutions under its control. However, the Bank has the statutory power, under section 4 of the Bank of England Act 1946, to enforce adherence to its directives.[117] To date, though, the Bank has not been compelled to resort to this power.

In studying the Bank's policy concerning monetary controls, it is necessary to note the existence of three separate periods in recent years: the years preceding 1971; the era of 1971–81; and the last few years. During the first period the Bank's policy was to attempt to exercise its controls mainly by the manipulation of the Bank Rate, a forerunner of the MLR. The approach to margins was simple. The banks had to place 8 per cent of their cash deposits in non-interest-bearing accounts with the Bank of England. Another 20 per cent had to be injected into liquid investments that could be converted into cash on demand or at short notice. When the supply of money on the market was too large, the Bank required the financial institutions under its control to increase their 'liquidity ratio' by placing with itself 'special deposits' in interest-bearing accounts. There were also often direct constraints on the rate of growth of the balance sheets of large banks.

Experience showed that this system tended to stamp out competition. Consequently, the Bank of England introduced in 1971 a new regime, which remained in effect until 1981.[118] In the wake of the Banking Act 1979, this regime was applied also to licensed deposit-takers.

The new regime—of the 'second period'—required the banks and other controlled institutions to keep a minimum ratio—12.5 per cent—of their 'eligible liabilities' in 'reserve assets'. Both terms require an explanation. The 'eligible liabilities' comprised deposits for periods not exceeding two years from customers other than banking institutions and, in addition, the bank's net foreign currency liabilities. Thus, the eligible liabilities represented an institution's immediate indebtedness to non-bank depositors and to foreign investors.[119] The 'reserve assets' in which a bank had to invest the above mentioned percentage, comprised: (*a*) a balance at the Bank; (*b*) money on call with listed discount market institutions and brokers; (*c*) United Kingdom and Northern Ireland Treasury bills; and (*d*) bills eligible

---

[116] Useful information is obtainable from 'The Measurement of Liquidity', Bank of England, July 1982. See also 'The Measurement of Capital', BEQB Sept. 1980, 240 et seq.; and Bank of England Notice BSD/1986/4 of June 1986.

[117] Cited above, p. 31.

[118] See generally 'Monetary Controls'—a discussion paper submitted by the Bank of England to the Chancellor of the Exchequer in Mar. 1980; Cmnd. 7858.

[119] On problems related to foreign currencies, see generally 'Foreign Currency Exposure', Bank of England, Apr. 1981.

for re-discount at the Bank of England such as bills of local authorities or those issued by the clearing banks. All such assets had to be in sterling.

Experience showed that the new system was not an adequate tool for guiding the economy and, further, that it failed to enhance competition. The Bank therefore introduced in 1973 a Supplementary Special Deposit Scheme (known as 'the corset'). The object was to control, where necessary, the number of interest-bearing deposits that could be accepted by any institution; if it exceeded the intended figure, it was required to lodge supplementary deposits—bearing no interest—with the Bank. Eventually, this scheme led to the depositing by the clearing banks of approximately 1.5 per cent of their eligible liabilities with the Bank.

But even the revised system proved inadequate. To start with, there were means to avoid the corset. In addition, it had the undesirable effect of curbing competition. So the system was revised yet again in 1981, with a view to encouraging competition and supporting free market forces.[120] The maintenance by banks of reserve assets was abolished. Instead, there has been a global move back to the maintenance of non-interest-bearing deposits with the Bank. At present these deposits with the Bank fall into two groups. First, the clearing banks have to maintain balances adequate for the daily clearing settlements. These are known as 'operational balances', and are calculated on the basis of estimated amounts required for the process involved.

Secondly, all institutions governed by the Banking Act 1979 which have eligible liabilities of not less than £10 million, as well as the trustee savings banks and the National Girobank, have to maintain with the Bank a balance equal to 0.5 per cent of these liabilities. The level of such a 'non-operational' balance to be maintained by an institution is set twice a year on the basis of its established liabilities for the preceding six months. Eligible liabilities were redefined so as to allow set-offs for, inter alia, money placed in the gilt-edged market. The special deposits scheme has remained operational, and constitutes an extra measure enabling the Bank to influence cash flows.

Instead of the requirement for the maintenance of reserve assets, the Bank widened considerably the discount facilities applicable to bills. Traditionally, the only bills discountable at the Bank were those issued by local authorities, Treasury bills and commercial bills issued by the clearing banks, by the accepting houses and by BOCBA members (such as the Hong Kong and Shanghai Bank).[121] This definition of bills has now been widened by the provision of a list of 'eligible banks', including most of the substantial financial institutions of the City. As the dealing rate for bills of this type is

---

[120] For full details, see 'Monetary Control: Next Steps', Bank of England, Mar. 1981; 'Monetary Control Provisions', Bank of England, 5 Aug. 1981; 'Discount House Multipliers', Bank of England, June 1982.

[121] P. 19 above.

favourable, banks are keen to be listed. All eligible banks have to maintain an average balance of 5 per cent of their eligible liabilities as secured money with members of the London Discount Market Association[122] or with gilt-edged jobbers. This balance is described as 'club money'.

The effect of the current scheme, just as of the preceding ones, is to secure both an adequate cash-flow and a fund of secured money for banking operations. The outcome aimed at is the maintenance of adequate liquidity of the banks. One change incorporated into the new scheme was the abolition of the direct determination by the Bank of the minimum lending rate. But interest rates continue to be affected by the setting of the discount rate for eligible bills.

That the scheme works satisfactorily emerges from a paper published by the Bank in 1983,[123] which explains the introduction of some minor modifications. The scheme is described in it as successful. The scheme functions without direct dependence on the supervisory powers introduced by the Banking Act 1979.[124] At the same time, it is clear that the existence of the supervisory powers of the Bank, and the necessity of furnishing information to it on a regular basis, are factors instrumental in inducing banks to adhere strictly to the existing scheme for monetary controls.

---

[122] The balance may not be less than 2.5% (4% until 1983) of eligible liabilities at any one day.

[123] 'Monetary Control Arrangements', Bank of England, 19 July 1983, basically reducing the percentages of the balances on eligible liabilities to be held by the banks involved.

[124] Under section 16; see pp. 42 et seq. above.

CHAPTER 3

Legal Definition and Privileges of Banks

1. BANKS AT COMMON LAW

(i) Problem of defining a bank

It has been shown in Chapter 1 that in the United Kingdom the banking industry is divided into a number of sectors. Each of these has its own characteristics and is therefore distinguishable from the others. As a result of this proliferation, the Legislature has not found it necessary to provide a functional definition that distinguishes banks from other financial institutions.[1] Separate Acts define a 'bank' for their specific purposes. An institution that is a bank in one context may not be so regarded for some other purposes.

First to be considered is the common law definition of a 'bank'. It is based on treating a bank as an institution engaged in banking business. The nature of this type of business has not been determined by Parliament. Its construction has accordingly remained in the hands of the courts.

The discussion of the common law definition is followed by a review of definitions found in specific Acts. The policy and objects of the relevant statutes is also considered. It will be shown that in many of these Acts the definition of a bank has been amended to reflect the policy of the Banking Act 1979.[2]

(ii) Banking business at common law

Under section 2 of the Bills of Exchange Act 1882:

'banker' includes a body of persons whether incorporated or not who carry on the business of banking.

Despite its patent circularity, this definition is not as unhelpful as it may

---

[1] In English law, a firm does not require a licence in order to engage in banking business. The only current restrictions are, first, that it needs to be licensed or recognized under the Banking Act 1979 before it accepts deposits from the public (see pp. 32 et seq. above) and, secondly, if it is not incorporated there can be no more than 20 owners: Companies Act 1985, s. 716(1).

[2] Discussed above, Chap. 2.

appear at first glance. It provides that, to determine whether or not an institution is a bank, the court has to review its business and must compare it with that transacted by banks generally. In this way, the definition furnishes a flexible guideline. At the same time, the definition has one disturbing feature. It treats the 'business of banking' as being carried on in a uniform manner by 'banks' generally. Chapter 1 demonstrates that this approach is misguided. The activities of a clearing bank differ in scope from those of an accepting house, and institutions of both these types carry on a business distinguishable from that of discount houses. The case law on the subject has side-stepped this inherent difficulty by assuming that some types of business are conceptually those carried on by a generic group of 'banks'.[3]

Three cardinal principles have been laid down by the courts in construing the common law definition. In the first place, the meaning of 'banking business' can change from time to time. In *Woods* v. *Martins Bank Ltd.*,[4] the issue was whether the giving of advice on financial matters constituted banking business. Holding that it did, Salmon J observed:[5]

the limits of a banker's business cannot be laid down as a matter of law. The nature of such a business must in each case be a matter of fact and, accordingly, cannot be treated as if it were a matter of pure law. What may have been true of the Bank of Montreal in 1918 is not necessarily true of Martins Bank in 1958.[6]

His Lordship relied, inter alia, on the fact that in the instant case the bank had held itself out as being in a position to advise its customers on their investments.

The second principle laid down by the courts is that a house regarded as engaged in 'banking business' in one place is not necessarily so considered elsewhere.[7] Thus it has been consistently held in Irish[8] and in Australian[9]

---

[3] This approach is reflected in works on the subject: H. L. Hart, *Law of Banking*, 4th edn., London, 1931, p. 1; Lord Chorley, *Law of Banking*, 6th edn., London, 1974, pp. 32–3; J. R. Paget, *Law of Banking*, 9th edn., pp. 5–6.
[4] [1959] 1 QB 55.
[5] Ibid., p. 70; see also *Davies* v. *Kennedy* (1869) IR 3 Eq. 668; *Re Shields' Estate* [1901] 1 Ir.R 173, 179; *Bank of Chettinad Ltd.* v. *Commissioners of Income Tax, Colombo* [1948] AC 378, 383.
[6] This a reference to the case of *Banbury* v. *Bank of Montreal* [1918] AC 626, in which it was held by the Privy Council on an appeal from Canada that the giving of advice on investments did not constitute banking business.
[7] This is implied in the above-quoted passage from *Woods* v. *Martins Bank Ltd.*, above. See also *Bank of Chettinad Ltd.* v. *Commissioners of Income Tax, Colombo*, above; *Commissioners of the State Savings Bank of Victoria* v. *Permewan, Wright & Co. Ltd.* (1914) 19 CLR 457.
[8] *Davies* v. *Kennedy* (1869) IR 3 Eq. 668; *Re Shields' Estate* [1901] 1 Ir.R 173; *Commercial Banking Co. Ltd.* v. *Hartigan* (1952) 86 Ir. LTR 109.
[9] *Commissioners of the State Savings Bank of Victoria* v. *Permewan, Wright & Co. Ltd.* (1914) 19 CLR 457; *Mason* v. *Savings Bank of South Australia* [1925] SASR 198, 204; *Melbourne Corporation* v. *Commonwealth of Australia* (1947) 74 CLR 31, 64–65; *Australian Independent Distributors Ltd.* v. *Winter* (1964) 112 CLR 443, 455 (where a co-operative society was held not to be a bank as it accepted deposits from members only).

cases that an institution which accepts money on deposit from the public for the purpose of relending it, carries on banking business even if it does not open for customers current accounts operable by cheques. It will be shown that the opposite view has been adopted in the United Kingdom. The distinction is explainable on the basis of the differences in the structure of banking in the countries concerned.

Thirdly, a number of cases stress the importance of an institution's reputation. If it is widely considered to be a bank, the courts will be inclined to adopt this view, and to treat the firm as engaged in banking business.[10]

Although the meaning of 'banking business' is subject to change, it is important to consider which types of transactions have traditionally been treated as characteristic of it. First and foremost is the acceptance of money on deposit from customers for the purpose of making a profit by re-investing it. FitzGibbon LJ explained the position succinctly in *Re Shields' Estate*:[11]

The business of banking, from the banker's point of view, is to traffic with the money of others for the purpose of making profit.

Similarly, in *Commissioners of the State Savings Bank of Victoria* v. *Permewan, Wright & Co. Ltd.*, Isaacs J described the essence of banking business as:[12]

the collection of money by receiving deposits upon loan, repayable when and as expressly or impliedly agreed upon, and the utilisation of money so collected by lending it again in such sums as are required.

The two cases emphasize that a bank's business is to borrow and lend to the public, whilst other financial institutions, such as co-operative societies, tend to borrow from, and to lend to, a limited group such as its members or shareholders.[13] On this point the two cases are supportable.[14] To date it has not been suggested that an institution may be regarded as a bank although it does not receive money on deposit from the public.

In the United Kingdom, the second essential type of banking business is the opening of current accounts operably by cheques and the collection of effects paid in by customers. In the landmark case of *United Dominions*

---

[10] *Re Birkbeck Permanent Benefit Building Society* [1912] 2 Ch. 183, 208; *Commercial Banking Co. Ltd v. Hartigan* (1952) 86 Ir. LTR 109; *United Dominions Trust Ltd. v. Kirkwood* [1966] 2 QB 431, discussed below.

[11] [1901] 1 Ir.R 173, 198.

[12] (1915) 19 CLR 457, 471.

[13] *Australian Independent Distributors Ltd. v. Winter* (1964) 112 CLR 443 (where a co-operative society was held not to be a bank as it did not accept deposits from the public but from members alone. But as it was as easy to join the society as it was to become the customer of a bank, the decision may be questioned.)

[14] It is, indeed, one of the types of business described as characteristic of banks in *United Dominions Trust Ltd. v. Kirkwood* [1966] 2 QB 431.

Trust v. *Kirkwood*[15] a finance company brought an action to recover a loan made to a dealer. The dealer pleaded that the company was an unregistered money-lender, and that the contract was accordingly illegal as it contravened the Money-lenders Act 1900.[16] The finance company claimed that under section 6(*d*) it was exempted from the registration provisions of the Act because it carried on, bona fide, the business of banking. It was proved that the finance company was regarded as a bank in the City, that it enjoyed some privileges given solely to banks, and that it had a clearing number. It was further established that in some cases the company credited amounts lent by it to a current account opened by it in the borrower's name. The finance company received deposits from the public, but these were invariably repayable on agreed maturity dates and not on demand. There was no evidence to suggest that the company collected cheques payable to its customers.

On these facts, Lord Denning MR doubted that the company carried on the business of banking. His Lordship described the main facets of banking business as follows:[17]

There are, therefore, two characteristics usually found in banks today: (i) They accept money from, and collect cheques for, their customers and place them to their credit; (ii) They honour cheques or orders drawn on them by their customers when presented for payment and debit their customers accordingly. These two characteristics carry with them also a third, namely: (iii) They keep current accounts, or something of that nature, in their books in which the credits and debits are entered.

Despite this description of banking business, Lord Denning held that the company was exempt from the provisions of the Money-lenders Act. He thought that, in cases of doubt, it was 'permissible to look at the reputation of the firm amongst ordinary intelligent commercial men. If they recognised it as carrying on the business of banking, that should turn the scale.'[18]

Diplock LJ's concurring judgment is based on a slightly different reasoning. In his opinion the finance company had a marginal banking business. In itself, it might not have brought it within the ambit of the definition. But the fact that the City considered the firm to be a bank established that it enjoyed

---

[15]   Above. And see *Joachimson* v. *Swiss Bank Corporation* [1921] 3 KB 110, 127; *Bank of Chettinad Ltd.* v. *Commissioners of Income Tax, Colombo* [1948] AC 378, 383–4 (although in this case the decision of the Privy Council was based on a statutory definition applicable in Sri Lanka).

[16]   Repealed by the Consumer Credit Act 1974, s. 192(4) and Sched. 5, Pt. 1, also repealing s. 123 of the Companies Act 1967, which empowered the Board of Trade (now the Department of Trade) to declare an institution a bank for the purposes of the Money-lenders Act. Note that, in view of the similarity between the definition of a banker in that Act and in the Bills of Exchange Act 1882, *Kirkwood*'s case remains of topical importance.

[17]   [1966] 2 QB 447.

[18]   Ibid., 454.

the reputation of carrying on banking business. This reputation, coupled with the firm's marginal banking business, sufficed to bring it within the definition.

Both Lord Denning MR and Diplock LJ thought they were confronting a borderline case. In reality, their Lordships were unwilling to put a major financial institution in jeopardy on the sole ground of its having failed to comply with the technicalities of the Money-lenders Act.[19] Harman LJ had no such qualms. In his dissenting judgment he expressed the view that the company was not carrying on the business of banking. It was, therefore, a mere money-lender.

It is clear that the three judgments in the *Kirkwood* case take divergent views regarding the importance of reputation for determining whether or not a given institution is a bank. As a rigorous analysis of law, Harman LJ's view is to be preferred. According to the common law definition, a bank is an institution that actually carries on banking business; not an institution which has the reputation of doing so or of being a bank. This definition postulates an objective test. Lord Denning, and to a lesser extent Diplock LJ, propounded a test based on subjective criteria. However, their view derives support from other cases.[20]

In *Kirkwood*'s case Diplock LJ inclined to the view that an institution would not be regarded a bank if its banking business was of a negligible size, or if its current accounts were opened as a mere cloak for lending transactions. This dictum was explained in *Re Roe's Legal Charge*.[21]

This recent case centred on the very issue concerning the interpretation of 'banking business' for the purposes of the Money-lenders Act that gave rise to *Kirkwood*'s case. In *Roe*'s case it was established that the lending institution opened current accounts for some customers and that cheques could be collected by it. It was further shown that the firm provided some other banking services, such as the sale of travellers' cheques, foreign currency dealings and facilities for the payments of customers' accounts by means of money transfer orders. The firm obtained daily print-outs showing the state of each account opened by it, and sent to its customers periodic statements. There were, however, four main differences between this firm's business and that of a regular bank. First, the firm's entire banking services were furnished through an agency bank, and not at premises maintained in its own name. Secondly, the number of the current and deposit accounts opened by the firm was less than 200, and in the course of 1984 only fifty-eight cheques had been cleared for customers. Thirdly, about 75 per cent of the firm's deposits were maintained by its shareholders and by its subsidiary and

[19] See Chorley, *Law of Banking*, p. 34 and in his *Gilbart Lectures* 1967; see also Megrah, (1967) 30 MLR 86.
[20] See also *Stafford* v. *Henry* (1850) 12 Ir. Eq.R 400; *Ex p. Coe* (1861) 3 De GF & J 335.
[21] [1982] 2 Lloyd's Rep. 370.

associated companies. Fourthly, the firm did not attempt to solicit deposits from the public by means of advertisements.

The Court of Appeal held that the firm was engaged in banking business. Lawton LJ said that it was immaterial that the size of the firm's banking business was negligible in comparison with that of a clearing bank. Thus, although the number of items cleared through the firm was very limited, it was wrong to conclude that is was not engaged in this type of banking business. The only question was whether the banking business carried on by the firm was real in terms of its entire business. Further, it was immaterial that the firm did not carry on all facets of banking business, and that its main business was in a different field.

On the last point, *Roe*'s case derives support from *Re Bickbeck Permanent Benefit Building Society*,[22] where a firm was held to be a bank although its banking business was not its main venture. Another important authority, *Re Bottomsgate Industrial Co-operative Society*,[23] supports the view that a firm may be a bank although it does not carry on all the facets of banking business. This view is reflected in the Banking Act 1979. It will be recalled that, for the purposes of this Act, an institution may be regarded as a bank although it does not carry on some types of banking business.[24]

It is thus possible that, even under the common law definition, a court will consider an institution a bank although it has ceased to carry on some types of banking business. *Kirkwood*'s case establishes, however, that the three types of banking business listed by Lord Denning MR form the essence of banking. If a firm does not carry on one of them, it is not regarded a bank at common law. One startling result is that institutions such as discount houses, which are considered specialized types of banks, fall outside the ambit of the common law definition. The same applies to many of the foreign banks, which do not open current accounts operable by cheques. From a practical point of view this may, however, be irrelevant, as such institutions do not require the defences conferred on banks by statutes using the common law definition.

(iii) *Defences conferred on banks under the Bills of Exchange Act*

The Bills of Exchange Act 1882, as augmented by the Cheques Act 1957, governs the banks' dealings in cheques.[25] Certain defences are conferred on banks as regards the payment of cheques drawn on them.[26] Other defences

---

[22] [1912] Ch. 183.
[23] (1891) 65 LT 712.
[24] See p. 36 above.
[25] For the discussion of cheques generally, see Ch. 9.
[26] See below, pp. 285 et seq. Note that some defences are available at common law.

are given to banks in respect of the discount and collection of such instruments.[27] In addition, the Act makes detailed provisions concerning the crossing of cheques.[28]

The defences in question are subject to two limitations. First, they are conferred solely on banks. Secondly, their application is confined to cheques and to some analogous instruments.[29] They do not apply to dealings by banks in other types of negotiable instruments such as promissory notes and commercial bills of exchange.

In reality, the definitions of the Act are circular. A bill of exchange payable on demand is a cheque only if it is drawn on a bank.[30] But the drawee of a bill is a bank only if he engages in 'banking business', an essential feature of which is the opening of current accounts operable by cheques. Thus, it is necessary to determine that the drawee is a bank in order to conclude that an instrument drawn on him is a cheque; but it is equally necessary to establish that the instruments drawn on a given institution are cheques before if can be asserted that this institution is a bank.

To date this circularity of definitions has not been the subject of judicial comment. It is believed that a court, confronted with this problem, would concentrate on the regularity in drawings and on the formal appearance of the instruments. If it were proved that the drawee regularly honoured instruments which appeared on their face to assume the form of cheques, the court would be inclined to regard him as a bank and to deem the instruments cheques, provided of course that the drawee engaged also in the other essential types of banking business.

It is interesting that the circularity in question was avoided in section 19 of the Stamp Act 1853. This section, which is the predecessor of section 60 of the 1882 Act, and which continues to confer the only defence available to banks that pay in-house drafts bearing forged indorsements, refrained from defining a cheque and a bank. It applied, originally, to given types of instruments, which were functionally defined in the section itself. Initially, this provision formed the basis of the paying bank's protection in cases of wrongfully paid cheques.[31]

(iv) Other privileges conferred on common law banks

Until recently the common law definition of a bank was widely used in Acts of Parliament. This has changed in the wake of the enactment of the Banking

---

[27] See below, pp. 421 et seq.
[28] See below, pp. 252 et seq.
[29] See below, pp. 309, 422.
[30] Bills of Exchange Act 1882, s. 73.
[31] See below, pp. 303–304.

Act 1979. Quite a number of definitions, contained in given statutes, have been replaced by definitions reflecting the approach of this Act to banking.[32] Apart from the Bills of Exchange Act 1882, only the Income and Corporation Taxes Act 1970 uses the old definition. Section 54 describes a bank as a body carrying on a bona fide banking business in the United Kingdom. Under subsection (2) a bank was not required to deduct income tax at source from interest payments made to depositors. The position was changed in respect of virtually all banks and similar financial institutions— at least for the time being—in 1982.[33] But section 54 has not been repealed, and may thus be brought back into effect.

2. DEFENCES CONFERRED ON BANKS BY STATUTES UTILIZING OTHER DEFINITIONS

(i) The right to receive deposits from protected customers

The Acts, to be discussed presently, purport to safeguard the interests of specific groups, such as beneficiaries of trusts, by restricting the manner in which funds belonging to them may be invested or deposited by those acting on their behalf. Organizations with whom such funds may be invested are, obviously, assured of having a certain cash-flow. Banks are invariably among the bodies with whom such funds may be invested. Originally, the Acts concerned either utilized the common law definition of a bank or introduced a regime under which certain houses were specifically authorized to transact the type of business prescribed.[34] But most relevant statutory definitions have been amended by the Banking Act 1979.

An important enactment in point is the Solicitors Act 1974. Section 32 confers on the Council the power to make rules requiring solicitors to deposit clients' funds with banks.[35] The definition of a bank for the purposes of this Act is currently based on the Banking Act 1979. It covers the Bank of England, the National Girobank, the recognized banks and any company which was treated by the Secretary of State as a 'building company' or a 'discount company' under the Protection of Depositors Act

---

[32] Banking Act 1979, Sched. 6, Pt. 1.

[33] By s. 26 of the Finance Act 1982 and s. 27(1) of the Finance Act 1984 under which tax on such payments has been made deductible. S. 54 has been made inapplicable to interest payments made by 'qualified lenders'.

[34] The Protection of Depositors Act 1963 is an example in point. The Act was repealed by the Banking Act 1979, which introduced a more sophisticated conceptual basis.

[35] As regards these rules see below, pp. 186–7.

1963.[36] A substantial number of financial institutions, currently licensed as deposit-takers, fall within the ambit of the last group.

A similar regime is applicable to insurance brokers. Rules made by the Insurance Brokers Registration Council[37] require that clients' funds be deposited with banks. The institutions covered by the relevant definition are the recognized banks (within the meaning of the 1979 Act), the licensed deposit-takers, the trustee savings banks, and the National Girobank.[38]

Provision for the payment of funds to the credit of a bank account is also made under the Trustee Act 1925. According to section 11, a trustee is permitted to pay trust funds into a bank account whilst he is looking for a suitable long-term investment.[39] Some authorities suggest that if the funds are left with the bank for a prolonged period, the trustee incurs liability to the beneficiaries if the bank fails. The word 'bank' is not defined in the Act.

The last statute in point is the Payment of Wages Act 1960. Section 1 provides that, with the employees' approval, their wages can be paid directly to the credit of their bank accounts. The work 'bank' is not functionally defined.[40]

(ii) The right to invest in protected or supervised transactions

Banks are empowered to lend money to certain groups which are given wide-reaching statutory protections. In addition, the banks are free to engage in certain types of centrally controlled business transactions. In these ways, banks are given preferential treatment in respect of the relevant investments. Two examples will suffice.

The first is the Agricultural Credits Act 1928, which restricts the power of farmers to grant mortgages or charges over farming assets. The object of the Legislature is to protect farmers against foolhardy borrowings. Mortgages and charges over their assets may, however, be given to 'banks',[41] which include the recognized banks, the licensed deposit-takers, the trustee savings banks, and the National Girobank.[42] A similar regime prevails in Scotland.[43]

---

[36] Banking Act 1979, Sched. 6, Pt. 1, para. 9, amending the definition of s. 87 of the Solicitors Act 1974. As regards Scotland, see Sched. 6, Pt. 1, para. 10.

[37] Under the Insurance Brokers (Registration) Act 1977, s. 11(2).

[38] Insurance Brokers Registration Council (Accounts and Business Requirements) Rules Approval Order 1979, SI 489, para. 11, as amended by SI 1630 of 1981, Sched., para. 6.

[39] *Rehden* v. *Wesley* (1861) Beav. 213; *Fenwicke* v. *Clarke* (1862) 4 De GF & J 240. The account must be separate from the trustee's personal one: *Re Gross, ex p. Kingston* (1871) LR 6 Ch. App. 632, 639.

[40] Although s. 7 defines a bank as including a savings bank.

[41] S. 5.

[42] Banking Act 1979, Sched. 6, Pt. 1, para. 2.

[43] Agricultural Credits (Scotland) Act 1929 and the Banking Act 1979, Sched. 6, Pt. 1, para. 3.

Secondly, under the Home Purchase Assistance and Housing Corporation Guarantee Act 1978, the Secretary of State may advance money to finance houses to enable them to grant loans to first-home purchasers.[44] The participants in the scheme include the recognized banks within the meaning of the 1979 Act, and institutions which had been recognized for the purposes of the Protection of Depositors Act 1963.[45] The position is similar in Northern Ireland.[46]

An important privilege, enjoyed by banks until 1986, was their right to deal in securities without having to qualify under the Prevention of Fraud (Investments) Act 1958. This privilege was conferred on them not as banks but by reason of their being entities carrying on some business other than the business of dealing in securities.[47] The position was changed by the Financial Services Act 1986, under which banks will have to seek the same authorisation as other financial institutions.[48]

(iii) The Bankers' Books Evidence Act

Frequently a bank's ledgers or its record books include information that is required as evidence in legal proceedings. Thus, statements of accounts may be of importance in actions for damages for breaches of contracts or in respect of income tax matters. Under the general principles of the law of evidence, information based on bankers' books could be received only if the originals were produced in court. Such a course would disrupt the running business of the bank concerned. Furthermore, the bank's employees would have to attend the court proceedings in order to submit the books or other information, and would have to give evidence about their source.[49] The Bankers' Books Evidence Act 1879 was passed in order to overcome the problems involved.

Originally the Act applied mainly to banks as defined at common law.[50] This position was radically altered by the Banking Act 1979. At present the 1879 Act applies to the recognized banks, to the licensed deposit-takers, to the municipal and trustee savings banks, to the National Savings Bank, and

[44] Home Purchase Assistance and Housing Corporation Guarantee Act 1978, s. 1.
[45] Ibid., Sched., Pt. 1, para. 7 as amended by the Banking Act 1979, Sched. 6, Pt. 1, para. 11.
[46] Home Purchase Assistance (Northern Ireland) Order 1978 as amended by the Banking Act, Sched. 6, Pt. 1, para. 12.
[47] Prevention of Fraud (Investments) Act 1958, s. 16 as amended by the Banking Act 1979, Sched. 6, Pt. 1, para 5. And see Prevention of Fraud (Investments) Act (Northern Ireland) 1940, s. 12 as amended by the Banking Act 1979, Sched 6. Pt. 1, para. 4.
[48] Repealing the 1958 Act; see 1986 Act, s. 377.
[49] See, generally, R. Cross, *On Evidence*, 5th edn., London, 1979, p. 184.
[50] But note the extension of the Act to other finance houses: Halsbury, *Statutes of England*, 4th edn., vol. 17, p. 106.

to the National Girobank.[51] The provisions of the Act are discussed in detail in Chapter 4.

3. THE MEANING OF 'BANK' WHERE THE TERM IS UNDEFINED

It has been shown that not all statutes conferring rights on, or regulating the position of, banks attempt to define the institutions affected. The Trustee Act 1925 is an instance in point.[52] Until the passing of the Banking Act 1979 it was safe to assume that, where undefined, the term 'bank' or 'banker' had to be given its common law rendering. This definition was prevalent and could, therefore, be regarded the most accurate legal description of a bank. The position changed in the wake of the 1979 Act.[53] It has been shown that the concept used in this Act in order to divide banks into functional groups has been incorporated into a considerable number of statutes affecting bankers. At present the approach of the Banking Act is more widely adopted than the common law definition.

It is thus difficult to decide which definition is to be resorted to where an Act does not determine the meaning of the word 'bank' or 'banker'. An attractive argument is that the date of such an Act is decisive. In an Act contemporaneous with the Bills of Exchange Act 1882, the common law definition ought to apply. In the case of a modern statute—especially one passed at about the same time as the Banking Act—the modern definition is in point.

Such a construction would, of course, have the advantage of construing each Act on the basis of the intention attributable to the Legislature at the time of its enactment. The proposed solution, however, ignores the cardinal principle which regards banking business as being of a transient nature. The case law construing the common law definition recognizes this fact. It enables the courts to determine each case in the light of the practice prevailing at the time it comes up for decision. The 1979 Act simply takes a further step in this direction. It provides guidelines for construing 'bank' and 'banker' in the light of the currently prevailing position. On this basis it is

[51] Banking Act 1979, Sched. 6, Pt. 1, para. 1(1), replacing s. 9 of the Bankers' Books Evidence Act 1879. The position concerning trustee savings banks will remain the same when their reorganization under the Trustee Savings Banks Act 1985 is complete, as they will then become recognized banks.

[52] See also the Race Relations Act 1976, s. 20 of which prohibits any discrimination in matters of banking. The word is not defined. Another Act which fails to define the word 'bank' is the Banking and Financial Dealings Act 1971.

[53] See above, pp. 32 et seq.

possible to treat the two definitions as complementary. The common law definition proclaims that a bank is a body engaged in banking business; the 1979 Act describes this business as transacted at present.

If this solution were accepted, then the meaning of 'bank' or 'banker' in a statute that failed to define the words would be determined with reference to banking business as envisaged in the 1979 Act. Unfortunately, one point would remain unclear. Is the work 'bank' or 'banker' to be construed as encompassing all the institutions brought under the regime of the 1979 Act or merely as covering the recognized banks? It is noteworthy that, where the definition of the Banking Act is introduced into a given statute, the Legislature spells out which institutions are banks in the relevant context. In some cases a privilege is conferred on the recognized banks alone; in most cases licensed institutions are also covered.

It is believed that, where a statute fails to define a 'bank', it is safest to examine, on the basis of the spirit of the Act as a whole, whether the word is to be understood in a narrow or in a wide sense. Where an Act exempts 'banks' from onerous provisions applicable in the case of particularly sensitive transactions, it stands to reason that the provision applies to a restricted group of outstanding bodies such as the recognized banks. Where the Act regulates a widely defined transaction, it is safe to construe the term 'bank' in its broader sense. To avoid ambiguity, it is desirable that Parliament clarify the position by adding suitable definitions to any Act with a lacuna.

THE CONSUMER CREDIT ACT

(i) Background

The object of this Act is to protect consumers—a term which comprises individuals, partnerships, and unincorporated bodies—in respect of certain types of transactions involving amounts not exceeding £15,000.[54] The Act introduces a licensing regime for persons and institutions engaged in the type of business covered and, in addition, makes provisions as to the form and content of credit agreements and the way in which consumer credit is carried on. It also combats certain practices such as misleading advertisements and unrestrained canvassing for business. The Act further regulates credit brokerage, debt adjusting and counselling, and the operations of

---

[54] See the definition of 'individual' in the Consumer Credit Act 1974, s. 189(1). The Act defined a 'consumer credit agreement' as a personal credit agreement for an amount not exceeding £5,000: s. 8(2). But as from 20 May 1985 the ceiling has been increased to £15,000: the Consumer Credit (Increase of Monetary Limits) Order 1983, SI 1878.

credit reference agencies. These, however, are only of marginal concern to banks.

The Act was passed to give effect to the recommendations made in the Report of the Crowther Committee, whose main concern was to stamp out abuses common in the consumer credit industry.[55] Sharp practices employed by some financial institutions in respect of hire purchase and hiring agreements and misleading information supplied to consumers by certain lenders were the main sources for concern. The Committee's study established that the Money-lenders Act 1900 was inadequate to protect consumers who required financial accommodation.

The Committee was, thus, concerned with the consumer credit industry generally. Banks were not among the financial institutions whose practices were the cause for alarm. It was, at the same time, thought that the reforms introduced by the Committee ought to apply across the board. Presumably it was envisaged that, if banks were generally excluded, there would be a rush of institutions purporting to qualify as such.

In accordance with the Committee's philosophy, the Consumer Credit Act 1974 does not aim specifically at regulating the activities of banks. Indeed, transacting with corporate customers and transactions for amounts exceeding £15,000—which constitute an important cross-section of banking business—are largely unaffected by it. But many of the provisions of the Act have a bearing on dealings by banks with individual customers and with unincorporated firms. However, the Act includes provisions which place banks in a favourable position as regards their most widely used lending facility: the overdraft.[56]

Clearly, the Act is relevant to bankers. Whilst a detailed review of it would be out of place in this work,[57] it will be useful to include a brief discussion of the aspects which concern banks. Specific sections, applicable to given types of banking business such as the issuing of credit tokens, are discussed where relevant.

(ii) Agreements covered

The Act uses a specialized terminology. Basically, it extends protection to consumers who enter into 'regulated agreements'.[58] These transactions

---

[55] Cmnd. 4596.

[56] Consumer Credit Act 1974, s. 74(1)(*b*), (3), and (3*A*) (inserted by the Banking Act 1979, s. 38(1); and see A. G. Guest and M. G. Lloyd, *Encyclopaedia of Consumer Credit Law*, London (looseleaf), para 2–075. See also pp. 485–8 below.

[57] The leading works are R. M. Goode, *Consumer Credit Legislation*, London (looseleaf); Guest and Lloyd, *Encyclopaedia of Consumer Credit Law*.

[58] Consumer Credit Act 1974, ss. 8(3), 15(2), 189(1). Note that 'credit' is widely defined in s. 9; it includes a 'cash loan, and any other form of financial accommodation'.

cover 'regulated credit agreements'[59] and regulated consumer hire agreements'.[60] In both types of contract, the debtor or hirer has to be a consumer; the financier, or 'credit provider' may be 'any other person'. Banks enter mainly into credit agreements, although some foreign banks enter into leasing agreements covering equipment.[61]

The Act treats certain transactions as 'exempt agreements'. These are unaffected by its provisions, except those concerning extortionate bargains.[62] Exempt agreements include those secured over land, provided they are effected by given bodies such as friendly societies and insurance companies.[63] Although some specific banks have secured an exemption, the banks as a group are not among the lenders specified for this purpose, which means that banks' loans secured over land are often subject to the provisions of the Act.[64] Other exempt agreements are certain types of trade credits involving not more than four repayments; low-cost consumer credit agreements, in which the interest does not exceed either 1 per cent above the prevailing clearers' base rate or a total of 13 per cent per annum;[65] and credit agreements made in the course of the regular financing of export and import transactions, including those in which the United Kingdom party acts as a merchant in a sale involving parties residing overseas.[66] Many loans extended by banks fall within the ambit of the last category.

Even where an agreement is regulated by the Act it is not necessarily subject to all its provisions. It has therefore been argued that some agreements ought to be treated as 'partially regulated agreements'.[67] Thus, certain provisions of the Act are excluded in respect of financial institutions engaged in the issuing of overdrafts; but other provisions are applicable.[68]

The Act applies both to agreements involving the extension of 'fixed credit' and to running account arrangements. The former type requires no

---

[59] Ibid., s. 8.

[60] Ibid., s. 15.

[61] Banks do not engage in hire purchase; but note that a tripartite agreement, comprising a hirer, a dealer, and a financier, is a credit agreement (of the 'fixed-sum credit' type under s. 10(1)(*b*)) from the financier's point of view, as he is treated as furnishing credit; a long-term lease without provision for transfer of property is a hiring agreement: Guest and Lloyd, *Encyclopaedia of Consumer Credit Law*, para. 2–016.

[62] Consumer Credit Act 1974, ss. 137–40. Extortionate bargains may be reopened by the court with a view to determining an equitable return.

[63] Ibid., s. 16 and see s. 189(1). For full details see the Consumer Credit (Exempt Agreements) Order 1985, SI 757.

[64] But see the Banking Bill of 1986. Under cl. 84, such agreements of banks could be excluded.

[65] SI 757 of 1985, regs. 3, 4, as amended by SI 1736 of 1985 and 1918, covering certain banks.

[66] SI 757 of 1985.

[67] The phrase is not used in the Act itself; see P. J. Cresswell, W. J. L. Blair, G. J. S. Hill, and P. R. Wood, *Encyclopedia of Banking Law*, London, 1982, vol. 1, para. 260.

[68] Such as those of Pt. 3.

explanation. It is best illustrated by a fixed-term interest-bearing loan. The latter type covers revolving credit agreements, under which the debtor is allowed to borrow amounts up to a given ceiling. The amount available to the debtor is automatically reduced whenever he withdraws an amount but is increased when he pays any amount to the credit of his account. Over-drafts granted on bankers' current accounts and the credit ceilings fixed in arrangements between issuers of credit cards and their customers are examples in point.

A running account credit agreement is within the ambit of the 1974 Act in any one of the following cases: (*a*) if the credit limit is £15,000 or less; (*b*) if, regardless of the credit limit, the debtor is precluded from drawing out at any one time an amount exceeding £15,000; or (*c*) if the credit charge, or any other provision favouring the creditor, is increased when the amount drawn exceeds £15,000,[69] Furthermore, the arrangement is 'regulated' if it is probable from the surrounding circumstances that the debit balance will not exceed £15,000 at any one time.[70]

(iii) Provisions to be complied with: licensing

One of the cardinal principles of the Act is that finance houses can engage in consumer lending and hiring agreements only if they obtain a licence from the Director General of Fair Trading.[71] The Director, who administers both the 1974 Act and the Fair Trading Act 1973, has a wide discretion to grant, vary, suspend, and revoke the required licence.[72] An appeal from his decision lies to the Secretary of State.[73] Anybody who engages in consumer hire agreements or consumer credit agreements without a licence commits an offence.[74] Agreements made by an offending house are enforceable only with the Director's consent.[75] Two of the points that the Director takes into consideration in such cases are, first, the extent to which the consumer has been prejudiced by the creditor's behaviour and, secondly, whether a licence would have been granted if applied for.[76]

Generally, the licensing scheme affects banks in two ways. First, they have to hold a licence if they wish to enter into the consumer credit business or to engage in ancillary business covered by the Act.[77] Secondly, a bank has

---

[69] Consumer Credit Act 1974, s. 10.
[70] Ibid., s. 10(3); and see s. 171(1).
[71] Ibid., s. 21.
[72] Ibid., ss. 25, 31–3.
[73] Ibid., s. 41.
[74] Ibid., s. 39.
[75] Ibid., s. 40.
[76] Ibid.
[77] Engaging in one of these activities without licence is an offence: Consumer Credit Act 1974, ss. 145, 147.

to be wary when it finances another financial institution that engages in regulated transactions. If the institution concerned is not duly licensed it may end up in financial difficulties, which are bound to affect the bank's ability to seek reimbursement from it for advances made.

(iv) Contractual disclosure

The licensing regime is not the only protective measure introduced by the Act. Certain formalities have to be observed when a regulated agreement is executed. Basically, the Act requires the full disclosure of the terms of the contract. Section 20 empowers the Secretary of State to make regulations for the disclosure of the true cost of credit incurred by the consumer. The regulations so made lay down a formula for the calculation of the total cost of credit and of a true percentage rate, known as the 'rate of the total charge of credit' or 'APR' (annual percentage rate).[78]

The Act itself prescribes further requirements. First, all the terms of a contract have to be embodied in a signed and legible document.[79] As from 19 May 1985 the contract has to disclose the total charge of credit and APR.[80] Secondly, the consumer must be given a copy of this document. This can be done either by supplying him with a copy of the proposed agreement before the date on which it is to be signed or by presenting the document for his perusal at the time set for its execution.[81] Thirdly, the consumer must usually be sent a further copy of the agreement within seven days of its execution.[82] Finally, the consumer must be given a notice, in a prescribed form, setting out his right of cancellation.[83] An agreement which is not properly 'executed' in compliance with these provisions is unenforceable except on a court order.[84]

The right of cancellation, to be referred to in the notice given to the consumer, is of limited application. It is exercisable where two conditions are fulfilled. First, the agreement must have been signed at a place other than the

---

[78] Consumer Credit (Total Charge for Credit) Regulations 1980, SI 51, regs. 2, 6.

[79] Consumer Credit Act 1974, s. 61.

[80] Consumer Credit (Agreements) Regulations 1983, SI 1553, reg. 2, and Sched. 1, paras. 9, 15, made under ss. 60–1 of the Act. Note that under Sched. 1, para. 10 of these regulations, disclosure of an interest rate and related charges suffices in the case of running accounts; the credit limit must also be shown: para. 8.

[81] Consumer Credit Act 1974, s. 62. And see Guest and Lloyd, *Encyclopaedia of Consumer Credit Law*, para. 2–063.

[82] Ibid., s. 63. But note that this is not required where the unexecuted copy of the agreement, signed by the creditor, becomes executed upon its signature by the hirer or debtor who had obtained a copy thereof.

[83] Ibid., s. 64.

[84] Ibid., s. 65.

business premises of the creditor, a negotiator, or a linked party. Secondly, a representation must have been made in the course of the antecedent negotiations by or on behalf of the creditor in the consumer's presence.[85] In practice this means that the debtor must have been subjected to 'face to face' pressure. The onus of proving the representation rests on the debtor, and his right must be exercised within five days of his receiving the required notice.[86]

But even if the debtor proves the necessary facts, the contract cannot be cancelled under this provision if it is secured over land, is a restricted-use credit agreement made to finance the acquisition of land, or is a bridging loan made in connection with the purchase of land.[87] However, in the case of some contracts pertaining to land, the debtor must be given a chance to withdraw before the execution of the agreement. To this end, he must be given, together with the draft agreement, a notice advising him of his right to withdraw from the transaction within one week.[88] This provision, though, does not apply to restricted-use credit agreements made to finance the acquisition of the mortgaged land or to bridging loans made in respect of the purchase.[89] Where the creditor fails to comply with these requirements of notice, the agreement is improperly executed.[90] Banks stand to benefit mainly from the third restriction to the debtor's right of cancellation.

The creditor's duty to supply information does not end when the agreement is executed. The debtor has the right to be kept informed about the state of his indebtedness to the creditor. Where the contract is for fixed sum credit, such as a bank loan, the debtor is entitled to a notice setting out the amounts repaid by him, the amounts due to be repaid at the time of the notice, and the amounts still outstanding.[91] In the case of running accounts, such as overdrafts, the debtor is entitled to a statement showing amounts outstanding and currently due.[92] Information of this type is supplied to the debtor on his request, and is usually accompanied by a copy of the agreement. During the period in which the creditor fails to comply with these requisites, he is unable to enforce the contract.

In addition, the debtor must be given notice if the creditor seeks to vary or modify the agreement under a power conferred on him in the contract.[93]

[85] Ibid., s. 67.
[86] Ibid., s. 68, which sets the cooling-off period at five days.
[87] Ibid., s. 67. And see Guest and Lloyd, *Encyclopaedia of Consumer Credit Law*, para. 2–068. Basically, where the contract is secured over the land or where it is signed at the creditor's business premises.
[88] Ibid., s. 58. And see the Consumer Credit (Cancellation Notices and Copies of Documents) Regulations 1983, SI 1557, reg. 4 and Sched. 1, Pt. 1; and amendment: SI 660 of 1985.
[89] Ibid., s. 58(2).
[90] Ibid., s. 61(2).
[91] Ibid., s. 77.
[92] Ibid., s. 78.
[93] Ibid., s. 82.

Undoubtedly, this provision is relevant to a bank that seeks to modify the terms on which an overdraft is extended to the customer.

(v) Default: termination and appropriation of payments

The Act seriously restricts the creditor's right of resorting to contractual remedies available upon the debtor's default. Thus, the creditor has to serve on the debtor a default notice before he seeks to terminate the contract, to demand early repayment of the outstanding balance, to utilize a security, or to restrict or defer the debtor's rights under the contract.[94] The debtor's right to any unused balance available to him may, however, be suspended. The default notice must state the nature of the breach and the method for remedying it or, if this is precluded, the amount to be paid as compensation. The debtor has to be given seven days in order to remedy the breach or pay the amount due. The consequences of the breach must also be spelt out.[95] The Act prohibits the charging of default interest, which means that the interest rate may not be increased on the debtor's breach.[96] Presumably, the provision can be avoided by a clause under which the penalty interest is stated as that ordinarily payable but the debtor is granted a reduction in respect of each instalment paid promptly.

By way of contrast, the Act sanctions early termination of the agreement by the debtor. He is always allowed to make early repayment[97] and, thereupon, becomes entitled to a rebate.[98] Any linked transaction is then also discharged.[99] The creditor is under a duty to advise the debtor of the amount to be paid upon the early discharge of the debt.[100] There is no doubt that the Act gives preferential treatment to the debtor. The policy involved is based on the consideration that the creditor ought to be able to re-invest his money at market rate. The debtor, on the other hand, could find it difficult to obtain finance from another source if the creditor were allowed to demand early repayment.

For this reason, the Act restricts the creditor's right to terminate the contract, even in cases where his decision is not motivated by the debtor's default but is based on a specific termination clause in the agreement. In

---

[94] Ibid., s. 87.
[95] Ibid., s. 88. Note that the non-compliance with a clause, such as one calling for repayment of the outstanding balance, which becomes effective on the initial default, is not an operative breach for the purposes of this section: subs. (3).
[96] Ibid., s. 93.
[97] Ibid., s. 94.
[98] Ibid., s. 95. And see the Consumer Credit (Rebate and Early Settlement) Regulations 1983, SI 1562.
[99] Ibid., s. 96.
[100] Ibid., s. 97.

such a case the creditor has to give the debtor seven days' notice, so as to enable him to search for another source of finance. The provision applies, however, only where the agreement covers a specific contractual period which has not ended by the time the creditor seeks to enforce his right.[101] It is believed that this provision does not apply to bank overdrafts which, conceptually, are regarded as repayable on demand rather than as available for a determined period.[102]

The Act modifies the common law rule of the appropriation of payments, under which amounts paid to the credit of an account are appropriated against the earliest debits outstanding.[103] Under the Act, the debtor has the right to indicate which debt due from him is to be discharged (or partly discharged) by an amount paid to him. If he fails to give an indication, the amount is pro-rated between debts due under his hire purchase agreements, his conditional sales and consumer hire agreements and his other *secured* agreements.[104] Obviously, an amount would not be appropriated against an unsecured overdraft or loan. It follows that, if a bank's customer pays in an amount without specifying to which account it is to be credited, it would be set off against his secured debts to the bank. In practice, however, such cases are unlikely to arise, as the customer's payment is accompanied by a deposit slip setting out details of the account to be credited.

(vi) Control of advertisements

The Act combats misleading advertisements. Under section 43, the relevant provisions apply to any advertisement in which a financial institution states that it is prepared to provide consumer credit.[105] Under section 46, the making of false or misleading advertisements, or of advertisements which do not include the required information, constitutes an offence. The details to be included in advertisements covered by the Act are set out in the Consumer Credit (Advertisements) Regulations 1980,[106] which distinguish between three types of advertisement: simple, intermediate and full. Under regulation 6, a simple advertisement may disclose only that the firm is engaged in credit extension business. Under regulations 7 and 8, an intermediate and full advertisement must contain certain specified details, which may include the rate of the total cost of credit.[107] Moreover, the reference to this rate

---

[101] Ibid., s. 98.

[102] See pp. 485–8 below.

[103] See 482–5 below.

[104] Consumer Credit Act 1974, s. 81.

[105] Under subs. (4)(2)(c), advertisements referring to contracts governed by a foreign proper law are not covered.

[106] SI 54 of 1980, made by the Secretary of State under s. 44.

[107] Ibid., reg. 11, and also reference in reg. 1(2) to the Consumer Credit (Total Cost of Credit) Regulations 1980, SI 51.

must be given certain prominence.[108] The relevant requirements apply even
to an advertisement displayed at the institution's premises, such as the
branch of a bank.[109]

Under regulation 12, an advertisement may refer to overdraft lending
only in respect of proper current accounts operable by cheques. The total
cost of credit applicable to an overdraft has to be shown in terms of the
interest rate charged and a statement of any specific charges made such as a
commitment fee.[110]

(vii) Canvassing

Section 48 of the Act prohibits the canvassing for regulated credit agreements if, basically, it is carried on at a place other than the business premises
of the would-be creditor, the canvasser, or the debtor. Section 49 makes
even more stringent requirements in respect of debtor–creditor agreements,
which are effectively personal loans. Here canvassing is prohibited in any
place except at trade premises. Canvassing means the soliciting of business
in the widest sense of the word. Under section 48, canvassing is permitted
where it is made in reply to an enquiry. In the case of a creditor–debtor
agreement, this exception applies, under section 49, only if the debtor's
request for the meeting, at which the canvassing took place, had been made
in writing.

The prohibition of canvassing applies only if the object of the meeting
was the soliciting of the agreement. Thus, a 'bank manager who, for
example, at a golf club suggests to a client that the client should enter into a
regulated agreement will not be canvassing unless he went to the club for
that purpose, and the same applies to a visit made to the client's home'.[111]

Section 49(3) makes a special exemption respecting overdrafts. It may be
asked why such an exemption is needed. Banks do not usually proffer their
overdrafts. However, banks encourage the opening of current accounts by
stating that customers are granted overdraft facilities on application. Canvassing of this type is permitted provided, first, that the person approached
already has some account with the bank and, secondly, that the canvassing
relates to an account current of a type covered by a Determination of the
Director of Fair Trading. The Determination so made applies to accounts

[108] Advertisements Regulations, reg. 20.
[109] Ibid., reg. 9.
[110] Ibid., sched. 2, para. 7(3).
[111] Guest and Lloyd, *Encyclopaedia of Consumer Credit Law*, para. 2–049. Note that canvassing for debtor–creditor–supplier agreements, such as credit sales, is allowed provided the
creditor holds a special licence under s. 23(3): ibid., para.2–050.

operable by cheques 'or similar orders', and sanctions canvassing only if effected by the creditor or his employees.[112]

(viii) Quotations

Under section 52 of the Act, a quotation is a document in which the creditor is to give 'prospective customers information about the terms on which he is prepared to do business'. The position is currently governed by the Consumer Credit (Quotations) Regulations 1980.[113] Under regulation 2, the provisions apply to any request for information made by a consumer to a credit broker or to a trader. Under regulation 4, the person approached is obliged to give the quotation.

Regulation 6 sets out the details to be shown. Included are the rate of the total cost of credit charged[114] and other details similar to those mentioned in the context of advertisements. Under regulation 6, the statement of the cost and of the rate of credit must be given greater prominence than any other rate shown, and at least as much as any other financial details. In the case of overdrafts, however, it is sufficient to show the same details as those required in such a case in an advertisement.[115]

(ix) Credit brokerage

Credit brokerage involves the introduction in the course of business of a would-be borrower to a credit provider. By and large, such agreements fall within the ambit of the Act if the credit limit or the cost involved does not exceed £15,000, or if a loan exceeding this figure is made for the acquisition of a dwelling which is to be occupied by the consumer or his relative and which serves as a security.[116] Banks are affected by the provisions of this Part of the Act where they refer a customer to another finance house, provided the introduction is not effected as a mere courtesy.

A credit brokerage business needs to be licensed.[117] Personal introductions, which are not made in the course of a person's business, are outside the ambit of the Act. Thus, the introduction of a new customer to a bank by

---

[112] Determination of Jan. 1977; Guest and Lloyd, *Encyclopaedia of Consumer Credit Law*, para. 4–4800.

[113] SI 55 of 1980.

[114] For details, see Quotations Regulations, Sched. 3.

[115] Quotations Regulations, Sched. 1, para. 2(6).

[116] Consumer Credit Act 1974, s. 145. But see Guest and Lloyd, *Encyclopaedia of Consumer Credit Law*, para. 2–146, who suggest that it is possible that credit brokerage exists even if the borrower seeks a loan of the non-consumer type.

[117] Ibid., s. 147.

an existing client does not constitute brokerage within the meaning of the Act.

(x) Debt adjusting and counselling

The Act covers the business of debt counselling and debt adjusting in respect of consumer credit and consumer hire agreements. Debt adjusting means the negotiation of new terms in existing agreements, for the taking-over of the debts involved, or for the discharge or liquidation thereof.[118] Credit counselling is the giving of advice to a consumer who has incurred debts under the type of agreement covered by the Act,[119] A person who engages in either of these two types of business requires a licence.[120]

The type of business which is primarily affected by this requirement is that of finance brokers and advisers, accountants, solicitors, mortgage and insurance brokers and other financial consultants. Neither the clearing banks nor the merchant banks engage in this type of business. The provisions of the Act are, however, relevant in the case of some small banks that do occasionally provide the service involved.

(xi) Credit reference agencies

A credit reference agency is an organization engaged in the business of collecting information on the financial standing of 'consumers' as defined in the Act.[121] A business that keeps credit information for its own purposes, such as a bank, is outside the definition. This is so despite the fact that banks give references on the standing of their customers at the request of other banks. Such references are given as a matter of courtesy, and are based on information available to the bank from its own records. The organizations covered by the Act are credit reference offices, detective agencies and similar types of bodies.[122]

(xii) Connected transactions

A regulated consumer hire agreement is not always one involving solely the hirer and the owner. Frequently, it is a 'debtor–creditor–supplier' arrangement, in which the creditor agrees to finance a contract between the debtor and the supplier. The supply of goods under a credit card is an example in

---

[118] Ibid., s. 145(5).
[119] Ibid., s. 145(6).
[120] Ibid., s. 147.
[121] Ibid., s. 145(8).
[122] Where the Act is applicable, the consumer is entitled to copies of the information pertaining to him: Consumer Credit Act 1974, ss. 157–9.

point.[123] Here the supplier of the goods or services provides them on the basis of his reimbursement arrangement with the issuer of the credit card (the 'creditor').

In cases of this type the Act imposes wide-ranging liability on the creditor. Thus, if the debtor has any claim against the supplier, which is based on breach of contract or on misrepresentation, he has a like claim against the creditor.[124] In many cases of this type the debtor is entitled to rescind his contract with the supplier. Accordingly, he is entitled also to withdraw from the connected credit agreement. The provision in point applies to transactions involving an item the cash price of which is less than £30,000 and more than £100.[125]

The Act uses an additional, extremely wide concept, which is that of 'linked transactions'. It applies even if a transaction is made between the debtor and a party other than the supplier or the creditor.[126] In its widest sense, a linked transaction is one into which the debtor enters in compliance with his main agreement. Two illustrations clarify the concept. First, a life policy effected by the debtor in pursuance of his main agreement with the creditor constitutes a linked agreement. Secondly, where a bank grants its customer a home renovation loan, the contract with the builders is a linked transaction. An ancillary agreement made in order to effect a security is, however, excluded from the definition of a linked transaction. It will be shown that the concept of linked transactions is relevant also in the case of credit cards.[127]

Under the Act, the validity of a linked transaction is subject to that of the main contract. A linked transaction entered into before the making of the principal agreement has no effect until this main contract is concluded.[128] Furthermore, the consumer's cancellation of the main contract operates also as his withdrawal from the linked transaction.[129] Sums paid under the linked transaction are, then, recoverable by the consumer.[130]

(xiii) Summary

Banks have to reckon with the hazards put in their way by the Consumer Credit Act 1974. In the first place, they are bound by the Act where they

---

[123] Ibid., s. 12.

[124] Ibid., s. 75(1).

[125] Ibid., s. 75(3) as amended by the Consumer Credit (Increase of Monetary Limits) Order 1983, SI 1878; and see also Consumer Credit (Exempt Agreements) (No. 2) Order 1985, SI 757 as amended by SI 1985 No. 1736 and SI 1985 No. 1918.

[126] Consumer Credit Act 1974, s. 19; and see Guest and Lloyd, *Encyclopaedia of Consumer Credit Law*, para. 2–020.

[127] P. 410 below.

[128] Consumer Credit Act 1974, s. 19(3).

[129] Ibid., ss. 57(1), 69(1).

[130] Ibid., s. 70.

enter into any regulated agreement or engage in a business requiring a licence. In the second place, banks have to keep a watchful eye on customers financed by them who are engaged in any business covered by the Act.

In addition, certain provisions of the Act have a direct bearing on specific types of banking business. Bank loans made to consumers, the issuing of credit tokens, and the taking of security in respect of consumer transactions are all examples in point. These provisions of the Act will be discussed where relevant. It is fortunate for the banks that the provisions of the Act have been relaxed in respect of overdrafts.

To protect themselves, most banks hold a licence issued by the Director General of Fair Trading. They also have departments whose sole business is to advise on implications of the Act on their activities. To date, no bargain made by a bank has been struck down under the 1974 Act.

5. ASSESSMENT OF THE STATUTORY TREATMENT OF 'BANKING'

The treatment of banks in English statutes lacks uniformity and harmony. Some Acts apply to banks as defined at common law, others to banks within the meaning of the Banking Act 1979, and others still fail to define the meaning of the term. The 1979 Act itself distinguishes between different categories of financial institutions, treating some as recognized banks, others as licensed deposit-takers, and the remaining ones as Schedule 1 bodies. There emerges a picture of a substantial number of institutions, each of which may be a bank for some purpose but not for others. An institution which is a licensed deposit-taker under the 1979 Act may be a bank at common law. Equally, an institution may be recognized as a bank under the 1979 Act but be considered not to engage in banking business as defined in the Bills of Exchange Act 1882. Discount houses are a good example of this last category.

In point of fact, the diversification is even more pronounced than has been described up to now. Two definitive Acts of Parliament have independent regimes for determining who is a bank for their purposes. The first is the Bank of England Act 1946, which empowers the Bank of England to issue directives for the purpose of controlling banking business. It defines a bank as a 'banking undertaking that may be declared by Order of the Treasury to be a banker for the purposes of this section'.[131] The second is the Exchange Control Act 1947, which empowers the Treasury to confer on 'authorized dealers' of its choice the authority to engage in foreign currency

---

[131] Bank of England Act 1946, s. 4(6).

transactions.[132] Although the Act is currently inoperative,[133] there was up to 1980 a special list of 'authorized currency dealers'.

It is tempting to argue that the existing legal position could be rationalized by the provision of a uniform functional definition of 'bank', and by subjecting all the houses covered to a single regime. A closer look at the City demonstrates that such a reform is unattainable. The word 'bank' has been traditionally used to describe a wide-ranging group of houses which are not united by a common thread. A clearing giant, like Barclays or National Westminster Bank, differs in its structure, business activities, and orientation from a discount house or a merchant bank. Undoubtedly, for given purposes all three types of institution can be treated in the same manner. The soliciting of deposits from the public is a case in point. Equally, it is realistic not to draw any distinction between them for the purposes of the Consumer Credit Act 1974. But for other purposes they have to be divided into separate groups. The defences conferred by the Bills of Exchange Act 1882 on banks as regards the collection of cheques are relevant to the clearers and the merchant banks, but are of extremely limited importance to discount houses and to some of the issuing houses.

It is thus clear that banks are treated as composing separate groups in view of the current structure of banking in the United Kingdom. The law rightly recognizes the existing diversification.

---

[132] The Exchange Control Act 1947, s. 42.

[133] Effected by a series of Statutory Instruments granting a general exemption from the provisions of the Act: Exchange Control (Authorized Dealers and Depositors) Amendment (No. 4) Order 1979, SI 1338; Exchange Control (Revocation) Direction 1979, SI 1339; and Exchange Control (General Exemption) Order 1979, SI 1660.

CHAPTER 4

The Bank and its Customer

1. THE LEGAL NATURE OF THE PROBLEM

In the present era, the statement that a person is the customer of a bank has no magic effect on his standing in everyday life. At least one half of the adult population of the United Kingdom maintains accounts with banks and is therefore within the definition of a 'customer'. The position differed in the nineteenth century, when the maintenance of an account with a bank enhanced a person's financial standing and creditworthiness as banks were particular in the selection of their customers. Indeed, until the end of the First World War banks were, fundamentally, acting for businessmen, for the professions, and for the landed classes. The relationship of a bank and its customer was a close one. Thus, banks were known to honour their customer's cheques as a matter of prestige even where these were drawn against inadequate balances.

Nowadays the fact that a person has an account with a bank leads, fundamentally, to three prosaic legal consequences. The first concerns the bank itself rather than its customer. Where a bank collects in good faith and without negligence cheques remitted to it by a 'customer', it is entitled to a statutory defence against the 'true owner'.[1] Secondly, it will be shown at the end of section 2 of this chapter that the bank owes a duty to obey its customer's instruction as regards the collection of cheques and other effects payable to him and, further, as regards the making of payments ordered by him. Thirdly, it will be shown that the bank owes certain incidental duties to its customer. Foremost of these is the duty of confidentiality, discussed in section 4. In addition, there are some situations in which the bank owes its customer a fiduciary duty of care akin to that owed by a trustee to the beneficiary of the trust. This problem is discussed in section 3 of this chapter. The analysis of these specific duties will be preceded by the discussion in section 2 of the meaning of the term 'customer'.

2. WHO IS A CUSTOMER?

The word 'customer' is not defined in the Bills of Exchange Act 1882 or in the Cheques Act 1957. At one time it was thought that a person became a

[1] Originally under the Bills of Exchange Act 1882, s. 82, now repealed and replaced by the Cheques Act 1957, s. 4.

customer only when banking services were habitually performed for him by the bank. The mere opening of an account by the bank in the customer's name was considered inadequate for this purpose.[2] This view was questioned in *Lacave & Co. v. Crédit Lyonnais*,[3] and discarded in *Ladbroke & Co. v. Todd*.[4] In the latter case, a rogue who stole a cheque opened with the defendant bank an account under the name of the ostensible payee of the instrument. The cheque was cleared and the rogue withdrew the funds. As a defence to the drawer's action for the conversion of the instrument, the bank relied on section 82 of the Bills of Exchange Act 1882. It was objected that section 82 was inapplicable, as the mere opening of the account did not constitute the rogue a customer. Bailhache J held that the rogue had become a customer when the bank agreed to open the account. The fact that the rogue had been advised that the proceeds could not be withdrawn before clearance was irrelevant in this regard.

A decision in the same spirit is that of the Privy Council in *Commissioners of Taxation v. English, Scottish and Australian Bank Ltd*.[5] A cheque, payable to the Commissioners of Taxation, was abstracted from their premises and paid by the thief to the credit of an account opened by him with the defendant bank. One of the questions raised in the course of the action in conversion, brought by the Commissioners of Taxation as true owners of the cheque against the collecting bank, was whether the rogue had become that bank's customer by reason of the single transaction involved. Lord Dunedin entertained no doubts on this point, observing:[6]

the word 'customer' signifies a relationship in which duration is not of the essence. A person whose money has been accepted by a bank on the footing that they undertake to honour cheques up to the amount standing to his credit is . . . a customer of the bank . . . irrespective of whether his connection is of short or long standing. The contrast is not between an habitué and a newcomer, but between a person for whom the bank performs a casual service, such as, for instance, cashing a cheque for a person introduced by one of their customers, and a person who has an account of his own at the bank.

Where a bank performs a casual service for a given person, that person does not become a customer even if the service is performed on a regular basis. In *Great Western Railway Co. v. London and County Banking Co. Ltd*.[7] a rate collector habitually cashed cheques at the counter of the defendant bank, with whom the rural authority maintained its account. In all these

---

[2] *Matthews* v. *Williams, Brown & Co.* (1894) 10 TLR 386, and authorities there cited.
[3] [1897] 1 QB 148, 154.
[4] (1914) 30 TLR 433. Cf. *Tate* v. *Wilts and Dorset Bank* (1899) 1 LDAB 286; 20 JIB 376.
[5] [1920] AC 683.
[6] Ibid., 687.
[7] [1901] AC 414, esp. 425.

cases he retained part of the amount and asked that the balance be credited to the authority's account. In one instance, where he cashed a cheque obtained from ratepayers by fraud, the bank was sued by them in conversion. Again, one of the questions was whether the cheque had been collected by the bank for a customer. It was held that, although the bank had regularly cashed cheques at the rate collector's request for a number of years, he could not be considered a customer as he maintained no account with the bank.

It is thus clear that a person becomes a customer of a bank when he opens an account with it. It is immaterial that the account is overdrawn,[8] and it is irrelevant whether the account is of the current type or of some other type such as a savings or a deposit account. There is only one case in which a firm is deemed a bank's customer although it maintains no account with it. This is where a clearing bank, as a matter of regular business dealings, collects cheques remitted to it by a non-clearing bank on behalf of that bank's customers. In the words of Bankes LJ in *Importers Co. Ltd.* v. *Westminster Bank Ltd.*, in which a clearer regularly collected cheques at the request of a foreign bank:[9]

In this case this class of business of collecting cheques was done between bank and bank, and it seems to me impossible to contend, as a matter of law, that the bank for which the [clearing bankers] were doing business were not, in reference to that business, their customer.

In some instances it is important to determine the very moment at which the relationship of banker and customer comes into existence. *Ladbroke & Co.* v. *Todd*[10] suggests that this occurs when the bank agrees to open the account in question. The same view was expressed in *Woods* v. *Martins Bank Ltd.*[11] The plaintiff, a young man without business experience who had inherited a considerable amount of money, was given careless advice concerning certain investments by a branch manager of the defendant bank. At the time at which the advice was given the plaintiff did not maintain an account with the defendant bank. However, when the plaintiff decided to act on the branch manager's opinion, he asked that the balance of an account, maintained with another financial institution, be collected by the defendant bank, that the bulk of the proceeds be utilized for the investment

---

[8]   *Clarke* v. *London and County Banking Co.* [1897] 1 QB 552.

[9]   [1927] 2 KB 297, 305. Atkin LJ thought that the foreign bank was the clearer's customer, as it maintained a 'drawing account' with the clearer. As regards such arrangements see pp. 235–6 below, showing that usually the clearer treats the other bank as if it were a branch. Note that the foreign bank's customer, on whose behalf the cheque is collected or on whose behalf money is deposited for a transfer, is not the clearer's customer: *Aschkenasy* v. *Midland Bank Ltd.* (1934) 50 TLR 209, affd. 51 TLR 34; *Kahler* v. *Midland Bank Ltd.* [1948] 1 All ER 811; affd. [1950] AC 24.

[10] (1914) 30 TLR 433.

[11] [1959] 1 QB 55.

concerned, and that the balance be credited to a new account to be opened with the defendant bank. In an action brought by him against the bank to recover the amount lost in the investment involved, the question arose as to whether the plaintiff had become the defendant bank's customer at the time at which the advice was given. Salmon J decided that the relationship of banker and customer had come into existence when the branch manager agreed to accept the plaintiff's instruction to open an account in his name. Finding on the fact that the advice to invest was reiterated on this occasion, his Lordship held that the defendant bank had failed to observe a duty of care which it owed to the plaintiff under the contract of banker and customer established between the parties.[12]

In some cases it is not easy to determine, at first glance, who is the bank's customer. Thus, in *Marfani & Co. Ltd.* v. *Midland Bank Ltd.*[13] a rogue, whose true name was K, opened with the defendant bank an account in the name of a wealthy businessman by the name of Eliaszade, who was a client of K's employers. In the context of an action in conversion, brought by the employers in respect of cheques paid by K to the credit of the 'Eliaszade' account, the Court of Appeal held that the bank's customer was K and not the genuine Eliaszade, who had never intended to enter into a banker and customer relationship with the defendant bank. Similarly, in *Stoney Stanton Supplies (Coventry) Ltd.* v. *Midland Bank Ltd.*,[14] in which A forged B's signature and opened an account in B's name without B's authority, it was held that no relationship of banker and customer came into existence between B and the bank. The bank therefore had no relationship of contract with B and did not owe him a duty of care. It follows that the mere opening of an account in a person's name does not establish a relationship of banker and customer between the parties. There is a need for the meeting of their minds.

There are, however, exceptional cases in which an account may be opened in B's name by A, B's consent being given tacitly thereto either before or after the event. Typical cases in point are those in which a local bank opens a foreign currency account with a foreign bank in the name of a British customer who is about to embark on a voyage or where a parent opens an account in his child's name. In the former case, the customer's consent to the opening of the new account is given tacitly when he instructs his own bank to remit the money overseas. The consent therefore precedes the actual opening of the account, although an application for the opening of

---

[12] Ibid., 63. His Lordship had to rest his decision on a finding of a breach of a contractual duty of care because in 1959, under the doctrine of *Candler* v. *Crane, Christmas & Co.* [1951] 2 KB 164 there was no room for an action in tort. The law was, of course, reformed in *Hedley, Byrne & Co. Ltd.* v. *Heller and Partners Ltd.* [1964] AC 465. *Woods*'s case has been followed in *Warren Metals Ltd.* v. *Colonial Catering Co. Ltd.* [1975] 1 NZLR 273.

[13] [1968] 1 WLR 956.

[14] [1966] 2 Lloyd's Rep. 373.

the account will be signed overseas by the British customer after his arrival at the foreign destination. In the second type of case, the child's consent to become the bank's customer may be given at a later time, such as the date at which it reaches the age of majority.

Situations of this second type are illustrated by the case of *Rowlandson* v. *National Westminster Bank Ltd.*[15] A businesswoman drew a cheque payable to a bank at which she was known, but with which she did not maintain an account, and explained that the proceeds were a gift meant for her grandchildren. The bank credited the proceeds to an account in the grandchildren's joint names and conferred the right to draw on their guardians. Although the guardians did not expressly approve this arrangement and were not specifically notified of the opening of the account, they did eventually learn of its existence and one of them drew a cheque on it. It was held that the bank owed a fiduciary duty to the grandchildren and, furthermore, that the bank had committed a breach of this duty when it permitted the guardian in question to draw on the account for the credit of his own personal account. It would appear to follow that a contract of banker and customer came into existence between the defendant bank and the grandchildren, presumably as a result of the tacit approval of the opening of the account by the guardians. The case may, undoubtedly, rest on its exceptional facts.

Three main conclusions follow from the analysis of the term 'customer'. The first is that the relationship of banker and customer comes into existence when the bank agrees to open an account in the customer's name. Habitual dealings are not, in themselves, a requisite. However, the fact that the bank agrees to open an account in a person's name signifies the bank's consent to enter into a regular business relationship with him. By opening the account the bank agrees to execute certain monetary transactions of the customer, which include the honouring of his cheques and the carrying out of periodic payments authorized by him. The bank further agrees to collect payments due under cheques or other effects made out to him. Secondly, by entering into the relationship of banker and customer, the bank agrees to act as the customer's agent in banking transactions and, in this context, to exercise the degree of care and skill to be expected of an agent, or banker, of this type. The exact scope of these duties and of additional fiduciary duties arising in specific situations are discussed subsequently. Thirdly, once the bank has accepted a person as a customer, it acquires certain defences *vis-à-vis* third parties in situations where the bank's operations on behalf of the customer expose it to common law actions. These situations, pertinent to the bank's position as payor and as collector of its customers' cheques and similar effects, are discussed respectively in Chapters 10 and 14.

[15] [1978] 1 WLR 798.

3. THE NATURE OF THE RELATIONSHIP BETWEEN BANKER AND CUSTOMER

It is clear from the preceding discussion that the relationship of banker and customer is contractual. But what sort of a contract is involved? It is believed that bankers developed from goldsmiths, who served the function of depositories of plate and gold belonging to clients. In these transactions the relationship was that of bailor and bailee. But such a contractual relationship does not explain the nature of a deposit of money to the credit of a customer's account with his bank. In the first instance, money does not easily lend itself to being the subject of bailment. Secondly, where a specific amount of money, such as coins in a bag, is deposited for safe custody, the bailee is expected to maintain the coins in specie. If he uses them as his own, the 'owner' is entitled to an account for any profits made by the bailee.[16] Such an arrangement would defeat the main object of the deposit of money with a bank.

The relationship of banker and customer is, likewise, not readily explained on the basis of the principles of the law of trusts. If the banker were a trustee of his customer's money, he would again be accountable for profits and, in addition, the customer would be entitled to a tracing order if the bank failed.

The relationship of banker and customer is most easily understood when one reflects on the nature of the agreement between them. It is agreed that an amount, equal to that deposited, has to be repaid by the bank. In the case of a current account, which is discussed in detail in Chapter 6, the amount is repayable, without interest, against the customer's demand. The right to draw on the funds by means of cheques and money transfers constitutes the benefit derived by the customer from his deposit of his money with the bank. In the case of a fixed deposit, or of money paid to the credit of a savings account, the amount is repayable either at a determined date or at call with the addition of interest. In all these cases the bank is entitled to co-mingle the amounts paid in by customers with its general funds and is, therefore, entitled to use the amount accumulated.

The essence of the contract of banker and customer is, therefore, the bank's right to use the money for its own purposes and its undertaking to repay an amount equal to that paid in, with or without interest, either at call or at a fixed time. This analysis of the nature of the contract of banker and customer has led the House of Lords, in the middle of the nineteenth century, to decide that fundamentally the contract was one of borrower and creditor. In *Foley* v. *Hill*[17] a customer paid an amount of money to the

---

[16] As regards the bank's position as bailee, see pp. 466 at seq. below.
[17] (1848) 2 HLC 28.

credit of an account opened with his bank on the understanding that it
would earn interest at the rate of 3 per cent p.a. As no interest was credited
to the account for approximately six years, the customer instituted an action
for an account in the Court of Chancery. He alleged that he was entitled to
the remedy sought either as the beneficiary of a trust or as the bank's principal. He further argued that as the relationship was of a fiduciary nature, his
claim was not barred by the Statute of Limitation then in force. It was held
that the customer was not entitled to an account, and that his correct course
was to institute a common law action in debt for the amount due. Empha-
sizing that the relationship between the parties was merely that of debtor
and creditor, Lord Cottenham said:[18]

The money paid into the banker's, is money known by the principal to be placed
there for the purpose of being under the control of the banker; it is then the banker's
money; he is known to deal with it as his own; he makes what profit he can, which
profit he retains to himself. . . .

His Lordship added that it was the bank's duty to 'repay to the principal,
when demanded, a sum equivalent to that paid into [his] hands'.[19] It is
important to note his Lordship's reference to the need of a demand. If the
relationship of banker and customer were an ordinary contract of debtor
and creditor, it would have been the bank's duty to seek out the customer
forthwith in order to repay the money.[20] *Foley* v. *Hill* further recognized
that the limitation period would commence to run from the date of an
unmet demand and not from the date of the deposit.[21]

The principle enunciated in *Foley* v. *Hill* was further illuminated in
Joachimson v. *Swiss Bank Corporation*.[22] A partnership, whose members
comprised English and German nationals, maintained an account with the
defendant bank. When the First World War broke out, the account had a
credit balance of £2,312. The partnership became at that time an alien
enemy, so that operations on the account became prohibited. At the end of
the war, the English partner sought to wind up the affairs of the partnership
and, in this context, brought an action claiming in the partnership's name
the repayment of the amount involved. As these proceedings were not preceded by a demand for payment, the Court of Appeal held that the action
was premature. Atkin LJ described the contract between the bank and its
customer in the following terms:[23]

---

[18] Ibid., 36.
[19] Ibid., 36–7.
[20] *Walton* v. *Mascall* (1844) 13 M & W 452, 457, 458; *Bradford Old Bank Ltd.* v. *Sutcliffe*
[1918] 2 KB 833, 848.
[21] This point was overlooked in *Pott* v. *Clegg* (1847) 16 M & W 321 (decided before *Foley*
v. *Hill*) and in *Re Tidd, Tidd* v. *Overell* [1893] 3 Ch. 154.
[22] [1921] 3 KB 110.
[23] Ibid., 127.

The bank undertakes to receive money and to collect bills for its customer's account. The proceeds so received are not to be held in trust for the customer, but the bank borrows the proceeds and undertakes to repay them. The promise to repay is to repay at the branch of the bank where the account is kept, and during banking hours. It includes a promise to repay any part of the amount due against the written order of the customer addressed to the bank at the branch, and as such written orders may be outstanding in the ordinary course of business for two or three days, it is a term of the contract that the bank will not cease to do business with the customer except upon reasonable notice. The customer on his part undertakes to exercise reasonable care in executing his written orders so as not to mislead the bank or to facilitate forgery.[24]

His Lordship concluded, on the basis of this analysis, that 'the bank is not liable to pay the customer . . . until he demands payment . . . '.

Four observations need to be made as regards the general principle derived from *Foley* v. *Hill* and the *Joachimson* case. First, the need for a demand exists only in the case of a current account or of a savings account which provides for payment at call. In the case of a fixed deposit, maturing at a predetermined time, the amount involved becomes payable on the designated day. If the customer has not asked that the deposit be renewed on maturity, the bank pays the amount involved to the credit of the customer's current account. This is acceptable banking practice.

Secondly, even in the case of a current account, the amount standing to the customer's credit becomes payable without a demand if the bank is being wound up[25] or if the banker–customer relationship is terminated due to the closure of the account. Thirdly, the period of limitation begins to run from the day on which the amount is payable.[26] This means that it commences on the day on which a demand is made and refused.

Finally, it is important to bear in mind that the analysis of *Foley* v. *Hill* and of the *Joachimson* case concentrates on the contract existing between banker and customer as reflected in the maintenance of an account. But there are many services, provided by the bank to the customer, which cannot be described in terms of a contract of debtor and creditor. Thus, where valuables are left for safe custody, the bank assumes the role of a bailee.[27] If it manages its customer's portfolio investments, it enters into a complex contract with him involving elements of an agency contract and a contract for services.[28] Even in a current account, the relationship of debtor and creditor

---

[24] Hinting, in this sentence, at the decision in *London Joint Stock Bank* v. *Macmillan* [1918] AC 777, discussed on pp. 292–3 below.

[25] *Re Russian Commercial and Industrial Bank* [1955] 1 Ch. 148.

[26] Cf. *Re Footman Bower & Co. Ltd.* [1961] Ch. 443. But where an account has been dormant for an excessive period of time, it will be assumed that the balance has been repaid: *Douglass* v. *Lloyds Bank Ltd.* (1924) 34 Com. Cas. 263.

[27] Pp. 466 et seq. below.

[28] As regards the liability of the bank under a contract involving the giving of advice, see pp. 463–6 below.

is augmented by that of agent and principal.[29] The bank undertakes to carry out orders for the payment of money issued by the customer, and to collect effects due to him. These duties are discussed in detail in Chapters 10 and 14. It is thus erroneous to describe the relationship of banker and customer as being merely that of debtor and creditor. Whilst it would be misguided to attempt to define the relationship of banker and customer in terms of status rather than of contract, it is realistic to concede that it constitutes a sui generis contract incorporating elements of specific, well-defined contracts, such as that of debtor and creditor.

Furthermore, the bank's role as debtor and the customer's role as creditor are reversed where the account is overdrawn. An overdraft may be granted either by an arrangement between the parties or simply by the bank's tacit agreement to the customer overdrawing the balance standing to the credit of his account. In both cases the overdraft is regarded as repayable on demand.[30] On this basis, the overdraft ought to be statute barred six years after the bank makes a demand for its repayment.[31] There is however authority for the view that the period of limitation begins to run from the time the overdraft is granted to the customer.[32]

4. THE BANK'S DUTY OF CARE AND POSITION AS FIDUCIARY

As the customer's agent, the bank has to adhere strictly to its mandate. The scope of the ensuing duties is discussed in the context of the bank's functions as the customer's paymaster and as the recipient of moneys payable to him.[33] Additional duties of care are imposed on the bank where it gives advice on financial matters to its customer,[34] where it accepts his valuables for safe custody,[35] and where it investigates, on his behalf, the standing of third parties such as potential business contacts.[36] The customer, in turn, owes his bank the general duty of a principal to an agent, which is to issue clear and unambiguous instructions, and a duty to issue his orders in a manner that does not facilitate their falsification.[37]

Apart from these general duties of care, special circumstances may constitute the bank a fiduciary. The bank is then subject to additional duties of

---

[29] Pp. 128–9 below.
[30] Pp. 478–9 below.
[31] Limitation Act 1980, ss. 5, 6; *Bradford Old Bank Ltd.* v. *Sutcliffe* [1918] 2 KB 833.
[32] *Parr's Banking Co. Ltd.* v. *Yates* [1898] 2 QB 468.
[33] Chs. 10 and 14, respectively.
[34] Pp. 463–6 below.
[35] Pp. 466–71 below.
[36] Pp. 466 et seq. below.
[37] Pp. 291 et seq. below.

care and also to a duty of full disclosure. These obligations go far beyond the bank's general duty which may, broadly, be described as a requirement to take care in the execution of its mandate. As fiduciary, the bank may have to question the validity of an instruction given to it by a person who is the representative of a customer. It also may be obligated to acquaint the customer with extraneous circumstances relevant to specific business transactions.

Three cases illustrate the circumstances that give rise to a fiduciary relationship between the bank and its customer. The first case, *Woods* v. *Martins Bank*,[38] has already been mentioned in a different context. Here the manager of a branch of the defendant bank induced the plaintiff to invest a substantial amount of money in shares of a company whose excessive overdraft was a matter of concern to the head office. The branch manager failed to disclose these facts to the plaintiff. The plaintiff, who was a young man without any business experience or acumen, lost the full amount invested in the shares. As a defence to the action brought by him, the bank pleaded that, at the time the advice was given by the branch manager, the plaintiff had not been a customer. The bank argued on this basis that it had not owed a duty of care to the plaintiff at the relevant time. Salmon J held that, even if a relationship of banker and customer had not been established at the time the advice was given, the bank, through its branch manager, had assumed a fiduciary obligation towards the plaintiff when it agreed to act as his financial adviser. His Lordship based this conclusion on a number of factors. First, he was impressed by the fact that, in his conversations with the plaintiff, the branch manager had emphasized the expertise of the defendant bank and, in effect, agreed on behalf of the bank to act as the plaintiff's general adviser in business matters. Secondly, his Lordship referred at length to a leaflet furnished to would-be customers, in which the bank held itself out as an expert in this field. Thirdly, Salmon J was evidently disturbed by the fact that the branch manager advised the plaintiff to invest his money in the shares of the company in question without disclosing the relevant conflict of interests arising because the plaintiff's money was going to reduce the company's overdraft. Although his Lordship found that there had been no fraud on the branch manager's part, he was of the view that the manager's conduct involved a breach of a fiduciary duty of care, arising from the trust placed in his judgment by the plaintiff.

In the second case, *Lloyds Bank Ltd.* v. *Bundy*,[39] the bank obtained from one of its customers a guarantee covered by a charge over land to secure an overdraft granted to that customer's son. The father was advanced in age and naive in business matters, and the property charged by him was his

[38] [1959] 1 QB 55, esp. p. 72; and see pp. 78–9 above.
[39] [1975] QB 326, followed in *Royal Bank of Canada* v. *Hinds* (1978) 88 DLR (3rd) 428.

home and only valuable asset. The branch manager did not disclose to him the extent of the financial problems faced by the son, and failed to suggest that the father seek independent legal advice before the execution of the guarantee in question. The transaction was advantageous from the bank's point of view as an earlier charge, executed by the father, did not adequately secure the overdraft incurred by the son at the time of the new arrangement. The Court of Appeal held the guarantee void, as the bank had not discharged the duty of fiduciary care owed to the customer. Conceding that such a duty did not usually exist when a customer agreed to guarantee the debts of a third party to his bank, Sir Eric Sachs emphasized that, in the present case, the guarantor—who was a customer of long standing—had placed his reliance on the bank's advice. The bank's failure to disclose the full facts was akin to the exercise of undue influence. His Lordship described the situations in which a fiduciary relationship would be created as follows:[40]

whilst disclaiming any intention of seeking to catalogue the elements of such a special relationship, it is perhaps of a little assistance to note some of those which have in the past frequently been found to exist where the court has been led to decide that this relationship existed between adults of sound mind. Such cases tend to arise where someone relies on the guidance or advice of another, where the other is aware of that reliance and where the person upon whom reliance is placed obtains, or may well obtain, a benefit from the transaction or has some other interest in it being concluded. In addition, there must, of course, be shown to exist a vital element . . . referred to as confidentiality.

This element of confidentiality exists, of course, in every contract of banker and customer.[41] The reliance on the bank's advice is usually the crucial matter for determining the presence of a fiduciary relationship. It must be shown that the customer placed the required degree of reliance on the bank's advice, and that the bank was aware of his attitude. The bank's mere failure to volunteer advice does not necessarily lead to the creation of a fiduciary relationship.

The law in point has been clarified in the third case: *National Westminster Bank Plc* v. *Morgan*.[42] The bank was asked to approve a refinancing arrangement for a customer whose improvident business ventures had led to his defaulting in payments under an existing mortgage, granted to a building society over the family home, owned jointly by the customer and his wife. As part of the proposed scheme, initiated in order to preclude the sale of the home by the building society, the bank required a charge over the same

[40] Ibid., 341. See also *Commercial Bank of Australia Ltd.* v. *Amadio* (1983) 46 ALR 402 (Aust.).
[41] Pp. 96 et seq. below.
[42] [1985] AC 686 reversing [1983] 3 All ER 85.

property. To this end, the branch manager called on the couple and asked the wife to execute the necessary documents. Although the wife, who was also a customer of the bank, expressed her unwillingness to execute a charge covering the husband's business ventures, the branch manager did not explain to her the wide-ranging nature of the security, reassuring her erroneously, though in good faith, that the charge only secured the amount advanced to refinance the original mortgage. The branch manager failed to advise the wife to seek independent legal advice. Upon the husband's demise it turned out that he had no business liabilities, but the bank sought to sell the property in order to recover the balance outstanding under the refinancing arrangement.

Reversing the decision of the Court of Appeal, which had ordered that the mortgage be set aside, the House of Lords held that the bank had not committed a breach of a duty of care or of a fiduciary duty owed to the wife. The relationship between the parties had remained that of banker and customer and, on the facts, the branch manager had not exercised undue influence to induce the wife to execute the charge. Lord Scarman reached this conclusion on three grounds. First, the bank had not derived any hidden or undue benefit from the transaction. The object of the arrangement was to save the customers from having their house sold by the building society. The wife was just as anxious to retain her home as the husband. Secondly, the branch manager's statement was incorrect technically rather than in substance. Although the charge was formally wide enough to secure the husband's business ventures, the bank had no intention of utilizing it in this manner. Indeed, it sought to levy execution solely in respect of the refinancing agreement. Thirdly, the wife understood the general nature of the charge and was aware that, unless she executed it, the house would be sold by the building society. His Lordship emphasized that the mere inequality between the bargaining power of the bank and of the wife was immaterial in the present case, and doubted that there was any need in modern law to establish a general principle of relief against inequality in the bargaining power of the parties to a contract.

Lord Scarman added that the relationship of banker and customer becomes confidential, or of a fiduciary nature, when the bank crosses the narrow line that gives rise to a special duty of care. He warned against attempts to provide an exhaustive definition of the circumstances in which such a duty arises. In the instant case, the bank had not made an unfair gain and had not acted in a manner that could be regarded as exercising undue influence over the wife. Under the circumstances, the bank was not obliged to suggest that the wife seek independent legal advice.

Morgan's case shows that the bank's failure to advise a customer to seek legal advice before he executes a guarantee is inconclusive. The principle in question has been applied by the Court of Appeal in *Cornish* v. *Midland*

Bank Plc.[43] This was another case in which a wife challenged the validity of mortgage given to the bank by herself and by her husband over a property owned by them jointly. When the spouses, who were both customers of the bank, signed the memorandum of mortgage, the branch manager failed to disclose to the wife that the mortgage covered further advances that could be made to the husband, and gave her the impression that the borrowings secured by the mortgage could not exceed a certain amount. During a period following the wife's separation from her husband, the bank allowed him to overdraw his account beyond the original express limit. The wife brought an action in which she asked that the mortgage be set aside and, alternatively, claimed damages for the loss sustained by her as a result of the bank's inaccurate advice.

The Court of Appeal reversed Taylor J's decision to set the mortgage aside on the ground of undue influence. Croom-Johnson LJ pointed out that *Morgan*'s case established that 'to raise undue influence it was necessary to show that the transaction had itself been wrongful in that it amounted to one in which an unfair advantage had been taken of another person.'[44] This had clearly not occurred in the instant case. But his Lordship concluded that the bank had been negligent when it advised the wife, originally, that the mortgage covered a single advance made in respect of the property involved. Kerr LJ explained the principle involved on the basis that if the bank gave the wife any explanation of the legal nature of the mortgage, it owed her a duty of care in formulating its advice. The Court of Appeal held that, as a bank had committed a breach of this duty of care, it had to pay damages to compensate the wife for her pecuniary loss. As the mortgage was not set aside, the bank could not establish a cause of action entitling it to recover from the husband the damages awarded to the wife.

It is important to bear in mind that in the *Cornish* case the advice given to the wife was misleading. If the advice is inaccurate in some technical manner but fundamentally correct, the customer is in all probability unable to recover. This follows from *Morgan*'s case and derives support from a Canadian authority: *Royal Bank of Canada* v. *Poisson*.[45] Here the bank agreed to grant a line of credit to the customer provided his wife executed a 'continuing guarantee'. When the wife signed the guarantee, she appreciated that she was committing herself as surety, but she did not fully comprehend the effect of the continuing nature of her undertaking. The High Court of

---

[43] [1985] 3 All ER 513.

[44] Ibid., 518. See also *James* v. *ANZ Banking Group Ltd.* (1986) 64 ALR 347 (Aust.). Cf. *O'Hara* v. *Allied Irish Banks Ltd.* [1985] BCLC 52, in which it was held that the bank did not owe any duty to give advice where the guarantee was furnished by a person other than a customer.

[45] (1977) 103 DLR (3rd) 735. See also *Royal Bank of Canada* v. *Savage* (1983) 126 APR 117 (Can.).

Ontario held the wife liable on her guarantee. Robbins J emphasized that here the bank was making a decision about the granting of a new credit facility to the husband. The wife was fully aware that her husband's request would be refused if she failed to execute the security. His Honour concluded that unless the bank exercised undue influence it was subject neither to an absolute duty to advise the wife—its customer—to obtain independent professional advice nor to an obligation to ensure that she fully comprehended the facts. It was adequate that she understood the general nature and purpose of the document signed. A later Canadian authority suggests that a remedy would have been granted if the bank had any knowledge of the erroneous assessment of the security by the customer.[46]

One conclusion that can be drawn from the foregoing cases is that a failure by the bank to disclose to its customer the existence of a conflict of interests places the bank in an awkward position. The customer's reliance on the incomplete advice furnished by the bank is more readily established in cases of this type, which are bound to raise questions in the mind of the judge, than in situations in which the customer is given all the required details. Thus, in *Woods* v. *Martins Bank Ltd.*, the plaintiff would have had little to complain of had he been informed of the defendant bank's wish to reduce the unduly large overdraft granted by the branch manager to the mushroom company in which he invested his money. If he went ahead with his investment whilst being in full command of the facts, he could be regarded as having resolved to take a gamble.

In both *Woods'* and *Bundy*'s case the respective bank had an interest and stood to derive some benefit from the transaction involved. The importance of this element is highlighted in *Morgan*'s case. A fiduciary duty of care, or a stringent duty of care and skill, may however be imposed on a bank even in the absence of these elements, provided there are some other circumstances that ought to put the bank on enquiry. *Selangor United Rubber Estates Ltd.* v. *Cradock* (No. 3)[47] is the leading case in point.

The case arose out of a scheme for the take-over of a company. The entire transaction was carried out in a meeting attended by the company's existing and new directors and by an officer of its bank, the District Bank. During this meeting a cheque for a very large amount, drawn on the account of the company, was exchanged for a bankers' draft issued by the District Bank. The effect of the arrangement involved was that the amount standing to the credit of the company's current account was to be lent to a middleman who, in turn, had undertaken to lend a similar amount to the makers of the take-over bid, who required the funds in order to pay for the shares. For this

---

[46] *Beaulieu* v. *National Bank of Canada* (1983) 124 APR 220 (Can.).
[47] [1968] 2 Lloyd's Rep. 289; the doctrine is based on *Barnes* v. *Addy* (1874) LR 9 Ch.App. 244.

reason, this elaborate scheme involved a contravention of a provision of the applicable company law. Whilst the District Bank knew that the company was being taken over, it was unaware of the illegal nature of the transaction. The only concern of the bank's officer, who was in attendance, was to ensure that the cheque was regularly signed and indorsed before he delivered the bankers' draft against it. When the company went into liquidation, the Official Receiver sought to recover the amount involved from the bank. The action was based on the bank's breach of its duty as a constructive trustee and, alternatively, in negligence for a breach of a duty of care owed by the bank to the company.

Ungoed-Thomas J gave judgment against the District Bank on both counts. He held that the bank knew, or ought to have known, that the plaintiff's money was used for the purchase of its own shares. As the bank was aware of the breach of trust committed by the directors of the company, it became a constructive trustee and, by issuing the draft, it committed a breach of the duty imposed on it in equity. His Lordship said:[48]

The knowledge required to hold a stranger liable as constructive trustee in a dishonest and fraudulent design is knowledge of circumstances which would indicate to an honest, reasonable man that such a design was being committed or would put him on inquiry, which the stranger failed to make, whether it was being committed. Acts in the circumstances normal in the honest conduct of affairs do not indicate such a misapplication, though compatible with it; and answers to inquiries are *prima facie* to be presumed to be honest. . . .

Ungoed-Thomas J stressed that, in his view, actual knowledge of the fraudulent design was not necessary in order to constitute the bank a constructive trustee. He thought that there can be circumstances which give rise to a duty to enquire and that if the bank fails to make enquiries it must be deemed to have knowledge of the facts. His Lordship was of the view that, in the case before him, there were such circumstances. It should be borne in mind that in this case the employee of the bank attended the meeting in which the scheme was put into operation, and was familiar with some aspects of the transaction.

Ungoed-Thomas J then turned to the question of negligence. He came to the conclusion that a bank owes a duty of care to its customer, which goes beyond the duty of verifying the genuiness of the signature and the regularity of the cheque. His Lordship referred to two types of cases. First, he considered authorities relating to situations where banks acted negligently when paying cheques, and arrived at the conclusion that these cases established that the bank owed a general duty of care under its contract with a customer. His Lordship reinforced his view by citing the second type of cases, namely those relating to actions by true owners of cheques against

---

[48] Ibid., 313. For recent comment see C. Harpum, (1986) 102 LQR 114, and 267.

collecting banks. He thought that these cases, although not relating to the relationship of paying banker and customer, indicated the type of careless acts for which any bank was liable. Ungoed-Thomas J then said:[49]

To my mind . . . a bank has a duty under its contract with its customer to exercise 'reasonable care and skill' in carrying out its part with regard to operations within its contract with its customer. The standard of that reasonable care and skill is an objective standard applicable to bankers. Whether or not it has been attained in any particular case has to be decided in the light of all the relevant facts, which can vary almost infinitely. The relevant considerations include the *prima facie* assumption that men are honest, the practice of bankers, the very limited time in which banks have to decide what course to take with regard to a cheque presented for payment without risking liability for delay, and the extent to which an operation is unusual or out of the ordinary course of business. An operation which is reasonably consonant with the normal conduct of business (such as payment by a stockbroker into his account of proceeds of sale of his client's shares) of necessity does not suggest that it is out of the ordinary course of business. If 'reasonable care and skill' is brought to the consideration of such an operation, it clearly does not call for any intervention by the bank. What intervention is appropriate in that exercise of reasonable care and skill again depends on circumstances. Where it is to inquire, then failure to make inquiry is not excused by the conviction that the inquiry would be futile, or that the answer would be false.

Four objections may be raised against this conclusion. First, the authorities cited by Ungoed-Thomas J do not support the wide conclusion which he bases on them. The cases relating to the negligence of the collecting bank concern a different point. A collecting bank does not owe an independent duty of care to the true owner of a cheque. The collecting bank has to prove that it has acted 'without negligence' solely for the purpose of relying on a defence conferred on it by the Cheques Act against strict liability to the owner of a converted cheque.[50] But where no action in conversion lies against the collecting bank, the true owner cannot sue it in negligence for the breach of a duty of care. The cases cited by Ungoed-Thomas J as regards the duty of care of a paying bank are all cases in which banks exceeded their actual mandate. Thus, in *Westminster Bank Ltd.* v. *Hilton*[51] a bank paid a cheque which had been countermanded by an ambiguous letter of its customer. The court examined whether a reasonable bank, acting carefully, would have stopped the cheque on the basis of this instruction. In *Curtice* v. *London City and Midland Bank Ltd.*,[52] owing to an oversight, a cable countermanding a cheque was not collected on time from the bank's letterbox. The court considered whether the bank acted negligently when paying

---

[49] Ibid., 324.
[50] Pp. 421–4 below.
[51] (1926) 43 TLR 124.
[52] [1908] 1 KB 293.

the cheque. Likewise, in the remaining cases cited by his Lordship, the question of the bank's duty of care to its customer was discussed in connection with the bank's failure to observe specific instructions. There does not appear to be a single case in which a bank was held negligent because it failed to examine the validity of instructions given to it by an authorized person.

The second objection to the rule formulated by Ungoed-Thomas J is based on the relationship between the bank and the customer. This, it will be recollected, is a relationship of debtor and creditor, as well as that of agent and principal. Normally, the bank is not a trustee of the customer and, while it is under a duty to obey instructions, it does not appear to be in a fiduciary position. It is therefore difficult to see why the bank should concern itself with anything apart from its instructions. It is to be doubted whether the bank should disobey its instructions and dishonour a cheque drawn on the customer's account by authorized persons because the bank fears that the signatories commit a breach of trust. If the suspicions are unfounded, the dishonour of a cheque may cause the customer considerable damage and the bank may then be sued in breach of contract. It is one thing to say that a bank that *knows* of a fraud committed by its customer's agent may be liable as constructive trustee if it participates in the transaction. To impose on a bank a general duty of care, which requires it to assess more than the apparent validity of instructions given to it, puts a heavy burden on it.

The third objection to the principle of Ungoed-Thomas J is based on the business exigencies of the banking world. Cheques have to be honoured or rejected promptly. This is the basis on which the clearing house functions. Undoubtedly, if a bank is aware that its customer is being cheated, it should dishonour the fraudently drawn cheque. This object is achieved by the constructive trust principle as applied by the learned judge. But it is submitted that the bank does not have the time, nor necessarily the experience, to investigate the regularity of acts of agents appointed by the customer. Thus, in the *Selangor United Rubber Estates* case, the employee of the District Bank who attended the relevant meeting had no experience in 'take-overs' of companies. Neither, in fact, did the branch manager. This ignorance was largely the cause of their failure to realize the irregularity of the transaction. Did this very ignorance constitute negligence? His Lordship held that it did. But it is difficult to agree with a proposition that may involve banks in an obligation to familiarize themselves with the details of transactions or with the type of business carried on by their customers. Their main function is to collect cheques, to receive deposits of money, and to pay cheques drawn by their customers. It is unrealistic to put banks under a duty to assist in securing that their customers are not defrauded by those trusted and appointed by them.

That the customer should not expect too much from his bank is a point stressed by Ungoed-Thomas J. It arose in connection with a second transaction in the case before him. C, the original 'investor' and purchaser, agreed to sell his newly acquired shares in the company to one of its directors. For this purpose the account of the company was transferred to a branch of the Bank of Nova Scotia with which the director concerned had his own account. The sale of the shares was effected by a process of drawing three cheques, resulting in debits and credits in the accounts of the director and of the company. As in the first transaction, this process was used to enable the director to purchase the shares with the money of the company. An employee of the branch of the Bank of Nova Scotia, who in point of fact made no enquiry, was told that the process was for 'internal accounting purposes'. Ungoed-Thomas J held that the Bank of Nova Scotia was not liable in negligence or as a constructive trustee. While the information given to its employee might not have satisfied a lawyer, a banker was entitled to treat it as a satisfactory explanation. The employee of the bank saw that, at the end of the three cheques operation, the balance in the accounts would be exactly the same as before. There was, thus, nothing to raise his suspicions. It is important to note that in this second transaction, the employee of the Bank of Nova Scotia did not attend a meeting concerning the transaction and was not in fact familiar with any details.

Thus, even in the view of Ungoed-Thomas J, the negligence principle propounded by him has a narrow scope of application. If the bank knows (or, in view of the facts, ought to know) of a fraud or a misapplication of funds, the constructive trust principle comes into operation. As the negligence principle does not appear to be more extensive, there is perhaps no need for it.

Finally, should a paying bank be liable as a constructive trustee merely because it 'ought to have known' of the fraud or irregularity committed by the customer's agent? Dicta of the Court of Appeal suggest that this is so only if the bank wilfully or recklessly shuts its eyes to the truth.[53] Moreover, the cases cited by Ungoed-Thomas J appear to base the bank's liability as constructive trustees on actual knowledge of the agent's act. This was also the view taken by the Supreme Court of New South Wales in *Dixon* v. *Bank of New South Wales*—a case directly in point.[54]

---

[53] *Carl Zeiss Stiftung* v. *Herbert Smith & Co.* [1969] 2 Ch. 276, 296, 299; *Belmont Finance Ltd.* v. *Williams Furniture Ltd.* [1979] Ch. 250, 276 and second proceedings: [1980] 1 All ER 393. Cf. *Baden, Delvaux et Lecuit* [1983] BCLC 325, 402–12, Peter Gibson J.

[54] (1896) 17 LR (NSW) Eq. 355. See also *Gray* v. *Johnston* (1868) LR 3 HL 1; *Gray* v. *Lewis* (1869) LR 8 Eq. 526 (for further proceedings in this case see (1873) LR 8 Ch. App. 1035); *Backhouse* v. *Charlton* (1878) 8 Ch. D 444; *Lawson* v. *Commercial Bank of South Australia* (1888) 22 SALR 74 (Aust.); *Thomson* v. *Clydesdale Bank Ltd.* [1893] AC 282; *Coleman* v. *Bucks and Oxon Union Bank* [1897] 2 Ch. 243; *McMahon* v. *Brewer* (1897) 18 LR (NSW) Eq. 88; *Bank of New South Wales* v. *Goulburn Valley Butter Co. Pty. Ltd.* [1902] AC 543; *Quistclose Investments Ltd.* v. *Rolls Razor Ltd.* [1970] AC 567, 582.

The principle in the *Selangor United Rubber Estates* case, which was followed in *Karak Rubber Co. Ltd.* v. *Burden*[55]—where the facts were similar—suggests that a bank can be regarded as a constructive trustee or fiduciary agent although it has not sponsored or encouraged the making of the transaction in question, and although the bank has not derived any benefit from it. The bank's duty of care, or liability as trustee or fiduciary, is based on its being in possession of knowledge relating to a dishonest design perpetrated on the customer by a person being in a position of trust. The same elements were emphasized in *Rowlandson* v. *National Westminster Bank Ltd.*,[56] discussed earlier, where the trustee of an account, which to the bank's knowledge was impressed with a trust, appropriated the funds to his own use. On the facts, it was held that the bank had been put on enquiry and, having failed to investigate, it was liable to the beneficiary of the trust, the customer.

However, a bank's knowledge that an account is impressed with a trust does not in itself render it liable to compensate the customer if his trustee commits a fraud. In an Australian case, *Bank of New South Wales* v. *Vale Corporation (Management) Ltd. (in Liq.)*,[57] the dispute concerned unit trusts issued for the purpose of acquiring properties belonging to a certain company. Under the trust deed, the manager was bound to hand over to the trustee any money received from investors on the understanding that, when the amount reached a given figure, the manager would request the trustee to purchase the properties in question. The defendant bank was appointed as the unit trust's bankers in the prospectus. Instead of using the trust money for the specified purpose, the manager paid the amounts received to different companies within the relevant group. The question was whether the bank was liable to compensate the beneficiaries of the trust. The Court of Appeal of New South Wales held that the bank was not liable. Street CJ referred to the fact that although the bank was aware that the account opened in this case was a trust account, there was nothing to show that the bank had a precise knowledge of the exact nature of the transaction involved. His Honour emphasized that the bank had no direct nexus with the subscribers of the unit trusts, and had no knowledge of the means by which the ultimate objects of the trust were expected to be attained by the use of the money paid into the account. Street CJ concluded that there were no special circumstances which ought to have awakened the branch manager's suspicions. The bank was not under a duty to supervise the managerial activities of the unit trust organization and, consequently, was not required to police its activities.

---

[55] [1972] 1 WLR 602.
[56] [1978] 1 WLR 798.
[57] Unreported, decision of 21 Oct. 1981.

It is clear that the decision in *Vale Corporation*'s case was partly based on the fact that no relationship of banker and customer existed between the beneficiaries of the trust and the bank.[58] But even as between banker and customer, there are limits to the extent that special circumstances can give rise to the creation of a fiduciary relationship or specific duty of care. *Morgan*'s case and *Royal Bank of Canada* v. *Poisson*[59] highlight some of the limitations of the principles involved. Another illustration is furnished by *Schioler* v. *Westminster Bank Ltd.*[60] The plaintiff, a Dutch national domiciled in Denmark but resident in the United Kingdom, maintained an account with the Guernsey branch of the defendant bank. Dividends due to the plaintiff from a Malaysian company were usually remitted by it directly for the credit of this account in sterling, an arrangement under which the plaintiff was not liable to taxation in the United Kingdom. On one occasion the dividend was remitted by a voucher expressed in foreign currency. In the absence of facilities in Guernsey for the negotiation of foreign currency drafts, the dividend voucher was forwarded by the Guernsey branch for collection to the bank's head office in England. The plaintiff, thereupon, became subject to payment of United Kingdom income tax, which was duly deducted by the bank. The plaintiff's action in breach of contract was dismissed by Mocatta J. His Lordship held that the bank had not acted negligently in failing to ask for specific instructions when the dividend was received in foreign currency. As the bank had acted in accordance with standard banking practice, it was not in breach of a duty of care.

It is clear that the case law in point is inconclusive. What are the main factors that will convince the court to hold that a fiduciary relationship has been established between a bank and its customer? The non-disclosure of a conflict of interests, in situations in which the bank has undertaken to advise its customer, is one example in point. But the type of case illustrated by the *Selangor United Rubber Estates* case is the one that causes difficulties in definition. It is one thing to say that a bank has to act fairly when it assumes direct or indirect management of its customer's affairs. It is a completely different matter to suggest that the bank's implied knowledge of special circumstances may place it under a fiduciary duty of care, even if the bank is unable to assess fully the meaning of the information possessed by it.

Any attempt to define the circumstances contemplated in *Selangor Rubber* would put a constraint on the cases in question. Thus, it is tempting to suggest that the principle applies only where the customer is a body corporate. But *Rowlandson*'s case militates against this construction. It may be equally alluring to propose a test based on an extra duty of care, owed by

[58] And see on this point, *Baxter Equipment Ltd.* v. *Canadian Imperial Bank of Commerce* (1981) 46 NSR (2d) 590 (Can.); and the *Baden Delvaux* case, n. 53 below, showing duty may exist.
[59] (1977) 103 DLR (3rd) 735.
[60] [1970] 2 QB 719.

banks to customers who have to act through trustees. This, however, would place an impossible burden on banks. They would then have to supervise regularly the activities of persons operating trust accounts.

It may be that the key to the solution is to be found in the practice of banks. Thus, in *Selangor Rubber*'s case the ordinary practice of the District Bank was to refer all matters involving take-over bids to the head office, which had personnel specialized in this field. In the case in question, this practice was not observed and the entire matter was handled through an ordinary branch. This fact was emphasized by Ungoed-Thomas J. In *Rowlandson*'s case, the ordinary practice of the bank was to credit the amount of a cheque, remitted for the purpose of the opening of an account in a name other than the applicant's, to an 'impressed account'. It was, thus, unusual for the bank to make its own decision to open the account in question in the name of the guardians. Equally, in *Wood*'s case and in *Bundy*'s case the respective banks departed from the practice prescribed in their own manuals. This was not the case in *Schioler* or in *Morgan*'s case. It is thus suggested that a special duty of care, be it based in contract or founded on a fiduciary relationship, arises where the bank fails to observe the degree of care prescribed by itself or by standard banking practice.

It has to be conceded that this solution is not supported by direct statements in the cases in question. It does, however, introduce a clear and consistent guideline. The proposed solution will have to be re-examined in the light of future cases.

5. THE CONFIDENTIAL NATURE OF THE CONTRACT

(i) General scope

To appreciate the confidential nature of the contract of banker and customer, it is important to recall that it comprises elements of agency.[61] As a general rule, an agent owes a duty of loyalty and confidentiality to his principal. This is so regardless of whether the agent is a solicitor, an estate agent, or a company director.[62] But the scope of the duty varies from one type of agent to another. Thus, in the relationship of client and solicitor the duty is absolute. A solicitor is even precluded from testifying in court about his dealings with his client.[63] Other types of agent are given a lesser degree of

---

[61] P. 84 above.

[62] *Regal (Hastings) Ltd.* v. *Gulliver* [1942] 1 All ER 378; *Boardman* v. *Phipps* [1967] 2 AC 46.

[63] *O'Rourke* v. *Darbishire* [1920] AC 581; *Minter* v. *Priest* [1930] AC 558.

immunity. Thus, a director may be ordered by a court to testify against his company's interests.

The entrenchment of the agent's duty of confidentiality is motivated by two considerations: the first is economic; the second is historical. Economically, a person whose calling involves confidential work has to be able to assure those engaging him—at law and in fact—that his discretion can be relied upon. The relationship of solicitor and client illustrates the point. If a solicitor could be compelled to divulge information, his client would not feel free to discuss his affairs openly. Historically, the agent has been consistently regarded as being in a position of trust.[64] He is accordingly bound to safeguard the principal's interests and confidences. The agent's duty of confidentiality is a facet of the principal's protection against unwarranted attempts by outsiders to enquire into his affairs.

In modern times, the policy considerations based on economic factors gained momentum. This explains why there is a variance in the extent to which the law recognizes the duty of confidentiality of different types of agents. In certain situations, the interest of the state is treated as being of greater importance than a given agent's duty of confidentiality. Again, regard is given in this connection to the actual degree to which it is desirable to enable the principal to place his full trust in the agent.

The connection between the bank's duty of secrecy and the general duty imposed in this regard on an agent was emphasised by Diplock LJ in *Parry Jones* v. *Law Society*:[65]

Such a duty [of secrecy] exists not only between solicitor and client, but, for example, between banker and customer, doctor and patient and accountant and client. Such a duty of confidence is subject to, and overridden by, the duty to the party to that contract to comply with the law of the land. If it is the duty of such a party to a contract . . . to disclose in defined circumstances confidential information, then he must do so, and any express contract to the contrary would be illegal and void.

It is clear that all the contractual relationships referred to by his Lordship embody elements of a contract of agency or of a contract of highly personal services.

In the case of banker and customer, the duty of secrecy is easily explained on the basis of economic policy. The bank has, in effect, a very detailed knowledge of its customer's financial affairs. All these details are acquired by the bank whilst it is acting as its customer's paymaster and receiver of amounts due to him and, frequently, in its role as the customer's major or sole financier.

The leading case, which defined the scope of the bank's duty of secrecy, is

[64] R. Powell, *Law of Agency*, 2nd edn., London, 1961, pp. 25–6.
[65] [1969] 1 Ch. 1, 9.

Tournier v. *National Provincial and Union Bank of England.*[66] The plaintiff, whose account with the defendant bank was heavily overdrawn, failed to meet the repayment demands made by the branch manager. On one occasion, the branch manager noticed that a cheque, drawn to the plaintiff's order by another customer, was collected for the account of a bookmaker. The branch manager thereupon rang up the plaintiff's employers, ostensibly to ascertain the plaintiff's private address, but, in the course of the conversation, he disclosed that the plaintiff's account was overdrawn and that he had dealings with bookmakers. As a result of this conversation, the plaintiff's contract was not renewed by the employers upon its expiration.

The Court of Appeal held that the bank was guilty of a breach of a duty of secrecy and awarded damages against it.[67] Atkin LJ pointed out that the information, which the bank was bound to treat as confidential, was not restricted to facts that it learnt from the state of the customer's account. Furthermore, the bank's duty remained intact even after the account had been closed or ceased to be active. The bank's duty to maintain secrecy encompassed 'information obtained from other sources than the customer's actual account, if the occasion upon which the information was obtained arose out of the banking relations of the bank and its customers'.[68] This happened in the instant case, as the information received by the branch manager was based on a cheque made payable to one of the bank's customers and drawn by another customer.

The Court of Appeal was, further, of the view that there was a need to recognize certain exceptions to the bank's duty of secrecy. These were most clearly stated by Bankes LJ, who said:[69]

On principle . . . the qualifications can be classified under four heads: (a) Where disclosure is under compulsion of law; (b) where there is a duty to the public to disclose; (c) where the interests of the bank require disclosure; (d) where the disclosure is made by the express or implied consent of the customer.

Each exception requires detailed analysis.

(ii) Compulsion at law

A bank may be compelled by law to disclose the state of its customer account in legal proceedings.[70] It is clear that, unlike a solicitor, a bank

---

[66] [1924] 1 KB 461.
[67] A Canadian authority suggests that there is no room for punitive damages; *Guertin* v. *Royal Bank of Canada* (1983) 43 OR (2d) 363.
[68] [1924] 1 KB 461, 485.
[69] Ibid., 473.
[70] *Bucknell* v. *Bucknell* [1969] 1 WLR 1204; *Eckman* v. *Midland Bank Ltd.* [1973] QB 519. Note that a subpoena, not backed by a court order, is inadequate: *Haughton* v. *Haughton* [1965] 1 OR 481.

cannot refuse to answer questions concerning its relationship with a customer on the ground of privilege. The courts, however, exercise their discretion carefully in requiring a bank to make disclosure.

A special procedure laid down for producing evidence of a customer's account with his bank is to be found in the Bankers' Books Evidence Act 1879.[71] Prior to this Act, the banks were required in appropriate cases to deliver in court their respective books which were then treated as any other evidence. This meant that the bank was deprived of the use of the ledger in question and this, of course, was inconvenient. Furthermore, a clerk had to attend the hearing in order to submit the documents.

The Act saves banks both from the need of producing their books and from the need of submitting the relevant evidence under the ordinary rules of procedure which would require the presence of the clerk. Under section 3, a copy of any entry in a bank's book is to be received in any legal proceedings as prima facie evidence of the entry involved. Under section 4, it has to be proved that the entry formed part of an ordinary book of the bank, and that it was made in the usual and ordinary course of business. The proof may be given by any officer of the bank, either orally or by means of an affidavit.[72] The person submitting the affidavit in question usually includes in it a confirmation that the copy agrees with the original. He is required to do so under section 5. These provisions are augmented by section 6, under which a bank is not compelled to produce a book, or to give oral evidence, in any action to which the bank is not a party except under an order of a judge 'made for special cause'. The submission of a copy, supported by an affidavit, is therefore the common means for obtaining evidence relating to entries in bankers' books.

Evidence submitted in compliance with the provisions of the Act can be used against any party to the proceedings, including the party who has called for them.[73] In certain cases a court may even draw conclusions from the bank's inability to produce documents concerning a given point. Thus, where the records of a bank did not disclose any reference to a deposit alleged to have been made a few years before the commencement of the proceedings, the court concluded that it had not been effected at all.[74]

The most important provision in the 1879 Act is section 7. On the application of a party to legal proceedings, a judge may authorize an inspection, and the taking of copies, of any entries in a bankers' book. An order may be made ex parte; but it must be served on the bank three clear days before it has to be obeyed. The object of this proviso is to ensure that the bank is

---

[71] As extended by the Banking Act 1979, Sched. 6, Pt. 1.

[72] This section, reflecting nineteenth-century banking structures, refers to a 'partner or officer'.

[73] *Harding* v. *Williams* (1880) 14 Ch. D 197.

[74] *Douglass* v. *Lloyds Bank Ltd.* (1929) 34 Com. Cas. 263.

given the opportunity of objecting to the order. The courts are careful in the exercise of their discretion under section 7.[75] They are guided by the decisions governing the inspection and discovery of documents.[76]

The basic rule as to when an order for inspection will be granted is thus clear. Where legal proceedings are commenced, an application under section 7 made solely to investigate an account in respect of which there are some suspicions will be refused.[77] But where there is prima facie evidence of foul play that may be established by an examination of the account, the order will be granted. Thus, in *Williams* v. *Summerfield*,[78] orders for the inspection of accounts belonging to a company's employees who were accused of misappropriating its funds, were granted to the police. The Divisional Court of the Queen's Bench Division, to whom a case was stated by the Magistrates, approved the orders, as there was independent evidence of the misappropriation and the only purpose of the order was to determine the amount involved.

The difficulty of drawing a clear borderline is demonstrated by two recent cases. In *R.* v. *Marlborough St. Metropolitan Stipendiary Magistrate, ex p. Simpson*,[79] the accused was prosecuted under section 30 of the Sexual Offences Act 1956 for living on the earnings of a prostitute. The Magistrate granted an order under section 7, permitting the inspection of the accused's bank account. The accused appealed on the ground that the order should not have been granted on an ex parte basis. Allowing the appeal, the Divisional Court of the Queen's Bench Division held that, although such an application could be granted on an ex parte basis, there was much to be said for giving notice to the other party. The court further thought that, when such an order was granted, it should be limited in time, as otherwise the investigation could continue indefinitely.

In the second case, *Bankers Trust Co.* v. *Shapira*,[80] two rogues obtained a substantial amount of money by presenting to the plaintiff bank in New York cheques purportedly drawn on it by a bank in Saudi Arabia. The plaintiff bank paid the amount of the cheques to the rogues and, at their request, credited a substantial amount of the proceeds to an account opened in their names by the defendant bank in London. When the cheques turned out to be forgeries, the plaintiff bank in New York reimbursed the amount

---

[75] *Emmott* v. *Star Newspaper Co.* (1892) 62 LJQB 77; *Ironmonger & Co.* v. *Dyne* (1928) 44 TLR 579. It must be exercised with great care: *South Staffordshire Tramways Co.* v. *Ebbsmith* [1895] 2 QB 669, 674. Cf. the Canadian case of *Sommers* v. *Sturdy* (1957) 10 DLR (2d) 269.
[76] *South Staffordshire Tramways Co.* v. *Ebbsmith*, above; *R.* v. *Bono* (1913) 29 TLR 635 (refusing to grant an order to support a 'fishing expedition' in a libel action).
[77] *Williams* v. *Summerfield* [1972] 2 QB 512; cf. *Sommers* v. *Sturdy*, above.
[78] Above.
[79] [1980] Crim. LR 305.
[80] [1980] 1 WLR 1274.

debited to the account of the Saudi Arabian bank and sought to recover its losses from the two rogues. In an attempt to locate them, the plaintiff bank applied for an order instructing the defendant bank to permit the plaintiff bank to inspect and take copies of all correspondence between the two rogues and the defendant bank, and further to photocopy all cheques drawn on that account. Mustill J refused to grant this relief, on the ground that the two rogues had not been served and that it would, in any event, be improper to make such an order in interlocutory proceedings.

Reversing this decision, the Court of Appeal stressed that the court would not lightly use its power to compel disclosure of information arising in the confidential relationship of a banker and a customer. But an order to this effect would be granted, even in interlocutory proceedings, where the plaintiffs sought to trace funds of which evidence showed that they had been fraudulently deprived. In particular, such an order would be made where delay might result in the dissipation of such funds before the action proceeded to trial. Lord Denning recognized that it was 'a strong thing to order a bank to disclose the state of its customer's account and the documents and correspondence relating to it'.[81] The plaintiff bank was, therefore, required to undertake that the information disclosed would be utilized solely for the purposes of the action to trace the funds.

Although the order is granted sparingly, it is generally available in any litigation. Obviously, such an order can be made in criminal proceedings.[82] Furthermore, it can be made against persons who are not parties to the litigation if they have a close nexus to it.[83] Thus, it would be made in respect of an account which was in fact owned by a party although it was formally maintained in the name of his spouse.[84] The order can also be made in the absence of the party against whom it is sought; but in such circumstances courts rarely grant it.[85] It has been held that the application for the order need not be served on the bank. It is sufficient if it is served on the party about whom the information is sought.[86]

The discussion of the disclosure provisions available under the 1879 Act would be incomplete without defining the type of document covered by the operative provisions. Under section 10, the words 'bankers' books' cover ledgers, day-books, cash-books and all other books used in the ordinary

---

[81] Ibid., 1282.

[82] *R. v. Kinghorn* [1908] 2 KB 949.

[83] *South Staffordshire Tramways Co. v. Ebbsmith* [1895] 2 QB 669.

[84] *Ironmonger & Co. v. Dyne* (1928) 44 TLR 579; see also *Howard v. Beall* (1889) 23 QBD 1.

[85] *Arnott v. Hayes* (1887) 36 Ch. D 731. But see *R. v. Marlborough Street Metropolitan Stipendiary Magistrate, ex p. Simpson* (1980) 70 Cr. App. Rep. 291. As regards the court's discretion, see *Pollock v. Garle* [1898] 1 Ch. 1; *L'Amie v. Wilson* [1907] 2 IR 130; *Staunton v. Counihan* (1957) 92 ILT 32.

[86] *Staunton v. Counihan*, above; contrast *L'Amie v. Wilson*, above.

business of a bank. A book used by the bank for reference and not for the object of making daily entries is included in the definition.[87] It has been held that even a casual record, such as a page from the bank's official day-book,[88] or the branch manager's diary,[89] fall within the definition.

During the nineteenth century and the first half of the twentieth, the definition spelt out in section 10 was adequate. All entries in the business of banking were made by means of some type of writing, be it typed or entered in ink. The position differs in the present era, when many entries are made electronically and records are kept on tapes. In *Barker* v. *Wilson*[90] it was held that the definition of 'bankers' books' included microfilms of a bank's record. Bridge LJ added that the definition included any permanent record made by means furnished by modern technology. It is believed that, on this basis, any entries made on tapes produced at BACS[91] or by means of a bank's individual computer, are subject to disclosure under a court order made in pursuance of section 7 of the Act. Undoubtedly, where inspection is ordered in respect of a magnetic entry, the bank would be obliged to furnish the equipment required to facilitate the inspection at its premises.

The provisions of the 1879 Act are general in nature. There are, in addition, instances in which orders for inspection and disclosure may be issued against a bank under specific statutes. Only two of these can be mentioned in the context of this treatment. First, a bank may be ordered to supply certain information on customers' affairs under sections 481 and 518(3) of the Income and Corporation Taxes Act 1970 and section 24 of the Taxes Management Act 1970.[92] Secondly, where the Department of Trade and Industry investigates the affairs of a company, agents of the company, including its bankers,[93] are obligated to produce books relevant in the prosecution of the company's directors or managers.

(iii) Duty to the public

The second exception to the bank's duty of secrecy, postulated by Bankes LJ in *Tournier*'s case, is where the disclosure is required in the public interest.

---

[87] *Asylum for Idiots* v. *Handysides* (1906) 22 TLR 573.

[88] *Re L. G. Batten Pty. Ltd.* [1962] QWN 2.

[89] *Elsey* v. *Federal Commissioner of Taxation* (1969) 121 CLR 99. But a deposit slip given to a customer is outside the definition: *Lever* v. *Maguire* [1928] VLR 262.

[90] [1980] 1 WLR 884.

[91] The banks' centre for electronic transfers generated by paper; pp. 354 et seq. below.

[92] And see *A-G* v. *National Provincial Bank Ltd.* (1928) 44 TLR 701, regarding the bank's duty to disclose interest paid out to the customer. An interesting Australian authority concerning the extent of the bank's obligation is *O'Reilly* v. *State Bank of Victoria* (1938) 57 ALJR 342.

[93] Companies Act 1985, ss. 434(2), 435, 452(1)(*b*); and see the Banking Act, 1979, s. 20(1)(*a*). And see *Australia and New Zealand Bank Ltd.* v. *Ryan* [1968] 3 NSWLR 118 concerning an Australian provision *in pari materia*.

Paget[94] rightly points out that this is the most difficult exception to define. In *Tournier*'s case, Bankes LJ relied on the words of Lord Finlay in *Weld Blundell* v. *Stephens*[95] to the effect that danger to the state may supersede the duty of secrecy owed by an agent to his principal. The application of the exception may, however, be subject to variations in different periods. Thus, in time of war a bank may be bound to disclose to the authorities information which it receives about the customer's dealings with an enemy alien.[96] But in *Tournier*'s case itself, Bankes LJ doubted that a bank was entitled to disclose to the police information which gives rise to suspicions that the customer was involved in a crime. The distinction, though, is arbitrary. Trading with an alien enemy, in a minor way and in respect of a product that has no direct bearing on the war machinery, may be of significantly less harm to society than the major trafficking in narcotics in a period of peace.

It is believed that one way for introducing harmony as regards the exception under consideration is to draw a distinction between misdemeanours and felonies. A bank may not be entitled to disclose information which leads it to suspect that its customer is involved in a misdemeanour. Where the bank discovers that the money deposited originated from blackmail or was paid in by a crime syndicate, the matter assumes a different proportion.

Up to now, there are no cases directly in point. The reason for this is clear. If the bank discloses to the police information leading to the arrest of a felon, proceedings against it for breach of contract are unlikely. If the bank turns a blind eye, it is unlikely that a prosecution will bring its guilt home to it. It is significant that the Swiss law,[97] which entitles a bank to make disclosure where money is received from crime syndicates, has not been invoked to date. Indeed, legislation of this type is practically cosmetic.

(iv) The bank's own interest

This is the third exception to the bank's duty of secrecy mentioned by Bankes LJ. The typical case is where the bank sues to recover an amount which it lent to its customer. The bank has to disclose in the pleadings the state of the customer's account and the amount owed by him to the bank. Obviously, such disclosure is sanctioned.[98]

A marginal case in point is *Sunderland* v. *Barclays Bank Ltd.*[99] The bank

---

[94] *Law of Banking*, 9th edn., p. 154.
[95] [1920] AC 956, 965.
[96] Chorley, *Law of Banking*, 6th edn., p. 23.
[97] For a review, see Comment, 15 Harv. Int. LJ 349, esp. 359 (1974).
[98] But, obviously, neither the bank nor its employees are entitled to use such information to further interests conflicting with the customer's: *Guertin* v. *Royal Bank of Canada* (1983) 43 OR 2d, 363.
[99] (1938) 5 LDAB 163.

dishonoured cheques drawn on it by a married woman, principally because the account had an insufficient credit balance, but also because the bank knew that the cheques were drawn in respect of gambling debts. When her husband interceded at her request, he was told by the branch manager that most of the cheques were drawn in favour of bookmakers. Du Parq LJ dismissed the wife's action for damages for the bank's breach of its duty of secrecy, as in his Lordship's opinion the disclosure was required in the bank's own interest. He further held that the wife had given her implied consent to the disclosure of the facts to her husband.

The second finding of the case may be doubted. The wife's complaint that the bank was dishonouring her cheques could not indicate that she was prepared to permit it to disclose the state of her affairs. The unjustified nature of the complaint, however, meant that the bank had an interest in advising the husband that it had good reasons for refusing to meet the wife's cheques. The bank had to do so in order to protect its own reputation. But it is difficult to see why the bank was justified in informing the husband that the cheques were related to gambling debts. It only had to show that the dishonour was justified by reason of want of funds. It is noteworthy that in *Tournier*'s case itself, the branch manager was held to have no justification for disclosing the plaintiff's gambling activities to his employer. It is suggested that the decision in *Sunderland*'s case is questionable, as it appears to entitle the bank to disclose more than is necessary for the purpose of protecting its own interests.

(v) *Information disclosed with customer's authority*

This is the last exception to the bank's duty of secrecy listed by Bankes LJ. The consent may be express or implied and may be general, in the sense that the bank is permitted to disclose the general state of the customer's account, or special, which means that the bank is entitled to supply only such information as is sanctioned by the customer.

The most common case of the former type is the giving of bank references. There is a well-established practice which authorizes banks to provide such information. The practice has probably become an established trade usage at this stage.[100] Customers will therefore be regarded as having consented to the giving of such information except if they have specifically indicated that they refuse to allow their banks to reply to such enquiries. Be this as it may, it can be stated with confidence that, where a customer refers to the name of his bank in the context of a business transaction or enquiry, he impliedly authorizes the request for and the giving of a reference by his bank.

---

[100] Cf. Paget, *Law of Banking*, 9th edn., p. 158.

GOTO
112

(vi) Secrecy and the intervention of foreign courts

A problem of conflict of laws concerning bank secrecy can present itself in the case of banks that maintain offices in countries around the world and look after the affairs of multinational customers. Frequently, a question concerning the affairs of such a customer arises in country A in respect of his operations in country B. The bank may then be required to testify about the matter in country A. Thus, an American branch of a British bank may be asked by a United States court to supply information maintained with the head office in London. Information may likewise be requested by the same court from the American office of a local bank in respect of operations conducted in the United Kingdom or in Switzerland. In all these cases, the information may be privileged under local law.

Two methods may be used in order to obtain the information. One is by means of 'letters of request' or 'letters rogatory'; the other by means of a subpoena. The former involves a request for the provision of the evidence made by a court in the country which seeks the information to a court in the place at which the records are maintained. The object of this procedure is to enable the requesting court to obtain the information in question without committing, directly or indirectly, an infringement of the sovereignty of another country. This question of comity is ignored where the court that seeks the information issues a subpoena. The order made by it frequently confronts the bank with the unpleasant choice of defying the subpoena at the risk of being held in contempt in the United States or obeying it at the cost of paying the price for infringing the secrecy laws of the country in which the information is maintained.

The use of letters of request, or letters rogatory, is regulated by the Hague Convention on the Taking of Evidence Abroad in Civil or Commercial Matters 1970,[101] which has led to the enactment of the Evidence (Proceedings in Other Jurisdictions) Act 1975.[102] Under section 1, the High Court may accede to the request and order that evidence be furnished, provided the evidence could be obtained in civil proceedings conducted before itself. The section further precludes the making of a general order for the global production of all documents that may be relevant to the proceedings. The request has to specify the particular documents sought to be produced. Obviously, the Act frowns on 'fishing' trips. Furthermore, it seems unlikely that a request will be met if it involves the infringement of a privilege recognized in English law.

The leading case in point is *Re Westinghouse Uranium Contract*.[103]

---

[101] Cmnds. 3991, 6272.
[102] Repealing and replacing the Foreign Tribunals Evidence Act 1856.
[103] [1978] AC 547.

American suppliers justified their failure to deliver uranium at the agreed price by pleading that the contract became frustrated as a result of the activities of a uranium cartel, of which they alleged that two British firms were members. The American District Court issued letters rogatory, requesting the High Court to order officers of these companies to produce certain documents to, and to give evidence before, the American consulate in London, although the companies were not cited as parties to the action concerning the supply contracts. It further appeared from the proceedings that the evidence so produced could become the subject of anti-trust proceedings to be instituted against members of the cartel in the United States.

The House of Lords held that the request ought to be denied. In the first place, the production of the evidence would have exposed the companies to fines under certain provisions of the EEC Treaty, so that they were entitled to claim privilege against self-incrimination. Secondly, their Lordships placed much weight on an intervention by the Attorney-General, who took the view that the wide investigatory procedures applicable under the United States anti-trust laws against foreign citizens constituted an infringement of UK law. It was noted in this regard that grand jury proceedings, involving the serving of a subpoena on the companies, had taken place in the United States,[104] which meant that the evidence procured would be available in penal proceedings. Summing up this aspect of the case, Lord Wilberforce said:[105]

if public interest enters on this matter on one side, so it must be taken account of on the other: and as the views of the executive in the United States of America impel the making of the order, so must the views of the executive in the United Kingdom be considered when it is a question of implementing the order here.

It may be safely assumed that the same weight would be given by the court to what it considered to be the national interest. The third reason for the refusal of the order is most succinctly expressed by Viscount Dilhorne:[106]

For many years now the United States has sought to exercise jurisdiction over foreigners in respect of acts done outside the jurisdiction of that country. This is not in accordance with international law. . . .

Although these words do not form the basis of the decision, they are echoed in other speeches delivered in this case.[107] It is clear that the House of Lords was perturbed by the fact that an order, giving effect to the District Court's request, would expose British subjects to proceedings conducted in

---

[104] For anti-trust investigatory proceedings, see *Re Westinghouse Electric Corporation Uranium Contracts Litigation* 563 F 2d 992 (1977); *Re Uranium Antitrust Litigation* 480 F Supp. 1138 (1979).
[105] [1978] AC 547, 617.
[106] Ibid., 631.
[107] Per Lord Wilberforce, *ibid.*, 610.

the United States in respect of acts performed outside that country. The case further suggests that a request would be denied if the order were to involve an infringement of a privilege recognized in English law. In the instant case, the privilege was the freedom of a person not to incriminate himself. It stands to reason that other privileges would be equally recognized. A bank's right and duty to maintain secrecy concerning its customer's affairs is unquestionably one of these. It is true that a bank may be compelled at law to disclose information. But it is to be doubted that the exception in point, recognized by Bankes LJ in *Tournier*'s case, is wide enough to force disclosure required in respect of British subjects or companies under foreign law.

Being aware of the hurdles placed in their way by the procedure involving letters of request, American courts frequently attempt to achieve their goal by ordering local officers of American and international banks to disclose details concerning operations of overseas branches. Where parol evidence is required, the bank or its officer is served with a subpoena. Where the object is to produce documents, resort is made to a subpoena *duces tecum*. If the bank officer refuses to obey the order, he faces contempt of court proceedings. Thus, in *United States* v. *Field*[108] a Canadian citizen, who was the manager of a bank in the Cayman Islands, appeared under subpoena before an American grand jury, and was compelled by the threat of contempt proceedings to answer questions concerning the account of a customer maintained with the home office.

However, the American courts take into consideration the prohibition imposed by the law prevailing at the place at which the required records are maintained. In *Société Internationale pour Participations Industrielles et Commerciales SA* v. *Rogers*[109] the United States Supreme Court refused to order a Swiss bank to produce documents, as their disclosure was contrary to Swiss banking law, and as the bank had not acted in bad faith in a manner aimed at bringing itself within the ambit of the law in question.

Although some decisions regard the prohibition of disclosure by foreign law an adequate reason for refusing to make an order,[110] the modern trend of American law is to emphasize the second element. Thus, in *United States* v. *First National City Bank*[111] the Circuit Court of Appeals refused to allow a bank to justify its refusal to disclose documents by reason of German bank secrecy laws. It was held that German law did not impose an absolute prohi-

[108] 532 F 2d 404 (1976).
[109] 357 US 197 (1958).
[110] *First National City Bank of New York* v. *IRS* 271 F 2d 616 (1959), cert. den. 361 US 948 (1960); *Ings* v. *Ferguson* 282 F Supp. 149 (1960); *Application of Chase Manhattan Bank* 297 F 2d 611 (1962).
[111] 396 F 2d 897 (1968), affg. 285 F Supp. 845 (1968), sub nom. *Re First National City Bank.*

bition and, further, that the bank had not taken bona fide steps to seek permission to disclose. A similar decision was reached in *SEC* v. *Banca della Svizzera Italiana*,[112] in which the District Court thwarted the attempt by a Swiss bank operating in the United States to rely on Swiss bank secrecy law to justify its refusal to disclose information required to prosecute some of its customers for offences involving insider trading. In both cases the courts balanced the hardship incurred by the bank if it revealed the information against the need to protect fiscal or economic laws of the United States. However, where a bank has made a genuine but unsuccessful attempt to seek the permission of local authorities to comply with the American order, or where it cannot be accused of seeking to use the foreign secrecy law as a mere shield, an order for a subpoena will be refused.[113]

Despite the purported restraint exercised by the American courts, their orders are invariably resented by the courts of the country at which the records are maintained. In the first place, such courts regard the American orders as an invasion of local jurisdiction. Secondly, the economic interests of the United States are often diametrically opposed to the other country's. Thus, in the *Westinghouse* case, discussed above, the United States sought to expose the uranium cartel whilst Britain's interest was to protect the privacy of the companies based in London.

That English courts will be guided by the national interest rather than by the policy of the United States is demonstrated by the recent decision in *X AG* v. *A Bank*.[114] A group of companies, engaged in the oil business, maintained their accounts with the London branch of an American bank. Although only one company had any dealings on the US market, the American Department of Justice sought information concerning all members of the group in respect of an investigation conducted into the crude oil industry. A subpoena was accordingly served on the bank's head office for the production in the United States of the London records concerning the affairs of the group. When the bank declared its intention to comply with the subpoena, the group obtained an interim injunction in which the High Court restrained the bank from disclosing the records. In disregard of a subsequent order of the United States District Court, seeking to compel disclosure, Leggatt J continued the injunction.

His Lordship held that, as the accounts of the companies were opened and maintained in London, the proper law of the contract was English law. Accordingly, the confidentiality of the contract of banker and customer,

[112] 92 FRD 111 (1981). See also *United States* v. *Field* 532 F 2d 404 (1976); *Arthur Andersen & Co.* v. *Finesilver* 546 F 2d 338 (1976).
[113] *Trade Development Bank* v. *Continental Insurance Co.* 469 F 2d 35 (1972); *US* v. *Bank of Nova Scotia* 691 F 2d 1384 (1982).
[114] [1983] 2 All ER 464.

recognized in English law, applied to the relationship of the members of the group with the bank. Leggatt J noted that, if obeyed, the District Court's order:

would take effect in London for the production of documents in breach of what might be termed a private interest in the sense that what is directly involved is a contract between banker and customer. But this indubitably is also a matter of public interest, because it raises issues of wider concern than those peculiar to the parties [in the instant case].[115]

Leggatt J then weighed all the relevant factors in order to consider whether, on a balance of convenience, the injunction ought to be vacated or continued. Paramount were the breach of secrecy required by the American order, and the fact that the District Court was unlikely to resort to contempt proceedings if the bank was enjoined from making disclosure by a court of competent jurisdiction at the place at which the records were maintained. Leggatt J concluded:[116]

I can summarise in a sentence the balance of convenience as I see it. On the one hand, there is involved in the continuation of the injunction impeding the exercise by the United States court in London of powers which, by English standards, would be regarded as excessive, without in so doing causing detriment to the bank: on the other hand, the refusal of the injunctions, or the non-continuation of them, would cause potentially very considerable commercial harm to the [group], which cannot be disputed, by suffering the bank to act for its own purposes in breach of the duty of confidentiality admittedly owed to its customers.

The injunction continued by Leggatt J restrained the bank from passing information concerning the companies' affairs to its head office in the United States or to any other person or branch.

A similar view was recently taken by the Court of Appeal of Hong Kong in *FDC Co.* v. *Chase Manhattan Bank*.[117] The plaintiffs—an American firm—maintained an account with the Hong Kong branch of the defendants, an American bank. In the course of an investigation of the plaintiffs' income tax statement, the American revenue authorities demanded information from the defendants' head office in New York about the plaintiffs' account in Hong Kong. The plaintiffs instituted proceedings in Hong Kong, to enjoin the defendants from complying with this request and to preclude them from transferring the information to the United States.

Affirming the trial court's decision to grant the injunction, the Court of Appeal took the view that a bank's duty of secrecy was not subject to territorial limits. The defendants, accordingly, were not entitled to divulge

---

[115] Ibid., 477.
[116] Ibid., 480.
[117] Unreported; nos. 65 and 131 (Civil) of 1984; judgment of 17 Oct. 1984.

information about the plaintiffs' account with the Hong Kong office either in the Colony or overseas. It was argued that the transfer of the information by the Hong Kong office to the head office in New York could not constitute disclosure, as the data would initially remain available to the defendants alone. Huggins VP conceded that this view might be correct if the information were transmitted to the United States office as a matter of routine. But he thought that:

it would be closing our eyes to the reality of the situation to allow the [defendants] to make an internal transfer of information which it would not make in the ordinary course of business when that transfer is designed for no other purpose than to bring the information within the jurisdiction of the foreign court.

The Court of Appeal was undeterred by the fact that the American order was on its face directed to the head office in the United States. The order was 'aimed unashamedly' at information which was within the jurisdiction of the Hong Kong courts and, accordingly, had an extra-territorial effect. His Lordship concluded:

The Hong Kong courts could enjoin the [defendants] against disclosing the information to the United States Government in Hong Kong and I am satisfied that they can restrain a transfer which is nothing more nor less than a device to avoid the enforcement in Hong Kong of the orders of a foreign court.

It is clear that, in reaching this conclusion, the Court of Appeal sought to protect the secrecy laws governing the interests of banks in Hong Kong. Huggins VP observed:

All persons opening accounts with banks in Hong Kong, whether foreign or local banks, are entitled to look to the Hong Kong courts to enforce any obligation of secrecy which, by the law of Hong Kong, is implied by virtue of the relationship of banker and customer.

The Court of Appeal expressed its sympathy for the defendants, who were given the Hobson's choice of either transferring the information to the United States at the risk of prosecution in Hong Kong or of refusing to do so at the risk of being held in contempt in New York. Nonetheless, the Court felt obliged to give effect to the laws of Hong Kong. The Court declined to assess the likelihood of the defendants being actually held in contempt under American law, holding that this matter was outside its competence. It treated this hazard as irrelevant for its own decision. In this regard, the Court of Appeal took a harder line than Leggatt J in *X AG* v. *A Bank*. Accordingly, the Hong Kong Court of Appeal appeared even more strongly motivated by the need to protect the local bank secrecy laws than the English High Court.

It is thus clear that the courts of the United Kingdom and of Hong Kong resist attempts by foreign courts to infringe the bank secrecy laws of the realm. The courts of the United Kingdom have, further, been unwilling to infringe the jurisdiction of foreign courts. Thus, in *R. v. Grossman*[118] the Court of Appeal discharged an order, made under section 7 of the Bankers' Books Evidence Act 1879, which would have enabled the Inland Revenue authorities to inspect records concerning the account maintained by the accused, who was prosecuted for tax evasion, with the Isle of Man branch of Barclays Bank. The order was vacated although it assumed the form of an instruction to the head office of the bank in London to obtain the required information from its branch in the Isle of Man. Lord Denning MR said that his refusal to affirm the order was motivated by the conflict of jurisdictions that would arise if it were allowed to stand.

This decision was followed in *MacKinnon v. Donaldson Lufkin & Jenrette Securities Corporation.*[119] A Bahamian company which was accused of committing a fraud concerning some international loans was struck off the Bahamian register. To acquire information about the persons involved, the victim obtained an order under section 7 of the 1879 Act, ordering the company's bank, a multinational with its head office in New York and with an office in London, to enable him to inspect certain documents. He also obtained a subpoena requiring the bank to attend by its proper officer to give evidence at the trial of the action and to produce all the relevant documents. Both the order and the subpoena were directed to and served on the bank at its London office but related to all the documents concerning the company. Discharging the order made by the Master, Hoffman J emphasized that the relevant order and the subpoena, which were to take effect in New York, infringed the sovereignty of the United States. His Lordship thought that the need to exercise with care the court's jurisdiction with regard to the sovereignty of other states was particularly important in the case of banks. The documents of a bank were usually concerned not only with the bank's own business but also with that of its customers. Bank secrecy laws in different states protected the confidentiality of such documents. 'If every country where a bank happened to carry on business asserted a right to require the bank to produce documents relating to accounts kept in any other such country, banks would be in the unhappy position of being forced to submit to whichever sovereign was able to apply the greatest pressure.'[120]

It seems unavoidable that cases involving the type of clashes of jurisdictions affecting bank secrecy laws, discussed in the foregoing paragraphs, will continue to occur from time to time. The expansion of the banking network throughout the world and the increase in the number of multi-

---

[118] (1981) 73 Cr. App. Rep. 302.
[119] [1986] 1 All ER 653.
[120] Ibid., 658.

national customers is bound to exacerbate the problem. It is believed that an international convention is the only means for avoiding this type of conflictual situation.

6. TERMINATION OF RELATIONSHIP

The relationship of banker and customer may, basically, be terminated in accordance with the terms agreed upon by the parties. Thus, in the case of a fixed deposit maturing at an agreed time, neither the banker nor the customer can terminate the agreement before the appointed day without the consent of the other party. The same applies where the customer has agreed to hire from the banker a safe-box for a fixed period. It follows that, in the context of the termination of the relationship, it is important to have regard to the specific aspect of the contract or relationship which the parties seek to sever.

In the majority of cases the customer maintains with the bank some account which contemplates payments on demand. This is the case in current accounts and in ordinary savings accounts. The customer is entitled to terminate the relationship at any time by drawing out the outstanding funds and by closing the account. The bank would not be under an obligation to pay cheques presented to it thereafter.

Where the bank wishes to sever the relationship, the position is different. The reason for this is that the customer may have asked his debtors to pay amounts due to him directly to the credit of his account. It would embarrass him if the cheques or other effects were returned to the drawers, accompanied by a note stating that the account had been closed.

This point was recognized in *Prosperity Ltd.* v. *Lloyds Bank Ltd.*[121] A course of business was established between the bank and its customer, an insurer, under which persons were required to pay premiums due to the customer directly to the credit of his account. The bank gave the customer one month's notice before closing the account. McCardie J said that the account could be closed only upon the giving of reasonable notice. In view of the course of dealings between the customer and his clients, one month's notice was considered inadequate. But his Lordship refused to grant a mandatory injunction ordering the bank to reopen the account, as such an order would constitute an instruction that the bank perform personal services. Damages were available, and their award subject to the customer's proof of loss.

The contract of banker and customer, being of a personal nature, termin-

---

[121] (1923) 39 TLR 372.

ates automatically where the customer dies or becomes bankrupt or, in the case of a partnership, where it is dissolved. The same applies where a corporation enters into liquidation. According to Wynn Parry J, in *Re Russian Commercial and Industrial Bank*,[122] the relationship is terminated when the legal personality of the body corporate ceases to exist. The balance in the hands of the bank thereupon becomes payable to the customer.

[122] [1955] 1 Ch. 148; see also pp. 281–285 below.

PART TWO

THE BANK AS A MONETARY AGENCY IN DOMESTIC TRANSACTIONS

CHAPTER 5

The Bank's Role as a Depository

1. ECONOMIC FUNCTION AND LEGAL CONCEPT

Banks serve two main functions in domestic transactions. The first is that of paying their customers' accounts by honouring their cheques and, generally, enabling customers to deposit their money in current accounts or in accounts bearing interest, such as savings accounts and fixed deposits. The second function of the banks is to act as lenders. This second function is discussed in Part III of this book (Chapters 16–22). The first function is discussed in this Part (Chapters 5–15).

To appreciate fully the bank's role as paymaster and as a recipient of its customer's funds, it is necessary to consider both the legal aspects of the subject and the basic economic concepts of banking. The present chapter attempts to do this, and also introduces the problems discussed in Chapters 6–15. It will be convenient to commence the analysis by reflecting on the nature of a bank's operations.

In a modern industrialized society, most transactions involving the payment of money on a regular basis are effected through banking channels. At present, most salaries and wages are paid by the employer's bank to the credit of his employees' accounts. Payment can be effected by means of cheques, but in the case of regular periodic payments of fixed amounts, such as salaries and wages, the sums due can be remitted through the payor's bank by means of a money transfer order. Moreover, even where the amount varies on each date of payment, as is the case with electricity or telephone bills, payment can be effected by means of a 'direct debit',[1] in which the payor authorizes his bank to remit to the payee on a regular date the amount charged by the payee on each occasion.

In the present era, payment by cash continues to be a widely used alternative to the settlement of accounts by means of banking channels. Thus, some consumers pay their electricity bills and telephone accounts in cash. In addition, most sales conducted in shops and many services supplied by entrepreneurs to consumers are settled by cash payments. Indeed, it seems unlikely that payments to grocers, to bookshops and to laundrettes will be effected by other means. But even in the area of consumer sales and services,

---

[1] Pp. 349–50 below.

payments of substantial amounts are frequently settled by means of credit cards or by cheques backed by bank cards.[2] Steps are currently being taken to facilitate the settlement of such payments by electronic transfers conducted by means of 'point of sale' computer terminals set at the supplier's premises and operable by a new type of card.[3] It is to be expected that the use of banking facilities for the discharge of amounts due from individuals will continue to increase in the next decade.

The payment of accounts is, of course, only one aspect of the bank's business. To be able to discharge his liabilities through his bank, a customer must either maintain an adequate credit balance with it or, alternatively, obtain overdraft facilities or loans. The availability of such facilities depends, in turn, on the regular flow of funds into the customer's account with the bank. Thus, an individual's ability to draw cheques for the payment of his electricity bills and telephone accounts may depend on his arranging for his salary or earnings to be paid into his bank account. Similarly, a corporation may be unable to arrange for the payment of its employees' wages by the bank unless its trade profits are paid into its account.

Banks act as agents for the receipt of amounts payable to their customers. Thus, customers can remit all cheques payable to them for collection to their banks. The process is arranged through the clearing house, and the legal problems involved are discussed in Chapter 14. Similarly, banks receive on behalf of their customers any amount remitted through the money transfer (or 'giro') system. Thus, when a consumer orders his bank to pay the monthly instalments due under his hire purchase agreement with a finance company, the amount remitted by his bank is received on behalf of the finance company by the latter's bank. This system is discussed in Chapter 12.

It follows that, apart from its activities as financier and as manager of business transactions, the bank's main business is that of acting both as the customer's paymaster and as the recipient of amounts payable to him. The word 'payment' must, in this context, be understood in its widest sense. It is not restricted to payments made in cash. This is not to say that banks are unable to handle cash on behalf of their customers. Indeed, a bank will receive cash payments made by the customer to the credit of his account. Equally, the bank will pay out cash if the customer presents a personal cheque for payment over the counter, or if an uncrossed cheque is presented in this manner by its payee or by a transferee.[4] Withdrawal of cash is further effected by means of encoded plastic cards utilized at computer terminals.[5] The majority of payments, though, are effected by means of debit and credit

---

[2] Pp. 391 et seq. below.
[3] Such tokens are in operation in other countries, such as Australia.
[4] As to crossings and their effect, see pp. 252 et seq.
[5] Pp. 399–401 below.

entries. Thus, where a cheque is cleared through a bank, the drawer's (customer's) account is debited with the amount involved and the payee's account is credited with it.[6] The transaction is completed without any cash being passed from hand to hand. The same is true in money transfer order transactions. Thus, in the case of a payroll settled by the giro operations of the banks, the employer's account is debited with the total amount, and the account of each payee is credited with the sum due to him. [7]

The constant flow of money into and out of each bank forms the basis of the economic concept used for describing the nature of banking. A bank is regarded as a reservoir of money.[8] The same definition is an apt description of the banking network as a whole. The concept highlights the fact that money flowing into the bank becomes part of a generic fund, and that money paid out by the bank flows, again, from the bank itself and not from an individual pool of money maintained by the customer.[9] In other words, the reservoir is that of the bank, not a reservoir comprising earmarked amounts owned by separate account holders.

Legal concepts accommodate this economic theory. It has been pointed out in Chapter 4 that money paid by the customer to the credit of his account with his bank is treated as being lent by him to the bank.[10] The amount involved is not earmarked or held in trust for him. It follows that the funds become the property of the bank. This concept is complementary to another well-known legal doctrine, namely, that money cannot be owned in the same way as corporeal property.[11] It is treated as a mere chose in action. It is, therefore, sound to regard any amount paid to the credit of the customer's account with his bank as a chose in action which has accrued to him. It is a debt which, in the case of a current account or a savings account, is payable to him on demand, whilst in the case of a fixed deposit it is repayable at an agreed future date.

An Australian authority, discussed in Chapter 4, further recognizes the validity of the economic definition of a bank. In the words of Isaacs J:[12]

[A bank] is, in effect, a financial reservoir receiving streams of currency in every direction, and from which there issues outflowing streams where and as required to sustain and fructify or assist commercial, industrial or other enterprises or adventures.

---

[6] For details, see pp. 230 et seq. below.
[7] Usually through BACS; see pp. 351 et seq. below.
[8] Lawyers' interest in defining a 'bank' arose at a late stage. Note that the term is not defined in the 1st edition of Paget, *Law of Banking*, published in 1904.
[9] Pp. 82–84 above.
[10] P. 82 above.
[11] *Miller* v. *Race* (1758) 1 Burr. 452.
[12] *Commissioners of the State Savings Bank of Victoria* v. *Permewan, Wright & Co.* (1914) 19 CLR 457, 471.

The very same case emphasizes two other elements in the definition of banking. The first is that a bank is prepared to trade with the public.[13] In other words, any member of the public whose character is established to the bank's satisfaction is entitled to open an account with it and, in appropriate circumstances, can obtain a loan or overdraft facilities. In the case of a building society and a credit union, a person usually has to be a member or a shareholder in order to be entitled to deal with it. In practice, though, the distinction is nebulous, as most members of the public can become members of credit unions or shareholders of building societies. Indeed, they are encouraged to do so. The other element emphasized by the Australian High Court is the generic nature of the bank's activities in the field of lending and of obtaining deposits.[14] Any amount may be paid in, and loans granted by the bank may be made for almost any purpose. In contrast, a building society or a friendly society has set guidelines as to the purposes for which it would lend. The point is, again, a questionable one as banks, too, tend to have a policy concerning the nature of their lending activities, even if this policy is not spelt out in their charter or memorandum of association.

It follows that from a purely economic point of view there is no magic distinction between the activities of a bank and those of other financial or lending institutions. It has been pointed out earlier that the Banking Act 1979 takes notice of this point. In reality, an institution is often treated as a bank because it enjoys the reputation of having such a status.[15]

2. PRACTICAL IMPLICATIONS OF THE ECONOMIC AND LEGAL CONCEPT

The main legal consequence of the economic concept which treats a bank as a reservoir of money is that the customer is deemed to have lent to the bank the amounts standing to the credit of his account. Three practical consequences follow from this analysis. The first is relevant where the bank becomes insolvent. The customer is regarded as an unsecured general creditor, whose claim is subordinate to those of preferential claim holders and to those of secured creditors.[16] As a general creditor, the customer acquires a dividend based on the amount of the surplus remaining after the settlement of secured and preferential claims. The amount of the dividend payable to

---

[13] Ibid., 479.
[14] Ibid., 471; and see further, pp. 52–54 above.
[15] The importance of this point emerges from the decisions of the majority in *Burnett* v. *Westminster Bank Ltd.* [1966] 1 QB 742 (and it is further emphasized in the Banking Act 1979: pp. 36–37 above.)
[16] For the general ranking of claims, see Chap. 18.

individual customers is pro-rated on the basis of the amount owed to each of them by the bank. The customer is not entitled to a tracing order, which would enable him to recover the amount due to him in specie.[17] Secondly, the balance due to the customer constitutes a mere claim available to him, whilst the money itself becomes that of the bank. It follows that the bank is free to use the money for its own purposes and dealings. It does not have to account to the customer for profits made by means of the money paid by him to the bank. All the customer is entitled to is the interest payable on deposits of the type involved. Moreover, in the case of a current account, he is obligated to pay bank charges, often without obtaining any interest on the balance standing to his credit.

The third practical consequence based on the economic analysis of a bank is that, as mere creditor of its customer, the bank is not in the position of a trustee. Subject to certain exceptions,[18] it does not owe the customer any fiduciary duty of care.

In view of these points, it may be rightly asked what induces members of the public to invest their funds with banks. The answer is, again, an economic rather than a legal one. From the eighteenth century, banks have attained a high reputation as regards creditworthiness and honesty in dealings. The trust engendered by their high standing induces members of the public to deposit their funds with banks even if the yield is marginally lower than that obtainable from other financial institutions. This public trust is enhanced by the fact that banks are strictly controlled and supervised by the Bank of England, which performs the function of a reserve bank in the United Kingdom.[19] Another factor is the size of the major banks and the phenomenal number of their branches throughout the United Kingdom. Members of the public are more inclined to invest with a branch of a financial giant than with a small concern that may not have the same economic power and standing.

3. THE BANK AS A DEPOSITORY OF ITS CUSTOMER'S FUNDS AND AS PAYMASTER OF HIS ACCOUNTS

The maintenance of an account with a bank confers on the customer two main benefits. First, in the case of any account except most current ones, he gains interest on amounts not required by him for immediate use. This aspect is discussed in detail in Chapter 8. Principally, the consideration for the bank's agreement to pay interest is its having the use of the customer's

[17] *Foley* v. *Hill* (1848) 2 HLC 28.
[18] Pp. 84 et seq.
[19] See Ch. 2.

money. The rate of interest depends on different factors. Thus, in fixed
deposits (i.e. deposits maturing at an agreed date) the rate is usually higher
in long-term deposits than in short-term deposits or in deposits payable 'at
call' (meaning 'on demand'). Furthermore, the rate may depend on the
amount deposited. Thus, certain types of accounts—which yield a high rate
of interest—are available only in respect of certain minimal amounts
deposited with the bank. Ordinary savings accounts, which carry the lowest
rate, can of course be opened for any amount.[20] From a practical point of
view, the bank's profit is, principally, the difference between the interest
that it pays to its customer and the amount which it earns by investing the
amounts deposited with it. The bank's own capital usually constitutes a
small fraction of the money available for business purposes.

The existence of current accounts—discussed in Chapter 6—is of particular importance to banks. The amounts which are regularly credited to such
accounts are predominantly available to the bank without its having to pay
any interest on the accrued balance. Experience shows that there is a certain
regularity in the cash-flow of current accounts, which means that banks can
predict with reasonable certainty the amounts that are likely to be standing
to their credit from time to time. By way of illustration, take the regularity
with which the balance standing to the credit of a wage-earner's account
increases when his salary is paid in and decreases throughout the month or
fortnight preceding the next payment. Similarly, the amounts standing to
the credit of accounts of business firms tend to vary on a cyclical basis,
showing a particular decrease when taxes are paid off. The bank's ability to
predict the fluctuations in the amounts standing to the credit of its customers' current accounts, and indeed other accounts, enables it to plan its
own investments.

The opening of current accounts for customers does, however, place an
important obligation on banks. This constitutes the second main benefit
derived by the customer from maintaining a current account. The bank's
duty is to observe the customer's instructions to pay amounts due from him
to third parties. The customer may order payment in two basic manners.
One is by the use of a cheque; the other is by executing a money transfer
order or by authorizing some third party to execute it on his behalf.

The use of cheques for the payment of the customer's account by the
bank is still the predominant method employed in the United Kingdom.
Usually, the payee remits the cheque to the credit of his account with his
own bank. His bank then 'clears' the cheque by acquiring payment from the
drawer's bank. The process is discussed in detail in Chapter 9. It is clear that
the drawer's bank acts as his agent in paying the cheque.[21] The payee's

[20] See Ch. 7.
[21] Pp. 264–6 below.

bank, too, acts as agent, except that its mandate is to seek payment rather than to make it.[22] The drawer's bank faces the hazards of paying cheques which have been tampered with or cheques which have been stolen from their genuine payees, and of paying cheques in disregard of a stop order. The bank's defences are discussed in Chapter 10. The payee's bank faces a different danger. If the payee is not entitled to obtain payment of the cheque, as is the case where he is a thief or a rogue who has forged his employer's signature, the bank that handles the instrument opens itself to a common law action in conversion.[23] The bank's position in such cases is discussed in Chapter 14.

The second method for paying the customer's accounts—that of money transfer orders—is discussed in Chapter 12. Again, both the payor's bank and the payee's bank act in a representative capacity. The former acts as a paying agent; the latter receives payment on the payee's behalf. One of the two main differences between the settlement of debts by the use of a cheque and by the use of a money transfer order is procedural. A cheque is sent by the drawer, who is the debtor, to the payee, who is the creditor. The presentment of the cheque for payment depends on the initiative of the payee. In the case of a money transfer order, the debtor's bank pays the amount involved directly to the payee's bank. This is so even in the case of 'direct debiting', where the periodic money transfer order is executed by an authorized payee, such as an electricity authority, on behalf of the payor who, in the given illustration, is the householder to whom the electrical power has been supplied.

The other major difference between the settlement of accounts by cheques and settlement by means of money transfer orders is that the cheque is a negotiable instrument whilst the money transfer order is not. The significance of this distinction, which is basically related to the fact that a cheque, unlike a money transfer order, is transferable, is discussed in Chapter 9. It is worthwhile adding that, in the future, the payment of accounts by means of money transfer orders may become a paperless operation. Thus, customers might be furnished with terminals installed in their premises, in which any instruction for the settlement of accounts could be given by electronic messages conveyed to a central computer by means of a keyboard.[24] Indeed, the use of cards, operating at points of sale,[25] came into operation on an experimental basis in 1985. Here again, the instruction to pay a given amount to the supplier of goods is executed by means of a card installed in a computer terminal and a paying message conveyed electronically. Again, both the remitting bank and the receiving bank face certain

[22] Pp. 418–21 below.
[23] Pp. 412 et seq. below.
[24] The so-called 'house terminals'.
[25] See n. 3 above.

hazards. The paying bank may remit the amount to the credit of the wrong account; the receiving bank may find that the wrong customer has been credited. In practice, the two situations arise simultaneously, as most money transfer orders are executed by an electronic operation which leads to both the crediting of the payee's account and the debiting of the payor's. The problems arising in such situations, as well as the question of the counter-mand of a money transfer order, are discussed in Chapter 12.

4. THE BANK AS ITS CUSTOMER'S AGENT FOR COLLECTION

Apart from paying cash to the credit of their bank accounts, customers are able to use the available banking facilities to effect the collection of items remitted to them by other parties. In the majority of cases, the item collected is a cheque payable to the customer or a similar type of document such as a dividend warrant. In addition, the bank receives on behalf of the customer amounts remitted to his credit by means of the money transfer system. The funds so collected are automatically lent by the customer to the bank. They form, therefore, part of the reservoir of money available to the bank itself.

The collection of cheques is discussed in detail in Chapter 14. Basically, the procedure involves hazards both as regards the bank's duties to its cus-tomer and as regards the bank's position *vis-à-vis* third parties.

As regards the customer, the bank has to be aware of two main requisites. The first is the need for the speedy collection of cheques and other instru-ments remitted by the customer to the bank for collection. If the bank does not act with due diligence, there is a delay in the presentment of the cheque to the payor's bank (the 'drawee' or 'paying' bank). If the drawer closes his account with the latter bank in the meantime, the cheque will be dis-honoured by that bank due to the collecting bank's dilatoriness. The collect-ing bank's customer may then be entitled to damages for the bank's failure to follow promptly the instructions given to it. Moreover, the collecting bank's failure to process on time the cheque payable to its customer may lead to a situation in which the customer's balance appears, on its face, inadequate for meeting cheques drawn by him on his account. These cheques may, then, be wrongfully dishonoured by his own bank in its capacity as 'paying bank'. In such cases, the customer may have an action for the wrongful dishonour of his cheque and, in certain cases, a concurrent action in defamation.[26]

The collecting bank may, further, be liable to the customer in conversion if a cheque payable to him is collected for the account of an unauthorized person. A case in point is where a cheque payable to a corporation is con-

---

[26] Pp. 310–4 below.

verted by an employee and paid to the credit of his own account which is maintained with the same bank as the corporation's. On the same basis, the bank may be liable to the owner of a cheque, who is not a customer, if the cheque is handled by the collecting bank for a thief, or for a person who has obtained it from the thief without acquiring a good title.[27] The bank's defences are discussed in Chapter 14.

The question of an action in conversion does not arise in the case of a money transfer order. The documents involved in such a transaction are not considered items of property, and there is no suggestion that their misappropriation involves conversion.[28] It is, further, unlikely that the bank can be sued for money had and received. As no tort is committed by it when it receives payment for the wrong party, there is no room for the quasi-contractual action based on waiver of tort.[29] For certain technical reasons related to the collecting bank's position as an agent, it is also unlikely that it can be sued by the genuine payee of the money transfer order in an action based on a generic claim in money had and received. These points are discussed in detail in Chapter 12.

There is, however, no doubt that mistakes can occur where money is remitted by means of a money transfer order. If the order is of the periodic type, the transfer is effected electronically through BACS which, it is believed, acts on behalf of the remitting bank and the receiving bank at different stages of the transaction. Each bank will be vicariously liable for its agent's negligence.[30] If the money transfer order is of a specific, non-recurrent nature, its collection is executed in a manner similar to that of the clearance of a cheque. Here, any mistake in crediting the customer's account will be made by the collecting bank itself. Thus, if the money is credited to the wrong account, the customer is entitled to claim that his own account be credited with it; he may, further, be entitled to an action in breach of contract if the bank's error leads to an apparent shortage of funds in his own account resulting in the dishonour of his own cheques on the bank. This question is discussed in Chapter 14.

The last problem that arises in the case of money transfer orders occurs where an amount is accepted by the bank on the payee's behalf, despite his instructions to the contrary. By way of illustration, a customer may instruct his bank to refuse to accept a payment due under a contract, such as a charterparty, if it is tendered out of time. If the bank accepts the money in contravention of this instruction, it may deprive the customer of an opportunity

---

[27] If the person has acquired a good title he will be a holder in due course, and hence the previous owner loses his rights over the cheque.
[28] Discussed on pp. 364–6 below.
[29] Pp. 412–8 below.
[30] Pp. 368 et. seq.

to rescind validly a contract with the charterer that has become unprofitable. The bank's liability in such cases is discussed in Chapter 12. It will be shown that, in practice, it is difficult for the bank to set into operation an order precluding the acceptance of funds remitted to the credit of the customer's account. Unlike an order countermanding payment, such a 'stop receipt' order is uncommon and there is, to date, no adequate machinery for setting such a request effectively into operation.

5.   CONCLUSION

As has been mentioned at the outset, this chapter is basically an introduction to Part II of the book. Chapters 6–14 will demonstrate that the legal principles defining the bank's liability as a paymaster, as a depository of funds, and as a collector of its customer's effects are closely related to the basic concept of the relationship of banker and customer. The bank, as a reservoir of funds, borrows amounts deposited with it by its customer and pays them out as his agent. Many of the legal principles discussed in the forthcoming chapters are, therefore, anchored in the basic rules of the law of agency. There is only one important rider to this fundamental principle. In its activities on behalf of its customer, the bank is involved both in paying the customer's cheques and in collecting cheques and other items payable to him. Most cheques, and some other similar items, constitute negotiable instruments which are readily transferable from hand to hand. The bank's position both as paying and as collecting agency is influenced by this fact.

CHAPTER 6

The Current Account

1. SPECIAL NATURE OF THE CURRENT ACCOUNT

Current accounts are used by a bank's customers for their regular financial transactions. Cheques payable to a customer are usually remitted by him to the credit of his current account. Some customers even ask their debtors to pay the amounts due to them directly to the credit of their account. A giro operation is used in such an instance.[1] In addition, the customer uses his current account for the purpose of discharging his liabilities. This can be done either by the drawing of cheques which are dispatched by him to creditors, or by means of giro forms, such as 'direct debits', issued by him to his bank.[2] It follows that the customer's current account can be loosely described as a reservoir of his money, used for paying funds both into it and out of it. At law, though, this description is inaccurate. When an amount is paid to the customer's current account, be it by means of cash, of a cheque payable to him, or of a giro transfer, the sum in question is forthwith regarded as being lent by the customer to the bank.[3] It follows that the amounts paid to the credit of the customer's account are converted into debts owed to him by the bank. In reality, the indebtedness of the payor of the amount remitted is substituted by a debt incurred by the bank.

This analysis is of importance in two respects. First, it is wrong to describe the amount standing to the customer's credit as his cash. It is an unsecured debt which, in the bank's insolvency, will rank as subordinate to preferred claims[4] and to secured debts.[5] The customer is thus in the position of a general creditor. Secondly, when the customer orders his bank to pay an amount of money to a third party, the bank discharges the instruction by

---

[1] See Ch. 12.

[2] Pp. 347 et seq. below.

[3] *Foley* v. *Hill* (1848) 2 HLC 28. It follows that usually the bank is not obliged to enquire of the source of the money paid to the customer's credit: *Thomson* v. *Clydesdale Bank Ltd.* [1893] AC 282. Furthermore, third parties cannot usually claim the money as their own: *Gray* v. *Johnston* (1868) LR 3 HL 1; cf. *John Shaw (Rayner's Lane) Ltd.* v. *Lloyds Bank Ltd.* (1945) 5 LDAB 396.

[4] Such as claims of employees for wages: Insolvency Act 1986, s. 175(1) and Sched. 6, paras. 9–12.

[5] Such as a loan secured by a floating charge over the bank's assets; but note that in some cases a floating charge is avoided: pp. 562–3 below.

paying out its own money.[6] It then reimburses itself by debiting the customer's account. It follows that, if the amount involved is paid to the wrong person, the customer does not have an action in money had and received against the payee.[7] The action would have to be brought by the bank. In practice, if payment is effected by means of a cheque which is paid to the wrong party, the customer attempts to recover his loss by suing the collecting bank in conversion.[8]

It has been shown earlier that an amount standing to the credit of the customer's current account is recoverable on demand. Traditionally, this demand is made by the drawing of a cheque. In modern banking it can also be effected by means of an automated teller machine operated by a cash-point card.[9] When the bank pays a cheque, it acts as its customer's agent.[10]

The bank's duty to carry out the instructions given to it is subject to four basic limitations. These, and some restrictions imposed on the bank's duty at law, are discussed in detail in Chapter 10; but an analysis of the basic limitations, which assists in defining the scope of the bank's duty, is topical at this point. The first limitation to the bank's duty is that the bank is not obliged to honour a cheque, or meet some other demand, if the customer's balance is inadequate.[11] An exception to this principle is that the bank has to meet the cheque or other demand, despite the inadequacy of the credit balance, if the bank has agreed to grant the customer an overdraft and the amount of the cheque does not exceed the prescribed ceiling.[12] The balance of a current account is calculated on the basis of the amounts actually standing to its credit at the time the customer's demand is made. The bank has a reasonable time for crediting amounts paid to the credit of a customer's account. If the funds remitted by the customer are drawn upon before the bank has had reasonable time to credit them to the account, the bank is not liable if it dishonours a cheque drawn by the customer.[13] Obviously, if the customer instructs the bank to collect cheques payable to him, he is not entitled to draw on them until the items have been cleared. However, here there is a telling difference between theory and practice. In effect, the proceeds are credited to the customer's account before the clearing of the instruments. There is authority for the view that, in the absence of agree-

---

[6] The point is made, convincingly, by Lord Denning MR in *Halesowen Presswork and Assemblies Ltd.* v. *National Westminster Bank Ltd.* [1971] 1 QB 1, 33–4, and see Buckley LJ, ibid., p. 46. The case was reversed on a different point: [1972] AC 785.
[7] Pp. 315–6 below.
[8] See Ch. 14.
[9] Pp. 399–401 below.
[10] Pp. 285–6 below.
[11] *Marzetti* v. *Williams* (1830) 1 B & Ad. 415, 424; *Bank of New South Wales* v. *Laing* [1954] AC 135, 154.
[12] P. 266 above. And see *Fleming* v. *Bank of New Zealand* [1900] AC 577.
[13] Pp. 267–9 below.

ment to the contrary, the very crediting of the account evidences the bank's readiness to permit the customer to draw against the balance as shown.[14] It follows that, in practice, it may arguably be possible to establish a usage under which the drawing against uncleared proceeds is permissible in the absence of express stipulation to the contrary. Many banks, though, include such a stipulation in their standard terms and conditions for the opening of current accounts.

The second limitation to the bank's duty to honour the customer's cheques is that the demand must be made at the branch with which the account is maintained. The customer is not entitled to demand payment at another branch.[15] If a cheque is cashed for the holder at some other branch, the bank is initially considered to have discounted rather than paid the cheque.[16] Thirdly, cheques should be paid only if presented during ordinary business hours. However, a bank does not commit a breach of its mandate by paying the cheque shortly after closure time.[17] Finally, as a matter of practice, banks dishonour cheques that have been outstanding for a long period of time. Usually, a cheque is dishonoured if presented after the lapse of more than six months from the date of its issue. Likewise, it is a practice not to pay an undated cheque.[18]

An important feature of the current account is that the role of the bank and of the customer can be reversed in given situations. If the account is overdrawn, the bank becomes the creditor and the customer the debtor. Whether or not the overdraft—like the credit balance standing to a customer's account—is repayable on demand is a delicate question which is discussed subsequently.[19] The agency relationship existing between the customer and his bank is not altered by the existence of the overdraft. The customer continues to be the principal and the bank remains the agent. It follows that no fiduciary duties of the type discussed in Chapter 4 are owed by the customer to the bank. At best, the customer owes the bank a duty of care;[20] but this duty is in existence regardless of whether the account is in credit or in debit.

The object of the current account is to enable the customer to pay by cheque amounts due from him, and to arrange for the collection of cheques payable to him and other receivables. Subject to certain exceptions, the

---

[14] *Capital and Counties Bank Ltd.* v. *Gordon* [1903] AC 240, 249; but see p. 268 below.
[15] *Woodland* v. *Fear* (1857) 7 El. & Bl. 519; *Arab Bank Ltd.* v. *Barclays Bank (DCO)* [1954] AC 495.
[16] Pp. 270, 44–8 below.
[17] *Baines* v. *National Provincial Bank Ltd.* (1927) 32 Com. Cas. 216; (1927) 96 LJKB 801.
[18] *Griffiths* v. *Dalton* [1940] 2 KB 264.
[19] Pp. 477–9 below.
[20] Pp. 291 et seq. below.

balance standing to the credit of a current account does not earn interest.[21] The main reason for this is that the customer is free to draw against it at any time. However, if a customer maintains his balance at a given minimum amount, many banks waive their regular charges.

2. THE STATEMENT OF ACCOUNT

(i) *The nature of the problem*

The initial practice was to provide the customer with a pass-book in which the bank recorded from time to time all the transactions concerning the account. To enable the bank to effect these entries, the customer occasionally left his pass-book with the bank for a few days. During the last fifty years pass-books ceased to be used for current accounts. They have been replaced by periodic statements, usually dispatched to the customer at the end of each month. It is obvious that both a pass-book and a periodic statement may contain inaccuracies, resulting from errors in additions or from wrong entries. The question arises whether the pass-book or the periodic statement can be used as evidence either against a customer who disputes an entry, or against the bank that wishes to rectify errors made to its disadvantage. By and large, the courts have tended to treat the pass-book and the periodic statement on one and the same basis. There are, however, distinctions between the customer's right to dispute the entries in the statement or pass-book and the bank's right to rectify errors made by it.

(ii) *The bank's right to rectify errors*

A person who pays another money without any reason usually acts under a mistake of fact. The payor, accordingly, is entitled to recover the amount involved by bringing an action in quasi contract, or by applying for a declaration that the amount involved was not due.[22] The procedure differs where a bank makes an error of the type discussed. In such a case the bank credits the customer's account with the wrong amount or with a sum not due to him. When the bank discovers the mistake it reverses the entry. If the customer disputes the bank's right to do so, he has to institute proceedings. Two pleas are open to him. The first is that the bank is estopped from disputing the correctness of the balance as shown in the pass-book or in the periodic statement. The other is based on a claim that the balance consti-

---

[21] It is understood that some of the remaining private banks continue to pay interest on current accounts provided the balance is maintained at not less than a given figure.

[22] See Chap. 11 below.

tutes an 'account settled' or an 'account stated'. This last plea is also relevant in respect of corrections demanded by the customer.

The success of the plea of estoppel depends on the effect that the wrongful payment has had on the customer's position. If he has changed his position to his detriment, the bank may find itself precluded from reversing the credit entry. This is the position, although the early decision of the Court of Chancery in *Clayton's Case*[23] suggests that a customer can be expected to examine the entries in his pass-book and to return it for correction where an error is discovered.

Skyring v. *Greenwood and Cox*,[24] decided in 1825, shows that an estoppel will be invoked where an error has lulled the customer into a false belief about his financial position. In that case the paymaster of a military corps credited an officer's account with money to which he was not entitled. The erroneous credits stretched over a period of five years, and the officer, who was unaware of the mistake, drew out the money regularly. When the paymaster discovered his error he continued to pay the officer's wages, failing to inform him of the need to rectify the position. When the officer died the paymaster purported to set off against credit entries some payments received for the officer's account. The estate's action, disputing the right of the paymaster to effect a set-off, was successful. It was held that the erroneous entries constituted representations to the effect that the amounts involved had been received for the officer's credit. As the officer had changed his position in reliance on the statements by spending more money than he would have otherwise done, the paymaster lost his right to reclaim the amounts credited. Abbott CJ observed:[25]

It is of great importance to any man, and certainly not less to military men than others, that they should not be led to suppose that their annual income is greater than it really is. Every prudent man accommodates his mode of living to what he supposes to be his income; it therefore works a great prejudice to any man, if after having had credit given him in account for certain sums, and having been allowed to draw on his agent on the faith that these sums belonged to him, he may be called upon to pay them back.

Similarly, in *Holland* v. *Manchester and Liverpool District Banking Co.*[26] the customer's pass-book showed a credit balance of £70 instead of the true amount of £60. In reliance on this entry, the customer drew a

---

[23] *Devaynes* v. *Noble* (*Clayton's Case*) (1816) 1 Mer. 529, 535–6. See, generally, Holden, 'Bank Pass Books and Statements', (1954) 17 MLR 41.

[24] (1825) 4 B & C 281. See also *Holt* v. *Markham* [1923] 1 KB 504; *Lloyds Bank Ltd.* v. *Brooks* (1950) 6 LDAB 161; (1951) 72 JIB 114.

[25] (1825) 4 B & C 281, 289.

[26] (1909) 14 Com. Cas. 241. It was observed that even if the bank was entitled to reverse entries it had to honour its customer's cheques up to the time it informed him of the correction of the balance.

cheque for £67, which was dishonoured when presented. The customer's action in breach of contract succeeded. Lord Alverstone CJ held that the bank was entitled to debit the customer's account with the amount erroneously credited. But the bank did not have the right to dishonour cheques drawn for sums within the balance conveyed to the customer 'until, at any rate, they [gave] him some notice'.[27]

The bank is always entitled to rectify the error within a reasonable time.[28] Furthermore, the customer could plead the estoppel in question only if he was misled, or had reason to be misled, by the erroneous balance. This principle was established in *British and North European Bank Ltd.* v. *Zalzstein,*[29] where the customer did not discover the wrong credit entry made in his favour until it had been reversed. It was, accordingly, held that he could not dispute the respective debit entries. At present, the principle is best illustrated by *United Overseas Bank* v. *Jiwani.*[30] A bank erroneously credited its customer's account twice with the amount of a single remittance. The amount involved was substantial, and the customer was not expecting any payment additional to the one genuinely received for the credit of his account. Despite this he drew on the balance accrued as a result of this windfall, and thereafter disputed the bank's right to reverse the undue credit entry. It was held that the customer ought to have known that the unduly high balance shown in his account was incorrect. He was not expecting any additional payment of a substantial amount to the credit of his account, and he was not entitled to shut his eyes to facts staring him in the face. A fortiori, the bank is entitled to rectify an error in the record if it is induced by the customer.[31]

(iii) The customer's right to demand corrections

In certain cases the customer, rather than the bank, is interested in having the wrong entry corrected. Thus, the customer's account may have been credited with an amount smaller than that of an item payable to him or debited with an amount larger than that for which he drew a cheque. In the majority of cases this occurs where the amount of the customer's cheque has been fraudulently raised. His position in such situations is governed by decisions discussed subsequently. In other cases such an error arises due to a computer fault.

---

[27] Ibid., 245.
[28] *Commercial Bank of Scotland* v. *Rhind* (1860) 3 Macq. HL 643; *British and North European Bank Ltd.* v. *Zalzstein* [1927] 2 KB 92.
[29] Above. See also, in Canada: *Collins* v. *Dominion Bank* (1915) 8 OWN 432; *Imperial Bank* v. *Kean* (1916) 10 OWN 80; *Hudson* v. *Royal Bank of Canada* (1920) 19 OWN 93.
[30] [1976] 1 WLR 964.
[31] *Saskatchewan and Western Elevator* v. *Bank of Hamilton* (1914) 18 DLR 411.

In most cases in which the customer demands the correction of a wrong entry the bank is prepared to accede to his wishes. In the first place, the bank's reputation is at stake. If customers cannot trust their banks they are unlikely to deposit the bulk of their liquid assets with them. Secondly, unless the amount involved is substantial, the bank prefers to shoulder the loss rather than to get involved in litigation. There are, however, cases in which the amount involved is large, and cases in which the error is notified to the bank after the lapse of a substantial time. In addition, there are cases in which the bank suspects collusion between the customer and the payee of the erroneously debited amount. In such situations litigation ensues. One of the questions then arising is whether the customer is entitled to demand rectification of entries in his account after the lapse of a reasonable time from the date of his receipt of the bank statement or the date of the entry in the pass-book. The basic answer in English law is that, in the absence of fraud, the customer is not precluded by the bank statement or by the pass-book from disputing an error or a wrong debit made by the bank.

The principle involved is based on the construction of the contract of banker and customer. It is thought that this contract does not place the customer under a duty to peruse his statement or the entries in a pass-book.[32] Even though he returns his pass-book or the counterfoil of his statement to the bank without referring to the error, he is able to dispute the entry subsequently.[33] This principle has been much criticized, on the basis that both common sense and good business practice require the bank's customer to verify the entries made in his account.[34] If such a perusal is not required, what is the object of the dispatch of a statement or of the making by the bank of detailed entries in a pass-book? If the object is merely to inform the customer of the amount standing to the credit of his account, it would be sufficient to provide him periodically with a statement of his balance. It may be retorted that such a statement is meaningless, as it does not acquaint the customer with the flow immediately preceding the date of the striking of the balance. In other words, such a bare statement does not inform the customer which cheques drawn by him have been presented and paid, and which of the items payable to him have been honoured by the drawee. This reply, however, presupposes that the customer is interested in this

---

[32] *Lewes Sanitary Steam Laundry Co. Ltd.* v. *Barclay & Co. Ltd.* (1906) 95 LT 444; *Kepitigalla Rubber Estates Ltd.* v. *National Bank of India Ltd.* [1909] 2 KB 1010, 1027–9; *Walker* v. *Manchester and Liverpool District Banking Co. Ltd.* (1913) 108 LT 728; *Lloyds Bank Ltd.* v. *Brooks* (1950) 6 LDAB 161, 72 JIB 114; *Brewer* v. *Westminster Bank Ltd.* [1952] 2 All ER 650, 656.
[33] *Kepitigalla Rubber Estates Ltd.* v. *National Bank of India Ltd.*, above.
[34] F. Pollock, (1910) 26 LQR 4; J. M. Holden, 'Bank Pass Books and Statements', (1954) 17 MLR 41; Chorley, *Gilbart Lectures*, 1954; cf. more recently, the powerful minority judgment of Laskin J in *Arrow Transfer Co. Ltd.* v. *Royal Bank of Canada* (1972) 27 DLR (3d) 81, 97–103.

information. If this is so , then surely the customer can be expected to peruse the statement submitted to him with a view to detecting errors or shortfalls!

The Uniform Commercial Code has, indeed, taken this view. Under section 4–406:

the customer must exercise reasonable care and promptness to examine the statement and items [attached to it] to discover his unauthorized signature or any alteration on an item and must notify the bank promptly after discovery thereof.

If the customer fails to comply with this duty and does not notify the bank of an error within fourteen days, he is precluded from disputing the regularity of the payments made. This estoppel does not apply if the customer establishes 'lack of ordinary care' on the bank's part. But even in such a case, the customer's right to dispute payment becomes barred after the lapse of one year[35] from the date of the statement.

A similar provision is unlikely to be enacted in the United Kingdom. This is due to the difference between the banking practice in this country and in the United States. In the United States, when the bank sends a statement to the customer it attaches to it all items drawn by him and debited to his account. The verification by the customer of his signature and the discovery of any tampering with an instrument becomes an easy task. In the United Kingdom the standard practice is that cleared effects are retained by the paying bank and are returned to the customer only if a specific request is made.[36] It follows that the checking of the correctness of a bank statement is a more arduous task in the United Kingdom than in the United States. In the United Kingdom the customer's only sources for verification are, usually, the counterfoils in his cheque-book and of giro forms.

If banks in the United Kingdom wish to tip the scales in their favour, they would have to do so by including a suitable term in their contract with the customer. This has been the practice of the Canadian banks for over fifty years. The clause in question should impose on the customer a duty to peruse his statement promptly and to notify the bank of any errors or irregularities within a specified time. Failure so to notify the bank should be deemed to constitute a verification by the customer of the balance struck.

Canadian courts have upheld the validity of such clauses. Thus, in *Columbia Graphophone Co.* v. *Union Bank of Canada*[37] the customer

---

[35] Three years in the case of a forged indorsement.

[36] Some firms require the return of all items drawn on the account for the purpose of the yearly audit. Note that under s. 3 of the Cheques Act 1957, a retired cheque constitutes a receipt of payment.

[37] (1916) 34 DLR 743, followed in *Rutherford* v. *Royal Bank of Canada* [1932] 2 DLR 332 (verification by agent bank's principal); *Mackenzie* v. *Imperial Bank* [1938] 2 DLR 764. Cf. *Ewing* v. *Dominion Bank* (1904) 35 SCR 133 (Can.) (case involved a specific notification of payment by the bank of a bill alleged to be drawn by customer but in reality forged); *Abbott* v. *Bank of Toronto* [1934] 3 DLR 256 (customer held not bound by statement in the absence of verification agreement). But the authorities emphasize the element of loss resulting from the delay.

completed a form in which he undertook to examine the statement and 'vouchers' accompanying it within ten days and to sign periodic receipts confirming the correctness of the balance. He did so for a time, but then ceased. Forged cheques had been debited to his account throughout the entire period. It was held that the customer was precluded from disputing entries in statements certified by him as correct; but he was free to refute entries in the statements he had not verified. He was able to challenge the later statements as his contract with his bank did not state that, upon his failure to notify an error, the entries were deemed to be correct.[38]

In a recent case decided by the Supreme Court of Canada, *Arrow Transfer Co. Ltd.* v. *Royal Bank of Canada*,[39] the customer had agreed, in a form executed when he opened his account, to verify all statements sent to him and to notify the bank of any errors and inaccuracies within a given period. Thereafter the account as kept by the bank was to constitute conclusive evidence of the correctness of the entries. A clerk, who occupied a responsible position in the customer's service, forged a number of cheques. The majority of the Court held that the customer was bound by the clause in question. As the customer had failed to notify the bank about the discrepancies, he was unable to contest the genuineness of the cheques. Laskin J's concurring judgment for the bank was based on a different ground. His Honour held that the customer's persistent failure to peruse the statements and to verify the state of his account precluded him from disputing the entries based on the forged cheques. Laskin J thought that the verification clause was inapplicable as it had to be construed narrowly and against the bank. Accordingly, the clause, which did not make any reference to the customer's duty to verify the genuineness of cheques which constituted the basis of debit entries made by the bank, did not exempt the bank from its liability for the payment of forged cheques even where the customer had failed to peruse the statements rendered to him.

Although these decisions are merely of persuasive authority, they should not be ignored. That the type of clause involved is in conformity with the spirit of English law is clear from cases concerning performance bonds and first demand guarantees. It has been held, in the context of cases concerning such facilities, that the conclusive evidence clause, which is similar to the

---

[38] See also *B & G Construction Co. Ltd.* v. *Bank of Montreal* [1954] 2 DLR 753, in which the customer was, surprisingly, held bound although the bank knew informally of the forgeries; *Syndicat des Camionneurs Artisans du Quebec Métropolitain* v. *Banque Provinciale du Canada* (1969) 11 DLR (3d) 610 (clause incorporated in contract at time of opening of account); *Booth Fisheries Canadian Co. Ltd.* v. *Banque Provinciale du Canada* (1972) 7 NBR (2d) 138 (same incorporation of clause); *Bad Boy Appliances and Furniture Ltd.* v. *Toronto-Dominion Bank* (1972) 25 DLR (3d) 257 (where a letter mentioning fears of forgery was held inadequate notification).

[39] (1972) 27 DLR (3d) 81 (Laskin J dissenting on this point).

clause here proposed, is not contrary to public policy.[40] The only reservation which needs to be expressed in respect of the proposed clause is that, to be effective, it has to be made an integral term of the contract of banker and customer. This cannot be done by adding such a clause at the foot of the bank statement, as this document does not evidence the terms of the contract between the parties. [41] Just as in Canada, the clause should be incorporated, as a cohesive term, in the contractual documents signed by the customer at the time the account is opened. The recent decision of the Privy Council in *Tai Hing Cotton Mill Ltd.* v. *Liu Chong Hing Bank Ltd.*[42] shows, further, that it is inadequate to include in the document signed by the customer when the account is opened an informal or precative verification clause, which falls short of imposing on him a definite duty to check his statements. To preclude the customer from disputing entries which he has not queried within the time prescribed for verification, the clause must convey to the customer that the entries will be conclusively binding on him if he fails to demand their rectification within the agreed period. If such a clause has not been agreed upon when the customer opened his account, its incorporation can subsequently be effected only by means of a valid variation of the contract.

(iv) Bank statements and pass-book entries as accounts stated

The plea that a bank statement or the pass-book constitutes an 'account stated' may be raised either by the bank or by the customer. Naturally, the argument is pressed by the party that seeks to deny the other the right to have an error or a wrong entry rectified.

The significance of the plea in question is that, in equity, an 'account stated' has to be settled by the debtor without further regard to the individual items involved. The right has been described as a 'convenient legal fiction which avoids the necessity, if recourse has to be had to legal proceedings, of suing upon the individual items in the account'.[43] From a practical point of view, when an account is stated it becomes similar to a

---

[40] *Bache & Co. (London) Ltd.* v. *Banque Vernes et Commerciale de Paris SA* [1973] 2 Lloyd's Rep. 437; *R. D. Harbottle (Mercantile) Ltd.* v. *National Westminster Bank Ltd.* [1978] QB 146; *Edward Owen Engineering Ltd.* v. *Barclays Bank International Ltd.* [1978] QB 159; *Howe Richardson Scale Co. Ltd.* v. *Polimex-Cekop* [1978] 1 Lloyd's Rep. 161; *Bolivinter Oil SA* v. *Chase Manhattan Bank* [1984] 1 Lloyd's Rep. 251.

[41] Cf. *Burnett* v. *Westminster Bank Ltd.* [1966] 1 QB 742, which concerned a clause printed on the folder of a cheque-book.

[42] [1986] AC 80; [1985] 2 Lloyd's Rep. 313, 322–3, adopting on this point the view of Hunter J in the Court of Appeal of Hong Kong: [1984] 1 Lloyd's Rep. 555 (and see further on this case pp. 295–7 below). See also *Lam* v. *Hang Lung Bank Ltd.* [1982] HKLR 215; *Asien-Pazifik Merchant Finance Ltd.* v. *Shanghai Commercial Bank Ltd.* [1982] HKLR 273.

[43] Chorley, *Law of Banking*, 6th edn., p. 175.

confirmation by the debtor that the creditor is claiming the correct amount. In the case of a current account, the customer and the bank would lose the right to query the correctness of given items once the bank statement or the pass-book became an account stated.

English law has refused to regard the pass-book and the statement submitted by the bank to the customer as constituting an account stated. It is true that, in *Blackburn Building Society* v. *Cunliffe, Brooks and Co.*,[44] Lord Selborne recognized that, in appropriate circumstances, a pass-book could be so regarded. But this proposition was doubted by the Court of Appeal in *Vagliano Bros.* v. *Bank of England*,[45] where Bowen LJ observed that there was no evidence to show that, as between a customer and his banker, the customer was under a duty to peruse his statement with a view to pointing out errors. Although Lord Halsbury, in the House of Lords, suggested that entries in the pass-book ought to have some effect, he did not hold that the pass-book would constitute an account stated where an error was not promptly discovered and notified.[46]

The view of the Court of Appeal was adopted in *Kepitigalla Rubber Estates Ltd.* v. *National Bank of India Ltd.*, where Bray J observed that it would be absurd to hold that the taking of the pass-book by the bank and its return to the customer established a settled account.[47] Bray J observed that, if the pass-book or statement of account were deemed an account stated, then the mere delivery of the document to the secretary of a company, who might be the very person defrauding it, would preclude the company from contesting the bank's right to debit its account with amounts paid against forged instruments. In the same vein, Lord Esher MR, in *Chatterton* v. *London and County Bank*,[48] thought that the pass-book would not constitute an account stated even if it was updated at regular intervals and returned to the customer accompanied by the paid effects, and although the customer ticked off all entries. His Lordship said that it was 'a hundred to one that [the bankers] never looked at the pass-book'. He thought, therefore, that they were unlikely to note that the customer ticked off the entries made from time to time.

It is submitted that the law in point is unexceptional. If either the bank or the customer is to be precluded from denying the validity of an entry made in the account, it is best to base the decision on all the circumstances of the case in question. The doctrine of estoppel, which would be invoked by the

---

[44] (1882) 22 Ch. D 61, 71–2, affd. sub. nom. *Brooks & Co.* v. *Blackburn and District Benefit Building Society* (1884) 9 App. Cas. 857.
[45] (1889) 23 QBD 243, 263.
[46] *Bank of England* v. *Vagliano Bros.* [1891] AC 107, 115–16, reversing the decision of the Court of Appeal, above, on other grounds.
[47] [1909] 2 KB 1010, 1029; 14 Com. Cas. 116.
[48] Unreported, *The Times*, 21 Jan. 1891.

inclusion of the type of clause used in Canada, comes closer to such a doctrine than a principle which treats the bank statement or the pass-book as an account stated.

(v) Customer's silence with knowledge of wrong entry

If the customer knows that an entry made in his pass-book or statement of account is wrong but keeps silent, he will be precluded from asserting the error once the bank has changed its position.[49] The typical case in which the point arises is where a customer knows that a cheque, paid by the bank, was issued by a forger, but for reasons of misguided loyalty or affection refrains from informing the bank. A question of some difficulty is whether such an estoppel would, likewise, be operative where the customer did not have actual knowledge of the irregularity involved, but on the basis of any reasonable practice or common sense ought to have known about it or to have suspected it.

The answer depends on the circumstances of each case. In *Morison* v. *London County and Westminster Bank Ltd.*,[50] Phillimore LJ hinted that, when a principal knows so much that it is 'a policy of an ostrich to know no more', the means for knowledge may be equated with actual knowledge. *Tina Motors Pty. Ltd.* v. *Australia and New Zealand Banking Group Ltd.*,[51] in which the customer assured the bank that any cheque signed by a specific agent could be taken to have been validly drawn, is an illustration in point. In this case the bank's enquiry should have put the principal—the customer—on notice.

Morison's case contemplates extreme situations. A good illustration is to be found in *Brown* v. *Westminster Bank Ltd.*[52] Here the servants of the customer, an old woman who was too frail to look after her affairs, forged her signature on cheques drawn on her account. The branch manager called on the customer on several occasions to ask whether the instruments were regular. Although the customer did not expressly verify the genuineness of the cheques, she likewise refrained from questioning their payment. She was, accordingly, held to be estopped from denying the bank's right to debit her account. It is to be doubted if conduct which did not lull the bank into safety to the same extent would be regarded as founding an estoppel.

---

[49] *Greenwood* v. *Martins Bank Ltd.* [1933] AC 51. See also *Leach* v. *Buchanan* (1802) 4 Esp. 226; and cases cited below, p. 291. In Canada see *Ewing* v. *Dominion Bank* (1904) 35 SCR 133 (Can.) showing that silence in the face of a written notification can result in an estoppel.

[50] [1914] 3 KB 356, 385. And see the more liberal principle in *Ewing* v. *Dominion Bank* (1904) 35 SCR 133 (Can.); *Abbott* v. *Bank of Toronto* [1934] 3 DLR 256.

[51] [1977] VR 205.

[52] [1964] 2 Lloyd's Rep. 187.

However, where the extent of the customer's disregard of ordinary standards of business practice and ordinary care is such as to invoke an estoppel, he cannot be heard to say that he has delegated the duty of examination to another person. After the lapse of a reasonable time, the customer is regarded as having the means of knowing what is being done by the person entrusted with the conduct of his affairs.[53]

3. COMBINATION OF ACCOUNTS

(i) Problem in practice

In many cases a customer maintains more than one account with his bank. Thus, a customer may use one account for strictly personal purposes and another one for his business. Similarly, a customer who has several enterprises may decide to maintain a separate account for each of them. In other cases, a customer may open some special type of account, such as a loan account or a savings account, in addition to his current account. Furthermore, some professional men are required to open special accounts for their business. Thus, solicitors are required to maintain clients' accounts.[54]

There are two situations in which the bank may wish to treat all the accounts maintained by a given customer as if they were one. The first is where the customer is unable or unwilling to repay an overdraft incurred in one account although another account is in credit. Predominant in this group are cases arising out of a customer's insolvency. The second type of situation in which the bank may wish to combine accounts is where the customer draws a cheque for an amount exceeding the balance standing to the credit of the account involved but the deficiency can be met out of funds deposited in another account. The two types of situation give rise to distinct problems.

In the first type of situation the bank seeks to combine the customer's accounts for its own purposes. If the customer is unwilling to pay an amount due in respect of an overdraft or of a loan, the bank can, of course, sue him for the debt. If, however, the bank is able to set off against the overdraft in account A a credit balance in account B, it obviates the inconvenience and expense involved in legal proceedings. Furthermore, it avoids the risk of a deterioration in the customer's financial affairs during the period of litigation.

The bank gains an even more substantial advantage from combining the

[53] *Jacobs* v. *Morris* [1902] 1 Ch. 816, 831; *London Joint Stock Bank Ltd.* v. *MacMillan* [1918] AC 777, 821, per Viscount Haldane.
[54] Pp. 186–8 below.

accounts of an insolvent customer. By way of illustration, take a case in which the customer's A account has an overdraft of £1,000 and his B account a credit of £2,000. If the bank were unable to effect a set-off by combining the two accounts, its position in the customer's bankruptcy would be unfavourable. The bank would be obliged to pay the amount of £2,000 standing to the credit of account B to the customer's trustee in bankruptcy. It would have to lodge a proof for £1,000 in respect of the overdraft. Being an unsecured creditor, the bank would be paid a dividend together with other general creditors. If the customer's assets yielded 30p in the pound, the bank would recover only £300 . The bank's position would be superior if it were entitled to combine the accounts. The bank would then set off £1,000 out of the £2,000 due to the customer in respect of the B account against his indebtedness to the bank, and would pay the balance of £1,000 over to the trustee in bankruptcy. The bank would, accordingly, receive repayment of the overdraft in full in priority to the claims of other general creditors.

In the second type of situation, where the bank seeks to combine its customer's accounts in order to meet a cheque drawn in excess of the available balance in the account on which it is drawn, the bank acts in the customer's interest. If the cheque is dishonoured, the main loss is to the customer's reputation. The bank is, basically, not obliged to meet an excessive demand.[55] It is, nevertheless, important to consider the bank's position in this type of situation.

Unsurprisingly, the analysis of the legal nature of the combination of accounts is based on authorities concerning the first type of situation. The main problems involved are the bank's right to combine accounts where there is an agreement or a manifestation of intention to the contrary; the question of whether the bank is obliged to give notice before it resolves to combine the accounts; and special questions related to the law of insolvency. These problems are discussed in this chapter in the light of the general common law principles. Specific contractual arrangements for a set-off are discussed in Chapter 21. The second type of situation which gives rise to a set-off has not been a frequent subject of litigation. The main problem is whether the bank either is under the duty or has the authority to combine the accounts in the customer's interest.

(ii) Legal meaning of 'combination of accounts'

One basic principle supports the doctrine that in certain situations the bank is entitled to combine the accounts of one customer. It is that the customer's

---

[55] P. 128 above.

underlying contractual relationship is with the bank and not with the branch at which the account is maintained.[56] Moreover, the basic relationship of banker and customer governs all the accounts of a customer regardless of their type. This is so despite the slight variations in the rights of the parties in different types of account. As there is only one contract of banker and customer, there is room for the argument that when the bank becomes the customer's creditor it can exercise a right of set-off as regards mutual dealings with him.

The significance of the doctrine involved is demonstrated by one of the first decisions in point. In *Re European Bank, Agra Bank Claims*,[57] the OC Bank maintained three accounts with the A & M Bank: a loan account; a discount account; and a general account. The A & M Bank gave the OC Bank securities to cover acceptances of bills of exchange, which were debited to the loan account. Shortly thereafter both banks failed. The dividend paid by the A & M Bank to its creditors discharged its indebtedness on the loan and the discount account, but was inadequate for meeting the overdraft incurred on the general account. The question was whether the securities given by the A & M Bank to the OC Bank could be utilized to discharge this remaining indebtedness or, having been appropriated to the loan account, were to be returned to the A & M Bank's liquidator. Malins VC held that the securities were available to cover the indebtedness in the general account. Affirming his decision, James LJ in the Court of Appeal in Chancery, emphasized that it would be wrong to treat the three accounts as 'distinct matters'. His Lordship said:[58]

It was only for convenience that the local account was kept separately. . . . In truth, as between banker and customer, whatever number of accounts are kept in books, the whole is really but one account, and it is not open to the customer, in the absence of some special contract, to say that the securities which he deposits are only applicable to one account.

This view has become well established.[59] Whilst it is indisputable that there is only one basic relationship between the banker and his customer, it has to be emphasized that its details vary from account to account. Thus, a current account is operable by cheques, whilst a savings account cannot be utilized in this way. Funds deposited in an ordinary savings account are usually repayable on demand; but amounts standing to the credit of an 'extra interest account' fall due at one month's notice. In reality, it is possible

---

[56] Pp. 81–84 above.
[57] (1872) LR 8 Ch. App. 41.
[58] Ibid., 44.
[59] *Garnett* v. *M'Kewan* (1872) LR 8 Ex. 10, 13 (per Martin B), 14 (per Pigott B); *James Kirkwood & Sons* v. *Clydesdale Bank Ltd.* 1908 SC 20, 24; *Re Sutcliffe & Sons Ltd., ex p. Royal Bank* [1933] 1 DLR 562.

to treat the contracts involved in separate types of accounts as distinct arrangements between the bank and its customer. *Re European Bank* and the cases following it do not overlook this point. All they suggest is that the parties to the contractual relationship, effected in respect of each account, are the customer and the bank. For this reason, debts accrued to the customer are due from the bank and not from an individual branch. Equally, debts due from the customer are recoverable by the bank and not by its branches. There is, thus, room for a set-off.

It is clear that in certain circumstances the bank is entitled to combine a customer's accounts. What is the legal nature of the bank's right? Some authorities suggested that when the bank combined distinct accounts of a single customer it exercised a lien.[60] This view was questioned in a number of English and Canadian[61] authorities, and was rejected by the House of Lords in the leading case of *National Westminster Bank Ltd.* v. *Halesowen Presswork and Assemblies Ltd.*[62] The decision is relevant as regards most questions respecting the combination of accounts and is, therefore, discussed in full at this point.

In *Halesowen*'s case the plaintiffs maintained a current account with the defendant bank. In April 1968, when this account showed a substantial debit balance, an account no. 2 was opened for the plaintiffs' trading operations. The bank agreed that, in the absence of a material change of circumstances, account no. 1 would remain frozen for a period of four months. On 20 May, the plaintiffs convened a meeting of their creditors. The defendants, who received a notice of the meeting, resolved to leave the arrangement of April in effect. On 12 June, the plaintiffs passed a resolution to wind up voluntarily. On 19 June, the bank informed the liquidator that it had determined to set off the credit balance in account no. 2 against the debit balance in the frozen no. 1 account. The liquidator objected, as in his view the bank was bound by the arrangement of April. Roskill J gave judgment for the bank. He thought that the bank had a right of set-off, which he treated as a lien. The bank's agreement to keep the two accounts separate was determined by the changed circumstances resulting from the plaintiffs' decision to wind up. This decision was reversed by the Court of Appeal.[63] All three judges were of the view that a bank's right to combine the customer's accounts constituted a setoff, and was not to be regarded as based

---

[60] *Re Keever (a bankrupt)* [1967] Ch. 182; Roskill J in *Halesowen Presswork and Assemblies Ltd.* v. *Westminster Bank Ltd.* [1971] 1 QB 1, 20–1, and see below for the further proceedings in the case (sub nom. *National Westminster Bank Ltd.* v. *Halesowen Presswork and Assemblies Ltd.*).

[61] *Re Sutcliffe & Sons Ltd., ex p. Royal Bank* [1933] 1 DLR 562; *Re E. J. Morel (1934) Ltd.* [1962] Ch. 21 (both cases describe the balance as the bank's money and the combination of accounts as a set-off); *Royal Trust Co.* v. *Molsons Bank* (1912) 8 DLR 478.

[62] [1972] AC 785.

[63] [1971] 1 QB 1 (reporting also Roskill J's decision).

on the exercise of a lien. The amounts deposited by a customer became the bank's money. All the customer had was the right to claim repayment of the debt by drawing a cheque on the account or by making a demand in some other manner. The bank could not have a lien over its own money or property. The majority of the Court of Appeal (Lord Denning MR and Winn LJ) further held that in the case in question the bank was not entitled to combine the accounts. The bank had agreed to keep the accounts separate, and if it wished to cancel this arrangement in view of the changed circumstances, it had to give notice to the customer. Buckley LJ dissented, as in his view the plaintiffs were entitled to combine the accounts under section 31 of the Bankruptcy Act 1914, the predecessor of section 323 of the Insolvency Act 1986.

The House of Lords restored Roskill J's decision. Their Lordships were, however, unanimous in adopting the view of the Court of Appeal to the effect that the bank's right to combine the customer's accounts was to be distinguished from a lien. Lord Cross observed: 'to describe the right to consolidate several accounts as an example of the banker's lien is . . . a misuse of language'[64] The House of Lords held that, on the facts, the defendant bank had the right to combine the accounts both in view of the nature of the arrangements made in April and under section 31 of the Bankruptcy Act. These aspects are discussed in further detail later on.

The distinction drawn in the *Halesowen* case between the bank's lien and its right to combine the customer's accounts appears well founded. Ordinarily, a person cannot have a lien over his own property. This is especially so where the property is also in his possession. Obviously, in the type of case here discussed, the bank both owns the money and has its use. How then can it exercise a lien in respect of it? There is room for only one argument to the contrary. A bank balance is not merely an amount of money which forms part of the bank's general funds. It also constitutes a debt due from the bank to the customer.[65] It therefore constitutes a chose in action, or an asset of the customer. It is clear that a third party, such as the customer's creditor, can seek recourse to this asset by such means as a garnishee order.[66] Whilst the customer's bank cannot exercise a lien over the money as such, can it possibly exercise a lien against the asset represented by the balance? It is true that the asset is a debt due from the bank. However, in the sale of goods an owner may in certain cases exercise a lien over his own property. By way of illustration, take a dealer who has disposed of a car under a hire purchase agreement. If the dealer subsequently effects repairs to the car at the purchaser's request and for his account, he can exercise a

[64] [1972] AC 785, at 810.
[65] Pp. 81–84 above.
[66] Pp. 271–5 below.

workman's lien over the property.[67] It is perhaps arguable that the bank should have an analogous right over a balance standing in its books to the credit of a customer, provided it had relied on this balance when it granted the customer an overdraft on another account or some special business loan. It will be considered subsequently whether such a right can be acquired by the bank by means of a charge over the balance in question.[68]

The question of whether the bank's right to combine accounts constitutes a set-off or may be also based on a lien is of practical significance. If it constituted a lien, it could be exercised over a balance standing to the credit of any of the customer's accounts. It would be immaterial whether the amount due was payable by the bank on demand or at some future time. Thus, where a customer was insolvent a lien could be exercised by the bank over funds standing to the credit of his fixed deposit account. The opposite would be true if the bank's right to combine accounts were regarded as a set-off. It would then be arguable that a debt due in the future, such as a fixed deposit, could not be set-off against an immediate liability. The trend of authority, admittedly, is to this effect.[69]

On the present state of the authorities, the bank's right to combine the balances of all the accounts of a single customer is to be regarded a right of set-off. It is a right conferred on the bank at law, but one which can be modified or restricted by agreement.[70] In *Garnett* v. *M'Kewan*,[71] Kelly CB thought that an important ground for recognizing the bank's right to combine accounts was the mutuality in the dealings of banker and customer. As the customer had the power to order his bank to transfer amounts from one of his accounts to another, the bank had a concurrent right. This dictum overlooks the fact that when the customer gives an instruction to his bank, such as an order to transfer funds from one account to another, he acts as a principal. The bank, as agent, does not have a similar right to issue instructions for the transfer of amounts from one account of its principal to another.

The right to set-off, or to combine accounts, is available only in respect of dealings between a bank and a person who is involved in the transactions concerned as a customer. In a Canadian case, *Rouxel* v. *Royal Bank of Canada*,[72] the plaintiff, who was owed an amount of $436 by the A Co., sent this firm an order to pay $80 to the M Co. Instead of obeying this

---

[67] See generally, *Tappenden* v. *Artus* [1964] 2 QB 185 and authorities there cited.
[68] Pp. 597–9 below.
[69] *Jeffryes* v. *Agra and Masterman's Bank* (1866) LR 2 Eq. 674, 680–1 (concerning set-off against amounts due on unretired bills); *Bower* v. *Foreign and Colonial Gas Co. Ltd.* (1874) 22 WR 740 (do.); cf. *Business Computers Ltd.* v. *Anglo-African Leasing Ltd.* [1977] 1 WLR 578, 585–6 (set-off in assignment situations).
[70] Pp. 593 et seq. below.
[71] (1872) LR 8 Ex. 10, 13. Contrast Bramwell B, at 14–15.
[72] [1918] 2 WWR 791.

simple instruction, the A Co. sent to the M Co. a cheque for $436 payable to the plaintiff. M Co. remitted this cheque to its own bankers, who in turn forwarded it to the defendant bank with an instruction that the cheque be released to the plaintiff against payment of the $80 which he owed to the M Co. The defendant bank asked the plaintiff to pay the $80 with disbursements and agreed to 'cash' the cheque for $436 on his behalf. To facilitate the clearing of the instrument the plaintiff was asked to indorse it. The bank subsequently decided to treat the indorsement as an implied request that the cheque be collected for the credit of a new account to be opened in the plaintiff's name. As against the credit balance accrued in this account upon the clearing of the cheque, the defendant bank set off a debit balance in another of the plaintiff's accounts.

It was held that the right of set-off could be exercised by the bank only in the context of the relationship of banker and customer. On the facts, the cheque in question was given to the bank merely to facilitate its presentment to the drawee bank. This was not a remittance of the cheque in the ordinary way, where a customer requests his bank to collect a cheque payable to him and to credit the account with the proceeds. The right to combine was, therefore, unavailable.

(iii) When may accounts be combined?

The general principle is well explained in *Greenwood Teale* v. *William, Williams, Brown & Co.*[73] The senior partner of a firm of solicitors opened three accounts: an office account, a deposit account, and a private account. The bank was initially told that clients' money would be paid to the credit of the deposit account. This account was subsequently closed, and thereafter both the firm's money and clients' funds were credited to the office account. As the private account was overdrawn for an amount far exceeding the credit in the office account, the bank resolved to combine the two accounts. Holding that the bank had acted properly, Wright J said that a bank had the right to combine a customer's separate accounts subject to three exceptions. First, the right to combine could be abrogated by a special agreement. Secondly, it would be inapplicable where a special item of property was remitted to the bank and appropriated for a given purpose: *Rouxel*'s case, discussed above, furnishes an example. Thirdly, a bank could not combine a customer's private account with one known to the bank to be a trust account or to be utilized for operations conducted by the customer as trustee. The bank's knowledge had to be express. The mere fact that an account was described

[73] (1894) 11 TLR 56.

as an office account was immaterial, as usually funds utilized by a firm through its office account were not trust property.

This analysis is unaffected by the decision of the House of Lords in the *Halesowen* case.[74] The decision of the Court of Session in *James Kirkwood & Sons* v. *Clydesdale Bank Ltd*[75] shows that the bank has the same right even if its customer is not insolvent but becomes unable to discharge a liability to the bank for other reasons.[76]

It is clear that the bank can combine the current accounts of a customer although they are maintained with different branches. In *Garnett* v. *M'Kewan*,[77] a customer's account with the B branch was overdrawn and, when he failed to discharge his liability, was frozen by the bank. Subsequently, the customer opened an account with the L branch of the same bank in order to facilitate the collection of cheques payable to him. The bank set off the credit balance in the account with the L branch against the overdraft in the account with the B branch. As it did not give notice to the customer, he continued to draw cheques on the L branch, and these were dishonoured by the bank. He sued the bank in breach of contract and in defamation.

Entering judgment for the bank, the Court of Exchequer held that, although there might be many accounts opened in a customer's name, there was only one contract between him and the bank. The bank was entitled to combine these accounts for its own purposes unless there was an agreement to keep them separate. Some doubts were, however, raised by Bramwell B, who observed:[78]

The bank is not liable to be called on to pay at one branch just because there is a balance at another. Why, then, may the bank without notice debit the customer's account at one branch with his deficiency on another?

His Lordship resolved his doubts by pointing out that it was unrealistic to allow a customer whose total balance was in debit to draw up to the credit balance maintained by the bank at any one branch. It was no hardship for the customer to be restricted to drawings within the net balance available to him from the bank. The customer was bound to know that he had a number of accounts with the bank, and was not entitled to ignore the overdrawn state of one of his accounts when drawing on another.

The assumption that a customer is, at any given time, familiar with the

---

[74] [1972] AC 785, discussed above.
[75] 1908 SC 20.
[76] Here the problems arose due to the customer's death and ensuing difficulties pertaining to his estate.
[77] (1872) LR 8 Ex. 10.
[78] Ibid., 14.

detailed state of all his accounts is questionable. A customer cannot know which cheques drawn by him and which cheques paid to the credit of one of his accounts have been cleared. At best, he can have a rough expectation concerning the state of his accounts. It seems advisable to rest the bank's right to combine accounts on the basic principles annunciated in *Re European Bank, Agra Bank Claim*,[79] and in the *Greenwood Teale* case.[80] The decision of the House of Lords in *Halesowen*[81] relies on the very same reasoning.

Of the three exceptions to the doctrine which recognizes the bank's right to combine accounts, it will be convenient to consider first the situations in which the bank agrees to keep the accounts apart. The decision of the Privy Council in *British Guiana Bank* v. *OR*[82] suggests that an agreement that the bank keep two accounts separate is usually determined if there are changed circumstances such as the customer's insolvency. As the accounts are no longer 'current' (in the sense of 'active') the bank is entitled to revert to its original position. An Australian decision, *Direct Acceptance Corporation* v. *Bank of NSW*[83] casts doubts on this point. The account of a company which was heavily indebted to the bank was frozen, and the bank agreed to open a no. 2 account for current operations. Shortly thereafter a debenture holder appointed a receiver. The bank thereupon sought to combine the company's two accounts so as to set off the credit balance in account no. 2 against the substantial debit balance in the frozen account. The liquidator disputed the bank's right to combine, and demanded the payment to him of the balance standing to the credit of account no. 2. Giving judgment against the bank, Macfarlan J said:[84]

The agreement . . . was that the main account should be frozen and there should not be a right to set off the credit balance of the working account against the debit balance of the main account. I cannot deduce or infer from the facts . . . any indication that it was also agreed that this agreement was to continue in operation only so long as the accounts . . . were current. Also I cannot accept that when a receiver and manager is appointed, a current account necessarily ceases to be a current account and operation upon it is void.

His Honour based this decision on two factors. First, he thought that an agreement to keep the accounts separate remained in effect despite the customer's insolvency. The position depended on the intention of the parties. Secondly, he held that the appointment of a receiver did not change the nature of the company's current account. This point is well taken, as the

---

[79] (1872) LR 8 Ch. App. 41.
[80] (1894) 11 TLR 56.
[81] [1972] AC 785.
[82] (1911) 104 LT 754 (JC, Guiana).
[83] (1968) 88 WN (NSW) (Pt. 1) 498.
[84] Ibid., 504.

appointment of a receiver does not necessarily mean that the company's business operations are to be suspended. The receiver may decide that the enterprise remain on foot.

A very different conclusion was reached in the *Halesowen* case. It was there held that a resolution to wind up constituted a material change in the circumstances, and that the bank's right to combine revived forthwith. Their Lordships were unanimous in holding that the words of the agreement for the opening of the working account made it clear that the arrangement would come to an end if there were materially altered circumstances.

The *Direct Acceptance* case and *Halesowen*'s case can be distinguished in two ways. First, the arrangement in *Halesowen* was of both a temporary and a contingent nature. It was to determine at the end of four months and even earlier than that if circumstances changed materially. In *Direct Acceptance* there was no restriction of this type. Secondly, in *Direct Acceptance* the company remained a going concern despite the appointment of a receiver. In *Halesowen*, the company was to cease operations for any purpose except its liquidation. The accounts, therefore, could be described as being no longer current.

It is believed that the first distinction is the more important one. It will be recalled that in *Halesowen*'s case the decision to wind up, passed on 12 June, was preceded by the calling of a meeting of creditors on 20 May. It was common ground that the calling of this meeting entitled the bank to treat the April agreement as at an end in view of the altered circumstances. The bank would have been justified in combining the accounts although the company's business was still a going concern at that time. The language of the clause used in *Halesowen*'s case was wide enough to confer on the bank such a power.

Does the mere fact that an account is designated as being something other than a current account imply that its balance may not be set off in the ordinary way? The point arose in *Re E. J. Morel (1934) Ltd.*[85] A company encountered financial difficulties whereupon it was arranged that it maintain three accounts with its bank: no. 1 was a frozen account representing the company's outstanding liabilities; no. 2 was a normal business account that the company was to use without regard to the no. 1 account; and no. 3 was a wages account. It was agreed that cheques for wages be drawn on account no. 2, but that after four months the debit be transferred to the wages account. When the company went into liquidation, account no. 1 had a debit balance of £1,839; no. 2 a credit balance of £1,544, and no. 3 a debit balance of £1,623. In the company's liquidation the bank lodged a proof for £1,917, which was the net debit balance left after the combination of all three accounts. It was claimed that £910 out of this balance constituted a

[85] [1962] Ch. 21.

preferential claim as it represented advances on wages. The liquidator disputed the claim for priority, as, in his opinion, it was necessary first to combine accounts nos. 2 and 3. This would have left a preferential claim of £78 only.

Adopting the liquidator's determination, Buckley LJ held that the doctrine of combination of accounts applied principally in respect of different current or general accounts of a given customer. Referring to *Bradford Old Bank Ltd.* v. *Sutcliffe*,[86] Buckley LJ observed:[87]

> there is an important difference between a case where a customer has several current accounts, and a case where a customer has an account which is not a current account, and one or more current accounts in the bank. In the first case where all the accounts are current, the banker can combine those accounts in whatever way he chooses, treating them all as being one account of his relationship with his customer. In the other case the accounts are of a different character, and the banker is not free to combine them in that way.

It is clear that *Morel's* case differs on this point from *Halesowen*. The distinction is, again, based on the facts. In *Halesowen* the bank reserved the right to combine the accounts in the event of a material change in the circumstances. *Morel's* case defines the position where the bank does not safeguard itself in this manner. The specific designation of the account as something different from a current account may, in such a case, support the argument that the account was meant to be kept apart.[88] The significance attributable to the name of an account, in a situation of this type, is further demonstrated by *Re Gross, ex p. Kingston*.[89] where it was held that an account opened by a customer as a 'police account' could not be combined with his personal one.

Whether or not the mere designation of an account is of significance is relevant where the question of combination arises in respect of a loan account. The circumstances leading to the opening of a loan account usually indicate that the parties have agreed that it be not combined with other accounts as long as the customer is able to carry on his business. Indeed, the customer could not engage in everyday transactions if he had to fear that a cheque, drawn by him on his working account, could be dishonoured as the bank had decided to set off the balance in that account against the amount due under the loan agreement. Thus, in *Bradford Old Bank Ltd.* v. *Sutcliffe*,[90] Pickford LJ held that the fact that one of the accounts was

---

[86] [1918] 2 KB 833.
[87] [1962] Ch. 21, 31–2.
[88] *Re Johnson & Co. Ltd.* [1902] 1 IR 439 supports the view that in such a case the accounts have to be kept apart even after the customer's insolvency.
[89] (1871) LR 6 Ch. App. 632.
[90] [1918] 2 KB 833, 839.

designated a loan account clearly showed 'that the accounts were to be kept distinct by arrangement' between the customer and the bank. This view is supported by Buckley LJ's decision in the *Morel* case,[91] and by the view of Lord Cross, in *Halesowen*'s case.[92] It is, therefore, submitted that a loan account and a current account are usually not meant to be combined. It would be unusual for the bank to exercise a right of set-off in respect of such an account whilst the customer's business was a going concern. The right may revive upon the customer's insolvency. When this happens, it is necessary to consider the arrangement between the parties.

According to the *Greenwood Teale* case,[93] the second exception to the bank's general right to combine accounts occurs in cases of specific appropriation. It will be recalled that the point arose in this very case. However, the Court of Appeal in Chancery held that there was insufficient evidence to show that the customer had appropriated the relevant securities for some specific purpose. The question came up again in *W. P. Greenhalgh & Sons v. Union Bank of Manchester*.[94] The plaintiffs, cotton brokers of Liverpool, sold a quantity of cotton to W. & Sons. The cotton was resold to spinners who issued to W. & Sons a bill of exchange for the price. W. & Sons remitted this bill to the defendant bank, with whom they had their business account. That bank credited the proceeds of the bill to W. & Sons' account where the funds reduced an existing overdraft. The plaintiffs claimed that the bills had been appropriated to their contract with W. & Sons, and were meant to secure payment of the price due to themselves. The plaintiffs further argued that notice of the appropriation of the bills had been given to the defendant bank. Entering judgment for the plaintiffs, Swift J said:[95]

If a person making a payment of money . . . to another, states definitely that such payment is to be used for a particular purpose, and the person to whom it is made does not dissent, he accepts it for the purpose and must use it . . . only for the purpose for which he receives it. . . .

His Lordship added that if the purpose was to arrange for payment to a third party and that person came to know of the appropriation of the funds, he was entitled to claim the amount involved. Presumably his rights would be those of an assignee.

Greenhalgh's case concerned primarily the rights of third parties. But the case is important where a bank wishes to combine a number of accounts maintained in the name of a single customer. It the bank knows that a given

---

[91] [1962] Ch. 21.
[92] [1972] AC 785, 809.
[93] (1894) 11 TLR 56, p. 145 above. See also *Mutton* v. *Peat* [1900] 2 Ch. 79.
[94] [1924] 2 KB 153.
[95] Ibid., 161.

sum or item has been appropriated for a specific purpose, the right of set-off cannot be exercised in respect of it.

The principle involved has been approved by the House of Lords in *Barclays Bank Ltd. v. Quistclose Investments Ltd.*[96] A company which was facing financial difficulties obtained a loan from the respondents in order to arrange for the payment of dividends declared by the general meeting. The amount of the loan was paid into a special account, opened for this purpose by the company with the appellant bank. Before paying out the dividends, the company went into liquidation. The bank thereupon sought to set off the balance in the special account against the overdraft incurred on the company's general account. The respondents instituted an action to establish that, as the object for which the money had been lent to the company had failed, it was held by the company as a resulting trustee for the respondents' benefit.

Lord Wilberforce held that, to succeed, the respondents had to establish two points. First, they had to show that the money lent could be utilized for a specific purpose only. Secondly, it was necessary to show that the bank had knowledge of the appropriation involved. His Lordship emphasized that the bank knew that the funds had been provided on the clear understanding that they could not be used for a purpose other than the payment of the dividends. Although the mere request to credit an amount to a special account would not have been fatal to the bank's right to combine, the bank here had been informed of the details of the transaction. The judgment of the Court of Appeal for the respondents was affirmed.

The third type of case in which, according to the *Greenwood Teale case*,[97] the bank does not enjoy the right to combine the customer's accounts, is where to the bank's own knowledge the account in credit is a trust account. The reason for this is plain: the bank cannot set off against the customer's personal debt an amount which is due—either legally or beneficially—to a third party such as the beneficiary of a trust. The leading case in point is *Union Bank of Australia v. Murray-Aynsley.*[98] A corporation maintained three accounts with its bank: a general account; a stock account; and a 'no. 3' account used for investments made by the corporation in the administration of a certain estate. The ledger of the no. 3 account, though, made no reference to the estate's interest. When the corporation had to be wound up, the bank sought to combine all three accounts. Dismissing the liquidator's objection, Lord Watson said that there was no evidence to show that the bank had been aware of the true nature of

[96] [1970] AC 567, affg. [1968] Ch. 540.
[97] (1894) 11 TLR 56, p. 145 above.
[98] [1898] AC 693. As regards solicitors' accounts, see the Solicitors' Act 1974, s. 85(2).

the no. 3 account. Unless the bank knew that the account was impounded with a trust, it retained the right of set-off in respect of the balance standing to its credit.

Although Lord Watson's decision derives support from other authorities,[99] it is open to criticism. In the *Murray-Aynsley* case there was no evidence to suggest that the bank had relied on the credit balance in account no. 3 in order to approve overdrafts granted to the corporation in respect of other accounts. Even if the corporation held out that the funds in account no. 3 belonged to itself, the bank could not rely on the misrepresentation involved unless it acted on it. It is difficult to see why an amount of money, due in equity to beneficiaries of an estate, should be used to satisfy the personal debts owed by the administrator or trustee to the bank.

Where a bank knows that an account is impounded with a trust, it cannot exercise a right of set-off against a balance standing to its credit to satisfy personal debts of the trustee. But can the bank set off against a credit balance in the trustee's personal account a debit balance in a trust account maintained by him? A Canadian authority, *Daniels* v. *Imperial Bank of Canada*,[100] suggests a positive answer. It was there held that, as the trustee had the right to draw on the trust account, he was to be regarded as having its control. On this basis, he was answerable with his own funds for a deficiency. The point may be questioned, as the trustee does not purport to transact trust business as a principal. Furthermore, if the bank requires his assurance, it can request him to furnish a personal guarantee. In the absence of such a facility it is difficult to see why the trustee's personal account should be utilized to cover a shortage in the trust account.

Usually the question of a set-off arises in respect of individual accounts maintained by a customer. But is there room for a combination of accounts if one is a personal account and the other a joint account? A Canadian authority suggests that a right of set-off may be available. In *Hill* v. *Bank of Hochelaga*,[101] a joint account was opened in the name of a married couple. The husband made the initial deposit and drew the bulk of the cheques on the account. Later on the wife notified the bank that the initial deposit came from the proceeds of the sale of some of her own properties. The question for decision was whether the bank could set off the husband's liability, incurred in respect of guarantees of advances made at his request to a certain corporation, against the credit balance of the joint account. It was held that a set-off could be exercised in respect of the balance of the joint account

---

[99] *Greenwood Teale* v. *William, Williams, Brown & Co.* (1894) 11 TLR 56; *Bank of New South Wales* v. *Goulburn Valley Butter Co. Pty. Ltd.* [1902] AC 543.
[100] (1914) 19 DLR 166.
[101] [1921] 3 WWR 430 (Ata. Sup. Ct.).

for any advances guaranteed by the husband before the bank was informed of the true source of the funds initially deposited. In respect of any later advances, the set-off could be exercised only against the husband's moiety in the joint account.[102]

Attractive as this decision may appear, it is open to criticism. An amount standing to the credit of a joint account constitutes a debt which is owed by the bank to the depositors jointly and severally. It is true that if the bank pays the amount standing to the credit of the account in violation of its mandate, as is the case where it honours a cheque that does not bear all the required signatures, the bank has to compensate the depositor who loses out.[103] The bank, therefore, has to pay an amount equal to this party's moiety in the account. But a bank that pays a cheque which bears the necessary signatures is not answerable to any of the depositors. This is so even if the depositors, who validly signed the cheque, issued it for improper purposes.

The same principle can be applied by analogy to the bank's right to combine a joint account with the personal account of one of the joint depositors. If the depositor in question has the right to draw cheques on the account on his own, it can be assumed that he also has the power to transfer money from the joint account to his own overdrawn account. In doing so, he would treat the money standing to the credit of the joint account as funds available for his own purposes. The bank would have no cause to question such a transfer. The bank, therefore, may justifiably assume that the amount standing to the credit of the joint account is available to either depositor, and that it is subject to a right of set-off in respect of such a depositor's personal account.

A point that has not been the subject of decision concerns the converse situation of that which gave rise to *Hill's* case. Can a bank set off against the credit balance in a customer's personal account an overdraft or loan incurred in respect of a joint account?[104] It is believed that the bank is entitled to do so. The debts incurred in respect of the joint account are due jointly and severally from all parties. As the banks could, accordingly, sue any depositor for the full amount of an overdraft of the joint account, it stands to reason that the bank also has the corresponding right of set-off.

---

[102] Cf. *Re Willis, Percival & Co. Ltd., ex p. Morier* (1879) 12 Ch. D 491, where it was held that an executor's indebtedness on his personal account could not be set off against the credit balance in the joint account maintained by him and his fellow executor. The decision, however, is largely based on the trust element in the joint account. And see *Bailey* v. *Finch* (1871) LR 7 QB 34, where, in similar circumstances, combination of accounts was allowed as the executor was, in effect, also the beneficiary of the estate.

[103] Pp. 161–171 below.

[104] But see *Watts* v. *Christie* (1849) 11 Beav. 546, which concerned the customer's right to request a set-off. In the course of the judgment it was held that the bank did not have a 'lien' over the personal account in respect of the overdraft on the joint account.

(iv) Is notice required?

Is the bank under an obligation to give notice to the customer before it combines his accounts in order to effect a set-off? This question was considered in *Garnett* v. *M'Kewan*,[105] where the Court of Exchequer answered it unanimously in the negative. In the words of Kelly CB:[106]

> In general it might be proper or considerate to give notice to that effect, but there is no legal obligation on the bankers to do so, arising either from express contract or the course of dealing between the parties.

An opposite conclusion was reached in *Buckingham Co.* v. *London and Midland Bank*.[107] A customer maintained with his bank a current account and a loan account, the debit balance of which was secured by a charge over his land. When property prices dropped sharply, the bank feared that its security had lost its value. It therefore set off without notice the credit balance in the current account against the sum due under the loan account. Consequently, some of the customer's cheques were dishonoured. Matthew J asked the jury to decide whether there was a course of dealings between the parties which permitted the customer to draw cheques on his current account without having regard to the state of the loan account and, further, whether he was entitled to reasonable notice if the bank decided to cancel this arrangement. The jury answered both questions positively and awarded damages of £500 against the bank.

Buckingham & Co.'s case is easily reconcilable with *Garnett* v. *M'Kewan*. In *Garnett* v. *M'Kewan* there was no agreement between the bank and its customer that the accounts be kept separate.[108] The bank could, therefore, exercise its right of set-off without notice. In *Buckingham & Co.*'s case the right was abrogated by an agreement based on a course of dealings. This agreement could be displaced solely by reasonable notice.

But even in such cases notice is not always required. An agreement to keep the accounts separate may be abrogated by subsequent developments. The classic case in point is where the customer becomes insolvent. His bankruptcy or winding-up usually abrogates the agreement, and may restore to the bank its right to combine the accounts without notice. Thus, in *British Guiana Bank* v. *OR*,[109] Lord Macnaghten held that an agreement to keep accounts apart remained in effect only whilst the accounts were current. It came to an end when they were frozen by the customer's insolvency.

---

[105] (1872) LR 8 Ex. 10.
[106] Ibid., 13.
[107] (1895) 12 TLR 70.
[108] See also *Irwin* v. *Bank of Montreal* (1876) 38 UCQB 375, 393; *Wallinder* v. *Imperial Bank of Canada* [1925] 4 DLR 390.
[109] (1911) 104 LT 754 (JC).

The point was considered in detail in *National Westminster Bank Ltd.* v. *Halesowen Presswork and Assemblies Ltd.*[110] It will be recalled that in this case the bank agreed to keep the current account and the frozen account apart for four months provided there was no material alteration in the customer's circumstances. Two changes took place. Initially the customer convened a meeting of creditors, and, subsequently, he decided to wind up voluntarily. The bank had resolved not to combine the accounts after the first event, but exercised its right without notice after the second event. Their Lordships were unanimous that the words of the agreement indicated that it was automatically avoided when the company decided to wind up. Notice by the bank of its decision to combine the accounts was therefore not required. Their Lordships indicated, however, that in the absence of clear language to such an effect, notice would probably be required. Viscount Dilhorne[111] said that, if the bank had made its decision to combine the accounts in the wake of the customer's decision to convene a meeting of creditors, the bank would have had to give reasonable notice. Lord Cross of Chelsea[112] said that, ordinarily, a bank would in the very least have to honour cheques drawn by the customer up to the time he was given notice of the combination of his accounts.

It follows that the question may still be open. From a commercial point of view it is necessary to take into account two conflicting considerations. On the one hand, the need of serving notice can do irreparable harm to the bank. Notice would enable the customer either to draw on his account until the 'reasonable time' given to him had expired or to divert cheques payable to him to some other bank accounts. On the other hand, it has been shown that the bank cannot close its customer's account, and thus terminate the contract between them, without serving notice.[113] In practice, the combination of accounts has the same effect as their closure. In both cases the customer is precluded from utilizing his account for ordinary trading purposes. Why, then, should the bank be required to give him notice of the closure of his account but not of its combination with other accounts? Still, it is believed that the solution proposed by Lord Cross of Chelsea presents an acceptable compromise.

(v) Special problems in insolvency situations

The most common situation in which a bank seeks to exercise its right of set-off is where an individual customer is adjudicated a bankrupt or a

---

[110] [1972] AC 785.
[111] Ibid., 807.
[112] Ibid., 810.
[113] Pp. 112–3 above.

corporate customer is being wound up. In such cases the bank's set-off is sanctioned not only by common law principles but also by section 323 of the Insolvency Act 1986, which has replaced section 31 of the Bankruptcy Act 1914. Section 323 provides for a set-off between amounts due to the creditor from the bankrupt and vice versa, provided the claims have been incurred in the course of 'mutual dealings' between the two parties.[114]

The scope of the original provision, section 31, was explained in *National Westminster Bank Ltd.* v. *Halesowen Presswork and Assemblies Ltd.*[115] One question that arose was whether the dealings between the defendant bank and the plaintiffs were 'mutual'. There was no doubt that any dealings between banker and customer on an account current would be so regarded. *Halesowen*'s case, however, involved one active account (no. 2) and one frozen account (no. 1). Their Lordships agreed with the view expressed in earlier cases[116] to the effect that dealings would cease to be 'mutual' within the meaning of the section where payments were made for specific or specially designated purposes. But the mere mention of a purpose was inadequate. Had it been sufficient, then any 'dealings' of a customer with his bank would cease to be mutual if their purpose was mentioned. Their Lordships considered this to be an unacceptable conclusion. Lord Simon defined the meaning of 'mutual' as follows:[117]

money is paid for a special (or specific) purpose so as to exclude mutuality of dealing within section 31 if the money is paid in such circumstances that it would be a misappropriation to use it for any other purpose than that for which it is paid.

In *Halesowen*'s case the dealings were mutual, as the agreement not to combine the accounts was made for a limited period and only insofar as the customer's circumstances remained materially unchanged.

The position has remained unchanged under the regime of section 323 of the Insolvency Act 1986. However, subsection (3) of this new provision clarifies one important point. Sums due from the bankrupt to the party seeking to effect the set-off are not to be included in the account taken 'if that other party had notice at the time they became due that a bankruptcy petition relating to the bankrupt was pending'.

A further question raised in *Halesowen*'s case was whether the parties

---

[114] S. 31 of the Bankruptcy Act 1914 applied to the winding-up of companies under s. 317 of the Companies Act 1948. S. 317 was replaced by s. 612 of the Companies Act 1985, which was, in turn, repealed by s. 438 of the Insolvency Act 1986. It is expected that regulations made under s. 411 and Sched. 8, paras. 12 and 14, of the 1986 Act will provide for the application of s. 323 of the winding-up of companies.

[115] [1972] AC 785.

[116] *Re Pollitt* [1893] 1 QB 455; *Re Mid-Kent Fruit Factory Ltd.* [1896] 1 Ch. 567; *Re City Equitable Fire Insurance Co. Ltd.* [1930] 2 Ch. 293.

[117] [1972] AC 785, 808.

could contract out of the provisions of section 31. Their Lordships were unanimous that, on the facts, the parties had not intended to exclude the section. Viscount Dilhorne and Lords Simon and Kilbrandon thought, in addition, that the section was of an imperative nature. They based their conclusion on the mandatory language of the section which provided that the creditor 'shall' have the right to set off. Lord Cross of Chelsea reached the opposite conclusion. In his opinion the word 'shall' was used in section 31 in order to confer a definite right of set-off on the creditor. His Lordship thought it incorrect to suggest that this right could not be abrogated by agreements.

Section 323 effectively supports Viscount Dilhorne's view. Subsection (2) does not confer the right to exercise a set-off on the creditor but enacts that 'an account shall be taken of what is due from each party to the other' and that the two amounts be set off against each other. It follows that the set-off in question is to be effected by the trustee in bankruptcy as a matter of course and quite regardless of the agreement between the parties. It is believed that this principle is undesirable and that Lord Cross's view is preferable. In many cases the bank's agreement to keep the accounts apart is motivated by the need of injecting confidence in the customer's business standing. When the bank seeks to abrogate its agreement and to combine the accounts upon the customer's insolvency, its interests do not conflict with the customer's but with the claims of his general creditors. The creditors involved are usually the very persons who have continued to trade with the customer as a result of the bank's agreement to keep him going by separating his accounts.

In *Halesowen*'s case the bank exercised a right of set-off in respect of amounts paid by the customer to the credit of his active account before the commencement of the winding-up. A Canadian authority suggests that the set-off cannot encompass amounts paid to the credit of the insolvent customer's account after the commencement of the bankruptcy or following the appointment of a receiver. Such amounts are 'not funds [deposited] to the credit of the bank's customer but [are] funds belonging to the . . . receiver', liquidator or trustee in bankruptcy.[118] A set-off in respect of amounts paid to the credit of the account before the relevant date may, of course, be exercised after the commencement of the bankruptcy or the winding-up.[119] Section 323 does not shed light on this problem.

One question which did not arise in *Halesowen*'s case was whether the

---

[118] *Re West Bay Sales Ltd.* (1979) 30 CBR (NS) 274, 280. See also *Re D. W. McIntosh Ltd.* v. *Royal Bank of Canada* [1940] 3 DLR 782. Cf. *Re T. C. Marines Ltd.* (1973) 34 DLR (3d) 489. For the converse problem, of whether a bank may exercise its right of set-off in respect of immatured claims due to it, see pp. 591–3 below.

[119] *Re D. W. McIntosh Ltd.*, above. That the right to combine accounts is not confined to bankruptcy situations, see *James Kirkwood & Sons* v. *Clydesdale Bank Ltd.*, 1908 SC 20.

remittance of amounts to the credit of an account, the balance of which can be impressed by a set-off, constitutes a 'preference' within the meaning of the Insolvency Act 1986. By and large, under section 239, which applies to the winding-up of companies, and under section 340, pertaining to the bankruptcy of individuals, a debtor gives one of his creditors a preference if the debtor does anything (or suffers anything to be done) which has the effect of putting the relevant creditor in a better position in the debtor's insolvency than if the thing had not been done. If such a preference is given to the creditor within the specified 'relevant time' (which in most cases is six months), a court has the power to make an order restoring the position to what it would have been if the debtor had not given that preference.

These new provisions originated, respectively, from section 44 of the Bankruptcy Act 1914 and from section 615 of the Companies Act 1985.[120] Section 44 was subject to a proviso—contained in section 45—under which a transaction could not be set aside in certain cases, one of which was where the creditor had furnished valuable consideration. In *Re Keever (a Bankrupt)*[121] it was held that where a cheque payable to a customer was remitted by him to his bank for the credit of his overdrawn account, the transaction was saved by this proviso because the customer's pre-existing debt constituted good consideration under section 27 of the Bills of Exchange Act 1882. The new Act does not have a similar proviso. But both in the winding-up of companies and in the bankruptcy of individuals an order restoring the original position is available only in so far as the debtor is influenced at the time he gives the preference by a desire to confer a benefit on the relevant creditor.[122] The effect of this rule is that, where the amount is paid to the credit of the insolvent customer's account without his having the intention of conferring a preference on the bank, an order ought to be refused. Where, however, the customer arranges for a sum to be remitted, or pays it in, under pressure, the rule is inapplicable.

It is interesting that this outcome is in harmony with views expressed in cases decided in common law jurisdictions other than the United Kingdom. Thus, Canadian cases support the view that payment to the credit of an account in respect of which the bank is entitled to exercise a right of set-off does not constitute an undue preference.[123] However, an Australian authority,[124] decided under a section *in pari materia* with section 45,[125] suggests

---

[120] Originally s. 320 of the Companies Act 1948.
[121] [1967] Ch. 182. Cf. *George Parker (Transport) Ltd.* v. *Eynon* [1973] 1 WLR 1461.
[122] Insolvency Act 1986, s. 239(6) (companies' winding-up); s. 340(4) (individual bankruptcies).
[123] *Re Sutcliffe & Sons Ltd., ex p. Royal Bank* [1933] 1 DLR 562; *Ross* v. *Royal Bank of Canada* (1965) 52 DLR (2d) 578; the cases were decided under s. 64 of the Canadian Bankruptcy Act, RCS 1952, which is *in pari materia* with s. 45 of the 1914 Act.
[124] *Richardson* v. *Commercial Banking Co. of Sydney Ltd.* (1952) 85 CLR 110.
[125] Bankruptcy Acts 1924–50 (Cth), s. 95.

that there are exceptions to this rule. A payment of the type discussed constitutes an undue preference if obtained under pressure, and with the knowledge that the customer's general creditors are likely to suffer a disadvantage as a result of it.

(vi) Combination of accounts in customers' interest

There is room for the combination of accounts in the customer's own interest where he draws a cheque for a sum exceeding the balance against which it is drawn but not the total amount deposited by him with the bank. Two separate questions arise. The first is whether the bank has the duty to combine the accounts in order to meet the cheque. Secondly, if the bank is not under such a duty, does it in the very least have the right to effect the necessary set-off?

It will be recalled that, although the customer's contract is with the bank as a whole, a demand for the repayment of amounts deposited by him must be made at the branch at which the relevant account is maintained.[126] It follows that the bank is not obliged to meet a demand made by the customer at another branch. Consequently, the bank cannot be called upon to combine accounts maintained by the customer at different branches in order to meet a cheque which is uncovered at the branch on which it is drawn. This conclusion derives support from an observation of Lord Denning in the Court of Appeal's judgment in the *Halesowen* case,[127] and from the decision of Bramwell B in *Garnett* v. *M'Kewan*.[128] But Bramwell B observed that, in practice, branch managers usually had a clear picture of their customers' dealings with the bank as a whole and were aware of accounts maintained by them with other branches. Despite the phenomenal development of branch banking in the twentieth century, the position has remained unaltered.[129]

A question on which there is no authority to date is whether or not the bank is obliged to combine different accounts maintained by a customer at one branch in order to refrain from dishonouring his cheque. By way of illustration, take the case in which a customer draws a cheque for £100 when his current account has a credit balance of £50 and his savings account a balance of £150. Is the bank obliged to transfer £50 from the savings account to the current account in order to meet the cheque? It is

---

[126] Pp. 129 above.

[127] [1971] 1 QB 1, 34. See also *Bank of New South Wales* v. *Goulburn Valley Butter Co. Pty. Ltd.* [1902] AC 543; *Houben* v. *Bank of Nova Scotia* (1970) 3 NBR (2d) 366.

[128] (1872) LR 8 Ex. 10, 14.

[129] In effect, the availability of computer searches and print-outs enables the bank to inform itself of a customer's total dealings with it.

believed that, as the customer does not expressly order the combination of his accounts, the bank is not obliged to effect a set-off. In theory, the branch manager may even resolve to dishonour the cheque. The justification for such a decision would be that the maintenance of different types of accounts by a customer manifests his intention that they be kept apart. In practice, the branch manager will permit his customer to overdraw his current account, leaving the savings account intact. The balance in the savings account serves as a security.[130]

The bank is thus not under an obligation to combine accounts in the customer's interest. But does the bank have the option of effecting such a set-off? Two authorities suggest that the bank has such a right.[131] This view derives support from a fundamental principle. Where an agent gives his principal an ambiguous instruction, the agent is entitled to reimbursement as long as he gives the instruction a reasonable construction which he believes to accord with the principal's genuine intention.[132] At first glance the drawing of a cheque which exceeds the credit standing to the customer's account appears to be unambiguous. It is a request that a certain amount be paid by the bank, regardless of the state of the customer's account. A closer look suggests that this is a simplification. A customer is aware of the fact that his bank is not obliged to meet a cheque drawn for an amount exceeding the available balance. He is, further, expected to be familiar with the state of his accounts.[133] If he draws an excessive cheque, he may be taken to request that the amount of it be paid out of any funds deposited with the bank. By effecting a set-off between the balances of different accounts, the bank obeys the spirit of this instruction.

Although the bank is not under a duty to effect a set-off in the customer's interest, it may have to do so, in the event of his bankruptcy, for the benefit of the general creditors. In *Mutton* v. *Peat*,[134] a stockbroker maintained with his bank a current account and a loan account. To secure the debit balance in the loan account, he gave the bank as a security some shares and bonds belonging to his clients. When the stockbroker was adjudicated a bankrupt there was a credit balance in his current account. The question was whether the bank was entitled to utilize the securities to recoup the full amount due under the loan account, or whether it had to set off against the indebtedness of the loan account the credit balance accrued in the current account. In the latter case the proceeds of the securities would have to be paid to the clients after the discharge of the net debt due. The Court of

---

[130]   As regards bank balances as securities, see pp. 590 et seq. below.
[131]   *Bank of New South Wales* v. *Goulburn Valley Butter Co. Pty. Ltd.*, above; *Houben* v. *Bank of Nova Scotia*, above.
[132]   Pp. 285–6 below.
[133]   Although he may in certain cases be unaware whether a certain cheque has been cleared.
[134]   [1900] 2 Ch. 79.

Appeal held that, as the securities were not specifically appropriated to cover the debit balance in the loan account, they could be utilized only for the satisfaction of the stockbroker's net indebtedness to the bank.

It is important to emphasize that in *Mutton* v. *Peat* the bank was unaware that the securities were not the customer's property. Furthermore, the bank's lien over the securities was not in issue. The decision that the lien was applicable only in respect of the net indebtedness of the customer to the bank is, it is submitted, unexceptional.

4. THIRD PARTY CLAIMS

(i) Definition of the problem

A bank's primary concern is its customer's interest. As long as it follows his instructions, it is safe. If the bank exceeds its mandate, it acts at its own peril.[135] There are, however, situations in which a bank has to take into account the possible claims of third parties. This occurs where the third party, be he an employer, an heir with a share of an estate, or the customer's spouse, has a claim based on breach of trust or arising from a conversion of his property. These cases can be divided into three classes.

The first type of case is where an employee, an agent, or a company's director misuses his power for his own benefit. Different types of situation give rise to cases of this sort. One of them is where the agent or employee draws a substantial cheque on the employer's account for the benefit of his own overdrawn account with the same bank. The other, less usual case, is that in which the director of a company utilizes its funds for inappropriate purposes. *Selangor United Rubber Estates Ltd.* v. *Cradock (No. 3)*,[136] discussed in Chapter 4, is a case in point.

The second type of case is where the bank seeks to set off a debit balance in the customer's personal account against the credit balance in some special account maintained by him. A third party may come forward and claim that the funds standing to the credit of the latter account are his property, either because they have been so appropriated or because the account in question is impounded by a trust of which he is the beneficiary.

The third type of case is where a third party claims the payment to himself of funds standing to the credit of a customer's account. The demand is usually based on the assertion that the claimant is entitled to the equitable property in the funds as beneficial owner under a trust.

From a legal point, one common thread runs through the three types of

[135] Pp. 128–9 above.
[136] [1968] 1 WLR 1555; [1968] 2 Lloyd's Rep. 289, discussed above, pp. 89–91.

case. In all of them the plaintiff asserts that a fiduciary duty or a duty imposed for his benefit under a trust has been violated either by the customer or by the bank. From a practical point of view, though, there is a telling difference between the three cases. The first type of case usually involves a dispute between the bank and its customer. The bank is sued in respect of losses which are said to have been sustained partly as a result of a breach of a duty of care or a fiduciary duty borne by the bank. In the second type of case the customer is, at best, a nominal party to the proceedings. In effect, it is a dispute between the bank and the customer's general creditors as to the distribution of the customer's assets in bankruptcy or in winding-up. The third type of case is generic. It encompasses disputes similar to those of the second group, except that they involve a claim by a specific third party rather than a denial by the customer's general creditors of the bank's right to exercise a set-off. The dispute, thus, is between a specific creditor or claimant and the liquidator or trustee in bankruptcy; the bank may be a nominal party to the proceedings.

One feature of all three types of case is that they arise in insolvency situations. In the first type of case, the customer would have a cause of action against the dishonest agent or employee in deceit, and, on occasions, in conversion. He sues the bank since an action against the rogue is unlikely to produce results. In the second type of case, the bank would not wish to consolidate the accounts if the legal owner of the funds were solvent. In the third type of case, the customer whose mishandling of trust funds is challenged by the beneficiaries would be sued personally if he had the financial ability to make good the loss.

The fact that, despite the common thread uniting the three types of case under consideration, they arise in separate practical situations means that their discussion has to be fragmented. The first type of case has been discussed in Chapter 4, which is concerned with the nature of the contract of banker and customer.[137] The second type of case has been discussed in this chapter as it arises in respect of set-off cases. Most of the problems respecting the third type of case occur in trust accounts. They are, therefore, raised in Chapter 7.[138] At this juncture it will be convenient to define further the third party's right and consider the main remedy available to him, namely, the tracing order.

(ii) Nature of the third party's right

Unlike other types of personal property, money is unspecific. Unless it is placed in an identifiable bag, or fund, where it is intact as an item of prop-

---

[137] Pp. 84 et seq. above.
[138] Pp. 181 et seq. below.

erty, it cannot be identified.[139] There is, therefore, no room for an action for the conversion of money. The only remedy available to a person who claims to have been deprived of a given amount of money which found its way into the hands of a third party is the tracing order. Such an order enables him to follow the money and to claim its payment to him by the recipient. But a tracing order is not available against a third party who has given value for the money in good faith. The claimant's only other course is to establish some wrongdoing which constitutes the bank a constructive trustee.[140]

The situations which give rise to this type of right were defined by the House of Lords in *Gray* v. *Johnston*.[141] A substantial amount of money was left by a testator to his wife for her lifetime and upon her death to their children. The wife, as executrix, drew a cheque on the bank account opened for the purposes of the estate and paid it to the credit of her personal account with the same bank. The children, suing as beneficiaries of the trust, attempted to recover the amount from the bank. Giving judgment for the bank, Lord Cairns LC emphasized the quandary which situations like that presented to a bank. His Lordship said:[142]

to hold a banker justified in refusing to pay a demand of his customer, the customer being an executor, and drawing a cheque as an executor, there must, in the first place, be some misapplication, some breach of trust intended by the executor, and there must in the second place . . . be proof that the bankers are privy to the intent to make this misapplication of the trust funds.

Lord Cairns stressed that, in the case before him, the bank did not stand to make a gain.

The same two elements were stressed in *Coleman* v. *Bucks and Oxon Union Bank*.[143] A firm of solicitors remitted a cheque for the credit of their agent's trust account. As no such account was in existence, the bank collected the cheque for the credit of the agent's personal account. At that time the account was in debit, but there was no suggestion that the bank was pressing for a reduction of the overdraft and, in effect, it allowed the agent to go on drawing. As there was no proof that the bank knew of the breach of trust or intended to be a party to it, and, further, as the bank did not benefit from the transaction, the solicitors' action was dismissed.

The trust which gives rise to the third party's rights need not be an express one. In *Re Kayford Ltd.*[144] a firm carrying on a mail order business opened a special deposit account with its bank, and paid to its credit all

[139] *Miller* v. *Race* (1785) 1 Burr. 452; *Moss* v. *Hancock* [1899] 2 QB 111, 118; *Banque Belge Pour L'Etranger* v. *Hambrouck* [1921] 1 KB 321, 326–7.
[140] Under the rule in *Barnes* v. *Addy* (1874) LR 9 Ch. App. 244, below pp. 89 et seq.
[141] (1868) LR 3 HL 1.
[142] Ibid., 11. See also *Bodenham* v. *Hoskyns* (1852) 2 De G M & G 903.
[143] [1897] 2 Ch. 243. See also *Thomson* v. *Clydesdale Bank Ltd.* [1893] AC 282.
[144] [1975] 1 WLR 279. See also *Baden, Delvaux et Lecuit* v. *Société General* [1983] BCLC 325, 402–12; *Re Montagu's Settlements*, unreported, 23.3.1985, Megarry V.C.

amounts received in respect of orders for goods that could not be supplied forthwith. When the firm went into liquidation the issue was whether the amounts credited to this account were due to the senders of the orders or to the liquidator. Giving judgment for the senders of orders, Megarry J said:[145]

The sender may create a trust by using appropriate words when he sends the money . . . or the company may do it by taking suitable steps on or before receiving money.

The opening of the account in question was a step of this type.

(iii) Tracing money

It has been pointed out that in certain cases a person who has been defrauded of a sum of money is able to recover his losses by means of a tracing order. Such an order enables him to follow the money into the 'fund' in which it is kept and to recover it in specie. In bankruptcy, the tracing order gives him priority over other creditors of the legal owner of the fund. In other cases he can obtain by means of such an order a remedy which is not available to him either in contract or in tort.

The basic principle emerges from *Re Hallett's Estate, Knatchbull v. Hallett*.[146] A solicitor paid to the credit of his personal account two sums which he held as trustee. One was an amount obtained under his own marriage settlement; the other comprised sums received by him on behalf of clients. The solicitor drew cheques on his account which reduced the balance from time to time to an amount smaller than the trust moneys; but he also regularly paid in cheques due to him. In his bankruptcy it was claimed by the trustees of the settlement and by the clients that they were entitled to follow the money to the bank account. The trustee in bankruptcy claimed that the funds held by the solicitor as fiduciary had been exhausted. Under the rule in *Clayton's Case*,[147] amounts paid out were to be appropriated against the earliest credit entries in the account. It was alleged that, as a result, the trust moneys had effectively been drawn out. Jessell MR held that the rule in *Clayton's Case* was inapplicable, as the solicitor was deemed to have utilized his own funds for his running payments. Accordingly, the trust funds were to be treated as still standing to the credit of the account. The claimants were, therefore, entitled to a tracing order. The fact that the money had been mixed up with the solicitor's private funds was irrelevant, as the trust fund had remained identifiable.

In *Hallett*'s case the money was traced to a fund under the control of the

[145] Ibid., 282.
[146] (1879) 13 Ch. D 696. See R. M. Goode, "Right to Trace and its Impact in Commercial Transactions" (1976) 92 LQR 360, 528.
[147] *Devaynes* v. *Noble (Clayton's Case)* (1816) 1 Mer. 529, 572; 35 ER 767, 781.

trustee. In appropriate cases money can be traced into the hands of a third party. But this right is lost where the third party receives the money in good faith and for a consideration. Thus, in *Banque Belge pour L'Etranger* v. *Hambrouck*,[148] an agent fraudulently drew cheques on his principal's account and paid them to the credit of his personal account. He then drew out the proceeds and paid them over to his mistress, who paid them to the credit of her account with her own bank. The principal initially claimed the money from the mistress's bank. But when this bank interpleaded he claimed it from the agent and from the latter's mistress. The Court of Appeal granted a tracing order. Bankes LJ pointed out that, as the money was unidentifiable, there was no room for an action in money had and received or in conversion. There was, however, room for a tracing order, as the agent had acquired money by means of a breach of trust. It could be followed into the hands of the mistress, as she had given no valid consideration for it, such as a contribution to household expenses.[149]

It is thus clear that trust property can be traced into the hands of donees who obtained an invalid gift of it.[150] The position has been authoritatively summarized in *Re Diplock*.[151] According to this case, money can be traced into a mixed fund although the co-mingling has been executed by an innocent volunteer. This principle is, however, subject to three limitations. First, the relationship between the claimant and recipient (or the person who obtained the property) must be such as to give rise to a fiduciary relationship of some sort. Secondly, the claimant's money must be fairly identifiable. Thirdly, the equitable remedy involved—the tracing order—must not work an injustice. In effect, the principle is still best explained by the classic statement of Viscount Haldane LC in *Sinclair* v. *Brougham*:[152]

So long as the money which the principal has handed to his agent to be applied specifically, and not on a debtor and creditor account, can be traced into what has been procured with it, the principal can waive his right of action for damages for tort, and, affirming the proceeding of the [agent], claim that his money is invested in a specific thing, which is his.

The right of an owner or of the beneficiary of a trust to trace his property may be exercised both against the third party who has acquired it and against that party's agent. It follows that, where money finds its way into a bank account, the tracing order is available both against the recipient and

---

[148] [1921] 1 KB 321.
[149] That such a contribution would constitute valuable consideration, see *Transvaal and Delagoa Bay Investment Co. Ltd.* v. *Atkinson* [1944] 1 All ER 579.
[150] *Ministry of Health* v. *Simpson* [1951] AC 251 (where trustees of a will distributed the trust property in good faith to the donees. The heirs were granted a tracing order against the donees when the will was set aside for uncertainty).
[151] [1948] Ch. 465.
[152] [1914] AC 398, 419.

against the bank. But the order is available against an agent only until such time as he repays the money to the recipient. Thus, if the money has been repaid by the bank to its customer—the recipient—the bank is not responsible to the beneficiary of the trust (or the original owner) unless it is privy to the breach of trust.[153]

The principle is of considerable importance to the bank. From the bank's point of view it would be intolerable to have to consider the possibility of being served with a tracing order whenever its customer disposed over, or paid in, amounts that could turn out to be trust money. The bank's position is further protected by the rule in *Tassell* v. *Cooper*.[154] A customer paid to the credit of his current account a cheque received in payment of merchandise sold on behalf of his employers. Although no fraud was involved, the employer requested the bank to retain the amount involved. As the employer furnished an indemnity, the bank consented and, subsequently, dishonoured one of its customer's cheques. Maule J held that the bank was not entitled to dishonour its customer's cheque at the request of a third party. It would appear that the employer's correct course was to apply for an injunction to restrain the employee from drawing against the funds involved.[155]

---

[153] *Transvaal and Delagoa Bay Investment Co. Ltd.* v. *Atkinson* [1944] 1 All ER 579. And see *Gowers* v. *Lloyds and National Provincial Foreign Bank Ltd.* [1938] 1 All ER 766, and pp. 329–333 below.

[154] (1850) 9 CB 509.

[155] *Fontaine-Besson* v. *Parr's Banking Co.* (1895) 12 TLR 121.

CHAPTER 7

Special Types of Account

1. TYPE OF PROBLEM

It has been shown in Chapter 6 that the relationship of banker and customer is primarily that of creditor and debtor. The amount deposited by the customer becomes part and parcel of the bank's own money. All that the customer has, therefore, is a chose in action, or a right to reclaim the debt from the bank by drawing a cheque or by issuing a giro form. When the customer makes such a demand, he issues an instruction to his bank. An agency relationship is in this way superimposed upon the contract of debtor and creditor.[1] Thus, when the bank pays the customer's cheque it performs two complementary functions. The first is that of discharging a debt due. The second is that of obeying its mandate.

Neither of these elements gives rise to problems in the ordinary relationship of banker and customer. There are, however, special types of accounts which present problems regarding the one or the other element. Thus, in some cases it may not be altogether clear to whom the debt, represented by the balance in the current account, is due. In other cases it is questionable who is entitled to issue the mandate. All these types of accounts require special consideration.

The joint account illustrates the type of difficulty that arises. In such an account it may be unclear who is entitled to draw cheques, and whether the debt is due to the two owners jointly or jointly and severally. In another type of account, namely that of a corporation, there is occasionally an element of doubt regarding the power of officers to draw cheques. Such a problem is one of capacity. Problems of power and capacity arise also in the case of accounts of executors and of trustees, and in the case of accounts of minors and of mentally incapacitated persons. In all these cases the question is whether the bank should promptly honour the customer's cheques or take some special steps before reaching a decision.

The payment of cheques drawn on such special accounts is only one of the problems faced by the bank. The other concern is the bank's approach to applications for loans or overdrafts. Is the bank safe if it follows the ordinary rules of commercial prudence, or is there a need for extra caution? Thus, in the case of a minor, does the bank have to satisfy itself that the loan

---

[1] Pp. 128–9 above.

is required for necessaries? Similarly, in the case of a corporation, does the bank have to ascertain that the loan is required for a valid purpose?

The problems raised will be discussed in this chapter. The first two sections deal with the joint account and with the somewhat similar partnership account. The next four types of account to be discussed are executors' accounts, trust accounts, solicitors' accounts and estate agents' accounts. The common thread in these types of account is the existence of an element of trust arising from the fact that the ostensible customer is the fiduciary of another. The bank has to remember in these types of account that, whilst the legal ownership in the funds is vested in the ostensible customer, the beneficiary of the trust has the equitable title. Discussion of these accounts is followed by an analysis of accounts of organizations and artificial bodies. These encompass accounts of local authorities, of companies, and of unincorporated associations. In all these accounts, the bank is primarily concerned with questions of capacity of agents and officers, and with the powers of the organization. The chapter concludes with an analysis of accounts of married women, of minors, and of the mentally incapacitated. The problems that arise are related to the special status of the customer.

2. JOINT ACCOUNTS

(i) Nature of the account

An account opened in the name of two or more customers is known as a joint account. It is to be distinguished from an account—such as an account of a company or an administrators' account—which stipulates that cheques have to be signed by more than one person. In the latter types of account, the authorized persons sign in a representative capacity, or as fiduciaries. In a joint account the owners, either jointly or severally, act on behalf of themselves.

(ii) Right to draw

When a joint account is opened, the customers instruct the bank whether each cheque has to be signed by all of them jointly, by two or more of them signing together, or by any one of them. The first two types of instruction give rise to disputes where the bank honours a cheque bearing a forgery of one of the required signatures or a cheque on which one of the mandatory signatures is missing.

In the leading case of *Jackson* v. *White and Midland Bank Ltd.*,[2] the plaintiff entered into negotiations for a contract under which he was to become a partner in, or joint owner of, the first defendant's business. An amount of £2,000 was paid by the plaintiff into a joint account at a branch of the defendant bank, opened by himself together with the first defendant and stipulating that cheques be signed by both parties. The first defendant forged the plaintiff's signature on several cheques, which were honoured in due course by the bank. The business negotiations between the plaintiff and the first defendant broke down. As the first defendant did not refund the amounts drawn, the plaintiff applied for an injunction ordering the bank to reverse the debit entries arising from the payment of the forged cheques and also for an injunction ordering the first defendant to authorize the bank to honour cheques for their amount drawn by the plaintiff alone. Giving judgment for the plaintiff, Park J said:[3]

the Bank made an agreement with the plaintiff and the first defendant jointly that it would honour any cheques signed by them jointly, and also a separate agreement with the plaintiff and the first defendant severally that it would not honour any cheques unless he had signed them. It follows, therefore, as the Bank has honoured cheques not signed by the plaintiff, the plaintiff is entitled to sue for breach of that separate agreement.

A similar view was expressed by Bingham J in *Catlin* v. *Cyprus Finance Corporation (London) Ltd.*[4] in which a bank, again, honoured a cheque which did not bear all the signatures stipulated in the agreement for the opening of the joint account. Although his Lordship regarded the mandate given to the bank as issued jointly by all the owners of the account, he held that the bank's duty to obey it was owed to each of them severally. This was so, as 'the only purpose of requiring two signatures was to obviate the possibility of independent action by one account holder to the detriment of the other'.[5]

In both the *Jackson* and the *Catlin* case it was established that the funds paid into the account were the plaintiff's property. The respective plaintiffs were accordingly allowed to recover the full amount paid out on cheques that ought to have been dishonoured by the bank. Where such facts cannot be proved, all the innocent joint owner of the account is entitled to recover

---

[2] [1967] 2 Lloyd's Rep. 68.
[3] Ibid., 79, following a dictum of Denning LJ in *Welch* v. *Bank of England* [1955] Ch. 508. See also *Baker* v. *Barclays Bank Ltd.* [1955] 1 WLR 822, and the Australian cases of *Ardern* v. *Bank of New South Wales* [1956] VLR 569, and *Simos* v. *National Bank of Australasia Ltd.* (1976) 10 ACTR 4; and note the much earlier case of *Twibell* v. *London Surburban Bank* [1869] WN 127. Contrast *Brewer* v. *Westminster Bank* [1952] 2 All ER 650, in which McNair J held that as the two owners, suing together, could not be heard to complain, the innocent party was precluded from proceeding as the bank's duty was owed to them jointly.
[4] [1983] QB 759.
[5] Ibid., 771.

is a moiety of amounts paid out wrongfully against cheques not signed by him.[6]

The innocent joint owner of an account is not entitled to recover payment of the amount of a cheque on which his signature has been forged if the cheque is drawn in discharge of a debt that can be enforced against him. Thus, in *Jackson*'s case, it was conceded that one of the cheques had been drawn to pay for the price of goods supplied to the plaintiff. Park J thought that the plaintiff's counsel was right in withdrawing the claim related to this item, as the bank was entitled 'to take advantage of the equitable doctrine by which a person who had in fact paid the debts of another without authority was allowed the advantage of his payments'.[7]

The doctrine referred to, which is based on *Liggett*'s case,[8] explains why a bank that honours a cheque which does not bear all the required signatures is liable to the innocent joint owner for a moiety, rather than for the full amount, of the instrument. A reasoning based on a strict application of the principles of agency would have led to the opposite conclusion. At common law, a bank which acts on an invalid mandate is not entitled to debit the account with any part of the amount paid out. The equitable doctrine referred to in *Jackson*'s case mitigates this harsh result. According to it, a principal on whose mandate the bank has purported to act cannot recover an amount exceeding the loss incurred by him due to the unauthorized payment made by the bank. Thus, where the owner of a joint account is the owner of one half of the balance, he is not entitled to recover more than 50 per cent of an amount paid by the bank without a valid authority.

The type of problem which has just been discussed does not arise where the bank is instructed to pay a cheque drawn on the account by any one of the joint owners. Unless there are facts which indicate that the account has been opened for a specific object, each party is entitled to draw on it for his own purposes. Thus, in *Re Bishop decd., National Provincial Bank Ltd.* v. *Bishop*,[9] a married couple opened a joint account and authorized the bank to honour cheques drawn by either of them. The husband drew several cheques for the payment of shares purchased in his own name. It was held that these shares became the property of the husband. They were not held by him in trust for his wife and himself.

A question that has not been the subject of decision to date is whether the

---

[6] *Twibell* v. *London Suburban Bank* [1869] WN 127; and see *Ardern* v. *Bank of New South Wales* [1956] VLR 569.

[7] [1967] 2 Lloyd's Rep. 68, 80.

[8] *B. Liggett (Liverpool) Ltd.* v. *Barclays Bank Ltd.* [1928] 1 KB 48, discussed on pp. 300–1 below.

[9] [1965] Ch. 450, followed in *Re Cameron* (1967) 62 DLR (2d) 389, 405; *Feaver* v. *Feaver* [1977] 5 WWR 271. Cf. *Jones* v. *Maynard* [1951] 1 Ch. 572, 575, where Vaisey J concluded from the method of dealings in a similar case that all investments had been acquired jointly for both parties to the account.

bank is entitled to dishonour a cheque if it has reason to suspect that it is drawn by one owner of the account in fraud of the other. By way of illustration, take the case in which a married couple maintains a joint account into which both of them pay their regular earnings. What is the bank's duty if one spouse draws a cheque payable to a travel agent and at about the same time withdraws the remaining balance in full? Can the bank pay the cheque without raising any questions, or does it become subject to a fiduciary duty to the other spouse? It is believed that the imposition of such a duty on the bank would put on it too onerous a task.

(iii) Survivorship

Who is entitled to a deceased party's moiety in the balance of a joint account: the surviving party or the estate? The question can arise in three different contexts. First, it arises if there is a dispute between the survivor and the deceased's heir. Secondly, the question can arise as between the survivor and the tax authorities. A case in point is where the survivor is also the deceased's heir. It may be asked whether or not the amount standing to the credit of the joint account is to be subject to capital transfer tax on the basis that it forms part of the deceased's estate. Thirdly, the question may arise in litigation between the bank and the survivor or the estate. This occurs if there is a dispute concerning the bank's decision to honour a demand.

Case law suggests that to answer the above problems it is necessary to draw a distinction between the legal title to the amounts involved and the beneficial or equitable interest therein. The former is important mainly as regards disputes between the bank and its customer. The latter is relevant in repsect of the remaining types of situation.

It is well established that the legal title in the deceased's moiety in the joint account vests in the survivor. In the leading case of *Russell* v. *Scott*, Dixon and Evatt JJ observed:

The right at law to the balance standing at the credit of the account on the death of [the deceased party] was thus vested in the [survivor].[10]

An equitable or beneficial title, which is quite separate from the legal one, may nevertheless vest in the estate. The position depends on the facts. If the amounts standing to the credit of the account were paid in by the two parties they would be regarded as having accrued to both of them. The estate of a deceased joint party is then unable to establish that it has a beneficial interest in the moiety.[11] The position differs if the amounts were paid in entirety

---

[10] (1936) 55 CLR 440, 451.
[11] The joint account may then be regarded as a genuine common pool: *Jones* v. *Maynard* [1951] 1 Ch. 572, esp. 575; *Gage* v. *King* [1961] 1 QB 188, 192–3, per Diplock J. And see *Plater* v. *Brealey* [1938] 4 DLR 765, affd. (no opinion) [1939] 2 DLR 767n.

or predominantly by the deceased. In such a case the rights of the estate depend on the deceased's intention in maintaining the funds in a joint account. The typical case in which the question arises is where one spouse transfers the credit balance of his personal account to a new joint account. Is he motivated by considerations of convenience, or is his object to effect a gift? The same problem arises where a parent or an aged relative transfers a personally owned balance to the credit of a joint account in the name of himself and a younger member of the family.

The solution depends on a consideration of all the facts. Thus, in *Marshal* v. *Crutwell*[12] a husband, who discovered that he was fatally ill, transferred the balance standing to the credit of his personal account to the credit of a new account opened in the joint names of his wife and himself. The bank was directed to honour cheques signed by either of the spouses. Cheques drawn by the wife up to the date of the husband's death were all issued under his direction and related primarily to household expenses. When the husband died, disputes arose between the widow and his remaining heirs concerning the balance standing to the credit of the joint account. Jessel MR held that no gift had been intended, and that the sole object of the arrangement was to provide a convenient method for managing the husband's affairs during his illness. On these facts, the assumption of survivorship was displaced and the estate was held to be beneficially entitled to the sum involved.

The opposite conclusion was reached on the facts in *Re Harrison*.[13] A husband opened an account in the joint names of his wife and himself. Initially the wife was informed neither of the existence of the account nor that she was entitled to draw on the funds. It was only when the husband's health declined that the branch manager advised her of the arrangement. When the husband died shortly thereafter, an envelope containing deposit receipts and indorsed with the wife's initials was discovered among his papers. In the bank's ledger it had been noted: 'Repayable to either or to survivor.' Russell J could find no motive for the opening of the joint account except the husband's wish that the wife take on survival. She was therefore the beneficial as well as the legal owner of the funds in question.

The two cases just discussed show that there is a need for a flexible approach to the problem of survivorship. The deceased's intention is discernible only from a careful assessment of the facts. Observations made by

---

[12] (1875) LR 20 Eq. 328. See also *Husband* v. *Davis* (1851) 10 CB 645; *Williams* v. *Davies* (1864) 3 Sw. & Tr. 437; *Re Potter* (1926) 39 OWN 327, 328; *McLean* v. *Vessey* [1935] 4 DLR 170.

[13] (1920) 90 LJ Ch. 186. See also *Young* v. *Sealey* [1949] Ch. 278, 295; *Re Bishop, decd., National Provincial Bank Ltd.* v. *Bishop* [1965] Ch. 450; *Re Figgis, decd., Roberts* v. *McLaren* [1969] 1 Ch. 123. The following Canadian authorities are of interest: *Re Reid* (1921) 50 Ont. LR 595; *Niles* v. *Lake* [1947] SCR 291; *Re Cameron* (1967) 62 DLR (2d) 389, esp. 405.

the deceased are given due weight. Thus, in *Russell* v. *Scott*[14] an old lady opened a joint account in the name of herself and her favourite nephew. During her lifetime this account was utilized solely for her own purposes. However, she mentioned to her solicitors that the nephew was to take as survivor. The High Court of Australia held that both the legal and the beneficial title to the funds vested in the nephew upon his aunt's death.

As pointed out above, the question of the survivor's beneficial title is relevant in cases involving disputes between heirs and, also, for tax purposes. It would appear that cases concerning the levying of capital transfer tax on joint account balances are determined on the same basis as cases involving disputes between competing parties claiming a right to the balance.[15] In contrast, the position of the bank is usually unaffected by questions related to the beneficial title to the funds. The bank's main concern is to meet the demands of the legal owner of the account. Moreover, most standard term contracts, executed when a joint account is opened, include a clause which requires the bank to honour cheques drawn by the survivor.[16] The accepted view is that, even in the absence of such a clause, the bank can obtain a good discharge by meeting demands made by the survivor.[17]

Lord Atkin's decision in *McEvoy* v. *Belfast Banking Co.*[18] supports the view that the bank is entitled to meet the survivor's demand. In this case a customer, whose health was failing, deposited with the bank £10,000 in the names of himself and his minor son. He specifically ordered that the amount be payable to either of them or to the survivor. The true object of this deposit was to save death duties that would be payable on the amount involved if it formed part of the father's estate. Shortly afterwards, the father made a will in which he left all his remaining assets to his executors in trust for his son, who was to acquire the property unconditionally on his twenty-fifth birthday. When the father died, the executors transferred the amount of £10,000 into their own names and frequently used the balance accrued to back and even to repay part of an overdraft granted to the deceased father's business. All this was done with the knowledge of the son, who took an active part in the business built up by his father. Moreover, the son made no demand for the payment of the £10,000 until the business failed and had to be liquidated. At that stage the son had reached the age of twenty-nine.

The bank claimed that it had validly paid the £10,000 to the executors,

[14] (1936) 55 CLR 440.
[15] Cf. *Thomson* v. *Federal Commissioner of Taxation* (1949) 80 CLR 344.
[16] It is noteworthy that no such clause is mentioned by H. L. Hart, *Law of Banking*, 3rd edn., London, 1914, pp. 250–1, and 4th edn., London, 1931, pp. 321 et seq.
[17] Paget, *Law of Banking*, 9th edn., p. 29; J. M. Holden, *Law and Practice of Banking*, 4th edn., London, 1986, vol. 1, para 11–85.
[18] [1935] AC 24.

and questioned the son's standing. The Court of Appeal of Northern Ireland gave judgment against the bank, holding that payment should have been made to the survivor, the son. The House of Lords reversed this decision. But although their Lordships were unanimous, they reached their conclusions on different grounds. Lord Warrington, with whom Lord Macmillan concurred, took the view that the executors were entitled to the payment of the amount involved by the bank as the father had not manifested an intention to donate it to the son. Lord Thankerton reached the same conclusion by applying principles of the law of contract. He regarded the contract as being solely between the father and the bank. The son, for whose benefit the contract had been made, was not a party and hence could not enforce the contract. Lord Atkin disagreed with this contractual analysis of the transaction. He observd that the father had manifested an intention of advancement as he clearly wished that upon his demise the sum involved be available to the son. The son therefore had the legal title to the amount involved. Furthermore, the contract was not just between the bank and the father but between the bank and the two parties in whose names the amount was deposited, namely the father and the son. Lord Atkin said:[19]

The suggestion is that where A deposits a sum of money with his bank in the names of A and B, payable to A or B, if B comes to the bank with the deposit receipt he has no right to demand the money from the bank or to sue them if his demand is refused. The bank is entitled to demand proof that the money was in fact partly B's, or possibly that A had acted with B's actual authority. For the contract, it is said, is between the bank and A alone. My Lords, to say this is to ignore the vital difference between a contract purporting to be made by A with the bank to pay A or B and a contract purporting to be made by A and B with the bank to pay A or B. In both cases of course payment to B would discharge the bank whether the bank contracted with A alone or with A and B. But the question is whether in the case put B has any rights against the bank if payment to him is refused. I have myself no doubt that in such a case B can sue the bank. The contract on the face of it purports to be made with A and B, and I think with them jointly and severally.

Lord Atkin emphasized that in cases of this type, B had to ratify the contract. A could not, on his own initiative and without B's consent, constitute B a party. Ratification, though, might be inferred from the circumstances. In the instant case there had not been ratification. To the contrary, the son's active participation in his deceased father's business both before and after he came of age, and the son's knowledge that the £10,000 in question were utilized to support the business, indicated that he agreed with the course adopted by the executors. He was, therefore, precluded from contesting the bank's right to pay to the executors.

Lord Atkin's judgment suggests that, under normal circumstances, the

---

[19] Ibid., 43.

bank is both entitled and obliged to meet the demands of the surviving party to a joint account. Indeed, where the survivor is of age when the account is opened, and has the capacity to enter into a contract, his agreement with the bank is made when he signs the forms requesting the opening of the joint account. It follows that, quite regardless of disputes that may arise between the survivor and the executors, the bank is authorized to honour the survivor's cheques.

It is noteworthy that Lord Atkin's judgment steers a course that avoids the need to adopt two other possible interpretations of the type of contract made in the *McEvoy* case. The first is that which leads to the conclusion of Lord Thankerton, to the effect that the contract is one between the bank and the original customer for the benefit of the other party to the joint account. The other possible view, which finds no echo in the case, is to regard the arrangement as involving an instruction given to the bank by the original customer for the payment of the amount standing to the credit of the joint account to the survivor. On both views the survivor would fail to obtain any contractual or beneficial rights. On the first view, he would be a third party to an agreement between the bank and the initial customer. On the second view, the bank would be precluded from paying the survivor's cheques as the original customer's instruction, or mandate, would determine upon his demise.[20] It is submitted that Lord Atkin's view is to be supported. If the customer's wish is either to enable another person to draw on his account or to confer on that person a non-enforceable benefit, the customer can achieve his object by means other than the opening of a joint account. To enable the other party to draw, he can execute a power of attorney conferring on his nominee the required authority. If he intends to make a gift on his death, he can do so by will or by creating a trust. When a person opens a joint account allowing for survivorship, he has the intention of achieving a specific object: he proposes to enable the other party (the survivor) to draw on the account both before and after his own demise. Lord Atkin's decision upholds this intention but provides the safeguards required to protect the bank where there are unusual circumstances, such as those of the *McEvoy* case.

3. PARTNERSHIP ACCOUNTS

(i) Opening and operating a partnership account

A partnership account resembles a joint account in that it is opened in the name of more than one person. As a partnership, unlike a corporation, does

---

[20] Pp. 278–80 below.

not have a legal personality separate from that of the partners, its account constitutes in effect a joint account of the partners.

Under section 5 of the Partnership Act 1890, each partner is his firm's agent and is therefore entitled to open an account on its behalf. Under section 6 he can operate the partnership's account in his own right, and is entitled to close it.[21] However, in *Alliance Bank* v. *Kearsley*,[22] it was held that a partner did not have the authority to maintain an account of the firm in his personal name. The other partners were therefore not liable to reimburse the bank in respect of losses incurred by the partner on the account in question although it was used solely for the purposes of the partnership. An argument against this decision is that, as the other partners would be liable if the account were opened by the partner in the firm's name, it was unreasonable to permit them to escape liability on the basis of a formality.

The rights conferred by the 1890 Act on each partner to operate the firm's bank accounts are frequently abrogated in the partnership agreement. Nowadays it is usual to stipulate that an account has to be opened and operated either jointly by all the partners or by two or three of them acting together.[23] The existence of such clauses is common knowledge. It is therefore arguable that, when a bank is asked to open an account in a partnership's name, it ought to consult the agreement. Ideally, a bank should require an authority executed by all the partners.

Forster v. *Mackreth*[24] demonstrates how important it is for the bank to consider, at each stage, the scope of a partner's authority. A partner indorsed some bills of exchange on behalf of the firm, and also drew in its name cheques post-dated by seven days. Martin B, in the Court of Exchequer, held that the other partners were not liable on the instruments. Dealing in bills was not a business in which the partnership—a firm of attorneys—could be expected to engage. The indorsements were, therefore, not within the partner's ordinary scope of authority. Similarly, although the drawing of cheques was within the partner's authority, the issuing of post-dated cheques was outside it. This was so although the cheques had been drawn in order to raise temporary finance for the firm by means of their discount.

It is to be doubted if Martin B's decision concerning the post-dated cheques would be followed today. His Lordship reaches his conclusion

---

[21] As to whether a partner is entitled to overdraw an account, see *Bank of Australasia* v. *Breillat* (1847) 6 Moore PC 152, 193.

[22] (1871) LR 6 CP 433.

[23] If the signature of two or more partners is required on a cheque, then the signature of one partner, purporting to act on behalf of the others, is inadequate: *Laws* v. *Rand* (1857) 3 CB (NS) 442. As regards the position where a cheque payable to a partnership is remitted for the credit of a partner's personal account, see *Souhrada* v. *Bank of New South Wales* [1976] 2 Lloyd's Rep. 444.

[24] (1867) LR 2 Ex. 163.

partly on the basis that 'we cannot in substance distinguish this [post-dated] cheque from a bill of exchange at seven days' date'.[25] More recent cases treat post-dated cheques both as valid and as regular on their face.[26] It is noteworthy that in *Guildford Trust Ltd.* v. *Goss*,[27] cheques drawn by one partner and indorsed by another were regarded as valid in the hands of the holder, despite their having been post-dated when he took them. Moreover, the partner who indorsed the cheques was held personally liable as he did not negate his personal responsibility by expressly signing in a representative form. The general principle which emerges from Martin B's decision in *Forster* v. *Mackreth* is, however, likely to stand the test of time. The partner's ability to bind the firm and his co-partners depends on what is considered to be the scope of his authority in ordinary trade. This authority is bound to vary from firm to firm. Thus, if the partnership in *Forster* v. *Mackreth* had carried on the business of banking, it would have been held bound by the partner's indorsement of the bills of exchange.

(ii) Borrowing through a partnership's account

A partner of a commercial or trading firm has the authority to raise credit and hence can make arrangements for an overdraft. It would appear to follow that the partner has the complementary power to give security for the loan involved. It is questionable whether in a professional partnership, such as a law firm or a medical practice, a partner is entitled to borrow money on behalf of the firm. Usually such a partnership enters into transactions involving the raising of credit only when all the partners are in agreement.

(iii) Dissolution of a partnership by death

The doctrine of survivorship is inapplicable to partnership accounts. Unless the partnership agreement provides to the contrary, the firm is dissolved upon the death of one of the partners. However, under section 38 of the Partnership Act 1890, the surviving partners have the power to continue to act for the firm for the purpose of winding-up its affairs. Case law suggests that the bank is not under an obligation to scrutinize carefully the surviving partners' actions in such a case. The bank is entitled to assume that they act within their statutory authority.

Thus, in *Backhouse* v. *Charleton*,[28] a partnership comprising a father and

---

[25] Ibid., 166.
[26] Pp. 248–50 below.
[27] (1927) 136 LT 725.
[28] (1878) 8 Ch. D 444.

his son instructed its bank that each partner was entitled to draw on the account both during the father's lifetime and after his demise. The son drew cheques on the partnership account and paid them to the credit of his personal account with the same bank. Malins VC held that the bank was not liable to the estate. He thought that, in respect of cheques drawn during the father's lifetime, the bank was under a duty to pay. On this point, the decision can be questioned. As the bank acted both as collecting bank and as paying bank, it could have been treated as liable in conversion if the son drew cheques in fraud of the other partner.[29] The main question in the case, however, was whether the bank was entitled to honour cheques drawn by the son in his role as surviving partner. Malins VC held that the bank was not called upon to make any enquiry concerning the payment of the cheques drawn after the father's death. He thought that to hold otherwise would be to deliver a blow to the business of banking. Far from being under a duty to investigate, the bank was bound to honour any of the cheques in question.

Similarly, in *Re Bourne*,[30] a partnership was dissolved by the death of one of the partners. The remaining partner continued to carry on the firm's business in order to wind up its affairs and, for this reason, refrained from closing its bank account. As the account was overdrawn and as an increase of the overdraft was required, the surviving partner deposited with the bank some title deeds as a security. The question was who had a priority over these deeds: the bank or the deceased partner's executors? Affirming Farwell J's decision, the Court of Appeal gave judgment for the bank. Romer LJ observed that the surviving partner had the power to give a good title to purchasers and mortgagees. Persons dealing with him were therefore entitled to assume that he was acting in good faith and within the scope of his authority to liquidate the partnership. This assumption safeguarded the rights of the bank. His Lordship said:[31]

When you find an account of that kind continued—and here it is only continued for something like nine months before the charge is given—the bankers . . . are entitled, in the absence of evidence showing the shewing the contrary, to assume and to be credited with the belief that the surviving partner is continuing it for the purpose of realization, and that sums paid into that account and sums drawn out of that account in the name of the partnership are paid in and drawn out for the purpose of the partnership.

On this basis, the Court of Appeal concluded that the account was to be treated as remaining in full effect.

---

[29] Pp. 444–8 below.
[30] [1906] 2 Ch. 427.
[31] Ibid., 433. Note that the rule of appropriation of payments, known as the rule in *Clayton*'s case (discussed below, pp. 482–5), was therefore inapplicable.

(iv) Problems of insolvency

Under sections 33 and 38 of the Partnership Act 1890, a partnership is dissolved by the insolvency of the firm or of one of its partners. After his adjudication, the insolvent partner is unable to bind the partnership. If, prior to the commencement of the bankruptcy, he has incurred any debts in the partnership's name, the other partners are liable. Their liability is usually joint and several.

An interesting point concerning partnership accounts arose in *Watts* v. *Christie*.[32] The account of a partnership of A and B was overdrawn whilst A's personal account with the same bank was in credit. When the bank failed, A assigned his personal credit balance to the partnership so as to facilitate a set-off of this credit balance against the partnership's debit balance. If such a set-off were exercised, the firm would have proved for the net credit balance rather than for the full amount of the credit balance, and would not have been obliged to pay the amount due under the overdraft to the trustee in bankruptcy. Lord Langdale MR held that the purported assignment was ineffective. The bank did not have a valid lien on the personal account of the partner in respect of debts incurred by the firm. Thus, the two accounts had to be kept apart; the bank could not have combined the two. It followed that, when the bank became insolvent, it was too late for the individual partner in question to effect a set-off by means of an assignment. The two balances had crystallized at the time of the commencement of bankruptcy.

4. EXECUTORS' ACCOUNTS

An account opened by executors or by administrators constitutes an account of the estate. The executors are the representatives of the estate and, unlike partners, have no personal interest in the account or in the estate's property. As each executor has the status of an agent, he is entitled to open an account in the name of the estate, and, equally, is entitled to countermand cheques drawn on it, be they drawn by himself or by another executor.[33] To avoid conflicts, banks usually ask for clear instructions concerning the drawing of cheques on an account of an estate. The bank's mandate is then spelt out in indisputable terms. To minimize the possibility of misappropriation of funds, the arrangement should provide that each cheque be signed by at least two executors.

---

[32] (1849) 11 Beav. 546; and see further, as regards the combination of accounts, pp. 152 et seq. above.

[33] *Gaunt* v. *Taylor* (1843) 2 Hare 413.

A problem that often arises in cases involving executors' accounts is whether or not the deceased's business can be carried on. The basic rule is that, in the absence of specific provisions in the will, the executors can carry on the business for the purpose of winding-up the estate; but they are not entitled to maintain it as a going concern.[34] Where the executors act within their authority, they are not liable if, in the course of the discharge of their duties, they make decisions which eventually lead to losses.[35] Furthermore, under sections 39 and 40 of the Administration of Estates Act 1925, the executors have the required incidental powers for carrying out their duties. This includes the power to borrow and to furnish security.

In some cases the will confers on the executors the power to continue the deceased's business either for a specified period of time or for such period as they consider advisable. In such a case the executors have both the power to conduct the busines and the required incidental or complementary powers. Thus, they are entitled to borrow for purposes of the business and, further, are able to give security over assets.[36] If the executor exceeds his powers, he is answerable in his personal capacity.[37]

Even if the will confers on the executors the power to continue to operate the deceased's business, it is advisable for a bank that is requested to grant the estate an overdraft or a loan to examine carefully the details of the transaction. It is, further, essential for the bank to ensure that the deceased's creditors have been paid or that they have given their approval to the transaction. Otherwise the creditors may take priority over the bank as regards the assets of the estate.[38] Undoubtedly, this advice is more easily given than followed in practice. Usually a bank does not wish to get involved in details concerning the winding-up of the estate of a deceased customer. The best solution is for the bank to obtain the executor's personal assurances regarding the purposes of the overdraft or loan. The bank is then in a position to recover from the executors any losses incurred due to the invalidity of the transaction.

If the executors have not given such an undertaking to the bank or are financially unable to make reimbursement, the bank may still succeed against the creditors provided it has a possessory as opposed to a non-

[34] Administration of Estates Act 1925, s. 49; and see *Marshall* v. *Broadhurst* (1831) 1 C & J 403; *Edwards* v. *Grace* (1826) 2 M & W 190; *Kirkman* v. *Booth* (1848) 11 Beav. 273; *Travis* v. *Milne* (1851) 9 Hare 141, 151–2; *Farhall* v. *Farhall* (1871) LR 7 Ch. App. 123. And see the Australian case of *Re Kerrigan* [1916] VLR 516.

[35] *Garret* v. *Noble* (1834) 6 Sim. 504.

[36] *Devitt* v. *Kearney* (1883) 13 LR Ir. 45. And see *Southwell* v. *Martin* (1901) 1 SR (NSW) Eq. 32; *Re Hammond* (1903) 3 SR (NSW) 270. The security is effective even if the executor acted in his personal interest, provided he remained within the scope of his general authority: *Attenborough* v. *Solomon* [1913] AC 76. And see the Trustee Act 1925, s 21.

[37] Cf. *Farhall* v. *Farhall* (1871) LR 7 Ch. App. 123.

[38] *Berry* v. *Gibbons* (1873) LR 8 Ch. App. 747, discussed below. There is often room for an argument that the executors' acts are ultra vires.

possessory security. In *Berry* v. *Gibbons*,[39] an executrix pledged with the bank a picture belonging to the estate so as to secure an overdraft. The bank granted the overdraft as it was not aware that administration proceedings had been successfully instituted against the executrix shortly before the transaction. As no receiver had been appointed at the time the bank obtained the pledge, it was held that the bank was entitled to enforce its security. However, the pledge in this case was, of course, a possessory security. It is questionable whether the bank could have enforced a non-possessory security, such as a floating charge or a bill of sale, in view of the determination of the executrix's appointment.

5. TRUST ACCOUNTS

(i) General principles

Trust accounts are opened mainly by executors appointed as trustees under a will, and by persons such as solicitors or trust companies who administer family or charitable trusts.

A trust does not constitute a legal entity separate from that of the trustees. Broadly, the principle is that the trustees have the legal title in the trust property and the *cestui que trust*, or beneficiary of the trust, acquires the equitable interest.[40] The trustees' function is to administer the trust in accordance with the deed under which they hold their appointment. In addition, certain powers and duties are conferred on them by the Trustee Act 1925.

Usually a trust deed requires the appointment of two or more trustees. The object of this arrangement is to ensure that the trust property is under the control of more than one designated person. Consequently, trustees are not usually permitted to delegate their authority.[41] For the same reason, and unless the trust deed makes a stipulation to the contrary, a cheque drawn on the trust account requires the signatures of all the trustees. Some mitigation to the principle that a trustee is not permitted to delegate his powers is, however, to be found in sections 23 and 25 of the Trustee Act 1925.[42] But even under this Act the absent trustee's powers cannot be delegated to a sole trustee, except to a trust corporation.

[39] (1873) LR 8 Ch. App. 747.
[40] D. B. Parker and A. R. Mellows, *The Modern Law of Trusts*, 4th edn., London, 1979, p. 8.
[41] *Re Flower and Metropolitan Board of Works* [1884] 27 Ch. D 592; *Green* v. *Whitehead* [1930] 1 Ch. 38.
[42] As amended by the Powers of Attorney Act 1971, s. 9(4); but *Green* v. *Whitehead* [1930] 1 Ch. 38, suggests that delegation of the power to sign cheques is excluded.

As the trustees have only the legal as distinct from the equitable title to the property, the problem of survivorship does not arise. When a trustee dies, another person is appointed either under the provisions of the will or by the court. Until such an appointment is made, section 18 of the Trustee Act 1925 authorizes the surviving trustee or trustees to carry on the business of the trust for the time being. It can also be carried on by personal representatives of the surviving trustee. It would appear to follow that in the event of the death of a trustee, the surviving trustee or trustees (or even the personal representatives of the last survivor) are entitled to draw cheques on the trust's account.

(ii) Borrowings by trustees

During any time at which an investment is being sought, the trustees are entitled to deposit trust money in a bank account.[43] Their right to borrow for the trust's purposes is restricted. Under section 16 of the 1925 Act, where the trustees are authorized either by law or under the trust deed to 'pay or apply capital money subject to the trust for any purpose or in any manner', they are deemed to have the power to raise the required amount by 'sale, conversion, calling in or mortgage of all or any part of the trust property'. Where the trustees have the power to mortgage they also have the complementary power of borrowing. There are specific statutory provisions which entitle the trustees to borrow money in given cases;[44] and, in certain situations, the power is spelt out in the trust deed. In addition, there is support for the view that the trustees have the power to borrow for the purpose of running the business of the trust.[45] Under section 17 of the 1925 Act, a purchaser or mortgagee who pays or advances money to the trust in reliance on the powers vested in the trustees in law or under the deed, is not 'concerned to see that such money is wanted, or that no more than is wanted is raised, or [concerned] otherwise as to the application thereof'.

It follows, therefore, that creditors or bona fide purchasers are protected provided they ensure that the transaction falls within the scope of the trustee's formal authority.

(iii) Duty of the bank

Does the same principle apply to transactions with banks? It will be recalled that the relationship of banker and customer may in certain cases be the

---

[43] Trustee Act 1925, s. 11; and see p. 59 above.
[44] Ibid., s. 16; and see also ibid., s. 28.
[45] *Dowse* v. *Gorton* [1891] AC 190; *Re Elijah Murphy Estate* (1930) 74 Sol. J 321.

subject of fiduciary duties owed by the bank.[46] To what extent is a bank thus liable if, in agreeing to grant a loan or in honouring a cheque, it has unwittingly assisted a trustee in carrying out an inappropriate transaction? It is, in this regard, important to distinguish between claims that may be raised against the bank by creditors of the estate and claims of the beneficiaries of the trust.

The question of the rights of creditors would arise only where, initially, the trustees were acting as executors of the deceased's will. It will be recalled that, in such cases, the bank is advised to ensure either that the creditors have been paid or that they have given their approval to the transaction. In these cases, the bank need concern itself solely with the initial creditors of the deceased. Debts incurred by the trustees in the course of the winding-up of the estate are not entitled to preference. It is obvious that the bank's concern with the propriety of the trustees' acts in cases of this type is based on their function as executors. In view of the narrow line of demarcation between executors and trustees, the bank is best advised to observe the proposed principle whenever it deals with representatives of an estate of a deceased person, be they executors, trustees, or administrators.

The bank's liability to the beneficiaries of the trust rests on a different basis. Equity protects the beneficiaries of a trust. Frequently it does so at the expense of innocent third parties who deal in good faith with a fraudulent trustee or with one who acts ultra vires.

The first basic rule for determining the bank's position is that no liability will be incurred by it to the beneficiaries unless it knows that the account involved is a trust account.[47] Naturally, the bank has knowledge if the account is expressly opened as such. Moreover, the words used to describe the account need not include the word 'trust'. Thus, in *Re Gross, ex p. Kingston*,[48] an official maintained two accounts with his bank. One was his personal account and the other was marked 'Police Account'. The official absconded whilst his personal account was in debit and the other account in credit. It was held that the bank could not combine the two accounts in order to set off the credit balance in the Police Account against the official's debit balance on his private account. Mellish LJ said that 'if an account is in plain terms headed in such a way that a banker cannot fail to know it to be a trust account, the balance standing to the credit of that account will, on the bankruptcy of the person who kept it, belong to the trust'.[49] Even if an account is not expressly marked or headed in a manner that proclaims its

---

[46] Pp. 84 et seq. above.
[47] *Thomson* v. *Clydesdale Bank Ltd.* [1893] AC 282; *Union Bank of Australia Ltd.* v. *Murray-Aynsley* [1898] AC 693; *Bank of New South Wales* v. *Goulburn Valley Butter Co. Pty. Ltd.* [1902] AC 543.
[48] (1871) LR 6 Ch. App. 632.
[49] Ibid., 640. Cf. *Re Wall* (1885) 1 TLR 522.

purpose, it will be treated as a trust account when there are some specific circumstances, such as the bank's familiarity with the will under which the trustees have opened the account. It is further thought that any knowledge of an officer of a bank, who has acquired it within the scope of his employment, is to be imputed to the bank.

It would be wrong, however, to conclude that whenever a customer maintains more than one account with his bank there is a presumption that one of them is a trust account.[50] The customer may open a number of accounts for the sake of convenience; he may, for example, wish to separate his personal or private transactions from those of a business carried on in his own name.

Thomson v. *Clydesdale Bank Ltd.*[51] is an interesting decision in point. The owners of certain shares ordered their stockbroker to sell them. The broker paid the cheque covering the price of the shares into his personal bank account, which was at that time overdrawn. Shortly thereafter the broker became insolvent, and the bank claimed priority in respect of the proceeds of the cheque. At the trial it was proved that the bank knew that the cheque covered the proceeds of the sale but did not know whether the money was in the stockbroker's hands as agent or in his own right. The House of Lords held that, under the circumstances, the bank was entitled to succeed. It did not have adequate notice of the transaction to be imputed with knowledge of the stockbroker's breach of trust. The decisions would have differed if the stockbroker had initially paid the cheque into his 'clients' account' and then withdrawn the funds by means of a cheque paid into his personal account.

The second general principle respecting liability in cases of breach of trust is that, primarily, the bank's concern is to ensure that the trustees act within the scope of their apparent powers. Thus, the bank has to ensure that a cheque drawn on the trust account carries all the required signatures. In the absence of express knowledge by the bank of an improper or a fraudulent design perpetrated by the trustees, the bank is not usually liable for their misconduct.[52] The bank is not required to assume the role of an amateur detective.

There are, however, situations in which a bank is not allowed to ignore a red flag that would suggest to a prudent businessman that something might be wrong. The typical case is that in which a trustee draws a cheque on a trust account and pays it to the credit of his personal account with the same bank. In *Foxton* v. *Manchester and Liverpool District Banking Co.*,[53] in

---

[50] Pp. 151–2 above.

[51] [1891] AC 282.

[52] *Re Gross, ex p. Kingston* (1871) LR 6 Ch. App. 632, 639; *Greenwood Teale* v. *William Williams, Brown & Co.* (1894) 11 TLR 56.

[53] (1881) 44 LT 406.

which such a cheque was drawn by the trustee in order to reduce his personal overdraft, Fry J held[54] that the bank had to establish that the payment was legitimate and proper. If the bank failed to discharge this onus of proof, it had to compensate the beneficiaries of the trust.

Some authorities have questioned this view.[55] They suggest that the onus of proof would be borne by the bank only if, before the collection of the cheque in question, the bank had struck a balance and became aware of the overdraft and pressed for payment. The opinion of Fry J has, however, been cited with approval by Farwell J in *Att.-Gen.* v. *De Winton,*[56] and is the one more likely to prevail. It is supported by *Rowlandson* v. *National Westminster Bank Ltd.,*[57] in which a bank was held liable to the beneficiaries where it permitted a trustee to draw cheques on the account for this personal purposes. It is noteworthy, in particular, that in this recent case the cheques were not even drawn to reduce an overdraft or an indebtedness of the customer to the bank.

The view expressed in an Australian authority,[58] to the effect that a bank would be liable only where it had actual knowledge of a fraudulent trustee's design, is thus believed to be too restrictive. Naturally, there are situations in which a trustee lawfully draws a cheque on the trust account to the credit of his personal account. Cheques drawn to reimburse expenses incurred by the trustees or to arrange for payment of his remuneration constitute good illustrations. But where the cheque is for a particularly large amount, or where the circumstances are out of the ordinary, the bank ought to be put on its guard.[59]

The circumstances that ought to give a bank notice of a breach of trust are best illustrated by *John* v. *Dodwell & Co. Ltd.*[60] A firm authorized its manager to draw on its bank account. The manager abused his power by drawing cheques for the payment of the price of shares purchased in his own name. His stockbrokers took these cheques in good faith; they were, however, aware of the fact that the manager was drawing the cheques on his employers' account. It was held that the employers were entitled to recover the amounts of the cheques from the stockbrokers, whose knowledge that the shares were to be acquired in the manager's own name put them on notice. This decision shows that an agent must exercise a degree of vigilance where a trustee appears to exercise his powers in an irregular manner. Undoubtedly, if the stockbrokers in *Dodwell & Co.*'s case had made an

---

[54] Ibid., p. 408.
[55] *Gray* v. *Johnston* (1868) LR 3 HL 1; *Coleman* v. *Bucks and Oxon Union Bank* [1897] 2 Ch. 243.
[56] [1906] 2 Ch. 106, 116.
[57] [1978] 1 W.L.R 798.
[58] *Fuglsang* v. *English Scottish and Australian Bank Ltd.* [1959] Tas. SR 155.
[59] See further, pp. 84 et seq. above.
[60] [1918] AC 563.

enquiry and been given a plausible explanation, such as that the shares were acquired in a nominee's name for tax purposes, they would have discharged their duty. A particular circumstance which ought to put a bank on notice is if the proceeds of a cheque drawn on a trust account are used to reduce the trustee's indebtedness to the bank. In *Gray* v. *Johnston*,[61] Lord Cairns observed that where the bank stands to benefit from the trustee's breach of trust, 'that circumstance, above all others, will most readily establish the fact that the bankers are in privity with the breach of trust'.[62]

6. SOLICITORS' ACCOUNTS

(i) Operation of the account

The term 'clients' account' or 'solicitors' account' describes an account opened by a solicitor in order to deposit clients' money. The need to treat a clients' account as a separate fund arises because such accounts have been the subject of legislation which lays down an accounting procedure that precludes the co-mingling of clients' moneys with the solicitors' own funds. The procedure seeks to combat both fraud and carelessness in the handling of the solicitors' trust funds. The provision conferring the power to make rules on the Law Society is section 32 of the Solicitors Act 1974. Under section 87, the rules are meant to apply to a solicitor's account regardless of whether it is opened in the name of a single member of the profession or as a joint account in the name of several practitioners. The rules made under the 1974 Act are the Solicitors' Accounts Rules 1975 and the Solicitors' Trust Accounts Rules 1975.

A detailed survey of the rules made by the Law Society is outside the scope of this work. From a bank's point of view, the only important provision is section 85 of the 1974 Act. According to this section, a bank is not under a duty to enquire into, and is not deemed to have any knowledge of, any right of a person to any money paid or credited to the clients' account 'which it would not incur or be under or be deemed to have in the case of an account kept by a person entitled absolutely to all the money paid or credited to it'. This section deals solely with the rights of persons to money paid or credited to the account; it does not refer to the bank's duties in respect of amounts drawn on the account by the solicitor. Thus, it can be safely presumed that the bank owes no duty to the solicitor's client as regards drawing on the account.[63] Indeed, under rule 7 of the 1975 Rules, a

---

[61] (1868) LR 3 HL 1.
[62] Ibid., 11.
[63] And note that the bank is under a less stringent duty to heed a red signal than any other agent: *Penmount Estates Ltd.* v. *National Provincial Bank Ltd.* (1945) 173 LT 344.

solicitor is entitled to draw on the type of trust account here discussed. Unless the cheque is drawn in circumstances which are clearly suspicious or which are out of the ordinary, the bank is not liable to the solicitor's client for a misappropriation of the funds.

(ii) Garnishee orders and related problems: who owns the balance?

Occasionally a creditor of a solicitor seeks to have a garnishee order applied both to the balance standing to the credit of a solicitor's personal account and to that of the clients' account. In *Plunkett* v. *Barclays Bank Ltd.*,[64] a clients' account was frozen by the bank when a garnishee order nisi was served on it. A cheque drawn by the solicitor on the clients' account was, accordingly, dishonoured by the bank and returned to the holder with the words 'refer to drawer' written on it. Dismissing the solicitor's action brought against the bank in defamation and in breach of contract, Du Parcq J observed:[65]

I find it impossible to say that money paid into a client account kept with a bank in the name of a solicitor is not a debt owing from the banker to the solicitor.

Thus, the account in question could be garnished by the solicitor's creditor. However, under O. 45 r. 5 of the Rules of the Supreme Court, the solicitor was entitled to notify the court that certain moneys attached by the garnishee order nisi were the property of a third party. The court would then make the order required to protect the client's interest.

Plunkett's case may be questioned. It has been shown that funds standing to the credit of a clients' account maintained by a solicitor are trust funds. It is accepted that the bank cannot set off against a credit balance standing to the credit of such an account, a debit balance in the solicitor's personal account.[66] Moreover, once the order nisi has been served, the solicitor is bound to notify the court that the balance in the clients' account does not comprise his own funds. Would it not have been more realistic to treat the balance as such also for the purposes of the order nisi? The garnishment of the account, followed by the release of funds by a court order, involves a wasteful and complex procedure.

The argument that it is unrealistic to regard the amounts standing to the credit of the clients' account as constituting the solicitor's money derives support from cases decided in respect of three problems. The first concerns

---

[64] [1936] 2 KB 107.

[65] Ibid., 118. But note that the order would not be made absolute except to the extent that the solicitor has a lien over the funds: *Loescher* v. *Dean* [1950] Ch. 491; *Re a Solicitor* [1952] Ch. 328.

[66] Pp. 151 et seq. above. Note also that funds standing to the credit of a client's account cannot be set off as against the solicitor's personal liability: Solicitors Act 1974, s 85(b).

the solicitor's bankruptcy. Under section 306(1) of the Insolvency Act 1986, only the 'estate' of the bankrupt vests in his trustee in bankruptcy. Under section 283(3)(a), property held by the bankrupt as a fiduciary or in trust is not treated as part of his estate. It has actually been held that the balance in the clients' account does not vest in the solicitor's trustee.[67] Secondly, in *Loscher* v. *Dean*[68] it was held that a solicitor was entitled to exercise a lien over funds standing to the credit of his clients' account in respect of amounts due for professional services rendered by him. If the amount standing to the credit of the clients' account constituted the solicitor's own property, how could he have a lien over it? Thirdly, it has been held that interest accrued on a clients' account cannot be retained by the solicitor. He has to account for the profit so made to his clients.[69] Obviously the balance on which the interest has accrued is not treated as beneficially owned by the solicitor.

It is submitted that these decisions are irreconcilable with the judgment of Du Parcq J in *Plunkett*'s case. It is preferable to regard the balance standing to the credit of the clients' account as unattachable by a garnishee order served on the bank in respect of a debt incurred by the solicitor in his personal capacity.

7. ESTATE AGENTS' ACCOUNTS

The business of estate agents resembles that of solicitors in one important regard. Estate agents handle large amounts of money on behalf of clients. Accounts opened by estate agents for the purpose of handling clients' money are regulated under the Estate Agents Act 1979. Under section 14(1) of the Act, estate agents are required to maintain clients' accounts. Under section 12, third parties' moneys, received by an agent in his capacity as bailee, as stakeholder, or in any other capacity, have to be paid to the credit of such an account. Banks are among the institutions with whom a clients' account may be opened.[70]

Section 13 of the Act provides that funds standing to the credit of a clients' account constitute trust money. It follows that the bank's position in respect of clients' accounts maintained by an estate agent is the same as its position in respect of solicitors' accounts. Moreover, it is arguable that the position is the same at common law. If an estate agent opens an account and

---

[67] *Re a Solicitor* [1952] Ch. 328.
[68] [1950] Ch. 491.
[69] *Brown* v. *IRC* [1965] AC 244.
[70] Estate Agents (Accounts) Regulations 1981, SI 1520, reg. 2 and Sched. The relevant provisions of the Act itself came into effect on 3 May 1982: Estate Agents Act 1979 (Commencement no. 1) Order 1981, SI 1517.

designates it a 'clients' account', he manifests the intention of using it in order to pay to its credit fund which he holds on behalf of customers. The fact that the funds are impounded with a trust is therefore brought to the bank's attention.

8. LOCAL AUTHORITIES

(i) *General principles*

A local authority constitutes a legal personality. Its employees are all in a position of trust. The bank of the local authority is conversant with this fact. Thus, it has to bear in mind that when the officers or employees of the authority enter into transactions on its behalf, they have to act within the powers exercisable by the authority itself and, further, have to remain within the scope of their individual mandate.

The law governing local authorities in the United Kingdom underwent substantial changes in the course of the last two decades.[71] At present the powers of local authorities are set out in three pieces of legislation: the Local Government Act 1972; the Local Government (Miscellaneous Provisions) Act 1976, which introduces certain amendments to the 1972 Act but which has no bearing on questions of banking law; and the Local Government Act 1985.

The bank's duty to honour cheques drawn by a local authority depends on the instructions given to it. Generally, the functions of the local authority may be discharged by a Council Committee or some other governing body.

(ii) *Operation of accounts and power to borrow*

Section 172 of the 1972 Act, as explained in Part 1 of Schedule 13, defines how payments are to be made to the credit of the local authority's account and out of it. The account itself can now be maintained in the authority's own name. It need not be opened in the treasurer's name, as used to be the practice in the nineteenth century.

Schedule 13 further regulates the power to borrow. Paragraph 1 authorizes borrowings for two purposes. First, a local authority has the power to borrow in order to relend the amount obtained to another local authority. Secondly, it may borrow money for any purpose sanctioned by the Secretary of State. However, under paragraph 10(1) of the same Schedule, a local authority does not require the approval of the Secretary of State if it wishes to apply to a bank for a temporary loan or overdraft for the purpose of

---

[71] For an excellent review of the general development, see Chorley, *Gilbart Lectures* 1968.

defraying certain expenses. Paragraph 2, which spells out the means that may be utilized in order to raise money, sanctions the granting of mortgages and of debentures.

(iii) Liability of the bank

The position of a bank that grants a local authority a loan or an overdraft for one of the above purposes is reasonably safe. Naturally, it is advisable for a bank to satisfy itself that the application for a loan is made by a duly authorized body of the local authority.[72] Primarily, the bank has to ascertain that the transaction is within the powers of the authority as defined by the Act and within the mandate of the officers with whom it deals. It further has to satisfy itself that the mandate has been duly issued by the Council or by the appropriate committee. However, even if the banks commits an error, it is not necessarily deprived of a remedy. Under paragraph 20 of Schedule 13, a person lending money to a local authority 'shall not be bound to inquire whether the borrowing of the money is legal or regular or whether the money raised was properly applied and shall not be prejudiced by an illegality or irregularity, or by the misapplication or non-application of that money'.

Paragraph 20 is of major importance in the case of borrowings made by local authorities in the short-term money market. Dealings in this market require to be conducted promptly. The careful perusal of a transaction, which is generally advisable where a bank considers extending a medium- or long-term loan to a customer, is out of place.

It has been suggested that paragraph 20 is of an all-embracing nature.[73] On this basis the section ought to apply to a transaction involving a loan made to a local authority by its own bank. The point, though, is questionable. Undoubtedly, the paragraph exonerates casual lenders, such as money market operators, from a duty to enquire into the powers of the persons approaching them on behalf of the local authority. A fortiori, it liberates the lender from any duty to examine the object of the loan and whether it is within the ambit of the legitimate powers of the authority. But can it be said with certainty that the same sweeping principle is applicable where the lender is the local authority's own bank? Whilst, in all probability, the bank is not bound to make any enquiries in its capacity as lender, the position is complicated by the bank's special relationship with its customer, the local authority. It has been shown that, in certain cases, a bank owes fiduciary duties to its customer. Moreover, it is clear that the contract of banker and

---

[72] *Southend-on-Sea Corporation* v. *Hodgson (Hickford) Ltd.* [1962] 1 QB 416. Note that the local authority must remain within the ambit of its powers: *William Bean & Son* v. *Flaxton Rural District Council* [1929] 1 KB 450.

[73] Paget, *Law of Banking*, p. 37.

customer is not merely one of lender and creditor.[74] In view of the nature of this agreement, it is believed that a local authority's own bankers ought to peruse with care any application for a loan made on its behalf.

9. COMPANIES' ACCOUNTS

(i) General principles

A company, like a local authority, has a legal personality of its own, regardless of whether it is a public corporation or a private company. This means that companies can enter into contracts in their given name and can sue and be sued.[75] In this way, companies differ from partnerships, which are identifiable with the partners.[76]

Until 1972, a bank dealing with a company had to satisfy itself that a transaction was not ultra vires the 'object clauses' of its memorandum of association or the powers conferred on its directors by the articles of association. Thus, a loan secured by a charge over the body corporate's assets was unenforceable where it was acquired for a purpose not sanctioned by the memorandum.[77]

The doctrine of ultra vires, which presented hurdles to banks dealing with companies, has been substantially modified by section 9(1) of the European Communities Act 1972 which has become section 35 of the 1985 Act:

(1) In favour of a person dealing with a company in good faith, any transaction decided by the directors is deemed to be one which is within the capacity of the company to enter into, and the powers of the directors to bind the company is deemed to be free of any limitation under the memorandum or articles of association.

(2) A party to a transaction so decided on is not bound to enquire as to the capacity of the company to enter into it or as to any such limitation on the powers of the directors, and is presumed to have acted in good faith unless the contrary is proved.

The object of this provision was to harmonize the law of the United Kingdom with that of the civil law jurisdictions within the EEC. But the section does not abolish the doctrine altogether.[78] First, section 9(1) applies only where the dealings are with directors. This, however, is a point that banks

---

[74] Chap. 4 above.

[75] See, generally, L. C. B. Gower, Modern Company Law, 4th edn., London, 1979, ch. 5.

[76] Pp. 175–6 above.

[77] For a case in modern times, see *Re Introductions Ltd.* [1970] Ch. 199. The general ambit of the doctrine of ultra vires and the power of the directors to bind a company is outside the scope of this book.

[78] See generally, Gower, *Modern Company Law*, 4th edn., pp. 178–9, who is critical of the provision and who regards ultra vires as remaining in effect to a certain extent. And see *Palmer's Company Law*, 23rd edn., London, 1982, pp. 126–7.

are inclined to observe as a matter of course. Secondly, the section applies only 'in favour of a person dealing with a company in good faith'. Thus, a person cannot rely on section 35 to enforce a contract which he knows to have been executed by a company whilst acting ultra vires its objects or by its directors acting in breach of their mandate. His position, it is believed, continues to depend on the common law principles which, of course, give prominence to the doctrine of ultra vires generally. It is true that under section 35 it is presumed that a party dealing with a company is acting in good faith. But it remains to be seen whether the close relationship of banker and customer may induce a court to treat the presumption as easily rebutted in this context. To avoid the danger of litigation, it remains a sound practice for the bank to study carefully a transaction which it is asked to finance, to satisfy itself that it is in the company's interests and for its objects. A particular consideration in point is that a company's business is, of necessity, transacted by agents acting on its behalf.[79]

(ii) Lending to a company

Generally, the memorandum of association confers on a company wide powers to transact business and to borrow money. Even whilst the ultra vires doctrine was in full effect, it was held that a trading company could borrow, although its power to do so was not spelt out in the memorandum. The reason for this was that, in the case of a trader, the power to borrow was considered incidental to the power to carry on business.[80] Up to 1972, banks had to satisfy themselves that the power was exercised for the purpose of the company's valid objects.[81] The position has been affected by the enactment of section 9(1) of the European Communities Act 1972, although it remains good banking practice to peruse carefully each transaction.

The power to borrow is not automatically conferred on a non-trading company, such as a holding company, whose only function is to own property on behalf of its shareholders. Non-trading companies do not usually require the power to borrow. Banks are aware of this. Despite section 35, they should examine the documents carefully before entering into an arrangement to grant a loan or overdraft to such a company.

[79] See, in this regard, pp. 84 et seq. above.
[80] *General Auction Estate and Monetary Co.* v. *Smith* [1891] 3 Ch. 432; cf. *Re Jon Beauforte (London) Ltd.* [1953] Ch. 131.
[81] *Re Jon Beauforte (London) Ltd.*, above. But even then, the problem was of restricted importance, as art. 79 of Table A of the Companies Act 1948 conferred on the directors very wide borrowing powers and also the power to grant security. Further protection was conferred by the rule in *Royal British Bank* v. *Turquand* (1856) 6 E & B 327, as applied to banks in *Mahoney* v. *East Holyford Mining Co. (in Liq.)* (1875) LR 7 HL 869, showing that it was not incumbent on a bank to investigate whether the directors of a company had been properly appointed.

(iii) Dealings in negotiable instruments and current account operations

The legal position concerning dealings in negotiable instruments issued by companies is governed by section 37 of the Companies Act 1985 which, for all practical purposes, is identical with section 33 of the Companies Act 1948. Section 37 reads:

A bill of exchange or promissory note is deemed to have been made, accepted or endorsed on behalf of the company if made, accepted or endorsed in the name of, or by or on behalf or on account of, the company by a person acting under its authority.

It has been pointed out that this provision has two major shortcomings.[82] First, it does not mention cheques. Secondly, it refers to the making, to the acceptance, and to the indorsement of negotiable instruments, but not to the drawing thereof. In truth, though, these shortcomings are of little significance. The draftsmanship of the section is explained by historical reasons. Section 37 originated as section 47 of the Companies Act 1862. At that time, the terminology applicable to negotiable instruments was considerably less uniform than it became twenty years later at the time of the enactment of the Bills of Exchange Act 1882. In practice, the reference to bills of exchange in section 37 is wide enough to cover cheques, which are bills of exchange drawn on a banker and payable on demand.[83] The word 'make', which in the 1882 Act is used only in respect of promissory notes, must, in the context of section 37, include the word 'draw', which is used to describe the issuing of bills of exchange including cheques. The reference to the company's 'name' in section 37 is believed to be to its registered name.[84]

Section 37, however, has a somewhat narrower scope than may be thought initially. In considering the exact effect of the section, it is important to distinguish between two types of dealings by a bank in negotiable instruments. The first is the discount or negotiation of such instruments. Basically this type of business is confined to bills of exchange (other than cheques) and to promissory notes. The bank may purchase a bill of exchange drawn by the customer, or it may purchase from the customer a bill payable to him. Moreover, in some cases the bank may simply add its indorsement on the back of the bill. In all these cases the discount, the negotiation or the indorsement has the object of enabling the customer to obtain funds forthwith against an instrument maturing at a future date. In the case of a discount or negotiation, he obtains funds from the bank itself;

---

[82] Paget, *Law of Banking*, 9th edn., p. 41.

[83] Bills of Exchange Act 1882, s. 73.

[84] *Maxform SpA* v. *Mariani and Goodville Ltd.* [1979] 2 Lloyd's Rep. 385, 389, decided under s. 108(4) of the Companies Act 1948, under which a director is personally liable to pay a company's bill, note, or cheque if its name is not accurately written on it in legible characters: *Chitty on Contracts*, 25th edn., London, 1983, vol. 2, para. 2477.

in the case of the bank's accommodation indorsement, he is able to discount the bill in the money market. He thus obtains the funds from a third party in reliance on the bank's promise. The same object is served by the discount, negotiation or indorsement of a promissory note. It could equally be the case if the instrument discounted were a post-dated cheque.

The second type of dealing by a bank in negotiable instruments is the honouring of cheques drawn on it by a customer. The object of such a transaction is completely different from that of the negotiation, discount, or indorsement of bills or notes. When a bank pays a cheque drawn by a customer, it obeys its mandate and, further, repays a debt accrued at the time of the deposit of the funds. Thus, when the bank honours its customer's cheques it acts as an agent and as debtor;[85] when it negotiates, discounts or indorses the customer's bills or notes, it acts as a credit provider or as a dealer in negotiable instruments.

It seems clear that section 37 protects a bank which negotiates, discounts or indorses bills of exchange or promissory notes. But does it apply to the honouring by a bank of cheques drawn on it by a corporate customer? Undoubtedly, the cheque purports to be 'made' or drawn on behalf of the customer. The payee or an indorsee thereof would thus be entitled to rely on section 37 in order to preclude the company from pleading an abuse of authority. But the drawee bank does not pay the instrument in view of its negotiable character. Provided the customer's account is in credit, the bank would honour a 'payment instruction' even if it were a non-negotiable instrument such as a conditional order or a non-tranferable cheque. It is believed that, as the bank which honours a cheque acts as an agent and not as a dealer in negotiable instruments, its position in this type of case depends on common law principles and not on section 37.

The common law doctrine which is applicable in cases of this type does not necessarily deprive the bank of protection. The usual type of circumstances that occur in practice are that a director or the company's secretary, who is by its article given the necessary authority to draw a cheque, exercises his powers in fraud of the company. The director or secretary may either abuse an actual authority validly conferred on him or may proffer to the bank a false document purporting to permit him to draw.

Some authorities treat an agent or purported agent who acts in this manner as having the implied authority to draw the instrument.[86] They protect

---

[85] Pp. 127–8 above.

[86] *Biggerstaff* v. *Rowatt's Wharf Ltd.* [1896] 2 Ch. 93, 102; *Hambro* v. *Burnand* [1904] 2 KB 10, 23; *Dey* v. *Pullinger Engineering Co.* [1921] 1 KB 77; *British Thomson-Houston Co. Ltd.* v. *Federated European Bank Ltd.* [1932] 2 KB 176. And see *Re Land Credit Co. of Ireland, ex p. Overend, Gurney & Co.* (1869) LR 4 Ch. App. 460, to which the doctrine is traceable. But note that the bill or cheque may be a total forgery and hence ineffective in the holder's hands: *Kreditbank Cassel GmbH* v. *Schenkers Ltd.* [1927] 1 KB 826.

the bank despite the abuse of the agent's powers. The rationale is that the bank's only duty is to demand a document which confers on the director or secretary the necessary authority. The bank need not verify the validity of the authorizing document or the agent's proper use of his powers.

Other decisions restrict the wide principle supported by the general body of authority. First, some cases suggest that the bank could not rely on the director's or secretary's implied authority unless the bank had good reason to believe that it existed. *Rama Corporation Ltd.* v. *Proved Tin and General Investment Ltd.*[87] is a case in point. Here Slade J held that a person could not plead an agent's implied or apparent authority unless he relied on it when he entered into the contract with the principal.

Secondly, it has been decided that a bank's ability to rely on an agent's apparent authority depends on what is being held out in respect of this agent by the company.[88] The bank is not entitled to assume[89] that the agent has an authority wider than that to be inferred from the position occupied by him or from the representation made in respect of him.[90]

Thirdly, the bank has to exercise care where the person with whom it deals is not a director. In the recent case of *British Bank of the Middle East* v. *Sun Life Assurance Co. of Canada*,[91] an undertaking of an insurance company to repay a bank amounts advanced to a property developer was held invalid as the senior officers of the company, who executed it, did not have the required express or implied authority.

Fourthly, it has been suggested in *Alexander Stewart & Son of Dundee Ltd.* v. *Westminster Bank Ltd.*[92] that suspicious circumstances should put the bank on enquiry. If the bank fails to observe a red signal, it cannot rely on an agent's implied authority which it has failed to investigate. A leading authority[93] has argued that this rule is wrongly decided as it conflicts with the decision of the House of Lords in *London Joint Stock Bank* v. *Simmons*.[94] It is true that in the last case Lord Herschell observed that the doctrine of constructive notice does not apply in the field of negotiable instruments. On this basis it is arguable that the concept of the bank's duty

---

[87] [1952] 2 QB 147.
[88] *A. L. Underwood Ltd.* v. *Bank of Liverpool and Martins* [1924] 1 KB 775, p. 786, per Bankes LJ, and 791–2 per Scrutton LJ.
[89] See, e.g., *Houghton & Co.* v. *Nothard, Lowe & Wills Ltd.* [1927] 1 KB 246, affd. on a different ground: [1928] AC 1.
[90] For a detailed analysis, see Gower, *Modern Company Law*, 4th edn., pp. 193–6, who considers also the effect of s. 9(1) of the European Communities Act 1972.
[91] [1983] 2 Lloyd's Rep. 9.
[92] [1926] WN 126 revd. ibid. 271; and see *B. Liggett (Liverpool) Ltd.* v. *Barclays Bank Ltd.* [1928] 1 KB 48, concerning suspicious circumstances surrounding the appointment of a director.
[93] Paget, *Law of Banking*, p. 43, who relies on *Bank of Bengal* v. *Fagan* (1849) 7 Moo. PC 61, 72; *Hambro* v. *Burnand* [1904] 2 KB 10; *Dey* v. *Pullinger Engineering Co.* [1921] 1 KB 77.
[94] [1892] AC 201.

to make such enquiries when it encounters suspicious circumstances is inapplicable in transactions involving cheques, bills of exchange and promissory notes. It is submitted that, where the bank merely deals in these instruments by discounting them, the point is well taken. But the position is different where the bank makes decisions concerning the handling of cheques drawn on the account of a corporate customer. Here the bank may owe the company—its customer—the type of duty of care discussed earlier.[95]

It is believed that the obvious difficulty in reconciling the cases in point elucidates the bank's correct course of action. The bank is best advised to exercise care when cheques are drawn on a corporate customer's account by an officer or employee. Usually the bank discharges its obligation by verifying that the instrument in question is drawn by duly authorized persons.[96] Thus, the document can be taken at face value, provided it is executed in the manner prescribed in the articles. The bank's duty may, however, be a more stringent one where a red signal manifests itself. The classic example is the drawing of a substantial cheque on the company's account for the credit of the fraudulent drawer's own overdrawn account.

Usually, though, it is clear that the absence of actual authority on the part of the person who purports to transact business on behalf of the company does not necessarily defeat the bank. In *Freeman and Lockyer* v. *Buckhurst Park Properties (Mangal) Ltd.*[97] it was held that in such a case a person who relies on the agent's authority is entitled to succeed if he is able to establish three points. First, it has to be shown that the party who relied on the agent's authority acted on a representation made to him. Secondly, the representation must have been made by a person who had the genuine or actual authority to manage the company's affairs. Thirdly, the transaction in question must not be ultra vires the memorandum of association. However, this last requirement has been rendered obsolete by section 9(1) of the European Communities Act 1972 (now s. 35 of the 1985 Act.)

The principles discussed above apply to trading companies. In the case of non-trading companies it is again necessary to draw a clear distinction between dealings in negotiable instruments and the use of cheques drawn on the company's account. Dealings in negotiable instruments are associated with financial institutions and commercial enterprises. It would be unusual for a non-trading company to draw or to indorse a bill or to make a promissory note unless it had the express power to do so under its memorandum

---

[95] And see, further, the special duty of care that may be imposed on a bank under the rule in *Selangor United Rubber Estates Ltd.* v. *Cradock (No. 3)* [1968] 1 WLR 1555, discussed above, pp. 89–91.

[96] Note that s. 9(1) of the European Communities Act 1972 does not free the bank from its duty to verify that the person with whom it is dealing is a director.

[97] [1964] 2 QB 480 explained in *Hely-Hutchinson* v. *Brayhead Ltd.* [1968] 1 QB 549. And see *British Bank of the Middle East* v. *Sun Life Assurance Co. of Canada* [1983] 2 Lloyd's Rep. 9.

of association. The opening of a current account and the drawing of cheques stands on a different footing. In modern practice, it is impossible for any body corporate, partnership or private firm to manage its affairs without a current account. The settlement in cash of outstanding accounts is not feasible in the present stage of an industrial economy. Thus, a non-trading firm, such as a holding company, has to use cheques to pay rates due in respect of its properties and, further, requires a bank account to facilitate the collection of rentals paid by cheques by its tenants. It is believed that, as regards the maintenance of a current account and the drawing of cheques on it, there is no longer any room for a distinction between trading and non-trading companies.

10. UNINCORPORATED ASSOCIATIONS' ACCOUNTS

Unincorporated associations are mainly bodies such as clubs, literary societies and charitable institutions. The objects of such bodies are primarily non-commercial. Frequently they decide not to incorporate in order to avoid the expense involved. The decision may also be motivated by a wish not to be mistaken for a trading enterprise. The funds of an unincorporated association are usually obtained from subscriptions and donations.

It is clear that an unincorporated association needs a bank account, to be utilized for the payment and collection of cheques. Moreover, in some cases it may need to borrow money in order to carry out its objectives. Thus, a club may wish to raise credit in order to arrange for the acquisition of its premises. A bank that accepts such a body as a customer and opens an account in its name has to be aware of some of the relevant fundamental principles.

The most important of these is that an unincorporated association does not have an independent legal personality. It follows that such an association can neither sue nor be sued in its own name.[98] Actions have to be brought against the committee that acts on behalf of the body. In reality, this involves an anomaly. An agent is sued on behalf of a principal who is known to all parties to be legally non-existent.

Who, then, is liable for the debts of the unincorporated association? Usually the liability of members is expressly restricted to the amount of the subscription or membership fee due from them. The action, which has to be brought against the committee, is basically instituted in order to recover the amount claimed from the funds of the association. But members of the committee may be personally liable as well. The point is best illustrated by

---

[98] But see, as regards the special problems of unregistered trade unions, *Taff Vale Railway Co.* v. *Amalgamated Society of Railway Servants* [1901] AC 426; *Willis* v. *Association of Universities of the British Commonwealth* [1964] 2 All ER 39.

Coutts & Co. v. *Irish Exhibition in London.*[99] An association was formed for the purpose of organizing an Irish arts exhibition. Initially the body was unincorporated and functioned through a committee. An overdraft of the association's current account was granted by the bank on the personal assurance of the committee members. Shortly thereafter the association was incorporated, but then had to be wound up due to the failure of the enterprise. The bank brought an action to recover the amount of the overdraft from the committee members. It was established that the account had not been officially transferred into the corporation's name and that the bank had not released the committee members from their liability. It was held that the committee members were the bank's customers and, accordingly, obliged to reimburse the amount involved.

The committee is not entitled to go beyond the powers conferred on it in the constitution of the association.[100] As long as it remains within the scope of its authority the committee has the power to delegate. In *Bradley Egg Farm Ltd.* v. *Clifford,*[101] it was held that the committee members were bound by the acts of a duly appointed agent. In *Fleming* v. *Hector,*[102] Lord Abinger CB held that the committee of an unincorporated club was entitled to delegate to an agent its power to draw and to indorse bills of exchange. His Lordship reached this conclusion on the basis of the terms of the constitution of the club in question. In modern practice it is common to include in the constitution of an unincorporated association an express power authorizing the committee to delegate such powers as it sees fit, including the power to operate its current account.

In its dealings with an unincorporated association the bank is advised to follow a few rules dictated both by prudence and by legal considerations. Where the bank accepts an unincorporated body as a customer, the bank should ask for clear instructions as to who is entitled to operate the association's account. Ideally, the bank should obtain a copy of the constitution or, failing that, a copy of a resolution concerning the opening of and drawing upon the association's account.

The bank has to be more cautious when the association requires an overdraft or a loan. It is clear that ordinary members of the association are not liable for its debts unless they have expressed their individual consent to the transaction. As pointed out above, the members of the committee are personally liable; but the bank's ability to recover from them depends, of course, on their financial standing. The best advice that can be given to the

---

[99] (1891) 7 TLR 313. As regards the committee members' right to be indemnified, see *Wise* v. *Perpetual Trustee Co. Ltd.* [1903] AC 139, 149.
[100] The position is the same as in the case of local authorities, as to which see *William Bean & Sons* v. *Flaxton Rural District Council* [1929] 1 KB 450.
[101] [1943] 2 All ER 378.
[102] (1836) 2 M & W 172.

bank is to extend credit to an unincorporated association only against adequate security.

11. MARRIED WOMEN'S ACCOUNTS

(i) Operation of account

A series of Acts commencing with section 7 of the Married Women's Property Act 1882, and culminating in the Married Women's Property Act 1964,[103] conferred on married women the power to enter into contracts and to bind their estates as if they were unmarried. It follows that, when a bank opens a current account in the name of a married woman, it need not have misgivings as regards its customer's ability to bind herself.

At one stage a bank had to exercise caution when it collected for the credit of a married woman's account a cheque payable to her husband. The concern was that the cheque in question might have been obtained by the husband by means of a fraud perpetrated on his employers.[104] It is believed that, in modern banking practice, this point is obsolete. It would be unrealistic to claim at present that a bank acts negligently if it fails to familiarize itself with the occupation of a married customer's spouse.

One danger faced in the case of married women's accounts is that money which in law is due to the husband may find its way into the wife's account. But it has been held that unless the bank is aware of an irregularity, it would incur no liability. Thus, *Re Montague, ex p. Ward*[105] decided that the husband's trustee in bankruptcy could not recover from the bank amounts paid out against cheques wrongfully drawn by the wife on his funds. However, a husband would undoubtedly be able to obtain a tracing order if money of his, acquired by his wife by means of a trick, was still standing to the credit of her account. The same rights would, of course, accrue to the wife where her husband had improperly acquired her property.[106]

(ii) Borrowing by married women

At present there is no room for a suggestion that a bank is under a special duty of care where a customer who is a married woman applies for a loan. The bank's decision as to whether to grant or refuse accommodation depends on commercial considerations. A problem arises, however, when a

---

[103] See, generally, *Chitty on Contracts*, 25th edn., vol. 2, paras. 593–4.
[104] *Lloyds Bank Ltd.* v. *Savory & Co.* [1933] AC 201, as to which see p. 425 below.
[105] (1897) 76 LT 203.
[106] See, generally, P. H. Pettit, *Equity and the Law of Trusts*, 5th edn., London, 1984, ch. 24.

spouse wishes to borrow money against what may turn out to be joint property, such as the family home or car. In such cases the bank has to be satisfied that the property to be charged is owned in full by the borrower. Where it turns out to be joint property, the bank has to acquire the consent to the charge of both spouses. The problem is a serious one, as it has been held that a spouse acquires an equitable interest in the family property by contributing some of the funds for its acquisition.[107] A mortgagee's rights would in such a case be subordinate to those of the contributing spouse unless both had acquiesced in the arrangement. It stands to reason that, in many cases, the contributing spouse's rights might be impaired by an estoppel. To raise this plea, it would be adequate to prove that the spouse in question knew about the mortgage arrangement and allowed it to go ahead.

(iii) Wife's guarantee of husband's debt

In certain cases a husband may ask his wife to guarantee to his bank a personal loan or overdraft. As a matter of practice the bank should in such cases suggest that the wife seek independent legal advice. Failure to suggest that such advice be sought is not, however, fatal. The question was discussed in Chapter 4.[108]

12. MINORS' ACCOUNTS[109]

(i) General principles relevant in the context of banking

The age of majority in the United Kingdom used to be twenty-one years. But under section 1 of the Family Law Reform Act 1969 the age was reduced to eighteen years. At common law, a contract made by a person who had not come of age (described as 'minor' or 'infant') was, basically, voidable at his option. This meant that a contract could be enforced by a minor but not against him.[110] The position was drastically changed by the Infants Relief Act 1874. Under section 1, three types of contract entered into by minors are void: contracts for the repayment of money lent, contracts for the supply of goods, and all accounts stated. Under subsection (2), a void contract of these types cannot be ratified when the minor reaches majority. The 1874

---

[107] *Williams and Glyn's Bank Ltd.* v. *Boland* [1979] Ch. 312; see also *Bristol and West Building Society* v. *Henning* [1985] 2 All ER 606; *Kingsnorth Trust Ltd.* v. *Tizard* [1986] 2 All ER 54.

[108] Pp. 85–89 above.

[109] See, generally, *Anson's Law of Contract*, 26th edn., ed. A. G. Guest, Oxford, 1985, pp. 183–203; G. H. Treitel, *Law of Contract*, 6th edn., London, 1983, pp. 409 et seq.

[110] But note that even now the view is that the contract is void at the minor's option: *Chitty on Contracts*, 25th edn., paras. 575 et seq.; G. H. Treitel, 'The Infants Relief Act 1874' (1957) 73 LQR 194.

Act is augmented by the Betting and Loans (Infants) Act 1892, which avoids any negotiable instrument issued or indorsed by a minor in the context of a betting transaction or a loan issued for its purposes.

The 1874 Act makes an important exception. A minor is bound by a contract under which he is supplied with goods or services that constitute necessaries. Lodgings, food, and, presumably, books required for study fall under this heading. Loans granted to enable a minor to acquire necessaries are also binding.[111]

The extent to which a minor is protected is illustrated by *R. Leslie Ltd.* v. *Sheill.*[112] A minor obtained a loan by misrepresenting his age. It was held that the amount lent could not be recovered in deceit or in quasi contract. The lender was not allowed to obtain by means of an indirect action a remedy not available in contract. The warning which this case spells out for banks is obvious. The one mitigation is that a minor cannot reclaim amounts paid by him under the void contract unless there has been a total failure of consideration. Consequently, he will usually be unable to reclaim instalments paid by him.[113]

Another general question that arises from time to time and which affects banks is whether an adult party to the void contract is entitled to set off against the minor's claim any amount due from the latter. The position is quite clear: a set-off is permitted only to the extent that the claim against the minor is legally enforceable.[114]

(ii) Specific problems faced by the bank: current account questions and lending

Three problems arise regularly when a minor wishes to have dealings with a bank. The first problem concerns the opening of a current account. Can it be in the minor's name? Secondly, is the bank entitled to honour cheques drawn on the account by a minor? Thirdly, what is the bank's position as regards the extension of credit to a minor?

The first two problems are related to a basic point: can a minor draw cheques on a current account? The answer depends on section 22 of the Bills

---

[111] *Re National Permanent Benefit Building Society* (1869) LR 5 Ch. App. 309, 313; *Lewis* v. *Alleyne* (1888) 4 TLR 560; *Chitty on Contract*, 25th edn., para. 547. But note, in contrast, that a bill or note is void even if issued for necessaries: *Re Soltykoff, ex p. Margrett* [1891] 1 QB 413. As regards the basis of a minor's liability for necessaries, note that contracts for their supply are excluded from the ambit of s. 1(1) of the Infants Relief Act 1874 and given further effect by s. 3 of the Sale of Goods Act 1979. As regards their binding effect at common law, see *Anson's Law of Contract*, 26th edn., pp. 183–4.
[112] [1914] 3 KB 607.
[113] *Valentini* v. *Canali* (1890) 24 QBD 166; *Hamilton* v. *Vaughan Sherrin Electrical Engineering Co.* [1894] 3 Ch. 589; *Pearce* v. *Brain* [1929] 2 KB 310.
[114] *Rawley* v. *Rawley* (1876) 1 QBD 460.

of Exchange Act 1882. Under subsection (1), a person's capacity to issue negotiable instruments is the same as his capacity to enter into simple contracts. Thus, a minor does not have the required capacity to bind himself by issuing bills of exchange, cheques and notes.[115] The signature executed by the minor does not, however, invalidate the instrument as a whole. Under subsection (2), '[w]here a bill is drawn or indorsed by an infant [or] minor . . . the drawing or indorsement entitles the holder to receive payment on the bill, and to enforce it against any other party thereto'. It is generally believed this section means that once a cheque has been paid the bank is discharged from its liability to pay the debt to the minor.[116] But the section does not refer to the bank. It entitles the holder to receive payment and to enforce the bill against the parties liable on it. The bank, which is merely the drawee, is not liable on the cheque. It is thus submitted that the suggestion that section 22 confers protection on a bank that pays a minor's cheque is erroneous. At the same time, common law principles enable a minor to give a valid discharge of a debt.[117] This view is supported by a number of early authorities which suggest that, when a bank honours the minor's cheque, it cannot be compelled to pay the amount over again when the minor comes of age.[118] It is thus arguable that, as between the bank and the minor customer, a cheque performs a specific function. It constitutes not merely a receipt but also a discharge of the bank's indebtedness to the minor.

It follows that a bank can safely open an account in a minor's name. The bank is entitled to honour the minor's cheques and, as long as the account is in credit, to treat it as an ordinary one. As a matter of caution banks tend, nevertheless, to open the account either in the name of the minor's guardians or in the minor's name, but on the understanding that it will be operated upon by the guardians.[119] In both cases the bank's customer is the minor.[120] In view of the trust element present in an account of this type, a

---

[115] *Re Soltykoff* [1891] 1 QB 413; *Levene* v. *Brougham* (1909) 25 TLR 265. A minor is not even liable on a post-dated cheque although its purported date of issue is subsequent to his coming of age: *Hutley* v. *Peacock* (1913) 30 TLR 42. Cf. *Belfast Banking Co.* v. *Doherty* (1879) 4 Ir. LR 124.

[116] Paget, *Law of Banking*, 9th edn., p. 32.

[117] *Re Brocklebank* (1877) 6 Ch. D 358, 360. Cf. *Ledward* v. *Hansells* (1856) 2 K & J 370.

[118] *Wilson* v. *Kearse* (1800) Peake Add. Cas. 196; *Valentini* v. *Canali* (1890) 24 QBD 166; *Pearce* v. *Brain* [1929] 2 KB 310. And see J. Grant, *Law Relating to Bankers*, 7th edn., London, 1924, p. 29, who argues that if the bank has met a minor's demand, it cannot be forced to pay over again. The cases of *R* v. *Inhabitants of Longnor* (1833) 4 B & Ad. 647; *Ewer* v. *Jones* (1846) 9 QB 623, cited, appear to support this view.

[119] Note that the appointment of an agent by a minor is fraught with difficulties: *Re Shephard, Shephard* v. *Cartwright* [1953] Ch. 728, 755. See also *Oliver* v. *Woodroffe* (1839) 4 M & W 650; *Calland* v. *Lloyd* (1840) 6 M & W 26, 31–2; *Doe d. Thomas* v. *Roberts* (1847) 16 M & W 778. But there are special cases where an agent may be validly appointed by a minor who runs a business: *Denmark Productions Ltd.* v. *Boscobe Productions Ltd.* (1967) 111 So. J 715.

[120] *Rowlandson* v. *National Westminster Bank Ltd.* [1978] 1 WLR 798.

bank may become subject to fiduciary duties to the minor. This is certainly the case where a drawing by a guardian is out of the ordinary.[121] Generally, though, the bank is safe in observing the instructions given to it by the guardians, and is entitled to pay cheques drawn by them on the account.

Problems arise where a minor requires financial accommodation. The bank is ill-advised to give any loan or to grant an overdraft to a minor. Under section 1 of the 1874 Act, such a contract is unenforceable. In *Nottingham Permanent Benefit Building Society* v. *Thurstan*,[122] a minor who was a member of a building society applied for a loan to enable her to purchase some land and to erect buildings on it. The society purchased the land from the owners and granted the minor the necessary loan needed to complete the buildings. The society retained the title deeds over the land and, in addition, obtained from the minor a mortgage over the property. When the minor came of age she brought an action for a declaration that the mortgage was void, and also claimed delivery of the title deeds. At the trial, Joyce J regarded the acquisition of the land and the execution of the mortgage as a single transaction and, as such, upheld it. He therefore dismissed the action. The Court of Appeal varied his judgment. It regarded the purchase of the land as separate from the loan granted by the society for the erection of buildings. As the mortgage was executed in respect of a loan it was avoided by the 1847 Act. The purchase of the land in the society's name was, however, held a distinct transaction. As this transaction was one between the original owners of the land and the society, it was valid. The House of Lords affirmed this decision, holding that the bank had a lien over the documents of title for the amount paid by it for the land. The mortgage was set aside and the loan granted for the building was held void.

A bank frequently obtains from an adult a guarantee of a loan or of an overdraft granted to the minor. This practice is fraught with dangers. In *Coutts & Co.* v. *Brown-Lecky*,[123] Oliver J held that where a loan was void due to the borrower's minority, a guarantee executed by an adult was equally inoperative. The reasoning in the case is unexceptional. As a guarantee is a secondary or ancillary undertaking, it cannot be more effective than the primary obligation which it aims to secure.

There are, however, two ways of avoiding the outcome of the *Brown-Lecky* case. The first is to phrase the guarantee in such a way that it constitutes an indemnity. In *Yeoman Credit Ltd.* v. *Latter*,[124] a finance company released a car to a minor under a hire purchase agreement. To back the minor's undertaking, an adult executed a document, entitled an indemnity,

---

[121] Ibid. Cf. *McEvoy* v. *Belfast Banking Co. Ltd.* [1935] AC 24.
[122] [1903] AC 6.
[123] [1947] KB 104; see also *Swan* v. *Bank of Scotland* (1836) 10 Bligh NS 627; *Heald* v. *O'Connor* [1971] 1 WLR 497, 505–6.
[124] [1961] 1 WLR 828.

in which he undertook to 'make good' to the finance company any loss incurred under the hire purchase agreement. The minor defaulted, whereupon the finance company brought an action to enforce its rights against the adult. It was argued, as a preliminary point, that the document in question constituted a guarantee and that it fell together with the hire purchase contract. The Court of Appeal held that the adult's undertaking constituted an indemnity, which was unaffected by the avoidance of the hire purchase agreement. Holroyd Pearce LJ observed:[125]

> the [issuer of the indemnity] was not purporting to guarantee or make good any particular obligation of the hirer. Under the terms of his agreement he had no liability to do so. His liability was to see that the [finance company] made their intended profit even though the hirer lawfully, without any default, terminated the hiring. [The issuer] was underwriting the profitable success of the transaction, he was not insuring against contractual breaches of it by the hirer.

The disinction between a guarantee and an indemnity, which is propounded in this case, accords with the general body of case law on the subject.[126] A guarantee constitutes a promise to compensate a creditor against loss incurred by the main debtor's default. An indemnity is a promise to reimburse to the beneficiary thereof any loss incurred in a given venture. It is true that, in practice, it is not always easy to distinguish between a guarantee and an indemnity. The loss in a given venture is frequently the direct outcome of the default of one of the parties to the underlying contract. Still, the court's determination is invariably based on the substance and not on the mere form of the undertaking. In the instant case, the court took one specific point into account. A guarantor is usually granted a right of subrogation, which enables him to recover from the debtor any amount paid under the guarantee to the creditor. No such right was conferred by the indemnity in *Latter*'s case.

The other way in which the bank can obtain a valid undertaking from a person who wishes to back a transaction with a minor is to use negotiable instruments. Thus, in *Wauthier* v. *Wilson*,[127] a father and his minor son jointly issued a promissory note in order to secure a loan granted to the son. When the son defaulted, the bank sought to enforce the promissory note against the father. At the trial, Pickford J treated the father as a guarantor but, despite this finding, held him liable. The Court of Appeal affirmed this decision on another ground. It treated the father as having entered into a joint obligation with his son. The fact that the son was not bound did not exonerate the father from his separate and distinct liability.

The rationale in *Wauthier* v. *Wilson* need not be regarded as confined to

---

[125] Ibid., 834.
[126] See Treitel, *Law of Contract*, 6th edn., pp. 137–8.
[127] (1912) 28 TLR 239, affg. (1927) 27 TLR 582.

liability incurred under a negotiable instrument. On the same basis, the father and son could have entered jointly into an agreement with the bank under which the loan was to be granted to the son. The father, as a separate party to the main agreement, would have been bound.[128] The consideration obtained by him would have been the extension of the loan to the son on the basis of the joint liability.

13. MENTALLY INCAPACITATED PERSONS' ACCOUNTS

(i) General principles

A person who becomes mentally incapacitated loses the legal ability to manage his own affairs. The Mental Health Act 1983 makes provision for the protection of such a person. One measure is that a judge of the Court of Protection appoints a receiver to take charge of the incapacitated person's affairs.[129] Banks can safely transact business concerning the customer with his receiver provided he remains within the scope of the authority conferred on him in his appointment.[130]

A mental disorder does not of itself free the disabled person from liability based in contract. The other party to the contract could enforce it if he was unaware of the true state of affairs. In *Imperial Loan Co.* v. *Stone*,[131] an action was brought by the payee of a promissory note against a party who had signed it as surety. It was proved that, at the relevant time, the surety was in a mental state that incapacitated him from comprehending the meaning of his act. But it was not established that the payee of the note had any knowledge of the surety's temporary insanity. The Court of Appeal held the surety liable. Lord Esher MR observed:[132]

When a person enters into a contract, and afterwards alleges that he was so insane at the time that he did not know what he was doing, and proves the allegation, the contract is as binding on him in every respect, whether it is executory or executed, as if he had been sane when he made it, unless he can prove further that the person with whom he contracted knew him to be so insane as not to be capable of understanding what he was about.

---

[128] *Lovell and Christmas* v. *Beauchamp* [1894] AC 607; *Wauthier* v. *Wilson*, above; *Chitty on Contracts*, 25th edn., para. 588.

[129] Mental Health Act 1983, s. 99(1). In the terminology of the Act, the incapacitated person is referred to as a 'patient'; under s. 96(1)(*h*) the judge may make an order declaring him to be incapable of entering into any contractual liability, in which case contracts made by him thereafter are probably void: *Anson's Law of Contract*, 26th edn., pp. 207–8.

[130] Mental Health Act, 1983, s. 99(2). The powers of the judge are spelt out in ss. 95–96.

[131] [1892] 1 QB 599.

[132] Ibid., 601.

(ii) Considerations relevant to banking operations

It is important to recall that when a bank deals with a customer it may perform either the function of an agent or that of a lender. In both types of transaction, the bank would find its contracts with a mentally disabled customer unenforceable, provided the bank had knowledge of his incapacity. In the case of current account operations the position is similar to that of the customer's bankruptcy. Under the rule in *Yonge* v. *Toynbee*[133] an agent's mandate is terminated by the principal's insanity. However, the contract of banker and customer is not purely one of agent and principal. The bank is under a duty to discharge its indebtedness to the customer by honouring his cheques. It is thought that the bank's mandate is terminated only when it receives notice of the customer's insanity.[134]

This view derives support from the principle in *Drew* v. *Nunn*.[135] The defendant represented to the plaintiff, a travelling salesman, that the defendant's wife was entitled to pledge his credit. Shortly thereafter the defendant became temporarily insane, whereupon the wife conducted his business. In the course of it she ordered goods from the plaintiff, who duly supplied them, being ignorant of the defendant's state of mind. When the defendant recovered, he repudiated the contract. The Court of Appeal upheld the trial judge's decision for the plaintiff. Brett LJ said that, fundamentally, the effect of a person's insanity was similar to that of his death or his bankruptcy. On this basis, an agent's mandate ought to be determined by the principal's insanity. The rule was, however, abrogated where the third party acted on the principal's representation or on his having held out that the agent was duly authorized to act for him. As long as the third party did not know of the principal's insanity, he could enforce the contract created by the agent.

As a general rule the bank should not honour cheques drawn by a customer who is known to have become mentally disabled, or by that customer's agent. The bank should also refuse to grant credit in such a case. The bank's proper course is to ask for an instruction of a duly appointed receiver. However, even if the bank has acted without having the authority of such a person, it may, in two types of case, hold the incapacitated customer to the contracts made on his behalf. The first case involves the supply of necessaries. The second case involves payments which, though made by the bank without authority, discharge a valid debt incurred by the customer.

The first type is illustrated by *Re Beavan, Davies, Banks & Co.* v. *Beavan*.[136] A bank, which knew that one of its customers had become insane,

---

[133] [1910] 1 KB 215.
[134] *Chitty on Contracts*, 25th edn., para. 2613, n. 45.
[135] (1879) 4 QBD 661; see also *Daily Telegraph Newspaper Co. Ltd.* v. *McLaughlin* [1904] AC 776.
[136] [1912] 1 Ch. 196.

allowed his son to draw cheques on the customer's account for necessaries. When the father died the account in question was overdrawn. In the administration proceedings the bank lodged a proof for the amount of the overdraft. The other creditors opposed this claim on the ground that the overdraft had been granted without authority. Giving judgment for the bank, Neville J held that the bank had lent the money involved to the son. Ostensibly, therefore, the alleged contract with the father could be rescinded. At the same time, the son, who had provided necessaries required by his father, was entitled to obtain reimbursement. The bank, which provided the required finance, was subrogated to the son's rights. The bank was entitled to claim the amount of the overdraft but neither interest thereon nor bank charges.

The case of unauthorized payments which benefit the mentally incapacitated customer was considered in *Scarth* v. *National Provincial Bank Ltd.*[137] The account of an insane customer was frozen by the bank. Initially, the customer's wife used her own money to discharge debts due from him. Subsequently, she induced the bank to transfer the balance standing to the credit of the husband's account to her own account. When the husband recovered, he brought an action to recover the amount involved. The wife relied principally on the equitable defence that the money was used for the discharge of the husband's debts.[138] Giving judgment for the wife on this ground, Humphreys J emphasized that, as she had a legitimate interest in protecting the husband's standing, it would be wrong to regard her as a mere volunteer. It seems clear that the bank was entitled to reap the benefit of this defence: the bank had provided the financial means which enabled the wife to pursue the course upheld by Humphreys J.

[137] (1930) 4 LDAB 241.
[138] *B. Liggett (Liverpool) Ltd.* v. *Barclays Bank Ltd.* [1928] 1 KB 48, discussed below, pp. 300–1.

CHAPTER 8

Interest-bearing Accounts

1. CLASSIFICATION AND COMPARISON WITH CURRENT ACCOUNTS

There are different types of interest-bearing accounts.[1] The savings account remains one of the most common ones. The customer can pay in any amount he chooses and is entitled to withdraw sums without notice. Interest is usually paid on the lowest balance in each calendar month, although some banks relate it to the daily balance. Another well-known variety is the fixed deposit. Here the customer deposits a given amount for a specified period of time at an agreed rate of interest. The deposit may, of course, be renewed at maturity. But a new rate of interest will then be determined, depending on the then prevailing market. In practice, a fixed deposit can be withdrawn before the agreed maturity date, provided the customer is prepared to lose part of the interest. Other types of interest-bearing account are the investment account and the extra interest account. In both types of account, the customer deposits certain minimum amounts; withdrawal is subject to an agreed period of notice.[2]

There are three main distinctions between interest-bearing accounts and current accounts. First, all interest-bearing accounts earn a return for the customer. Although some banks pay interest on current accounts maintained at not less than a specified credit balance,[3] most banks, including the clearers, do not subscribe to an arrangement of this type. A customer who maintains a certain minimum balance on a regular basis obtains only one advantage from such banks:[4] he is not required to pay banking charges.

Secondly, the amount deposited by the customer to the credit of his current account is withdrawable by cheques. Although two nineteenth-century authorities suggest that cheques may also be drawn on an interest-bearing account,[5] this view is insupportable in modern law. The automation of the

---

[1] The nomenclature is constantly changing; the one here adopted does not accord with technical banking terminology.

[2] The terminology varies from bank to bank. Some of the smaller banks have a unique structure of accounts, including some current accounts which also earn interest for the holders. The complexity of the arrangement is usually reflected in their nomenclature.

[3] This is the case as regards some banks in Scotland and some of the smaller banks of England and Wales.

[4] The figure used to be £500 but now varies considerably from bank to bank.

[5] *Stein* v. *Ritherdon* (1868) 37 LJ Ch. 369; *Hopkins* v. *Abbott* (1875) LR 19 Eq. 222. And see *Dixon* v. *Bank of New South Wales* (1896) 12 WN (NSW) 101.

clearing system resulted in the printing of personalized cheque-books, the forms in which set out, in magnetic ink, details concerning the customer and his account. A cheque is accordingly meant to be used solely in respect of the account for which the form is provided.[6] The fact that cheque books are not furnished in respect of interest-bearing accounts is a clear indication that there is no practice permitting the drawing of cheques on the balance.

Thirdly, a current account may be either in credit or, with the bank's consent, overdrawn. In the former case, the customer is the creditor; in the latter, he is the debtor. Interest-bearing accounts are opened on a different understanding. It has been held that the law does not recognize an overdrawn interest-bearing account.[7] If a customer who maintains such an account with his bank requires accommodation, he has to apply for a personal loan. But this principle is occasionally departed from in modern practice. Cheques payable to the customer may be collected for the credit of an interest-bearing account. If he is permitted to withdraw the funds before clearing and the cheques are returned unpaid, the account has to show a temporary debit balance.

The distinction between a current account and an interest-bearing account is far from new. It was explained in a similar manner by Lopes LJ in *Re Head, Head* v. *Head (No. 2)*:[8]

While the money was on a current account it was payable on presentation of a cheque, and it carried no interest; when it was placed on deposit it bore interest, and was no longer payable on a cheque, but it was only payable after twenty-one days' notice.[9]

There is a further, economic, distinction between current accounts and interest-bearing accounts. The object of a current account is to enable the customer to have access to the nation-wide system of money transfers provided by the banks. He can utilize it by drawing cheques payable to his creditors and by requesting his bank to collect cheques sent to him by his debtors. He also has access to the giro system. The banks furnish the facility in order to obtain, on a short-term basis, money that does not cost them interest. The interest-bearing account enables the customer to earn interest on his money and provides the bank with funds that it can invest for a period of time. Although all deposits paid to a bank are maintained as a co-mingled fund, it is correct to describe the amounts standing to the credit of current accounts as liquid funds maintained by customers for everyday use. Funds maintained in interest-bearing accounts are best regarded as investment deposits.

---

[6] For a detailed discussion, see pp. 231 et seq. below.
[7] *Barclays Bank Ltd.* v. *Okenarhe* [1966] 2 Lloyd's Rep. 87, 94.
[8] [1894] 2 Ch. 236, 238.
[9] Referring to the special arrangement in that case. Currently, the tendency is to make withdrawals subject to one month's notice.

2. LEGAL NATURE OF THE ARRANGEMENT

(i) Creditor-debtor relationship

The balance standing to the credit of a customer's interest-bearing account is a debt due to him from the bank. Just as in the case of a current account, the amount is not held by the bank as trustee and the arrangement does not involve a secured debt. In *Hopkins* v. *Abbott*[10] the question was whether a clause in a will, making a bequest of 'all bonds, promissory notes and other securities for money', covered a balance standing to the credit of a deposit account. Holding that it did not, Malins VC observed that the deposit receipt issued to the testatrix was merely evidence of the debt incurred by the bank. As this debt was unsecured, it did not fall within the ambit of the word 'securities'.

A similar conclusion was reached by Lord Atkin in *Akbar Khan* v. *Attar Singh*, where his Lordship observed:[11]

A deposit of money is not confined to a bailment of specific currency to be returned in specie. As in the case of a deposit with a banker it does not necessarily involve the creation of a trust, but may involve only the creation of the relation of debtor and creditor, a loan under conditions.

In most types of interest-bearing account, it is clear that there is only one contract between the customer and the bank. It is made at the time the account is opened, and both withdrawals from and payments into the account are effected in performance of this contract. Some doubts were raised at one stage with regard to the application of this analysis to fixed deposits. It was pointed out that in this type of account each deposit is the subject of separate arrangements and may be made on distinct terms. Despite this, the prevailing view is that fixed deposits made by a single customer are the subject of but one contract between the parties. In *Hart* v. *Sangster*, Lord Goddard CJ said:[12]

I cannot agree that where a deposit account is kept between a customer and a banker there is a new contract every time money is paid in; . . . it is one continuing contract . . .

On this basis it is arguable that a bank that agrees to accept one fixed deposit from its customer is obliged to accept further amounts, provided they are not less than the prescribed minimum. Usually this principle would not give rise to any problems. But there might be the odd case in which a bank would prefer to refuse to accept a deposit from a given customer.

---

[10] (1875) LR 19 Eq. 222.
[11] [1936] 2 All ER 545, 548.
[12] [1957] 1 Ch. 329, 337.

The balance due under an interest-bearing account may be payable on demand, at an agreed time, or upon giving notice of an agreed length. In the last case, the notice is a condition precedent to the bank's duty to pay.[13] Under the old practice, another condition precedent to payment used to be the production by the customer of the pass-book or of the deposit receipt. This clause is discussed subsequently,[14] but it is worth while mentioning at this stage that most banks have discontinued the practice of issuing pass-books and deposit receipts. Where the production of such a document is not required and the balance is payable on demand, the balance is considered 'ready money'.[15] Practically, it is then equated with a balance in a current account.

Every interest-bearing account is maintained with a given branch of the bank. In this regard, it is similar to a current account. It follows that the balance is a debt situated at the branch in question.[16] The customer has to make his demand at that place. Where the bank does not issue a deposit receipt or a pass-book, it tends to insist that this rule be observed. Where either of these two documents is furnished to the customer, the bank may be prepared to make repayments at other branches against the relevant document. The customer may, in such a case, be asked for an identification.

(ii) Payment to the wrong person

Payment of the balance to the wrong person occurs mainly in cases in which a deposit receipt or a pass-book supplied to the customer falls into the wrong hands. Although these documents are treated merely as evidencing the debt incurred by the bank[17] and not as negotiable instruments, customers tend to misunderstand their legal nature. They tend to write a transfer instruction, addressed to the bank, at the foot of the document and then deliver it to the intended transferee. If the document falls into the hands of an imposter, the bank's payment is bound to be queried. The same problem could conceivably arise under the modern practice, which has seen the abolition of pass-books and deposit receipts by most banks. By way of illustration, take the case in which a rogue presents to the bank a letter of instruction for the payment of the balance which he has abstracted from the rightful transferee.

---

[13] *Bagley* v. *Winsome and National Provincial Bank Ltd.* [1952] 2 QB 236. Although the decision regarding garnishee proceedings (as to which see pp. 271–5 below) is no longer good law in view of s. 38 of the Administration of Justice Act 1956, the analysis of the bank's duty in cases involving interest-bearing accounts remains valid.

[14] Pp. 221–222 below.

[15] *Stein* v. *Ritherdon* (1868) 37 LJ Ch. 369.

[16] *R.* v. *Lovitt* [1912] AC 212.

[17] Pp. 220–1 below.

The basic principle is that the bank makes any payment to a third party at its peril. In *Wood v. Clydesdale Bank Ltd.*,[18] the plaintiff executed an indorsement on a deposit receipt for £100 and sent it to his brother. In addition, he sent a letter to his bank, ordering it to pay £60 of the accrued balance to his brother against the production of the receipt. The deposit receipt, which was accompanied by a copy of the plaintiff's letter to the bank, was stolen from the mail. The thief presented it to the bank and obtained payment. Upholding the plaintiff's claim disputing the payment made, the Court of Session held that the bank had not obtained a valid discharge by its payment to the imposter. Lord Mackenzie said:[19]

If a deposit-receipt bearing a genuine endorsement is presented to the bank, say by a stranger, there is no absolute rule in regard to the liability of the bank to pay over again if it be ascertained that the person asking for the payment had not the authority of the true holder.

In the instant case, the bank had failed to satisfy itself of the payee's identity. As it had been instructed to pay £60 to the plaintiff's brother, it could not obtain a valid discharge from another person.

It stands to reason that the position would have differed if the plaintiff had asked the bank to pay the amount involved to any person tendering the deposit receipt. The bank would then have been in a position to argue that it had followed the instructions given to it. There may also have been room for pleading an estoppel based on the generality of such a mandate.

However, the plea of estoppel is unlikely to be widely available in practice. In *Evans v. National Provincial Bank of England*[20] the plaintiff delivered a deposit receipt to X so as to enable him to obtain the interest due on the account involved. X abused her trust and obtained payment of both the interest and the capital. Collins J held that, as the plaintiff had not intended to transfer the balance, the bank could not obtain a valid discharge from X. A crucial fact in this case was that the plaintiff had not written on the face of the receipt any words manifesting an intention to assign the debt due from the bank. If she had written such words, without indicating that X was to obtain payment of the interest alone, she would, in all probability, have been estopped from challenging the bank's payment.

(iii) Terms of contract

An interest-bearing account is governed by a set of standard terms. The customer agrees to observe these conditions, which impose on him a duty to

---

[18]   1914 SC 397.
[19]   Ibid., 402–3.
[20]   (1897) 13 TLR 429.

exercise a certain degree of care. He further agrees to be bound by the provisions concerning the repayment of the amount deposited.

Additional conditions are occasionally printed at the foot of a deposit receipt or in a pass-book. In an Australian authority, Pape J described the effect of such terms:[21]

the provisions set out in the passbooks are part of the terms of the contract between the bank and its customers and do constitute conditions precedent to any obligation by the bank to repay the money at credit . . .

This view is to be supported in respect of any situation in which the customer is made aware of the terms on which the bank is prepared to open the account. It is immaterial whether these are contained in a deposit receipt, in a pass-book, or in a set of standard terms and conditions proffered to the customer when the account is opened. Unless he objects to the terms involved, he is to be regarded as contracting on their basis.[22] The converse is applicable where the customer is not advised of the existence of the relevant terms until after the time of the creation of the contract. Thus, a customer has been held not to be bound by terms set out on the folder of a cheque-book, as these had not been effectively incorporated into his contract with the bank.[23] This reasoning retains its validity in respect of terms set out in any documents relating to bank accounts. On this basis, it seems crucial whether the customer is informed, at the time he opens an interest-bearing account, that the relevant conditions are printed in the pass-book.

(iv) Joint deposits

The problems arising in respect of joint deposits are, for most purposes, identical with those arising in respect of joint current accounts.[24] However, two interesting problems, which would appear to be inapplicable in the case of current accounts, arose in two early cases respecting deposit accounts. First, in *Innes v. Stephenson*,[25] the parties to a joint savings account, which under contemporary practice was operable by cheques, failed to specify who was entitled to withdraw the funds. Lord Tenderden CJ held that, as the owners were not partners, they were unable to act on behalf of each other. The signatures of all of them were therefore required on each cheque or withdrawal form. If the bank paid out against an instrument bearing the

[21] *Re Australia and New Zealand Savings Bank Ltd., Mellas v. Evriniadis* [1972] VR 690, 693.
[22] Assuming the customer studied the form of the statement when applying for the account.
[23] And see pp. 264–6 below.
[24] Pp. 168–175 above.
[25] (1831) 1 M & Rob. 145.

forged signature of one of the owners, it was liable to compensate the innocent owners for their losses.

Secondly, in *Husband* v. *Davis*[26] the question for decision was whether
the bank was entitled to pay a matured deposit to any one of the owners of a
joint account or had to obtain their joint discharge. Maule J observed:[27]

there can be no doubt that a man may pay a debt to one of several to whom he is
indebted jointly. The case of bankers stands upon special grounds. Where trustees of
others have a joint account with them as bankers, it is usual to require the authority
of the whole to pay the money. But that arises from the peculiar contract and relation between bankers and their customers.

This conclusion is supportable. It would be unacceptable to draw a distinction between the nature of the bank's mandate during the currency of
the deposit and the nature of the mandate when payment becomes due.

3. DISPOSITIONS OVER BALANCE

(i) Problems concerned

The balance standing to the credit of a current account is universally known
to be payable on demand. Although it constitutes a debt, it can effectively be
used as cash. The position is more complex in the case of interest-bearing
accounts. As regards dispositions over the available balance, such accounts
can be divided into two groups: those in which the balance is payable on
demand, and those in which it matures on any other basis. The latter group
encompasses 'extra interest accounts' and 'investment accounts', in which
the balance is payable subject to notice, and fixed deposits, in which it
matures at an agreed future time. Savings accounts are the most common
type of account in which the funds are payable on demand. This distinction
between the types of accounts has to be borne in mind in respect of dispositions over the balance, which are the assignment of the funds involved,
the bank's exercise of a right of set-off, and the garnishment of the balance.

(ii) Assignment of balance or of part thereof

The balance standing to the credit of any interest-bearing account is a debt
and hence a legal chose in action. It accrues when the deposit is effected,

---

[26] (1851) 10 CB 646.
[27] Ibid., 650.

and matures either on demand or at a specified future time. A legal chose in action can be assigned both in equity and under the Law of Property Act 1925.[28] As the Act prescribes a certain procedure and some specific requirements for an assignment, it is common to use in respect of bank balances the less formal equitable assignment. This practice has not led to legal problems. The reasons for this are discussed in Chapter 21.

The balance standing to the credit of an interest-bearing account may be assigned even if the pass-book or deposit receipt describe it as non-transferable.[29] Where the balance is assigned, the customer is no longer entitled to payment.[30]

There used to be a widely held misconception to the effect that the balance of an interest-bearing account could be assigned by the delivery of the respective deposit receipt or pass-book. Whilst one mid-Victorian authority supported this view,[31] it was overturned in a subsequent nineteenth-century decision.[32] The latter view is to be preferred. As neither a deposit receipt nor a pass-book constitutes a negotiable instrument, their transfer by delivery is ineffective.

The more difficult question is whether the delivery of such a document, with words evidencing an intention to assign the balance entered in it, confers any rights on the transferee. This type of transaction was used, when deposit receipts and pass-books were common, to effect a *donatio mortis causa* (a gift to mature on the assignor's demise), and has on a number of occasions been upheld by the courts. Thus, in *Re Griffin, Griffin v. Griffin*[33] the testator left his residual estate to his two sons in equal shares but handed to one of them a deposit receipt on which he had written: 'pay my son'. The other son contested the validity of the gift. Byrne J thought that the testator had done everything required to effect a gift by delivering the receipt, with the words written on it, to the first son. His Lordship said:[34]

[The testator] gave an order to pay, indorsed on the document without the production of which the bank would not pay, and he handed over the document itself to his son, thereby putting it out of his own power to claim the money.

The point emphasized by Byrne J was that, in the instant case, the testator had forfeited his right to claim the balance in his own name. The gift, or

---

[28] S. 136. Under this provision most choses in action that are assignable in equity are also assignable under the Act; see pp. 580 et seq. below.
[29] *Re Griffin, Griffin v. Griffin* [1899] 1 Ch. 408; *Elliott v. Elliott* (1899) 15 WN (NSW) 186.
[30] *Partridge v. Bank of England* (1846) 9 QB 396.
[31] *Woodhams v. Anglo-Australian and Universal Family Assurance Co.* (1861) 3 Giff. 234.
[32] *Moore v. Ulster Banking Co.* (1877) 11 IR CL 512; *Re Griffin, Griffin v. Griffin* [1899] 1 Ch. 408.
[33] [1899] 1 Ch. 408.
[34] Ibid., 412.

assignment, was therefore complete. The same element is stressed in other authorities.[35] The argument, though, is circular. The assignment is complete, as the donor has lost his rights over the debt. But, by the same token, he loses these rights as the assignment (or gift) has been completed!

The thrust of the reported decisions is that the customer is entitled to assign the balance standing to the credit of his interest-bearing account. But can he assign a part of the amount due? A statutory assignment would be ineffective for such a transaction. A part of debt can, however, be assigned in equity.[36]

(iii) Set-off by bank

An assignee who demands the payment of the balance of an interest-bearing account may find that the bank seeks to exercise against him a right of set-off which it has against the assignor. Such a case involves a conflict of claims, and the court has to decide who is entitled to priority. *Jeffryes* v. *Agra and Masterman's Bank*[37] suggests that the answer depends on two factors: the date on which the debt matures and the date on which notice of the assignment was given to the bank.

The facts of the case were complex. A merchant of Liverpool dispatched goods to a purchaser in India and negotiated the shipping documents to the AM Bank. His account with the bank was credited forthwith with a substantial part of the amount due. He was given a 'memorandum of receipt' for the balance and advised that the amount covered by it was 'retained' by the bank as a security. As the merchant required additional funds without delay, he indorsed the receipt to another bank—the R Bank—as a security for an advance. The R Bank advised the AM Bank of this transaction and asked to be advised about the 'fate'[38] of the receipt. The AM Bank refused to comply with this request, and notified the R Bank of its own rights over the balance and that the receipt was not negotiable. Shortly thereafter the merchant suspended payment.

The issue was which of the two banks had the superior claim. The AM Bank purported to exercise a right of set-off which it had against the merchant. The R Bank claimed to be entitled to payment as assignee. Wood VC emphasized that the amount covered by the receipt was payable subject to a

---

[35] *Re Pinto Leite, ex p. Olivaes* [1929] 1 Ch. 221. And see *Elliott* v. *Elliott* (1899) 15 WN (NSW) 186; *Anning* v. *Anning* (1907) 4 CLR 1049.

[36] See pp. 580 et seq. below.

[37] (1866) LR 2 Eq. 674.

[38] Meaning: whether the balance became unconditionally due, which event would take place when the Indian purchaser paid the price.

contingency, namely the payment of the price by the purchaser of the goods. It followed that the debt, evidenced by the receipt, had not matured when the merchant suspended payment. His Lordship observed:[39]

you cannot retain a sum of money which is actually due against a sum of money which is only becoming due at a future time.

In the instant case, the receipt evidenced a debt of the latter type: it was to mature when the condition precedent was performed. If the merchant claimed payment of the debt when it became due, the AM Bank would be entitled to set off any sums payable by him. But this set-off could not be claimed by the bank in respect of his contingent liabilities.

The AM Bank's rights against the R Bank were basically the same as those which it had against the merchant. The AM Bank could exercise against the R Bank a set-off based on 'liabilities actually accrued before [it] had notice of the assignment, not matured when [it] had notice of the assignment, but matured when the debt became payable'.[40] But no right of set-off could be exercised in respect of liabilities incurred by the merchant to the AM Bank after it had notice of the assignment.

Wood VC concluded that the R Bank was entitled to the payment of the amount covered by the receipt. But its right was subject to the AM Bank's set-off of amounts payable to it by the merchant at the time the debt evidenced by the receipt fell due, provided the merchant's liability had been incurred before the date of the notification of the assignment to the AM Bank.

A similar view was expressed by Clauson J in *Re Pinto Leite, ex p. Olivaes*:[41]

when the debt assigned is at the date of notice of the assignment payable in futuro, the debtor can set off against the assignee a debt which becomes payable by the assignor to the debtor after notice of assignment, but before the assigned debt became payable, if, but only if, the debt so to be set off was debitum in praesenti at the date of the notice of assignment.

His Lordship emphasized that the debt to be set off against the assignee must have accrued before the date of the notification of the assignment to the debtor. The fact that the debt had matured after the date of the notification was irrelevant. The crucial point was that it did not remain contingent at the time payment was claimed by the assignee. If it were a conditional or immature liability at that stage, it could not have been the subject of a set-off.

---

[39] (1866) LR Eq. 674, 680.
[40] Ibid.
[41] [1929] 1 Ch. 221, 236.

(iv) Garnishee proceedings

A debt can be garnished by a judgment creditor if it is 'accrued and payable' at the time the order nisi is made.[42] Up to 1956 there were doubt as to whether deposits for fixed periods and deposits repayable at a minimum notice could, thus, be garnished.[43] These doubts were removed by section 38 of the Administration of Justice Act 1956. The position is discussed in detail subsequently.[44]

(v) Limitation of action

When a debt becomes barred by limitation, the creditor is unable to enforce payment. Contractual debts become barred after the lapse of six years. The period begins to run from the day on which the action accrues,[45] which in the case of an interest-bearing account is the date on which the debt becomes payable. This date depends, of course, on whether the funds are due on demand, at a fixed future date, or upon the giving of notice of a pre-scribed number of days.

To protect their reputation, banks are disinclined to plead limitation even in cases in which the debt is clearly barred. A bank may, however, plead limitation as a last resort where it suspects collusion or dishonest behaviour on the customer's part.

Atkinson v. *Bradford Third Equitable Benefit Building Society*[46] was an interesting case in point. A customer maintained with a building society a deposit repayable subject to notice and to the production of the pass-book. Two days after the customer's demise, in January 1879, an unidentified per-son obtained payment of the balance against the production of the pass-book and a withdrawal form on which he forged the deceased's signature. The administrators, who were appointed by the court in May 1889, brought an action for the full balance of the account before the end of the month. One of the defences pleaded by the building society was that the debt had, by then, become statute barred.

Rejecting this defence, the Court of Appeal held that the period of limi-tation started to run on the day of the granting of the letters of administra-tion. This was the earliest date on which the estate could make a valid demand for the payment of the balance. Although the conclusion that the debt was not statute barred appears unexceptional, it is arguable that the

---

[42] RSC, O. 49, r. 1; CCR, O. 27, r. 1.

[43] *Joachimson* v. *Swiss Bank Corporation* [1923] 3 KB 110 suggests that where a balance is payable at call, the serving of the order constitutes a demand.

[44] Pp. 271–5 below.

[45] Limitation Act 1980, s. 5.

[46] (1890) 25 QBD 377.

period of limitation started to run from an even later date, namely the day on which the administrators made their demand for the payment of the balance.

Presumably, the Court regarded the debt as having fallen 'due' on the day of its wrongful discharge to the imposter. It thus treated the payment involved as a breach of the contract between the bank and the deceased. On this basis, the period of limitation would start to run against the customer as from the date of the wrongful payment although, as against the estate, the cause of action was treated as having accrued on the first day on which it could be pursued in a court. But it is difficult to see why the action, brought either by the customer or by his estate, should be regarded as based on a breach of contract which took place when the bank made payment to the imposter. The action was for the repayment of a debt that had not been discharged by the bank when the estate made its valid demand. The period of limitation should not have started to run until this demand was made.[47]

It is clear that, in cases of this type, a bank is usually suspicious. It is bound to wonder how the pass-book or deposit receipt fell into the wrong hands. Its doubts are exacerbated if it is not advised promptly of its customer's demise.

4. DEPOSIT RECEIPTS AND PASS-BOOKS

(i) Problems involved

In modern practice, most banks, including all the clearers, have abandoned the use of pass-books and deposit receipts. This move was dictated by two considerations. First, the banks were perturbed by the tendency of their customers to treat pass-books and deposit receipts as convenient means for effecting informal assignments of the balances covered by them. As a result of this misconception, banks were frequently faced with the quandary of either making payment to a 'holder' at their peril[48] or invoking the customer's wrath by refusing to meet a transferee's demand. The position was exacerbated by the fact that the defences available to banks in cases involving the wrongful payment of cheques[49] were not extended to the wrongful payment of balances of interest-bearing accounts.

Secondly, the loss of a pass-book or of a deposit receipt was a common occurrence but frequently remained undetected by the customer for a con-

---

[47] Limitation Act 1980, ss. 5, 6; and see generally pp. 82–83 above.
[48] See pp. 212–2 above.
[49] See Chap. 10 below.

siderable period of time. This led to obvious problems if the document fell into the hands of a rogue. The problem does not arise as frequently in the case of current accounts, as the constant use of cheque-books means that their loss is usually spotted without delay. Thirdly, the need to supply deposit receipts and to replace them whenever a deposit was renewed entailed considerable clerical work. So did the need to update the pass-book.

The computer-produced periodic statement, which has replaced the deposit receipt and the pass-book, is a time-saving device. Further, it is universally understood that it does not constitute a negotiable instrument, and that its delivery does not have any legal consequences. As some banks continue to use deposit receipts and pass-books, it is necessary to discuss the two documents briefly. It will be convenient to discuss, principally, the case law concerning deposit receipts and to apply it to pass-books.

(ii) Legal nature of deposit receipt and pass-book

A deposit receipt does not constitute a negotiable instrument.[50] In *Akbar Khan* v. *Attar Singh*,[51] Lord Atkin pointed out that, unlike a promissory note, a deposit receipt did not include an express promise by the bank to pay the amount involved. The sole object of the receipt was to constitute a record of the transaction involved. His Lordship thus treated the receipt as a document issued to evidence the existence of a debt.[52] The same object was ascribed by Lord Evershed MR to a savings pass-book in *Birch* v. *Treasury Solicitor*.[53]

It follows that, ordinarily, a deposit receipt is not transferable by delivery. But is a bank entitled to issue deposit receipts which are expressly made negotiable? It would appear that some banks issue instruments of this type.[54] Moreover, it has been argued forcefully that the negotiable character of such receipts ought to be recognized.[55] But the argument is dubious. It is well established that parties cannot create at will new forms of negotiable

---

[50] The view to the contrary, expressed in *Woodhams* v. *Anglo-Australian and Universal Family Assurance Co.* (1861) 3 Giff. 234 is no longer to be regarded as good law.

[51] [1936] 2 All ER 545, 548. See also *Hopkins* v. *Abbott* (1875) LR 19 Eq. 222; *Moore* v. *Ulster Banking Co.* (1877) 11 IR CL 512. And see Grant, *Law Relating to Bankers*, 7th edn., London, 1924, p. 219; H. L. Hart, *Law of Banking*, 4th edn., London, 1931, p. 268.

[52] See also *Pearce* v. *Creswick* (1843) 2 Hare 286; *Jeffryes* v. *Agra and Masterman's Bank* (1866) LR 2 Eq. 674, 680; *Hopkins* v. *Abbott* (1875) LR 19 Eq. 222; *Birch* v. *Treasury Solicitor* [1951] 1 Ch. 298, 313.

[53] Above.

[54] *National Bank of Australasia Ltd.* v. *Scottish Union and National Insurance Co.* (1951) 84 CLR 177.

[55] G. A. Weaver and C. R. Craigie, *Banker and Customer in Australia*, Sydney, 1975, pp. 62 et seq.

instruments.[56] If they wish to use an instrument in a given transaction, they have to employ one of the recognized forms. Principally, these are bills of exchange, cheques and promissory notes.

The only exception to the rule that negotiable instruments form a closed list is that a new form of instrument may be sanctioned by a commercial usage.[57] Such a usage need not be of a long standing.[58] But it has to be certain,[59] notorious,[60] and generally recognized by the City.[61] The fact that deposit receipts have largely fallen into disuse in the United Kingdom militates against any assertion that, where they are expressed to be transferable by delivery, they are deemed to be negotiable instruments by usage.

It follows that the delivery of a deposit receipt does not, in itself, confer on the transferee any rights of ownership. To claim the amount involved, he must be able to establish that it has been validly assigned to him. It has been shown that appropriate words, written on the receipt, may have such an effect. The principles involved apply a fortiori to pass-books, which are not generally regarded as negotiable instruments.

As deposit receipts and pass-books do not constitute negotiable instruments they are not, in themselves, good securities.[62] The reason for this is that their possession does not confer on the holder a good title to either the document involved or the funds. Despite this, the custody of the deposit receipt or pass-book can give some protection to a creditor. This is the case where the production of the document involved is made a condition precedent to the bank's duty to repay the amount deposited. The validity of this type of clause has been upheld in a number of cases.[63] Thus, in *Kauter* v. *Hilton*, Dixon CJ, delivering the judgment of the High Court of Australia, said:[64]

The passbooks contain a notice that withdrawals may be made by the depositor personally on production of the passbook and the necessary completed withdrawal

---

[56] *Crouch* v. *Crédit Foncier of England Ltd.* (1873) LR 8 QB 374.

[57] *Goodwin* v *Robarts* (1875) LR 10 Ex. 337, affd. (1876) 1 App. Cas. 476; *Bechuanaland Exploration Co.* v. *London Trading Bank Ltd.* [1898] 2 QB 658; *London Joint Stock Bank* v. *Simmons* [1892] AC 201.

[58] *Bechuanaland Exploration Co.* v. *London Trading Bank Ltd.*, above; *Edelstein* v. *Schuler & Co.* [1902] 2 KB 144.

[59] *Sewell* v. *Corp* (1824) 1 Car. & P 392, 393; *Devonald* v. *Rosser & Sons* [1906] 2 KB 728, 743.

[60] See, e.g., *Tucker* v. *Linger* (1883) 8 App. Cas. 508. The word 'notorious' in this context, refers to the clear understanding of the usage by businessmen affected by it.

[61] *Picker* v. *London and County Banking Co. Ltd.* (1887) 18 QBD 515.

[62] *Hopkins* v. *Abbott* (1875) LR 19 Eq. 222.

[63] *Atkinson* v. *Bradford Third Equitable Benefit Building Society* (1890) 25 QBD 377; *Re Dillon, Duffin* v. *Duffin* (1890) 44 Ch. D 76; *Re Tidd, Tidd* v. *Overrell* [1893] 3 Ch. 154; *Re Griffin, Griffin* v. *Griffin* [1899] 1 Ch. 408; *Anning* v. *Anning* (1907) 4 CLR 1049; *Re Australia and New Zealand Savings Bank Ltd., Mellas* v. *Evriniadis* [1972] VR 690.

[64] (1953) 90 CLR 86, 101.

form or to the bearer of a completed withdrawal form signed by the depositor and presented with the passbook. The presentation of the passbook is therefore required before any moneys can be withdrawn from an account.

At the same time, it is important not to overestimate the benefit derived by a creditor by obtaining the custody of a pass-book or of a deposit receipt of his debtor. The custody of the documents does not entitle the possessor to demand payment. In point of fact, the debtor, or 'depositor', may be able to obtain payment despite his having parted with the document. Thus, he may be able to convince the bank that the deposit receipt or pass-book has been lost.[65] The holder will have no action against the bank if it replaces the instrument and, eventually, pays the amount deposited to the customer!

The best advice that can be given to the holder is to advise the bank of his being in possession of the pass-book or deposit receipt for security purposes. The bank may then refuse to release the funds to the customer unless the document involved is surrendered.[66] The ensuing delay may give the holder the time required to obtain judgment against the depositor and to serve on the bank a garnishee order nisi.

(iii) Loss of deposit receipt or pass-book

The loss by the customer of a deposit receipt does not free the bank from its duty to pay. The bank has to replace the lost receipt subject to its obtaining from the customer an indemnity against claims by third parties.[67] However, as the possession of the receipt does not entitle a third party to claim the proceeds, the object of the indemnity is unclear. Indeed, the customer is entitled to payment even if the bank has made payment to an imposter against the wrongfully acquired receipt. In such a case, the production of the receipt by the customer ceases to be a condition precedent to the bank's duty to pay.[68] He may, thus, decide to claim payment at the appropriate date of maturity without insisting on having the lost receipt replaced.

The very same principles should be applicable where the lost document is a pass-book.

---

[65] The bank's duty where a deposit receipt or pass-book is lost is discussed below. Note that, according to *Wood* v. *Clydesdale Bank Ltd.* 1914 SC 397, the bank has to pay the amount of the deposit to the customer even where it has been paid to an impostor against the production of the required deposit receipt or pass-book.

[66] *Quaere* whether such a transfer of a deposit receipt or pass-book constitutes an equitable assignment for security purposes. The point has not been the subject of decision.

[67] This appears to be supported by *Pearce* v. *Creswick* (1843) 2 Hare 286; *Atkinson* v. *Bradford Third Equitable Building Society* (1890) 25 QBD 377; *Re Dillon, Duffin* v. *Duffin* (1890) 44 Ch. D 76. And see *Conflans Stone Quarry Co. Ltd.* v. *Parker* (1867) LR 3 CP 1 concerning a circular note lost in the mail.

[68] *Wood* v. *Clydesdale Bank Ltd.* 1914 SC 397.

(iv) The deposit receipt and the pass-book as the subject of a
donatio mortis causa

A *donatio mortis causa* is a gift which is to take effect upon the donor's
death. Deposit receipts and pass-books are occasionally handed over by an
owner whose health is failing, in order to effect such a donation. Frequently,
he makes his object clear by saying such words as: 'This is yours when I go.'
In such cases it is clear that the object of the donor is to effect a gift of the
funds covered by the document. He uses the receipt or pass-book in the misguided belief that its delivery involves a transfer of the funds. This mistake is
not made by customers of banks that have adopted the modern practice. To
date, there is no reported case in which the customer purported to donate
the funds standing to the credit of his interest-bearing account by handing
over the periodic statement.

The type of *donatio mortis causa* here under discussion was frequently
effected in the hope of avoiding death duties. It has been seen that, for the
same reason, funds might occasionally be deposited to the credit of a joint
account opened in the name of the donor and his heir. That such a design is
not necessarily successful was demonstrated in *McEvoy* v. *Belfast Banking
Co.*[69] At present, a gift, effected by the handing over of a deposit receipt or a
pass-book with an instruction that the donee receive the funds upon the
donor's demise, probably incurs capital transfer tax under section 22 of the
Finance Act 1975.

It is accepted that the mere handing of the deposit receipt to the donee
does not necessarily constitute a valid *donatio mortis causa*. The crucial
question is whether the gift has been completed. The answer depends on
whether the donor has manifested the intention of effecting an irrevocable
gift, and on whether he has relinquished his control over the funds involved.
The conclusion depends on the exact words uttered or written by the donor
at the time he delivered the receipt.

The main object of the courts is to give effect to the donor's wishes. But
whilst the basic principle is clear, the cases in point are not easily reconcilable. In *Re Dillon, Duffin* v. *Duffin*[70] the donor, who was seriously ill, completed a cheque form printed at the foot of a deposit receipt and delivered it
to a relative. The donee was to retain the document if the donor died, but
was asked to return it if he survived his illness. Rejecting the estate's claim
for the payment of the funds, the Court of Appeal upheld the validity of the
gift. It recognized that the filling out of the cheque form and the delivery of
the receipt did not necessarily constitute an irrevocable assignment of funds.

[69] [1935] AC 24. And see *Thomson* v. *Federal Commissioner of Taxation* (1949) 80 CLR
344.
[70] (1890) 44 Ch. D 76. See also *Re Griffin, Griffin* v. *Griffin* [1899] 1 Ch. 408; *Re Ward,
Ward* v. *Warwick* [1946] 2 All E R 206.

But by parting with the document, the donor lost his control over the funds. The reason for this was that the production of the receipt was made a condition precedent to the bank's duty to pay. Cotton LJ added that the donor's demise completed the gift.

A telling argument against this conclusion is that, on the facts, the donor had retained an interest in the amount involved. If he had had no such intention, why did he insist that the document be returned to him if he recovered from his illness? In an Australian case in which a donor retained an interest in the account in a similar manner, it was held that the gift had remained revocable and hence invalid.[71] Modern case law emphasizes the significance of the relinquishment of control. The gift is effective only if the donee acquires the unconditional right to dispose of the funds.[72] *Dillon*'s case may thus be doubted.

A *donatio mortis causa* is valid only if the deposit receipt reaches the hands of the donee. If it is retained by the donor or by his agent for delivery, the gift remains incomplete.[73] However, the gift is not destroyed if the donor regains possession of the receipt from time to time following its initial delivery. But, in such a case, the gift is effective only if the receipt is delivered back to the donee before the donor's demise.[74]

Whilst the case law in point is primarily concerned with deposit receipts, it ought to be equally applicable to gifts effected by means of the delivery of a pass-book. The determination of the donor's intention and the completeness of the gift are also the main considerations in cases involving this type of document.

5. ASSESSMENT

The main development respecting interest-bearing accounts in recent years was the replacement of pass-books and deposit receipts by periodic statements similar to those used in the case of current accounts. This modern practice is in line with the tendency to regard the contract of banker and customer as a continuous relationship, which does not require separate records or memoranda of individual entries.

It is believed that this is a satisfactory development. In the first place, the abolition of deposit receipts and of pass-books has enabled the banks to achieve greater efficiency in their day to day work. Secondly, from a legal point of view, the deposit receipt and the pass-book did not serve a useful

[71] *Thomson* v. *Federal Commissioner of Taxation* (1949) 80 CLR 344.
[72] *Birch* v. *Treasury Solicitor* [1951] 1 Ch. 298; *Kauter* v. *Hilton* (1953) 90 CLR 86; *Haythorpe* v. *Rae* [1972] V R 633.
[73] *Moore* v. *Ulster Banking Co.* (1877) 11 IR CL 512.
[74] *Watts* v. *Public Trustee* (1949) 50 SR (NSW) 130.

object. As they were considered mere records, evidencing the existence of a debt, their function could always have been performed just as effectively by a periodic statement. Thirdly, the misconception about the nature of the documents in question had led to undesirable litigation concerning *donationes mortis causa* and questionable assignments. It is believed that the modern practice is more readily understood by the public.

CHAPTER 9

The Bank's Role as Paying Agent: Cheques

1. CHEQUES AND THEIR BACKGROUND

In everyday life, cheques serve two main objectives. The first is to enable a customer who has a current account to obtain repayment of the funds lent by him to the bank.[1] In such a case, the customer draws a cheque payable to his own order and cashes it at the bank's counter. The use of cheques is fortuitous in this context. On the Continent, the same objective is achieved by the use of a special form known as a 'withdrawal voucher', which is similar to the form used in the United Kingdom for the withdrawal of funds standing to the credit of a savings account. The second function of a cheque is to facilitate the payment of an amount due from the drawer to a third party. Here the cheque is drawn to the order of the person involved and is either dispatched to him by post or handed to him personally. The cheque constitutes the customer's request that the bank pay a specified amount to the payee or to his transferee.[2]

It is significant that the two transactions just described can be effected by means other than the drawing of cheques. Thus, instead of the personal cheque drawn by the customer to obtain money standing to the credit of his account, the withdrawal of funds can be effected by the use of a card inserted in an automatic teller machine. Similarly, instead of paying a debt by the sending of a cheque to the creditor, the customer can utilize the 'bank giro'. In such a transaction, in which the customer completes a form other than a cheque, payment is effected by means of a direct transfer from the customer's account into a designated account maintained by the payee. Both the automatic teller machine operable by cards and the money transfer system utilize a computerized, or electronic, system. Details of these transactions are discussed in Chapter 12.

Despite the availability of alternative methods of payment, cheques have remained the major instrument employed in the United Kingdom for the discharge of debts. The reason for this phenomenon is, basically, historical. To explain it, a brief discussion of the background of cheques is required.

---

[1] As regards the creditor–debtor relationship involved, see pp. 81–84 above.

[2] The bank's duties in paying cheques drawn on it are discussed in Ch. 10; its position as a collecting bank is discussed in Ch. 14.

In England, cheques developed during the seventeenth century[3] as a facility akin to the negotiable instruments then in the market, which were bills of exchange and promissory notes.[4] The bill of exchange provided a more suitable model than the promissory note. The reason for this emerges when one compares the two instruments. In a bill of exchange, one person—the drawer—orders another person—the drawee—to pay, at a given future time or on demand, a specified amount of money to a designated third party or to bearer.[5] A promissory note is an instrument in which one person, the maker, promises to pay a given amount, at a future time or on demand, to the order of a named person or to bearer.[6] The function of a cheque, which is an order given by the customer to his bank, is thus closer to that of a bill of exchange than of a promissory note. Cheques therefore followed the pattern provided by bills of exchange. To this day, a cheque is defined as a 'bill of exchange drawn on a banker payable on demand'.[7]

There is little information regarding the banking practice prevalent in respect of cheques during the eighteenth century. During the first half of the nineteenth century, cheques were usually payable to bearer. The practice changed in the wake of the Stamp Act 1853, which abolished the *ad valorem* duty on order cheques, introducing in its stead a fixed duty of one penny.[8] As from that period, most British banks have provided their customers with books containing cheque forms payable to order.[9] The use of cheques has steadily increased during the second half of the nineteenth century, a trend that has continued right up to the present era.

From a legal point of view, a cheque has two separate roles. One determines its basic nature and the rights of a person who obtains it either as ostensible payee or by way of transfer; the other defines the effect of the cheque as regards the relationship of the customer who draws it with the bank on which it is drawn.

In their former role, cheques are regarded as negotiable instruments. Such instruments differ from other types of legally binding contracts in three regards. First, a negotiable instrument confers a right of action on the person

---

[3] J. M. Holden, *History of Negotiable Instruments in English Law*, London 1955, ch. 7. Chorley, *Gilbart Lectures*, 1955, p. 40.

[4] Holden, *History of Negotiable Instruments*, pp. 206–16.

[5] Bills of Exchange Act 1882 (BEA), s. 3. The definition can be traced back to the sixteenth century at least.

[6] BEA, s. 83. The battle for the recognition of promissory notes as valid negotiable instruments took place at the end of the seventeenth century and at the beginning of the eighteenth. See *Williams* v. *Williams* (1693) Carth. 269; *Potter* v. *Pearson* (1702) 2 Ld Raym. 759; *Clerke* v. *Martin* (1702) 2 Ld Raym. 757; *Buller* v. *Crips* (1703) 6 Mod. 29. Promissory notes were given statutory recognition in the Bills of Exchange Act 1704.

[7] BEA, s. 73.

[8] For the implications, see Holden, *History of Negotiable Instruments*, pp. 221–4.

[9] S. 19 of the Stamp Act 1853 conferred on them a defence in cases of forged indorsements: see pp. 303–4 below. And see now BEA, s. 60.

who has its lawful possession.[10] Such a person, who is known as the 'holder', may be the payee of the instrument, an indorsee or the bearer.[11] In other types of contract, the physical possession of the documents evidencing its terms does not, in itself, confer a right of action. A simple contract is enforceable only by the parties to it or, in certain cases, by an assignee.[12] Secondly, a negotiable instrument is transferable. If it is payable to bearer, it can be negotiated—or transferred—by mere delivery.[13] If the cheque is payable to order, negotiation is effected by its indorsement by the payee followed, again, by delivery.[14] Contracts other than negotiable instruments may also be assigned, but the procedure laid down is more cumbersome.[15] Thirdly, the transferee of a negotiable instrument may obtain a better title than the transferor's. This occurs where the instrument is transferred to a 'holder in due course', who is, basically, a person who acquires an instrument, regular on its face, in good faith and for valuable consideration.[16] Under the general law of contract, an assignee usually does not acquire a title better than the assignor's. In other words, the assignee's rights against the debtor are subject to the 'equities' available to the debtor against the assignor.[17] In effect, a negotiable instrument is a specific item of property, and its possession confers certain rights on the 'true owner', such as the right to bring an action for the conversion of the instrument.[18]

These attributes of negotiable instruments are applicable to cheques. Usually cheques are transferable and, subject to certain exceptions,[19] the holder acquires a right to sue the drawer. If the holder falls within the definition of a holder in due course his action is, in effect, indefeasible.[20] The fact that the cheque is countermanded by the drawer does not defeat an action brought against him by a holder in due course.[21]

As regards the second role of a cheque, which defines its function in the relationship of banker and customer, the negotiability of the instrument is of little relevance. Here the cheque constitutes an instruction, or order, given by the customer, who is regarded as the principal, to the bank, which

[10] BEA, s. 38(1).
[11] Ibid., s. 2.
[12] See, generally, *Chitty On Contracts*, 25th edn., vol. 1, paras. 1273, 1289–90.
[13] BEA, s. 31(2).
[14] Ibid., s. 31(3).
[15] See Chap. 21 below, and *Chitty On Contracts*, 25th edn., paras. 1272–3, 1278.
[16] BEA, s. 29. See further, pp. 504–7 below.
[17] See pp. 585–6 below.
[18] See pp. 507–8 below.
[19] Mainly where a cheque is made non-transferable: see pp. 246–7 below.
[20] But not where a cheque bears a crossing accompanied by the words 'not negotiable': see pp. 255–6 below. But note effect of s. 123 of Consumer Credit Act 1974, discussed below, p. 262.
[21] Note, though, that if the holder was aware of the countermand of the cheque when he acquired it, he is not a holder in due course: pp. 246–8 below.

is his agent.[22] The bank is, therefore, under a duty to observe the terms of the authority, or mandate, conferred on it by the customer. Thus, if the customer countermands payment, the bank has to obey his instructions and must therefore dishonour the instrument.[23] The bank cannot be sued by the holder, as it is a mere drawee and as such not liable on the instrument itself.[24] Moreover, the issuing of the cheque by the customer does not constitute an assignment to the payee of the amount for which the instrument is drawn.[25] It follows that the payee does not have any right against the bank in contract. The negotiability of the instrument is, however, relevant as regards the contract of banker and customer where the cheque is drawn as payable to bearer, or becomes so payable as a result of a valid indorsement of the initial payee.[26] By honouring such an instrument when it is presented by the bearer, the bank remains within the scope of the authority conferred on it by the customer. It is then irrelevant how the bearer acquired the cheque.

As pointed out above, one of the main functions of a cheque is to effect payment of amounts due from the drawer to a third party. The person who receives a cheque drawn to his order or to bearer can utilize it in one of three ways. First and foremost, if the cheque is uncrossed he can present it for payment at the counter of the branch on which it is drawn. The bank must then decide promptly whether to pay or to dishonour the instrument. The matters with which the bank is concerned are the genuineness of the drawer's signature and the adequacy of the balance against which the cheque is drawn.

The holder's second way of obtaining payment of a cheque is to remit it for collection to the credit of his own bank account. The payee's bank, which assumes in such a case the role of a 'collecting bank', presents the cheque to the drawee bank (the 'paying bank') through the clearing system.

The holder's third way of obtaining payment is to transfer, or 'negotiate', the instrument to another person who is prepared to pay him the amount thereof. This method is often utilized by reason of tax considerations or in cases in which the initial payee of the cheque does not maintain an account with a bank. Where a cheque is negotiated, the transferee has, again, the ordinary three options for obtaining payment thereof.

The collection of cheques through the clearing system is by far the most common procedure for the payment of cheques in the United Kingdom. It has the advantage of saving any person who maintains an account with a

---

[22] This point was finally determined in *London Joint Stock Bank* v. *Macmillan* [1918] AC 777, but can be traced back to *Young* v. *Grote* (1827) 4 Bing. 253.
[23] BEA, s. 75(1) and pp. 299–300 below.
[24] BEA, s. 53(1).
[25] Ibid.
[26] As to which cheques are payable to bearer, see pp. 243–7 below.

bank the need of presenting each cheque payable to him in person to the drawee bank. Furthermore, most cheques issued in the United Kingdom are crossed by the drawer. The details of the procedure involved and its object are discussed subsequently. At this point, however, it is important to emphasize that the drawee bank is not permitted to pay a crossed cheque over the counter.[27] It can honour it only when presented by 'a bank'. It is true that a crossing does not preclude the payee from negotiating the instrument. Subject to one possible exception,[28] such a cheque remains transferable. But a transferee is, again, precluded from demanding payment by presenting the instrument over the drawee bank's counter. He, too, must either negotiate the instrument or arrange for its collection through a bank.

Recent estimates suggest that at least 75 per cent of all cheques drawn in the United Kingdom are paid through the clearing systsem. A detailed discussion of this system is, therefore, of importance for the understanding of the functioning of banks in this country.

2. THE CLEARING PROCESS

The process used for the clearing of cheques is based on a procedure developed in the eighteenth century, when the use of cheques became common. Initially, each bank obtained payment of cheques remitted to it by its customers by presenting them by messenger to the drawee bank. To save time, the bank messengers gathered in a meeting-place in which they exchanged their respective cheques in the morning. They reconvened in the afternoon, when dishonoured cheques were returned to the messengers who had brought them, and a balance was struck between the messengers of the different banks in respect of 'cleared' effects, i.e. cheques which had been honoured by their offices. This system, originally confined to cheques drawn and payable within the boundaries of the City of London, was modified from time to time to meet the demands of the constantly developing banking network. In 1833, the then clearing banks hired premises in a building at 10 Lombard Street, which was eventually acquired by a company owned by them.[29]

The clearing house has remained at these premises up to now. Despite the recent restructuring, discussed in Chapter 1, of the companies which own the clearing systems, the clearing of cheques remains divided into two main sections: the general clearing and the town clearing. The town clearing is basically the venue for the exchange of cheques for amounts of not less than £10,000 drawn on and collected by branches within the boundaries of the

---

[27] BEA, s. 79.
[28] See pp. 256–8 below.
[29] For details, see 'The Clearing System', Study Booklet Series, BiS, London, 1982.

City. In terms of volume, the items there collected are approximately 1 per cent of all cheques collected on a single day. In terms of the amounts involved, the town clearing accounts for over 90 per cent of the total of daily transactions. Apart from cheques, the town clearing is used for the exchange of bankers' payments, issued likewise for substantial amounts.[30] All other cheques drawn on branches in England and Wales are exchanged at the general clearing section. Their volume is in the millions. In addition to the clearing of cheques, the clearing house is also the venue for the clearing of paper-originated giro transfers.[31]

One significant development in the twentieth century was the granting of access to the clearing facilities to non-clearing banks. Originally, these banks continued to present cheques for payment through messengers. The new system enables these banks to use the services of a clearer for the exchange of their cheques at the clearing house. By now, most banks of the United Kingdom have such an arrangement.

The main modification of the clearing process in the second half of the twentieth century was the introduction of a partially computerized process. A contemporary development was the signing of the 'Golden Memorandum',[32] in which all the clearing banks of the United Kingdom agreed, inter alia, to act as agents for each other in respect of the clearing of cheques. One innovation introduced by the Memorandum was that, in its wake, cheques were no longer required to be remitted by the holder to the branch at which he maintained the account to be credited with the proceeds. The instrument could be paid in at any branch of one of the participating banks. Although the Memorandum is no longer in force, it has been replaced by individual agreements made between the clearing banks. For all practical purposes the position has remained unchanged under these agreements.

The general clearing process is based on the use of two separate documents handed by the payee or the holder of the cheque to the collecting bank. The first document is the cheque. The second is the credit slip, filled in by the payee or holder. Each document contains certain printed details, which include the name of the bank and the respective branch, and blank spaces to be filled in by the respective customer. In addition, each document has a line printed in magnetic ink and readable by the reader–sorter machines used by the banks.

The printed blank form of a cheque includes a number of lines which are to be filled in by the drawer.[33] The first is meant for the insertion of the date

---

[30] See p. 354 below.

[31] See Ch. 12.

[32] The Memorandum, originally issued in 1967, was reprinted from time to time under the title of 'Bank Money Transfer Services'. Its main object was to introduce the Bank Giro systems; its provisions concerning the collection of cheques were incidental.

[33] For the form of a cheque, see Appendix of Forms.

on which the cheque is issued. The second line, which reads 'Pay to . . . or order' (or 'or bearer'), is meant for the insertion of the payee's name. The third line is meant for the insertion of the amount in figures and in words. In addition, most forms contained in British cheque-books have the drawer's name printed on each cheque. The drawer's signature will be executed just above it. The additional line, printed in magnetic ink at the foot of the form, sets out the clearing number of the bank and of the branch on which the cheque is drawn, the number of the drawer's account, and the number of the cheque in question.

Like a cheque, the credit slip contains a line meant for the insertion of the date of the transaction. It also has a box in which the payee lists the amounts of cheques, of other effects, and of cash paid by him to the credit of his account, and a space meant for the insertion of the name of the person who actually hands the credit slip to the bank. In the majority of cases, the name inserted in this space will be that of the customer whose account is to be credited with the amount involved. But in certain instances the name may be that of an agent who is asked to arrange for the clearance of cheques payable to the customer. A line printed in magnetic ink at the foot of the credit slip[34] sets out the clearing number of the bank and of the branch with which the account to be credited is maintained, the number of that account, and the number of the credit slip. The back of the form includes a schedule in which the customer lists details of individual cheques paid in.

In the clearing process, the two documents, the cheque and the credit slip, serve different functions. The credit slip is used to effect the credit entry in the payee's account. The cheque is used to arrange for the debiting of the drawer's account. The actual procedure involved in the clearing of a cheque is subject to some variations. The most common process is that used where the drawer and payee maintain their accounts with different banks and the cheque and credit slip are paid in at the branch with which the payee maintains his account. The same basic procedure applies where the drawer and the payee maintain their respective accounts with two separate branches of the same bank. The procedure is modified if the cheque and the credit slip are paid in at a branch or bank other than that with which the payee maintains his account,[35] and where the bank engaged by the payee is not a clearer. An entirely different procedure is used where the payee and the drawer maintain their accounts with the very same branch of a single bank. Such a transaction is known as an 'in-house' payment.

It will be convenient to commence with a description of the ordinary

---

[34] At the date of going to press, not all banks furnish personalized deposit form books to their customers; most banks, though, make them available on request.

[35] Note that such payment in, at a branch other than that with which the payee maintains his account, is sanctioned by the agreements between the banks which have replaced the 'Golden Memorandum'.

clearing procedure. By way of illustration, assume that the payee maintains his account with the Piccadilly Branch of the L Bank and the drawer's account is with the Oxford (High Street) Branch of the B Bank. In the ordinary course, the clearing of the cheque takes three days. On the first day, the credit slip and cheque are processed by the Piccadilly Branch. The amount of the cheque is encoded in magnetic ink on the cheque and a credit entry is made by means of a computer in the customer's account. If the slip is accompanied by a number of items, the payee's addition of the sums is verified. In addition, a special crossing to the Piccadilly Branch is inserted on the cheque. At present, the main object of this crossing,[36] which is added even where a general crossing has been executed by the drawer, is to identify on the cheque itself the branch which has arranged for its clearing. The credit slip accompanying the cheque remains at the branch. The cheque itself is placed in a bundle of cheques drawn on the B Bank.

In the evening, all bundles of cheques to be collected for the customers of the Piccadilly Branch are forwarded to the L Bank's clearing department in London. The next morning, each bundle is perused by the L Bank's clearing department to ensure that the cheques are not physically damaged and that each item has all the required details encoded on it. The bundle containing the cheque in question is then placed in a box labelled with the name of the B Bank, which is either delivered at the clearing house to employees of that bank or placed on racks allocated to it. The box is then taken to the B Bank's clearing department.

At the B Bank's clearing department, the cheques in the box are again fed into an electronic reader-sorter machine, which performs three functions. First, it places the cheque in question in a box of items drawn on customers of the Oxford (High Street) Branch. Secondly, the machine reads the details encoded on the cheque in magnetic ink. This information is passed on to the B Bank's computer, which will take it into account in the calculation of the balance in the drawer's account at the close of the subsequent day, unless an advice to the contrary is received on that day from the Oxford (High Street) Branch. Obviously, the decision as to whether to pay or to dishonour the cheque is not taken at the clearing department. However, if the balance in the drawer's account is inadequate for meeting the cheque, the computer will place the cheque on an 'out of order list', comprising items specially drawn to the Oxford (High Street) Branch manager's attention. The third function performed by the reader-sorter machine relates to the settlement between the L Bank and the B Bank. The B Bank's clearing department verifies the total amount of cheques presented each day for the customers of every clearer. The cheque in question will constitute part of the amount due from the B Bank to the L Bank.

---

[36] For the ordinary object of such a crossing, see pp. 254–5 below.

The actual settlement between the B Bank and the L Bank takes place at the end of each trading day. The figure, which is based on setting off the balances of all items exchanged in the clearing house on that day, is confirmed the following morning. The settlement, though, is based on the provisional, or uncleared, balances. Adjustment required as a result of the dishonour of individual items is made subsequently. It is considered realistic to strike a balance on the assumption that all cheques cleared on a given day will be honoured as, in practice, the dishonoured items are minimal.

The cheque described in the illustration is forwarded by the B Bank's clearing department to the Oxford (High Street) Branch at the end of the second day of the clearing cycle, i.e. the day after its receipt by the Piccadilly Branch of the L Bank. The cheque is processed at the Oxford (High Street) Branch the next day. Theoretically, the branch is supposed to verify both the adequacy of the funds available and the regularity of the cheque. 'Regularity', in this context, means the authenticity of the drawer's signature, the proper dating of the cheque, and the agreement between the amount in words and in figures. In practice, the need to verify the balance arises only where a cheque is placed on the 'out of order list'. The branch manager or some authorized officer must then decide whether to grant the customer an overdraft or to dishonour the cheque. The verification of the regularity of the cheque is carried out only if its amount exceeds a certain figure, which varies from bank to bank.

If the Oxford (High Street) Branch resolves to dishonour the cheque in question, it has to perform two tasks. First, it has to key the information into its computer terminal. Secondly, it has to return the cheque by first class mail to the Piccadilly Branch of the L Bank. This branch is identified by means of the crossing executed by it before it set the cheque into transmission. The cheque has to be sent out before the close of the day on which the Oxford (High Street) Branch received it, which is the third day of the clearing cycle. A notation explaining the reason for the dishonour is executed on the cheque.[37] The Clearing House Rules make provision for the return of cheques after the close of the third day of the cycle, under a clause known as the 'inadvertence rule'.

If the cheque is honoured, it is retained by the Oxford (High Street) Branch. However, some customers—predominantly small businessmen— require their banks to return 'cancelled' cheques. The main reason for this is that cheques serve as receipts.[38] They may, therefore, be required by a firm's auditors. In this type of arrangement, cheques paid by the customer's bank are returned to him periodically, usually once a month.

---

[37] The reason may, for example, be: 'amount in words and figures differ', or the notorious formula: 'refer to drawer' denoting inadequacy of funds in the drawer's account.

[38] Cheques Act 1957, s. 3.

Where the Oxford (High Street) Branch has resolved to honour the cheque, it need not supply any information to the clearing department's computer centre. This is so even if the cheque was included in the 'out of order list'. If the computer centre does not receive an advice of dishonour by the end of the third day of the clearing cycle it will carry out the necessary entries.

The clearing procedure just described is used even if the two branches—that which collects the cheque and that on which it is drawn—are of the same bank. In such a case, the cheque is processed initially by the collecting branch and then remitted, through the clearing department, to the drawee branch. Although there is no need for the exchange of the cheque at the clearing house, the processing of the cheque in the bank's own clearing department and its dispatch to the drawee branch can take just as long as the process involved in the clearance of cheques where two banks are involved.

The clearing process has to be modified where a cheque drawn on the Oxford (High Street) Branch of the B Bank and payable to the credit of an account maintained with the Piccadilly Branch of the L Bank is paid in at a branch of a third bank, such as the Leicester Square Branch of the N Bank. In such a case, the Leicester Square Branch executes on the cheque a special crossing to itself and then sends the cheque and the credit slip to the N Bank's own clearing department, which delivers the credit slip through the clearing house to the L Bank's clearing department and the cheque to the B Bank's. The respective clearing departments execute the required computer entries; the credit slip is forwarded to the Piccadilly Branch and the cheque to the Oxford (High Street) Branch. If the latter branch decides to dishonour the cheque, it returns it to the Leicester Square Branch of the N Bank, which advises the Piccadilly Branch.[39] One result of this procedure is that the notification of the dishonour to the Piccadilly Branch may take one extra day. As this delay is sanctioned by prevailing banking practice, the payee is not in a position to complain.[40] Moreover, if the cheque was paid in by a transferee, he retains the right to give notice of dishonour to previous parties.[41]

Another variation in the clearing process takes place where the payee of a cheque maintains his account with a bank that is not a member of the clearing house. The payee's bank processes the cheque as if it were, for all practical purposes, a branch of the clearer that it uses as agent, except that most non-clearing banks keep their own records of their customers' accounts and do not convey these to the computer centre of the agent bank. The

---

[39] A basically similar procedure is followed where the cheque is paid in at the Leicester Square Branch of the L Bank itself. The cheque and credit slip are sent directly to the clearing department of the L Bank.

[40] As regards notice of dishonour generally, see p. 261 below.

[41] BEA, s. 49(13).

customer's credit slip is accordingly retained by his own bank. The cheques alone are forwarded in bundles by the payee's bank to the clearing department of the agent. The same department receives, through the clearing house, the cheques drawn on customers of the non-clearing bank in question, and forwards them in the same way as cheques drawn on its branches. It is understood that in the case of non-clearing banks with networks, each branch sends its cheques directly to its agent's clearing department and, in turn, receives from the centre cheques drawn on it.

The clearing procedure is simplified to a considerable extent where both the drawer and the payee maintain their accounts with the same branch of a given bank. In such a case, both the crediting of the payee's account and the debiting of the drawer's account are effected at the computer terminal of the branch in question. The required processing takes place on the very day on which the in-house item is paid in.[42]

The complexity of the operations of the general clearing system is largely due to the volume of the cheques exchanged every day. The procedure is simplified in the case of the town clearing. First, the operations are carried out manually in their entirety. Secondly, the items continue to be exchanged as individual bundles in the clearing house. To this end, each participating bank has a desk in the clearing house which is manned for a few hours on each afternoon of a business day. Each City Branch sorts the town clearing items payable to its customers into bundles of items drawn on other clearers, and these have to reach the clearing house by 3.15 p.m. They are there and then delivered by the employees at the payee (collecting) bank's desk to the employees of the drawee bank. At the latter desk, the itemized list attached to the bundle is verified. All cheques received at this desk are then sorted into individual bundles for each of its branches. These bundles are immediately taken physically to the respective branches, where each cheque is examined forthwith. An instrument which is dishonoured has to be returned to the collecting bank's desk at the clearing house before closing time.

The third characteristic of the town clearing is that both the crediting of the payee's account and the debiting of the drawer's account take place on the day the cheque is delivered to the collecting branch. The town clearing cycle is therefore one day. Settlement is, again, effected through the Bank of England. It is based on the itemized lists exchanged in the clearing house; the amounts of dishonoured items are refunded to the drawee (paying) bank in the following day's settlement. These items cannot be taken into account on the day of exchange as they are usually returned to the clearing house too late to initiate immediate reconciliation. It is clear that, just as in the general clearing, the decision concerning the fate of individual town clearing items is taken at the branches.

---

[42] As regards the legal position of the bank in cases of this type, see pp. 444–8 below.

The procedures used for the clearing of the cheques and other items used by banks are based on an agreement made between the clearing banks. The details thereof are set out in the Clearing House Rules, the original version of which can be traced back to the early nineteenth century. At present there are three operative sets of rules—the General Clearing Rules, the Town Clearing Rules, and the Credit Clearing Rules—which regulate the clearing of giro items. The legal nature of these rules has been considered in a number of cases, the two most recent of which are *Royal Bank of Ireland Ltd.* v. *O'Rourke*,[43] and *Barclays Bank plc* v. *Bank of England*.[44] In both cases, the question was whether the presentment of a cheque by the collecting bank to the paying bank took place at the time of its delivery at the clearing house or when the cheque actually reached the branch on which it was drawn.

In *O'Rourke*, Murnaghan J took the view that presentment took place at the later time, as presentment had to be made to a person entitled to decide whether to pay or dishonour the instrument. His decision was reversed by the Supreme Court of Ireland, where Lavery J held that presentment took place when the cheque was delivered to the paying (drawee) bank's employees at the clearing house. In the *Bank of England* case, Bingham J adopted Murnaghan J's view. His Lordship regarded the paying bank 'as being, from the time of receiving the cheque [in the clearing house] until the time of presenting it, a sub-agent of the [collecting] bank, which is itself the agent of the payee'.[45] In reaching this conclusion, Bingham J relied on the fact that 'the delivery of the cheque to the branch was the physical presentment to the banker for his decision whether to dishonour the cheque or not'.[46] Of paramount importance is his Lordship's analysis of the standing of the Clearing House Rules:

If it is to be said that the drawer loses that right [i.e. to have the cheque duly presented] as the result of a private agreement made between the banks for their own convenience, the very strongest proof of his knowledge and assent would be needed, not only because of the general rule that an individual's rights are not to be cut down by an agreement made between others but also because, in this particular case, the rights of additional parties (such as indorsers) could be affected.[47]

---

[43] [1962] Ir. R 159.

[44] [1985] 1 All ER 385.

[45] Ibid., 392. His Lordship relied on *Bailey* v. *Bodenham* (1864) 16 CB (NS) 288, 290; *Prince* v. *Oriental Bank Corp.* (1878) 3 App. Cas. 325, 328; *Bank of British North America* v. *Haslip* (1914) 30 OLR 299, 301–2.

[46] Ibid., 394. His Lordship relied on *Hare* v. *Henty* (1861) 10 CB (NS) 65, 59; *Prideaux* v. *Criddle* (1869) LR 4 QB 455; *Bank of British North America* v. *Haslip* (1914) 30 OLR 299, affd. 31 OLR 442; *Riedell* v. *Commercial Bank of Australia Ltd.* [1931] VLR 382; *H. H. Dimond (Rotorua 1966) Ltd.* v. *Australia & New Zealand Banking Group Ltd.* [1979] 2 NZLR 739.

[47] Idem.

It is clear that Bingham J refused to treat the Clearing House Rules as constituting an independent customary source of law binding on all persons transacting business with banks. The contracts of adhesion, signed by customers when opening their ordinary accounts with banks, do not make express reference to these rules.

One practical problem is faced by the branch manager in each case in which it is necessary to decide whether to honour or to dishonour a cheque drawn against inadequate funds. The balance communicated to the branch manager by the computer terminal is not that of the day in question but the balance struck at the close of the previous day. The manager, therefore, has to reach his decision on the basis of a balance which is known to be marginally out of date. In practice, though, the problem is of minor significance. An experienced branch manager is familiar with the record and with the credit-worthiness of each customer. He is, therefore, in a good position to assess the situation, and to decide whether to honour or to dishonour a cheque drawn by the customer against an inadequate balance comprising uncleared effects. Thus, if the customer's cheque were presented towards the end of the month, the branch manager would be aware of the fact that a deficiency resulting from the payment of the cheque in question could be met when the customer's monthly wage was paid by the employer to the credit of the account involved.

The discussion of the clearing system shows that, throughout the process, the cheque is treated as a mere instrument issued to effect payment. As has been mentioned, the role of the cheque as a negotiable instrument remains of limited importance where it is cleared through the banking system. That role is relevant only in the rare cases in which a cheque is remitted for the collection of an account maintained by a person other than the ostensible payee. Moreover, even in these cases only one attribute of negotiability is of significance, namely the fact that the instrument is transferable by indorsement and delivery. The most important aspect of negotiability, which is that the transferee may acquire a better title than the transferor, remains irrelevant as regards the clearing process.[48] The role of the cheque as a negotiable instrument is, however, of importance in the relationship of the drawer and the payee, and as regards the rights of a holder.

3. THE CHEQUE AS NEGOTIABLE INSTRUMENT

(i) Introductory

It has been pointed out that a cheque serves two functions. In the relationship between the bank and its customer, it constitutes an instruction to pay a

[48] See, generally, p. 228 above.

certain amount of money to the payee's order or to the bearer. As between the drawer of the cheque, who is the bank's customer, and the payee or a subsequent holder, the cheque constitutes a negotiable instrument. The payee or indorser is, therefore, entitled to enforce it against the drawer.[49] The bank, as drawee, is not a party to the cheque, and the instrument is unenforceable against it by the holder.[50] The mutual rights and obligations arising from the cheque as between the bank and its customer, the drawer, are discussed in Chapter 10. Certain elements of the cheque's negotiability, which are relevant to this relationship, are, of course, referred to in that context. The position of a bank that collects the cheque for the holder is discussed in Chapter 14.

In this chapter, the discussion centres on the cheque as a negotiable instrument which is enforceable by the holder. In this context, it is necessary to consider the legal nature of a cheque and its form, its negotiability and restrictions imposed thereon, the special problems of the post-dating of cheques, the marking of cheques, and the crossing of cheques. A brief analysis of the dishonour of a cheque and of duties of the holder arising thereafter is presented in the last part of this chapter.

(ii) Definition and attributes of a cheque

A cheque is defined in section 73 of the Bills of Exchange Act 1882, as a bill of exchange, drawn on a banker payable on demand. On reading this definition together with that of a bill of exchange in section 3(1) of the Act, the following composite definition emerges: a cheque is an unconditional order in writing, drawn by one person upon another person who is a bank, signed by the drawer, requiring the bank to pay on demand a sum certain in money to or to the order of a specified person or to bearer. The cheque need not use the words 'on demand', but may use instead the synonymous expressions 'on sight' or 'on presentation' or, simply, may not specify a time for payment. In all three cases, the instrument is deemed to be payable on demand under section 10(1); cheques issued in the United Kingdom follow the last pattern.

Two features which are common to cheques are not spelt out in the definition. First, the definition does not require that a cheque be drawn on the bank by a customer. In practice, though, cheques are drawn against balances maintained in current accounts. A person who maintains such an account becomes the bank's customer.[51] The only cases in which a cheque is drawn on a bank by a person other than a customer is where there is fraud

[49] BEA, s. 38(1).
[50] Ibid., s. 53(1).
[51] See pp. 76–80 above.

in the transaction, such as the case in which the signature of the drawer is executed by a forger or by a person without authority to draw on behalf of the owner of the account. Such an instrument constitutes a cheque, and may confer rights against the indorsers on a holder who takes it without knowledge of the fraud.[52] But the instrument is not a valid mandate given by the customer, so that the bank is under a duty to dishonour it.

Secondly, the definition does not require the cheque to disclose the date on which it is drawn. The date is, however, material,[53] as a cheque which has been outstanding for a prolonged period is considered stale and is dishonoured by the drawee bank as being 'out of date'.[54] An unauthorized alteration of the date of the cheque has the effect of discharging it.[55] The usual form of a cheque sets out a space in which the drawer is expected to fill in the date of issue.

In all other regards, the form of a cheque accords with the detailed provisions of the definition of the Bills of Exchange Act. Thus, the cheque forms issued in the United Kingdom include the imperative instruction 'pay' rather than a less direct command. Accordingly, the cheque constitutes an order. Case law suggests that the order could be couched in polite language, such as 'please pay', as long as the request remained imperative rather than precative.[56]

An important requisite based on the definition is that the order has to be unconditional. However, the demarcation between a conditional and an unconditional order is not always clear. An illustration is furnished by section 3(3) of the Act. An order to pay out of a particular fund is conditional; but if the order itself is unqualified it remains unconditional although it is coupled with an indication of a particular fund out of which the drawee is to reimburse himself, with a particular account to be debited with the amount, or with a statement of the transaction which gives rise to the drawing of the instrument. This rule is of practical importance. It will be recalled that an ordinary cheque, contained in a personalized cheque book, sets out certain details, including the drawer's account number, in magnetic ink. But this information is inserted solely for the purpose of identifying the account against which the cheque is drawn. It does not qualify the drawer's demand that the bank pay the cheque. The instrument is, therefore, unconditional.

---

[52] BEA, s. 55(2).

[53] Ibid., s. 64(2); and see *Vance* v. *Lowther* (1876) 1 Ex. D 176.

[54] The Clearing House Rules have no specific provision determining when a cheque becomes stale. An analogy can be drawn from BEA, s. 36(3), which provides that a bill payable on demand is to be regarded as overdue when it has been outstanding for an ureasonable time. It is clear that eight days appears too short a period to render a cheque stale; cf. *London and County Banking Co.* v. *Groome* (1881) 8 QBD 288.

[55] BEA, s. 64(1).

[56] *Little* v. *Slackford* (1828) 1 M & M 171; of *Hamilton* v. *Spottiswoode* (1849) 4 Exch. 200, 210.

Certain cheques, such as those issued by some social security authorities, contain a receipt form printed either on the front or at the back of the cheque. If the request for the signing of the receipt qualifies the drawer's order, the instrument ceases to be an unconditioned order. Thus, in *Bavins Jnr. & Sims* v. *London and South Western Bank*,[57] it was held that a cheque which read 'Pay to B. Bavins the sum of sixty-nine pounds; provided the receipt at the foot hereof is duly signed, stamped and dated', was conditional. The instruction for the signature of the receipt was in this case directed to the drawee. If the instruction is not directed to the drawee, but to the payee, it does not necessarily qualify the order to pay. Thus, in *Nathan* v. *Ogdens Ltd.*,[58] a cheque was issued to effect payment of a debt. It was in the ordinary form but at the foot were printed the words 'the receipt at the back hereof must be signed, which signature will be taken as an indorsement . . . '. It was held that this instrument remained unconditional despite the clause at its foot. The request for the receipt was directed to the payee and, therefore, did not qualify the order issued by the drawer to the drawee.

The distinction between the decisions in the two cases is based on the nature of the request for the receipt. To determine whether such a request falls under the umbrella of the first or of the second decision, it is important to examine whether it is inserted or printed above or beneath the space meant for the drawer's signature. Any words appearing in front of the signature constitute part and parcel of the instruction given to the bank. They do, therefore, qualify the order. Words appearing beneath the signature are more likely to be regarded as auxiliary to the order part of the cheque. They are therefore directed to the payee and not to the drawee. An exception to this general rule is formed by cheque which bear on their front the letter 'R'. This letter serves as an indication to the bank that its customer, the drawer, requires the bank to satisfy itself that the receipt form, provided either at the front or at the back of the cheque, is completed. This suggests that if such a signature is missing, the bank is expected to dishonour the cheque. Thus, the execution of the payee's signature is a prerequisite to the payment of the instrument by the bank. The order is, therefore, conditional.[59]

The condition which qualifies the order is not always a request for the execution of a receipt. It can, for example, be a note on the face of the instrument to the effect that the cheque will not be honoured if presented later than, say, the lapse of six months from the date of issue. Whether such an instruction qualifies the order to the bank or is directed to the payee is a question of fact. It is strongly arguable that the very inclusion of a note to

---

[57] [1900] 1 QB 270.

[58] [1905] 93 LT 553: affd. (1905) 94 LT 126. See also *Thairlwall* v. *Great Western Ry. Co.* [1910] 2KB 509.

[59] Note that the clearing banks regard such an instrument as conditional: p. 309 below.

this effect is an implicit request to the bank not to pay the instrument if presented at a later date. But in *Thairlwall* v. *Great Northern Ry.*,[60] it was held that where such a note appeared at the foot of a dividend warrant, which constituted a cheque, the instrument was unconditional.

Two further requisites based on the definition of a cheque need to be emphasized. The first is that a cheque has to be in writing. Written, for the purposes of the Act, includes 'printed'.[61] It is not clear whether this provision encompasses the signature, and whether a signature may accordingly be executed by means of a rubber stamp. The word 'signature' is not defined in the Act. In *Goodman* v. *J. Eban Ltd.*,[62] the majority of the Court of Appeal thought that a signature affixed by a solicitor on his bill of costs was an adequate signature within the meaning of section 65(2) of the Solicitors Act 1932. In his dissenting judgment, Denning LJ expressed the view that a document could not be signed by means of a rubber stamp, although a mark executed by an illiterate person would be adequate. The difference between a mark and a facsimile signature is not easy to discern. His Lordship expressed the view that a facsimile signature, unlike the mark, was a 'thoughtless impress of an automaton, in contrast to the reasoned attention of a sensible person'.[63] But a facsimile signature imprinted by means of a rubber stamp can be just as thoughtfully executed by a person as can a mark. In reality, the main distinction between a written signature and a mark on the one hand and a facsimile signature on the other is that the rubber stamp can be readily utilized by an unauthorized person whilst a signature, or even a mark, is more difficult to forge. But this, in itself, is not a good ground for doubting the general validity of a facsimile signature.

There is authority for the view that 'written' includes writing in pencil.[64] A cheque written in pencil is, however, unusual in terms of modern banking practice. It is believed that banks will honour a cheque written in pencil, but will then request the customer to abandon the practice.

The second point emphasized in the definition is that a cheque has to be drawn by one person on another person being a bank. This means that if one branch of a bank draws a cheque on another branch or on the head office of the same bank, the instrument is not within the definition as it is drawn by the bank on itself. It will, however, be seen that certain defences conferred on the collecting bank and on the paying bank in respect of cheques are specifically extended to encompass dealings in such 'bankers'

---

[60] Above.
[61] BEA, s. 2.
[62] [1954] 1 QB 550.
[63] Ibid. 561. See also *Lazarus Estates Ltd.* v. *Beasley* [1956] 1 QB 702. Denning LJ's view is supported by the decision of the Supreme Court of Ceylon in *Meyappan* v. *Manchanayake* (1961) 62 NLR 529.
[64] *Geary* v. *Physic (1826) 5 B & C 234.* But see *Importers Co. Ltd.* v. *Westminster Bank Ltd.* [1927] 1 KB 869, 874, affd. [1927] 2 KB 297.

drafts'.[65] In addition, the holder of a banker's draft is in as good a position as the holder of a negotiable instrument. This is so as, under section 5(2), where the drawer and the drawee of an instrument are one and the same person, the holder has the option of treating the instrument either as a bill of exchange or as a promissory note. In both cases the holder is entitled to enforce the instrument.[66]

(iii) The negotiability of a cheque

The method for the transfer of a cheque depends on whether it is payable to a specific person's order or to bearer. A bill is payable to bearer either if it is expressed to be so payable or if the last indorsement on it is executed in blank.[67] A bill is payable to order either if it is expressed to be so payable or if it is expressed to be payable to a particular person and does not include words prohibiting transfer or indicating an intention that it should not be transferable.[68]

The problem that arises in respect of a cheque which is initially made payable to bearer is whether it may be converted into an order cheque by means of a special indorsement, in which the indorser specifies the name of a designated indorsee. An Australian authority suggests that the cheque remains payable to bearer despite the execution of the special indorsement.[69] But this view is questionable. Under section 34(4), 'any holder may convert [a] blank indorsement into a special indorsement by writing above the indorser's signature a direction to pay the bill to or to the order of himself or some other person'. Although this provision does not apply to a bill or cheque drawn initially as payable to bearer but only where the instrument has been indorsed in blank, it reflects the policy of the Act. As a cheque which becomes payable to bearer by reason of the blank indorsement can be converted into an order instrument, it is difficult to see why a cheque, drawn originally as payable to bearer, may not be equally converted into an order cheque by the execution of a special indorsement. Some support for this view can be derived from section 8(5), under which a cheque that 'either originally *or by indorsement*, is expressed to be payable to the order of a

---

[65] Pp. 308–9 below.

[66] *Williams* v. *Ayers* (1877) 3 App. Cas. 133, 142–3; *Re Commercial Bank of South Australia* (1887) 36 Ch. D. 522, 525; *Capital and Counties Bank Ltd.* v. *Gordon* [1903] AC 240, 250. Cf. *Commercial Banking Co. of Sydney Ltd.* v. *Mann* [1961] AC 1, 7 where Viscount Simonds described bankers drafts as promissory notes issued by banks.

[67] BEA, s. 8(3).

[68] Ibid., s. 8(4). And see subs. (5), under which a bill is payable to a specified person's order even if made payable to him without the addition of words indicating that it is payable to order.

[69] *Miller Associates (Australia) Pty. Ltd.* v. *Bennington Pty. Ltd.* (1975) 7 ALR 144; W. J. Chappenden, 'Liability of Signatories to Indorsers of Cheques', (1981) 55 ALJ 135.

specified person, and not him or his order, is nevertheless payable to him or his order at his option'. This provision envisages that the eventual tenor of an instrument may depend either on the manner in which it is drawn or, following its negotiation, on its last indorsement. The provision does not assume that, if in its original tenor the cheque is payable to bearer, it cannot be changed to an order instrument by a special indorsement.

Where a cheque or bill is payable to order, it must specify the identity of the payee with reasonable certainty.[70] A cheque which is made out for a specific purpose, such as 'cash or order', is not a bill of exchange, as it is not payable to a specific payee and is therefore not a cheque.[71] Difficulties arise when the drawer leaves the payee's name in blank. It has been suggested that such an instrument should be treated as payable to bearer 'because that is the natural legal effect'.[72] But it cannot be argued that, where the space between the printed words 'pay . . . *or order*' is left blank, the cheque should be construed in this manner. The words 'or order' militate against such an interpretation. The fact, though, is that the drawer of such an instrument intends to create a valid bill or cheque. One manner of giving effect to his intention is to treat the bill as payable to himself. Thus, in *Chamberlain* v. *Young and Tower*[73] it was held that an instrument reading 'pay . . . order' should be construed as meaning 'pay my order' and, thus, considered a valid bill. But in *R.* v. *Randall*,[74] an instrument reading 'pay . . . or order' was held not to be a bill. An attempt has been made to distinguish the two cases on the basis that the addition of the word 'my' to the phrase 'pay . . . or order' would be meaningless. But the line could be easily construed as 'pay myself or order', which formula is commonly used in personal cheques cashed over the counter. A Scottish decision, in which such a bill was treated as a promissory note, provides an acceptable solution, as it gives effect to the drawer's intention of issuing a negotiable instrument.[75]

Under section 7(3), where a bill or cheque is made payable to a fictitious or non-existing person, it may be treated as payable to bearer, which means that it is transferable by mere delivery. It also means that the bank has the mandate to pay such a cheque to bearer. A difficulty arises, however, because the terms 'fictitious' and 'non-existing' are not defined in the Act. In the leading case of *Bank of England* v. *Vagliano Bros.*,[76] the plaintiffs were

---

[70] BEA, s. 7(1).

[71] But the bill would be valid if payable to 'cash or bearer': it is, then, a bearer bill. Note that under s. 3–111 of the Uniform Commercial Code, a bill payable to 'cash or order' is deemed a valid bill.

[72] *Daun and Vallentin* v. *Sherwood* (1895) 11 TLR 211, 212.

[73] [1893] 2 QB 206.

[74] (1811) Russ & Ry. 195.

[75] *Laurence Henderson, Sons & Co. Ltd.* v. *Wallace and Pennell* 1902, 40 SLR 70, 71, per Lord Trayner. The Lord Justice-Clerk, Lord Macdonald, treated the instrument as a bill.

[76] [1891] AC 107.

in the habit of accepting bills drawn on them by X and payable to the order of P & Co. G, a clerk of the plaintiffs, forged such a bill. The plaintiffs, who did not discover G's forgery of X's signature as the purported drawer, accepted the bill and made it payable at the defendant bank. G then added a forged indorsement in P & Co.'s name, presented the bill to the defendant bank, and obtained payment. The plaintiffs' action for a declaration that the defendant bank was not entitled to debit their account with the amount of the bill was dismissed. The House of Lords held that the bill was payable to a fictitious or non-existing person, and that the defendant bank was, therefore, entitled to pay it when presented by a bearer. Although a firm known as P & Co. was in existence, the person who actually drew the bill—the forger G—had no intention that the bill should be paid to this firm.

Thus, a fictitious or non-existing person may be not only the creation of fiction, such as 'Ivanhoe', or a person who has ceased to exist at the time the bill is drawn, such as a deregistered company, but also a real payee whose name is put on the bill as mere pretence. Whether or not the payee is fictitious or real depends, accordingly, on the intention of the person who actually draws the bill. Whilst this view is supportable in the case of cheques in which the drawer determines the tenor of the bill and is, in effect, the main party to be charged in the event of its dishonour, it is difficult to see that the principle of the *Vagliano* case is appropriate in the case of bills of exchange. In such an instrument, the main obligor is the acceptor[77] and not the drawer. If the acceptor—e.g. the plaintiffs in the *Vagliano* case—intends the instrument to be payable to a designated payee, such as P & Co., why should the court be guided by the intention of a person whose name does not even appear on the bill, such as the forger G? This argument is reinforced in the case of a bill of exchange because the order to pay the bill is given to the designated bank, the defendants in the *Vagliano* case, by the acceptor!

The principle of the *Vagliano Bros.* case was applied to cheques in *Clutton* v. *Attenborough & Son*.[78] A clerk induced his employers to draw a cheque payable to John Brett by falsely representing that a person of that name was entitled to a remuneration for certain work done for the employer. It was held that the payee, John Brett, was a non-existing person. As the employer who drew the cheque intended to make it payable to a 'John Brett' who had completed some work for him, and as there was in reality no such person in existence, the decision appears unexceptional. The position, however, is different if the drawer is induced by another person's fraudulent misrepresentation to make a cheque payable to a designated real

---

[77] BEA, s. 54.

[78] [1897] AC 90. As regards an instrument payable to a person known to have died before its issue, see *Cando Trust Co.* v. *The Queen* [1982] 2 FC 722 (Can.).

person. Such a cheque is not payable to a fictitious or non-existing person and hence is not payable to bearer.[79] The reason for this is that, although the motive that induces the drawer to draw the instrument is the misrepresentation concerning his liability to a third party, he has nevertheless the intention of making the cheque payable to the very person concerned.[80]

In a Canadian authority, *Royal Bank of Canada* v. *Concrete Column Clamps (1961) Ltd..,*[81] Laskin CJC, in a forceful dissenting judgment, pointed out that in the instant type of case 'the discovery of the real or imaginary character of the payee is post facto: and ordinarily the drawer, induced by the fraud, would intend that the cheque take its effect in favour of the named payee'. Implicit in his Honour's judgment is a well-founded criticism of the principle derived from the relevant cases. Indeed, if a cheque is treated as payable to a fictitious or non-existing payee, it is deemed, under section 7(3), to be a bearer cheque. It is therefore enforceable by the transferee against the drawer. If it is treated as payable to a particular person, then the instrument is unenforceable by a transferee who holds it under an indorsement which is not executed by that person.[82] His Honour implies that it is unreasonable that the holder's rights should depend upon the exact intention of, or on the nature of, the misrepresentation attributable to the person who induced the drawer to issue the instrument. It may be that Laskin CJC would prefer basing the outcome on the drawer's fault. At present, this view is not favoured.[83]

Under section 8(1) of the Act, the drawer can restrict the negotiability of a cheque. This is done by inserting in the instrument words which prohibit transfer or which indicate an intention that the instrument be not transferable. When the drawer employs such a procedure, his main object is to prevent the drawee bank from paying the cheque to a person other than the ostensible payee. Understandably, banks discourage their customers from adopting such a course, as it tends to impose extra liability on them. The most effective way of restricting the negotiability of a cheque is by inserting after the payee's name the word 'only'. It has been held that, in such a case, there cannot be a holder, let alone a holder in due course, capable of enfor-

---

[79] *Vinden* v. *Hughes* [1905] 1 KB 795; *North and South Wales Bank Ltd.* v. *Macbeth* [1908] AC 137.

[80] Can a cheque be treated as payable to bearer if the payee is fictitious or non-existent but the words 'or bearer' in the printed form have been struck out and a crossing has been added, accompanied by the words 'not negotiable—a/c payee only'? See, *Rhostar (Pvt.) Ltd.* v. *Netherland Bank of Rhodesia Ltd* [1972] 2 SALR 703, 709–11.

[81] (1976) 74 DLR (3d) 26, 31–2. Cf. *Paul* v. *Western Canada Lottery Foundation* (1981) 127 DLR (3d) 502.

[82] P. 504 below.

[83] It is not favoured even in Canada, where the view of the majority, based on the *Vagliano Bros.* case, was adopted in *Fok Cheong Shing Investments Co. Ltd.* v. *Bank of Nova Scotia* (1981) 32 OR (2d) 705.

cing the instrument.[84] The same object can be achieved by writing the words 'not transferable' on the face of the cheque. The apparently similar words 'not negotiable' have a special meaning when accompanying a crossing, [85] and their meaning when written on an uncrossed cheque is unclear.[86]

Under section 8(1), negotiability is restricted only if the instrument contains words to this effect. This means that the mere cancellation of the words 'or bearer' or 'or order' on a printed cheque form does not have the effect of restricting the negotiability of the instrument. Under section 8(4), a bill which is payable to a particular person remains payable to that person's order. The conclusion is that the cancellation of the words 'or order' is ineffective to change the tenor of the instrument. The cancellation of the words 'or bearer' renders the bill payable to the order of the particular payee named therein.

Where the 'negotiability' of a cheque is restricted, the instrument is in all probability non-transferable. The point is a difficult one, as the Act does not explicity distinguish between transferability and negotiability. Transferability has, however, been shown to be only one attribute of negotiability.[87] The decision in *National Bank* v. *Silke*[88] fails to throw light on whether a non-negotiable instrument is also non-transferable. It is believed that the better view is that a restriction of a cheque's negotiability affects all three aspects of its character as a negotiable instrument. Support for this view is to be found in that an instrument which is rendered non-negotiable by the inclusion of suitable words cannot be enforced by a holder.[89] The first attribute of negotiable instrument therefore ceases to apply in respect of it. The third aspect, namely that a transferee may obtain a better title than the transferor, is explicitly excluded by the reference in section 8(1) to 'negotiability'. It is, therefore, difficult to see why the second attribute of negotiability, which is the transferability of the instruments, should remain intact.

Does the payee of a non-negotiable cheque have to present it for payment in person at the counter of the drawee bank? It has been suggested that such a cheque may be crossed and presented for payment through clearing channels by the payee's bankers.[90] As the collecting bank acts as a mere agent of the payee and not as a transferee in his own right, this view deserves sup-

---

[84] *Hibernian Bank Ltd.* v. *Gysin and Hanson* [1939] 1 KB 483, affg. [1938] 2 KB 384, where a bill of exchange, which was not a cheque, contained the word 'only' and 'not negotiable' on its face.

[85] Pp. 255–6 below.

[86] *Hibernian Bank Ltd* v. *Gysin and Hanson* [1939] 1 KB 483, 488, shows that the words, when written on an instrument other than a cheque, restrict negotiability. On a cheque, the words have their special meaning only when accompanied by a crossing. When written without, they may arguably be given their natural construction.

[87] Pp. 227–8 above.

[88] [1891] 1 QB 435.

[89] *Hibernian Bank Ltd.* v. *Gysin and Hanson* [1939] 1 KB 483.

[90] Paget, *Law of Banking*, 9th edn., p. 193.

port.[91] On the same argument, though, the payee should be entitled to present the cheque for payment at the drawee bank's counter through a personal agent, such as a relative or business associate. In the absence of case law in point, it is difficult to determine the construction likely to be given to the drawer's intention by a court.

It has been pointed out above that a negotiable cheque is transferable either by indorsement and delivery or by mere delivery, depending on whether it is payable to order or to bearer. As negotiation is rare in the case of cheques and common in the case of other types of bill of exchange, it will be convenient to discuss details of the form of an indorsement and the distinction between a special indorsement and an indorsement in blank in Chaper 17. Two points need, however, to be made at this stage. The first is that, in the case of cheques, an indorsement frequently serves the function of a receipt. This aspect of the law of cheques is illustrated by cases in which the ostensible payee of an uncrossed cheque cashes it over the drawee bank's counter. The bank has the intention of honouring, and hence of discharging, the instrument, and not that of becoming a transferee. An indorsement for transfer or negotiation purposes is, therefore, unnecessary. But under current banking practice, the payee is asked to sign his name on the back of the cheque.[92] The signature, which assumes the form of an indorsement in blank, simply evidences payment of the cheque by the bank to a person who claims to be the payee.

The second point is that, where a cheque is transferred, the transferee is well advised to demand the payee's indorsement even if the cheque is payable to bearer. The reason for this is that, by executing an indorsement, the 'indorser' warrants that the cheque will be paid on presentment.[93]

(iv) Post-dated cheques[94]

A cheque is an instrument payable on demand. The blank line meant for the insertion of the date of issue at the top of the form does not have the object of enabling the drawer to determine the date of the presentment of the instrument for payment. There are, however, cases in which the drawer wishes to ensure that a cheque is not presented before a certain date, such as the day on which his monthly salary is due to be paid into his account by his employers. In such a case, the drawer can post-date the cheque, which then gives the impression of having been issued at the postponed date. After that date the cheque appears on its face to be an ordinary instrument which is

[91] Pp. 418–21 below.
[92] Pp. 309–10 below.
[93] BEA, s. 55(2).
[94] See J. M. Holden, 81 *JIB* 253, and 85 *JIB* 41; C. R. Craigie, 'Post Dated Cheques', (1983) 11 A Bus. LR 107 (Aust.).

payable on presentment to the drawee bank. Post-dated cheques were used instead of bills of exchange payable at fixed future dates during periods in which the stamp duty on cheques was lower than on bills. At present, however, the stamp duty differential is no longer in effect.[95]

Does a post-dated cheque fall within the definition of section 73 of the Act? In an Australian authority, *Brien* v. *Dwyer*,[96] Barwick CJ suggested that a post-dated cheque constituted a bill of exchange payable at a future date, rather than a cheque which had to be payable on demand. On this basis it was decided that the furnishing of a post-dated cheque did not comply with a contractual term in a contract of sale which required payment by cheque. The decision, however, is questionable, as under section 10(1)(*b*) an instrument is payable on demand if no time for payment is expressed in it. Although a post-dated cheque bears an incorrect date of issue, it does not designate any date for payment.

English law inclines to the view that a post-dated cheque is valid in all regards. The reasoning is based on section 13(2) of the Act, under which a bill is not invalid by reason of its being post-dated, ante-dated or undated. Although the section does not refer specifically to the validity of the instruments as a cheque, but only as a bill, it has been held that this provision validates a post-dated cheque.[97]

The English authorities further conclude that the holder of a post-dated cheque is entitled to enforce payment of it. Moreover, a transferee who obtains a cheque for value and in good faith becomes a holder in due course on the date on which he acquires the instrument, and not only as from the date on which it purports to be made. In the authority in point, *Hitchcock* v. *Edwards*,[98] it was expressly held that the post-dating of the cheque does not render the instrument irregular on its face.

Certain disadvantages are, however, attached to a post-dated cheque. They stem from the fact that, as between the drawer who is the customer and the drawee bank, the post-dating of the instrument has the effect of instructing the bank to refuse payment if the cheque is presented before the purported date of its issue. It follows that if the customer countermands the cheque during the period in which it is post-dated, the instrument will be dishonoured by the bank.[99] The holder's only remedy in such a case is to sue

---

[95] Up to 1961 bills were subject to an *ad valorem* duty whilst cheques were subject to a fixed duty of 2p. The Finance Act 1961 equated the duty payable on bills with that payable on cheques. At present bills and notes are exempt from duty under the Finance Act 1970, s. 32; see Byles, *Bills of Exchange*, 25th edn., London 1983, p. 8.

[96] (1979) 22 ALR 485, 491–2, and see Aickin J at 508.

[97] *Hitchcock* v. *Edwards* (1889) 60 LT 636; *Royal Bank of Scotland* v. *Tottenham* [1894] 2 QB 715.

[98] Above.

[99] *Morley* v. *Culverwell* (1840) 7 M & W 174, 178; *Pollock* v. *Bank of New Zealand* [1902] 20 NZLR 174; *Keyes* v. *Royal Bank of Canada* [1947] 3 DLR 161. Contrast *Magill* v. *Bank of North Queensland* (1985) 6 QLJ 262.

the drawer. In addition, the bank will be bound to dishonour the cheque if the drawer dies or becomes insane while the cheque is post-dated.[100] For these reasons it is inadvisable for a payee to take a post-dated cheque in satisfaction of an outstanding debt.

From an analytical viewpoint, it is clear that the case law on the subject is inconsistent. As between the holder and the drawer, a post-dated cheque is regarded as valid and as regular from its genuine date of issue. As between the drawer and his bank, the very same cheque is treated as unissued until the arrival of the fictitious day of drawing. It is believed that it would be preferable to treat a post-dated cheque on an equal basis in all the relevant relationships. This could be attained by a provision under which a cheque were to be deemed payable on demand irrespective of its purported date of issue.[101]

(v) Marking of cheques

There are two types of situations in which a bank on which a cheque is drawn is asked to mark or 'certify' it as good for payment. The first is where the request is made by the drawer or by the holder. The second is where the cheque reaches the hands of the collecting bank too late for presentment through the clearing house on the same day. In such a case, the collecting bank may request the drawee bank to mark the cheque as good for payment on the understanding that the cheque will be cleared the next day. In both types of case, the object of the request made to the drawee bank is based on the presentor's wish to ascertain the fate of the instrument. Furthermore, only one basic formula, which is 'marked good for payment', is in use. But the effect of the marking differs to a considerable degree in the two situations.

Where a cheque is marked at the request of the collecting bank, the certification is recognized under the custom of bankers as constituting a promise to pay. This was initially settled at the beginning of the nineteenth century.[102] Currently it is recognized that such a marking is equivalent to payment, and that a marked instrument cannot be returned as dishonoured.[103] However, the marking is valid for one day only, which means that the instrument must be cleared by the collecting bank without delay.

A certification requested by the drawer or by the payee of a cheque is not

---

[100] Pp. 278–80 below.

[101] But see, by way of contrast, s. 73(*b*) of the Bills of Exchange Ordinance of Israel, under which a post-dated cheque is payable or acceptable only after the purported date of issue.

[102] *Robson* v. *Bennett* (1810) 2 Taunt. 388. And see *Goodwin* v. *Robarts* (1875) LR 10 Ex. 337, 351–2; affd. (1876) 1 App. Cas. 476.

[103] Initially this was settled in a circular of the Bankers Clearing House of February 1927.

a request for immediate payment. The drawer who requests the bank to certify the cheque wishes to give it extra currency by the addition of the bank's name to his own. The payee or holder, who could get payment forthwith by presenting the cheque, wishes for reasons of his own to defer payment, but at the very same time wants to obtain assurance thereof. A specific case in which he may wish to obtain such an assurance for due payment is where he holds a cheque while it is still post-dated.

Some legal systems make provision for the certification of a cheque at the request of the holder or the drawer. Section 3–411 of the Uniform Commercial Code (USA) is an example in point. Under this provision the certification of a cheque constitutes an acceptance. The bank is not obliged to give such a certification, but if it does, the drawer of the cheque and any indorsers are discharged from liability. The bank which has certified a cheque is entitled to earmark the amount required for meeting it out of the balance standing to the drawer's credit. Obviously, the balance available for meeting other cheques drawn by the drawer would be reduced accordingly.

In the United Kingdom, a cheque is regarded as not being a proper instrument for the bank's acceptance under section 18 of the Bills of Exchange Act 1882. Although it was at one time suggested that a bank could accept a cheque if it so desired,[104] there is clear authority for the view that such a course would be unusual[105] and, further, that certification does not constitute an acceptance. In *Bank of Baroda Ltd.* v. *Punjab National Bank Ltd.*,[106] Lord Wright observed that 'the marking of a cheque has so far been only judicially recognized to import a promise or undertaking to pay as between banker and banker for the purpose of clearance'.[107] As between other parties, the certification was a mere 'representation, as to the genuineness of the cheque and of the signature. If the cheque had not been post-dated, the certification might also be held to include a representation as to the then sufficiency of the drawer's account.[108]

It seems unlikely that the holder of a marked cheque could sue the drawee bank on the basis of the representation made when the bank certified the cheque. The holder's difficulty would be to establish a valid cause of action. It will be recalled that the drawing of a cheque does not constitute an assignment of funds against which it is drawn by the drawer to the payee. The bank, as mere drawee, is not bound as against the holder to meet the cheque, even if it is drawn against an adequate balance. Under the

[104] *Robson* v. *Bennett* (1810) 2 Taunt. 388, 396. Note that the acceptance of a cheque payable to bearer would, in any event, be contrary to the Bank Charter Act 1844, s. 11.
[105] *Bellamy* v. *Marjoribanks* (1852) 7 Exch. 389, 404; *Bank of Baroda Ltd.* v. *Punjab National Bank* [1944] AC 176, 188.
[106] Above. See also *Gaden* v. *Newfoundland Savings Bank* [1899] AC 281; *Southland Savings Bank* v. *Anderson* [1974] 1 NZLR 118.
[107] [1944] AC 176, 187.
[108] Ibid., 191.

certification, the bank might be estopped from denying the validity of the drawer's signature or even from denying that, at the time the cheque was certified, his account had a sufficient balance for meeting the instrument. But an estoppel based on such a representation does not in itself constitute a valid cause of action. It is, further, unlikely that the action could be based on negligence imputable to the bank in respect of its representation on the basis of the principle initially laid down in *Hedley Byrne & Co. Ltd.* v. *Heller and Partners Ltd.*[109] The reason for this is that the bank's representation cannot be taken to imply that the instrument would be paid when presented. It is well understood that the decision as to whether a cheque is to be dishonoured must invariably depend on the circumstances existing at the time of its presentation for payment, and not on the position prevailing at any earlier point of time.

The limited effect of the certification of a cheque is highlighted by the fact that the instrument can be countermanded by the customer at any time before it is paid. The bank is then bound to dishonour the cheque.[110] The certification is thus without any binding effect.

At present, the practice of marking cheques at the request of the holder or the drawer is not used by the clearing banks. Indeed, certification has been discouraged by the Committee of London Clearing Bankers since 1920.[111] The usual procedure is that, instead of marking a cheque as good for payment at the request of the drawer or of the holder, the bank exchanges it for a bankers' draft issued by itself. However, it is understood that the marking of cheques is still practised by some merchant and private banks in this country.

4. CROSSED CHEQUES

(i) Background and types of crossings

The crossing of cheques is a feature of the law of the United Kingdom and of countries which have adopted its system. It is unknown in the United States, and though known in some Continental jurisdictions, has a different effect there.

In the United Kingdom, the practice originated in the eighteenth or early nineteenth century in the context of the procedures of the clearing house.

---

[109] [1964] AC 465, discussed on pp. 459–60 below.
[110] *Keyes* v. *Royal Bank of Canada* [1947] 3 DLR 161; *Southland Savings Bank* v. *Anderson* [1971] 1 NZLR 118, 121; cf. *Gibson* v. *Minet* (1824) 2 Bing. 7.
[111] Paget, *Law of Banking*, 9th edn., p. 248.

The employees of different banks, who brought to the clearing house cheques remitted for collection by customers, wrote the name of their banks on each cheque so as to facilitate the settlement of the acccounts at the clearing house.[112] There is no suggestion that at the time the name of the collecting bank was written between the presently common transverse parallel lines. The crossing of cheques by the drawers is later in origin. It was certainly known by the middle of the nineteenth century.[113]

Crossed cheques became the subject of legislation for the first time in the Crossed Cheques Act 1856,[114] which made the fraudulent obliteration and alterations of a crossing an offence. The next step was taken in the Crossed Cheques Act 1876, which repealed and replaced the earlier legislation. The two main innovations of this Act were, first, that a bank which paid a cheque in contravention of a crossing was rendered liable to compensate the 'true owner',[115] and, secondly, that statutory recognition was given to crossings accompanied by the words 'not negotiable'. The Act further provided a general defence for banks as regards the collection of crossed cheques. This defence became the subject of section 82 of the Bills of Exchange Act 1882, and was subsequently widened in section 4 of the Cheques Act 1957. Other provisions of the 1876 Act are currently reproduced, subject to minor variations, in sections 76–81 of the 1882 Act.

The 1882 Act recognizes two basic types of crossings. The first, which in known as a general crossing,[116] consists of the placing of two parallel transverse lines across the cheque. These lines may stand on their own or may be accompanied by the words 'and company' or an abbreviation thereof, which usually assumes the form of '& Co.'. In modern practice, it is uncommon to add these words to a general crossing. Their origin can, again, be traced back to the early practice of the clearing house. Where the drawer crossed a cheque in this manner, the collecting bank could add its own name in front of the symbol '& Co.', and in this way identify itself for the clearing process. At present, this specific function is served by the encoded crossing executed at the collecting branch's computer terminal.

The second type of crossing, known as a special crossing,[117] is executed by placing on the front of the cheque the name of a specific bank. This bank is, obviously, not the drawee bank but the bank which is expected to collect

[112] See the discussion in *Bellamy* v. *Majoribanks* (1852) 7 Exch. 389, 402; *Carlon* v. *Ireland* (1856) 25 LJQB 113.

[113] See the discussion in *Smith* v. *Union Bank of London* (1875) 1 QBD 31.

[114] As amended by the Crossed Cheques Act 1858. Apart from specific provisions, such as s. 19 of the Stamp Act 1853, this was the first Act dealing specifically with aspects of cheques. And see *Simmonds* v. *Taylor* (1857) 27 LJCP 248.

[115] The earlier decision in *Smith* v. *Union Bank of London* (1875) 1 QBD 31, centring on the earlier Acts, was inconclusive.

[116] BEA, s. 76(1).

[117] Ibid., s. 76(2).

the cheque. This type of crossing was the one originally executed by banks for the purposes of the clearing procedure. As a crossing executed by either the drawer or the holder of the cheque, a special crossing has become obsolete.

Both a general and a special crossing may be accompanied by the words 'not negotiable'.[118] In practice, it is common to add to these words the phrase 'account payee only'.

(ii) Execution of crossing and its effect

According to section 77 of the 1882 Act, a cheque may be crossed generally or specifically either by the drawer or by the holder. The holder is entitled to cross a cheque even if an original crossing, usually printed on the cheque, has been 'opened' by the drawer. Furthermore, the holder may turn a general crossing into a specific one by adding the name of a bank, and can also add the words 'not negotiable'. The word 'holder' includes, in this context, an agent for collection,[119] so that a collecting bank is entitled under the Act to alter a general crossing in the same manner as a transferee who acquires the instrument in his own right. In this way, the Act gives effect to the procedures of the clearing house. Section 77 further provides that where a cheque is crossed specifically, the bank to whom it is so crossed may again cross it specifically to another bank for collection. The object of this provision is to enable banks that are not members of a clearing house to remit cheques payable to their customers to one of the clearing banks. Where an uncrossed cheque, or a cheque crossed generally, is sent to a bank for collection, it may cross it specifically to itself.

There are some misconceptions in the business world about the effect of a crossing. It is often asserted that a crossing restricts the transferability of a cheque. This is incorrect. The effect of a crossing is best understood when one recalls the two main methods for obtaining payment which are available to the holder of an uncrossed cheque. In the first place, the holder can send the uncrossed cheque for collection to his own bank, which will then present it to the drawee bank through the clearing channels. Secondly, the holder may present the uncrossed cheque for payment at the drawee bank's counter. When a cheque bears either a general or a specific crossing, this second mode of realization is unavailable to the holder. If the cheque bears a general crossing, it must be presented for payment through a bank; if it bears a specific crossing it must be presented for payment through the desig-

---

[118] Ibid., s. 76, and see s. 81.
[119] *Akrokerri (Atlantic) Mines Ltd.* v. *Economic Bank* [1904] 2 KB 465, 472; *Sutters* v. *Briggs* [1922] 1 AC 1; *Baker* v. *Barclays Bank Ltd.* [1955] 1 WLR 822.

nated bank.[120] The holder of a crossed cheque also has the option of negotiating it to a third party.

Under section 79(2) of the Act, if the drawee bank pays a cheque otherwise than in the manner authorized by the crossing, it is liable to compensate the true owner of the instrument for any loss sustained by the latter due to the improper payment of the cheque. It is, however, provided that when a cheque is presented for payment and does not at that time appear to be crossed or to have had a crossing which has been altered or obliterated, the drawee bank does not incur any liability to the true owner, provided it has paid the cheque in good faith and without negligence. This proviso should not give the impression that it is legitimate to obliterate a crossing. Under section 78, a crossing is a material part of a cheque and, except where an addition is authorized by the Act as explained above, it is unlawful for any person to alter a crossing or to tamper with it.[121]

Thus, one of the declared objects of a crossing is to protect the rights of the true owner of a cheque. Another effect of a crossing is to protect the rights of the drawer. A bank that pays a cheque in a manner prohibited by the crossing executed on it exceeds its authority and is not entitled to debit the drawer's account.[122] Payment without negligence in accordance with the tenor of a crossing does, on the other hand, confer on the drawee bank a defence against an action by the drawer or by the true owner of the cheque.[123]

(iii) Crossing accompanied by the words 'not negotiable'

Section 81 of the 1882 Act defines the effect of the words 'not negotiable' where these are added to a crossed cheque. A person who takes a cheque with such a crossing cannot obtain a better title than that of the transferor and cannot confer a better title on a subsequent transferee. It follows that the third characteristic of negotiable instruments, discussed earlier in this chapter,[124] is inapplicable where a cheque is crossed 'not negotiable'. Although the cheque remains transferable, each transferee takes it subject to the defects in the title of all previous parties. A person cannot become a holder in due course of the instrument. In *Great Western Railway Co. v. London and County Banking Company Ltd.*, Lord Lindley said: 'Everyone who takes a cheque marked "not negotiable" takes it at his own risk, and

---

[120] BEA, s. 79(2). Under s. 79(1), if a cheque is crossed specially to more than one bank, the drawee bank has to refuse payment. But this does not apply where the second bank is the first bank's agent for collection.

[121] See also s. 64(1), which defines the details which are material.

[122] *Bobbett* v. *Pinkett* (1876) 1 Ex. D 368, 372–3.

[123] BEA, s. 80, discussed pp. 306–7 below.

[124] Pp. 227–8 above.

his title to the money got by its means is as defective as his title to the cheque itself.'[125]

(iv) Cheques crossed with the words 'account payee only' added

It is a well-established practice to add the words 'account payee only' to a general crossing. The Act itself is silent as regards the effect of these words. At first glance they appear to direct the drawee bank to pay the cheque only if it is presented for the account of the payee. In practice, though, such a construction would place an impossible task on the drawee bank. The crossing which accompanies these words means that the cheque has to be collected through clearing channels so that it cannot be presented for payment by the payee. But when the cheque is received through the clearing process the drawee bank has no direct means for ascertaining whether it is being collected for the account of the ostensible payee or for some other account. It is true that, where a cheque is collected for the account of such other person, the collecting bank as a matter of practice requires the original payee's indorsement. But in many cases the payee indorses the cheque even if it is collected for his own account. The appearance of the payee's indorsement, or signature, at the back of the cheque is therefore not conclusive evidence that the instrument is collected for another person. It has been held that the words 'account payee only' should not be treated as directed to the drawee bank.[126]

A separate question is whether or not the words 'account payee only' preclude the transfer of the cheque. Do they constitute words prohibiting transfer or indicating an intention within the meaning of section 8(1) of the Act that the cheque be not transferred? A South African authority, *Dungarvin Trust (Pty.) Ltd. v. Import Refrigeration Co. (Pty.) Ltd.*,[127] suggests that although the words 'account payee only' are not an express prohibition of the transfer of the cheque, they preclude it by implication, as they indicate that the instrument should be paid only to the account of the ostensible payee. A later South African authority[128] takes the opposite view, which is also that expressed in the English cases in point.[129] According to these authorities, the words in question constitute a direction to the collecting bank.

---

[125] [1901] AC 414, 424. See also, *Universal Guarantee Pty. Ltd. v. National Bank of Australasia Ltd* [1965] 1 Lloyd's Rep. 525, 531. Cf. *Miller Associates (Australia) Pty. Ltd. v. Bennington Pty. Ltd.* (1975) 7 ALR 144 (Aust.).

[126] *National Bank v. Silke* [1891] 1 QB 435, 439.

[127] [1971] 4 SALR 300, followed in *Rhostar (Pvt.) Ltd. v. Netherlands Bank of Rhodesia Ltd.* [1972] 2 SALR 703, 705.

[128] *Standard Bank of South Africa Ltd. v. Sham Magazine Centre* [1977] 1 SALR 484 (App. Div.).

[129] *National Bank v. Silke* [1891] 1 QB 435; *Universal Guarantee Pty. Ltd. v. National Bank of Australasia Ltd.* [1965] 1 Lloyd's Rep. 525.

This bank is warned that if it were to collect the cheque for an account other than the ostensible payee's, it would act at its own peril.[130] If the collecting bank ignores this warning, it would in all probability lose the defence conferred on it under section 4 of the Cheques Act 1957 against an action by the true owner of the cheque.[131]

The weight of authority is thus opposed to the view that the words 'account payee only' restrict the transferability of a crossed cheque. This leads to an anomaly. On the one hand, the collecting bank is warned not to collect the cheque unless it is remitted for the credit of the ostensible payee's account. On the other hand, the cheque remains transferable. But as the collecting bank is expected to refuse to handle the cheque at the request of a transferee, and as the cheque, being crossed, cannot be paid over the counter, how can it be regarded as transferable in practice? Undoubtedly, a collecting bank may agree to handle the cheque for the account of a third party, such as the ostensible payee's spouse or parent, if the payee does not have an account of his own.[132] However, these are exceptional circumstances. In the ordinary course, the collection of the cheque will be refused unless it is remitted for the credit of the ostensible payee's account. The instrument is therefore transferable in theory alone.

The prevailing view has the further disadvantage of treating the words 'account payee only' as having a completely different effect than the other components of a crossing. It will be recalled that the general crossing itself restricts the manner in which the cheque is to be discharged. Payment over the counter is precluded. The accompanying words 'not negotiable' have a further restrictive effect on the instrument itself. A transferee cannot acquire a better title than the transferor. The words 'account payee only' are, under the bulk of authority regarded as a mere warning to the collecting bank. Unlike the other elements of a crossing, the words 'account payee only' are not supposed to affect the nature of the cheque itself.

It may be retorted that, whilst the effect of a general crossing and of the accompanying words 'not negotiable' is governed by the Act, the words 'account payee only' have no statutory recognition and do not constitute a component of the crossing. But it is clear that, in practice, these words are invariably written on a cheque as part and parcel of a crossing. Indeed, in the majority of cases the entire crossing is executed by means of a rubber stamp, which includes the transverse parallel lines, the words 'not

---

[130] And see *Akrokerri (Atlantic) Mines Ltd.* v. *Economic Bank* [1904] 2 KB 465, 472; *Morison* v. *London County and Westminster Bank Ltd.* [1914] 3 KB 356, 373–4.

[131] *House Property Co. of London Ltd.* v. *London County and Westminster Bank* (1915) 84 LJKB 1846; *Universal Guarantee Pty. Ltd.* v. *National Bank of Australasia Ltd.* [1965] 1 Lloyd's Rep. 525, 531. Cf. *Morison* v. *London County and Westminster Bank Ltd.*, above, 373.

[132] For some support for the view that the payee may authorize collection for a third party's account, see *Souhrada* v. *Bank of New South Wales* [1976] 2 Lloyd's Rep. 444, 452 (Aust.).

negotiable' and the words 'account payee only'. It is, therefore, artificial to treat the different components of the crossing as being directed to separate parties, the first two elements being directed to the world at large and the third as being a mere warning to a specific person—the collecting bank—which is not intended to be a party to the instrument.

It is believed that the opinion expressed in the *Dungarvin* case, discussed above, is to be preferred, although to date it is contrary to the general view. Furthermore, it is arguable that as the words 'account payee only' manifest an intention that the bill be collected only for the credit of the ostensible payee, they constitute a 'red flag'. A person who takes such a cheque as transferee cannot therefore hold it in due course.

(v) Crossing of instruments similar to cheques

The provisions of the Act concerning the crossing of cheques apply to four types of instruments which, though similar to cheques, are not encompassed by the definition of a bill of exchange. First, under section 95 of the 1882 Act, the relevant provisions apply to dividend warrants. Secondly, the sections on crossings are extended to 'any document issued by a customer of a banker which, though not a bill of exchange, is intended to enable a person to obtain payment from that banker of the sum mentioned in the document'.[133] This provision was introduced to facilitate the crossing of cheques made payable to 'cash or order',[134] which are not bills in the strict sense of the word as they are not payable to a specific person or to bearer. Thirdly, section 5 of the Cheques Act 1957 applies the provisions on crossing to 'any document issued by a public officer which is intended to enable a person to obtain payment from the Paymaster General or the Queen's and Lord Treasurer's Remembrancer of the sum mentioned in the document'.[135] Finally, a crossing may be executed on a draft drawn by a banker on himself and payable on demand.[136] Such drafts do not fall within the definition of a bill, as they are not drawn by one person on another.

5. THE HOLDER'S DUTIES IN RESPECT OF CHEQUES

(i) The meaning of duty and to whom it is owed

It is inaccurate to speak of 'a holder's duties' as regards the handling of the cheque. If the holder retains the cheque for good, or decides to destroy it, he

---

[133] Cheques Act 1957, s. 4(2)(*b*), read with s. 5.
[134] *Orbit Mining and Trading Co.* v. *Westminster Bank Ltd.* [1963] 1 QB 794.
[135] Cheques Act 1957, s. 4(2)(*c*), read with s. 5.
[136] Ibid., s. 4(2)(*d*), read with s. 5.

does not commit a breach of a duty owed to any person. In the context of this discussion, 'duty' means an obligation which the holder has to perform if he wishes to enforce the cheque against the drawer and against any indorser. As the drawee bank does not commit a breach of its contract with the holder be dishonouring the cheque—to which the drawee bank is not even a party—it would be fallacious to suggest that the holder owes any duty which is a condition precedent to the drawee bank's duty to perform. This is so even as regards the due presentment of a cheque. It is true that a cheque which is presented for payment after the lapse of an unreasonable time from the date of its issue is considered stale, and that the drawee bank will dishonour it on this ground alone. But the bank's decision is based on the fact that its mandate from the drawer, who is the bank's customer, sanctions the payment of a cheque only if it is presented for payment within a reasonable time.

The duties to be performed by the holder as a condition precedent to his right to enforce a dishonoured cheque against the drawer and the indorsers are defined in the Act in respect of bills of exchange generally. There are, however, some modifications which apply only in the case of cheques. In this chapter the general duties of the holder are discussed broadly, emphasis being placed on the special problems arising in respect of cheques. The holder's three duties are, first, to present the cheque for payment; secondly, to send timely notice of dishonour if the instrument is unpaid; and, thirdly, to note and protest the dishonoured cheque if it falls within the definition of a foreign bill.[137]

(ii) Presentment for payment of a cheque

Like other types of bills of exchange payable on demand, a cheque has to be presented for payment within a reasonable time.[138] Section 74(2) provides that in 'determining what is reasonable time regard shall be had to the nature of the instrument, the usage of trade and of bankers, and the facts of the particular case'. The emphasis in this provision is on the usage of bankers. Cases decided before the enactment of this provision may be regarded as out of date.

It is clear that, under both the Act and the practice of bankers, a crossed cheque has to be presented through clearing channels. Moreover, the holder may decide to add a crossing to an open cheque, which is then treated as being crossed. At present, the ordinary clearing cycle is three days, although an extra day is sanctioned under the 'inadvertence rule'.[139] Thus the

---

[137] The meaning of these phrases is explained below, pp. 261–2.
[138] BEA, s. 45(2); and see s. 74(1).
[139] P. 234 above. Note also that presentment is effected when the cheque reaches the branch on which it is drawn.

collection of a cheque through a collecting bank is invariably sanctioned by usage, although the procedure involved may take a number of days. In practice, it is impossible to generalize as regards the number of days required.

The more difficult question concerns the speed with which the payee of the cheque has to either present it or arrange for its clearing. At common law, a distinction was drawn between cases in which the payee lived in the same place as the drawee bank and cases in which he resided in a different place. In the former case, he was expected to present the cheque for payment by the end of the day following its receipt.[140] In the latter case, he had one day to arrange for the dispatch of the cheque to his own bank for collection.[141] But this practice is obsolete. In the present era, it is common for businessmen to remit cheques payable to them for collection just once or twice a week. In the absence of recent authority, it is advisable to regard the question as open. It is noteworthy that presentment of a cheque to the drawee bank through the post office is regarded as anomalous. The payee is expected to use clearing channels.

Delay in presentment has a different effect on the position of the indorser than on the position of the drawer. The indorser is discharged quite regardless of whether or not he sustains loss as a result of the delay.[142] The principle here is the same as that applicable to bills other than cheques. The position of the drawer of a cheque is governed by section 74(1):

Where a cheque is not presented for payment within a reasonable time, and the drawer or the person on whose account it is drawn had the right at the time of such presentment as between him and the banker to have the cheque paid and suffers actual damage through the delay, he is discharged to the extent of such damage, that is to say, to the extent to which such drawer or person is a creditor of such banker to a larger amount than he would have been had such cheque been paid.

The section applies in situations in which the drawer's account had the required credit balance for meeting the cheque, but the bank became insolvent while the cheque was outstanding. A similar rule applies under section 3–502 of the Uniform Commercial Code. Under section 74(3) the holder of the cheque is subrogated to the drawer's rights against the bank. Thus, if the cheque were dishonoured because the bank became insolvent during the delay, and the bank paid a dividend of 30p in the pound to its creditors, the drawer would be discharged to the extent of 70 per cent of the amount of the cheque. The holder could then prove for the amount involved in the bank's winding-up.

Where a debtor takes a third party's cheque from his creditors in satisfac-

---

[140] *Alexander* v. *Burchfield* (1842) 7 Man. & G 1061; 3 Scott NR 555.
[141] *Hare* v. *Henty* (1861) 10 CB (NS) 65, 30 LJCP 302. Note that dispatch by post to the drawee bank was contrary to practice.
[142] BEA, s. 45.

tion of the debts and fails to present the cheque without delay, the failure of the bank discharges the debtor from further liability. The creditor is treated as a person who has wasted a security given to him by the debtor.[143]

(iii) Notice of dishonour

The rules concerning the dispatch of notice of dishonour by the holder of a bill of exchange to previous parties apply in the case of cheques.[144] If the holder fails to send notice in the manner prescribed and within the time provided for in the Act, the indorser and drawer are discharged.[145]

For the purposes of the dispatch of notice of dishonour, an agent is regarded as a party to the bill and, therefore, discharges his duty by sending it to the principal from whom he received the instrument.[146] A collecting bank is thus entitled to give notice of dishonour to its customer and is not required to inform previous parties to the bill. The mere return of the instrument with a notation indicating dishonour is adequate.[147]

In practice, notice of the dishonour of a cheque is not usually required in order to safeguard the holder's rights against the drawer. In the first place, the drawer is not entitled to notice of dishonour if, as between the drawee and himself, the drawee is not obligated to meet the instrument.[148] Thus, if a cheque is dishonoured for want of funds, the drawer is not entitled to notice of dishonour.[149] Secondly, the drawer is not entitled to notice of dishonour where he has countermanded payment.[150]

The indorser is in a different position from that of the drawer, as the indorser is not aware of the likely fate of the cheque. He is entitled to notice of dishonour from the holder and, if notice is not given to him in accordance with the provisions of section 49 of the Act, he is discharged.[151]

(iv) Noting and protest

The noting and the protest of a cheque are governed by section 51 of the Act, which applies to all bills of exchange. Fundamentally, protest and noting—the meaning of which is explained in chapter 17—is required only

---

[143] *Polak* v. *Everett* (1876) 1 QBD 669; *Hopkins* v. *Ware* (1869) LR 4 Ex. 268; *Sawyer* v. *Thomas* (1890) 18 OAR 129.

[144] The rules are set out in BEA, s. 49; and see pp. 518–20 below.

[145] BEA, s. 48.

[146] Ibid., s. 49(13).

[147] Ibid., s. 49(*b*).

[148] Ibid., s. 50(2)(*c*).

[149] For a review of the position at common law, see Byles, *Bills of Exchange*, 25th edn., pp. 166–8; before the Act it depended on whether the drawer could expect the drawee to pay.

[150] BEA, s. 50(2)(*c*).

[151] Ibid., s. 48.

in the case of a foreign instrument.[152] The term 'foreign bill' includes any instrument which is either drawn or payable outside the United Kingdom, or one the payee of which resides abroad.[153] Thus a cheque drawn on a British bank by a foreign correspondent or customer, or even a cheque drawn by a local customer while he is abroad, is a foreign instrument. However, whether a bill is of the inland or of the foreign type depends on its appearance.[154] Thus, if a customer draws a cheque on his account with a British bank while he is abroad and does not insert the foreign place of drawing in the instrument, the cheque is to be treated as an inland instrument.

In practice, the majority of cheques are inland bills on their face, and hence are not noted and protested. It should be emphasized that a cheque drawn by a resident of the United Kingdom on his bank and payable to a creditor overseas in discharge of a debt constitutes an inland bill, because it is to be presented and paid at the counter of the local bank.

6. IMPLICATIONS OF THE CONSUMER CREDIT ACT 1974

The 1974 Act does not restrict the use of cheques as instruments issued to effect payment. But section 123(3) prohibits the taking of any negotiable instrument, including a cheque, by way of security. Section 123(2) prohibits the transfer of a cheque by a creditor to a person other than a bank. The object of this provision is to preclude dealers and finance houses from defeating a valid claim asserted by a consumer by the transfer of the cheque issued by him to an associated company which would claim to be a holder in due course. The transfer of a cheque to a bank for clearing purposes is unaffected.

Naturally, the provisions of the Act apply only to transactions which fall within its ambit.[155]

7. TRAVELLERS' CHEQUES

Travellers' cheques are misnamed. They constitute cheques neither in form nor in substance. In a travellers' cheque, the issuer undertakes to pay the specified amount of money to the order of the original holder (the purchaser) of the instrument or to a transferee, provided the signature, executed by the original holder when he purchased the instrument, tallies with the

---

[152] Ibid., s. 51(2); and see p. 520 below.
[153] BEA, s. 4(1).
[154] Ibid., s. 4(2).
[155] For further details, see pp. 527–8 below.

countersignature executed by him at the time he cashes it. This requisite constitutes the common feature of all travellers' cheques, although the actual form assumed by them differs from issuer to issuer.

The promise or order that appears in the travellers' cheque is usually conditional. The issuer undertakes to pay the instrument only if there is correspondence between the two signatures executed by the original holder. The issuer's undertaking is therefore conditional. Travellers' cheques, accordingly, do not fall within the definition of one of the established forms of negotiable instruments, which are bills of exchange, cheques and promissory notes. They are, in all probability, a new species of negotiable instrument established by a general mercantile usage. The principles governing travellers' cheques, which are largely based on North American decisions, are discussed in detail elsewhere.[156]

---

[156] For a detailed discussion, see *Chitty On Contracts*, 25th edn., paras. 2555 et seq.

CHAPTER 10

The Paying Bank

1. THE BANK'S DUTY TO PAY CHEQUES

(i) Form of cheques and scope of duty to pay

One of the most important functions of a bank is the payment of cheques drawn by customers on their current accounts. Although conceptually a cheque can be drawn on any piece of paper,[1] it is customary for banks to provide their customers with cheque-books and to insist that cheques be drawn on forms contained therein. Moreover, where a customer has more than one current account with his bank, he is furnished with a separate cheque-book for every account and is advised to utilize the forms in each book for the respective account only. This request is motivated by practical considerations. First, the name of the account and the address of the branch at which the account is kept are printed on the forms contained in each cheque-book. Any alteration requires extra checking by the bank. Secondly, the forms include a box with numbers printed in magnetic ink which set out the clearing number of the bank and of the relevant branch, and the numbers of the account and of the cheque itself. This data is automatically decoded in the computerized clearing process applicable since the 1960s, and facilitates the clearing of the cheque.[2] An alteration made on the form, such as a change effected in ordinary ink of the name and of the address of the branch on which the instrument is drawn, is bound to lead to confusion, as the computer is unable to cope with it.

The point is illustrated by *Burnett* v. *Westminster Bank Ltd*.[3] A customer had two current accounts with Westminster Bank: one with the X Branch and the other with the Y Branch. At the relevant time, the Y Branch had become linked to the computer network of Westminster Bank, which meant that cheques drawn on this branch were cleared by a process based on the decoding of the details imprinted in magnetic ink. The X Branch had not been linked to the network, remaining subject to the manual clearing process. Despite a request set out in the folder of the cheque-book issued by the

---

[1] *Roberts & Co.* v. *Marsh* [1915] 1 KB 42.
[2] The clearing procedure is discussed above, pp. 230 et seq.
[3] [1966] 1 QB 742.

Y Branch to the effect that forms contained in the book be used only for drawing cheques on the relevant account, the customer used one form to draw a cheque on his account with the X Branch. To this end, he struck out the address of the Y Branch on the cheque and substituted that of the X Branch. On the following day he gave notice of countermand to the X Branch. The cheque, however, was forwarded by means of the computerized clearing process to the Y Branch, where it was honoured. It was held that the request set out in the folder did not constitute a term of the contract between the bank and its customer, as the accounts in question had been opened before the computerization of the Y Branch. The notice printed in the folder was, accordingly, given to the customer after the contract between him and the bank had been concluded. The bank could not vary its contract with the customer by a unilateral act. The cheque in question was, therefore, treated as drawn on the X Branch, and the countermand given to that branch was held to be effective.

Burnett v. *Westminster Bank Ltd.* shows that the paying bank's contract with its customer cannot be abrogated unilaterally by the bank, even when there is a change in banking practice occasioned by such factors as technological developments. The contract can, however, be varied by express agreement. Undoubtedly, a variation of a contract is valid only to the extent that it is supported by consideration.[4] In the case in question, the notice given in the folder could have been constituted a term of the contract if it had been made the subject of an agreement by means of a circular letter issued to customers and offering them some concession in consideration of their acceptance of the new practice. It could, further, be made the basis of contracts with new customers.[5] To date this has not occurred in the United Kingdom.

Burnett's case reflects a further point. The bank's duty to pay a cheque, or to refuse its honour, is owed to the customer alone. In English law the drawing of a cheque does not involve an assignment by the customer to the payee or holder of the instrument of a chose in action owed by the bank.[6] Furthermore, the bank does not accept the cheque, and hence it does not engage to honour it when presented.[7] The cheque itself is unenforceable against the bank.

This does not mean that a bank can dishonour cheques drawn on it with

---

[4] *Re Williams Porter & Co. Ltd.* [1937] 2 All ER 361; *Anson's Law of Contract*, 26th edn., p. 434.

[5] The point was raised in *Burnett*'s case, above, 763.

[6] The Bills of Exchange Act 1882 (BEA), s. 53(1); and see *Schroeder* v. *Central Bank of London Ltd.* (1876) 34 LT 735; *Shand* v. *Du Buisson* (1874) LR 18 Eq. 283, 288–9; *Hopkinson* v. *Forster* (1874) LR 19 Eq. 74. The position differs in Scotland: s. 53(2).

[7] In the United Kingdom cheques are not 'certified'; see above, pp. 250–2. That cheques are not meant to be accepted has been establised since the middle of the nineteenth century: *Bellamy* v. *Marjoribanks* (1852) 7 Exch. 389, 404. And see *Bank of Baroda Ltd.* v. *Punjab National Bank Ltd.* [1944] AC 176, 188.

impunity. A wrongful dishonour constitutes a breach of the contract between the bank and its customer. But the bank's duty to its customer is subject to certain limitations. The first is that the amount of the cheque must not exceed either the balance standing to the credit of the customer's account or the ceiling of agreed overdraft facilities. The second restriction applies to the place of payment. The bank's duty to pay its customer's cheques arise only if the instrument is presented at the branch at which the account is kept. Thirdly, the bank's duty to pay the customer's cheques may be abrogated by law. This occurs in the following cases: (*a*) upon the issuing of a garnishee order or an injunction restraining payment; (*b*) upon the making of a '*Mareva*' injunction; (*c*) upon the customer's death or his development of a mental disorder; and (*d*) upon the customer's bankruptcy or, in the case of a company, upon its winding-up. Finally, an irregularity in the cheque may justify its dishonour by the bank.

The limitations to the bank's duty to pay assist in defining the scope of its actual mandate. The relevant restrictions are discussed forthwith. The actual process used by banks for the clearance of cheques is discussed in Chapter 9. The last two sections of the present chapter deal respectively with the bank's liability for the wrongful payment of a cheque and with the converse situation, in which the bank wrongfully fails to honour its customer's cheque.

(ii) Availability of funds

The bank's duty to pay cheques depends on the availability of adequate funds on which the customer is entitled to draw. These may accrue either on the basis of an actual credit balance standing to the credit of the account,[8] or on the basis of an arrangement for an overdraft.[9] In some cases it is difficult to assess at first glance whether or not a given cheque is covered when presented. The reason for this is that the balance shown in a current account at a given time depends, principally, on the amount of the cheques processed at the close of the previous day plus any periodic payments made by that time through BACS. Thus, an account might show a balance of, say, £500, although in reality cheques totalling at an extra amount of £1,000 plus periodic payments were lodged at an hour which made it impossible to commence their processing on the same day. This fact is well known in the banking community. In practice, branch managers tend to be lenient in the

---

[8] *Joachimson* v. *Swiss Bank Corporation* [1921] 3 KB 110; *Bank of New South Wales* v. *Laing* [1954] AC 135, esp. 154. See also *Inglis* v. *Commonwealth Trading Bank of Australia* (1973) 47 ALJR 234.

[9] *Fleming* v. *Bank of New Zealand* [1900] AC 577; *Pyke* v. *Hibernian Bank Ltd.* [1950] IR 195; *Bank of New South Wales* v. *Laing* [1954] AC 135.

exercise of their discretion to dishonour a cheque which appears uncovered when presented. Usually, the customer's record and station in life are taken into account and, furthermore, banks maintain a list of questionable accounts which require extra caution. A cheque drawn on an account not mentioned in this list will frequently be met, even if it is for an amount exceeding the available balance.

From the purely legal point of view, however, the position is clear. The bank's duty to honour the customer's cheques depends on the actual state of the account at the time of presentment.[10] The bank is given a reasonable time to credit to its customer's account any amounts paid in by way of cash, of periodic payments, or by means of cheques payable to the customer's order. Thus, in *Marzetti* v. *Williams*,[11] a customer's balance amounted to £69. 19s. 6d. on the morning of 18 December 1828. At 11.00 a.m. the customer paid an amount of £40 in cash to the credit of his account, so that the actually available balance became £109. 19s. 6d. Despite this, a cheque drawn by the customer for £87. 7s. 6d. was dishonoured when presented at the bank's counter at 3.00 p.m., as the amount of £40 had not been entered into the customer's ledger by then. The cheque was paid when presented again on the next day, but the customer brought an action in breach of contract based on the initial dishonour of the instrument. Lord Tenderden CJ said that a bank committed a breach of contract when it failed to pay a cheque if the customer's account had an adequate balance for meeting it; but the bank was entitled to a reasonable time to credit funds paid in. A delay of four hours was held to be unreasonable.

The decision in *Marzetti* v. *Williams*, to the effect that a four-hour delay in the crediting of an amount paid to the credit of an account constituted an unreasonable time, was based on the finding of the jury. In modern banking practice it is unlikely that such a short lapse of time between the moment at which the amount is paid in and that at which it is shown in the customer's ledger constitutes an unreasonable delay. Even in the case of the crediting of an account with an in-house payment, the amount may not be entered before the end of the day. The amount is shown in the customer's balance in the statement of the subsequent day.

In *Marzetti* v. *Williams* the amount of £40 was paid by the customer in cash. Different problems arise when the customer's balance is based on amounts of cheques payable to him and remitted to the bank for collection. It will be recalled that the customer's account is credited before the cheque is cleared. Accordingly, the presentment of the cheque to the branch on which it is drawn occurs thereafter.[12] In this respect there is no difference between

---

[10] *Bank of New South Wales* v. *Laing* [1954] AC 135, 154.
[11] (1830) 1 B & Ad. 415.
[12] For a full discussion of the practice concerned, see pp. 233–5 above.

the old clearing practice and the new one. The outcome is that if a cheque is dishonoured by the drawee bank, the payee's balance with his own bank is reduced as the initial credit entry is reversed.

It is thus obvious that an amount entered in the customer's account has not irreversibly accrued until the completion of the clearing process. The problem that arises as a result is whether or not the customer is entitled to draw against funds which have been credited to his account subject to the possibility of the reversal of entries upon dishonour. Usually banks inform their customers, in clauses printed on deposit forms or on the folder in which these forms are contained, that the proceeds of cheques paid into the account cannot be withdrawn before clearance. On this basis, it is forcefully arguable that the bank is entitled to dishonour the customer's cheque if it is drawn against uncleared effects.[13] In practice, though, banks tend to honour a customer's cheque even if the available credit balance is based on such uncleared effects. It is believed that this practice may have established a course of dealings which defines the scope of the contract of banker and customer. The early case of *Rolin* v. *Steward*[14] decided that it is a question of fact whether or not the crediting of an account with the proceeds of an uncleared cheques demonstrates that the bank has permitted its customer to draw on the amount involved. The later case of *Capital and Counties Bank Ltd*. v. *Gordon*[15] suggested that usually the crediting of the customer's account with the amount of a cheque gives him such a right. But this view has been doubted.[16] The better view is that the answer depends on the intention of the parties. This is discernible from both the express terms of the contract, as evidenced by a clause in a deposit slip, and from the prevailing banking practice, which is to be established by evidence. It is submitted that if the two are in conflict, the established practice prevails.

Where the customer's balance is adequate, the holder may be tempted to pay the difference between this balance and the amount of the cheque to the credit of the drawer's account so as to facilitate the payment of the cheque. It has been held that if the bank discloses the balance to the holder, it commits a breach of the duty of secrecy owed to the customer.[17] But if the holder discovers the state of the account from other sources, modern banking practice enables him to cover the deficiency.[18] Under the 1967 agree-

---

[13]   Note that *A. L . Underwood Ltd*. v. *Bank of Liverpool* [1924] 1 KB 775 emphasizes that the mere crediting of the customer's account does not in itself indicate that he is permitted to draw against the uncleared component of the balance; and see *Westminster Bank Ltd*. v. *Zang* [1966] AC 182; and pp. 128–9 above.

[14]   (1854) 14 CB 595.

[15]   [1903] AC 240, 249.

[16]   *A. L. Underwood Ltd*. v. *Bank of Liverpool*, above. And see pp. 418–21 below.

[17]   *Foster* v. *Bank of London* (1862) 3 F & F 214; and see pp. 96 et seq. above.

[18]   The question of the holder's right to do so is much debated; see Paget, *Law of Banking*, 9th edn., p. 233; *Questions on Banking Practice*, Institute of Bankers, 10th edn., quest. 417.

ment, which, though not in effect in its original form remains operative in spirit, the holder is able to pay the necessary amount at a branch of any participating bank for the credit of the relevant account. The procedure, however, involves a certain risk, based on the fact that banks usually pay cheques in the order in which they are processed. If the holder makes up the deficiency in the account but the cheque payable to him is accidentally processed after some other outstanding cheque drawn on the same account, his cheque may be dishonoured. The amount paid by the holder into the drawer's account cannot be earmarked.

The modern automated clearing process will in due course eliminate the problem of the simultaneous presentment of cheques totalling at an amount exceeding the balance available in the customer's account. Under the old procedure, where payment was effected by a fully manual process executed at each branch, banks developed individual practices for dealing with situations of this type. Some banks paid the cheques in the order in which they were presented until the outstanding balance became inadequate for the payment of the remaining cheque for the smallest amount. Other banks preferred to honour the cheques for the highest amounts, basing their practice on the assumption that the customer's reputation would be harmed to the greatest extent by the dishonour of a substantial cheque. Under the current practice, which involves a semi-automated clearing process, the practice has remained essentially the same. But the introduction in the future of the fully computerized clearing of cheques, where the entire process of debiting and crediting would be effected by a data bank, would introduce a change. Cheques would then be met strictly in the order in which the entries were made. The first cheque to be dishonoured would then be that drawn for an amount exceeding the balance available at the time of processing. This cheque would be forwarded to the branch on which it was drawn with a request for instructions. In the meantime, cheques for smaller amounts, drawn for a sum not exceeding the outstanding balance, would probably be met. The simultaneous presentment of cheques would cease to occur.

Although a bank has a single legal personality, accounts are deemed to be domiciled at the branch at which they are kept. This principle is explainable by the banking practice of the nineteenth century. In the absence of expeditious means, such as the telephone, to enable a teller to verify a balance kept in an account maintained with a branch other than that at which the cheque was presented, and in the absence of facilities for the verification of a signature in any place other than at the drawee branch, it was impossible to develop a practice that would facilitate the payment of cheques at a place other than the branch on which they were drawn. Modern banking facilities have introduced new possibilities. A balance can be verified instantaneously by an enquiry made through the computer facilities linked to the bank's central computer. A signature can be printed in invisible infra-red ink when a document, such as a cheque form, is furnished to the customer, so that any signature executed can be compared with the 'hidden' one. At present, it is uncommon to print signatures in infra-red ink on cheque forms, but such signatures are widely used in savings books and similar documents. Moreover, in some countries, such as West Germany, a signature can be telephotoed from branch to branch. The days in which cheques had to be regarded as payable solely at the drawee branch are over from a practical point of view.

The nineteenth-century law has, however, remained unaltered. In *Woodland* v. *Fear*,[19] a cheque was drawn on the G Branch of the S Bank. The holder, whose place of residence was near the B Branch of the same bank, presented it at this branch and received payment. When the B Branch forwarded the cheque to the G Branch, it turned out that it had been drawn against an inadequate balance. The S Bank brought an action to recover the amount paid to the holder. It was held that the B Branch had not been under a obligation to honour the cheque as the instrument was not drawn on it. Presentment for payment could be made only at the G Branch. The B Branch was, accordingly, treated as having taken up the cheque for collection. When the cheque was dishonoured by the G Branch, the S Bank, as the collecting bank, had a right of recourse.

The principle that a cheque has to be presented for payment at the branch at which the account is kept has been approved in *Joachimson* v. *Swiss Bank Corporation*,[20] which, further, lays down that a cheque need be honoured only in so far as it is presented during ordinary business hours. The bank, however, is not in breach of its duty to the customer if it pays a cheque within a reasonable time after closing hour.[21]

The fact that a cheque needs to be presented for payment at the branch at which the account is kept can, in certain cases, have far-reaching effects. Thus, in *Arab Bank Ltd.* v. *Barclays Bank (DCO)*[22] the A Bank maintained an account with the Jerusalem Branch of the B Bank. When hostilities broke out between the Jewish and the Arab communities, that branch had to be provisionally closed. Shortly after the end of the Independence War the branch, which by then fell within the Israeli part of Jerusalem, was reopened. But under Israeli law the funds standing to the credit of the A Bank's account became payable to the Custodian for Absentee Property. As the A Bank was accordingly unable to make a valid demand at the Jerusalem branch, it claimed repayment of the amount involved from the B Bank's head office in London. The House of Lords held that the A Bank was not entitled to make a demand in London, as the amount standing to the credit

[19] (1857) 7 E & B 519.
[20] [1921] 3 KB 110, 127, per Atkin LJ.
[21] *Baines* v. *National Provincial Bank Ltd.* (1927) 32 Com. Cas. 216; (1927) 96 LJKB 801.
[22] [1954] AC 495.

of the customer's account was repayable only at the branch at which the account was kept. The debt was situated at this place. The A Bank's right to demand payment was, accordingly, governed by the laws of the State of Israel, which also formed the proper law of the contract.

It follows that a cheque is to be regarded as payable by the branch on which it is drawn rather than by the bank as a whole. A customer who opens an account with a bank in a foreign country has to realize that payment is subject to the provisions of local laws.

(iii) Garnishee proceedings

The balance standing to the credit of the customer's account can be attached by way of a garnishee order issued under the Rules of the Supreme Court,[23] or by means of a garnishee summons issued under the Rules of the County Court.[24] Proceedings of this type are usually instituted by a judgment creditor whose claim against the bank's customer has not been satisfied. The creditor applies to the court for an order under which all debts 'owing and accruing' from the bank to the customer are to be attached for the purpose of satisfying the creditor's judgment against the customer. Initially the court issues a garnishee order nisi, under which the bank may show cause why it should not pay the amount owed by the customer to the creditor. If the bank does not show cause, the court issues a final order requiring the bank to pay over an amount adequate to satisfy the customer's debt to the creditor.[25] Payment to the creditor or into court of the amount involved discharges the bank's debt to the customer.

At one stage there were some doubts regarding the applicability of garnishee proceedings to accounts maintained with banks. In the case of current accounts the doubts were based on the fact that payment was due on demand. It was argued that before the customer made such a demand the debt was not 'owing and accruing' within the meaning of the provisions concerning garnishee proceedings.[26] The point was resolved in *Joachimson* v. *Swiss Bank Corporation*, where Bankes LJ observed that the service of the garnishee notice on the bank operated as a demand.[27] This ruling militates against the literal construction of the provisions in point, as the garnishee debt ought to be 'owing and accruing' at the very time the proceedings are instituted. From a commercial point of view, however, it is sound to enable a judgment creditor to levy execution against the balance standing to the

[23] RSC, Ord. 49, r. 1.
[24] CCR, Ord. 27, r. 1.
[25] *Choice Investments Ltd.* v. *Jeromnimon (Midland Bank, Garnishee)* [1981] QB 149, 155.
[26] Paget, *Law of Banking*, 1st edn., London, 1906, p. 136. The view is not supported in the current 9th edition.
[27] [1921] 3 KB 110, 115; and see Warrington LJ, 131.

credit of his debtor's current account, as in practice the funds serve the same function as cash.

Up to 1956 the position was less clear in the case of deposit accounts. For the purpose of garnishee proceedings such accounts were traditionally divided into fixed deposits maturing at an agreed time, and deposit and savings accounts the balance of which was repayable subject to the giving of a minimum period of notice by the customer. Moreover, in both types of deposit, repayment was subject to the surrender by the customer of the deposit receipt or book. There was authority for the general view that a debt owed by a bank to a customer and maturing at a given future date was 'owing and accruing' and could be garnished, but that the amount could not be claimed by the garnishment creditor from the bank before the agreed maturity date.[28] At first glance a debt due under a deposit account would fall within the ambit of this ruling. But the need for producing the deposit receipt or book and, in the second type of account, the need for giving minimum notice to determine the maturity of the debt were considered to pose obstacles.[29] The law was clarified by the passing of section 38 of the Administration of Justice Act 1956, under which amounts standing to the credit of savings accounts, deposit accounts, and fixed deposits with banks may be garnished. The provision is wide enough to encompass modern deposit accounts which often do not fall fairly and squarely into one of the two categories outlined above.[30]

It follows that at present any amounts deposited by a customer with his bank are subject to garnishee proceedings. The order nisi attaches all the accounts opened by the customer with his bank, including accounts opened for special purposes such as solicitors' 'clients' accounts'.[31] The debt, however, must be situated within the United Kingdom. A garnishee order will not attach a balance maintained with a foreign branch of the bank and repayable in foreign currency.[32]

The order nisi attaches the full amount standing to the credit of the customer's account. The bank is unable to honour cheques drawn by the customer even if their payment would not reduce the balance in the account beneath the figure required to discharge the debt due to the garnishment

---

[28] *Webb* v. *Stenton* (1883) 11 QBD 518, per Brett MR, 524, and Lindley LJ, 527.

[29] *Bagley* v. *Winsome and National Bank Ltd.* [1952] 2 QB 236, 241. See also *Bank of New South Wales Savings Bank* v. *Freemantle Auto Centre Pty. Ltd.* [1973] WAR 161; *Music Masters Pty Ltd.* v. *Minelle* (1968) Qd. R 326; *Re Australia and New Zealand Savings Bank Ltd.*; *Mellas* v. *Erriniadis* [1972] VR 690, 696–7.

[30] The provision is to be read with SCR, Ord. 49, r. 1a, which encompasses deposit receipts. The 1956 Act does not, however, apply to deposit accounts with the Post Office Savings Bank.

[31] *Plunkett* v. *Barclays Bank Ltd.* [1936] 2 KB 107.

[32] *Richardson* v. *Richardson* [1927] P 228. Further, it will not attach a balance maintained by a foreign embassy for its usual operations: *Alcom Ltd.* v *Republic of Colombia* [1984] AC 580.

creditor.[33] In some garnishee orders nisi, however, a specified amount is expressed as the ceiling attachable. In such a case the bank earmarks the prescribed amount plus an additional sum to cover estimated costs, and permits the customer to draw on the remaining balance.[34]

The garnishee order nisi does not attach amounts paid to the credit of the customer's account after the date on which the order is made and served on the bank. This rule, decided in *Heppenstall* v. *Jackson (Barclays Bank, Garnishee)*,[35] poses problems as regards the attachment by an order nisi of the balance credited to the customer's current account. Does the order attach amounts of cheques credited to the account before clearance? In *Jones & Co.* v. *Coventry*[36] it was held that the order attaches, prima facie, the balance as it stands, including the component based on uncleared cheques. An Australian authority, *Bank of New South Wales Ltd.* v. *Barlex Investments Pty. Ltd.*,[37] takes the opposite view, holding that the order does not attach amounts based on uncleared cheques as these are only provisionally credited to the customer's account. It is believed that the Australian authority is to be preferred. The order nisi attaches only debts owing and accruing to the garnishment debtor in the hands of the garnishee. The amount of a cheque paid into the customer's account does not become a debt due and accruing to him from the bank until the instrument is cleared. The proceeds of an uncleared cheque are, therefore, not affected by the garnishee order unless the customer is able to draw against them.

Another Australian authority, *Universal Guarantee Pty. Ltd.* v. *Derefink*,[38] suggests further that the date on which the balance is attached is not the date of the service of the order nisi but the date on which the order is actually made. The order attaches the balance available at that moment less the amount of cheques paid by the bank after that time but before the service of the order. The difficulty with this test is that the balance standing to the customer's account at a given moment is not easily ascertainable at a later point of time. Balances are struck as at the closing hour of the relevant day. The better view is that the garnishee order nisi attaches the balance available at the time the order is served. Indeed, when the order is served the bank may decide to freeze the customer's account forthwith and open a new account for his running operations.

The garnishee order nisi affords the bank the opportunity of raising objections to the making of an absolute order for the payment over of the

---

[33] *Rogers* v. *Whitley* [1892] AC 118. See also *Edmunds* v. *Edmunds* [1904] P 362.
[34] As regards the garnishee bank's right to deduct its expenses from the amount attached, see *Webb (Genny) Transport* v. *Brenner* [1985] 5 CL 19.
[35] [1939] 1 KB 585, 592.
[36] [1909] 2 KB 1029.
[37] (1964) 64 SR (NSW) 274.
[38] [1958] VR 51.

funds into court or to the creditor. There are a number of situations in which the bank may wish to raise such an objection.

First and foremost is the case in which there is a clash of priorities between the garnishee order and an assignment by the customer of the balance standing to the credit of his account. *Rekstin* v. *Severo Sibirsko Gosudarstvennoe Akcionernoe Obschestro Komseverputj*,[39] a case concerning money transfer orders, establishes that when an amount due to the customer from the bank is effectively assigned, the customer is no longer entitled to dispose of the chose in action involved. Thus, when an assignment of the amount standing to the credit of the account has been completed before the serving of the garnishee order nisi, the assignee's claim prevails over that of the garnishment creditor. A statutory assignment, made under section 136(1) of the Law of Property Act 1925, is complete when notice of it is served on the 'debtor', who, in the type of case considered here, is the bank.[40] It follows that, where the clash is between a statutory assignment and a garnishee order nisi, priority is determined by the date of notification to the bank. The position differs in the case of an equitable assignment, which becomes effective when it is executed and quite irrespective of the notification to the debtor.[41] It follows that an equitable assignment would take priority over a garnishee order nisi provided the assignment was executed in good faith before the order was served on the bank. This is so even if the notification of the equitable assignment were given to the bank after the service of the order nisi.

The second situation in which the bank may wish to apply for a discharge of the order nisi is where it has a right of set-off or a right to combine the credit balance in the garnished account with a debit balance accrued in another account maintained by the same customer. Where the debit balance is accrued by way of an overdraft of a current account, the bank is entitled to exercise its right of set-off, as the amount is either known or readily ascertainable.[42] Furthermore, an overdraft is in essence repayable on demand. The position differs in the case of loans payable at a future date, as the amount is not due and claimable at the time the order is served.[43] However, most modern lending agreements confer on the bank a right to demand repayment in full if a garnishee order nisi is issued against the customer. The right of set-off would thereupon accrue forthwith.

The third situation in which a bank tends to raise objections to the gar-

---

[39] [1933] 1 KB 47; and see *Carran* v. *Newpark Cinemas Ltd.* [1951] 1 All ER 295, and the Australian authority of *Cossill* v. *Strangman* (1962) 80 WN (NSW) 628.

[40] See pp. 581 et seq.

[41] See p. 583 below.

[42] *Tapp* v. *Jones* (1875) LR 10 QB 591.

[43] See Weaver and Craigie, *Banker And Customer in Australia*, p. 164, citing the view of Sir John Paget in his *Gilbart Lectures*, 1913, JIB vol. 34, p. 255.

nishee proceedings is where the balance is standing to the credit of a trust account. In such cases the bank is aware that the customer, the garnishment debtor, is not entitled to the money in question in his own right. The bank is, therefore, under a duty to raise the matter in court. Although the order nisi attaches the balance initially and precludes the bank from paying cheques drawn on the account,[44] it will be discharged when it is established that the accrued balance comprises amounts deposited with the customer as a trustee. Clients' funds standing to the credit of a stockbroker's trust account[45] constitute an illustration in point.

The fourth case in which the order nisi may be discharged is where the balance standing to the credit of the customer's account is owned jointly by himself and by other parties. Moneys standing to the credit of a joint account are not attachable by means of a garnishee order[46] issued against one of the owners of the account unless it is proved that, in reality, the funds are the property of the garnishment debtor.[47] However, where there is a judgment debt, due jointly and severally from a number of debtors, it is possible to garnish a balance standing to the credit of an account maintained by only some of them.[48]

Finally, it is in the bank's interest to raise objections if the garnishment debtor is described in the order nisi under a name which differs from that under which he has opened the account. If the garnishment debtor and the customer are not one and the same person, and the bank overlooks this fact and dishonours a cheque in reliance on the order nisi, the bank may be liable for the wrongful dishonour of the cheque. There is authority for the view that, in the case of a discrepancy in the names, the bank is entitled to disregard the order nisi.[49]

(iv) Mareva injunctions

In the course of the last decade, a bank's duty to obey its customer's instructions for the payment of money and for the transfer of funds has frequently been abrogated by *Mareva* injunctions. This novel type of order, named

---

[44] *Plunkett* v. *Barclays Bank Ltd.* [1936] 2 KB 107.

[45] *Hancock* v. *Smith* (1889) 41 Ch. D 456.

[46] *Macdonald* v. *Tacquah Gold Mines Co.* (1884) 13 QBD 535; *Hirschorn* v. *Evans (Barclays Bank Ltd., Garnishee)* [1938] 2 KB 801. And see *Hoon* v. *Maloff (Jarvis Construction Co. Ltd., Garnishee)* (1964) 42 DLR (2d) 770, showing that a partnership account cannot be garnished to satisfy the debts of one of the partners.

[47] *Harrods Ltd.* v. *Tester* (1937) 157 LT 7.

[48] *D. J. Colburt & Sons Pty. Ltd.* v. *Ansen (Commercial Banking Co. of Sydney Ltd., Garnishee)* (1966) 85 WN (NSW) (pt. 1) 64.

[49] *Moore* v. *Peachey* (1842) 8 TLR 406; *Koch* v. *Mineral Ore Syndicate (London and South Western Bank Ltd., Garnishee)* (1910) 54 Sol. Jo. 600.

after the first case that attempted to define it,[50] has been given statutory recognition in section 37 of the Supreme Court Act 1981. Under this provision,
the High Court's power to grant an interlocutory injunction restraining any
party from removing from the jurisdiction, or otherwise dealing with, assets
located within the jurisdiction is exercisable regardless of whether or not the
party is domiciled, resident, or present within the jurisdiction. But although
the *Mareva* injunction is accordingly available in disputes respecting both
international and domestic transactions, its main domain remains the former type of case. In the context of domestic banking transactions, it merits a
general rather than a detailed discussion.[51]

The object of the *Mareva* injunction is to prevent a defendant from
defeating a judgment that may be given against him by dissipating his assets.
Accordingly, an order is granted if the plaintiff is able to establish two
points. First, he must be able to show that he is likely to obtain judgment.
This means that he has to establish a good arguable case.[52] Secondly, the
plaintiff must show that there is a real danger that the defendant will
transfer the assets out of the jurisdiction or that he may otherwise deal with
them so as to make them unavailable or untraceable.[53] It is clear that these
guidelines confer on the court a wide discretion. Broadly speaking, the court
considers whether it is just and convenient to grant the order.[54] One of the
considerations taken into account is the defendant's record and standing.
Thus, in the context of a substantial international dispute, the Court of
Appeal refused to grant a *Mareva* injunction against a bank, as the Court
did not believe that there was a danger that the bank would remove its
assets from the jurisdiction.[55] Whilst at one stage the *Mareva* injunction was
regarded purely as an interlocutory order, available principally before the
giving of the final judgment in the relevant case, it is now established that
the court has the power to grant it between final judgment and execution.[56]

---

[50] *Mareva Compania Naviera SA* v. *International Bulk Carriers SA (The 'Mareva')* [1975] 2
Lloyd's Rep. 509; for an earlier case see *Nippon Yusen Kaisha* v. *Karageorgis* [1975] 1 WLR
1093.

[51] A detailed analysis will be included in the relevant chapter of the volume devoted to international banking.

[52] *Z Ltd.* v. *A-Z* [1982] QB 558, 585; *Ninemia Maritime Corp.* v. *Trave Schiffahrtsgesellschaft (The 'Niedersachsen')* [1984] 1 All ER 398, 402, 415; see also *Rasu Maritima SA* v. *Perusahaan Pertambangan Minyak Dan Gas Bumi Negara (Pertamina)* [1978] QB 644.

[53] *Rahman (Prince Abdul)* v. *Abu-Taha* [1980] 1 WLR 1268, 1272; *Searose Ltd.* v. *Seatrain
(UK) Ltd.* [1981] 1 All ER 806, 808; *Ninemia Maritime Corp.* v. *Trave Schiffahrtsgesellschaft
(The 'Niedersachsen')*, above, 406.

[54] *Ninemia Maritime Corp.* v. *Trave Schiffahrtsgesellschaft (The 'Niedersachsen')*, above,
418.

[55] *Etablissement Esefka International Anstalt* v. *Central Bank of Nigeria* [1979] 1 Lloyd's
Rep. 445.

[56] *Orwell Steel (Erection and Fabrication) Ltd.* v. *Asphalt and Tarmac (UK) Ltd.* [1985] 3
All ER 747. The defendant may, further, be enjoined from leaving the jurisdiction: *Bayer AG* v.
Winter [1986] 1 All ER 733, 737.

The *Mareva* junction is usually addressed not only to the defendant but also to third parties who are believed to hold any of his assets. Accordingly, such an order usually instructs the defendant's bank to freeze his account or to ensure that the balance is not reduced beneath a given figure. A bank that disobeys such an order faces contempt proceedings. Furthermore, the order is usually not made in respect of a single specified account but is extended to the global balance due to the customer. Indeed, the bank may be ordered to search its records so as to ascertain all the defendant's accounts. The plaintiff is ordinarily asked to give security to cover the costs incurred by the bank in this manner.[57]

The bank has to remain vigilant as regards all the dealings of the customer as from the time of the service of the order. The reason for this is that the order attaches both to existing assets and to property acquired by the defendant after the date on which the order is made;[58] any funds paid to the credit of the customer's account thereafter are caught by the order. It follows that the bank cannot rule off the customer's old account and permit him to open a new account to be freely utilized for new operations.

When granting a *Mareva* injunction, the court is careful not to impinge on rights of third parties. Thus, if a third party claims that any of the defendant's assets are in reality his own, the court will set the order aside as regards the property involved. This principle ought to apply where a third party proves that amounts standing to the credit of the defendant's account with a bank are trust funds. However, the court is not bound to act on the basis of a mere allegation. It may require the third party to establish his claim.[59] Here too the court exercises its jurisdiction on the basis of what appears just and convenient. If the court refuses to set the order aside in respect of property claimed by a third party, it may require the plaintiff to furnish security to protect the third party against loss.[60] The plaintiff's offer to furnish such security does not, however, necessarily preclude the court from setting the order aside in respect of the property involved. A *Mareva* injunction is set aside if its maintenance would involve hardship, such as unwarrantable interference with the third party's freedom to transact his business.[61]

The courts' policy to refrain from affecting third parties' rights by the granting of a *Mareva* injuction is a reflection of the nature of this order. It is a procedural device, which aims at protecting the plaintiff against sharp

[57] *Searose Ltd.* v. *Seatrain (UK) Ltd.*, above.
[58] *TDK Tape Distributor (UK) Ltd.* v. *Videochoice Ltd.* [1985] 3 All ER 345, 349.
[59] *SCF Finance Co. Ltd.* v. *Masri* [1985] 2 All ER 747. The third party, or a bank that makes the claim on behalf of the trust, is entitled to costs: *Project Development Co. Ltd.* v. *KMK Securities Ltd.* [1982] 1 WLR 1470.
[60] *Clipper Maritime Co. Ltd.* v. *Mineralimportexport (The 'Marie Leonhardt')* [1981] 3 All ER 664.
[61] *Galaxia Maritime SA* v. *Mineralimportexport* [1982] 1 WLR 539.

practices employed by the defendant. The correct view is that a *Mareva* injunction acts *in personam*.[62] The order does not confer new rights *in rem* on the plaintiff at whose request it is granted. Satisfaction of debts owing to other creditors is not precluded by the granting of such an order. If their claims are established, the court usually allows the discharge of the debts out of the assets attached by the *Mareva* injunction. The order, thus, does not confer any priority on the plaintiff and is not aimed at constituting him a secured creditor.[63] This principle is of considerable importance to banks, whose right of set-off against a customer will be upheld by a court which has issued a *Mareva* injuction.[64]

It is clear that there are some similarities as well as distinctions between the *Mareva* injunction and a garnishee order nisi. From the bank's point of view, both preclude the payment of the customer's cheques and giro transfers. The account is frozen to the extent prescribed by the court. Furthermore, neither order has the effect of defeating the bank's own rights against the customer or of conferring new rights on the plaintiff. The two major distinctions between the orders are procedural. First, a garnishee order nisi is available only to a judgment creditor; a *Mareva* injunction is generally used to freeze the defendant's account whilst the proceedings are pending. Secondly, the garnishee order nisi is available to a judgment creditor as a matter of right, whilst the *Mareva* injunction is a discretionary remedy.

(v) Customer's death or insanity

Under section 75(2) of the Bills of Exchange Act 1882, the bank's duty and authority to pay cheques is terminated when it obtains notice of the customer's death. This section overrides in the case of cheques the principle that the mandate of an agent is automatically determined by the principal's death, and that the agent is liable to the estate for any acts performed thereafter.[65]

Section 75(2) is applicable only in the case of cheques. It is an important provision, as banks do not have any means for obtaining immediate notice of the customer's death. A decision handed down in the year in which the Act was passed applied a similar principle in a case in which the bank paid a

---

[62] *Cretanor Maritime Co. Ltd.* v. *Irish Marine Management Ltd. (The 'Cretan Harmony')* [1978] 1 WLR 966. Cf. *Z Ltd.* v. *A-Z* [1982] QB 558.

[63] *Iraqi Ministry of Defence* v. *Arcepey Shipping Co. SA* [1981] QB 65, 71–2; *Admiral Shipping* v. *Portlink Ferries Ltd.* [1984] 2 Lloyd's Rep. 166, 168.

[64] *Oceania Castelana Armadora SA* v. *Mineralimportexport (The 'Theotokos')* [1983] 2 All ER 65.

[65] *Campanari* v. *Woodburn* (1854) 15 CB 400.

bill of exchange which the customer, who was the acceptor of the instrument, had domiciled at the bank's premises. As the bank paid the bill after the customer's death but before obtaining notice thereof, the Court of Common Pleas held that the bank was entitled to debit the account.[66]

When the bank obtains notice of the customer's death it has to stop acting on his behalf. The bank is no longer entitled to pay cheques drawn by the customer before his death, even if their amounts are trivial and it is clear that they were drawn for essential services rendered to the customer in his lifetime, such as the supply of electricity or of gas. Payments made by means of money transfers must, equally, cease upon the customer's death. It is clear that, in practice, this principle leads to difficulties, as payments due to tradesmen, professional men, and suppliers of services have to be deferred until the completion of the necessary probate or administration procedures. In some countries, such as the United States and New Zealand, the law has been amended to authorize the bank to pay cheques presented within ten days after it receives notice of the customer's death.[67] A person who claims to be entitled to a grant of letters of administration, or to be an executor of the deceased's will, is entitled to order the bank to refrain from paying cheques presented within this period. It is believed that the reform was well conceived.

A question on which there appears to be no authority is whether or not the bank is obliged to refuse to accept any payments received for the credit of an account after the customer's death. As the bank accepts such payment as the customer's agent, it would appear that the bank's mandate is terminated either when the customer dies or, by analogy with section 75(2), when the bank receives notice thereof. Payments made into the customer's account by tenants, by business associates, and by financial houses managing his portfolio investments, have, therefore, to be rejected! A particularly acute problem relates to cheques paid by the customer to the credit of his account but which have not been cleared by the time the bank receives notice of his death. On a strict common law analysis, the bank's mandate to receive the funds is terminated, at the latest, when it obtains notice of the customer's death! It is, however, to be doubted if the law would be strictly construed in such cases.

One further principle results from the fact that a cheque constitutes a mandate given by the customer to the bank for the payment of the amount involved. A cheque does not constitute a *donatio mortis causa*, even when it is given by the customer to the payee with knowledge of impending death.[68]

There is no direct authority regarding the effect of insanity on the bank's

---

[66] *Rogerson* v. *Ladbroke* (1822) 1 Bing. 94.

[67] Uniform Commercial Code, s. 4–405(2); Bills of Exchange (Amendment) Act 1971 (NZ), s. 2.

[68] *Re Beaumont; Beaumont* v. *Ewbank* [1902] 1 Ch. 889.

duty to pay its customer's cheques.[69] It has been held in *Young* v. *Toynbee*[70] that an agent's authority is determined by the principal's insanity. The relationship of banker and customer, however, is not purely one of principal and agent, and it is therefore uncertain that the principle in question is applicable. The generally held view is that notice of the customer's insanity terminates the bank's authority to pay.[71] This principle is supportable by drawing an analogy from section 75(2).

(vi) Bankruptcy and winding-up

The general effect of the bankruptcy of a natural customer, or the winding-up of an incorporated one, on his relationship with the banker, is discussed in Chapter 6. At this point it is necessary to consider the effect of the customer's bankruptcy or winding-up on the bank's duty to pay his cheques.

The basic effect of the customer's bankruptcy is to vest his property in his trustee in bankruptcy.[72] The customer's estate includes, for bankruptcy purpose, all property belonging to or vested in him at the commencement of the bankruptcy or acquired by him before his discharge.[73] It will be recalled that the amount standing to the credit of the customer's account constitutes a debt owed to him by the bank. For the purposes of bankruptcy proceedings such a debt is deemed to be an asset due to the customer. The bank, however, is entitled to set off against the amount due to the customer any amount due to the bank from him, such as a sum accrued on an overdraft. This right of set off, which is known as the right to combine the customer's account, is discussed in detail in Chapter 6. The balance which remains payable to the customer has to be paid over by the bank to the trustee.[74]

Under the regime of the Bankruptcy Act 1914, problems used to arise in respect of the bank's obligation to pay to the trustee the net balance due to the insolvent customer. This amount was calculated as it stood at the date of the 'commencement of the bankruptcy', which date was 'related back' to the first 'act of bankruptcy', e.g. the non-payment of a judgment debt, committed by the bankrupt within the three months preceding his adjudication.[75] Consequently, transactions made by the bankrupt during the relation back period, including dealings on his current account, could be challenged by his

---

[69] But see *Drew* v. *Nunn* (1879) 4 QBD 661; *Daily Telegraph Newspaper Co. Ltd.* v. *McLaughlin* [1904] AC 776.

[70] [1910] 1 KB 215.

[71] Hart, *Law of Banking*, 4th edn., p. 302; F. H. Ryder, 'Bankers and the Law Relating to Lunacy', (1934) 55 JIB 14; Megrah, *The Banker's Customer*, 2nd edn., p. 76. And see pp. 205–7 above.

[72] Insolvency Act 1986, s. 306.

[73] Ibid., s. 283, and see s. 307(1) as regards after-acquired property.

[74] Ibid., s. 312(4); and see *Re Bumpus, ex p. White* [1908] 2 KB 330.

[75] Bankruptcy Act 1914, s. 37.

trustee.[76] This problem does not arise under the new regime. According to section 278 of the Insolvency Act 1986, the bankruptcy of an individual 'commences with the day on which the bankruptcy order is made'. Unless the bank obtains an undue preference[77] from the bankrupt, it need not be concerned about transactions preceding the date of the bankruptcy order.

An exception to this general principle occurs in respect of any payment made by the customer before the date of the order but after the presentations of the petition for his adjudication. Under section 284(1)–(3) such a payment is void unless it is made with the consent of the court or is ratified by it subsequently. If this is not the case, the payee holds the sum paid 'for the bankrupt as part of his estate'. However, under subsection (4) this provision is inapplicable if the payment is received by the payee in good faith, for value, and without knowledge of the presentation of the petition. Section 284 does not grant an express remedy against a bank that obeys its customer's instruction to pay a cheque drawn after the date of the presentation of the petition. But the knowledge that such a payment is, generally, void if made without the sanction of a court order, means that the bank's correct course is to defer payment until the proper procedural steps have been taken.

A more difficult problem arises if a bank pays a cheque drawn by its customer after the date of the making of the order. This happens, occasionally, if a cheque is presented for payment after this date but before the gazetted order is noted by the bank. Under the old regime, the bank's position was precarious. In *Re Wigzell, ex p. Hart*,[78] in which the court had actually suspended publication of the order, the bank was held liable for all payments made after the issuing of the unpublished receiving order. Furthermore, it could not set off against these payments the amount of cheques paid into the customer's account after the relevant date, as any combination of accounts had to be based on the state of the account as at the time of the adjudication. This decision was reached notwithstanding an observation by Lord Sterndale MR, to the effect that it would be improper for a trustee to impeach a transaction if it were not honourable or high-minded to do so.[79] A subsequent case, *Re Wilson, ex p. Salaman*,[80] attempted to confine the rule in *Wigzell*'s case. Here the Official Receiver granted the bankrupt leave to deal with certain moneys, although a receiving order had been issued. The court refused to allow the Official Receiver to adopt a course which would have enabled him, on the one hand, to reap the profit of payments made to the

---

[76] Some protection was conferred on persons, such as banks, who dealt with the bankrupt during this period without notice, under ss. 45 and 46 of the Bankruptcy Act 1914. The leading case was *Re Dalton, ex p. Harrington and Carmichael* [1921] 2 KB 835.

[77] Pp. 158–9 above.

[78] [1921] 2 KB 835.

[79] Ibid., 850.

[80] [1926] 1 Ch. 21.

bankrupt whilst impeaching payments made by him. The court, however, held that the bankrupt's transactions had been contracted in accordance with the power granted by the Official Receiver. The cases were, therefore, distinguishable.

Some protection was conferred on banks by section 4 of the Bankruptcy (Amendment) Act 1926 which is reproduced, subject to certain changes, in section 284(5) of the Insolvency Act 1986. Under the new provision, where, after the commencement of the customer's bankruptcy, a cheque is honoured by the bank or some other payment is made by it at the customer's order, the debit is maintainable except in two cases. The first is where the bank had notice of the bankruptcy before it paid the cheque or made the payment involved. The other is where it is not reasonably practicable to recover the amount involved from the payee. At first glance, subsection (5) confers on the bank an adequate protection. But the second exception presents problems. It has been argued that, under the 1926 Act, any abortive demand made by the trustee in an attempt to obtain reimbursement is an adequate proof that it is not reasonably practicable to recover the amount involved from the payee.[81] Section 284(5) leaves the position unchanged.

One additional practical problem connected with the commencement of the bankruptcy arises from the fact that an adjudication order is not necessarily made at the very beginning of the relevant day. Under the old regime, there was authority for the view that the order was, nevertheless, to be treated as having been made at the start of the day.[82] Section 278 appears to adopt this principle as the bankruptcy commences with the day on which the order is made. It follows that if, before it receives notice of the order, the bank pays one of its customer's cheques in the course of the day, it requires the protection of section 284(5).

Where one of the owners of a joint account is adjudicated a bankrupt, the bank is best advised to dishonour any further cheques drawn on the account, regardless of whether they are drawn by both owners jointly or by one of them entitled to sign on his own. As the mandate given to the bank as regards the payment of cheques emanates jointly and severally from all the owners, the notice of the bankruptcy of one of them may be regarded as terminating the bank's authority to pay. It has been suggested that the bank may in such cases resort to interpleader proceedings, in so far as there is any dispute between the trustee of the bankrupt owner of the account and the other parties as regards the genuine ownership of the funds involved.[83]

The effect of the winding-up of a company on the bank's duty to pay its

[81] R. L. B. V. Williams and Muir Hunter, *On Bankruptcy*, 19th edn., London, 1979, pp. 365–7.
[82] *Re Pollard* [1903] 2 KB 41, 45.
[83] Paget, *Law of Banking*, 9th edn., p. 96.

cheques is similar to that of the bankruptcy of an unincorporated customer. Under section 127 of the Insolvency Act 1986 (section 227 of the Companies Act 1948), any disposition of property made after the commencement of the winding-up by the court is void. According to section 129, which has replaced section 229 of the Companies Act 1948, the date of the commencement of a winding-up by the court depends on whether the proceedings were preceded by a resolution of the company to wind up or started with the presentation of the petition. In the former case, the winding-up commences at the date of the resolution. In the latter case, the relevant date is that of the presentation of the petition.

In *Re London and Mediterranean Bank, Bolognesi's Case*,[84] it was held that cheques drawn by the directors after the commencement of the winding-up of a company could not be attributed to it. Under section 127 of the 1986 Act, the court has a discretion to validate a transaction made after the commencement of the winding-up. The bank's ability to obtain an order validating a transaction under this section probably depends on its not having had notice of the true facts. Moreover, an Australian decision, *Re Mal Bower's Macquarie Electrical Centre Pty. Ltd.*[85] casts some doubts on the scope of this section. Street CJ expressed the view that the Australian counterpart of section 127 had no application where the bank paid a cheque to the company itself or to one of its clerks; the provision was, in his opinion, confined to transactions in which the property of the company passed from the its control into other hands.

The leading decision on section 127 was handed down by the Court of Appeal in *Re Gray's Inn Construction Co. Ltd.*[86] A company had a current account with its bank which was overdrawn to the extent of £5,332. A winding-up petition was presented by one of the company's creditors. The bank followed its usual practice, which was to permit the company to continue operating its account until the date on which the petition was granted. As between these two dates an amount of £4,824 was paid out to creditors for goods and services supplied before the commencement of the winding-up and, in addition, the company sustained an extra trading loss of £5,000. The Court of Appeal held that any payment made into the account during the relevant period as well as any sum paid out of it constituted a disposition under section 127. Cheques should therefore not have been honoured without the sanction of a validating order. The Court refused to exercise its discretion to validate payments made out of the account, as the 'dispositions' involved were effected for the purpose of discharging certain pre-liquidation debts in priority to claims of other creditors. The fact that the bank had

[84] (1870) LR 5 Ch. App. 567.
[85] [1974] 1 NSWLR 254.
[86] [1980] 1 WLR 711.

acted after obtaining some information about the nature of each payment involved did not absolve it from liability, and was no reason for the exercise of the court's discretion. Furthermore, the bank could not set off against the overdraft incurred by the company the amount of cheques collected after the commencement of the winding-up.

At the same time, the Court of Appeal felt it would be unjustified to penalize the bank. It observed that any amounts paid out in respect of pre-liquidation debts ought whenever possible to be recovered from the payees. The bank was made unconditionally liable to reimburse the £5,000 of the trading loss incurred due to the continued operations of the company. Buckley LJ added that, even if it was in the interest of the general body of creditors that the company be permitted to continue its trading operations, the proper course was to freeze its current account as at the date of the presentation of the petition and, if necessary, to obtain the court's authorization to open a new account for all subsequent dealings. An important conclusion from this decision is that all transactions on current accounts made after the commencement of the winding-up are caught by section 127.

The general test to be applied by the courts in the exercise of their discretion under section 127 is simple. They are to be guided by the points set out in section 284(4)–(5) of the Insolvency Act 1986 and by a general consideration of what is fair and equitable in the circumstances.[87] A good illustration is provided by *Re T. W. Construction Ltd.*[88] A bank agreed to extend overdraft facilities to a company after the presentation of a winding-up petition to enable the company to pay wages, on the understanding that certain sums, due to the company under letters of credit opened to finance the export of machinery, would be paid into the company's account with the bank. Wynn-Parry J validated the arrangement, as in his Lordship's view it would have been unconscionable to permit the liquidator to rescind it.

Dispositions, such as the payment or collection of cheques, made in the ordinary course of business before the hearing of the petition, are not affected by the winding-up order.[89] It follows that the bank need not stop the clearing of a cheque presented for payment or for collection before the issuing of the order even if the process is not completed when the order is made.

---

[87] *Re Perpetoire Opera Co. Ltd.* (1895) 39 Sol. Jo. 505 (decided in respect of a comparable provision in the Companies Act 1862). See also *Re Steane's (Bournemouth) Ltd.* [1950] 1 All ER 21 (referring to the court's general discretion); *Re Clifton Place Garage Ltd.* [1970] Ch. 477.

[88] [1954] 1 WLR 540.

[89] This follows from *Re Operator Control Cabs Ltd.* [1970] 3 All ER 657. Cf. *D. B. Evans (Bilston) Ltd.* v. *Barclays Bank Ltd.* (1961) 7 LDAB 283.

2. THE BANK'S LIABILITY FOR WRONGFUL PAYMENT: NATURE OF THE PROBLEM

It has been shown in Chapter 9 that a cheque serves two functions. In the first place it constitutes a negotiable instrument utilized to effect the payment of a sum due from the drawer. This is the cheque's main function as an instruments which can be circulated instead of cash. The second function of a cheque, which defines its legal nature as between the customer and the bank, is that it constitutes an order or an instruction issued by the former to the latter. A cheque is therefore an instrument in which the customer, acting as principal, instructs the bank—his agent—to perform a specific act, which is the payment of a definite sum of money to the order of the payee or to the bearer.[90] This means that, as between the bank and the customer, the contractual relationship arising from the drawing of the cheque is primarily governed by the principles of the law of agency. Consequently, the bank's duty is to adhere strictly to the terms of its mandate. If the bank deviates therefrom, it does so at its peril. The point has been explained most clearly by Devlin J in a case relating to the liability of a bank that departed from the instructions given to it by the customer as regards the opening of a letter of credit:[91]

It is a hard law sometimes which deprives an agent of the right to reimbursement if he has exceeded his authority, even though the excess does not damage his principal's interests. The corollary . . . is that the instruction to the agent must be clear and unambiguous.

When this statement is applied to the unauthorized payment of a cheque, it means that the bank is not entitled to debit its customer's account with the amount involved unless it can plead one of the recognized defences. These include, in the first place, the common law defences that can be raised by an agent who disobeys his principal, such as estoppel, ratification, and the ambiguity of the mandate. In the second place, the bank is entitled to rely on a specific equitable defence applicable where the unauthorized payment of a cheque by the bank has benefited the customer. By way of illustration, take a cheque paid by the bank despite its countermand. If the payment of the cheque has, nevertheless, the effect of discharging a valid debt due by the customer to the payee, it would be inequitable to allow the customer to reap this benefit and at the same time to refuse to permit the bank to debit his

---

[90] *London Joint Stock Bank Ltd.* v. *Macmillan and Arthur* [1918] AC 777; *Westminster Bank Ltd.* v. *Hilton* (1926) 43 TLR 124.

[91] *Midland Bank Ltd.* v. *Seymour* [1955] 2 Lloyd's Rep. 147, 168, following the decision of the House of Lords in *Ireland* v. *Livingston* (1872) LR 5 HL 395. Cf. *European Asian Bank AG* v. *Punjab and Sind Bank (No. 2)* [1983] 1 WLR 642, 656, suggesting certain limitations to Devlin J's dictum.

account. This equitable defence is discussed in conjunction with the bank's common law defences.

Both the common law defences and the equitable defence fail to confer on the bank a fully adequate defence for all instances of the wrongful payment of a cheque. To appreciate this point, it is necessary to consider the different situations in which a bank pays a cheque without a valid mandate. First and foremost is the case of cheques bearing a forged signature of the drawer, or signed in excess of an agent's authority. Secondly, there are those cases in which a third party, such as a holder, executes an unauthorized alteration of the instrument, such as the raising of the amount, which invalidates the cheque.[92] In both types of case the bank has a good common law defence provided the customer has either facilitated the fraud or has led the bank to believe that all is well. In the third place, banks do occasionally pay cheques despite countermand orders. Common law protects the bank if it can be shown that the stop order was ambiguous or issued at too late a time to be acted upon by the bank. The fourth case, which involves cheques on which the payee's endorsement is forged by a third party, is one in which the bank does not obtain any defence at common law. At the same time, the bank is unable to verify the genuineness of the payee's signature, especially where the cheque is presented through the clearing house. If the cheque is not paid to the genuine payee or to a person holding under that payee's indorsement, the cheque is not paid to the order of the designated person and hence is not discharged in accordance with the terms of the mandate conferred on the bank. A defence is conferred on banks, in cases of this type, under the Bills of Exchange Act 1882 and under the Cheques Act 1957.[93]

The drawer's action for the wrongful payment of the cheque, which is based on the bank's breach of mandate, is not necessarily the only hazard faced by the bank where a cheque has been paid for the credit of a person who is not entitled to the proceeds. A cheque is considered an item of property with a value equal to the amount for which it is made out.[94] It follows that the true owner can bring an action in conversion provided he is entitled to the immediate possession of the instrument.

Can such an action in conversion be brought by the true owner against the paying bank where the cheque has been paid by it to a person other than himself? An action in conversion usually lies for the misappropriation of a chattel or for its destruction.[95] The paying bank, of course, does not appropriate the chattel either in its own name or on behalf of a principal. It simply purports to obey an instruction for payment, embodied in the cheque and

---

[92] BEA, s. 64, discussed below, p. 518.
[93] Pp. 303–9 below.
[94] Pp. 413–4 below.
[95] See, generally, P. H. Winfield and J. A. Jolowicz, *On Torts*, 12th edn., London, 1984, pp. 479 et seq.

issued by the customer. It is, however, arguable that the payment of the cheque discharges the instrument and hence has the effect of destroying the value of the cheque as a negotiable instrument. The purported conversion is, thus, the destruction of the instrument as an item of property. There is, indeed, a specific situation in which such an action, based on the payment of the cheque, is conferred on the true owner by the Bills of Exchange Act 1882. It arises where the bank pays a cheque in a manner that contravenes a crossing executed on it.[96]

The existence of a general action in conversion by the true owner against a paying bank which has paid any type of cheque to the wrong person derives support from *Smith* v. *Union Bank of London*.[97] The payee of a cheque, drawn on the defendant bank, crossed it specially to the C Bank with which he maintained his account and indorsed the instrument in blank. The cheque was stolen thereafter and was remitted by an innocent third party, who became its holder in due course, to the credit of his account with the L Bank. The defendant bank, the drawee, paid the cheque when presented by the L Bank, despite the special crossing.[98] It was held that, as the crossing did not restrict the negotiability of the cheque, the payee had ceased to be its true owner when the instrument came into the hands of a holder in due course. Accordingly, the payee was not entitled to the immediate possession of the cheque and his action in conversion failed. But Blackburn J, whose decision was affirmed by the Court of Appeal, observed that if the bank had paid the cheque to a person other than the holder in due course, it would have laid itself open to an action in conversion by the true owner.[99]

On closer examination, the dictum in *Smith* v. *Union Bank of London* requires a narrow construction. The paying bank's act of conversion is supposed to be the destruction of the negotiable character of the cheque resulting from its discharge. But under section 59 of the Act, a bill, including a cheque, is discharged only upon its 'payment in due course'. This occurs where the instrument is paid by the drawee in good faith to a holder of whose defect in title the drawee has no knowledge. It follows that payment in due course does not occur where a cheque is paid to a person who has acquired it under a forged indorsement, as such a person is not a holder.[100] It further follows that payment to such a person does not discharge the cheque or destroy its negotiability. The paying bank is therefore not subject to an action in conversion by the true owner.

In reality, the literal construction of the Act leads to a paradox. To succeed in an action in conversion, the plaintiff has to establish both that he

[96] BEA, s. 79(2).
[97] (1875) LR 10 QB 291; affd. (1875) 1 QBD 31.
[98] Such payment was prohibited under s. 2 of Act 21 & 22 Vict. c. 79.
[99] (1875) LR 10 QB, p. 195.
[100] P. 504 below.

himself is the true owner of the instrument, and that payment was made in due course; he has, therefore, to establish that the instrument was paid to a holder! If the plaintiff establishes this second fact, he runs the risk that the paying bank, the defendant in the action, may take the matter one step further and establish that the person to whom the payment was made was the holder in due course of the instrument and hence acquired its title. Alternatively, the paying bank can avoid liability in conversion to the true owner by pleading the forgery of the initial payee's indorsement, in which case the payment of the cheque does not constitute an act of conversion. In effect, the true owner's action in conversion is available only where payment of the cheque is made to a holder who, for some technical reasons,[101] cannot be regarded as a holder in due course!

Doubts concerning the availability of the action in conversion whenever a cheque has been improperly paid are to be found in the decision of the Court of Appeal in *Charles* v. *Blackwell*.[102] This case, which was heard before the enactment of the 1882 Act, decided that where a cheque was properly paid no action in conversion was maintainable against the bank. Cockburn CJ observed:[103]

A cheque taken in payment remains the property of the payee only so long as it remains unpaid. When paid the banker is entitled to keep it as a voucher till his account with his customer is settled. . . . If the cheque was duly paid, so as to deprive the payees of a right of action . . . they no longer have any property in it.

These words suggest that the payee, or true owner, loses his property in the cheque when it is paid. Notably, his Lordship referred specifically to a situation in which a cheque was 'duly paid'. In terms of the 1882 Act, these words are to be understood as referring to the proper mode of payment, which is payment in due course. This, as has been pointed out, is the only situation in which the action would arise at all. It is with respect suggested that the observation that the true owner loses his right when the cheque is paid is unfounded. The very discharge of the cheque is the basis of his complaint. If the argument were correct, it could be pleaded in any action in which a collecting bank was sued in conversion where a cheque had been paid to it by the paying bank.

Does the true owner have against the paying bank an alternative action in quasi contract? There is no doubt that, where the true owner is entitled to sue in conversion, he can waive this tort and sue in money had and received. This point has been well established since the decision of the House of Lords in *United Australia Ltd*. v. *Barclays Bank Ltd*.[104] But this type of quasi con-

---

[101] For example, if the cheque is irregular on its face.
[102] (1877) 2 CPD 151.
[103] Ibid., 162–3.
[104] [1941] AC 1. See *Morison* v. *London County and Westminster Bank Ltd*. [1914] 3 KB 356.

tractual action does not lie if the plaintiff, the true owner, does not have a tort to waive.

The more pertinent question is whether the true owner has an action in money had and received, such as an action based on payment made under a mistake of fact, or on total failure of consideration, which can be brought against the paying bank independently of the purported action in conversion.[105] The point is a difficult one, and does not appear to be covered by direct authority. Some indirect support for the availability of such an action can be derived from a dictum of Vaughan Williams LJ in the decision of the Court of Appeal in *Bavins Junr. and Sims* v. *London and South Western Bank Ltd.*[106] But analysis suggests that the true owner of a cheque is not entitled to bring an action in money had and received against the paying bank where the cheque has been paid to a person without a title. The main reason for this becomes apparent when one recalls that the relationship between the paying bank and its own customer, the drawer of the cheque, is one of debtor and creditor. The bank does not hold its customer's money in specie. It follows that when a bank pays a cheque it utilizes its own funds and seeks reimbursement from the customer by debiting his account. It is therefore inaccurate to suggest that the paying bank discharges the cheque by paying upon its presentment any specific funds earmarked for the true owner's use by the customer. Moreover, even if the paying bank were regarded as discharging the cheque by paying the customer's money, it would not incur the risk of a quasi contractual action by the true owner if it remitted the funds to the wrong party. The drawing of a cheque does not involve an assignment to the payee of the funds against which it is drawn.[107] Indeed, if the drawee dishonours the cheque the true owner has no action against him. How then can the payee, who claims to be the true owner of the cheque, be heard to complain that the money paid by the bank is either received or standing to his credit?

In conclusion, it is clear that the paying bank's main risk in cases of wrongful dishonour is the customer's action for breach of mandate. The true owner appears to have an action only in cases involving payment in violation of a crossing, and in cases in which any cheque payable to his order has been paid to a holder other than a holder in due course. This would usually occur where the cheque came into the hands of a holder after it was stolen from the true owner who had indorsed it in blank. The true owner's action would be brought in conversion and, concurrently, in waiver of tort. An independent action in money had and received is, it is submitted, unavailable to the true owner.

---

[105] The nature of which is explained in detail in *Fibrosa Spolka Akcyjna* v. *Fairbairn Lawson Combe Barbour Ltd.* [1943] AC 32, esp. 62. And see, generally, Ch. 11 below.
[106] [1900] 1 QB 270, 278.
[107] BEA, s. 53(1).

3. THE PAYING BANK'S DEFENCES FOR WRONGFUL PAYMENT
AT COMMON LAW AND IN EQUITY

(i) Outline

Common law and equity confer on the bank certain defences applicable
where the customer disputes the validity of the payment of a cheque. Cases
of this type occur where the bank has paid a cheque in a manner that contravened the customer's instructions. The situations involved can be classified
into three groups.

The first group involves cases in which the cheque has been altered by an
unauthorized party who may, for example, have raised the amount of the
cheque or changed the name of the payee. If the bank pays the altered
instrument, it exceeds the authority conferred on it by the customer. In
addition, the unauthorized alteration avoids the cheque if it affects a
material part of it.[108] The amount of the cheque, the name of the payee, the
date on which the cheque is purported to be drawn, and any crossing are
such material details.[109] When a bank honours a materially altered cheque,
it not only fails to observe its mandate but also pays a void instrument. The
customer is entitled to object to the debiting of his account with such
unauthorized payment unless the bank has a specific defence. Common law
confers such a defence on the bank either where the customer facilitated the
alteration by his carelessness or where his conduct was such as to induce the
bank to believe that all was well. Basically the customer's conduct gives rise
to an estoppel.

The second type of case in which the bank obtains a defence for the
wrongful payment of a cheque is where the customer ratifies an unauthorized signature or alteration of a cheque. The third type of case in which
common law confers on the bank a defence is where the customer's ambiguous instruction misleads the bank. A typical case is where the customer
countermands payment of a cheque without supplying the necessary details
or describes the instrument wrongly and as a result the bank fails to identify
the cheque to be stopped.

Apart from the defences conferred on the bank at common law, there is
the equitable defence based on the bank's discharge of a valid debt. This
partial and extremely limited defence, already mentioned earlier on, is discussed after the three common law defences.

---

[108] BEA, s. 64.
[109] P. 255 above as regards crossing.

(ii) Customer's carelessness and cases giving rise to estoppel

This type of defence may be based either on the customer's conduct before the cheque is forged or altered, or on his behaviour after he has obtained knowledge thereof. The basic principle is best illustrated by *Brown* v. *Westminster Bank Ltd.*[110] The servants of an aged woman forged her signature on cheques drawn on her current account. The branch manager called on the woman on several occasions to enquire about the genuineness of the cheques but was assured by her that all was well. Although the branch manager had doubts about her mental capacity, it was held that her conduct precluded her from asserting, subsequently, that some of these cheques had been forged.

In *Brown* v. *Westminster Bank Ltd.* the bank was able to plead an estoppel on the basis of the customer's explicit representation. A mode of conduct which lulls the bank into safety has a similar consequence. This principle applies where the customer fails promptly to inform the bank about forgeries of his cheques. In *Greenwood* v. *Martins Bank Ltd.*[111] a wife forged her husband's signature on cheques drawn on his account with the defendant bank. Initially, the husband accepted his wife's explanations for her conduct and, at her request, agreed not to disclose the forgeries to the bank. Some time thereafter he discovered that the wife's explanation had been false. When he threatened her with exposure, she committed suicide. The husband's action, disputing the bank's right to debit his account with the forged cheques, failed. It was held that he was under a duty to make full disclosure to the bank as soon as he discovered the initial forgeries. His silence had lulled the bank into the belief that the signatures executed by the wife were genuine. The husband's silence further precluded the bank from instituting proceedings during the wife's life. Upon her death, the husband's liability for her frauds terminated. In effect, the bank lost a right of action as a result of the husband's silence.

This last element, in *Greenwood* v. *Martins Bank Ltd.*, was based on the law applicable in the 1930s.[112] The case suggests that, if the customer's

---

[110] [1964] 2 Lloyd's Rep. 187. See also *Leach* v. *Buchanan* (1802) 4 Esp. 226; *Brook* v. *Hook* (1871) LR 6 Ex. 89; *Ontario Woodsworth Memorial Foundation* v. *Grozbord* (1964) 48 DLR (2d) 385; *Mutual Mortgage Corporation Ltd.* v. *Bank of Montreal* (1965) 55 DLR (2d) 164; *Tina Motors Pty. Ltd.* v. *Australia and New Zealand Banking Group Ltd.* [1977] VR 205. Cf. *M'Kenzie* v. *British Linen Co.* (1881) 6 App. Cas. 82, which was, however, a Scottish appeal.

[111] [1933] AC 51. See also *Ewing & Co.* v. *Dominion Bank* (1904) 35 Can. SCR 133, leave to appeal denied: [1904] AC 806; and particularly *Ontario Woodsworth Memorial Foundation* v. *Grozbord*, above, in which the customer's silence prevented the bank from bringing an action before the date on which the forger absconded.

[112] [1933] AC 59. At present the husband is not liable for the wife's tort: Law Reform (Married Women and Tortfeasors) Act 1935; Winfield and Jolowicz, *On Torts*, 12th edn., p. 690.

silence does not cause any loss to the bank, he is entitled to dispute the debits based on the forgeries. Moreover, the customer is entitled to dispute the genuineness of signatures on his cheques even if forgeries, executed without his knowledge, were perpetrated over a long period of time. In *National Bank of New Zealand Ltd.* v. *Walpole and Patterson Ltd.*,[113] it was held that a customer was not under an obligation to keep a vigilant eye on his business with a view to detecting forgeries expeditiously. This view has been recently approved by the Judicial Committee in *Tai Hing Cotton Mill Ltd.* v. *Liu Chong Hing Bank Ltd.*[114]

The type of estoppel pleaded in cases like *Greenwood* v. *Martins Bank Ltd.*, or in *Brown* v. *Westminster Bank Ltd.*, can be asserted only in so far as the customer's representation or silence is not induced by pressure emanating from the bank. In *Brook* v. *Hook*,[115] a father, some of whose cheques had been forged by his son, asserted that they had been executed by himself in order to avoid the son's prosecution. As the bank was aware of the true facts, it was not allowed to plead an estoppel when the father contested the debiting of his account.

A specific mode of conduct by the customer which defeats his action against the bank is carelessness related to the drawing of the cheque. Where he signs a cheque in blank, the position is covered by statute. Under section 20(1) of the Bills of Exchange Act 1882, a person in possession of a blank cheque has 'prima facie authority to fill up the omission in any way he thinks fit'. The main object of this provision is to protect a subsequent holder who takes the completed cheque. Furthermore, it has been held that where the paying bank pays such a cheque in good faith, the customer is estopped from disputing payment, notwithstanding that the cheque has been completed in an unauthorized manner.[116]

A more complex principle applies where the customer does not sign the cheque in blank but draws it in a manner that enables a rogue to perpetrate a fraud. Basically the customer is liable if his conduct involved negligence. This principle can be traced back to *Young* v. *Grote*,[117] in which the amount of a cheque was written out in a manner which enabled the payee to raise it. The bank was held entitled to debit the customer's account with the altered amount. The principle of this case remained confined to the careless drawing of cheques. In *Scholfield* v. *Earl of Londesborough*,[118] it was held to be inapplicable where the acceptor of a bill of exchange, who had made it

---

[113] [1975] 2 NZLR 7.
[114] [1986] AC 80.
[115] (1871) LR 6 Ex. 89.
[116] *London Joint Stock Bank Ltd.* v. *Macmillan and Arthur* [1918] AC 777, 881. And see *Lloyds Bank Ltd.* v. *Cooke* [1907] 1 KB 794; *Smith* v. *Prosser* [1907] 2 KB 735; *Wilson and Meeson* v. *Pickering* [1946] KB 422.
[117] (1827) 4 Bing. 253.
[118] *Scholfield* v. *Earl of Londesborough* [1896] AC 514.

payable at his bank, contested the bank's right to debit him with the amount which had been fraudulently raised by the holder. The basis of this rule is to be found in a significant difference between the issuing of a cheque and the acceptance of a bill. When a bill is accepted, the blank spaces left by the drawer already appear in it. It is therefore difficult to impute negligence to the acceptor.

Scholfield's case induced the Privy Council in *Colonial Bank of Australasia Ltd.* v. *Marshall*[119] to depart from the ruling in *Young* v. *Grote*. That principle was vindicated, however, in the leading case of *London Joint Stock Bank* v. *Macmillan and Arthur*.[120] A clerk prepared a cheque for £2 payable to bearer. There was no sum in words then written on the cheque, but after it had been signed by the employer the clerk altered the figure to £120 and inserted the words 'one hundred and twenty pounds' in the space provided. The bank was held entitled to debit the customer's account with that amount. Lord Finlay LC said:[121]

A cheque drawn by a customer is in point of law a mandate to the banker to pay the amount according to the tenor of the cheque. It is beyond dispute that the customer is bound to exercise reasonable care in drawing the cheque to prevent the banker being misled. If he draws a cheque in a manner which facilitates fraud, he is guilty of a breach of duty as between himself and the banker and he will be responsible to the banker for any loss sustained by the banker as a natural and direct consequence of this breach of duty.

The principle of *Macmillan*'s case was irreconcilable with the doctrine of *Marshall*'s case. But even in Australia, where the Privy Council's decision remained binding, the High Court has recently adopted *Macmillan*'s principle. In *Sydney Wide Stores Pty. Ltd.* v. *Commonwealth Trading Bank*,[122] a cheque, prepared by the customer's clerk for the alleged purpose of discharging a debt owed to a company known as 'Computer Accounting Services', was made payable to this firm under its initials 'CAS'. After the cheque was signed by the authorized persons, the clerk added the letter 'H' to the payee's name so that the cheque became payable to 'cash or bearer'. The employee then obtained payment for himself. Relying on the *Marshall* case, the Supreme Court of New South Wales struck out the bank's defence, alleging the customer's negligence in drawing the cheque, as being bad in law. An appeal from this order was allowed by the High Court, which decided to adopt the ruling in *Macmillan*'s case. Murphy J pointed out the policy considerations which induced the High Court to depart from the principle of *Marshall*'s case. His Honour said:[123]

---

[119] [1906] AC 559.
[120] [1918] AC 777.
[121] Ibid., 789.
[122] (1981) 55 ALJR 574.
[123] Ibid., 579.

there is a real question whether it would be better to let the loss continue to fall on the banking industry. Although the standard of care habitually observed by cheque drawers may fairly be described as low, I am not satisfied that any considerable burden has been imposed on banks by the application of the *Marshall . . .* decision. If in practice the losses, which to individual bank customers would be onerous, are cumulatively only slight for the banking system in comparison with the vast amount of business done by cheque, a sensible system of loss spreading would be to continue as before. Further, if the cumulative losses are now slight, it would be absurd to impose a standard of care such that every drawer of cheques would have to regard employees and associates as potential forgers.

In the *Sydney Wide Stores* case the High Court did not decide that the customer was negligent. This question was left for determination by the trial court, to whom the case was remitted. The question undoubtedly is one of mixed fact and law. The answer depends on whether or not the feasibility of the alteration involved would have been foreseen by a reasonable man. The decision of the Court of Appeal in *Slingsby* v. *District Bank Ltd.*[124] suggests that not every blank space or incomplete detail left in a cheque when drawn involves negligence on the customer's part. In this case the customer left a blank space between the name of the payee and the printed words 'or order'. A fraudulent third party utilized this space and made the cheque payable to the payee 'per pro' himself. He then negotiated the cheque by indorsing it in his own name. It was held that the customer had not been negligent and that, although the alteration was not apparent, the customer was entitled to dispute the debiting of his account with the amount of the cheque.

It is clear that the customer's duty of care, based on the principle of *Macmillan*, is a narrow one. Negligence which is not connected with the actual drawing of a cheque does not usually afford a defence to a bank that has wrongfully honoured a cheque. In *Bank of Ireland* v. *Evans' Trustees*,[125] which related to the negligent keeping of a seal, Parke B expressed to the House of Lords the unanimous opinion of the judges: 'If there was negligence in the keeping of the seal it was very remotely connected with the act of transfer'. His Lordship went on the explain:[126]

If such negligence could disentitle the plaintiffs, to what extent is it to go? If a man should lose his cheque book, or neglect to lock the desk in which it is kept, and a servant or stranger should take it up, it is impossible in our opinion to contend that a banker paying his forged cheque would be entitled to charge his customer with that payment.

It would appear that, while a customer must be careful not to facilitate fraud when drawing cheques, he is not under a duty to his banker to

---

[124] [1932] 1 KB 544, affirming [1931] 2 KB 588.
[125] (1855) 5 HLC 389.
[126] Ibid., 410–11. See also *Welch* v. *Bank of England* [1955] Ch. 508.

exercise care in organizing his business so as to prevent opportunities for others to forge his cheques.

This view derives support from *Lewes Sanitary Steam Co. Ltd.* v. *Barclay & Co Ltd.*[127] A company's secretary, who to the knowledge of the chairman of the board of directors had been convicted of forgery, was made a joint signatory and was entrusted with keeping the company's cheque-book and pass-book. It was held that the company's bank was not entitled to debit its account with the amount of a cheque on which the secretary had forged the signature of one of the directors, and that the company was not estopped by its conduct from alleging the forgery.

This principle was adopted in *Tai Hing Cotton Mill Ltd.* v. *Liu Chong Hing Bank Ltd.*[128] The plaintiffs maintained current accounts with three different banks in Hong Kong. An employee, L, who was in a position of trust, committed a series of frauds. Initially, he tricked one of the plaintiffs' directors into signing cheques, which L converted. Subsequently, L resorted to the cruder method of forging the director's signature on cheques. During the entire period of six years in which L perpetrated the frauds, the plaintiffs failed to make any security checks, and did not properly peruse the periodic statements furnished by the banks. When the frauds were detected the plaintiffs did not contest the banks' right to maintain the debits based on the cheques signed by the director; but they demanded that their accounts be re-credited with the amounts of the forged cheques. The banks disputed this claim, alleging that the plaintiffs were in breach of a duty of care owed both in contract and in tort, and that they were estopped from contesting the entries.

The decision of the Hong Kong Court of Appeal vindicating the banks' stand was reversed by the Judicial Committee. Lord Scarman pointed out that, on the facts, none of the contracts between the plaintiffs and the three banks included an express term imposing on the plaintiffs a duty to conduct their business in a manner that would obviate the type of fraud that had taken place or precluding them from contesting entries based on forged items. The implied term in the contract of banker and customer, based on *Macmillan*'s case and on *Greenwood* v. *Martins Bank*, was confined to what could 'be seen to be plainly necessary incidents of the relationship. Offered such a service, a customer must obviously take care in the way he draws his cheque, and must obviously warn his bank as soon as he knows that a forger is operating the account.'[129]

Lord Scarman rejected the view that a wider duty than that could be owed in tort. He thought that it would be confusing to formulate a tortious

[127] (1906) 95 LT 444. See also *Kepitigalla Rubber Estates Ltd.* v. *National Bank of India Ltd.* [1909] 2 KB 1010.
[128] [1986] AC 80.
[129] Ibid., 106.

duty, imposed on the customer, when the parties were free to define their mutual obligations on a contractual basis. Obviously, the banks could have imposed more onerous duties on their customers, the plaintiffs, in the contracts governing the current accounts. Thus, the banks could have stipulated that, if entries were not queried within a given period of time, the statements in which they were included would be deemed correct. The clauses incorporated in the three contracts between the plaintiffs and the bank fell short of this. Lord Scarman concluded that as the plaintiffs had not been in breach of a duty of care they were not precluded from pleading the forgeries. The banks were ordered to reverse the debit entries and, further, to pay interest on the amounts involved, as the plaintiffs could have placed these sums in interest-bearing accounts.

The principle of *Tai Hing*, which redefines and clarifies the principles of *Macmillan*'s case and *Greenwood v. Martins Bank Ltd.*,[130] has a narrow scope of application. In many cases it is difficult for the bank to bring itself within its ambit. In some cases, however, the bank may be able to plead a third and related defence based on the specific relationship between the customer and the person who has committed the fraud. Thus, in *Greenwood v. Martins Bank*, the customer was estopped from pleading the forgery because his silence had deprived the bank of its right of action. Under the law as then applicable, if the forgeries had been notified to the bank before the wife's death, the bank could have sued the wife in deceit and joined the husband. The husband's liability would have been similar to the vicarious liability borne by an employer for the act of his employees.

The possibility of pleading vicarious liability in appropriate cases was mentioned in *National Bank of New Zealand Ltd. v. Walpole and Patterson Ltd.*[131] This was another case in which a series of forgeries and fraudulent alterations affecting cheques drawn on a company's account were carried out by an agent. Although the point was not pleaded, Richmond J observed that a customer might in cases of this type be liable vicariously for the employee's fraud. This dictum deserves consideration. It is true that the employee's fraud, in cases of this type, is contrary to the employer's interests. This aspect, however, is irrelevant, as is demonstrated by the rule in *Lloyd v. Grace, Smith & Co.*[132] The question is whether the type of fraud here considered is perpetrated in the employee's course of employment. Where the employee's function is to prepare cheques for the employer's signature—as is the case where he is engaged as an accountant or a bookkeeper—the answer may be affirmative.

[130] [1933] AC 51, discussed above.
[131] [1975] 2 NZLR 7, 14. This defence was pleaded but not pursued in the *Tai Hing* case, above.
[132] [1912] AC 716.

(iii) Ratification

Where an agent exceeds his authority in drawing a cheque, his act may be ratified, or adopted, by the principal. Ratification precludes the principal from disputing the paying bank's right to debit his account with the proceeds of the cheque. Cases of this type occur mainly where the bank honours a cheque drawn by the agent for an amount exceeding his authority, or where the instrument is paid although a director, who is authorized to draw on a company's account jointly with other officers, draws a cheque without obtaining an additional signature.

The latter type of case arose in *London Intercontinental Trust Ltd.* v. *Barclays Bank Ltd.*[133] Here the cheques, which were honoured by the bank although they bore the signature of one director instead of the required two signatures, were drawn principally in order to transfer funds from one of the company's accounts into another. Initially, when the board of directors discovered the irregularity, it resolved to take no action. Subsequently, the company ran into financial difficulties and a new board was appointed. It was then decided to bring an action against the bank, alleging that the cheques in question had been paid in breach of mandate. Slynn J gave judgment for the bank on three grounds. First, he held that the director in question had had the actual authority to transfer the relevant amounts, which meant that he could have issued an oral or written instruction to this effect on his own. The bank was, accordingly, entitled to act on the director's specific instructions although he gave them by means of cheques signed by him alone. His Lordship observed:[134]

The bank as a result of its failure to observe the discrepancy took a risk in honouring the cheque that [the director] was not in fact authorized. In the case of both these cheques . . . he was so authorized.

Secondly, Slynn J concluded on the facts that the original board of directors had adopted the director's act with the full knowledge that the cheques had been improperly drawn. The company had, in this way, ratified the payment of these cheques by the bank. Thirdly, his Lordship noted that before the company brought its action against the bank it had pursued a claim in liquidation before the Stock Exchange on the basis that the transactions, the subject of the transfer of the funds by cheques, were valid. The company had thereby made its election and was bound by it.

Ratification can thus be pleaded either where the principal expressly ratifies the unauthorized drawing or where his conduct indicates that he has adopted the agent's act. An interesting Australian authority concerning the

---

[133] [1980] 1 Lloyd's Rep. 241.
[134] Ibid., 249.

latter type of case is *West* v. *Commercial Bank of Australia Ltd.*[135] A customer opened an account with a bank for the purposes of a business managed by his son, and instructed the bank to pay cheques only if these were signed jointly by the son and by the customer's wife. After a few months the son arranged with one of the bank's tellers to honour cheques signed solely by himself. The customer became aware of the arrangement but took no steps to preclude the honouring of such cheques. Moreover, on one occasion, when a promissory note was executed for the purposes of the business and made payable at the bank, the customer indorsed it although it was not signed by the wife. The High Court of Australia held that, under these circumstances, the customer was estopped from denying the bank's authority to honour cheques signed by the son alone. The customer could not acquiesce in the practice and then elect to repudiate the son's authority to the detriment of the bank. Although the High Court based its decision on an estoppel, the case manifests all the elements needed for ratification. In essence, the customer could not at one and the same time adopt and repudiate the act of the son.

Ratification, however, applies only in the relationship of principal and agent. It does not apply where a person who signs the cheque belonging to another has no authority at all. The prevailing view is that a forgery cannot be ratified.[136] This principle gives rise to a difficulty. Under section 9(1)(*d*) of the Forgery and Counterfeiting Act 1981, a document is false, and hence counterfeit, 'if it purports to have been made . . . on the authority of a person who did not in fact authorize its making in those terms'. This language suggests that a signature placed on a cheque by an agent who intends to misuse the instrument, rather than to utilize it in the course of his employment, constitutes a forgery. The decision in *Kreditbank Cassel GmbH* v. *Schenkers Ltd.*[137] decided under section 1(1) of the Forgery Act 1913 which used similar language, lends support to this view. In this case a manager fraudulently drew and indorsed bills on his company's behalf for his own purposes. It was held that his signatures on the bills were, therefore, forgeries within the meaning of the 1913 Act. This led the court to conclude that the bills were void as the agent's 'forged' signatures were inoperative under section 24 of the Bills of Exchange Act 1882.

The question of ratification did not arise in *Kreditbank*'s case, but it could be concluded that, as the signatures constituted forgeries, they could not be ratified. Section 24, however, distinguishes between a forged signa-

---

[135] (1935) 55 CLR 315.
[136] *Brook* v. *Hook* (1871) LR 6 Ex. 89. See also *Williams* v. *Bayley* (1866) LR 1 HL 200; *Imperial Bank of Canada* v. *Begley* [1936] 2 All ER 367, 374; *Stoney Stanton Supplies (Coventry) Ltd.* v. *Midland Bank Ltd.* [1966] 2 Lloyd's Rep. 373. Contrast *M'Kenzie* v. *British Linen Co.* (1881) 6 App. Cas. 82, 99 (a Scottish case in which the earlier English authorities were not mentioned).
[137] [1927] 1 KB 826.

ture and an unauthorized signature. This suggests that, for the purposes of the Bills of Exchange Act 1882 which governs the law of bills and of cheques, an agent's unauthorized signature differs from a mere forgery. The proposed distinction accords with the law as it stood when the 1882 Act was passed. Under section 22 of the Forgery Act 1861, which was then in force, an unauthorized signature of a bill or of a note was outside the definition of 'forgery'.[138]

It is believed that, for the purposes of litigation between banker and customer, it is preferable to give effect to the distinction, made in section 24 of the 1882 Act between forged and unauthorized signatures, rather than to conclude that the Forgery Act 1913, followed on this point in the 1981 Act, introduced an implicit reform equating the two. It is unrealistic to render the bank liable for the agent's abuse of his authority where the principal, the customer, is prepared to adopt the agent's act!

(iv) Customer's ambiguous instructions

It is a general principle of agency law that an agent is not liable for disobeying the customer's intended instruction if this was so ambiguous as to mislead a reasonable man. The agent is entitled to reimbursement as long as he acted on what he honestly considered to have been the principal's intention.[139] This principle applies only where the ambiguity is not apparent. In *Cunliffe, Brooks & Co.* v. *Blackburn and District Benefit Building Society*,[140] it was held that a banker was under a duty to obey his customer's instructions given in the cheque only if these were clearly expressed. In practice, banks dishonour cheques which are written in an illegible manner or which manifest an irregularity in the mandate, such as a difference between the words and the figures denoting the amount to be paid.

The most common type of ambiguous instruction is the unclear countermand of a cheque. In *Westminster Bank Ltd.* v. *Hilton*,[141] the customer drew a cheque on 31 July 1924, the number of which was 117285, and post-dated it to 2 August. On 1 August he sent a cable to his bank in which he ordered it to stop 'cheque 117283', quoting the correct amount and name of the payee. Cheque no. 117285 was presented for payment on 6

---

[138] And see *Morison* v. *London County and Westminster Bank Ltd.* [1914] 3 KB 356, 366. Although the Court of Appeal's decision was delivered after the 1913 Act came into effect, this Act was not relied upon as it had not been in force at the time of the trial. On the basis of the 1861 Act, cheques drawn in excess of the agent's authority were held not to be forgeries.

[139] This is known as the principle of *Ireland* v. *Livingston* (1872) LR 5 HL 395. And see *London Joint Stock Bank Ltd.* v. *Macmillan and Arthur* [1918] AC 777. And see footnote 91 to this chapter.

[140] (1884) 9 AC 857, 864.

[141] (1926) 136 LT 315.

August, and the bank paid it in the belief that it was a replacement of the countermanded cheque no. 117283. Subsequently, another cheque, drawn by the plaintiff for £7, was dishonoured by the bank, as the payment of cheque 117285 had exhausted the balance standing to the credit of the customer's account. The latter's action for the wrongful dishonour of the cheque for the £7 was disallowed by the House of Lords. It was held that the customer's instruction was ambiguous because of the reference to the wrong number of the cheque. The bank had made a reasonable inference from the facts.

The principle illustrated by *Westminster Bank Ltd.* v. *Hilton* is applicable only where the instruction given by the bank to the customer is unambiguous on its face. If the instruction is patently capable of more than one interpretation, or is unclear, the customer is under a duty to seek better particulars or simply to disobey the order.[142]

(v) The equitable doctrine

Usually, a person who decides to pay the debts of another cannot claim any remuneration. He is a mere volunteer and has no cause of action. A bank that pays a cheque in the mistaken belief that it does so under a mandate is, however, in a position different from that of a volunteer. It does not act on its own resolve but on the basis of a mistake made by it. It has been suggested that, in cases of this type, the bank should be able to rely on the equitable principle of subrogation, which would entitle it to step into the shoes of the customer to the extent that he has derived some benefit from the payment made.[143] It has been further suggested that this principle should apply where the bank has paid an instrument that bears a forged signature, or less than the required number of signatures, to the extent that the customer has derived benefit as a result of the payment involved. The payment of a countermanded cheque is another illustration if its payment confers a benefit on the customer such as the discharge of a debt.

The doctrine was explained by Wright J in *B. Liggett (Liverpool) Ltd.* v. *Barclays Bank Ltd.*[144] Here the bank paid a cheque drawn on the account of a company although the instrument bore only one instead of the required two signatures. The cheque had been drawn for the payment of amounts due to tradesmen for the supply of goods to the company. His Lordship emphasized that the payment of the cheque had discharged the company's

---

[142] *European Asian Bank AG* v. *Punjab and Sind Bank (No. 2)* [1983] 1 WLR 642, 656.
[143] F. R. Ryder, 'Forgery on a Drawer's Cheque', *Gilbart Lectures* (1972), pp. 23–4.
[144] [1928] 1 KB 48.

debt to the tradesmen. At common law this would, of course, be irrelevant. The bank would be treated as a mere volunteer. But the position differed in equity. Wright J said:[145]

The equitable doctrine had been applied beyond question over and over again to cases where an agent not having the authority of his principal has borrowed money on behalf of his principal. Under these circumstances at common law the agent cannot be sued and cannot be made to repay the amount so borrowed, but in equity it has been held that to the extent that the amount borrowed has been applied in payment of the debts of the principal, the quasi lender is entitled to recover from the quasi borrower.

His Lordship added:[146]

the general principle of equity, that those who pay legitimate demands which they are in some way or other bound to meet, and have had the benefit of other people's money advanced to them for that purpose, shall not retain that benefit so as, in substance, to make those other people pay their debts.

His Lordship was of the view that this principle applied not only where the advance was made by means of actual payment but also where it involved a series of credits and debits.

The principle in question was referred to in *Lloyds Bank Ltd.* v. *Chartered Bank of India, Australia and China*,[147] and in *Re Cleadon Trust Ltd.*,[148] where it was, however, held that it would apply only to the extent that the payment discharged the debt of the customer. It would not apply where it discharged the debts of a connected business, such as a subsidiary company.

Liggett's case explained the principle on the basis of subrogation. The paying bank is subrogated to the payee's rights against the customer, and is entitled to rely on these rights when the customer disputes the payment involved. The principle can be more readily explained as an independent doctrine that precludes the customer from reaping the benefit of the payment involved whilst demanding a reversal of the debit entry made by the bank. Thus, a recent Australian decision suggests that the doctrine may be raised even as a partial defence to an action in conversion if part of the proceeds of the instrument were applied to reduce an indebtedness of the true owner.[149]

---

[145] Ibid., 60.
[146] Ibid., 61. See also *Jackson* v. *White and Midland Bank Ltd.* [1967] 2 Lloyd's Rep. 68. For a detailed analysis see E. P. Ellinger and C. Y. Lee, 'The Liggett Defence' [1984] LMCLQ 459.
[147] [1929] 1 KB 40.
[148] [1939] Ch. 286, 302–5, 316.
[149] *Associated Midland Corporation* v. *Bank of New South Wales* [1980] 1 NSWLR 533.

4. THE PAYING BANK'S DEFENCES FOR WRONGFUL PAYMENT: STATUTORY PROTECTIONS

(i) Outlay

The common law protects the paying bank that has made an unauthorized payment mainly where the customer's conduct is such as to estop him from denying that there has been a departure from his mandate. The cases covered were those of forged signatures, of inadequate signatures, and of material alterations which the customer has facilitated. Apart from estoppel, the customer's inability to proceed against the bank may be based either on his having ratified the bank's act or on the ambiguity of the instruction given by him. Statute confers on the bank additional defences, applicable mainly where the customer's mode of behaviour cannot be described as faulty. The cases involved are primarily those of payments made despite the forgery of the payee's indorsement, and certain cases of material alterations such as the skilful obliteration of a crossing. Usually, the bank's protection depends on its having acted either in the ordinary course of business or 'without negligence'. In certain other cases the bank obtains a valid defence if it has paid a cheque 'in due course'. The different defences require detailed consideration. Payment in due course is the basic principle involved, although such payment does not necessarily confer on the bank a defence against its customer.

(ii) Payment in due course

Under section 59, 'payment in due course' means payment made at or after the maturity of the bill to the holder thereof in good faith and without notice that his title to the bill is defective. The effect of such payment is to discharge the bill. As a cheque is a bill of exchange payable on demand, the question of its 'maturity' does not arise.

In most cases payment in due course entitles the bank to debit its customer's account with the amount of the cheque. The reason is obvious. The customer instructs the bank to pay the instrument to A's order, or to 'A or bearer'. This is what the bank usually does when it pays a cheque to the holder. But not every person who obtains the possession of a cheque is a holder. In this respect, it is important to recall the distinction between a cheque payable to order and one payable to bearer. A cheque payable to bearer, which includes a cheque payable to a specified person or to bearer, is transferable by the mere delivery thereof.[150] Any person who obtains its

---

[150] BEA, s. 31(2).

possession by delivery is a bearer and hence the holder of the instrument. It follows that when the drawee bank pays such a cheque to a person who has its possession, it acts in accordance with the terms of its mandate.[151]

The position differs in the case of a cheque payable to the order of a specific payee. Such an instrument is deliverable by the payee's indorsement completed by the delivery of the instrument.[152] If the payee's indorsement is forged on the cheque, a subsequent party is not the holder of the instrument. The reason for this is that the holder of a bill or of a cheque is defined as 'the payee or indorsee of a bill ... who is in possession of it, or the bearer thereof'.[153] A person who takes a cheque under the forged indorsement of the payee does not fall within any one of these categories and, therefore, is not a holder of the instrument.[154] Payment to him is not made in due course and does not constitute a discharge. The cheque is not paid in accordance with the drawer's instruction, as it is not paid to the payee or to his order. Moreover, even where a cheque is paid to the holder thereof—be he the payee, the indorsee, or a bearer—the bank does not necessarily honour the instrument in accordance with the drawer's instruction. Thus, the transferee of a stopped bearer cheque and the indorsee of a countermanded order cheque are 'holders' within the meaning of the Act. But the bank's duty is to obey the stop order given by the drawer and to dishonour the instrument!

(iii) Payment in the ordinary course of business

The Act does not confer a defence on a bank that disobeys a stop order. But the problem of payment against a forged indorsement had to be tackled when the use of cheques became popular. A bank has no means of verifying the genuineness of the payee's indorsement. The payee is a stranger and the bank is not familiar with his signature. Furthermore, as a cheque may be negotiated several times before it is presented for payment, the task of verifying the genuineness of an indorsement is beyond the powers of the paying bank.

The first defence conferred on banks in cases of this type was to be found in section 19 of the Stamp Act 1853. This Act abolished the *ad valorem* duty on cheques, replacing it by a fixed amount. It was envisaged that this would lead to an increase in the use of cheques, and the need for the bank's protection in cases of payment against forged indorsements became paramount. Section 19 provides that, where a bank pays any draft or order drawn on it for a sum of money and payable to order on demand and the instrument purports to be indorsed by the payee, it is not incumbent on the paying bank

[151] *Charles* v. *Blackwell* (1877) 2 CPD 151, 158.
[152] BEA, s. 31(3).
[153] Ibid., s. 2.
[154] *Lacave & Co.* v. *Crédit Lyonnais* [1897] 1 QB 148.

to show that the indorsement of the payee, or any subsequent indorsement, was made by or under the authority of the person whose indorsement it purports to be, and the bank obtains a valid discharge. This provision is still in effect in respect of bankers' drafts and other instruments which are not encompassed by the definition of a bill.[155] In the case of cheques, this provision has been superseded by section 60 of the Bills of Exchange Act 1882, which adopts the pattern of section 19.

Section 60 applies, and deems the payment to have been made in due course, if the bank is able to show that it has acted in good faith and in the ordinary course of business. In an Australian authority, *Australian Mutual Provident Society* v. *Derham*,[156] it was decided that the last phrase means the mode of transacting business which is adopted by the banking community at large. It has been held that, where the bank pays a crossed cheque over the counter, or where it honours a cheque bearing an irregular indorsement, it is not acting within the ordinary course of business.

A question of some difficulty is whether a bank that acts with negligence may nevertheless be considered as paying a cheque in the ordinary course of business. In *Carpenters' Co.* v. *British Mutual Banking Co. Ltd.*,[157] Greer LJ expressed the view that when a bank acts negligently it deviates from the ordinary course of business. Slesser LJ, who concurred with Greer LJ on other grounds, thought that a bank may be acting in the ordinary course of business despite its negligence. This view was supported by Mackinnon LJ, who delivered a dissenting judgment. The question thus remains open. In practice, the question is not likely to arise again. The ordinary course of business is determined on the basis of the business methods of a reasonably careful banker. A departure from this standard establishes negligence.

A question of some doubt is whether section 60 protects the bank only in cases in which the forged indorsement was placed on the cheque before its presentment for payment, or even where it was executed when the cheque was tendered to the bank. The section does not expressly distinguish between the two cases. All it says is that, where payment is made by a bank in the ordinary course of business and in good faith, the bank need not show that an indorsement placed on the cheque is genuine. Obviously, if the indorsement is not required, as in the case of a cheque payable to bearer, the question is irrelevant. Furthermore, an indorsement is really not necessary where a cheque is presented to the bank by the ostensible payee. The paying bank does not wish to obtain a transfer to itself of the instrument, and hence a negotiation to it is not necessary. The bank's function is simply to pay the

---

[155] P. 242 above and 496 below. For details, see *Benjamin's Sale of Goods*, 2nd edn., London, 1981, paras. 2005 et seq.
[156] (1979) 39 FLR 165, 173.
[157] [1938] 1 KB 511.

cheque. However, it is customary for banks to request the payee to sign a cheque presented over the counter, as his indorsement serves as a receipt.

South African cases suggest that, where payment is made to the payee over the counter, section 60 has no application.[158] A similar view was taken by an Australian authority, *Smith* v. *Commercial Banking Co. of Sydney Ltd.*,[159] where a thief signed his name twice on the back of a bankers' draft in the presence of the teller. It was held that the forged signature did not absolve the bank from liability, and that the Australian counterpart of section 60 (which applies also to drafts) conferred no defence. At first glance, it may appear that the case of *Brighton Empire and Eden Syndicate* v. *London and County Banking Co. Ltd.*,[160] decided by the English High Court, went in the opposite direction. Here a director forged his company's indorsement on a cheque and thereafter negotiated it to another employee who presented it to the bank for payment. It was held that, as the bank had acted in good faith, it was entitled to plead the defence of section 60. This case is, however, distinguishable from *Smith*'s case, as in the present case the indorsement was utilized for the transfer of the cheque and not merely as a receipt of its payment by the bank.

It is submitted that the South African and Australian authorities are good law. The object of section 60, as that of section 19 of the Stamp Act 1853, is to protect the bank where it has paid a cheque to a person holding it under a forged indorsement. Where the person who presents the instrument purports himself to be the payee of the instrument, the bank is able to verify his identity.

The main requirement in section 60 is that the cheque be paid in the ordinary course of business. The words of Lord Halsbury in *Bank of England* v. *Vagliano Bros.*[161] are significant. His Lordship doubted that 'it would be possible to affirm that any particular course was either usual or unusual in the sense that there [was] some particular course to be pursued'.[162] The question is, basically, one of fact. Thus, the payment of a large cheque presented by a scruffy-looking individual may dictate a different 'ordinary course' than the payment of a cheque for an ordinary amount presented by a person with a usual appearance. As regards other circumstances, the bank is not at fault if it pays a cheque slightly after the official closing time.[163] An indorsement executed in a foreign language, unreadable by the average Englishman, is in all probability irregular; if a cheque with such an

---

[158] *National Bank of South Africa Ltd.* v. *Paterson* [1909] 2 LDAB 214; *Sapelberg* v. *Barclays Bank (DCO)* 3 SALR 120.

[159] (1910) 11 CLR 667.

[160] *The Times*, 24 March 1904.

[161] [1891] AC 107.

[162] Ibid., 117. See also *Auchteroni & Co.* v. *Midland Bank Ltd.* [1928] 2 KB 294.

[163] *Baines* v. *National Provincial Bank* (1927) 96 LJKB 801.

indorsement were honoured, this would be outside the ordinary course of business.[164]

(iv) Complementary defence of payment without negligence

In addition to section 60 of the Act, there is a specific provision confined to crossed cheques. Under section 80, where the cheque has been paid in accordance with the tenor of its crossing, in good faith and without negligence, the paying bank is placed in the same position as if the cheque had been paid to the true owner thereof. Furthermore, the protection is also conferred on the drawer, provided the cheque was indorsed by a forger after it had reached the hands of the payee. For all practical purposes, the phrase 'without negligence' in section 80 replaces the pharse 'in the ordinary course of business' of section 60.

The existence side by side of sections 60 and 80 is explainable by historical reasons. As already pointed out, section 60 can be traced back to section 19 of the Cheques Act 1853. Section 80 stems from section 9 of the Crossed Cheques Act 1876; this explains why it is applicable only to cheques of such a type.

In the United Kingdom, the need to have two provisions has been questioned by Holden.[165] Undoubtedly, unlike section 60, section 80 confers a protection not only on the paying bank but also on the drawer whose cheque was received by the payee. But the two provisions could have been amalgamated. However, a recent Australian authority suggests that section 80 is useful in its own right. In *Australian Mutual Provident Society* v. *Derham*,[166] an assured, who had decided to surrender his policy, lodged a form requesting the company to remit the proceeds to an agent. This agent completed the surrender form by inserting his own post office box as the assured's address. When the agent received the company's crossed cheque payable to the assured, he forged on it the latter's indorsement and paid the cheque to the credit of his own bank account. McGregor J held, inter alia, that the paying bank was protected by the Australian equivalent of section 80. As the bank was not concerned with the regularity of the indorsement, it had paid the cheque in question 'without negligence'. That the bank was not concerned with the regularity of the indorsement followed from the Australian counterpart of section 1 of the Cheques Act 1957, discussed subsequently. His Honour, in effect, read section 80 together with the

---

[164] *Carlisle and Cumberland Banking Co.* v. *Bragg* [1911] 1 KB 489, 496 (unaffected as regards this point by *Saunders* v. *Anglia Building Society (Gallie v. Lee)* [1971] AC 1004); *Arab Bank Ltd.* v. *Ross* [1952] 2 QB 216.

[165] Holden, *History of Negotiable Instruments*, p. 268. And see Chalmers, *Bills of Exchange*, 13th edn., London, 1964, p. 268.

[166] (1979) 39 FLR 165.

Australian equivalent of section 1. The decision in *Derham*'s case could have been reached even if payment were not made 'in the ordinary course of business', provided it had been made without negligence.

(v) *Irregularity in or absence of indorsement*

Section 60 and the complementary section 80 protect the paying bank only where the indorsement of an order cheque, which appears regular on its face, turns out to be forged. Payment against an absent or irregular indorsement is both outside the ordinary course of business and, on the same reasoning, negligent. The indorsement of the payee is irregular whenever it differs materially from the name by which he is described by the drawer. If a cheque is payable to 'John Williams', an indorsement by 'J. Williams' is regular. But if the payee is described on the face of the instrument under a misnomer (e.g. W. Williams) and then indorses it in his correct name (e.g. John Williams), the discrepancy between the front and the back of the instrument renders the indorsement irregular, although it may be effective for the purpose of negotiation.[167] Similarly, if a company indorses a cheque without adding the word 'company' or 'Ltd.', which forms part of its description as the payee of the cheque, the indorsement is irregular.[168]

A special problem concerning the regularity of an indorsement arises where it is executed by an agent. Where A is B's agent, usually he will indorse a cheque as 'A on behalf of B', or 'A *per pro* B' (*per pro* meaning *per procuratorem*, or by procuration). The drawer himself may make the cheque payable to 'A *per pro* B', which often occurs in cases such as settlements of claims, in which a cheque is made payable to the creditor through his solicitor. There is a view that the agent must indicate that he is signing on behalf of the principal and not merely that he is assuming the role of an agent. Thus, it has been suggested that where a cheque payable to 'John Brown' is indorsed 'John Brown, W. Robinson (agent)', the indorsement is irregular as the word 'agent' contextually signifies the signer's business rather than status.[169] But this view is pedantic. Banks accept such indorsements as valid.

The agent has to show that he is signing in representative capacity even if the cheque is made payable to him as an agent. In *Slingsby* v. *District Bank Ltd.*,[170] an executor of a will instructed his solicitors, Messrs. C. & P., to draw a cheque payable to stockbrokers. One of the partners of the firm of

---

[167] *Arab Bank Ltd.* v. *Ross* [1952] 2 QB 216.

[168] Ibid., 234.

[169] Chorley, *Law of Banking*, 6th edn., p. 85. And see the dictum of Piggott CB in *O'Reilly* v. *Richardson* (1865) 7 ICLR 74; Scrutton LJ in *McDonald (Gerald) & Co.* v. *Nash & Co.* [1922] WN 272, revsd. on a different point: [1924] AC 625.

[170] [1931] 2 KB 588, affd. [1932] 1 KB 544.

solicitors initially made the cheque payable to the stockbrokers, obtained the required signatures, and then utilized a gap left after the stockbrokers' name as payee in order to make the cheque payable to these payees 'per pro C & P'. The partner then indorsed the cheque merely as 'C & P', and paid it into an account of a company in which he had a personal interest. It was held that the indorsement was irregular, and hence the paying bank could not plead the protection of sections 60 and 80 of the Act.

In the case of a company, section 37 of the Companies Act 1985 provides that a negotiable instrument is deemed to be made, accepted or indorsed in the firm's name 'if . . . [signed] in the name of, or by or on behalf or on account of, the company by any person acting under its authority'. It follows that a company's indorsement is regular if its name is written out, or impressed with a rubber stamp. However, banks insist that the person who executes the indorsement should identify himself. In practice, therefore, a regular indorsement in the company's name should read 'X Ltd. per A B, director', 'A B on behalf of X Ltd.', or words to a similar effect.

It is obvious that cheques are frequently indorsed in an irregular manner. This stems from the misnomer of the payee's name on the front of the cheque, or from inaccurancies in the description of corporate bodies. The best advice that could be given to the payee was to indorse the cheque in the name in which he was described and then to add his genuine signature. The extent of the problem, in particular in the case of corporate bodies with a large clientele, can be best appreciated if one bears in mind that, at one stage, the firm of Thomas Cook & Sons had several rubber stamps with different names to be employed for the indorsement of cheques payable to them under different variations of their proper corporate name![171]

Up to 1957, the paying bank's correct legal course was to dishonour any cheque that was irregularly indorsed or on which the indorsement was missing. This was the case also where the cheque was presented for payment through the clearing system, as the collecting bank was expected to demand the payee's indorsement even where the cheque was not negotiated to a third party. Undoubtedly, such an indorsement served as a mere receipt rather than for the proper function of an indorsement, namely for the negotiation of the instrument. But an irregularity was considered to render the cheque as being paid with negligence and outside the ordinary course of business. This meant that, unless the paying bank was prepared to forego the protection of sections 60 and 80, it had to reject a substantial number of cheques. This situation was undesirable and, eventually, led the Committee on Cheque Indorsements (the Mocatta Committee), in its report of

---

[171] This procedure is described in *Bird & Co.* v. *Thomas Cook & Son Ltd.* [1937] 2 All ER 227. And note that if a director signs a cheque or accepts a bill which describes the company incorrectly, he is personally liable on the instument: the Companies Act 1985, s. 394(4), discussed in *Chitty on Contracts*, 25th edn., vol. 2, para. 2477.

November 1956,[172] to recommend that indorsements be no longer required as a pre-condition for the payment of cheques other than those presented over the counter. The Cheques Act 1957, enacted in the wake of this report, went further than that. Under section 1(1), where a banker in good faith and in the ordinary course of business pays a cheque drawn on him and the cheque is not indorsed or is irregularly indorsed, the bank does not, in doing so, incur any liability by reason only of the absence of or the irregularity in the indorsement. The bank is, further, deemed to have paid the instrument in due course. Subsection (2) extends the application of this provision to documents which, though not bills of exchange, are intended to enable a person to obtain payment from the bank of the sum mentioned in the instrument. Instruments of this type include 'cheques' payable to 'cash or order' which, as has been pointed out,[173] do not constitute bills of exchange. Subsection (2) further extends the provision of subsection (1) to bank drafts which, likewise, are not bills within the definition of the Act.

Section 1 had the effect of eliminating the need of an indorsement of a cheque as as prerequisite to the bank's right to invoke the protection of sections 60 and 80 of the 1882 Act. But the Committee of London Clearing Banks took the view that the public interest would be best served by retaining the need for indorsements in certain circumstances. These circumstances are stated in a circular of 23 September 1957, sent by the Committee to clearing bank managers. Despite the lapse of time, the practice laid down in the circular has remained unaltered. The procedure prescribed in the circular can thus be taken to establish the 'ordinary course of business' to be observed by banks when paying cheques. If this procedure is disregarded, the bank is deprived of the protection conferred on it by section 1. This follows from the language of the section, which states that a bank does not incur liability 'by reason only' of a missing or of an irregular indorsement. When a bank pays an irregularly indorsed cheque, although the practice based on the circular regards it as one on which a regular indorsement is required, the paying bank honours it not only despite the relevant defect but also in disregard of standard banking practice.

The situation in which the circular requires the paying bank to insist on an indorsement are (a) where cheques are presented for payment over the counter; (b) in respect of combined cheques and receipt forms marked 'R'; and (c) where cheques payable to joint payees are paid into an account which is not maintained in the name of all of them. It is understood that, in this last type of case, the indorsement of one payee is sufficient if the cheque is payable to them in the alternative. Otherwise, the indorsement of all of them is required.

[172] Cmnd. 3.
[173] P. 244 above.

It is important to note that in most of the cases an indorsement, which is required under the circular, serves the function of a receipt rather than the negotiation of the cheque. This is the case in all combined cheques marked 'R', and whenever the person who presents any cheque for payment over the counter is the ostensible payee. But if the cheque is presented by a subsequent holder, the bank will insist on having indorsements of both the holder and of the ostensible payee. The object is to ensure the apparent regularity in the line of indorsements. In reality, though, the usefulness of the practice is questionable. If a cheque, payable to X's order, is stolen by Y and presented by Y for payment over the counter, Y can easily forge X's indorsement before he goes to the bank; he can then add an indorsement in his own name! Under section 60, the paying bank will be protected in such a case if the forged indorsement is regular. *Smith* v. *Commercial Banking Co. of Sydney Ltd.*,[174] discussed above, does not deprive it of its defence, as the forged signature is that of X and not of Y, to whom the cheque is paid. However, under the terms of the circular, the protection would be lost if X's indorsement were not only forged but also irregular.

5. THE CUSTOMER'S REMEDIES FOR WRONGFUL DISHONOUR OF HIS CHEQUES

(i) Scope of problem

It will be recalled that the bank's duty to honour a cheque is owed to the customer alone.[175] A wrongful dishonour of a cheque constitutes a breach of contract on the bank's part. In certain cases the customer may have an additional action in defamation. This action is usually based on the reply that the bank writes on the cheque when it returns it unpaid. In certain cases, the reason stated is meant to save the customer's reputation. Thus, the bank may explain its dishonour of a cheque by the words 'amount in words and in figures differ'. Another instance, which occurs in the case of companies, is an indication by the bank that the cheque does not bear all the required signatures. The situation which leads to actions in defamation arises where a cheque is dishonoured due to a supposed inadequacy of funds standing to the credit of the customer's account. Where the bank's answer on the cheque gives the impression that this is the case, the customer's reputation may be harmed. He is then tempted to sue both for breach of contract and defamation.

---

[174] (1910) 11 CLR 667.
[175] Pp. 238–9 above.

(ii) Action in breach of contract

Under the basic principles governing actions for breach of contract, the innocent party is entitled to recover damages from the party in breach. But unless the innocent party has sustained a loss, he is confined to recovering nominal damages.[176]

This general rule is applicable where the bank dishonours a cheque without a justifiable reason. A distinction is drawn in this context between a person who is in business and other members of the public. In the case of the latter group, the amount of damages recoverable for wrongful dishonour is nominal, unless special loss can be proved. This basic principle is best illustrated by *Evans* v. *London and Provincial Bank*.[177] The customer was the wife of a naval officer. When her cheque for groceries was wrongfully dishonoured by the bank, she sued in breach of contract. It was held that she had suffered no loss and she was, therefore, awarded one shilling by the jury. Similarly, in *Gibbons* v. *Westminster Bank Ltd.*,[178] where the bank dishonoured a cheque drawn by a tenant in favour of a landlord, it was held that the customer had to prove loss in order to recover substantial damages. Lawrence J observed that such loss would have to be pleaded and proved as special damage.

The converse is true in the case of people engaged in trade. From the beginning of the nineteenth century, a stigma attached to the reputation of a merchant whose bills (including cheques) were not met by the bank at which they were domiciled. This damage to reputation was recognized as early as 1830 in *Marzetti* v. *Williams*.[179] The principle involved is most clearly stated in *Rolin* v. *Steward*, where a merchant's cheque was wrongfully dishonoured by his bank, by Williams J in the Court of Common Pleas:[180]

when . . . the [customer] is a trader . . . the jury, in estimating the damages, may take into their consideration the natural and necessary consequences which must result to the [customer] from the [bank's] breach of contract: just as in the case of an action for slander of a person in the way of his trade, or in the case of an imputation of insolvency on a trader, the action lies without proof of special damage.

This basic principle has remained unchanged. It is still based on the same rationale.[181] It is assumed that a tradesman's reputation suffers from the dishonour of his cheque, as it implies that his bank, which is the entity most familiar with his financial standing, has no trust in his creditworthiness. The

---

[176] *Anson's Law of Contract*, 26th edn., p. 491.
[177] *The Times*, 1 March 1917; 3 LDAB 152.
[178] [1939] 2 KB 882.
[179] (1830) 1 B & Ad. 415.
[180] (1854) 14 CB 595, 607; and see *Bank of New South Wales* v. *Milvain* (1884) 10 VLR (Law) 3.
[181] *Jayson* v. *Midland Bank Ltd.* [1968] 1 Lloyd's Rep. 409.

amount of damages to be awarded is, fundamentally, a matter for the assessment of the judge, or for a jury where he is not sitting alone.[182] Undoubtedly, the bank's prompt apology for the mistake, conveyed in writing to the ostensible payee, will be taken into consideration.[183]

The distinction between the award of damages to tradesmen and other persons does, however, pose a question. It was, undoubtedly, suitable in a period in which the significance of credit to traders and its meaning to ordinary members of the public were clearly distinguishable. It may be asked if this is still the position at present. In the first place, the demarcation between traders and other members of the community is no longer clear-cut. In addition to solicitors, accountants and money brokers, who are clearly akin to businessmen,[184] there is the intermediary class which comprises such persons as physicians and dentists, whose reputation in financial matters is of considerable significance to their ability to obtain supplies for their surgeries. Secondly, the average consumer, in the present era, depends to a very substantial extent on the availability of credit. A civil servant whose cheque is dishonoured is likely to suffer the same type of loss as that sustained by a trader such as a grocer or a builder. The latter may have difficulty in obtaining supplies. The former may have a problem as regards the supply to him on credit of petrol for his car or of books needed for the furthering of his professional career. A re-examination of the basic principle is timely.

The hazard of the wrongful dishonour of a cheque has not been eliminated by the introduction of the semi-automated clearing process of cheques, and by the system used in respect of money transfers.[185] Although a cheque sets out in magnetic ink the number of the account to be debited, and although the deposit slip used by the payee identifies his own account in the same manner, mistakes can occur when the amount of a cheque, initially written in ordinary ink by the drawer, is encoded in magnetic ink by the clerks who effect the respective debit or credit. As a result the balance in a specific account, against which a further cheque is drawn, may be shown inaccurately. Furthermore, the computerized process itself is fallible: the encoded details can be misinterpreted by the computer if the cheque has been folded or otherwise handled carelessly. The risk of error is even greater

---

[182] 'Reasonable damages' are to be awarded: *Wilson* v. *United Counties Bank Ltd.* [1920] AC 102, 112, per Lord Birkenhead LC. And see *Szek* v. *Lloyds Bank* (1908) 2 LDAB 159.

[183] For a telling argument in point, see Weaver and Craigie, *Banker and Customer in Australia*, pp. 380–1.

[184] Thus, in *Davidson* v. *Barclays Bank Ltd.* [1940] 1 All ER 316, a bookmaker was treated as a tradesman. In contrast, a firm engaged in kite-flying was treated as a non-trader in *Ellow Co. Ltd.* v. *Lloyds Bank Ltd.* (1934) 4 LDAB 455, although the court also took into consideration the poor record of the firm which frequently drew uncovered cheques.

[185] As regards the clearing of cheques, see pp. 231 et seq. above; as regards money transfer, see pp. 351 et seq. below.

in the case of individual money transfer orders. It will be recalled that, at the time of going to press, such orders are not processed by BACS, and further, that such individual orders continue to be written out by hand and do not always include the identifying details set out on cheques in magnetic ink. The end result is that the danger of inaccurate balances in current accounts continues to be a real one.

This danger means that the bank has to compose with care its grounds for the dishonour of what appears to be an uncovered cheque. If it gave an answer such as 'insufficient funds' and it then turned out that the balance in the customer's account was adequate, the bank would face the hazards of an action, especially where the customer was a trader or a professional man.[186] The difficulty, however, is that standard formulas that may appear innocent have acquired a certain notoriety and indicate that the cheque is drawn without cover. Thus, in New Zealand, the words 'present again' have been held to indicate an inadequacy of funds simply because that was the meaning attributed to the phrase generally.[187] The formula 'refer to drawer' is another one which, at this stage, has become associated with uncovered cheques.[188] It is believed that almost any phrase that became associated with uncovered cheques would, in due course, acquire such an ulterior meaning. The safest course that can be adopted by the bank is the return of the unpaid cheque, accompanied by a note which confirms its dishonour but does not give any specific reason therefore.[189]

(iii) Action in defamation

Any carelessly composed answer written on a dishonoured cheque is capable of being construed as defamatory provided it is susceptible to such an interpretation by a reasonable man. The question is one of mixed fact and law. The legal question is whether the words are at all open to such a construction.[190] If they are, it is a question of fact whether or not the words have conveyed such a meaning in the case in question. The innocent appear-

---

[186] *Davidson* v. *Barclays Bank Ltd.* [1940] 1 All ER 316. And see *Miles* v. *Commercial Banking Co. of Sydney* (1904) 1 CLR 470.

[187] *Baker* v. *Australia and New Zealand Bank* [1958] NZLR 907.

[188] This was not so initially: *Szek* v. *Lloyds Bank Ltd.* (1908) 2 LDAB 159; *Flach* v. *London and South Western Bank Ltd.* (1915) 31 TLR 334; *Plunkett* v. *Barclays Bank Ltd.* [1936] 2 KB 107. It is believed that the position differs today, as cheques are not 'referred to drawer' in other types of cases, and this fact is common knowledge. And note that in a more recent Irish case, *Pyke* v. *Hibernian Bank Ltd* [1950] IR 195, the words were held defamatory by a jury; and see *Jayson* v. *Midland Bank Ltd.* [1968] 1 Lloyd's Rep. 409.

[189] *Frost* v. *London Joint Stock Bank Ltd.* (1906) 22 TLR 760.

[190] The mere dishonour of the cheque, without the giving of a reason, is probably not the basis for an action in defamation: *Bank of New South Wales* v. *Milvain* (1884) 10 VLR (Law) 3; *Kinlan* v. *Ulster Bank Ltd.* [1928] IR 171.

ance of the words is irrelevant, as they may convey an innuendo. Thus, in *Baker* v. *Australia and New Zealand Bank Ltd.*,[191] Shorland J, in the Supreme Court of New Zealand, held that the words, 'present again' were both legally capable of such a meaning and that, in fact, they had conveyed that effect in the case before him. In *Pyke* v. *Hibernian Bank Ltd.*,[192] Black J reached a similar conclusion as regards the words 'refer to drawer', and his decision was upheld by the Irish Court of Appeal. In *Jayson* v. *Midland Bank Ltd.*,[193] an English jury, which found that the dishonour of a cheque was justified on the facts, found nevertheless that the last quoted words could lower a person's reputation and were defamatory if untrue.

In practice, therefore, it is possible to bring an action for the wrongful dishonour of a cheque under the complementary causes of action of breach of contract and of defamation. The customer is, however, unlikely to be awarded a separate amount of damages in respect of each plea. Indeed, in some cases juries awarded substantial damages for the one cause and nominal damages for the additional second cause of action.[194] There are, however, advantages to the bringing of the action in the alternative under both causes. If the action in defamation fails but the action for breach of contract suceeds, the plaintiff has, in the very least, vindicated his right to have drawn the cheque. This may be important as regards his financial standing. It is, therefore, inadvisable to abandon the action in breach of contract. If, on the other hand, the action is confined to one in breach of contract, the action is to be heard by a judge sitting alone. If the action is brought in defamation, the plaintiff, subject to the court's discretion, is entitled to trial by jury. Tactically, the plaintiff may see an advantage in having the action tried in this way.

---

[191] [1958] NZLR 907.
[192] [1950] IR 195.
[193] [1968] 1 Lloyd's Rep. 409.
[194] Thus, in *Szek* v. *Lloyds Bank Ltd.* (1908) 2 LDAB 159, the jury awarded £250 for breach of contract and nil for defamation. Grantham J, indeed, suggested to the jury that one sum should be awarded for both claims. In *Baker* v. *Australia and New Zealand Bank Ltd.*, above, a nominal amount was awarded for the breach of contract involved, but £100 for defamation.

CHAPTER 11

Recovery of Money Paid by Mistake

1. THE PROBLEM IN PRACTICE AND THE BASIC PRINCIPLE

It was shown in Chapter 10 that, in certain cases, banks which pay their customer's money without having his valid mandate are nevertheless entitled to debit his account. The defences conferred by the Bills of Exchange Act and the common law defence of estoppel are relevant in this context. There are, however, cases in which the bank does not have a defence against the customer. Thus, because of a computer error, a giro payment may be effected twice instead of once, or a bank may honour a cheque despite an effective countermand issued by the customer.[1] In such a case, the bank's only course is to attempt to reclaim the money from the payee. Moreover, even where the bank is entitled to debit its customer's account with a wrongfully made payment, it may prefer—for reasons of policy—to recover the amount from the payee.

The word 'payee' has to be understood in this context in a wide sense. Usually, the amount involved is paid by the paying bank to the collecting bank engaged by the ultimate payee. If payment is made because of an error, recovery may be claimed either from the ultimate payee or from his bank. In many cases the two may be sued jointly. It will be shown that the action against the collecting bank is, however, subject to certain limitations which are inapplicable to actions brought against the ultimate payee. The distinction stems from the fact that the collecting bank receives payment in a representative capacity, whilst the payee obtains payment for himself.[2] When the collecting bank acts for itself, e.g. where it discounts an instrument, its position is similar to the ultimate payee's.

The action instituted in cases of this type is a quasi-contractual action, or action in restitution, brought to recover money paid under a mistake of fact.

---

[1] See pp. 299–300 above. For an authoritative and lucid analysis of the subject, see H. Luntz, 'Bank's Right to Recover on Cheques Paid by Mistake', (1968) 6 Melb. Univ. L Rev. 308.

Note that an action in restitution is not usually brought by a collecting bank, which can in most cases rely on the right of recourse conferred on it by the BEA (p. 511 below). For an extraordinary case in which the collecting bank sought to recover money paid under a mistake, see *Deutsche Bank (London Agency) v. Beriro & Co.* (1895) 1 Com. Cas. 255.

As regards the connection between the bank's right to debit the customer's account and its right to recover from the payee money paid in cases of lack of mandate, see *Commercial Bank of Australia Ltd. v. Younis* [1979] 1 NSWR 444.

[2] Pp. 329–33 below.

It is brought by the paying bank, and not in its customer's name, as the money paid over is the bank's.[3] It will be recalled that the relationship of banker and customer is that of debtor and creditor, and that money deposited by the customer with his bank is co-mingled with the bank's remaining funds. Even if the bank grants the customer an overdraft in order to meet his instruction for payment, the bank pays out its own funds to the payee or his bank. The customer simply incurs a debt equal to the amount involved. It follows that a quasi-contractual action brought against the payee by the customer could be resisted on the ground that the money was not his.[4]

The practical situations in which there is room for the paying bank's action in restitution fall into two main groups. The first encompasses cases in which the paying instruction is set out in a document other than a negotiable instrument. The second group relates to the wrongful discharge of negotiable instruments, especially of cheques. Cases involving instruments rendered non-negotiable, such as fraudulently altered cheques, are conceptually within this second group.

The first group covers all cases involving the wrongful discharge of giro orders and other instructions for payments, such as CHAPS (Clearing House Automated Payment System) and SWIFT (Society for Worldwide Interbank Financial Telecommunications) transfers. Reported decisions are scarce. They include instances in which a given payment was erroneously effected twice, and cases in which payments were completed although the customer revoked his instruction or the payee became insolvent before receiving payment. It is conceivable that cases of forged or unauthorized giro instructions will arise eventually.

The second group is well covered by authorities. Factually, the cases fall into the following categories: (*a*) the wrongful payment of a countermanded cheque; (*b*) the payment of a cheque bearing a forged signature of the payee or the signature of an agent executed in excess of his authority as conveyed to the bank; and (*c*) the payment of cheques bearing a false indorsement of the ostensible payee. In addition, the bank may pay a cheque although its amount has been fraudulently raised or may make a mistake as to the identity of the payee. The same type of case can arise in respect of bills of exchange. Thus, the bank may erroneously pay a bill which is on its face domiciled at its premises but which the bank has been ordered to dishonour

---

[3] But note that there is here an element of inconsequential reasoning in the case law. On the one hand, the bank is deemed to pay its own money (pp. 81–84 above); on the other hand, it pays this amount as its customer's agent (pp. 127–8 above). If it pays money as an agent, should the principal not be entitled to reclaim it in cases of error quite regardless of whether the money involved was his or, initially, the bank's?

[4] See generally on the bank's rights. See R. Goff and H. Jones, *On Restitution*, 2nd edn., London 1978, pp. 88–9.

or on which the instruction to pay has been forged by the acceptor's unscrupulous employee. The bank may, further, pay an instrument due to a mistake as to its customer's available balance.

In the majority of cases the action involved is brought to enable the bank to recover payment of an amount which it cannot debit to its customer's account. In some cases, though, the action has the object of giving the paying bank an advantage over the payee's general creditors. This is the case where the paying bank has remitted an amount twice over. Normally, the amount would of course be refunded by the collecting bank without demur. But if the collecting bank becomes insolvent before the error is discovered, the position is complicated by the existence of the claims of the general creditors which, usually, cannot be satisfied in full. Is the bank that made the erroneous payment entitled to recover the amount in specie or is it confined to claiming it as an amount paid under a mistake of fact, in which case the bank would rank as general creditor in respect of it? It will be shown that the bank may be able to recover the amount involved in specie by means of a tracing order.

2. RECOVERY WHERE THE MISTAKE IS KNOWN TO THE PAYEE

Even in cases where the bank's only object is to recover from the recipient an erroneously made payment, it is necessary to distinguish between two situations. The first is where the payee is aware of the bank's error in making payment. The second is where the payee, too, is under a mistake of fact. The distinction is best illustrated by the wrongful payment of a countermanded cheque. The payee may be aware of the stop order when he presents the cheque; he is therefore not a party to the bank's mistaken belief. But he may be equally ignorant of the circumstances. The same distinction applies to cases concerning payments made in respect of documents other than negotiable instruments. Thus, the recipient may be either aware or ignorant of the fact that a bank giro credit has been wrongfully issued by the payor's employee, or that a payment received to the credit of his account was in reality due to an associate or to a namesake.

Cases involving mistakes common to the bank and to the payee require a careful analysis, as the authorities are not altogether conclusive. Cases in which the payee is aware of the bank's error are clear-cut. It is considered unconscionable for the payee to retain an amount of money which he knows to have been paid in error. The bank is entitled to reclaim the money in a quasi-contractual action or, possibly, in an action based on a fraudulent misrepresentation made by the payee.[5] The argument in respect of the

---

[5] This alternative is supported in Quilliam J's judgment in *Southland Savings Bank* v. *Anderson* [1974] 1 NZLR 118.

second type of action is that the payee tacitly represents that he is entitled to the money. It, is, however, questionable if he is rightly regarded as making any statement, be it express or tacit. When he presents an instrument for payment, he is merely seeking an answer. Where payment is by giro or by some other money transfer order, all he does is to receive payment.

The payor's right to reclaim payment where the payee is aware of his error can be traced back to nineteenth-century cases. Thus, in *Martin* v. *Morgan*[6] the payee of a cheque, who presented it to the drawee when he found out that the drawer was facing insolvency, failed to mention that the instrument had been post-dated at its inception. Dallas CJ ordered the payee to refund the amount paid, as there had been an 'inequality of knowledge' of the relevant facts.[7] In *Holt* v. *Ely*[8] a solicitor, who had been charged with the payment of certain bills by the drawer thereof, was allowed to recover the amount paid to bill brokers who had mis-stated the nature of a bill held by them. Lord Campbell CJ said that the solicitor was entitled to recover as the bill brokers had induced an error pertaining to his mandate. Erle J thought that the misrepresentation formed the basis of a valid action for money had and received.

It is now accepted that the payee's knowledge of the payor's error forms the basis for an action in restitution. Thus, in *Kendal* v. *Wood*[9] the payees knew that partnership funds were used to discharge a personal debt of one of the partners. Allowing the partnership to recover the amount involved, Cockburn CJ in the Court of Exchequer Chamber observed that the payee had received the partnership's money at his peril. To be able to retain the funds, he would have had to establish the payor's authority. In *John* v. *Dodwell & Co.*,[10] stockbrokers were ordered to repay the amount of a cheque drawn by a company manager on his employers' account for the payment of shares purchased in his own name. Lord Haldane held that it was sufficient that the brokers knew that the funds involved were owned by the company; it was not necessary to show that the brokers were aware of the fraud. In *Reckitt* v. *Barnett, Pembroke and Slater Ltd.*,[11] where the facts were basically the same, Lord Hailsham LC emphasized that the action was based on the payee's receipt of funds known to him to be paid without proper authorization.

It may be argued that the recovery of the amounts paid in the cases discussed up to now is based on the payee's knowledge that the funds are paid

---

[6] (1819) 1 Broad. & B 290.
[7] But the decision was influenced by the fact that a post-dated cheque was illegal under contemporary law: The Stamp Act 1815 (55 Geo. 3 c. 184), s. 12. Contrast now BEA, s. 13.
[8] (1853) 1 El. & Bl. 795.
[9] (1871) LR 6 Ex. 243, 248.
[10] [1918] AC 563.
[11] [1929] AC 176.

to him under circumstances involving a breach of trust. On this basis they could be distinguished from cases in which the payee received payment of a cheque known by him to have been countermanded by the drawer. The analogy between the two types of case, though, is the payee's knowledge that the instrument is paid under a mistake of fact. Both in cases involving a breach of trust and in cases such as the payment of a countermanded cheque, the instrument would be dishonoured if the bank were aware of the true position. The payee, who is aware of the bank's error, ought in all honesty to familiarize it with the true facts. That the payee's knowledge constitutes the basis of the action emerges from *Larner* v. *London County Council*.[12] Here a serviceman was ordered to refund to the municipal authority excessive amounts paid to him due to a misconstruction of his record. The authority's quasi-contractual action succeeded in view of the serviceman's knowledge of the mistake that had taken place.[13]

3. RECOVERY IN CASES OF PAYMENTS NOT INVOLVING NEGOTIABLE INSTRUMENTS

(i) Payor's liability and payee's entitlement

The basic principle was stated in *Kelly* v. *Solari*,[14] in which an insurance company paid out the sum due under a life policy as it overlooked that the policy had been cancelled before the death of the assured. The Court of Exchequer held that, unless the directors had paid out without caring whether the policy was valid or rescinded, the company was entitled to recover. A new trial was, accordingly, ordered to determine whether or not payment had been voluntary. The ratio of the case is to be found in the words of Parke B:[15]

where money is paid to another under the influence of a mistake, that is, upon the supposition that a specific fact is true, which would entitle the other to the money, but which fact is untrue, and the money would not have been paid if it had been known to the payer that the fact was untrue, an action will lie to recover it back, and it is against conscience to retain it; though a demand may be necessary in those cases in which the party receiving may have been ignorant of the mistake.

---

[12] [1949] 2 KB 683.
[13] For a somewhat different approach, see *Southland Savings Bank* v. *Anderson* [1974] 1 NZLR 118. See also *Bank of New South Wales* v. *Deri* (1963) 80 WN (NSW) 1499, 1503. Cf. *Westminster Bank Ltd.* v. *Arlington Overseas Trading Co.* [1952] 1 LLoyd's Rep. 211 (where fraud was not found as it had not been pleaded).
[14] (1841) 9 M & W 54.
[15] Ibid., 58. The wording of the passage differs in the report of the case in (1841) 11 LJ (NS) Ex. 10. See Luntz, 'Bank's Right . . . ', p. 312.

This passage is regarded as defining the nature of an action for the recovery of money paid under a mistake of fact.[16] It has, however, given rise to problems. The main one is that Parke B refers to a mistake which induces the payor to believe that he is legally liable to satisfy the payee's demand. If these words were to be taken literally, a bank would not usually be able to recover money paid under a mistake of fact. The reason for this is that a bank's duty to make payment is rarely owed to the payee. This is well understood in the case of cheques and is equally correct in respect of giro payments. However, Luntz[17] has pointed out that the relevant words are not included in the report of the case in the *Law Journal*. Whilst they derive support from some later cases,[18] the better view is that they are unduly restrictive.

Thus, in *Kerrison* v. *Glyn, Mills, Currie & Co.*,[19] a Mexican mining company drew bills of exchange on a New York bank. To facilitate payment, the plaintiffs, who had an interest in the Mexican company, remitted an amount of £500 to the defendant bankers, who were the London agents of the New York bank. The defendant bankers credited the New York bank's overdrawn account with the amount involved. Both the plaintiffs and the defendant bankers were, at that time, unaware that the New York bank had just failed and, accordingly, was unable to meet the bills of exchange. The plaintiffs demanded the repayment of the amount as money paid under a mistake of fact. Restoring Hamilton J's[20] decision, the House of Lords held that the plaintiffs were entitled to recover the amount paid although they would not have been under an obligation to remit it even if the New York bank had remained solvent. The mistake was operative as the plaintiffs had made the payment involved in anticipation of the proper winding-up of a transaction in which they had a commercial interest. The insolvency of the New York bank meant that this object was unattainable.

Another instance is to be found in *Jones (RE) Ltd.* v. *Waring & Gillow Ltd.*[21] B, who falsely introduced himself as an agent of a firm of car manu-

---

[16] It is described as one that has withstood attacks, by Lord Shaw of Dunfermline in *Jones (RE) Ltd.* v. *Waring and Gillow Ltd.* [1926] AC 670, 689.

[17] 'Bank's Right . . . ', pp. 311–12.

[18] *Aiken* v. *Short* (1856) 25 LJ Ex. 321, 324 (but note that in the report of the same case in (1856) 1 H & N 210, the ratio emphasizes the payee's entitlement to receive payment; see below; *Morgan* v. *Ashcroft* [1938] 1 KB 49, per Sir Wilfrid Greene MR; Scott LJ, who concurred on other grounds, *dubitante*; *Commonwealth Trading Bank* v. *Reno Auto Sales Pty Ltd.* [1967] VR 790. Cf. *South Australian Cold Stores Ltd.* v. *Electricity Trust of South Australia* (1957) 98 CLR 65, 75 cited by Luntz, 'Bank's Right . . . ', p. 311.

[19] (1911) 17 Com. Cas. 41. And see the judgment of Scott LJ in *Morgan* v. *Ashcroft* [1938] 1 KB 49, 72–3.

[20] (1910) 15 Com. Cas. 1, reversed by the Court of Appeal in ibid., 241

[21] [1926] AC 670, rev'ng [1925] 2 KB 612 and restoring the decision of Darling J. And see Luntz, 'Bank's Right . . . ', p. 316. See also *Imperial Bank of Canada* v. *Bank of Hamilton* [1903] AC 49, concerning the erroneous payment of a fraudulently raised instrument, and discussed below, pp. 321–3.

facturers, purported to arrange on their behalf for the plaintiffs' appointment as franchise holders, provided the plaintiffs agreed to pay a deposit of £5000 for the purchase of 500 cars. B asked that the cheque be made payable to the defendants who, he claimed, were financing the manufacturers. In reality, B's story was a fabrication. He delivered the cheque to the defendants in order to obtain the release of chattels which they had seized when he defaulted under a hire purchase agreement. Restoring Darling J's decision in favour of the plaintiffs, the majority of the House of Lords held that the £5000 were recoverable as money paid under a mistake of fact. No reference was made to the fact that, when the plaintiffs drew the cheque, they were not under the mistaken belief that they had a relationship of contract with the defendants, who were the payees. The plaintiffs' mistake related to their supposed contractual relationship with the car manufacturers or with the rogue B.

Where a transaction is confined to two parties, the payor's liability is a reflection of the payee's right. Luntz,[22] though, rightly points out that the two are not necessarily concurrent. In certain cases the payee may be entitled to demand the money not from the payor but from a third party, who instructs the payor to make payment. The payee does not, then, have any rights against the payor. This is invariably the case where debts are paid through banking channels. The payee of a bank giro credit or of a cheque may have rights against the issuer or drawer but none against the bank. The payee may, thus, be entitled to the money although the payor is not liable to him.

An argument that comes to mind is that under *Kelly* v. *Solari* the payee has the right to retain the money whenever he is entitled to it at all, be it as against the payor or as against a third party such as the payor's principal. This view derives support from Parke B's reference to the unconscionability of the behaviour of a payee who purports to retain money to which he has no entitlement. This element is missing where he can establish some valid claim. Most authorities, though, take a view contrary to this argument.[23]

Thus, in *Imperial Bank of Canada* v. *Bank of Hamilton*[24] the amount of a cheque, which had been 'marked' by the drawee bank at the drawer's request, was fraudulently raised by him thereafter from $5 to $500. The bank was allowed to recover the excess from the holder in due course, to the credit of whose account the cheque had been paid. It was held that the 'marking' or 'certification' did not bind the bank. The Privy Council did not consider whether the holder was 'entitled' to receive the full amount from a party other than the bank, such as the drawer. The bank's mistake about the

[22] 'Bank's Right . . . ', p. 314.
[23] Ibid., p. 315.
[24] [1903] AC 49.

validity of the cheque formed the basis of its action in restitution against the holder. The mistake was operative although the bank had not made a mistake about its liability, and despite the fact that the holder in due course might have been entitled to obtain the amount from the drawer.

Similarly, in *Colonial Bank* v. *Exchange Bank of Yarmouth, Nova Scotia*[25] the plaintiff bank, which had been instructed by a customer to pay an amount of money to the X Bank, paid it by mistake to the defendant bank. As the customer in question had a heavily overdrawn account with the defendant bank, it purported to retain the money and apply it in reduction of the overdraft. It was clear that the plaintiff bank did not believe that it was under any liability to the defendant bank; but it could have thought that the defendant bank was entitled to the money. In the outcome, the plaintiff bank made no mistake about its own liability or about the defendant bank's rights because the customer was, indeed, indebted to this bank. Nevertheless, the plaintiff bank was allowed to recover the amount paid. Luntz concludes that this case shows 'that mistake as to the recipient's "entitlement" . . . is not a necessary condition for the recovery of money paid in such circumstances.'[26] Likewise, in *Jones (RE) Ltd* v. *Waring & Gillow Ltd.*,[27] the plaintiffs, who made a mistake concerning their liability to pay B or the car manufacturers, did not make a mistake about the payee's entitlement to receive the money.

The conclusion is that the payor's mistake, which forms the basis of his action in restitution, need concern neither his own liability to pay the amount involved nor the payee's entitlement to the money. His right to recover the amount is unaffected by a claim that the payee may have against a third party. It is adequate that the payor is under an operative mistake concerning his own motive or reasons for making payment. A mistake made by a paying bank is operative whenever it has been the cause of its performance.

Only one authority runs counter to this view. In *Barclay & Co. Ltd* v. *Malcolm & Co.*,[28] a bank erroneously paid twice an amount which it had been ordered to transfer. The payee, however, was in effect entitled to obtain from the payor a substantial part of the amount overpaid. He, therefore, repaid the balance which had not been owing to him and purported to retain the amount due. The bank's action in restitution was dismissed on the ground that the payee, who was entitled to the amount involved, could not be regarded as acting unconscionably in purporting to retain the amount due to him.

This decision has been questioned by Goff J in *Barclays Bank Ltd.* v.

---

[25] (1885) 11 App. Cas. 84.
[26] 'Bank's Right . . . ', p. 315.
[27] [1926] AC 670, discussed above.
[28] (1925) 133 LT 512.

W. J. Simms Son & Cooke (Southern) Ltd.[29] on the basis that the bank's mistake about the existence of a valid mandate for the extra payment by the payor was an adequate cause for ordering restitution. His Lordship further pointed out that the decision conflicted with the House of Lords decision in *Jones (RE) Ltd.* v. *Waring & Gillow Ltd.*,[30] where recovery was allowed although the payee was entitled to be paid by B, from whom he had acquired the cheque. It is clear that the prevailing view is as stated by Goff J. The attraction of the principle of *Malcolm & Co.*'s case is that it enables the payee to retain an amount to which he has a claim. It remains to be seen which view will prevail.

(ii) Nature of operative mistake

It is clear that not every mistake made by the payor is operative. Some authorities suggest that the mistake must relate to some misconception affecting the payor's relationship with the payee. A typical case in point is *Kleinwort, Sons, & Co.* v. *Dunlop Rubber Co.*[31] The vendor of rubber assigned the price due to him to M1. Due to an error, the buyers paid the amount involved to M2, who had been the assignees in other transactions. M2 actually received the amount involved in the belief that it was due to them. After the purchasers were ordered to pay the amount over again to M1, who was entitled to the amount as equitable assignee,[32] they brought an action to recover the amount paid by them to M2. The House of Lords held the purchasers were entitled to succeed as the mistake, which concerned the relationship of payor and payee, was the sole cause of the payment involved.

Doubts about the conclusiveness of this analysis were, however, raised by Barwick CJ in *Porter* v. *Latec Finance (Qld.) Pty. Ltd.*[33] His Honour pointed out that if, to be operative, the mistake had to be between the payor and the payee, recovery would be ruled out unless the mistake was common to both parties. The inadequacy of the test is further highlighted by the fact that, if strictly applied, it precludes a bank from recovering the amount of a stopped cheque, as the bank's mistake is its oversight of the customer's instruction.[34] The mistake, therefore, is between the bank and its customer and not as between the bank and the payee.

[29] [1980] QB 677.

[30] [1926] AC 670.

[31] (1907) 97 LT 263. See also *Colonial Bank* v. *Exchange Bank of Yarmouth, Nova Scotia* (1885) 11 App. Cas. 84; *Commonwealth Trading Bank of Australia* v. *Kerr* [1919] SASR 201; *Commonwealth Trading Bank* v. *Reno Auto Sales Pty. Ltd.* [1967] VR 790. Cf. *Bank of New South Wales* v. *Deri* (1963) 80 WN (NSW) 1499; *Southland Savings Bank* v. *Anderson* [1974] NZLR 118.

[32] *William Brandt's Sons & Co.* v. *Dunlop Rubber Co. Ltd.* [1905] AC 454.

[33] (1964) 111 CLR 177, 178.

[34] *Commonwealth Trading Bank* v. *Reno Auto Sales Pty. Ltd.*, above. Contrast *Bank of NSW* v. *Deri*, above; *Southland Savings Bank* v. *Anderson*, above.

In effect, the proposed test is supportable only if it is conceded that the mistake has to relate to the mutual rights and duties of the payor and the payee: it would then follow that it must be 'between them'. But it has been shown that the former test, based on Parke B's words in *Kelly* v. *Solari*, is too narrow. If the mistake need not concern the liability of the payor to the payee, it is difficult to see why, to be operative, the mistake has to be 'between them'. It is thus not surprising that in both *Kerrison* v. *Glyn, Mills, Currie & Co.*[35] and *Jones (RE) & Co. Ltd.* v. *Waring Gillow Ltd.*[36] recovery was allowed, although the mistake was between the payor and a third party.

Any doubts in point were settled by Goff J in *Barclays Bank Ltd.* v. *W. J. Simms, Son & Cooke (Southern) Ltd.*[37] The drawer countermanded payment of his cheque when he discovered that a receiver had been appointed under a mortgage debenture issued by the payee. Due to a clerical error, the bank paid the cheque to the receiver on the day following the delivery of the stop order. When the bank discovered its mistake, it recredited the drawer's account and demanded repayment. Giving judgment for the bank, Goff J emphasized that, if the mistake was otherwise operative, it did not have to be between the bank, or payor, and the payee. It was adequate that it was a fundamental mistake which had induced the payment involved.

The reference to a fundamental mistake is conceptionally clear. A mistake which has the effect of inducing the payor, or bank, to make a payment which it would otherwise decline to execute is fundamental. An attempt to augment the rule was made in *Commercial Bank of Australia Ltd.* v. *Younis.*[38] Hope JA expressed the view that, to be fundamental, a bank's mistake has to relate to its mandate. Further support for this view is to be found in the decision of Goff J in *Barclays Bank Ltd* v. *W. J. Simms, Son & Cooke (Southern) Ltd.*,[39] It is, however, possible to envisage cases in which a bank's error is not directly related to the authority conferred on it by the customer. Thus, a bank may honour a cheque in persuance of its mandate and in the belief that it is, further, bound to do so. If in reality the bank is not obliged to pay, it acts under a mistake of fact.[40] Why should such a mistake not be regarded as fundamental?

At the same time, it is true that the test of 'fundamentality' may lead to practical difficulties in interpretation. The room for doubt left by it is illustrated by *Porter* v. *Latec Finance (Qld.) Pty. Ltd.*,[41] mentioned above. Here

---

[35] (1911) 17 Com. Cas. 465.

[36] [1926] AC 670.

[37] [1980] QB 677.

[38] [1979] 1 NSWR 444. And see *Bank of New South Wales* v. *Murphett* [1983] 1 VR 489.

[39] [1980] QB 677, 699–700.

[40] E.g., if the customer's balance was based on a cheque converted by him and wrongfully collected by the bank; see below.

[41] (1964) 111 CLR 177.

LHG obtained a loan from P by pretending that he was his own father—HHG—and by fraudulently executing a mortgage over his father's property. At LHG's request, P paid part of the amount advanced in discharge of a genuine mortgage granted by HHG to a third party. Subsequently, LHG, again posing as his father, obtained an advance from LF Finance, part of which was, at his instruction, paid by this firm directly to P in discharge of the amount due to him. Upon the discovery of the fraud, LF Finance sought to recover the amount involved from P as money paid under a mistake of fact.

The High Court of Australia held that the claim failed, as the amount was paid by LF Finance to P on behalf of LHG. But the nature of the mistake was also considered. Barwick CJ, who delivered one of the majority judgments, thought that the mistake as to LHG's identity was not fundamental between payor and payee because the object of the payment involved was simply to discharge a specific mortgage.[42] Taylor and Owen JJ, who concurred on the other grounds, did not consider the question. Kitto and Windeyer JJ, who delivered dissenting judgments, concluded that the mistake was fundamental, as payment would have been refused if the payor had been acquainted with the true facts.[43]

Clearly, it is not always easy to determine whether a mistake which has induced a bank to make payment is fundamental or incidental. If the mistake misleads the bank about its mandate, it is fundamental. A mistake is, further, fundamental if it leads the bank to believe that it is under a duty to make payment although, on the true facts, it is not obliged to do so.[44] In most other cases it is essential to consider the entire circumstances surrounding the payment involved. If the mistake was the direct reason for the bank's erroneous payment, it is fundamental.

(iii) Defence of change in position and of consideration for payment

Two defences that are occasionally raised where the payor seeks to recover money paid under a mistake of fact are, first, that the payee had changed his position in reliance on the payment involved and, secondly, that the payee had given consideration for the amount remitted to him. The two defences are not identical. A change in the payee's position takes place subsequent to the payment involved, as is the case where the payee releases a security when a giro payment has been effected. Consideration has to move at the time the contract is made or the payment is remitted. It is furnished, for example, where the payee agrees to release securities against an assurance that the

---

[42] Ibid., 188.
[43] Ibid., 204 per Windeyer J; 189–91 per Kitto J.
[44] See further on this point, as regards 'uncovered' cheques p. 336 below.

amount will be paid. In the case of a negotiable instrument, the consideration may further be given before the payment involved is effected.[45] Although the two defences are frequently pleaded in the alternative, they ought to be discussed separately.

The defence of the change of the payee's position is, in reality, based on considerations of common justice. It appears inequitable to demand that a person repay money where he has, in reliance on its receipt, incurred a liability or given up an advantage. The argument, though, is not clear-cut. When taken to its extreme, a payee can always plead that a windfall, which he thought was due to him, has encouraged him to incur a liability. Thus, a person who believes himself to be the donee of a valid gift may on its basis enter into a contract for the purchase of a house. It is well recognized that the instant defence is not applicable in cases of this type.[46] In its more limited sense, the defence is applicable to a detriment incurred directly as a result of the payment. The release of a security is the classic example.

But even in this restricted sense, the defence is not generally available against a claim for the recovery of money paid under a mistake of fact. This has been the position since the decision of the House of Lords in *Jones (RE) Ltd* v. *Waring & Gillow Ltd* . Although Lord Sumner thought[47] that it was harsh to render the payee liable for the payor's mistake, he, and the other majority judges, concluded that this was the law.

A similar view was expressed more recently by Kerr J in *National Westminster Bank Ltd.* v. *Barclays Bank International Ltd.*[48] A blank cheque, stolen in Nigeria from the cheque-book of the plaintiff bank's customer, was offered in London to the second defendant in the context of a transaction involving the illegal exchange of Nigerian currency for pounds sterling. At that stage, the thief had inserted in the cheque the amount of £5,000 and all other material details except the payee's name. The second defendant filled in his own name in the remaining space and arranged for his own bank—the first defendants—to present the cheque for a special answer. Due to the skilful forgery of the drawer's signature, the cheque was honoured by the plaintiff bank. The second defendant thereupon authorized the release of funds in Nigeria to the parties with whom he was dealing. When the first defendant discovered the forgery, it recredited its customer's account and brought an action to recover the amount involved. In fact, the action was pursued only against the second defendant.

Giving judgment for the plaintiff bank, Kerr J held that the money was paid by it under an operative mistake of fact. He thought that the object of

---

[45] BEA, s. 27(1).
[46] *Standish* v. *Ross* (1849) 3 Exch. 527; Luntz 'Bank's Right . . . ', p. 323.
[47] [1926] AC 670, 695–6. See also *Commonwealth of Australia* v. *Kerr* [1919] SASR 201; *Transvaal & Delagoa Bay Investment Co. Ltd.* v. *Atkinson* [1944] 1 All ER 579.
[48] [1975] QB 654.

the presentment of a cheque for a special answer was to remove doubts about cover. By paying the cheque, the plaintiff bank had not made any tacit representation concerning the authenticity of the drawer's signature. The mere change in the second defendant's position was, in itself, no defence to the plaintiff bank's claim. The only valid defence would have been an estoppel, precluding the plaintiff bank from asserting the forgery of the cheque. Finding that this defence was not established, Kerr J said that a bank was not under a duty to the payee of a cheque to 'recognize its customer's signature'. He held that the plaintiff bank had not been negligent in failing to detect a skilful forgery.

Kerr J emphasized that the second defendant had not been candid in his dealings with the banks. He had failed to relate that the cheque was utilized for a transaction contravening Nigerian exchange control laws and that he had doubts about its authenticity. These circumstances reinforced his Lordship's view that the second defendant could not establish an estoppel. It is clear that this aspect of the case is one of the keys to his Lordship's decision. But the case supports the general proposition that a change in the payee's position is not a defence to the payor's action in restitution.

Kerr J's decision does not focus on the cases concerning restitution of money paid under a mistake of fact relating to negotiable instruments. On the contary, his Lordship held that the special principles applying to such a situation were confined to cases involving genuine negotiable instruments. In the instant case, the cheque was a forgery and therefore not a negotiable instrument.[49] The decision, therefore, concerns mistaken payments made by banks generally.

Kerr J's decision thus follows that of the majority of the House of Lords in *Jones (RE) Ltd.* v. *Waring & Gillow Ltd.*[50] It is noteworthy that in the other leading recent decision—*Barclays Bank Ltd.* v. *W. J. Simms Son & Cooke (Southern) Ltd.*[51]—Goff J thought that a change in the payee's position would be a bar to the payor's action for the recovery of money paid under a mistake of fact. But *Simms'* case concerned a genuine cheque, which was accordingly a negotiable instrument. The decision may possibly be treated as confined, on this point, to cases of that type.[52]

Kerr J's decision in the *National Westminster Bank* case clarifies yet a further point. Usually, negligence would not preclude the payor from seeking recovery. In this regard it is important to distinguish the type of case under consideration from those in which the payor owes a duty of care to

[49] And see *Bank of England* v. *Vagliano Bros.* [1891] AC 107, holding that total forgeries are not negotiable instruments *strictu sensu*.
[50] [1926] AC 670.
[51] [1980] QB 677.
[52] Goff J (ibid., 695–6) stated the defence in general terms, citing *Kleinwort, Sons & Co.* v. *Dunlop Rubber Co.* (1907) 97 LT 263, which, however, is inconsistent on this point with *Waring & Gillow's* case. His Lordship referred, however, to the special authorities concerning change in the payee's position following payment to the payee of a negotiable instrument.

the payee or makes a representation to the effect that payment is due. Thus, a public authority, which makes a mistake in the calculation of emoluments payable to pensioners, will not be able to recover excessive payments effected by it over a period of time where the payee has accepted the money in good faith and has geared his standard of living on the basis of the mistake.[53] However, a bank that pays an amount in reliance on what appears to be its customer's instruction, is not considered to make a representation about its duty to pay, and does not owe the payee a duty of care. It would be precluded from demanding recovery of an amount paid under an operative mistake of fact only where the payee was able to establish all the ingredients of an estoppel.

In some cases the payee may argue that he ought to be allowed to retain the amount erroneously paid to him because he has furnished consideration for it. *Barclays Bank Ltd. v. W. J. Simms Son & Cooke (Southern) Ltd.*[54] suggests that this plea is more effective than the defence based on a change in the payee's position. Goff J said that recovery would fail if the payment was made for good consideration, 'in particular if the money [was] paid to discharge, and [discharged], a debt owed to the payee (or a principal on whose behalf he [was] authorized to receive the payment) by the payer or by a third party to whom he [was] authorized to discharge the debt'.[55]

It is believed that this dictum would be suitable in the case of some payments erroneously made by a bank on behalf of its customer. If such a payment discharges an obligation owed by the customer to a third party, the bank is entitled to debit his account with the amount involved.[56] The decision in this regard is, however, to be made by the bank. In certain cases, such as the erroneous execution of a countermanded payment order, the bank may prefer to recredit the customer's account and leave any dispute to be settled between the customer and the payee. As a general principle, Goff J's dictum remains to be tested. It is appropriate to consider its two branches separately.

Where the consideration given for the payment involved is between the payee and the bank (payor), it is analytically correct to treat it as irrevocable. The payment may then be described as one effected in discharge of a contract made tacitly between the bank and the payee. An example in point is the delivery by the payee to the bank of shares or bonds over which he has been granted a pledge by the bank's customer.

---

[53] *Skyring* v. *Greenwood* (1825) 4 B & C 281, 290; *Holt* v. *Markham* [1923] 1 KB 504 per Bankes and Warrington LJJ; Scrutton LJ., though, based his concurring judgment on an estoppel.
[54] [1980] AC 677.
[55] Ibid., 695. Goff J relied on dicta in *Aiken* v.*Short* (1856) 1 H & N 210 and *Kerrison* v. *Glyn, Mills, Currie & Co.* (1911) 81 LJKB 465.
[56] Under the doctrine of *B. Liggett (Liverpool) Ltd.* v. *Barclays Bank Ltd.* [1928] 1 KB 48, discussed above, pp. 300–2.

The principle is not as readily applicable where the consideration is furnished in a contract made between the payee and the bank's customer. It is arguable that the matter is one between these two parties. As between the bank (payor) and the payee, the payment is one made voluntarily. If it is made as a result of an operative mistake of fact, such as the oversight of the customer's countermand, the bank ought to be able to recover. In reality, the furnishing of consideration under the contract between the bank's customer and the payee involves a change of position on the payee's part. It ought to preclude recovery only if a change in the payee's position is recognized as a valid defence.[57]

4. ACTION AGAINST A COLLECTING BANK

The payment made by the bank under a mistake of fact may, in certain cases, be made directly to the payee. This occurs where a cheque is presented by the payee over the counter, or where the bank pays him in cash an amount remitted from overseas. In the majority of cases, though, the amount is credited to the payee's account with his own bank, that is, the 'collecting bank'. If the paying bank acted under a mistake of fact, it may then wish to sue both parties or, where the payee is impecunious or has absconded, may have no option but to concentrate its efforts on an action against the collecting bank alone.

The basic principle has been clear since Lord Mansfield's decision in *Buller* v. *Harrison*.[58] Where money is paid to an agent, it can be recovered from him up to the time at which he remits it to his principal. In a modern case, *Gowers* v. *Lloyds and National Provincial Foreign Bank Ltd.*,[59] a retired army officer's widow fraudulently continued to receive his pension by representing that he was still alive. The relevant payments were obtained by means of certificates, presented through the defendant bank, which included an attestation by an alleged medical practitioner to the effect that the army officer was well. The sums involved were remitted directly to the bank, which paid them out to the widow.

Affirming the decision of the trial judge, the Court of Appeal held that the amounts were not recoverable from the bank. Sir Wilfrid Greene MR said

---

[57] But contrast *Bank of Montreal* v. *R.* (1907) 38 SCR (Can.) 258, which holds that payment cannot be recovered from a payee who was a holder in due course of the instrument. It is, with respect, questionable if this principle is correct where the bank paid the cheque due to the oversight of a countermand. If the bank had refused to pay the cheque, the holder could not enforce it against the bank, which is a mere drawee. Why then should the bank be unable to reclaim payment?

[58] (1777) 2 Cowp. 565.

[59] [1938] 1 All ER 766.

that money paid to an agent under a mistake of fact could be recovered from him as long as he had it in his hands. He went on: 'If, on the other hand, he has paid it away to his principal, then it cannot be recovered from the agent, and the only remedy is to go against the principal'.[60] It was held irrelevant that the bank had believed that its principal was the army officer whilst, in reality, it was acting for the widow. It was adequate that the funds had been remitted to its genuine principal—the widow.[61]

It is interesting to note, at this point, that the practical effect of the doctrine involved leads to an inconsistency respecting the general question of the collecting bank's liability where it acts for a fraudulent customer. If the customer requests it to collect a stolen cheque, or some other negotiable instrument, the bank will initially be liable to the true owner in conversion and, in the alternative, in a quasi-contractual action based on waiver of tort.[62] From a practical point of view, it is thereupon liable to damages equal to the amount of the instrument. The bank's only effective defence is that provided by section 4 of the Cheques Act 1957, under which, inter alia, it has to establish that it had acted without negligence.[63] The fact that the bank has paid the proceeds of the converted instrument to the customer is no defence! But where payment is received by the collecting bank in a transaction which does not involve a negotiable instrument (or some other item that may be the subject of an action in conversion), its liability in a quasi-contractual action expires when it pays the amount over to the fraudulent customer. The bank's negligence is quite immaterial in such a case.

Even in cases which do not involve negotiable instruments, the bank's defence of having paid the amount out to the customer operates in a narrow area. It is inapplicable in all cases in which, in reality, the money is received by the bank as a principal. Thus, in *Continental Caoutchouc & Gutta Percha Co.* v. *Kleinwort Sons & Co.*[64] K, a firm of rubber merchants, was regularly financed by two banks: the defendants and B & Co. The purchasers of some of K's rubber, who were ordered to remit part of the price to the defendants and the balance to B & Co., erroneously paid the full amount to the defendants, who received the money in good faith and credited K's account therewith.

Affirming Bingham J's decision, the Court of Appeal held that the amount was recoverable by the payors, the purchasers. Collins MR distinguished two types of case. The first was where a bank received payment

---

[60] Ibid., 773.

[61] Note that an amount may be deemed to have been paid out to the principal even where, at his request, the agent purchases items meant for his own use: *Transvaal & Delagoa Bay Investment Co. Ltd.* v. *Atkinson* [1944] 1 All ER 579. Here the agent purchased household effects and settled bills which her husband, the payee, was bound to pay.

[62] Pp. 412 et seq. below.

[63] Pp. 421 et seq. below.

[64] (1904) 9 Com. Cas. 240; 90 LT 474.

as a mere agent. Here the amount could not be recoverd from the bank once it was paid out to the principal. The other was where the bank received payment for itself. It would then be in the same position as any other party to whom money was paid under a mistake of fact. In the instant case, the defendants were generally entitled, under the financing agreement made with K, to the proceeds of rubber sales financed by them. They, thus, received the money in the belief that it was due to them in their own right. In reality it was received under mistake, as the proceeds related to a transaction financed by the second bank, B & Co. The money was therefore recoverable.[65]

Support for this view is to be found in the decision of the New Zealand Court of Appeal in *Thomas* v. *Houston Corbett & Co.*[66] It was there held that whether an amount of money is received by the payee as agent or as principal depends on his understanding of the transaction and the capacity in which he purports to act.

In some cases, it may not be easy to determine whether the bank receives payment as principal or as agent. Undoubtedly, if the bank pays the customer cash or allows him an overdraft against an uncleared cheque, it is considered to act as a discounting bank. When the cheque is cleared, the funds are received by the bank for itself or as a principal.[67] In such a case, the bank would be just as open to an action in restitution by a payor as any other payee.[68] But in some cases the bank allows the customer an insignificant overdraft against an uncleared balance, e.g. £10 (required to meet a cheque drawn by him) against an uncleared balance of £100. In such a case, the bank is deemed to act concurrently as a collecting and as discounting bank.[69] It is therefore difficult to decide in which capacity it receives the funds involved.

In *Continental Caoutchouc*, Collins MR referred to a difficulty that arose where an amount of money was received by the bank as an agent but applied in reduction of an existing overdraft extended to the principal. Here the money is effectively used to discharge a debt due from the principal to the agent. His Lordship observed:[70]

[Such agent] has no doubt benefited by getting his debt paid, but he has done so in discharging his primary duty of passing the money on to his principal. He has

---

[65] 9 Com. Cas, 248–9, 90 LT, 476. See also *Holland* v. *Russell* (1863) 4 B & S 14, 8 LT 468; *Newall* v. *Tomlinson* (1871) LR 6 CP 405.
[66] [1969] NZLR 151. See alo *Transvaal & Delagoa Bay Investment Co. Ltd.* v. *Atkinson* [1944] 1 All ER 579, where a wife was held to have received as an agent amounts paid into her account by her husband in fraud of his employers and for his own use.
[67] Pp. 418–21 below.
[68] See the decision of the Supreme Court of Canada in *Dominion Bank* v. *Union Bank of Canada* (1908) 40 SCR 366.
[69] P. 421 below.
[70] (1904) 9 Com. Cas 240, 248–9; 90 LT 474, 476.

constructively sent it on and received it back, and has done nothing incompatible with his position as conduit-pipe or intermediary. He was entitled to be paid, and has been paid by his debtor, who has no doubt put in funds to do so by the receipt of the money, and who therefore, and not the intermediary, has had the benefit of the windfall. Hence the care with which the courts have considered whether the sum has in fact been effectually passed out of the hands of the agent into those of the principal, no entry by the agent in his books sufficing until the assent of the principal has completed the transaction.[71]

His Lordship's reference to the principal's assent is, unfortunately, unhelpful where the funds are used to reduce an existing overdraft. It is in the nature of a current account that an amount paid to the credit of an overdrawn account is automatically set off against the existing debit balance. The customer's assent is given when an account of this type is opened. It is noteworthy that in *Kleinwort, Sons & Co* v. *Dunlop Rubber Co.*, which involved another transaction of the same merchant and a similar type of mistake, Lord Loreburn LC expressed the view that an amount received by the bank in reduction of the customer's overdraft had not been paid over.[72] It was further held, on the facts, that is was immaterial that the payment involved induced the bank to extend the customer's overdraft. This finding, though, was based on the verdict of the jury, which concluded that the bank would have extended the facility in any event. Generally, the conclusion is questionable. Where the bank increases the customer's overdraft ceiling in reliance on the payment made, it gives him, in effect, a new facility.

A related problem arises in all cases in which the customer's current account it operated upon for a considerable time before the payor demands repayment. It is in the nature of a current account that amounts are paid in and out on a running basis. What is the position if, subsequent to the erroneous payment, the customer withdraws funds in excess of the amount involved but also pays in money to the credit of his current account? Is it then possible to say that the bank has paid the erroneously received sum over to the customer? A positive answer is supported by a strict application of the rule in *Clayton's Case*,[73] under which debit items are to be set off against credit items on a basis of first in first out. The erroneous payment would, therefore, be exhausted before any items were set off against amounts paid into the account later on. But if the credit balance in the customer's account is not exhausted or reduced to an amount lower that that of

---

[71] His Lordship referred to *Buller* v. *Harrison* (1777) 2 Cowp. 565, which, however, is weak authority in point.

[72] (1907) 97 LT 263, 264; the dictum though, is based on the finding of the jury. For the full facts, see p. 323 above. See also *Admiralty Commissioners* v. *National Provincial and Union Bank of England* (1922) 127 LT 452.

[73] *Devaynes* v. *Noble, Clayton's Case* (1816) 1 Mer. 529, 572, discussed below, p. 483.

the erroneous payment, it is difficult to see why the payor should be prevented from seeking recovery from the bank. The bank is a reservoir of money,[74] and the accrued balance is a debt owed by it to the customer. Moreover, it holds the funds as an agent. As the money is still available to the customer—who benefited from the windfall—why should it not be reclaimable from the bank—the customer's agent and debtor?

Support for the last argument is to be found in two cases which suggest that the bank, or agent, should be answerable to the payee as long as the credit entry remains reversible.[75] It is true that in one of the cases, *Holland* v. *Russell*,[76] Cockburn CJ, who delivered the decision of the Court of Queen's Bench, suggested that the amount was to be regarded as paid over when it had been made the subject of a 'settled account' or an account stated. But it will be recalled that a bank's periodic statement does not constitute a settled account.[77] The bank is precluded from reversing payment only where the customer is able to invoke an estoppel based on the change in his position .[78] As long as the credit entry remains subject to reversal by the bank, payment ought to be recoverable from it. It should, therefore, be possible to join it as a party in an action in restitution brought against the customer by the payor.

It is interesting that, on a strict analysis of the relationship of banker and customer, there is room for a forceful argument in an entirely different direction. The cases discussed up to now presuppose that the funds standing to the credit of the customer's account are held by the bank on his behalf. Theoretically, this is inaccurate. It is, indeed, true that any amounts drawn by the customer are paid out by the bank as his agent. But until the customer makes a demand, the funds standing to his credit are co-mingled with the bank's other funds and hence are its own money. The customer's only asset is a debt, or chose in action, due to him from the bank. On this basis it is arguable that a collecting bank ceases to hold any funds as the customer's agent from the moment at which these are credited to his account, and not from the time at which the customer withdraws them. The money may therefore be regarded as paid over by the bank when the amount becomes available to the customer on clearance. The action in restitution against the collecting should be lost at that time. This argument is untested, and is in conflict with the generally held view. But it cannot be dismissed as running counter to any authority or to an established principle.

---

[74] P. 119 above.
[75] *Holland* v. *Russell* (1861) 30 LJ (NS) QB 308, affd. (1863) 4 B & S 14; *Admiralty Commissioners* v. *National Provincial and Union Bank of England* (1922) 127 LT 452.
[76] (1863) 30 LJ (NS) QB, 313.
[77] Pp. 133–6 above.
[78] Pp. 136–8 above.

5. RECOVERY PROBLEMS IN CASES OF NEGOTIABLE INSTRUMENTS

(i) Special problems

As pointed out at the outset, some special problems arise where money is paid by a bank under a mistake of fact pertaining to the discharge of a negotiable instrument. In the first place, it is necessary to define the meaning of 'operative mistake' in cases of this type. Secondly, there is a controversy concerning the effect of a change in the payee's position on the bank's right to demand repayment. There is an inconsistency in the case law as regards the result of a delay in the bank's demand for repayment. It is, occasionally, said that the payee's position is automatically affected, as the delay precludes him from giving notice of dishonour to his transferee.

The two questions require separate treatment. It is, however, important to define the scope of the relevant doctrines. It can now be regarded as well established that the principles involved apply only to genuine negotiable instruments. Where an instrument is avoided as a result of forgery,[79] or of material alterations made to it,[80] or is non negotiable due to a technicality,[81] the position is governed by the general principles of the law of restitution discussed earlier.[82] The cases, however, are not altogether consistent, as in a number of instances the point was not raised.

(ii) Nature of operative mistake

Basically, two types of mistake may induce a bank to pay a negotiable instrument. The first relates to the bank's mandate. The second relates to its liability to pay.

As has been pointed out at the outset, different circumstances may mislead a bank as regards it mandate. First, it may fail to recognize the forgery of its customer's signature.[83] Secondly, its mandate may be vitiated by a fraudulent alteration of a material detail, such as the raising of the cheque's amount.[84]

---

[79] BEA, s. 24; *Bank of England* v. *Vagliano Bros.* [1891] AC 107.

[80] BEA, s. 64.

[81] E.g. if a conditional order is included instead of an unconditional order, in which case it may, however, be valid between the parties.

[82] See *Imperial Bank of Canada* v. *Bank of Hamilton* [1903] AC 49; *National Westminster Bank Ltd.* v. *Barclays Bank International Ltd.* [1975] QB 654, pp. 000–000 above.

[83] *Price* v. *Neal* (1762) 3 Burr. 1354; *Smith* v. *Mercer* (1815) 6 Taunt. 76; *Cocks* v. *Masterman* (1829) 9 B & C 902; *Imperial Bank of India* v. *Abeyesinghe* (1927) 29 NLR (Ceylon) 257; *National Westminster Bank Ltd.* v. *Barclays Bank International Ltd.* [1975] QB 654.

[84] *Imperial Bank of Canada* v. *Bank of Hamilton* [1903] AC 49. The bank here claimed back the difference between the genuine amount of the cheque and the amount to which it had been raised. As the instrument was, however, avoided the bank would appear to have paid without any mandate; it should therefore have been allowed to recover the full amount.

Thirdly, it may pay the cheque to a person who holds it under a forged indorsement of the ostensible payee's signature.[85] Fourthly, it may pay a cheque because it overlooks the customer's countermand. Here, too, the bank pays in the belief that it has the authority to do so whilst, in reality, its mandate has been revoked.

There can be no doubt that a mistake due to the bank's failure to recognize a forgery or material alteration is fundamental. Accordingly, such a mistake is operative.[86] Moreover, the bank is not under a general duty to 'recognize its customer's signature'.[87] There is therefore nothing to prevent the bank from pleading the mistake. The only question that arises, and on which there is conflicting authority,[88] is whether the bank loses its right of recovery if the payee changes his position.

At one time it was uncertain whether the bank could recover payment where it overlooked its customer's countermand. In *Commonwealth Trading Bank* v. *Reno Auto Sales Ltd.*,[89] Gillard J thought that recovery would be disallowed, as such a mistake was between the bank and the drawer and not, as required, between the bank (payor) and the payee. It has been pointed out above that this analysis is wrong.[90] The better view is that the bank's mistake is operative as it concerns the very motive of its payment, namely its belief in the existence of the customer's mandate. Recent authorities have consistently held that such a mistake entitles the bank to recover the amount paid in an action in restitution.[91] Again, the payee may possibly resist the action where he has changed his position.

It may be argued that the principle in point is decidedly slanted in the bank's favour. Why should the bank be allowed to recover an amount paid by it owing to a mistake incurred as a result of its own carelessness? Despite

---

[85] *London and River Plate Bank Ltd.* v. *Bank of Liverpool Ltd.* [1896] 1 QB 7.
[86] But see dicta in *Hart* v. *Frontino and Bolivia South American Gold Mining Co. Ltd.* (1870) LR 5 Ex. 623, 652 per Bramwell B; *Simm* v. *Anglo-American Telegraph Co.* (1879) 5 QBD 188, 196 per Lindley J (who restricted his dictum to the impossibility of recovering the money from a bona fide holder for value); *Dominion Bank* v. *Jacobs* [1951] 3 DLR 233 (mistake as to forgery held not to be between payor and payee). Contrast, as regards Canada, *Royal Bank of Canada* v. *R.* [1931] 2 DLR 685.
[87] *London and River Plate Bank Ltd.* v. *Bank of Liverpool Ltd.*, above; *National Westminster Bank Ltd.* v. *Barclays Bank International Ltd.*, above.
[88] Pp. 338–41 below.
[89] [1967] VR 790; on the facts, his Honour decided that the countermand had been ineffective and that, accordingly, no mistake had been made by the bank. But he thought that, even if the countermand had been effective, the action would fail. See also *Royal Bank of Canada* v. *Boyce* (1966) 57 DLR (2d) 683. *Barclays & Co. Ltd.* v. *Malcolm & Co.* (1925) 133 LT 512, discussed above, supports the same view but, undoubtedly, turned on its special facts.
[90] Pp. 323–5 above.
[91] *Southland Savings Bank* v. *Anderson* [1974] 1 NZLR 118; *Barclays Bank Ltd.* v. *W. J. Simms, Son & Cooke (Southern) Ltd.* [1980] QB 677; *Commercial Banking Co. of Australia Ltd.* v. *Younis* [1979] 1 NSWR 444; *Bank of New South Wales* v. *Murphett* [1983] VR 489. See also *Commonwealth of Australia* v. *Kerr* [1919] SASR 201; *Bank of New South Wales* v. *Deri* (1963) 80 WN (NSW) 1499. Luntz, 'Bank's Right . . .', p. 310, refers also to a South African case: *Natal Bank Ltd.* v. *Roorda* 1903 TH 298.

the convincing thrust of this rhetorical question, there are three strong arguments in favour of the bank's right of recovery. First, the payee gains a windfall. If the bank obeys the countermand order and dishonours the cheque, the payee is without any remedy against it. He has to settle his dispute with the drawer. It follows that, when he is required to refund the amount paid due to the bank's oversight, he is in no worse a position than he would have been if the bank had followed the drawer's instructions. Secondly, except where the *Liggett* doctrine is applicable,[92] the bank may be unable to debit the drawer's account. It is unreasonable to expect the bank to bear a loss occasioned as a result of the dispute that has induced the drawer to stop the cheque delivered by him to the payee. Thirdly, the very notion of an action in restitution is that money paid due to a mistake of fact is recoverable despite the payor's negligence.[93]

There is an uncertainty as regards the bank's right to recover an amount paid due to an error concerning the drawer's balance. In *Chambers* v. *Miller*,[94] the payee was in the process of counting the money paid to him against a cheque he had just presented to the bank, when the teller discovered that the drawer's account had an inadequate balance. The teller attempted to take the money back from the payee by force. The payee's action in assault was successful. Furthermore, all the judges in the Court of Common Pleas held that the bank was not entitled to recover the money. Byles and Williams JJ expressed the view that the bank's mistake as to the customer's balance was immaterial.[95] Erle CJ rested his decision on the fact that the error was not between the payor and the payee.[96] The ratio of the case, however, concerned the action in assault.

In *Pollard* v. *Bank of England*,[97] a bank paid a bill of exchange domiciled at its premises because it overlooked that the acceptor's account had insufficient funds and, further, that he had countermanded payment.[98] It was held that under these circumstances the mistake was inoperative. This decision is no longer good law as regards the mistake relating to the stop order. The finding that the mistake concerning the insufficiency of funds was likewise inoperative was based on the fact that it was not an error between the payor and the payee. This argument has been shown to run counter to modern authority.

A different reason for the principle suggested in *Pollard*'s case is to be found

---

[92] Pp. 300–2 above.

[93] P. 330 above.

[94] (1862) 13 CB (NS) 125; 32 LJ (NS) CP 30.

[95] Ibid., at 13 CB (NS), 136 and at 32 LJ (NS) CP, 33 respectively.

[96] Ibid., at 13 CB (NS), 134 and at 32 LJ (NS) CP, 33 respectively.

[97] (1871) LR 6 QB 623. See also *Woodland* v. *Fear* (1857) 7 El. & Bl. 519, which has been generally doubted in *Prince* v. *Oriental Banking Corporation* (1878) 3 App. Cas. 325.

[98] The domicile bank was, thus, in the same position as if a customer had stopped a cheque drawn on it for which, further, his account had inadequate funds.

in *Barclays Bank Ltd.* v. *W. J. Simms, Son & Cooke (Southern) Ltd.*[99] Here Goff J pointed out that where the bank pays a cheque due to a mistake as to the available balance, it still acts within the scope of its mandate. It therefore remains entitled to debit the customer's account. The bank may, presumably, be regarded as having assented to a request made by the customer for the extension of overdraft facilities.[100]

There are, however, two difficulties with this reasoning. One is that the bank's right to debit its customer's account is of little value where he becomes insolvent.[101] This, of course, is the very case in which the bank seeks to recover the money from the payee. The other is that it is unrealistic to regard a bank that pays a cheque because of a mistake relating to the customer's balance as assenting to a request for an overdraft. Undoubtedly, the bank does not make a mistake concerning its mandate. But it makes a mistake concerning its duty to pay. Thus, the customer's balance may be incorrectly stated due to his account having been credited twice with a single payment received by the bank. Alternatively, the balance may be based on the proceeds of forged or converted cheques which are reclaimable from the bank. In all these cases, the bank is under the genuine impression that the customer has adequate funds for meeting his cheques. The bank therefore erroneously believes that it is bound to honour them.

It is difficult to see why such a mistake is to be regarded as inoperative. The mistake is fundamental in that it is the sole cause of the bank's decision to make payment. In effect, it is as compelling as a mistake concerning the bank's mandate. Both types of mistake mislead the bank as regards its proper course of business or its legal obligations. Undoubtedly, the position differs where the 'swelled up' balance is based on uncleared effects remitted to the bank by the customer. The bank takes a calculated risk when it obeys his orders and pays cheques drawn by him against uncleared funds. It is certainly not bound to do so.[102] On the basis of Goff J's dictum, the bank cannot, thereafter, be heard to plead a mistake. But where the bank does not act as a volunteer, its mistake as to the customer's balance appears a fundamental one.

It is, therefore, believed that the proposition that a bank's error as to the sufficiency of the customer's balance is inoperative is too sweeping. Where the mistake misleads the bank about its duty to obey the customer's instruction, the amount paid ought to be recoverable.

---

[99] [1980] QB 677.
[100] Ibid., 699–700. And see Luntz, 'Bank's Right . . . ', p. 329.
[101] Cf. Luntz, 'Bank's Right . . . ', p. 330.
[102] Pp. 266 et seq. above.

(iii) Payee's change of position

It has been shown earlier that, under the prevailing view, a change in the payee's position does not in itself defeat the payor's action in restitution.[103] Special considerations apply, however, where the payment is made against, or in discharge of, a negotiable instrument. Dealings in such instruments require prompt handling. The drawee of a bill of exchange has to decide promptly on presentment whether or not to accept it. Equally, a bank at whose premises a bill is domiciled has to give its reply promptly when the instrument is presented for payment by the holder. The same is true about a bank to whom a cheque, drawn on it, is presented for payment.[104] Speed is, further, required in respect of the procedures to be followed upon the dishonour of a negotiable instrument. Both notice of dishonour and, in the case of a foreign instrument, protest have to be effected promptly.[105]

The need to act promptly in dealings in negotiable instruments has led to one important result. A holder who presents a bill for payment or for acceptance expects to have a prompt advice of its fate. In practice, if not in law, he tends to regard the answer given to him as final.[106] The legal consequences of this attitude require a careful analysis. This, in turn, will facilitate a review of the general question of the effect on an action in restitution of a change in the payee's position.

At one stage, the courts took the view that, because of the nature of dealings in negotiable instruments, an action would not usually lie for the recovery of money paid against them under a mistake of fact. In *Price v. Neal*,[107] Lord Mansfield said that an action of restitution was barred by the payment of the instrument. In a somewhat later case, *Cocks v. Masterman*,[108] the position was explained in a different manner. In that case, a bank paid a bill which had been domiciled at its premises by the acceptor. Although the acceptor was a customer, the bank did not recognize that his purported signature was a forgery. Bayley J, in the Court of King's Bench, held that recovery was barred. His Lordship pointed out that the holder was entitled to give notice of dishonour on the very day on which a bill was not met. The parties

---

[103] Pp. 325–9 above. But note the view to the contrary of Goff J in *Barclays Bank Ltd.* v. *W. J Simms, Son & Cooke (Southern) Ltd.* [1980] QB 677.

[104] Chap. 9 above.

[105] Pp. 518–20 below.

[106] Note that in *National Westminster Bank Ltd.* v. *Barclays Bank International Ltd.* [1975] QB 654 Kerr J thought that the special presentment of the cheque involved a tacit enquiry about cover but not about the authenticity of the instrument. In his view, a bank would not expect such a presentment to be related to the holder's doubts about the drawer's signature. As cheques are rarely negotiated in practice, there is force in this view. However, cheques are transferable by nature. It is believed that, from the holder's point of view, there is room for a forceful argument to the contrary.

[107] (1762) 3 Burr. 1354.

[108] (1829) 9 B & C 902.

'who pay the bill ought not by their negligence to deprive the holder of any right or privilege'.[109] He concluded that the holder was entitled to know the fate of the bill on the day of presentment. Once this day was over, payment was final and irrecoverable.[110]

A similar view was expressed in *Mather* v. *Maidstone*[111] by Jervis CJ, who thought that the bank ought to be deprived of the right to recover where it had had the means of satisfying itself of its liability to pay the instrument. Obviously, this would have been a narrower principle than that suggested either in *Price* v. *Neal* or in *Cocks* v. *Masterman*. But in *London and River Plate Bank Ltd.* v. *Bank of Liverpool Ltd.*,[112] in which a bank attempted to recover a few months after payment the amount of a bill bearing forged indorsements, Mathew J reverted to the reasoning of the earlier cases. His Lordship thought that, if a mistake was discovered promptly, the money paid under it could possibly be recovered. But if 'the money is paid in good faith, and is received in good faith, and there is an interval in time in which the position of the holder may be altered, the principle seems to apply that money once paid cannot be recovered back'.[113] Mathew J thought that such a change in position was bound to take place due to the lapse of time.[114]

It was at this stage of the authorities that the matter came up again before the Privy Council in *Imperial Bank of Canada* v. *Bank of Hamilton*.[115] A cheque for $5 was presented by its drawer to the drawee bank, who agreed to 'mark' it. In Canada, the effect of this procedure was similar to an acceptance.[116] The drawer then fraudulently raised the amount of the cheque to $500 and remitted it for collection to another bank. Initially, the cheque was paid by the drawee bank. The fraud was, however, discovered the next morning, whereupon notice of it and a demand for repayment of the excessive amount was served forthwith on the collecting bank. Lord Lindley observed that, under the circumstances, the collecting bank was not adversely affected by the delay in notice. He then pointed out that, in any event, the instrument in question was a total forgery and hence not a negotiable instrument. Moreover, the drawer who had committed the forgery was not entitled to notice of dishonour. He held, therefore, that the rule propounded in the earlier cases was inapplicable.

[109] Ibid., 908–9.
[110] Cf. *Wilkinson* v. *Johnson* (1823) 3 B & C 428, where repayment was demanded on the very day of dishonour.
[111] (1856) 18 CB 273, 295.
[112] [1896] 1 QB 7. See also *Morison* v. *London County and Westminster Bank Ltd.* [1914] 3 KB 356.
[113] [1896] 1 QB 11.
[114] Mathew J thought that the change in position could take place even where the mistake was drawn to the payee's attention on the same day.
[115] [1903] AC 49.
[116] See pp. 321–2 above.

Lord Lindley's point concerning the question of the notice of dishonour is unexceptional. In virtually all the cases in which the bank reclaims money paid in respect of a negotiable instrument, the payee is not required to give notice of dishonour to the party from whom he obtained it. Thus, if the instrument is a cheque that has been countermanded, the payee need not give notice of dishonour to the drawer.[117] As against a previous indorser, notice of dishonour may be given when repayment is claimed. The delay occasioned by circumstances beyond the payee's control is excused.[118] This is also the case where repayment is demanded on the basis of a forgery which is not noticed when the instrument is presented for payment, or because of any other operative mistake made by the bank. Moreover, it is questionable whether the instrument may be regarded as having been dishonoured at the time of payment when, in reality, the bank purported to discharge it! It is true that in *Barclays Bank Ltd.* v. *W. J. Simms Son & Cooke (Southern) Ltd.*, Goff J thought that, where the money is recovered, the bill is to be regarded as not having been paid at all so that it would have to be treated as dishonoured on presentment. It is, however, hard to see how a subsequent development can change what has taken place at the time of the presentment of the bill.[119]

Recent decisions affirm that the mere delay in the bank's claim for repayment does not preclude the action for the recovery of the money. There is, however, some inconsistency between them as regards the effect of a change in the payee's position. In *National Westminster Bank Ltd.* v. *Barclays Bank International Ltd.*,[120] Kerr J took the view that a mere change in the payee's position does not constitute a bar. The payor's action would be defeated only where the payee was able to establish all the elements of an estoppel. The case, however, concerned a forged cheque, and his Lordship therefore considered himself governed by the general principles affecting the law of restitution rather than by the special rules in point relating to negotiable instruments. In the *W. J. Simms* case, which concerned a countermanded instrument, Goff J inclined to the view that a change in the payee's position would defeat an action for the recovery of the money paid under a mistake of fact.[121] Although the case concerned a negotiable instrument, his Lordship stated the principle as having a general scope of application. In *Bank of New South Wales* v. *Murphett*[122] the point was left open as, on the facts, there was no detrimental change in the payee's position. Starke J was of the view that a mere delay was not in itself an adequate change in position.

---

[117]   BEA, s. 50(2)(c) (case 5).
[118]   Ibid., s. 50(1).
[119]   [1980] QB 677, 702. See also *Bank of New South Wales* v. *Murphett* [1983] 1 VR 489.
[120]   [1975] QB 654.
[121]   [1980] QB 677, 695.
[122]   [1983] 1 VR 489.

It is clear that the point awaits a final decision. Up to that time it is arguable that the position remains governed by the view of the majority of the House of Lords in *Jones (RE) Ltd.* v. *Waring & Gillow Ltd.,*[123] to the effect that a change in the payee's position does not preclude recovery. The fact that the House of Lords was divided three to two shows, however, that the answer is uncertain. A few points may aid in clarifying the area of controversy.

First, what is meant by a 'change in position'? It is clear that a mere delay in the discovery of the mistake and its notification to the payee is irrelevant. The question of the payee's duty to give notice of dishonour to the party from whom he took the instrument does not usually arise. It is also irrelevant that the payee spends the funds. His making use of a windfall is not, ordinarily, a good argument for releasing him from his duty to restitute the money.[124] The position differs where the payee performs some specific act in reliance on the payment involved. Thus, if the payee releases securities deposited by the transferor of the instrument or furnishes value, he changes his position in the belief that the payment made to him is final.

Secondly, ought this last type of change in position bar an action for the recovery of the money? On balance, Goff J's view in the *W. J. Simms* case appears supportable. In ordinary trade there is need for finality in dealings. If a party receives payment of a negotiable instrument in good faith, why should he be expected to speculate on the motives of the payor? Is it realistic to expect the payee of a cheque to investigate the genuineness of the document or the validity of the bank's decision to effect payment? It is believed that, in the final analysis, the most appropriate view is that expressed by Lord Mansfield in *Price* v. *Neal.*[125] Whilst it is wrong to preclude an action for recovery on account of a mere delay in the discovery of the error, or an indirect change in the payee's position, Lord Mansfield's view makes good sense where the payee has relied on the payment to his detriment. It noteworthy that section 3–418 of the Uniform Commercial Code (USA) provides that payment is final in favour of a person who has changed his position in reliance on the payment of a negotiable instrument.[126] It is believed that this provision presents a suitable solution.

6. TRACING ORDERS

Where the payee of an amount paid under a mistake of fact is insolvent, the bank may wish to obtain a tracing order. This will enable it to recover the

---

[123] [1926] AC 670, discussed above pp. 320–1.
[124] See p. 326 above.
[125] (1762) 3 Burr. 1354.
[126] The provision further precludes recovery from a holder in due course. But this may be questioned in regard to cheques and bills which are not accepted by the bank, as these do not embody the bank's undertaking.

amount in specie and, effectively, in priority to the general creditors.[127] Thus, in *Chase Manhattan Bank NA* v. *Israel–British Bank (London) Ltd.*,[128] the plaintiff, a New York bank, was asked by one of its correspondents to pay a given amount to the M Bank, another New York bank, for the account of the defendant, an English bank. Due to an error, the plaintiff paid the amount twice. Granting a tracing order, Goulding J observed that such an order would be available under both the law of New York and that of England. His Lordship rejected the argument that a tracing order would be granted only where a fiduciary relationship existed between the payor and the payee at the time of payment. It was 'enough that . . . the payment into the wrong hands itself gave rise to a fiduciary relationship'.[129] Such a relationship eventuated because a person who paid money to another under a factual mistake retained an equitable property in it, and the payee's conscience would be subjected to a fiduciary duty to respect this property right.

It is interesting to note that, where a tracing order is not available on the facts, the bank's position may be a difficult one. In *Re Byfield, ex p. Hill Samuel & Co. Ltd.* v. *Trustee of the Property of a Bankrupt*,[130] the bank transferred an amount of £19,500 from the customer's account to that of her mother at another bank. This payment was effected because the bank was unaware that a receiving order had been issued against the daughter on the previous day. The mother used about £12,000 to discharge some of the daughter's debts and paid the balance over to the trustee. The question was whether the bank could lodge a proof for the amount transferred as money paid under a mistake of fact.

Goulding J held that the bank was not entitled to be subrogated to the claims of the creditors paid by the mother. He further held that the bank could not prove for the amount involved in its own right. It is noteworthy that, on the reasoning in *Chase Manhattan,* the bank should have been allowed to trace the money into the hands of the mother before she paid it over. It is obvious that she received the amount involved with full knowledge of her daughter's financial position.

---

[127] See pp. 164–6 above.
[128] [1981] 1 Ch. 105.
[129] Ibid., 119.
[130] [1982] Ch. 267.

CHAPTER 12

The Giro System and Electronic Transfers of Funds[1]

1. INTRODUCTION AND BASIC CONCEPTS

The word 'giro', which is used to describe money transfer operations, is derived from the Greek word for circle. Giro denotes the cyclic operation involved in the transfer of credit balances from one bank account into another. On the Continent such systems have been used successfully for a considerable period of time as an alternative to the payment of accounts by cheques. Even in the United Kingdom, where payment of cheques has been predominant for a considerable period of time, the money transfer system is no novelty. In an elementary form it has been operable for a long time by means of individual letters in which customers instructed their banks to pay given amounts of money to the credit of designated payees. As a fully operative system providing an alternative to the settlement of accounts by cheques, the bank giro came into operation in the 1960s, in the wake of the introduction of the national giro, operated by the Post Office.[2] At present the bank giro and the National Girobank are linked so that an amount can be transferred from an account maintained with a clearing bank to an account maintained with the National Girobank, and vice versa. Most of the banks involved in current account transactions in the United Kingdom participate in the bank giro.

Both the national giro and the bank giro are money transfer systems which operate either on the basis of a written instruction or, in some cases, on the basis of orders encoded on a tape. Another development is the introduction of plastic tokens, known as 'cashpoint cards', which are used to obtain cash from an automatic teller machine or in order to carry out other transactions keyed into the computer terminal of the computer. These tokens are discussed in the next chapter.

---

[1] For other treatments of the subject, see J. M. Holden, *Law and Practice of Banking*, 3rd edn., London, 1982, vol. 1, ch. 10; Chorley, *Law of Banking*, 6th edn., pp. 265 et seq. And see F. R. Ryder, 89 *JIB* 323. The American system is exhaustively discussed by N. Penney and D. I. Baker, *Law of Electronic Fund Transfers*, New York, 1980 (plus supps.).

[2] In operation since the beginning of the 1960s. At present the Post Office (Banking Services) Act 1976 confers on the Post Office the power to provide full banking services for its clients. And see the British Telecommunications Act 1981, s. 58(1).

In the case of giro transactions, a uniform set of forms is used throughout the entire banking system. Four main variants are employed: individual money transfer forms (known as 'bank giro credits'), standing orders, traders' credits, and direct debits. However, one basic method of transfer is operable in all giro transactions. A specific terminology is required so as to avoid confusion between the roles of the different parties in giro transfers and in the clearing of cheques.

In a giro operation, the person who wishes to effect payment—the payor—instructs his bank (the 'transferring bank') to pay a specified amount to the credit of a designated account, maintained either in the payor's own name or, more usually, in the name of a third party. The bank to whom the amount is to be remitted is best described as the 'recipient bank' and the person whose account is to be credited as 'the payee'. Where a payor wishes to use the bank giro he has to complete a standard form, on which the only printed details are the name of his own bank—the transferring bank—and the operative branch. The payor inserts, in blank spaces provided in the instrument, the date of the instruction, the number of his own account,[3] the name of the payee, and details concerning the recipient bank (name of bank, details of branch, and number of account to be credited), the amount and, in some forms, the object of the payment involved (e.g. 'rent' or 'invoice no. xx'). The form is signed by the payor and, usually, is either delivered by him to the branch with which he maintains his account or posted to it.[4] However, under arrangements prevailing in the banking network, he can also hand the form for transmission to any one of the banks participating in the giro system.

The procedure described above is that employed in the case of individual money transfer orders. In the case of other variants there are some modifications, although the basic concept is the same. The main variation occurs in direct debits. Here the payee is authorized to issue to the 'transferring bank' orders for the payment of money on the payor's behalf. This method is used primarily for the settlement of insurance premiums, or of regular accounts where a varying amount is due from the payor from time to time. The payee is authorized to request the transfer of funds as the payor's agent.

The very nature of giro operations anticipates the existence of a suitable clearing system. Obviously, when a bank is asked to transfer an amount standing to the credit of an account maintained with itself to another account opened with it, the operation takes place by suitable debit and credit entries in the accounts of the payor and the payee. Similarly, where two banks are involved, the settlement between the transferring and recipient

---

[3] Banks supply personalized or encoded giro form books to customers on request.

[4] Although, in practice, he can deliver the form to other branches of his own bank, which will then set it into the course of transmission.

bank is not made by delivery of cash but by the striking of a balance between the total of amounts transferred on a given day. At present there are a number of clearing systems in operation for these procedures. The first is used in the case of all transfers made on a periodic basis. These are effected through the Bankers' Automated Clearing Services Ltd (BACS), which is a computer centre utilised by the clearing banks. The second is used in the case of individual money transfer orders and, basically, is similar to the clearing of cheques. A third system is operative in respect of amounts to be transferred from an account maintained within a branch operating within the boundaries of the City of London to another account in a bank in the same place. Such payments can be effected on the day the order is issued by means of instruments known as 'bankers' payments'. The procedure used is a settlement through the town clearing or through bank messengers. A fourth, electronic, system for substantial payments was introduced in 1984. It is known as CHAPS[5] and is operated by means of 'gates' utilizing a network of British telecommunications.

Finally, two entirely separate systems are used for the electronic transfer of funds overseas. An electronic transfer system, known as SWIFT,[6] facilitates the transfer of amounts by a telecommunications system operable for bankers' international transactions throughout the world. An alternative method for such transfers remain telex and the mail transfers. In operations of this type, the transferring bank communicates to the recipient bank, either directly or through an intermediary, details of the account to be credited with the amount involved and the method by which the recipient bank is to reimburse itself. Usually, this will be by debiting the transferring bank's account with the recipient bank; if this account is in debit, or if no such account is maintained, the recipient bank is authorized to draw for the amount due on a designated third bank.

It is clear that in SWIFT, and in international money transfers executed by mail or by telex, the transfer is again effected by a process of debiting the payor's account and by crediting the payee's account. A physical handling of currency is avoided. This is so although the parties talk about the transfer of a stipulated amount in a designated currency, such as $US2,500.00.

In all the various types of money transfer operations, be they domestic or international, the guiding legal principles are derived from the law of agency. The payor gives a mandate to the 'transferring bank'; the latter issues a specified order to the recipient bank. The transferring bank may do so directly, as is the case where the payor issues an individual 'giro credit'

[5] Clearing House Automated Payments Systems. For useful background information, see R. T. Clark, 'CHAPS—A New Approach to Payment Systems', Interbank Research Organization, London, 1982.
[6] Society for Worldwide Interbank Financial Telecommunications. The organization's headquarters are in Brussels. See further, pp. 361–3 below.

form directed to a clearing bank. In other cases, intermediary banks are involved. Thus, if the payor issues his individual 'giro credit' form to a bank that is not a member of the clearing house, the instruction will be transmitted to the recipient bank through a correspondent bank, with which the payor's bank maintains an account. The exact nature of the principles involved is discussed in section 5. Two troublesome issues are the determination of the time of payment of the amount transferred and the status of the recipient bank. The answer to the former question is relevant where the payor wishes to countermand his order to transfer. The second question is important for defining the recipient bank's duty to observe instructions given to it. Its position will frequently depend on whether it is acting at a given moment as an agent carrying out the instruction of the transferring bank or as an agent acquiring the relevant credit on behalf of the payee.

The significance of the law of agency in giro operations and international money transfers is demonstrated by the memorandum to the public, published by the clearing banks and the Scottish banks in 1967, which has been discussed in Chapter 9. In this important document, known as the 'Golden Memorandum' and setting out the advantages of the money transfer system, the participating banks gave notice that each one of them was authorized to act on behalf of all others in giro transactions. Under this memorandum, a person could pay an amount of money to any one of the participating banks for the credit of a designated account with the same bank or with any other bank within the system, regardless of whether or not he had a bank account in the United Kingdom. This meant that any person who maintained an account with one of the participating banks could use any bank within the system in order to pay an amount of money to the credit of his own account or of any other person's account with a participating bank. He could, likewise, hand to any bank cheques or similar instruments to be collected for the credit of his own current account. A person who did not have a current account of his own with one of the participating banks was allowed to use the bank giro in order to pay cash to the credit of any account maintained either with the bank to whom the money was paid or with any other participating bank.

Although the Golden Memorandum is no longer in effect as a general agreement between all the banks participating in the giro system,[7] it has been effectively replaced by agreements made between individual banks within the system. From a practical point of view, the position has therefore remained unaltered. The legal implications of the system are discussed subsequently. Three salient points need, however, to be made at the outset. First, where a person uses a bank with which he does not have an account in order to carry out a giro operation, it is difficult to state categorically

---

[7] It is understood that the agreement was cancelled in view of problems arising under the Restrictive Trade Practices Act 1956.

whether this bank, to be described as the 'pay-in bank', is acting as the payor's agent or on behalf of the payor's bank.

Secondly, it is essential to recognize that, even where the payor pays cash to the pay-in bank, the transaction is carried out by the transfer of balances and not by the transfer of money. When the cash is paid to the pay-in bank, the banknotes or coins become part of that bank's own pool of money. The payor's request is carried out by an instruction, issued through the pay-in bank, that a specified bank account be credited with the amount involved.

Thirdly, it is inadvisable for banks to handle cheques or negotiable instruments at the request of a payor who is not a customer of the bank. It will be shown, in Chapter 14, that where the payor is not the true owner of the effects involved, a bank that collects them on his behalf opens itself to an action in conversion. It may be argued that no such action is maintainable where the documents are simply transmitted or delivered to another bank.[8] But the point has not been the subject of decision. Moreover, the statutory defence applicable in this type of case is available to a bank only where it has acted for a customer.[9] In giro transactions the pay-in bank may, nevertheless, be able to plead the defence in question if the payor remits the effects to it for the credit of an account with one of the participating banks. The pay-in bank may, possibly, claim that it received the instrument as an agent of that bank, and that it is therefore entitled to rely on the defences available to its principal. The point is a dubious one because, as pointed out above, it is uncertain on whose behalf the pay-in bank acts in giro transactions.

A detailed analysis of the practice and law concerning money transfer orders is provided in the remaining sections of this chapter. Section 2 discusses the variants of money transfer orders used for giro operations within the United Kingdom, and compares these giro operations with the payment of money by cheques. Section 3 discusses the clearing methods used in domestic money transfer operations. Section 4 discusses international money transfers, including SWIFT transfers. The section further deals with specific problems related to the risk of rate fluctuations. The last section provides a legal analysis of money transfer operations, and discusses the problems arising in this context.

2. DOMESTIC GIRO FORMS AND THEIR COMPARISON WITH CHEQUES

(i) Individual money transfer forms (bank giro credit transfers)

The bank giro credit, or the individual credit transfer form, is the basic facility used by the banks in money transfer operations. The standard form,

---

[8] As the pay-in bank does not make any proprietary disposition affecting the instruments involved; but see pp. 442–3 below.
[9] Pp. 421–2 below.

reproduced in the Appendix of Forms, is straightforward. It is entitled 'bank giro credit' and has blank spaces provided for the insertion of the details concerning the transfer: the name of the payee's account and the other details concerning it; and the amount involved. Notably, the form sets out neither the payor's express request that the bank execute the transfer nor his authorization for the debiting of his account. The payor is, however, required to sign the form; his mandate to the bank as regards the remittance of the funds is based on his executing, in this manner, a standard bank giro credit. But the bank giro credit does not, even by implication, confer on the bank the authority to reimburse itself. The payor has to remit to the bank the required cash, a personal cheque, or cheques of third parties payable to himself. In this regard the Bank Giro in the United Kingdom differs from the giro systems used on the Continent, where the giro docket performs the dual function of authorizing the bank both to transfer the amount involved and to debit the customer's account.

(ii) Standing orders

Standing orders are used to arrange for periodic payments of fixed amounts, such as monthly rents, instalments due under hire purchase agreements, and annual subscriptions. The payor's instruction is executed on a form with blank spaces in which he inserts the details found in the bank giro credit as well as a direction concerning the frequency of payments. No specific funds are earmarked by the bank at the time it receives the instructions in order to enable it to reimburse itself. Instead, the payor impliedly authorizes the bank to debit his account with the amount of each payment when it is made. The standing order is thus a self-contained instruction which need not be accompanied by the customer's cheque or by cash. Obviously, it can be used only by persons who maintain an account with the transferring bank.

In practice, organizations, such as charitable bodies, arrange for the printing of standard forms which set out the details of their account. The payor completes this form by inserting the details concerning his account with the transferring bank. The order is transmitted to this bank by the payee. From a legal point of view, the practice does not lead to a departure from the principles to be discussed subsequently. The payee transmits the form as the payor's agent.[10] In other cases, the creditor simply conveys the details of his bank account to the debtor, who can then pay the account by means of a money transfer order. Local authorities have used this method for some time. Here the order is executed and transmitted by the payor.

---

[10] The legal nature of the relationships arising in the transaction is discussed in s. 5 of this chapter.

(iii) Traders' credits

Traders' credits appear to have been in use in an elementary form from the beginning of this century.[11] Their object is to simplify the payment of accounts rendered to a trader in connection with goods or services supplied to him for his business. Such accounts do not have to be paid forthwith but are settled on a periodic basis, such as once a fortnight. The traders' credit is used instead of the dispatch of individual cheques or money transfer orders in respect of each account due.

The system operates as follows. The trader lists all the amounts to be paid by him in a standard form obtained from his own bank and sets out details concerning the identity of each payee and the account to be credited with each amount. In addition, he fills in for each item a credit voucher, which is used for notifying the recipient bank of the details of the credit; a copy of the respective voucher is forwarded by the latter bank to the payee. The payor posts or delivers the list (viz. traders' credit) and vouchers to his own bank accompanied by a single cheque, drawn on his account with this bank and covering the total amount to be paid out. In practice, the cheque serves the function of authorizing the payor's bank—the transferring bank—to debit the payor's account with the amounts transferred. This instruction could just as easily be included in the list itself.

It will be shown that traders' credits can be encoded on a tape, in which case they are cleared through the data bank—the BACS. Some major British corporations, such as ICI and Marks and Spencer, have direct access to this institution. This means that they can issue their traders' credit, or standing order, directly to BACS and not to their own bank. BACS is given an instruction as to the bank account to be debited with the amount involved and also the identity of the accounts to be credited. In such an operation there is no need to issue a cheque covering the amount to be paid out by means of the 'transfers', and the entire operation is electronic. BACS acts as the transferring bank's agent; instructions transmitted by a customer are, as regards BACS, transmitted for his bank.

(iv) Direct debiting

The direct debiting system, introduced in 1967, was initially advertised in the Golden Memorandum. It facilitates the prompt payment of amounts due under commercial and consumer contracts by enabling the supplier, dealer, or other creditor to obtain payment of amounts due to him by issuing a direct demand for payment to the debtor's bank. The procedure

---

[11] Holden, *Law and Practice of Banking*, 4th edn., vol. 1, p. 314; Chorley, *Law of Banking*, 6th edn. p. 271.

involves some extra paperwork at the initial stages but saves time thereafter. The creditor asks the debtor to sign a standard form, which is lodged with the debtor's bank (the 'transferring bank'). The form authorizes this bank to pay amounts demanded by the creditor; there is no need to require on each occasion the confirmation of the indebtedness by the debtor. However, to avoid disputes some creditors send their accounts to the debtor before claiming payment from his bank. A notice, printed at the foot of the invoice, states that if no objection is raised by the debtor within seven days a direct debiting form will be presented to the transferring bank.

In practice, creditors do not send the direct debiting form directly to the transferring bank, but remit them to their own bank (the 'recipient bank'), which makes arrangements for clearance. In the majority of cases, direct debiting is used to arrange for the payment of varying amounts falling due at regular or irregular intervals, such as amounts payable in respect of the supply of different quantities of a commodity ordered by a purchaser from a supplier from time to time as old stock is used up.

It is obvious that direct debiting is open to abuses. To protect themselves, the banks demand from each firm that wishes to utilize this method for obtaining direct payment of its accounts an indemnity, addressed to all the banks participating in the money transfer system, and covering each of them against all losses and expenses incurred directly or indirectly as a result of direct debiting. The indemnity authorizes the banks to compromise any claim on the creditor's (payee's) behalf.

(v) Comparison of giro forms with cheques

Both giro forms and cheques are used for the settlement of accounts by means of the issuing of a written instruction to the bank. The legal question of whether or not a giro form constitutes a cheque is discussed subsequently. At this point it is important to compare the practice involved in the two systems. The discussion aims at highlighting the relative advantages and disadvantages inherent in each of them.

It has been shown in Chapter 9 that cheques lend themselves to sharp practices. The main danger is that the payee, who obtains the possession of a cheque, may alter it by raising the amount involved. Frauds by agents, such as employees, who fraudulently complete cheque forms signed by their principals in blank are equally common. Even if such a fraud does not cause financial loss to the bank, it may involve it in expensive litigation. The danger of fraud is increased if the drawer fails to cross the cheque or overlooks the practical need of adding the words 'not negotiable' and 'A/C Payee Only' to a crossing.[12] It would be wrong to assert that the danger of fraud is

---

[12] Pp. 256–8 above.

altogether eliminated in the case of giro transactions. However, as bank giro forms are generally posted or delivered to the transferring bank and not to the payee, the danger of fraud or of conversion is reduced. A giro fraud will have to be perpetrated by one of the payor's clerks or agents.

Another disadvantage of the payment of debts by cheques manifests itself where an instrument, presented for payment through a bank, is dishonoured by non-payment. Under the existing clearing procedure, the payee's account is credited before the cheque is set into transmission for its presentment to the drawee bank. If the cheque is dishonoured by the latter bank, due to an irregularity or to the inadequacy of funds standing to the drawer's account, the cheque has to be returned to the collecting bank, which returns it to the payee and reverses the credit entry made in his account. In giro operations, the form is processed initially by the transferring bank. It is only when this bank has satisfied itself of the regularity of the form and that payment is in order that the recipient bank becomes involved in the transaction. The transferor's account is debited before the crediting of the payee's account; the latter step usually completes the cycle and is final. It is important to emphasize that the giro clearing procedure does not rule out the need for occasional reversals of ledger entries. But the problem arises only where an amount is credited to a wrong account as a result of an error in decoding or of the insertion of inaccurate details in the bank giro credit.

The giro system is not superior to payment by cheques in all regards. First and foremost, the filling out of the giro forms is cumbersome in comparison with the drawing of a cheque. In addition to the writing out of the name of the payee and the amount—both of which appear also in a cheque—the trans- feror has to insert in the giro form all the details concerning the payee's bank account, and in some cases a reference explaining the object of the payment made. Secondly, the use of giro forms in the place of cheques generates extra work for both the transferring bank and the recipient bank compared with their involvement with cheques. The transferring bank has to deliver a credit voucher to the recipient bank in the clearing house, and some of the leading banks undertake the burden of advising the transferor about the execution of his instruction. The recipient bank has to notify the payee. Thus, the giro sys- tem involves multiple notices and postage. In comparison, a cheque serves in itself the purpose of notice. Except where it is dishonoured, its clearance involves a minimum of paperwork for all concerned.

3. THE CLEARANCE OF GIRO TRANSFERS

(i) Paper clearing and electronic clearing

At present there are two main clearing methods for money transfer oper- ations in the United Kingdom. The one which is similar to the clearing of cheques involves a manual transmission of giro forms. The settlement of accounts by bankers' payments is a variant of this procedure. The other procedure involves the electronic clearing of money transfers through BACS,[13] which has already been described as the data centre of the United Kingdom's clearing banks. A new electronic system, known as CHAPS and introduced in 1984 after some controversy, is used for the same day transfer of substantial amounts. This system may eventually replace the 'bankers' payments' system.

Although the clearing techniques are basically a matter of practice rather than of law, certain aspects of the procedure involved are relevant for defining the legal roles assumed by the parties. Before embarking on the description of the practices involved it is necessary to refer to one fundamental distinction between the clearance of cheques and of giro forms. In the case of cheques, the clearing process is initiated by the collecting bank, which sets into motion the machinery for obtaining the payment of an amount due to one of its customers. The process can, therefore, be described as the collection by an agent of a debt due to his principal. In giro operations the process is initiated by the transferring (or paying) bank which remits an amount payable by one of its customers.[14] The object of this bank is, thus, to effect payment on behalf of its customer, not to demand it. Nonetheless, the notion of settling debts by means of the transfer of bank balances is essentially one and the same regardless of whether the instrument used is a cheque or a giro form. In both cases a series of ledger entries is substituted for the payment of cash. The word 'clearing' describes both types of operation.

(ii) The manual clearing procedure

The procedure involved in the clearing of bank giro credits is fundamentally the same as that used in the case of cheques. The customer delivers to his bank a bank giro credit accompanied by a cheque or a withdrawal form. At the branch of the transferring bank with which the payor maintains his account, the relevant data is entered on the bank giro credit form in magnetic ink. The figures printed set out the clearing numbers of the transferring bank and the relevant branch, the number of the recipient bank and its branch, the numbers of the accounts of the payor and of the payee, and the amount to be transferred. The payor's account is debited by means of a message, keyed into the computer terminal at his branch. One copy of the

---

[13] Pp. 354–7 below.

[14] Except that in certain cases, initially covered by the Golden Memorandum and at present under individual agreements, the machinery may be set in motion through a third bank to whom the customer hands his giro form; pp. 231–2 above.

bank giro credit form (as well as the cheque or withdrawal form) is retained at this branch; the other is dispatched to the transferring bank's clearing office. On the next day, the head office delivers this form through the clearing house to the recipient bank's clearing office. In the case of some banks, the amount involved is there credited to the payee's account and, on the same day, the form is then forwarded to the payee's branch. In the case of other banks, the crediting of the payee's account is carried out at the branch and not at the head office of the recipient bank, as the payee may have instructed his branch to reject the payment proffered.[15] If this is not the case, the payee is informed by his own branch of the credit received.

The procedure varies slightly if the bank giro credit is delivered at a bank other than that with which the payor maintains his account. In such a case both the giro credit form and the attached cheque are transmitted through the respective clearing channels. The end result is that the payor's cheque reaches his own branch.

A special procedure is used where a member of the public who is not a customer of a bank utilizes the money transfer system in order to settle a debt due to a third party. The payor, who in such a case makes use of the clearing banks' general offer initially contained in the Golden Memorandum,[16] pays cash at any branch of one of the participating banks for the credit of a designated account of a third party. In such a case the amount involved becomes part of the funds of the pay-in bank and a credit balance accrues for the benefit of the payee's account. The details of this account will be set out in the bank giro credit form filled in by the payor. Obviously, there is no need for the pay-in branch to debit any account. All it has to do is to send the form to the recipient bank through the clearing house.

The manual clearing system of money transfer orders is, obviously, cumbersome and slow. The ordinary cycle takes three days and, if the account to be credited is maintained in a remote part of the United Kingdom, it may take yet another day even if the form is handed to the payor's own branch.[17] Despite this, the manual clearing system of money transfer orders continues to be used for individual bank giro credits. It is also used in the case of some payments falling into the class of traders' credits. Thus, a small business firm may find it advisable to pay its accounts by means of one form, setting out the details of all the credits to be made and accompanied by individual vouchers for each transaction. The vouchers, which are in a form similar to that of individual bank giro credits, are then used for the clearing process. The same applies in the case of payrolls of small firms such as bookshops or

---

[15] At present there appears to be no method for recording this instruction at the computer centre. A manual perusal of credit forms is required where an instruction for the rejection of a payment has been received by a bank.

[16] P. 231 above.

[17] Note the unavoidable delay provision in the Clearing House Rules; p. 234 above.

grocers. In effect, the manual clearing of money transfers is just as cumbersome as the payment of each debt incurred by a trader, or each monthly salary due from an employer, by means of an individual cheque. The main advantage of the use of the money transfer system in these cases is that it obviates the risk of the loss of the payment instrument inherent in the dispatch of cheques through the post.

A special type of money transfer form, knows as a bankers' payment, is used for the transfer of substantial amounts of money from one bank to another. The bankers' payment is sent by the transferring bank to the recipient bank, which presents it for payment on the same day through the town clearing system. A bankers' payment may be drawn by any one of the clearing banks, or by any bank that uses a clearer as an agency bank.[18] Although all operations are carried out manually, the clearing cycle is completed on the day of exchange.[19] A bankers' payment is executed on a form similar to that of a bank giro credit.[20]

Another speedy means for effecting inter-bank transfers is provided by the new electronic system known as CHAPS. As this system is used only for payments of not less than £10,000, bankers' payments are likely to remain in use for some time. The operations of CHAPS are discussed in the next section, following the description of the BACS procedures.

(iii) Clearance through BACS and CHAPS

'Bankers' Automated Clearing Services' provide an alternative to the manual transfer of funds. Automated clearings are used for periodic payments, certain traders' credits, direct debitings, and similar types of transfers. The firm which operates BACS has approximately 8,000 clients. These are the clearing banks, other financial institutions, and substantial trading firms sponsored by the clearing banks.

The main difference between the automated system and the manual clearance of cheques and of bank giro credits is one of method. There is no distinction as regards the element of time. The procedure used by BACS involves electronic transfers which obviate the need for a great deal of paperwork and for the physical transmission of documents. The automated

---

[18] The procedure can be traced back to the eighteenth century, when cheques were likewise 'cleared' by presentation by the collecting bank's messenger to the paying bank.

[19] The significance of a special arrangement for speedy clearance of 'within town' transfers is demonstrated by statistics. In 1984, the daily average of amounts collected within the City amounted to £5,291,926, as compared with £479,425 collected in the general clearing. But the picture changes in respect of the number of items involved: 4,848 in the case of town clearings as compared with 1,559,997 in respect of general clearings. Thus, City clearings accounted for 90% of the total amounts cleared but for only 0.3% of the total number of items involved.

[20] See Appendix.

process substitutes for the exchange of paper at the clearing house an electronically effected transfer system executed with the aid of the central agency: BACS. The cycle involved in this procedure is spread over three days.

The typical clearing procedure is best explained by referring to payments made directly between banks. In such a case the transferring bank prepares a tape which sets out the relevant data respecting each amount to be remitted. Basically, the details involved are the same as those shown in bank giro credits. Transactions covered by the tape are classified on the basis of the identity of the different payors.

The tape is manually delivered to the BACS's premises in London by the close of the first day of the clearing cycle. Its processing at BACS begins during the evening, when the computer converts the tape in question into tapes classified with reference to the relevant recipient banks and the payees. The practical importance of this process can be illustrated by referring to a university's payroll. The tape delivered to BACS will show the payments made by the university to each employee and details of the relevant accounts to be credited. In the conversion process in BACS, the new tapes will be arranged for delivery to each recipient bank and will show the name and account number of the respective employees and the amounts payable to them. BACS's tapes, which are expected to be ready by 3.00 a.m. the next morning, are sent out by courier to the head offices of the recipient banks involved.

The tapes received from BACS are processed by the recipient bank's computer centre on the second day of the clearing cycle. Each amount is credited to the account of the respective customer. The information so processed is made available to branches on the third day of the cycle. Where notification is required, it is dispatched to customers by the branch on that day. The global settlement made between each bank and the remaining clearing banks at the end of each day takes into account the figures reached through the head offices which utilize the records of their computer centres.

There is, of course, room for errors in the procedure. If there is a request for the reversal of an entry after the close of the third day of the clearing cycle, it is necessary to issue a 're-debit request' explaining the error. Rectification is effected subject to the agreement of all the parties involved.

Where payment is directed not by a bank but by one of BACS's 'sponsored' clients, the process involves some duplications. The initial tape, used for effecting the debits, is prepared by the computer centre of the client. It is delivered directly to BACS; the sponsoring bank figures as transferring bank in the tape, and the total of the amount covered by the tape is debited to the client's account with his bank. In all other regards the process is the same as in the case of tapes emanating from banks. The sponsoring bank obtains the information required by it through BACS.

An important exception to the general pattern of the system used by BACS occurs in the case of direct debits. It will be recalled that, in such an operation, a trading firm is authorized by a client, or 'debtor', to demand from his bank payments of accounts posted to him from time to time. The trading firm acts, in such a transaction, as the client's agent. If the demand is made through BACS, the creditor's bank (the 'transferring bank') issues a demand for payment and not an order to transfer or to pay.[21] The procedure involved is, however, the same as in the case of a payment instruction. The only difference is that the 'recipient bank' is required to pay rather than to receive payment. This request can be refused, without any reason being given, before the close of the third day of the respective clearing cycle.

The main shortcoming of BACS is that its use is confined to the transfer of periodic or regular payments made by substantial firms. Another disadvantage is that the clearing cycle continues to spread over three days. By way of contrast, the manual clearing of bankers' payments involves a one day cycle. But this system, too, has shortcomings. It is a costly process, effective mainly in respect of payments made within the City of London, and, primarily, of inter-bank settlements. An attempt to provide a new, effective, and speedy system for individual transfers has been made by the launching of CHAPS.[22]

CHAPS became operative in 1984. Its function can be defined as the automated transfer of payments for 'same day clearing'. At this stage the transactions are still confined to the transfer of amounts of not less than £10,000. But it is expected that in due course the operations will encompass all 'same day settlements' by the British clearing banks and eventually also of the other banks.[23] Even at this stage, the operations are not confined to transactions within the City.

The procedure used by CHAPS differs from that of BACS in two important aspects. First, BACS operates through one main centre located in Edgware, which uses its own computer system. CHAPS operates through terminals—known as 'gateways'—maintained either individually by one of the major banks (a 'settlement bank') or jointly by some smaller banks. Secondly, the operations of BACS involve the composition of tapes which are delivered manually by the participating banks to the centre, and vice versa. In the case of CHAPS, the operation is totally automated or, in other words, effected by means of direct electronic messages.

A short description of the process is warranted. When a customer wishes to make a same day settlement by means of CHAPS, his bank (the 'transfer-

---

[21] If the creditor is a firm sponsored by its bank, it can issue the instruction directly to BACS.

[22] See note 5 to this chapter.

[23] The Trustee Savings Bank England and Wales and the City branches of the Scottish banks are already linked.

ring bank') transmits an appropriate message to its gateway. From there the message is sent by cypher, through 'British Telecom Switching Service', to the recipient bank's gateway.[24] When the message is received at the recipient bank's gateway, it is transmitted forthwith to the relevant branch or head office. The payee's account is credited in due course. This last operation is not governed by the guidelines of CHAPS as it is an aspect of the relationship of individual banks with their customers.

CHAPS is used not only by the banks which own the gateways, but also by other participating banks which use 'settlement banks' as agents. The participating banks are treated by the settlement bank to which they are affiliated as if they were a branch of that bank itself. They have direct access to the gateway and, of course, can both transfer and receive funds through it.

The settlement of the daily balance accrued as a result of CHAPS transfers is effected through the Bank of England which has its own CHAPS gateway. The amount involved is speedily determined at the close of each trading day as each gateway keeps records of amounts received from and of amounts paid to each settlement bank operating through it. If the records of the gateways involved agree, a message for settlement of the balance is dispatched to the Bank of England.

The settlement of amounts transferred through CHAPS gateways is conclusive. All participating banks have undertaken to refrain from disputing transfers effected by them through the system. The effectiveness of security methods used to preclude frauds remains to be tested with the passage of time.

4. INTERNATIONAL MONEY TRANSFERS

(i) Methods in use

The international transfer of money is an essential facet of free trade. In many countries it is restricted by exchange control legislation, the object of which is to safeguard the stability of the national currency and to prevent the undue outflow of local capital. In the United Kingdom, exchange control was abolished in 1980,[25] so that there are at present no restrictions on the

---

[24] If the recipient bank is a participating bank the 'destination gateway' is apparent. But where the recipient bank is not one of the participants in the CHAPS system, the 'dispatching gateway' has to determine which one of the participating banks is to be used as a correspondent for effecting transfer to the recipient bank. A routing table, updated from time to time, is kept to aid gateway operators to make this decision.

[25] See the Exchange Control (Authorised Dealers and Depositaries) (Amendments) (No. 4) Order 1979 (SI 1338); the Exchange Control (Revocation) Directions 1979 (SI 1339); the Exchange Control (General Exemption) Order 1979 (SI 1660). The orders have the effect of suspending the operation of the Exchange Control Act 1947.

amounts that may be transferred overseas or on the inflow of funds into the country.

In practice, all international money transfers, except the very limited importation and exportation of currency notes, are effected through banking channels. Four main methods are in use: the bankers' draft; the mail transfer, which is in the process of becoming obsolete; telegraphic transfers, effected mainly by means of telex messages; and SWIFT transfers. In addition, travellers' cheques and travellers' letters of credit facilitate the provision of foreign currency to individuals who travel abroad. But even in the use of these facilities, settlement is effected by means of banking channels: travellers' cheques are cleared through banks and travellers' letters of credit involve the drawing of cheques by the holder on the issuing bank.

Travellers' cheques are discussed elsewhere in this book.[26] So is the legal nature of bankers' drafts.[27] It will be recalled that a bankers' draft constitutes a negotiable instrument only if it is drawn by one bank on another. This applies regardless of whether the draft is issued to effect payment in the United Kingdom or overseas. The legal distinction between drafts that are negotiable instruments and those that fall outside the definition is, however, irrelevant as regards the applicable clearing or collection procedure.

(ii) The use of bankers' drafts

Bankers' drafts are used in two main situations. One is where a person who travels overseas wishes to transfer a large amount to the credit of a bank account which he intends to use on his arrival. The expense involved in the acquisition of travellers' cheques makes the use of a bankers' draft attractive. The other case is where a person wishes to remit money to someone residing overseas but does not know the identity of the payee's bank. The bankers' draft, in which the payor's bank orders his correspondent (or its own overseas office) to pay a specified amount to the payee's order, is remitted by the payee to his own bank for collection. That bank presents the bankers' draft for payment to the drawee bank through the usual clearing channels available for cheques.[28] The drawee bank obtains reimbursement either by debiting the drawing bank's account with itself or, if this account is overdrawn, by drawing for the required amount.

The main risks involved in the use of a bankers' draft are its theft, or, if sent by mail, its loss in transmission. The payee, though, is protected. In the United Kingdom, a collecting bank that acts for the thief of the draft opens itself to an action in conversion and may, frequently, be without any

---

[26] See pp. 262–3 above.
[27] Pp. 242–3 above.
[28] This is the practice in the United Kingdom; but it is applicable in other countries as well.

defence.[29] Furthermore, the payee, as holder, is entitled to have the draft replaced by his bank against an indemnity. As that indemnity can be enforced by the issuing bank only if the draft comes into the hands of a holder in due course,[30] the payee is usually protected. The reason for this is that bankers' drafts are made payable to the payee's order, which means that transfer can be effected only by means of the payee's genuine indorsement.[31] A person acquiring the instrument under a forged indorsement is not a holder.[32] However, this rule is applicable only under British and North American law. In other jurisdictions, an indorsement which is regular on its face is effective to transfer title even if it is forged.[33] The risk of the loss or of the theft of a bankers' draft dispatched overseas is, therefore, not to be dismissed lightly in such cases.

(iii) Mail and telegraphic transfers

Mail transfers and telegraphic transfers can be discussed together, as the procedure used is the same in both cases, except that in the former the customer's instruction is executed by letter whilst in the latter it is carried out by a telegram or by telex. In both types of transaction the customer requires his own bank—the transferring bank—to remit a specified amount to a designated person or firm overseas. Ideally, the payor should be able to provide his bank with details of the payee's bank account. Where these details are furnished, the transferring bank instructs its correspondent in the payee's place to arrange to credit the relevant account with the amount involved.

If the correspondent bank happens to be the payee's bank, the procedure is straightforward. The payee's account is credited and the transferring bank's account with its correspondent is debited with the amount in question. If the payee's account is maintained with a bank other than the transferring bank's correspondent, the transfer can be executed in two ways. In most cases the transferring bank still uses the services of its correspondent, which will then remit the amount involved through local clearing channels to the credit of the payee's account with the recipient bank. Alternatively, the transferring bank may send a message directly to the recipient bank, requesting it to credit the payee's account with the amount involved and authorizing it to reimburse itself by drawing either on the transferring bank

[29] See pp. 308–9 below.

[30] This is the case where the draft is a negotiable instrument; BEA, ss. 69–70.

[31] Bills of Exchange Act 1882, s. 31(3). This section applies only to drafts that are negotiable instruments. As regards in-house drafts, see pp. 242–3 below.

[32] P. 504 below.

[33] See, for example, Uniform Law on Bills of Exchange and Promissory Notes, promulgated by the Geneva Convention No. 3313 of 7 June 1930, 143 LNTS 257, art. 16.

or more frequently on its local correspondent. In some cases the recipient is asked to draw on an overseas bank. By way of illustration, take a case in which an amount expressed in US dollars is remitted from London to a bank in Kuwait, which is asked to reimburse itself by drawing on the transferring bank's account with its correspondents in New York.

The procedure differs where the payor is unable to furnish to the transferring bank the details concerning the payee's account. In such a case, the transferring bank engages its correspondent overseas, who informs the payee about the receipt of the funds and asks for his instructions. Usually the payee will thereupon request that the amount involved be paid to the credit of his account with a specific bank. This instruction is, again, carried out through the clearing house.

It is clear that international money transfers usually involve at least two currencies: that of the country from which the funds are remitted and that of the country to which the money is being transferred. By way of illustration, take a telegraphic transfer of funds from the United Kingdom to Australia. The amount involved may be transferred either as a sum expressed in pounds sterling or in Australian dollars. In the former case, the conversion of the amount from one currency into the other takes place when the amount transferred is received in Australia. It will then be converted into Australian dollars on the basis of the banks' buying rate for telegraphic transfers ('T/T'). In the latter case the conversion takes place in London. In other words, the payor's account is debited with the amount of pounds sterling required to issue the telegraphic order in question.

In some cases a telegraphic transfer involves three rather than two currencies. This takes place where a contract stipulates payment on the basis of a currency other than that of the country of the seller or of the buyer.[34] Thus, in a sale of oil by an exporter in Kuwait to an importer in Brazil, the price is usually expressed in US dollars. Here the purchaser will have to arrange for a telegraphic transfer of the amount expressed in US currency.[35]

The difference between the selling rate and the buying rate for a specific type of transaction in a given currency is maintained by banks for two main reasons. The first is the need to maintain a margin of profit for dealings in foreign currency. For this reason, the selling rate of a currency is invariably higher than the banks' buying rate thereof. Secondly, the difference involved is meant to act as a partial hedge against fluctuations in currencies. As banks

---

[34] The question of whether the currency is the currency of account, which is merely used to calculate the amount payable, or the currency of payment, which is the legal tender in which payment is to be rendered, is discussed in works concerning the conflict of laws. See, for example, Dicey and Morris, *Conflicts of Laws*, 10th edn., London, 1980, vol. 2, pp. 999 et seq.

[35] Where a price expressed in foreign currency is due at a future date, the seller can protect himself by a forward exchange contract for the purchase of the currency. The buyer, too, can protect himself by selling the foreign currency due to him on a 'forward' basis.

are unable to match completely their purchases and sales of a specific currency during every trading day, the difference between the selling and the buying rate is meant to cover them against daily fluctuations. Consequently, the difference between the selling rate and the buying rate increases as a currency's stability declines.

The currency fluctuations that may occur where payment is made in a foreign currency is not unique to settlements arranged by telegraphic transfers. Such fluctuations manifest themselves also if payment is to be made by a bankers' draft or by the drawing of a bill of exchange accompanied by documents of title. This practical problem has been explained at this stage because it is most clearly discernible in the case of telegraphic transfers, which are inter-bank transactions.

In general terms, telegraphic transfers constitute a satisfactory method for rendering payment of amounts due overseas or for transferring funds abroad. The main risk is that the funds can erroneously be credited to an account other than that specified by the payor. The mistake is usually rectified within a few days, but the delay involved can have serious consequences. Thus, where the initial error in transfer leads to a delay in the payment of an amount due under a charterparty, the shipowner may be entitled to withdraw the vessel.[36] This type of loss is incurred not only in the case of an error in transmission but also in cases in which transfer is delayed as a result of faults in the telecommunication system used. Regardless of whether a transfer is made by telegram or by a telex message, breakdowns and technical problems are known to have taken place. These problems have encouraged the development of the banks' own network for international money transfers.

(iv) SWIFT transfers

The Society for Worldwide Interbank Financial Telecommunications is an organization maintained by banks and financial institutions throughout the world.[37] It operates a network of communications which can be used by banks and other financial institutions for money transfers, for the opening of letters of credit, and generally for the transmission of messages from institution to institution.

The system operates through three main centres, situated respectively in Brussels, in Amsterdam, and in Culpepper, Virginia, in the United States.

---

[36] See cases discussed below, pp. 384 et seq.

[37] Operations commenced in the summer of 1977. For further details, see H. F. Lingl, 'Risk Allocation in International Interbank Electronic Fund Transfers: CHIPS & SWIFT (1981) 22 Harv. Int'l. LJ 621; E. U. Byler and J. L. Baker, 'SWIFT: A Fast Method to Facilitate International Financial Transactions' (1983) 17 J World Trade L 458; and see brochure published by SWIFT's Headquarters in Brussels, obtainable from clearing banks in the United Kingdom.

Each country in which the banks have joined the system has a national terminal connected primarily to one of these three major centres. The national terminal of the United Kingdom is situated at BACS's premises at Edgware, and is connected to the Amsterdam centre. However, all three major centres are inter-linked, and as a result, interchangeable. If one of them closes down temporarily, transactions can continue to be carried out through another one of the centres.

In practical terms, the method of operation of SWIFT is similar to that of CHAPS, except that a single national centre is used instead of a number of gateways.[38] When a customer instructs his bank to carry out a money transfer or some other SWIFT operation, his instruction is conveyed by the bank's terminal to the national centre. This can be done by a special SWIFT link or by means of a telex message. The national centre encodes the message and dispatches it to the applicable major centre. The message has to set out all the relevant details concerning the transfer, including the name of the correspondent whom the transferring bank wishes to use overseas, in order to complete the transfer. This latter bank is not necessarily the payee's bank, which may not have a SWIFT link.[39] The centre which receives the message transmits it, after verifying some encoded security numbers, to the national terminal in the country of destination, where the message is decoded and transmitted to the chosen correspondent of the transferring bank. If the correspondent is not the recipient bank, it completes the transaction by using the facilities available for domestic transfers. Reimbursement of amounts transferred is attained in the same way as in telegraphic transfers.

SWIFT operations are transmitted by the transferring bank on the day they are received from the customer, and are expected to reach their destination on the same date. However, the time zone differential has to be taken into account in this regard. Obviously, a message dispatched from London to Melbourne will reach its destination after business hours, even if it is executed immediately. To cope with this problem, messages are stored at the receiving terminal if they arrive after it has closed for the day. They are processed on the next day in the order in which they have been received, except that 'priority' messages, which involve extra cost, are placed at the head of the queue.

SWIFT transfers have four advantages over telegraphic transfers. First, a telegram or telex may be garbled as a result of a failure in operations. As the banks have no control over the transmission agency, the hazard is a serious one. By contrast, SWIFT is attuned to the special needs of banks and other financial institutions which are in a position to control operations.

---

[38] Note that SWIFT, too, can be used for domestic transfers. A deterrent is the cost involved.

[39] In SWIFT terminology the payee's bank is called the 'account with' bank.

Secondly, in telex or telegraphic transfers there is no standard formula or text used to convey a message. As a result, there is room for confusion. In SWIFT operations, the banks use standard forms. This harmonization obviates ambiguities and misconstructions. Thirdly, there is no universal language for telegraphic transfers. In the case of SWIFT, English has been adopted as the language of operations. Finally, a telegraphic or telex message is not recorded, except by the transferring and recipient banks. There is no certainty that a message which appears as transmitted on the transferring bank's telex has in fact reached its destination. This danger is avoided in SWIFT operations, as each national terminal stores all messages received by it. Furthermore, each message received on a SWIFT terminal is automatically acknowledged.

At present there is a growing conviction in the banking world that the safest and fastest way to effect transfers is by means of SWIFT. The popularity of the system has increased enormously during the last four years.

5. THE LEGAL NATURE OF MONEY TRANSFER ORDERS

(i) The problem area

It is difficult to define the legal nature of money transfer orders. Despite the popularity which operations of this type have attained in the course of the last decade, there remains a dearth of case law in point. Moreover, the discussion in the foregoing pages demonstrates that it is erroneous to regard money transfer orders as comprising a single type of transaction. There is a marked difference between the methods used in domestic and in international money transfers, and even these two types of transfer have to be divided into different categories.

The divergence in the transactions covered under the umbrella of 'money transfer orders' contrasts with the system built around cheques and their clearance through banking channels. It is true that the rights of the parties to a cheque may vary from case to case, on account of the different types of crossing or of other words appearing in the instrument.[40] But the nature of the cheque itself is clearly defined. To date, no certainty of this type prevails in respect of money transfer orders. Only three points can be asserted with confidence. The first is that the documents used in money transfer transactions are not negotiable instruments. The second is that the law of assignment is, in all probability, inapplicable. The third, and only positive, rule is that for most purposes the relationships of the parties to money transfer orders are governed by the law of agency. But whilst it is clear that the

---

[40] See pp. 255–8 above.

banks involved in the transaction act in a representative capacity, it is frequently difficult to determine on whose behalf a given bank is acting at a particular moment. Thus, if an amount is transferred by means of a telex, does the recipient bank receive the message as the agent of the transferring bank or of the payee? This question may be of considerable importance for determining the point of time at which the payor loses the right to countermand the payment order issued by him. The answer applicable in the case of telegraphic transfers may not necessarily be applicable to a transfer executed through SWIFT or CHAPS.

In the United Kingdom, money transfer operations have not been made the subject of specific legislation. Neither the law of negotiable instruments nor the principles of assignment are applicable. The legal position differs in the United States, where many aspects of money transfers, particularly consumer protection problems, are governed by the Electronic Fund Transfer Act 1978.[41] But this Act is not exhaustive, and many problems remain subject to other statutory provisions and to principles of American common law.[42]

(ii) Are money transfer orders negotiable instruments?

This question has been raised in the United States, where the definition of a negotiable instrument is wider than in the United Kingdom. Under section 4–104(g) of the Uniform Commercial Code, some of the principles of the law of negotiable instruments apply for certain purposes to 'any instrument for the payment of money'. These words encompass a money transfer order.[43] By contrast, section 3 of the Bills of Exchange Act 1882 provides that a document is a bill of exchange only if it meets the following requirements: it has to be an 'unconditional order' in writing[44] addressed by one person to another, instructing the addressee to pay a certain sum in money to the order of a specified payee or to the bearer. Payment may be due on demand or at a fixed or determinable future time. Clearly, this definition does not cover electronic orders which do not involve a written or typed instrument. Thus, a transfer executed through CHAPS or SWIFT cannot, on the very face of it, be regarded a negotiable instrument.[45] The position differs if some order is issued in a written form, as is the case in respect of bank

---

[41] 15 USCA, s. 1693a.

[42] Penney and Baker, *Law of Electronic Fund Transfers*, paras. 10–02 et seq.

[43] Ibid., pp. 10–18. Such an 'item' is subject to art. 4 of the Code, governing collection. The basic definition in section 3–104 is similar to that of the English Act.

[44] Note that 'writing', under section 1–201(46) UCC, is defined as 'any . . . intentional reduction to tangible form'. This may include an electronic message. English law does not have a similar provision.

[45] The written order is given to the transferring bank. It is not a negotiable instrument for the reasons given hereafter as regards the bank giro credit.

giro credits, traders' credits, direct debits, and telegraphic transfers. There are, however, three grounds for asserting that the orders issued in these types of transactions do not constitute negotiable instruments. These are best explained by examining the form of a bank giro credit in the light of the definition of a bill of exchange.

The first distinction between a negotiable instrument and a bank giro credit is that the giro form is not payable at a determinable future time or on demand. The words 'payable on demand' in section 3 of the 1882 Act refer to payment at sight or on presentment,[46] which means that payment is to be effected when demanded by the payee or holder. The bank giro credit, which is delivered to the drawee bank and not to the payee, is payable as soon as the drawee, viz. the transferring bank, can make payment. It may be argued that a bill of exchange is deemed to be payable on demand if no time for payment is expressed in it,[47] and that this is the case in a bank giro credit. The answer, as regards the bank giro form, is that an instrument can be treated as payable on demand only if the payee is afforded the opportunity to claim payment. The same argument is applicable to all giro forms, such as direct debits, traders' credits, and telegraphic transfers, which do not stipulate a payment date.[48]

The second ground for regarding a bank giro credit as being outside the definition of a negotiable instrument is that the giro form is not payable to the order of a specified person or to bearer. It is true that the form nominates a specific payee to whom, or to whose account, the money is to be paid. But the amount is not payable to that payee's order in the sense of section 3 of the 1882 Act. It is true that a bill is payable 'to the order of a specified payee' even if it is made payable to him alone without the addition of the words in question.[49] However, it must be clear from the nature of the instrument that the payee is to be given the opportunity of deciding that the bill be paid to the order of a person other than himself. To this end, he must be able to transfer the bill in the appropriate manner. Any other construction of the words 'or order' in section 3 would render them meaningless. In a bank giro credit, the payee is not given the opportunity of transferring the instrument or, in other words, of determining to whose order it is to be paid.

The third and most important ground for denying that a bank giro credit is a negotiable instrument is that the giro form does not include any words that can be construed as a formal instruction given by the payor to the transferring bank. Accordingly, the form is not an order. This point is true in respect of all giro forms used in the United Kingdom. It follows that these forms do not constitute negotiable instruments.

[46] Bills of Exchange Act 1882, s. 10(1)(*a*).
[47] Ibid., s. 10(1)(*b*).
[48] But note 'value date' in SWIFT transfers; pp. 385–6 below.
[49] Bills of Exchange Act 1882, s. 8(4).

The conclusion that giro forms do not constitute negotiable instruments is of considerable practical importance in instances of deceit. Where a giro form is fraudulently issued or altered, the rights of the parties depend on the principles of the law of contract and of agency alone; the law of negotiable instruments is inapplicable.

(iii) Is a money transfer order an assignment?

The answer to this question is of considerable practical importance.[50] If a money transfer order constitutes an assigment, it is complete when the assignor (the transferring bank) acts on the debtor's (the payor's) instruction to assign the amount involved to the assignee (the recipient bank). In the case of a statutory assignment, made under section 136 of the Law of Property Act 1925, notification to the debtor—the transferring bank—completes the assignment.[51] In the case of an equitable assignment, the transaction is complete when the debt is assigned. Notification to the debtor is advisable but not a prerequisite to validity.[52] It follows that, if a money transfer order is an assignment, revocation becomes impossible once the assignor, the transferring bank, puts the necessary machinery for transfer into motion.

It has been argued that a money transfer operation constitutes an assignment of debt. In an American decision, the Circuit Court of Appeals (Second Circuit) observed that the amounts deposited by the payor with the transferring bank constituted a chose in action and were therefore assignable.[53] Moore J added[54] that, under the law of the United States,

In order for there to be a valid assignment of a chose in action, there must be a specific direction to transfer by the assignor and notice to the assignee.

The order to transfer was given by the payor to the transferring bank, and the credit slip, delivered to the recipient bank, was adequate notice. The Court treated the recipient bank as an assignee who received the amount transferred as the payee's agent.

It is submitted that, despite the persuasive character of the authority in question, the better view is that, in English law, a giro operation does not involve an assignment. English law differs from that of the United States in that it distinguishes between statutory and equitable assignments. Two arguments demonstrate that a money transfer operation does not constitute a statutory assignment. In the first place, a money transfer order does not

---

[50] See, Generally, Chorley, *Law of Banking*, 6th edn., pp. 268–9; *Chitty On Contracts*, 25th edn., vol. 2, paras. 2654–6.

[51] This is clear from the words of the section; and see *Hockley* v. *Goldstein* (1922) 90 LJKB 111.

[52] *Brandt's Sons & Co.* v. *Dunlop Rubber Co. Ltd.* [1905] AC 454, 462.

[53] *Delbrueck* v. *Manufacturers Hanover Trust Co.*, 609 F 2d 1047, 1051 (1979).

[54] Ibid.

usually involve the transfer of the total debt due to the payor from his debtor, the transferring bank. The assignment of part of a debt is, of course, not sanctioned by section 136.[55] Secondly, a money transfer order does not always relate to funds standing to the credit of the payor's account with his bank at the time the instruction is issued. A standing order is a typical example in point. Undoubtedly, the payor assumes that the required funds will be available at the time the transfer is to be effected. It is, nevertheless, unrealistic to regard the debt to be owed by the bank to the payor at a future time as anything but an expectancy. As such it is not assignable under section 136.[56]

The points raised do not rule out the classification of a money transfer operation as an equitable assignment of a legal chose in action. However, to attribute to the payor an intention to effect an assignment militates against the nature of the transaction. The one and only object of all the different types of money transfer operations is to instruct the transferring bank to perform a service on behalf of the payor, who is that bank's customer and principal. This instruction need not relate to a debt due to the customer, the payor, from the bank but may involve a request for the extension of an overdraft. In other words, the bank is not always the payor's debtor. Moreover, it is frequently difficult to decide whether any instruction given to a bank for the transfer of an amount of money constitutes an assignment or is a mere order issued by the customer as a principal.[57] In most money transfer orders it is assumed by the parties that the instruction may be revoked at least until the time it reaches the recipient bank. This emerges from the explanation of the giro system originally included in the Golden Memorandum of 1967, from the language of the forms used for traders' credits and standing orders, and, above all, from the phraseology of forms signed by the payor in direct debiting arrangements. None of the forms used in money transfer orders, be they domestic or international, discloses an intention of conferring on the payee the right to claim payment of the amount involved from the transferring bank or from the recipient bank. Also, there is accordingly no intention that part of a balance which constitutes a debt payable by the transferring bank to the payor be made over to the payee as a chose in action claimable by him. It is submitted that, on the facts, money transfer operations are inconsistent with the machinery and with the objectives pertaining to the assignment of debts.

On this analysis, money transfer orders involve a string of operations

---

[55] *Williams* v. *Atlantic Assurance Co. Ltd.* [1933] 1 KB 81, 100; *Walter and Sullivan Ltd.* v. *Murphy & Sons Ltd.* [1955] 2 QB 584.

[56] *Durham Bros.* v. *Robertson* [1898] 1 QB 765; cf. *Walker* v. *Bradford Old Bank Ltd.* (1884) 12 QBD 511.

[57] See, for example, *Morrell* v. *Wooten* (1852) 16 Beav. 197, esp. 204; cf. *Williams* v. *Everett* (1811) 14 East. 582.

carried out by the different banks acting in a representative capacity. This view has been adopted in *Royal Products Ltd. v. Midland Bank Ltd.* by Webster J, in the following words:[58]

[Money transfers] are to be regarded simply as an authority and instruction, from a customer to its bank, to transfer an amount standing to the credit of that customer with that bank to the credit of its account with another bank, that other bank being impliedly authorized by the customer to accept that credit by virtue of the fact that the customer has a current account with it, no consent to the receipt of the credit being expected from or required of that other bank, by virtue of the same fact. It is, in other words, a banking operation, of a kind which is often carried out internally, that is to say, within the same bank or between two branches of the same bank and which, at least from the point of view of the customer, is no different in nature or quality when, as in the present case, it is carried out between different banks.

(iv) Position of the transferring bank

The transferring bank is engaged in giro transactions in a representative capacity. In the majority of cases it is employed by a customer—the payor— who orders the transfer of a given amount of money, usually to a third party but occasionally to the credit of the payor's own account with an overseas bank. It follows that the transferring bank, as agent, is obliged to carry out the instruction given to it with reasonable skill and care.[59]

The transferring bank's main duty is to adhere strictly to the instruction given to it. This principle is forcefully stated in the context of a different type of transaction by Devlin J in *Midland Bank Ltd. v. Seymour*:[60]

It is a hard law sometimes which deprives an agent of the right to reimbursement if he has exceeded his authority, even though the excess does not damage his principal's interests. The corollary . . . is that the instruction to the agent must be clear and unambiguous.

The harshness of this doctrine has been mitigated in respect of money transfer orders by Webster J in *Royal Products Ltd. v. Midland Bank Ltd.*[61] In this case it was argued that the doctrine of strict compliance, pertaining to documentary credit transactions, applied equally to a transferring bank's duty to carry out its customer's instruction to transfer money. His Lordship said:[62]

---

[58] [1981] 2 Lloyd's Rep. 194, 198. And see *FIDC v. European American Bank and Trust Co.* 576 F Supp. 950, 957 (1983).

[59] See *Royal Products Ltd v. Midland Bank Ltd.* [1981] 2 Lloyd's Rep. 194, 198.

[60] [1955] 2 Lloyd's Rep. 147, 168. Cf. *European Asian Bank AG v. Punjab and Sind Bank (No. 2)* [1983] 1 WLR 642, 656, where Goff LJ observed that an agent could rely on an ambiguity to justify the construction given by him to the mandate only if the ambiguity was not patent.

[61] [1981] 2 Lloyd's Rep. 194.

[62] Ibid., 199.

I reject the submission . . . that in construing those instructions [for the transfer of money] I should, as a matter of law or banking practice, give a legal implication to each detail of them, for it seems to me that the doctrine which would lead to that result has little application to the facts of the present case, having received its first authoritative recognition . . . in the context of confirmed credits.

Webster J concluded that the doctrine of strict compliance had no application in the case of money transfer orders. This meant that the transferring bank was not in breach of its mandate as long as it carried out its instruction with skill and in a manner sanctioned by current banking practice.

The transferring bank's duty of care and skill imposes on it three specific obligations. The first is that the amount has to be transferred on time. Thus, if a specific time for transfer is expressly specified in the order, the bank has to comply with the deadline prescribed if it accepts the instruction to transfer. Usually, the time of transfer is discernible from the circumstances of the transaction. If the customer orders that the money be transmitted by a telegraphic transfer or by telex, it is to be assumed that he requires the transaction to be carried out on the same day. The same applies, a fortiori, if the bank is asked to effect the transfer by the use of SWIFT. The need for a speedy execution of the order may, further, be conveyed to the bank by familiarizing it with the object of the transfer involved. Thus, where the amount to be transferred is known to be a rental due on a given day under a charterparty, the bank has to exercise all the means at its disposal to ensure that the amount reaches its destination on time.

The transferring bank's second duty is to engage a reliable correspondent in the payee's country. Obviously, the problem does not arise in every transfer of funds. If the payee maintains his account with one of the transferring bank's correspondents overseas, then a direct transfer is possible. In many cases, though, there is a need for an intermediary bank. This problem is not confined to international transfers. It may arise in domestic money transfer operations if the payee maintains his account with a bank that does not participate in the giro system.

At common law the transferring bank is vicariously liable for the negligence or default of its correspondent. The point was settled by the House of Lords in 1927, in *Equitable Trust Co. of New York* v. *Dawson Partners Ltd.*,[63] in respect of the engagement of a correspondent by a bank issuing a letter of credit. The principle is applicable also to the engagement of a correspondent by a bank charged by its customer with the collection of a bill of exchange drawn on a merchant overseas.[64] In modern practice, banks

---

[63] (1927) 27 Ll. LR 49.
[64] *Mackersy* v. *Ramsays, Bonars & Co.* (1843) 9 Cl. & F 818, 846, 851.

engaged in transactions requiring the assistance of an intermediary stipulate in their contract with the customer that the correspondent is employed at the customer's expense and risk. Exemption clauses of this type have been upheld by courts,[65] and, as they appear reasonable, are highly unlikely to be affected by the provisions of the Unfair Contract Terms Act 1977. They are frequently included in the contract in which the customer instructs its bank to transfer an amount of money by means of a giro operation. This contract will usually include also a clause reserving the bank's right to act through a correspondent. But even in the absence of such a clause, the bank's right to use a correspondent has been recognized by the courts.[66] By and large, the payor's chances of holding his bank liable for the negligence of its correspondent are slim. In view of modern standard forms, he would have to prove that the bank had failed to exercise reasonable care and skill in choosing its correspondent. This is a formidable task.

It is important to note that the problems related to the transferring bank's liability for its correspondent arises only if the bank engages an entity other than its own overseas branch or office. The bank is, of course, liable to the payor for the negligence of any of its own branches and offices. The reason for this is obvious. Although the customer, the payor, is expected to make his demand at the branch with which he maintains his account,[67] his contractual relationship is with the bank, which, despite its numerous branches, has only one legal personality.[68]

The third principle concerning the bank's duty of care is that its obligation is owed only to a payor or transferor who is a customer. It will be recalled that, in certain cases, the transferring bank carries out a giro operation at the request of a member of the public who is not its customer. In acceding to his request, which normally involves the transfer of an amount paid in cash to the credit of a third party's account, the transferring bank acts in accordance with the spirit of the Golden Memorandum as embodied in the individual agreements made between the participating banks.[69] If the amount is paid by the payor to the credit of a customer of the bank which he approaches, the sum transferred is received on behalf of the payee. But if the money is to be transferred to the account of a customer of another bank, the position is unclear. Does the transferring bank act, for this specific transaction, as the agent of the payor or of the recipient bank? If it acts on behalf of the payor, it is subject to the duty of care owed by an agent to his princi-

---

[65] *Calico Printers' Association Ltd.* v. *Barclays Bank Ltd.* (1931) 36 Comm. Cas. 71; affd. do. 197, (1931) 145 LT 51.
[66] *Royal Products Ltd.* v. *Barclays Bank Ltd.* [1981] 2 Lloyd's Rep. 194, 197.
[67] P. 129 above.
[68] Pp. 81–84 above.
[69] P. 231 above.

pal. If it effects the transfer on behalf of the recipient, it owes no duty to the payor except that of acting honestly. It is believed that the better view is that, in cases of this type, the transferring bank has no contractual relationship with the payor. It has not accepted him as a customer, has received no consideration for effecting the transfer, and, above all, has no intention of entering into a contract with him. It accepts the money for transmission solely in order to comply with the spirit of the arrangement made in the Golden Memorandum. That document made it clear that the participating banks were acting as agents of each other, which would rule out their acting as agents for strangers wishing to utilize the system. It is believed that in cases of this type there is no privity of contract between the payor and the transferring bank.[70]

(v) Position of the correspondent bank

It will be recalled that the correspondent bank is employed only where the transferring bank is unable to transmit the funds directly to the recipient bank. As the correspondent is engaged by the transferring bank, there is no privity of contract between the correspondent and the payor. In *Calico Printers' Association* v. *Barclays Bank Ltd.*,[71] the plaintiffs engaged Barclays as their agent for the presentment of a bill of exchange, accompanied by commercial paper for goods, to the buyers. Barclays, in turn, engaged its correspondent, the AP Bank. As the bill was dishonoured, the plaintiffs ordered Barclays to arrange for the storing and insurance of the goods. This instruction was transmitted by Barclays to the AP Bank, which stored the goods but failed to insure them. When the goods were destroyed by fire, the plaintiffs sued the two banks for breach of contract and in negligence for their failure to adhere to their mandate. It was held that Barclays was not liable, as an exemption clause included in the contract between it and the plaintiffs exonerated it from liability for the negligence of its correspondents. The AP Bank was held not to be liable to the plaintiffs as there was no privity between them. Wright J observed that as a general rule there was no privity of contract between a principal and his agent's sub-agent. This ruling has been adopted by Webster J in *Royal Products Ltd.* v. *Midland Bank Ltd.*,[72] as regards the question of the

---

[70] For a different view, see Chorley, *Law of Banking*, 6th edn., pp. 277 et seq. Note further the possibility of liability in tort: cf. *London Borough of Bromley* v. *Ellis* [1971] 1 Lloyd's Rep. 97; *The Zephyr* [1984] 1 Lloyd's Rep. 58, revd. [1985] 2 Lloyd's Rep. 529. The question has to be examined in the light of the doctrine of *Hedley Byrne & Co.* v. *Heller and Partners Ltd.* [1964] AC 465.
[71] (1931) 36 Comm. Cas. 71; affd. do. 197, (1931) 145 LT 51.
[72] [1981] 2 Lloyd's Rep. 194, 198.

relationship of the issuer of a money transfer order (the payor) and his bank's correspondent.

The fact that under English law there is no privity between the payor and the transferring bank's correspondent should not, however, lull British banks that have offices abroad into a sense of safety. The point is illustrated by two American authorities. In the first, the transferor was held to have privity of contract with his bank's correspondent as the latter had been expressly selected by him.[73] In the second case, *Evra Corporation v. Swiss Bank Corporation,*[74] a rental was due under a charterparty at the Banque de Paris in Geneva at a predetermined time. The charterer ordered his bank in Chicago to effect the transfer. A telex message was duly transmitted by the London branch of the Chicago bank to its correspondent in Geneva, the defendants. Owing to the fact that the defendants' telex terminal in Geneva ran out of paper, the message was not received, although the terminal automatically acknowledged the message to the transferring bank's branch in London. When the breakdown was discovered, the time for the payment of the amount to the shipowner's bank, the Banque de Paris in Geneva, was over. The shipowner accordingly withdrew the ship. The charterer then brought an action against the correspondent bank, the defendants, in Illinois.

The United States District Court held that bank liable in damages for breach of contract and in negligence. It concluded, by an analogy from article 4 of the Uniform Commercial Code, that under the common law of the United States there was privity of contract between the charterer—the payor—and the defendants, his bank's Swiss correspondents. The same conclusion would undoubtedly have been reached if the correspondents had been a British bank. This decision was reversed by the Circuit Court of Appeals (Seventh Circuit), on the ground that the defendants, who had not been familiarized with the special circumstances of the case, were not liable for consequential loss. The loss sustained by the charterers as a result of the withdrawal of the ship was too remote. But the appellate court did not question the existence of privity between the charterers or transferors and the correspondent bank.

Although this decision may be questioned on the basis of considerations of private international law,[75] it constitutes a cause for alarm. The United States is not the only country in which a corrrespondent bank is deemed to have privity of contract with the customer of the bank by which it is engaged.

---

[73] *Silverstein* v. *Chartered Bank* , 392 NYS 2d 296 (1977).

[74] 522 F Supp. 820 (1981); revd. on another ground 673 F 2d 951 (1982). The decision of the District Court was followed in *Securities Fund Services Inc.* v. *American National Bank and Trust Co.*, 542 F Supp. 323 (1982).

[75] Was the alleged contract between the charterer and the correspondent governed by Swiss or by American law? The District Court accepted American law with impunity.

(vi) Position of the recipient bank

Unlike the transferring bank and the correspondent bank, whose legal functions are conceptually well defined, the recipient bank's position may vary from one giro operation to another. Thus, in direct debiting, the recipient bank acts as the payee's agent. It is true that when the payee initiates the direct debit operation he acts as the payor's agent. But when he selects the recipient bank and nominates the account into which payment is to be made, he consciously designates the receiving station at which he expects to obtain a payment due to him. Whilst the order to the transferring bank is executed by the payee of the direct debit in a representative capacity, he proposes to accept the payment involved in his own right. The recipient bank is designed as the payee's agent for that purpose.

By the same token, the recipient bank obtains the funds on behalf of the payee whenever the payor transfers the funds to the credit of an account designated by the payee. By way of illustration, take a case in which an employer pays a wage to the credit of a bank account nominated by the employee.

The position differs where the money transfer order is initiated by the payor without the express consent of the payee. Thus, a tenant may pay rent due under a lease to a bank with which he happens to know that his landlord maintains an account. In such a case, the recipient bank acts solely at the request of the payor or of the payor's agent—the transferring bank. The landlord is not obliged to accept payment of the rent by way of a money transfer order, or even by a cheque, but may insist on payment in 'legal tender', viz. cash. If the landlord does not reject the credit entry, he adopts the bank's act in accepting payment.

In some transactions it may be difficult to decide on whose behalf the recipient bank has been acting. Cases in which an attempt is made to pay an amount due out of time furnish an interesting example. Thus, a charterparty or a commercial lease frequently require payment by a definite date to the credit of a designated account of the payee with a given bank. The payee, who may wish to use a delay in payment as an excuse to withdraw the ship, may instruct his bank to reject any payment tendered after the stipulated date. Despite this instruction, the practice prevailing at the recipient bank may lead to a situation in which a payment made out of date is credited to the unwilling payee's account. Is it arguable that the amount accepted by the recipient bank in such a case is received by it as an agent of the transferring or of the correspondent bank, and that the crediting of the payee's account has been effected *per incuriam*? There is no direct authority in point. It is submitted that the answer depends on the payor's knowledge of the payee's attitude to the late payment. If the payor is unaware of the payee's intention to refuse payment, he is able to argue that the recipient bank has accepted payment under the ostensible or apparent authority conferred on it by the payee. If the payor is aware of the payee's order that the bank reject payment, this contention is untenable.[76]

It is fortunate that, in some types of money transfers, guidance is provided by the contracts made between the banks involved in the transaction. Thus, in SWIFT transfers, the master agreement between the banks participating in the network makes detailed provisions concerning the allocation of losses in cases of breakdowns and of improperly executed instructions. Where this is not so, the question has to be decided by reference to basic common law principles. *Evra Corporation* v. *Swiss Bank Corporation*,[77] discussed above, furnishes an interesting illustration of the type of problem that may arise. It will be recalled that in that case the breakdown in communications occurred when the telegraphic transfer was transmitted by telex to the faulty machine of the correspondent bank. Under the circumstances, it could not be argued that payment was received by the payee, the shipowner. But what would have been the position if the breakdown had taken place at the premises of the recipient bank, the Banque de Paris? Presumably, as that bank was nominated by the shipowner, it would be arguable that, by transferring the amount involved when due, the correspondent bank had rendered payment on time. In other words, it would then be arguable that the shipowner was precluded from denying timely payment, as the liability for the recipient bank's negligence was borne by himself.

Another question which has not come up for decision in the United Kingdom is whether the recipient bank owes a duty of care to the payor. The existence of such duty is not ruled out by the absence of privity between these two parties. An American authority illustrates the type of case which gives rise to this problem. In *Securities Fund Servicess Inc.* v. *American National Bank and Trust Co. of Chicago*,[78] an unknown person forged an instrument which misled a trustee into selling shares deposited with him, and into ordering his own bank (the transferring bank) to remit the proceeds to Account no. 204471 described as maintained with the recipient bank by J B. The latter bank accepted payment of the amount involved for the credit of Account no. 204471, although it was in the name of an entirely different person. Giving judgment for the transferor, Leighton DJ held that 'the loss of the transferred funds is the reasonably foreseeable result of a deposit made where the name on the transfer instructions differs from the name on the account into which the funds are deposited'.[79]

---

[76] The payor's position is analogous to that of a payee of a cheque who requests and obtains payment although he is aware that it has been countermanded; the amount is recoverable from him: pp. 317–9 below.

[77] 522 F Supp. 820 (1981) revd. on a different ground: 673 F 2d 951 (1982); p. 372 above.

[78] 542 F Supp. 323 (1982).

[79] Ibid., 327.

6. TIME OF PAYMENT AND COUNTERMAND

(i) Complexity of problem

The analysis of the legal relationships of the parties to money transfers does not furnish a decisive answer to the question of when the order is executed. An attractive argument is that the order is performed when payment is complete, in the sense that there is no longer room for a countermand. Unfortunately, this answer leads to circularity, as, on the same basis, payment is complete and a countermand precluded when the order is executed upon the receipt of the funds by the payee or his agent, the recipient bank. The object is to find a test for determining the moment at which the funds are so received. The difficulty is that, as shown above, the position of the recipient bank varies from transaction to transaction. This uncertainty means that it is impossible to give a general answer as to when a money transfer is complete. In each situation a number of factors have to be taken into account. First and foremost, it is essential to have regard to the nature of the money transfer operation involved. Thus, the moment at which a SWIFT transfer is complete may differ from the moment at which a telegraphic transfer is deemed to have been executed. Similarly, a transfer executed through BACS becomes irreversible at a time different from that at which a bank giro credit is completed. In some of these cases the master agreement between the banks determines the time at which an instruction to transfer becomes irrevocable.[80] This moment could, then, be regarded as the time of payment. In others, the analysis has to proceed on the basis of common law rules.

Secondly, the time of payment may depend on the number of parties involved in the transaction and on the role assumed by each of them. At the one end of the scale there is the in-house transfer, in which the payor and the payee maintain their accounts with the same branch of a given bank.[81] At the other end of the scale there is an international transfer involving up to five parties: the payor, the transferring bank, the correspondent bank, the recipient bank, and the payee. To these parties may be added the computer centre or transmission network, such as the CHAPS gateways, the Post Office in telegraphic transfers, and the SWIFT centres. It is conceivable that, although a specific instruction may be 'executed' as between two parties in the chain, it remains executory as regards some other party. An example is furnished by a telex dispatched by the transferring bank to its correspondent

---

[80] Thus, the American CHIPS master agreement provides that an order cannot be revoked after its release; however, the order is thereafter conveyed to the recipient bank within a few minutes. For an excellent analysis of this system, see *FDIC* v. *European American Bank and Trust Co.*, 576 F Supp. 950 (1983).

[81] If the transfer involves two branches of the same bank, it usually involves transmission through the bank's computer centre; payment is, thus, 'cleared'.

with a request that the funds be credited to the payee's account with the recipient bank. As between the transferring bank and the correspondent bank, the transaction may arguably be complete and executed when the correspondent dispatches its own message to the recipient bank. The payee, however, may not be regarded as having been 'paid' until the amount is credited to his account by the recipient bank.[82]

Thirdly, it is important to note that the answer to a problem of the type under discussion is influenced by the practical situation in which it arises. Thus, in cases in which the transferring bank wishes to stop payment, or to reverse a credit entry, the payee is likely to maintain that payment has been completed before the attempt to countermand is made.[83] If any question arose in such a case as regards the recipient bank's authority to obtain payment on behalf of the payee, the latter would proffer arguments supporting the validity of the mandate, including the plea that he had given his consent to the receipt of the amount involved in advance. The payee will take a different stand where a contract entitles him to invoke an attractive forfeiture clause if payment is out of time. In such a case the payee has an interest in disputing the recipient bank's authority to obtain payment on his behalf, and in raising arguments to the effect that payment was late. He might even attempt to establish that, although payment was complete as between the transferring bank and the recipient bank, it was revocable or reversible as between himself and the payor.

The courts are unlikely to suceed in developing a uniform rule for the determination of the time at which a money transfer is complete. In every case coming up for decision there are, basically, six points of time at which the payment may be regarded as executed.[84] The first is the time at which the payor's instruction is transmitted by the transferring bank. The second is the time at which the instruction reaches the recipient bank or its agent. The third is the time at which the recipient bank sets into motion the internal machinery for crediting the payee's account. The fourth is the time at which the payee's account is credited with the amount involved. The fifth is the time at which the payee is notified of the receipt of the funds. The sixth is the time at which the payee agrees to receive the amount involved, either expressly or by implication.

The case law in point, comprising mainly American and English authorities based on international transfers, is not easy to reconcile. This is not

---

[82]   For elaboration, see pp. 385–7 below.

[83]   For example, consider cases in which the payor dies or becomes bankrupt after the issuing of the payment order, whereupon the mandate to pay is determined: *Pool* v. *Pool* (1889) 58 LJ P 67 (death); *Drew* v. *Nunn* (1879) 4 QBD 661, 665–6 (bankruptcy). And see *Salton* v. *New Beeston Cycle Co.* [1900] 1 Ch. 43 (knowledge of revocation).

[84]   Cf. Penney and Baker, *Law of Electronic Fund Transfers*, pp. 24, 16–17, who suggest six similar points of time.

surprising, as the cases arose in respect of different methods of transfer and in different situations. It will be convenient to divide the cases into two groups: those dealing with attempts to countermand money transfer orders or to reverse payment, and those concerning the completion of payment before a specified deadline.

(ii) Cases involving countermand of payment and reversals of credit entries

Attempts to countermand money transfers, or to question their execution, arise in different circumstances. The earliest English decision in point is *Rekstin* v. *Severo Sibirsko Gosudarstvennoe Akcionernoe Obschestvo Komseverputj*.[85] A customer instructed his bank to transfer the total balance standing to his credit to an account maintained with the same branch by another customer. After the bank had effected the transfer by making the required ledger entries but before notification was given to the payee, a judgment creditor served a garnishee order nisi attaching the transferor's balance. It was held that, at the time the order nisi was served, the amount transferred was still accruing to the transferor. However, in reaching this decision Talbot J, in the Court of Appeal, emphasized that the transferor did not owe any debt to the transferee, and that there was nothing to indicate that the transferee had anticipated payment. As there was no evidence to establish the transferee's assent to the transfer of the amount involved, the bank could not be regarded as having the authority to hold the amount involved as a debt accrued to him. It is submitted that this decision, which favours the view that payment is incomplete until the transferee manifests his consent to the transfer of the funds, has a narrow scope of application. In most modern money transfers, where an amount is transmitted to the payee's account at his own request, the recipient bank is given the authority for the crediting of the payee's account by implication.

That the payee's readiness to accept payment can be inferred from circumstances preceding the execution of the money transfer can be demonstrated by two American authorities concerning remittances of funds from Japan made on the eve of the attack on Pearl Harbor. In *Singer* v. *Yokohama Specie Bank*,[86] the plaintiff, who was owed an amount of approximately $US557,561 by the Tokyo office of the YS Bank, instructed that the amount be remitted to him in the United States. The Tokyo office thereupon ordered its agency in New York to make such an amount available to the plaintiff. The agency notified the plaintiff and requested him to obtain the Treasury licence required to authorize the payment over of the funds. Before

---

[85] [1933] 1 KB 47.
[86] 47 NYS 2d 881 (1944); affd. 48 NYS 2d 799 (1944) but revd. 58 NE 2d 726 (1946). For further proceedings in the case, see 85 NE 2d 894 (1949).

this was granted, the agency was put into liquidation by the Alien Property Custodian. The Supreme Court of New York held that the amount involved had not accrued to the plaintiff at the time the agency was taken over. A recipient bank would be liable to the payee only 'upon its making an enforcible [sic] promise to pay the sum' involved.[87] A mere representation that funds were held at the payee's disposal was inconclusive, even if it was complemented by a permission to draw against the funds. The Appellate Division affirmed this judgment but it was reversed, on the point in question, by the New York Court of Appeals. It was held that the notification of the transfer to the plaintiff 'served to create an enforcible legal obligation by the New York Agency to make such payment'.[88]

This decision was followed by the New York Court of Appeals in *Guaranty Trust Co. of New York* v. *Lyon*,[89] in which the facts were similar, except that the funds were remitted to the payee at the order of a third party. It was held that the New York Agency of a Japanese bank—acting as the recipient of funds transferred from Tokyo—obtained the amount involved on behalf of the payee. When the payee was advised of the amount standing to his credit, the funds were available to him and payment was regarded as irreversible.

The two decisions of the New York Court of Appeals suggest that the transfer of the amount involved to the recipient bank, acting as the payee's agent, is tantamount to the receipt of the funds by the payee himself. The basic principles of the law of agency support this conclusion, provided the agent has acted within the scope of his authority in accepting payment. It can thus be argued that payment becomes complete and irrevocable at the moment it reaches the hand of the agent (the recipient bank). Unfortunately, it is not always clear at which point of time the recipient bank makes its decision to accept the amount involved on the payee's behalf.

The importance of determining the moment at which payment is accrued to the payee is demonstrated by the leading English decision in point, *Momm* v. *Barclays Bank International Ltd.*[90] On 26 June 1974, the defendant bank received a telex instruction from one of its customers, the Herstatt Bank of Frankfurt, to credit the account of the plaintiff, another customer of the same branch, with an amount of £120,000. Although Herstatt's account did not have an adequate credit balance, the assistant manager decided to credit the plaintiff's account. The necessary forms were accordingly prepared and processed forthwith by the defendant bank's computer operators. Later in the day Herstatt suspended payment. On the next day the defendant bank

---

[87] 47 NYS 2d, 882.
[88] 58 NE 2d, 728.
[89] 124 NYS 2d 680 (1953).
[90] [1977] QB 790, sub nom. *Delbrueck* v. *Barclays Bank International Ltd.* [1976] 2 Lloyd's Rep. 341.

reversed the credit entry which had appeared in the plaintiff's account. The plaintiff, who was notified neither of the credit entry nor of its reversal, discovered the facts through a perusal of the defendant bank's books. He thereupon brought an action for a declaration that his account had been wrongfully debited on 27 June. Giving judgment for the plaintiff, Kerr J observed:[91]

The issue is whether or not a completed payment had been made by the defendants to the plaintiffs on June 26. This is a question of law. If the answer is 'Yes,' it is not contested that the plaintiffs have a good cause of action. If there were no authorities on this point, I think that the reaction, both of a lawyer and a banker, would be to answer this question in the affirmative. I think that both would say two things. First, that in such circumstances a payment has been made if the payee's account is credited with the payment at the close of business on the value date, at any rate if it was credited intentionally and in good faith and not by error or fraud. Secondly, I think that they would say that if a payment requires to be made on a certain day by debiting a payor customer's account and crediting a payee customer's account, then the position at the end of that day in fact and in law must be that this has either happened or not happened, but that the position cannot be left in the air. In my view both these propositions are correct in law.

His Lordship distinguished *Rekstin*'s case as having been decided on its special facts. It is noteworthy that Kerr J treated the credit entry in the plaintiff's account with the defendant bank as a final settlement, or payment, although there was no proof that the plaintiff had authorized the defendant bank to receive payment. His Lordship emphasized that the payment would be final only if it stood undisturbed at the end of the 'value date', which is the date on which funds are to be made available to the payee. Presumably an entry is not to be considered as final before the close of the day in question, as the bank can correct errors or reverse payment until then.

Herstatt's collapse also led to litigation concerning money transfers in the United States. In *Delbrueck & Co.* v. *Manufacturers Hanover Trust Co.*,[92] the plaintiffs, a German bank which maintained an account with the defendant bank in the United States, entered into exchange contracts with Herstatt. An amount of $US12.5 million was payable by the plaintiffs to Herstatt under these contracts on 26 June. On 25 June the plaintiffs sent a telex message to the defendant bank requesting it to credit Herstatt's account with the Chase Manhattan Bank with the amount involved. At 10.30 a.m. on 26 June (at Eastern Standard Time prevailing in New York), Herstatt was closed down by the German Reserve Bank. At approximately 11.40 a.m. the defendant bank transferred to Chase the amount of $12.5 million, by using the American CHIPS system. Within the next thirty

---

[91] Ibid., 799–800.
[92] 609 F 2d 1047 (1979), affirming 464 F Supp. 989 (1979).

minutes the plaintiffs called the defendant bank in order to stop this payment, and immediately thereafter confirmed the countermand by telex. At 9.00 p.m. on the same day, Herstatt's account with Chase was formally credited with the amount involved.

The plaintiffs based their action on negligence. They claimed that the defendant bank committed a breach of a duty of care when it failed to act on the countermand order, given to it at 11.40 a.m., in the course of the remaining business hours of 26 June. The District Court dismissed this action and its decision was affirmed by the Second Circuit Court of Appeals. Moore J reviewed the technology involved in CHIPS transfers, pointing out that a transfer executed through this autonomous network invariably reached the recipient bank almost as soon as it was released or executed by the computer terminal of the transferring bank. It was the understanding of all the banks participating in the system that funds transferred by means of CHIPS could be drawn upon by the payee as soon as the electronic message was received by the recipient bank. His Honour concluded accordingly that the transfer of funds to the credit of Herstatt's account was complete as soon as it was effected by the defendant bank. The fact that the credit was not entered in Herstatt's account until 9.00 p.m. on 26 June was merely a matter of bookkeeping and hence irrelevant. Moore J observed:[93]

Based on the nature of the CHIPS system, and the fact that the member banks viewed the transactions as irrevocable . . . we hold that the CHIPS transfers were irrevocable when made.

For this reason, the defendant bank had not acted negligently when it failed to revoke the transfer of the funds to Chase. Moore J, therefore, held that a money transfer executed by means of CHIPS could not be revoked or stopped once it was set into transmission by an electronic message executed on the 'value date'. His Honour further concluded that Herstatt's bankruptcy did not revoke Chase's mandate to receive funds on its behalf.[94]

At first glance there appears to be an inconsistency between the English decision and its American counterpart. Kerr J held that payment became irrevocable at the close of the value date. Moore J thought that payment was complete, and hence irreversible, when executed by means of a CHIPS transfer. The distinction between the two conclusions, however, is explainable by the difference in the respective methods of transfer employed in the two cases and by the banking practices related thereto. Kerr J based his decision on the finding that banking practice related to in-house transfers made provision for a reversal of entries on the day of execution. Moore J

---

[93] Ibid., 1051. For a full description of CHIPS, see the decision of the District Court, 464 F Supp., p. 992.

[94] Note that Moore J further supported his decision by invoking the law of assignment of debt; see on this point pp. 366–8 above.

gave effect to the practice developed in respect of CHIPS transfers, which precluded revocation once the transfer was 'released' by the computer terminal of the transferring bank. It is, therefore, arguable that as regards the question of countermand both cases support the view that the position is governed by banking practice rather than by an abstract application of legal principles. Obviously, the position may vary from transaction to transaction depending on the technology used for transfer.

The importance of banking practice in respect of money transfers is further illustrated by the most recent authority in point, *Royal Products Ltd. v. Midland Bank Ltd.*[95] The plaintiffs, Maltese merchants, maintained their account in the United Kingdom with the defendant bank. In Malta they had two current accounts: one with the B Bank, and the other with the N Bank. The plaintiffs, who wished to transfer an amount of £13,000 from their account with the defendant bank to the credit of their account with the N Bank, were deterred from ordering a direct transfer by the high banking charges of the N Bank. The plaintiffs therefore ordered the defendant bank to remit the amount involved to the credit of their account with the B Bank, intending to complete the cycle by eventually remitting the amount involved from the B Bank to the N Bank.

The plaintiffs issued their instruction to the defendant bank on 23 November 1972. On the same day, the defendant bank sent a telex message instructing its correspondent in Malta, which by sheer coincidence happened to be the N Bank, to credit the amount in question to the plaintiff's account with the B Bank. The N Bank received the telex on 24 November. Usually the N Bank would have completed the transfer by delivering a bankers' payment to the B Bank. But as there were rumours on the morning of the day in question that the B Bank was facing liquidity problems, the N Bank departed from this procedure and credited the amount involved to a suspense account opened by it in the B Bank's name. The N Bank, which recognized that the plaintiffs were its own customers and was aware that the ultimate destination of the funds was the plaintiffs' account with the N Bank itself, contacted the plaintiffs and suggested that the funds be diverted directly to the credit of this account. However, as the N Bank did not disclose its reasons for making this suggestion, the plaintiffs mistook that bank's motives, and insisted that the amount be transferred as instructed. On the evening of 24 November it was thought that the B Bank had overcome its financial crisis. On the same evening, or possibly on the morning of 25 November, the N Bank notified the B Bank, by means of a credit note, that it had passed a remittance for the amount involved to the credit of the plaintiffs' account.

On the morning of 25 November, the B Bank was forced to suspend operations and, in due course, was put into liquidation. As general creditors, the plaintiffs were unable to recover any part of the amount involved. Initially they instituted proceedings against the N Bank in Malta, based on breach of contract and on negligence. When this action failed, the plaintiffs attempted to recover their loss from the defendant bank in the United Kingdom.

The plaintiffs based their action on two main contentions. The first was that their instruction for the transfer of the funds to the credit of their account with the B Bank had not been carried out. The defendant bank in the United Kingdom was therefore bound to reimburse the amount involved and, if necessary, had to do so by revoking its instruction to the B Bank. In support of this point, the plaintiffs argued that on 28 November—which was well after the dispatch of the N Bank's order to the B Bank—they had instructed the N Bank to divert the funds to the credit of the plaintiffs' account with itself. The plaintiffs' second contention was that the N Bank had been negligent in effecting payment to the credit of their account with the B Bank. To start with, the N Bank should have warned the plaintiffs, its customers, of the rumours concerning the B Bank's shaky financial position. In addition, it was argued that the N Bank's knowledge of the true circumstances of the transaction imposed on it a fiduciary duty. The defendant bank, it was argued, was vicariously liable for these breaches.

Webster J gave judgment for the defendant bank. His Lordship held that the defendant bank was entitled to use the services of a correspondent to effect the transfer ordered by the plaintiffs. His Lordship conceded that the defendant bank owed the plaintiffs a duty of care and skill in choosing the correspondent involved, and that the defendant bank was vicariously liable for any negligence committed by the correspondent. The sub-agent himself—the N Bank—had no privity of contract in respect of the instant transaction with the 'payor', the plaintiffs.

His Lordship then examined the transfer. Explaining its legal nature and the manner in which it was carried out, his Lordship observed that a recipient bank, such as the B Bank, was

impliedly authorized by the customer to accept that credit by virtue of the fact that the customer [had] a current account with it, no consent to the receipt of the credit being expected from or required of the same bank, by virtue of the same fact.[96]

Webster J concluded on this basis that there was no need for an express consent by the B Bank to the transfer ordered by the plaintiffs.

Having made these preliminary findings, Webster J turned to the main issues of the case: the time of payment and the bank's duty of care. He concluded that three events had to take place before payment was complete. First, the B Bank had to be put in a position where it was entitled to draw on

[96] Ibid., 198.

the funds made available for transmission to the plaintiffs' account. Secondly, the B Bank had to be informed that the funds were to be made available to the plaintiffs. Thirdly, the transfer was complete even before the payees, the plaintiffs, were notified that the funds had been credited to their account. Here the B Bank obtained definite notice that the funds were available to it for drawing when it obtained the payment order on the evening of 24 November (or early on the morning of 25 November). The transfer was then complete. In determining the time at which the B Bank was deemed to have received the necessary notification, his Lordship relied on the course of dealings used by reputable banks.

On the other issue, his Lordship held that the N Bank had not been in breach of a duty of care in carrying out the instruction to transfer the amount involved to the credit of the plaintiffs' account with the B Bank. The N Bank was precluded, by a duty of secrecy owed to the B Bank, from disclosing to the plaintiffs the disturbing information received by it. Moreover, there was, in his Lordship's opinion, no evidence to show that transfer should have been delayed or refused. The plaintiffs 'called no evidence to the effect that a reasonably competent bank in the position of [the N Bank], with the information that it had received . . . would or should, as a result of any such doubts, have refrained from passing the credit to [the B Bank] or, indeed, that it would have been entitled to have done so'.[97] The instruction to transfer had to be completed on the day following its receipt, and the N Bank was entitled to act accordingly. His Lordship further mentioned that, in carrying out the instruction to transfer, the N Bank was acting at the order of the defendant bank. Being thus the agent of the defendant bank for the purposes of this specific transaction, the N Bank was not in breach of a duty, arising under its general contract of banker and customer with the plaintiffs, in executing the transfer in question.

Webster J thus concluded that the plaintiffs' order to reverse payment was issued after the transfer of the funds had been completed. The execution of the order in question did not involve any negligence on the part of the N Bank; the question of the defendant bank's vicarious liability therefore did not arise. It is clear that Webster J reached his conclusion by relying on the banking practice prevailing in respect of the type of money transfers involved. His Lordship analysed the legal nature of the operation in the following words.[98]

the remittance made was not a remittance of a distinct fund lodged with the [defendant bank] but was a transfer of part of the amount standing to the credit of [the plaintiffs'] account with [the defendant bank], that is to say of a fund which, in ordinary banking practice, is treated not as the customer's money but as money lent by the customer to the bank which the bank may use in any way it chooses.

[97] Ibid., 205.
[98] Ibid., 209–10.

This analysis led his Lordship to the conclusion that the amount paid by the N Bank into the suspense account opened by it prior to the dispatch of the payment order to the B Bank was not the plaintiffs' money but that of the defendant bank. In the instant case, this conclusion did not lead to any major consequence as regards the judgment delivered. It may, however, be of importance in cases in which a transferor, who finds himself in a position similar to that of the present plaintiffs, attempts to obtain a tracing order.

The conclusion to be derived from the two cases resulting from Herstatt's collapse and from the case involving the banks in Malta is that a money transfer is complete when the funds are made available to the recipient bank on behalf of the payee. All three decisions took into account the respective banking practice. As the question of countermand is primarily one that arises between the payor and his bank, or between the payee and the recipient bank, the emphasis on banking practice is understandable. The decision of the Circuit Court of Appeals in *Dulbrueck* is the most important authority in point. It is to be expected that further cases of this type will arise in due course.

(iii) Cases involving payments out of time

Cases of this type arise under different types of contract. A good example is an agreement under which a forfeiture clause can be invoked if payment is not rendered by a given date. Generally speaking, such clauses are included in contracts in which time is made the essence. To date all the cases in point concerned withdrawals by shipowners of vessels on the ground that a rental due from a charterer was paid out of time.

In cases of this type the question relates, in essence, to the contract between the payor and the payee. As pointed out above, different considerations may be applicable in determining what constitutes due or timely payment in this type of case from considerations in respect of disputes concerning the contract of banker and customer. The basic rule was formulated by the Court of Appeal in '*The Brimnes*'.[99] Here it was held that, to determine whether an amount due under a charterparty was paid on time, an analogy had to be drawn from cases concerning the question of when payment was complete if made in cash. Edmund-Davies LJ concluded:[100]

The owners' contention, however, that the tendering of the commercial equivalent of cash would suffice found favour with Brandon J [the trial Judge]. In particular, he concluded that any transfer of funds to [the recipient bank] for the credit of the owners' account so as to give them the unconditional right to the immediate use of the funds transferred was good payment. In my judgment, that was clearly right . . .

---

[99] *Tenax Steamship Co. Ltd* v. *Brimnes (Owners of)* ('*The Brimnes*') [1975] QB 929.
[100] Ibid., 948.

Megaw LJ, who delivered a concurring judgment, said that payment by means of a credit entry was complete when the creditor was bound to treat it as the equivalent of cash, in the sense that he was able to draw on the balance accrued.

Unfortunately, it is not always easy to determine the time at which the credit balance, entered in the payee's account, becomes the equivalent of cash. Thus, in *Mardorf Peach & Co. Ltd.* v. *Attica Sea Carriers Corporation of Liberia (The 'Laconia')*,[101] the recipient bank received a telex message requiring it to credit the shipowners' account with an amount due under the charterparty. This telex was received at the recipient bank's centre after the date appointed in the charterparty but shortly before the bank was given an instruction by the shipowners to refuse late payment. The bank commenced taking the steps required for the crediting of the shipowners' account with the amount remitted, but, on receiving the instruction to refuse payment, it refunded the amount to the transferring bank before executing the actual entry. One of the questions in the case was whether the transfer of funds to the recipient bank had the effect of completing the payment due from the charterer. Giving judgment for the shipowners, the House of Lords held that the transfer had not been completed before the amount was refunded, as the recipient bank had not taken a conscious decision to accept payment. The steps taken by it for processing the telegraphic transfer were purely provisional and procedural.

If this reasoning were to be applied to giro operations in general, it would lead to the conclusion that the recipient bank has an opportunity to reject payment, if ordered to do so by the payee, within a reasonable time. But once the amount has been credited, the payee has obtained payment, as he is then free to draw on the accrued balance. It is arguable that if the payee has ordered his bank, in advance, to reject a late payment, then the bank acts outside the scope of its actual authority in receiving it thereafter.

The 'Laconia' was explained recently by the House of Lords in *'The Chikuma'*.[102] In this case a rental was due in Rome, on 22 January 1976. On the preceding day the charterers instructed their bank to remit the funds. By a telex message, dispatched on the due date, the transferring bank remitted the funds to the recipient bank. The amount was received on the same day, but it was noted that the 'value date' was shown as Monday 26 January. Under Italian law the funds became available to the shipowners on 22 January, although interest was to accrue only as from the value date of

---

[101] [1977] AC 850, questioning on this point *Astro Amo Compania Naviera SA* v. *Elf Union SA ('The Zographia M')* [1976] 2 Lloyd's Rep. 382; and overruling *Empresa Cubana de Fletes* v. *Lagonisi Shippint Co. Ltd. ('The Georgios C.')* [1971] 1 QB 488. For the basic rule, see *Tankexpress A/S* v. *Compagnie Financière Belge de Pétroles SA* [1949] AC 76.

[102] *A/S Awilco of Oslo* v. *Fulvia SpA di Navigazione of Cagliari ('The Chikuma')* [1981] 1 WLR 314.

26 January. Thus, if the shipowners had withdrawn the amount on the day of transfer they would have probably incurred interest to the bank for the period of four days ending 26 November. On 23 January the shipowners, who decided to treat this remittance as being out of date, instructed their Italian bank to reject payment.

Giving judgment for the shipowners, Lord Bridge conceded that 'payment' in the context of money transfers encompassed settlement not only by legal tender but also by means of final credit entries. Broadly speaking, payment was effected when the transferee—or payee—had the unconditional use of the amount settled by means of the ledger entry. His Lordship stressed that, although payment by legal tender was not expected in cases of this type, the payee was entitled to expect the full equivalent of it. An amount which could not be used for investment purposes, e.g. for obtaining interest on it, was not the equivalent of cash. His Lordship said:[103]

The book entry made by the owners' bank on January 22 in the owners' account was clearly not the equivalent of cash, nor was there any reason why the owners should have been prepared to treat it as the equivalent of cash. It could not be used to earn interest, e.g. by immediate transfer to a deposit account. It could only be drawn subject to a (probable) liability to pay interest. In substance it was the equivalent of an overdraft facility which the bank was bound to make available.

On this basis the amount remitted could not be regarded as the equivalent of cash as the payees—the shipowners—did not have the unconditional use of it on the due date.

Lord Bridge's judgment has been forcefully criticized by Dr Mann[104] on the ground that the case should have been regarded as governed by English law, under which the funds would have accrued to the shipowners unconditionally when credited to their account. In his opinion the 'value date' would have been irrelevant under English banking law and practice. It is believed that this criticism is unfounded. Even if the case were decided on the basis of English law, the payment should not have been regarded as equal to cash. The reason for this is that the majority of English banks would regard the stipulation of a 'value date' in a money transfer order as an indication that the payee's account ought not to be credited before that date. Thus, it is believed that, under the prevailing English banking practice, the amount in question would not have been entered in the shipowners' account until 26 January. This would, without a shred of doubt, have been payment out of time. Any earlier crediting of the amount involved to the credit of the shipowner would have been coupled, in English banking practice, with an indication that the amount might not be drawn upon before the date in

---

[103]   Ibid., 320.
[104]   F. A. Mann, 'Uncertain Certainty' (1981) 97 *LQR* 379.

question, although most banks would have followed the simpler practice of entering the amount in a suspense account until 26 January.

In summary, it is arguable that the cases decided on the point in question emphasize the need to make the funds available to the payee by the stipulated date. They are so available only if the payee can utilize them without any restrictions as if they constituted amounts in cash.

(iv) Comparison of the two types of case

The cases concerning the payor's attempt to countermand a money transfer order have to be regarded as distinct from the cases concerning the payment of money within a due date stipulated in a contract between the payor and the payee. In the former type of case, the authorities suggest that there is no room for countermand of payment, or for reversal of entries, once the funds have been made available to the recipient bank and that bank has agreed, expressly or impliedly, to receive payment thereof. A key to the determination of the issue involved is to be found in prevailing banking practice. This is understandable, as the litigation invariably involves one of the banks participating in the money transfer operation. On this basis, it is realistic to suggest that the practice developed over the years in the banking community furnishes the necessary clues regarding the payor's right to countermand payment or to demand a reversal of entries. Undoubtedly, the courts use as an analogy the completion of the clearing cycle of cheques which, it will be recalled, is determined exclusively by banking practice.

In the second type of case, the parties are the payor and the payee. Here the question is one of the discharge by a commercial firm of a contractual obligation. The analogy must therefore be taken from cases determining the time at which payment by cash or by legal tender is complete between the payor and payee.

This demarcation has led to an interesting difference in the basic principles applicable in the two types of case. Between the banks, or between a bank and one of its customers, the transfer is complete when the credit balance is irrevocably available to the recipient bank. Between payor and payee, payment is complete when it stands to the unconditional order of the payee. It remains to be seen if the House of Lords will eventually be able to find a general principle applicable to all the cases in point.

7. CONFIDENTIALITY OF INFORMATION

Computer centres, such as BACS or SWIFT acquire in the course of their operations a great deal of information respecting the customers of the participating banks. This is so regardless of whether the information is obtained from a tape or message initiated by the cutomer himself, as is the case in some BACS transactions, or from tapes or messages transmitted by the banks. The data or computer department of the bank, too, has access to information recorded on each customer.

In the United Kingdom, information or data of this type is rendered confidential by the Data Protection Act 1984, passed in part to give effect to the Council of Europe Data Protection Convention.[105] The Act makes provision for the appointment of a Registrar of Data Protection, with whom 'data users' and 'computer bureaus' have to register.[106] In this book, there is room only for a few general observations concerning the Act and its effect.

The definition of data in section 1(2) covers the type of information or details stored by the computer departments of banks and by such organizations as BACS. The bank's computer centre, and hence the bank itself, is a 'data user' within the meaning of section 1(5). BACS, which provides others with services respecting data stored by it, is a 'computer bureau' within the meaning of section 1(6). The customers about whom the information is stored are 'data subjects'.

The Act has two basic provisions concerning confidentiality. Under section 5(2), a person who is registered either as a data user or as both a data user and a computer bureau is precluded from disclosing any data held by him to any person who is not described in the relevant entry. It is presumed that entries made in respect of banks and such centres as BACS will describe other banks and participants in the respective clearing systems as persons to whom disclosure may be made in the course of ordinary operations.

The second provision concerning confidentiality, which applies only to data relating to living individuals ('personal data', as defined in section 1(3)), is section 15. It precludes a computer centre from disclosing any such data except with the prior authority of the person for whom the data is provided. The reference would appear to be to the banks or other data users that require the bureau to process the information. Disclosure may of course be made to servants or agents who carry out the relevant transactions.

In view of the detailed rules concerning bank secrecy, discussed in Chapter 4, the new Act is unlikely to affect the duties of a bank towards its customer. Furthermore, section 43(5)–(6) makes specific exemptions which are broadly similar to those discussed in respect of bank secrecy. Thus, disclosure of data may be sanctioned by a court order and is allowed where the data subject has consented to it. The importance of the Act as regards banking law is that it precludes organizations such as BACS, with whom an individual bank's customer does not have privity of contract, from disclosing information concerning him.

---

[105] And see 'Data Protection—The Government's Proposals for Legislation', Cmnd. 8539.
[106] As regards commencement, see s. 42(1) of the 1984 Act and the Data Protection Act 1984 (Appointed Day) Order 1985, SI 1055 and the Data Protection Tribunal Rules 1985, SI 1568.

CHAPTER 13

Credit Tokens

1. AVAILABLE TOKENS REVIEWED AND CLASSIFIED

Credit tokens are widely used in various types of transaction. The oldest form is a token which a department store or chain of petrol stations supplies to its clients to enable them to obtain goods or services against its production. In such a bipartite arrangement the card is used to charge the client's account with the issuer.[1] At present, these cards have been largely replaced by modern tokens. These fall into four groups.

First and foremost is the 'credit card' issued by a bank or financial institution. The card-holder can utilize it to purchase goods or to acquire services from dealers who display the issuer's insignia. The dealer supplies the relevant items against a docket, in which the card-holder authorizes the issuer to debit his account with the amount due. The dealer thus receives payment from the issuer, who obtains reimbursement from the card-holder. Settlement by the card-holder may be made either when the account is submitted, in which case he does not incur a finance charge, or by instalments, each of which must be not less than a given percentage of the balance outstanding at the time of payment. Where payment is made by instalments, interest is charged on the balance due at the end of each billing cycle (usually a calendar month).[2]

The second card—frequently described as a T & E (Travelling and Entertainment) card—is a variant of the credit card. The procedure for its use is the same as that described, except that the holder is expected to settle promptly each account submitted to him by the issuer. Such a card, which is also known as a charge card, differs from the orthodox credit card in that the holder is not expressly granted credit facilities.[3]

The third type of token is the 'cheque card' or the 'cheque guarantee card'. In such a card the issuer, who is usually a clearing bank, undertakes to pay cheques drawn by the customer, provided certain conditions are complied with.[4] Cheque cards differ from credit cards in that

---

[1] For an excellent historical review, see E. E. Bergsten, 'Credit Cards—A Prelude to a Cashless Society', (1967) 8 BC Ind. & Com. L Rev. 485.

[2] Access and Barclaycard fall into this group.

[3] Diners' Club and American Express issue such cards.

[4] Ordinary cheque cards are used for cheques drawn within the United Kingdom. Where a customer requires a card for use abroad, he is issued a Eurocheque card, which guarantees the payment of cheques drawn within Europe.

the issuer undertakes to honour a negotiable instrument drawn by its customer, rather than to pay for his purchases or to reimburse advances made to him.

The last type of token is the 'cashpoint' card, which is used by the customer in order to obtain cash from automated teller machines. The token can, further, be used to make a balance enquiry and, in the case of some banks, for paying cheques to the credit of their customers' accounts. Cashpoint cards differ from the other three types of token in one important respect. In credit, charge and cheque cards any transaction between the card-holder and the third party is evidenced by a document or docket. Authentication is based on the comparison of the card-holder's signature on the relevant paper with the signature placed by him on a space provided for this purpose in the card. He may, further, be asked to produce an identification. In the case of cashpoint tokens, the customer identifies himself by typing a number, disclosed only to himself and known as the 'personal identification number' (PIN), on the keyboard of the terminal. The entire operation is, therefore, carried out through the machine.[5]

Despite the differences between the four types of token, there is a similarity in the practical problems arising in all of them. Disputes concern, basically, questions of liability for the misuse of the card by unauthorized persons, especially where the card-holder fails to notify the issuer of its loss or conversion. Another problem, which is likely to arise eventually, concerns the dealer's right to enforce his claim against the issuer of one of the first three types of card in cases of its misuse by the holder. In the case of cashpoint cards, which involve bipartite arrangements, the last problem is inapplicable.

Two additional problems arise in respect of all four types of token. The first is the card-holder's criminal liability for the abuse of the token by excessive drawings or purchases. In credit, T & E, and cheque cards, this type of problem arises where an extravagant holder refuses to return a card for cancellation and embarks on a shopping spree. With cashpoint cards, such a case manifests itself only in extreme situations, where a holder who is aware of the delay in the sifting of information by the computer centre, withdraws excessive amounts by relying on a recorded credit balance which he knows to be out of date. The second, and particularly complex, problem is the application to all four types of token of the consumer credit legislation. The discussion of these two subjects follows that of the analysis of the four types of card.

---

[5] Cashpoint cards are issued by the clearers, although one building society—the Halifax—has also introduced a card. Further initiatives by building societies are contemplated. It is further expected that some banks will unite their networks of teller machines.

2. TRIPARTITE CREDIT TOKENS

A credit card transaction involves three contracts. First is the contract between the issuer and the card-holder. Basically, the issuer undertakes to pay for the purchases made by the card-holder within a specified credit limit. A wrongful refusal by the issuer to stand by this promise would thus constitute a breach of this contract. The issuer further agrees to the settlement of the amounts outstanding from time to time by minimum payments to be made upon the presentation to the holder of each monthly statement. The holder agrees to reimburse the issuer in the prescribed manner, and undertakes to pay the applicable credit charge.

It will be shown that the agreement between the issuer and the card-holder usually constitutes a regulated credit agreement within the meaning of the Consumer Credit Act 1974. The card itself is a credit token as defined. In terms of general common law principles, the contract resembles that made between a bank and the applicant for a traveller's letter of credit. In such a transaction, the customer requests the bank to issue to him a letter of credit in which correspondents are invited to provide him with cash on the strength of the bank's promise to reimburse. The contract involves the extension of credit by the bank (issuer); the customer undertakes to reimburse it and to pay the agreed charge.[6]

The second contract is between the issuer and the dealer. It is based on a master agreement in which the issuer agrees to pay to the dealer amounts due from card-holders, provided the goods or services are supplied on the agreed terms. Basically, this means that the dealer cannot supply goods or services without making a credit enquiry if the price exceeds a given figure. The dealer is, further, expected to compare the signature appearing on the sale docket with the holder's signature on the card. The issuer obtains an agreed percentage of each amount paid under the card as a consideration for the service rendered to the dealer.

It has been suggested that the transaction is to be regarded as an assignment by the dealer to the issuer of the amount due from the card-holder. This analysis is unacceptable as the dealer supplies the goods or services to the card-holder with a view to obtaining payment from the issuer. The debt, therefore, is due in the first instance from the issuer and not from the card-holder.[7] The better view is that the issuer makes a direct promise of reim-

---

[6] As regards travellers' letters of credit, see *Benjamin's Sale of Goods*, 2nd edn., London, 1981, para. 2142. And see R. M. Goode, *Consumer Credit Legislation*, London, looseleaf, para. 828.2, who compares the transaction with a documentary credit.

[7] Bergsten, 'Credit Cards', pp. 511 et seq.; W. B. Davenport, 'Bank Credit Cards and the Uniform Commercial Code', (1968) 85 Banking LJ 941, 961; R. E. Brandel and C. A. Leonard, 'Bank Charge Cards: New Cash or New Credit', (1971) 69 Mich. L Rev. 1033, 1047–9; R. A. Reiter, 'Bank Credit Cards and Enterprise Liability', (1973) 21 UCLA L Rev. 278.

bursement to the dealer in their master agreement.[8] The issuer's promise to the dealer is thus similar to that made by a bank in a traveller's letter of credit.

The third agreement is between the dealer and the card-holder. This agreement remains a contract of sale or a contract for the provision of a service, although payment is expected from the issuer. A difficult question arises in respect of this contract where the issuer becomes insolvent. Is the dealer's only right to lodge a proof for the amounts outstanding or can he demand payment from the card-holder? The answer depends on whether the docket, signed by the card-holder, constitutes absolute or conditional payment of the amount for which it is made out.

Cases decided in respect of letters of credit suggest that the docket constitutes a conditional discharge, and that the card-holder remains liable to pay the price of the goods to the dealer upon the issuer's insolvency.[9] But this analogy was rejected recently by Millett J. in *Re Charge Card Services Ltd.*[10] His Lordship held that the contract between a card-holder and a dealer was distinguishable from the contract of sale stipulating for the furnishing of a banker's documentary credit covering the price of the goods. The buyer, who effected the documentary credit, had the right to select the issuing bank. He could therefore be expected to bear the loss if the bank chosen by him became insolvent and, consequently, defaulted. By way of contrast, in cases involving credit cards, the parties agree that a specified procedure, namely payment by the specified issuer, is a valid means for the discharge of the debt incurred by the card-holder. When the card is used to effect payment, the dealer agrees to accept the docket in lieu of the holder's personal payment obligation. The parties further agree that the docket signed by the card-holder is furnished to the dealer in full discharge of the amount for which it is made out.

The contract between the card-holder and the dealer does not require further consideration. The rights of the card-holder and the issuer are, at present, predominantly governed by the Consumer Credit Act 1974. It will be shown that the Act makes provisions concerning the vexed question of liability for the misuse of the card by a stranger. The Act also governs questions such as the acceptance of the card by the holder, its cancellation, and the supply of information by the issuer. The Act, further, renders the issuer liable to the holder for certain acts and representations of the dealer.[11] The

---

[8] And see the analysis of Lord Diplock in *Metropolitan Police Commissioner* v. *Charles* [1977] AC 177, 182, which, though concerning a cheque card case, appears applicable also in the context of credit cards. And see A. P. Dobson, 'Credit Cards', [1979] JBL 331.

[9] See, e.g., *Sale Continuation Ltd.* v. *Austin Taylor & Co. Ltd.* [1968] 2 QB 849; *W. J. Alan & Co. Ltd.* v. *El Nasr Export and Import Co.* [1972] 2 QB 189, 212; *Maran Road Saw Mill* v. *Austin Taylor & Co. Ltd.* [1975] 1 Lloyd's Rep. 156, 159, noted in (1977) 40 MLR 91.

[10] [1986] 3 All ER 289.

[11] See below, pp. 408 et seq.

delivery of unsolicited cards is prohibited. One question which is not covered by the Act is the holder's power to countermand a payment instruction issued by him to the issuer. The problem is discussed in the context of T & E cards, which in certain cases fall outside the ambit of the Act.

There is a dearth of authority concerning the contract between the issuer and the dealer. It is clear that, in the master agreement, the issuer undertakes to pay the amount accrued on sale dockets less a given percentage. The issuer is under a duty to perform this promise even if the card-holder absconds or fails. Indeed, the object of the transaction is to enable the holder to obtain goods and services on the issuer's credit.

Two problems might eventually come up for decision. The first concerns the issuer's liability where a dealer supplies goods or services to an imposter, who has converted the token and forged the true holder's signature on the docket. The second concerns the issuer's liability to reimburse the dealer where the card has been used by the holder (or by an impostor) for a purpose other than that contemplated by the parties. For example, would the issuer be liable to reimburse an appointed restaurant which made a cash advance to the holder or sold him a second-hand radio? As the answers to both problems depend on the application of common law principles, they are discussed in the context of T & E cards.

3. T & E CARDS

Certain T & E (or 'charge') cards are outside the ambit of the Consumer Credit Act 1974. The rights of the parties to such T & E cards are governed by common law principles.[12] As there is a dearth of authority in point in English law, reference is made to some American decisions. Most of these are from the 1960s, as cases decided later on are usually based on the provisions of statutory law which is not *in pari materia* with the applicable common law.[13]

As between issuer and card-holder, the principal problem has always been that of responsibility for loss resulting from the misuse of the card by a third party. Cases of this type occur where the card is stolen and the holder fails to notify the issuer, or where a member of his household or business surreptitiously uses the token without his knowledge. An early American

[12] Although even in such cases there is an argument that the agreement between the card-holder and the issuer is a regulated agreement, and hence governed in certain regards by the Act; pp. 403–5 below.

[13] The Uniform Commercial Code, the Uniform Consumer Credit Code, and the Federal legislation in point. See, generally, Davenport, 'Bank Credit Cards and the UCC', 941; A. G. Cleveland, 'Bank Credit Cards', (1973) 90 Banking LJ 719, esp. 725–7 (discussing the Uniform Consumer Credit Code); L. B. Orr and J. H. Tedards, 'Bank Credit Cards and the Right of Setoff', (1975) 26 SC L Rev. 89.

authority suggests that, where there is no express term in point in the contract between the parties, the risk of loss is borne by the issuer. The reason is simple: he can seek reimbursement only if a transaction has been sanctioned by the genuine card-holder.[14]

There was no uniformity in the approach of the courts when the contract in question absolved the issuer from liability where the holder failed to give prompt notice of the loss of the card. Some decisions took the view that the card-holder was bound by his contractual undertaking.[15] In one case it was held that, despite the clause, the issuer owed a duty of care to the card-holder. It was incumbent on him to prove that this duty was discharged before he could invoke the clause.[16] In another case, where the thief went on a shopping spree with the converted card, the court refused to give effect to the clause. The issuer should have been alerted by the obvious pattern of the frauds. However, in that case the dealers were clearly at fault, as they supplied to the thief items which were not within the legitimate purpose of the card.[17]

The reasoning in the authorities cited may not strike a chord in an English court. It does, however, suggest one possible avenue for assailing the exemption clause. In English law, the only argument against the validity of such a clause is to be found in section 3(2) of the Unfair Contract Terms Act 1977. Under this provision, a party whose standard conditions form the basis of the contract cannot rely on a term in order to excuse a contractual performance substantially different from that undertaken by him, except to the extent that the term meets the test of reasonableness of the Act.[18] It is, of course, clear that the honouring of an instruction issued by an impostor is a performance not contemplated by the parties to the credit card transaction. The American authorities support the view that a term which excuses such a performance is not reasonable, as it frees the issuer from the underlying duty of care. However, it has to be conceded that a term which exonerates the issuer from liability where the holder fails to report the loss of the card is justifiable on the basis that forgeries are hard to detect.

The other main problem concerning the contract between the issuer and the holder is that of countermand of payment. It will be recalled that a drawer has the right to instruct his bank to dishonour a cheque even if the payee is entitled to its payment.[19] The reason for this is that as against the bank, which acts as an agent, the drawer is entitled to cancel his instruction.

---

[14] *Thomas v. Central Charge Service Inc.*, 212 A 2d 533 (DC Cir. 1965).
[15] *Magnolia Petroleum Co. v. McMillan*, 168 SW 2d 881 (Tex. Civ. App. 1943); *Texaco Inc. v. Goldstein*, 229 NYS 2d 51 (Mun. Ct. 1962), affd. 241 NYS 2d 495 (Sup. Ct. 1963) (clause held fair).
[16] *Union Oil Co. of California v. Lull*, 349 P 2d 243 (Ore. 1960).
[17] *Gulf Refining Co. v. Williams Roofing Co.*, 186 SW 2d 790 (Ark. 1945).
[18] As to which, see Consumer Credit Act 1974, s. 11.
[19] P. 229 above.

Can the same reasoning be applied to the payment, or charge, order in a docket completed when the holder uses his T & E card?

It is believed that such an analogy would be misguided. A cheque can be countermanded, as the bank does not make a promise to the payee. The position of the issuer of a token is different. Under his contract with the dealer, the issuer is bound to pay the amount of dockets signed by the holder. Moreover, the holder enters into his contract with the issuer on the basis of this understanding. He knows that his execution of the docket involves the creation of a binding payment undertaking on the issuer's part. For this reason, the holder is not entitled to countermand his instruction in the docket any more than the applicant for a documentary credit is entitled to demand that the bank revoke its binding promise to the beneficiary of the facility.[20]

It remains to consider whether, at common law, the issuer may be liable for the dealer's default or misrepresentation. One American authority sought to achieve such a result by subjecting the issuer to product liability, on the ground that the display of his insignia conferred an aura of dependability and reliability on the dealer.[21] The point is a questionable one. It is believed that in English law the connection will be regarded as too tenuous.

The contract between the issuer and the dealer is carefully defined in the master agreement. Usually the dealer is granted the right to be paid provided the card-holder's signature on the docket tallies with the one displayed on the card. The dealer is therefore entitled to recover against a skilful forgery. There are, however, two exceptions. First, the dealer may not recover payment if he has rendered services or provided goods under a card which has been put on a stop list communicated to him. Secondly, the card has to be used for the purposes for which it is issued. Thus, if a card is issued with an indorsement to the effect that it can be used only for 'travelling and entertainment', the dealer cannot seek reimbursement from the issuer for the price of a radio sold to the holder.[22]

4. CHEQUE CARDS

In a card of this type, the issuer warrants to the payee that a cheque, drawn by the holder for not more than a stated maximum amount, will be paid on

---

[20] For a discussion, see *Benjamin's Sale of Goods*, 2nd edn., para. 2204. But note that, in the case of cards governed by the Consumer Credit Act 1974, the holder can make effective against the issuer most of the claims which he has against the dealer (pp. 408–10 below). This is an even more effective remedy than the power to countermand payment!

[21] *Connor* v. *Great Western Savings & Loan Association*, 447 P 2d 609 (1969); contrast *Bradler* v. *Craig* 79 Cal. Reptr. 401 (2d Dis. 1969); *Sherlec* v. *Wells Fargo Bank*, 96 Cal. Reptr. 434 (1st Dis. 1971). And see Reiter, 'Bank Credit Cards and Enterprise Liability'.

[22] *Gulf Refining Co.* v. *Williams Roofing Co.*, 186 SW 2d 790 (Ark. 1945).

presentment. The undertaking is subject to four conditions. First, the cheque must be signed in the presence of the payee and the signature has to correspond with that on the card. The object of this requirement is to combat the misuse of the card, although the condition emphasizes the correspondence in appearance rather than the genuineness of the payee's signature. Secondly, the cheque must be drawn on a form bearing the code number shown on the card. Usually this number is the sorting code of the branch with which the customer maintains his account. In effect, this means that the cheque has to be drawn on a form itemized to the payee's branch. Thirdly, the cheque has to be drawn before the stated expiry date. Fourthly, the card number has to be written on the back of the cheque by the payee. By doing so, the payee shows that he has accepted the cheque in reliance on the token.

There are two significant differences between a cheque card and a credit or T & E card. The first, as mentioned above, is that in a cheque card the bank undertakes to honour its customer's cheque rather than to make payment for goods sold or for services provided to him. Secondly, the bank's undertaking in a cheque card is addressed to the world at large. Any bank, merchant, or private person is entitled to act on it. In the case of credit and T & E cards, the bank's promise is directed only to the appointed merchants and financial institutions with whom the issuer has an agreement and who display his insignia. The reimbursement promise in arrangements of this type is therefore specially addressed, and not a unilateral offer to enter into a contract with anybody who accepts it.

A bank's promise in a cheque card is comparable with the undertaking given in a traveller's letter of credit.[23] In such a facility the issuer undertakes to reimburse advances made to the holder (beneficiary) against cheques drawn by him for up to a specified maximum amount.[24] The beneficiary's signature is usually set out in a separate letter of introduction, which the traveller is required to keep apart from the letter of credit. The letter itself may be addressed either to the world at large, in which case it is a general letter of credit, or to a given person or persons, such as the issuer's correspondents, in which case it is 'specially advised'.[25] A person who acts on the bank's promise in such a letter of credit can enforce it provided he is a promisee within the contemplation of the instrument, and provided further that he complies with the conditions set out in it.[26]

The cheque card clearly resembles the general variety of a traveller's letter

---

[23] Brandel and Leonard, 'Bank Charge Cards: New Cash or New Credit', 1047.

[24] Ellinger, *Documentary Letters of Credit—A Comparative Study in Law*, pp. 5–7; *Benjamin's Sale of Goods*, 2nd edn., para. 2142.

[25] *Birckhead and Carlisle* v. *Brown*, 5 Hill (NY) 634, 642–3 (1843) affd. 2 Den. (NY) 375 (1845); *Evansville National Bank* v. *Kaufman*, 93 NY 273, 280 (1883), both of which include an interesting analysis.

[26] *Northumberland County Bank* v. *Eyer*, 58 Pa. St. 97, 103 (1868).

of credit. The bank's undertaking in a cheque card was described by Lord Diplock in *Metropolitan Police Commissioner* v. *Charles*[27] as one that—

gives the payee a direct contractual right against the bank itself to payment on presentment, provided that the use of the card by the drawer to bind the bank to pay the cheque was within the actual or ostensible authority conferred upon him by the bank.

A cheque card is considered not to fall within the ambit of the Consumer Credit Act 1974.[28] The rights of the parties to the transaction depend, therefore, on common law principles. The problems arising in respect of the contract between the banker and the holder are mainly the holder's right to countermand payment and the question of the liability for the misuse of the card by an impostor. Cases of the misuse of the card give rise also to problems regarding the contract between the bank and the issuer.

The terms and conditions on which the bank agrees to furnish the cheque card include a clause in which the holder's right of countermand is effectively withdrawn. But is this term conclusive? When the customer draws a cheque on his account, he instructs the bank, which is his agent, to make payment thereof.[29] The bank's mandate to pay is terminated if the customer countermands his order.[30] Is a clause in a contract of principal and agent effective to restrict the principal's right to cancel an instruction?

It is believed that the answer is to be gleaned from the law pertaining to letters of credit. Where the customer instructs his bank to open an irrevocable credit, he foregoes his right to order the bank to refuse to perform its promise to the beneficiary.[31] Conceptually, the explanation is that, when a principal orders his agent to give an independent undertaking to a third party, the relationship ceases to be one of pure agency. The agent, who binds himself to the third party, becomes in effect an independent contractor. Courts will not make orders which preclude banks from performing irrevocable undertakings given at a customer's request.[32] In a cheque card transaction, the customer—the card-holder—is aware of the fact that, when he uses his cheque card, he confers on the payee an irrevocable right to seek payment directly from the bank.

As cheque cards are, in all probability, outside the ambit of the Consumer

---

[27] [1977] AC 177, 182.

[28] P. 403 below.

[29] Pp. 228–9 above.

[30] Bills of Exchange Act 1882, s. 75.

[31] See, e.g., *Sovereign Bank of Canada* v. *Bellhouse, Dillon & Co. Ltd.* (1911) 23 Que. KB 413 and, generally, *Benjamin's Sale of Goods*, 2nd edn., para. 2184 and authorities there cited. The principle is essential as otherwise the bank would be in a quandary where its own undertaking would be binding *vis-à-vis* the beneficiary but subject to objections by the customer.

[32] See, especially, *Harbottle (RD) (Mercantile) Ltd.* v. *National Westminster Bank Ltd.* [1978] 1 QB 146, 155–6 per Kerr LJ; *Edward Owen Engineering Ltd.* v. *Barclays Bank International Ltd.* [1978] 1 Lloyd's Rep. 166, 171 per Lord Denning MR.

Credit Act 1974, questions concerning liability for their misuse are governed by the common law principles discussed in respect of T & E cards. There is, however, one additional consideration where the misused token is a cheque card. The underlying relationship between the bank and its customer, the card-holder, is more closely grounded on agency principles than is the relationship between the issuer of a T & E card and its holder. It is therefore arguable that, quite regardless of the terms on which the card is issued, the bank is not entitled to debit its customer's account with a cheque, or order, which has not emanated from him. The bank has no genuine mandate in such cases.[33] The answer, probably, is that the question here is not one of the determination of scope of the bank's authority but that of the allocation of risks connected with the use of cheque cards. If the parties agree that in a given situation the risk is to be borne by the holder, the arrangement ought to be binding on him.

As a matter of practice, banks do not impose absolute liability on the holder of a cheque card. He is to bear a loss only if he fails to give notice to the bank of the loss or misappropriation of the token. Further, customers are asked not to carry the card and the cheque-book together. Obviously, if only one of the items is stolen, the thief does not have the immediate means for perpetrating a fraud.[34] Customers are well advised to observe these requirements which, it is submitted, are reasonable and fair.

The contract between the bank and the payee of the cheque can give rise to problems only where the drawer's signature is a forgery. Where it is genuine, the bank has to pay the cheque provided the terms and conditions set out in the card are met. Thus, the cheque and card have to tally; the amount may not exceed the prescribed maximum (usually £50); the cheque has to be drawn before the expiry date of the card; and the payee has to write the number of the card on the back of the cheque. If all these requirements are complied with, the bank has to pay the cheque regardless of the availability of adequate funds standing to the drawer's account.

Difficulties arise where all conditions appear to be met but the drawer's signature is a forgery. The terms printed on the card require the drawer's signature on the cheque to 'correspond' with that displayed on the card. A forged signature may, of course, correspond in its appearance with the one of which it is a fake. It is believed that, as a matter of practice, banks pay skilful forgeries in order to retain the viability of the cheque cards system.

Whether, as a matter of law, 'correspondence' refers to similarity in form or to genuineness is open to controversy. On the one hand, it stands to reason that, if the bank were held not to be entitled to debit the drawer with

[33] Pp. 286 et seq. above.
[34] Although it is understood that professional criminals are frequently able to fake cheque forms so as to match the card and the cheque!

forged items, the courts would be disinclined to require the bank to make payment thereof. On the other hand, the different contractual relationships in a cheque card transaction are as autonomous as those of a documentary credit transaction.[35] On this basis, it is arguable that the bank's inability to debit the customer's account with the amount of a cheque with a forged signature, has no bearing on the bank's duty *vis-à-vis* the payee. Moreover, the terms of the cheque card are stipulated by the bank. In cases of ambiguity they are, therefore, to be construed *contra proferentem*.

5. CASHPOINT CARDS

In terms of technology, there are two types of cashpoint cards: off-line and on-line. Off-line cards operate by means of an identification of the PIN, which is encoded on the card itself, by the automatic teller machine. The transaction is thus scrutinized by the program used by the terminal, and there is no direct link, for individual transactions, with the central computer of the bank. The danger, of course, is that a person who misappropriates the card may succeed in decoding the PIN. In contrast, an on-line card does not have any record of the PIN. Instead, the number is retained by the central computer, to which the terminal is linked (or 'on-line'). When the customer keys the PIN into the terminal and requests to withdraw a given amount in cash, the computer verifies the correctness of the number and the availability of an adequate balance. In on-line cards the PIN remains safe. The disadvantage is that the 'line' between terminals and the computer centre is, of course, subject to mechanical disturbances and breakdowns.

Originally, Midland Bank and National Westminster used the off-line type of card and the other banks the on-line type. Recently, there has been a general shift to on-line cards. Moreover, some banks have just launched a card that can be operated in the terminals of each of them. It is clear that, the wider the network, the more useful is the card. It is further understood that a number of building societies are contemplating the introduction of a joint card.

If the card-holder memorizes his number, the danger of abuse is minimal. Unfortunately, many holders, who find it difficult to remember their PIN, carry a record with them. If this falls into the hands of a thief together with the card itself, misuse becomes easy. It is likewise facilitated where the holder 'lends' his card to a friend, even if the main object is to obtain funds for himself through that person's use thereof. Liability for misuse has to be considered both in the light of common law principles and under the Con-

[35] See, on this point, *Benjamin's Sale of Goods*, 2nd edn., paras. 2204, 2277.

sumer Credit Act 1974. The reason for this is that it is not certain that all cards of this type fall within the ambit of the Act.

The common law approach is best illustrated by an American authority, *Judd* v. *Citibank*.[36] The card-holder disputed the debiting of her account with an amount of $800, which was shown on her statement as having been withdrawn by the use of her cashpoint card. The teller machine involved was programmed to effect a withdrawal only if the card was verified and the numbers on it were matched with the PIN keyed in. The card-holder testified that at the time of the withdrawals she had been at work, that she had not entrusted her card to anybody, and that she had kept her PIN to herself. The Civil Court of the City of New York gave judgment for the card-holder. The relevant issue was identified as follows:[37]

Has [the card holder] proven her case by a fair preponderance of the credible evidence? In this case we are met with a credible witness on the one hand and a computer printout on the other.

The Court took into consideration that machines were subject to breakdowns and concluded:[38]

this court is not prepared to go so far as to rule that where a credible witness is faced with the adverse 'testimony' of a machine, he is as a matter of law faced also with an unmeetable burden of proof. It is too commonplace in our society that when faced with the choice of man or machine we readily accept the 'word' of the machine everytime. This, despite the tales of computer malfunctions that we hear daily.

The Court, thus, preferred the card-holder's testimony to the evidence based on computer printouts. Obviously, the court was free to reach this conclusion as it had to choose between two diametrically opposed pieces of evidence.

An English court, faced with a similar problem, would have to reckon with an additional consideration. The master agreement between the bank and the card-holder includes a clause under which the bank's record is deemed conclusive proof of transactions effected through the use of the teller machine. Clauses of this type have been held valid in the context of performance bonds and first-demand guarantees, where the term usually states that a demand made by the beneficiary of the facility constitutes conclusive proof of the happening of the event on which payment is due.[39] There is, however, a difference between the object of a conclusive evidence clause in a performance bond agreement and the comparable clause in a cashpoint agreement. In the former case, the object of the clause is to enable

[36] 435 NYS 2d 210 (1980).
[37] Ibid., 211.
[38] Ibid., 212.
[39] See, e.g., *Bache & Co. (London) Ltd.* v. *Banque Vernes et Commerciale de Paris SA* [1973] 2 Lloyd's Rep. 437, 440; *Benjamin's Sale of Goods*, 2nd edn., para. 2280.

the bank to honour its undertaking without getting embroiled in disputes between the beneficiary of the performance bond and the 'account party' at whose request the facility was furnished. In the latter case, the object of the clause is to preclude the bank's customer—the card-holder—from disputing inaccuracies in his statement. The cases are, therefore, distinguishable. The clause in cashpoint card agreements may yet be held contrary to public policy or unreasonable under the Unfair Contract Terms Act 1977.[40]

The risks inherent in the use of cashpoint cards is further demonstrated by a later American authority. In *Ognibene* v. *Citibank NA*,[41] a rogue, who was standing near the bank's terminals, memorized the PIN of a card-holder who was using a machine. The rogue, who pretended to be engaged in the servicing of the terminals, used an adjacent telephone in order to conduct a fictitious conversation with his employers, after which he asked the card-holder to let him have the use of the card so as to ensure that the terminal was in order. After withdrawing money by keying in the number, the rogue returned the card to the holder saying all was well. The card-holder contested the bank's right to debit his account with the amount extracted by the rogue, claiming that the bank had failed to introduce a safe method for the use of the card. Giving judgment in his favour, Thorpe J, in the Civil Court of the City of New York, held that the bank had been negligent in not taking measures to combat a ruse of which it had been aware. The bank ought to have provided the card-holder with information sufficient to alert him to the danger when he was confronted by a rogue.

Again, it is difficult to predict whether an English court would adopt a similar approach. The card-holder may be regarded as having committed a breach of his contract with the issuer by allowing an unknown person to use his card. But in the instant case the card-holder did not disclose his PIN to the rogue. Is he to be held liable for his failure to prevent a person from looking over his shoulder?

6. THE PROVISIONS OF THE CONSUMER CREDIT ACT 1974

(i) Tokens affected

A credit token is defined in section 14(1) of the Consumer Credit Act 1974. The token may be a card, a check, a voucher or some other 'thing' which is issued to an individual, i.e. not to a company. The issuer must undertake either that on production of the token he will supply cash, goods, or services

---

[40] S. 11 and hence avoided under s. 3(2) (by debiting the customer's account with an amount never withdrawn, the bank renders a performance different from that contemplated.)
[41] 446 NYS 2d 845 (1981).

on credit or that, where a third party supplies cash, goods, or services against the production of the token, the issuer will pay the third party for them. The first heading covers bipartite credit tokens. These fall within the definition only if the issuer undertakes to supply cash, goods or services *on credit*. This requirement is not found in the case of the second heading. Such a credit token, therefore, falls within this heading even if the relevant items are not actually supplied on credit; under section 14(3), a provision of credit is deemed to arise when the cash, goods, or services are supplied. It is irrelevant whether or not the issuer deducts a discount or commission from the amount paid to the supplier. It is, further, irrelevant whether the cash, goods, or services are to be supplied against the mere production of the token or whether 'some other action is also required'.

This definition was clarified in *Elliott* v. *Director General of Fair Trading*,[42] where a token was held to fall within its ambit although all that had been furnished was a provisional card, to be exchanged for the final token when the holder supplied some financial details about himself and completed an application form. These requirements were held to constitute 'some other required action' which did not exclude the token from the ambit of section 14. It was further held immaterial that the undertaking given in the token was not binding in law.

The definition of a credit token is a wide one. It encompasses a book of vouchers that the issuer may use under a credit agreement in order to draw on his account, provided the issuer undertakes to meet these. But ordinary cheque forms, supplied by a bank to its customer, are not covered. The reason for this is that the bank's undertaking to the customer is for the payment of the instruments, not for the supply of cash, goods, or services.[43] Cheques are outside the definition even if the customer's name and his account's number are set out on them, and regardless of whether they are 'open' cheques or include a printed crossing.

It is clear that credit cards fall within the ambit of section 14. They involve tripartite arrangements for the supply of cash, goods, or services to the holder by appointed dealers at the issuer's expense. T & E cards, on the other hand, are not necessarily covered. This is not due to the fact that the issuer of such tokens requires the holder to settle accounts promptly and in full on presentment (which takes place at the end of each calendar month) and that the card-holder, accordingly, does not effectively obtain credit. If the issuer regularly carries on a consumer credit business, the card nevertheless falls within the definition of section 14(1)(*b*). But if the issuer does not engage in consumer credit business, then his T & E card is not a credit

---

[42] [1980] 1 WLR 977. And see generally Goode, *Consumer Credit Legislation*, I/1007 et seq. (paras. 2261 et seq.); Guest and Lloyd, *Encyclopaedia of Consumer Credit Law*, paras. 2–015 et seq.

[43] Guest and Lloyd, *Encyclopaedia of Consumer Credit Law*, para. 2–015.

token,[44] unless it enables the holder to obtain cash against its production. At the same time, even if a T & E card constitutes a credit token, there is no 'credit token agreement' within the definition of section 14(2), unless there is a regulated agreement as defined in the Act.[45]

Section 14 does not cover cheque cards. In such tokens, the issuer promises to honour cheques drawn by his customer for up to a specified amount and provided certain conditions are met. The issuer does not promise to reimburse third parties who trade with the holder.[46] The distinction, undoubtedly, is a technical one, as the holder invariably acquires cash, goods, or services against the cheque guaranteed under the card.

Cashpoint cards constitute credit tokens. This is so because in most arrangements pertaining to them there is an understanding that the automatic teller will supply cash to the customer even if the withdrawals involve an overdraft of the account. Cash is thus supplied on the issuer's credit within the first limb of the definition of section 14. Moreover, even if the machine is programmed to refuse a request involving an overdraft, the card falls within the definition if, subsequently, cash is made available by the machine when the account is overdrawn.[47] As all machines function on the basis of the balance at the close of the day preceding the transaction, a customer may in certain circumstances obtain cash although his account is at that time effectively overdrawn.[48]

It is believed that the position has remained unaltered in respect of cashpoint cards which, under mutual arrangements between specific banks, can be used by the holder in terminals belonging to a bank other than the card issuer. If the A Bank furnishes cash through one of its terminals to a holder of a B Bank card, the A Bank acts as an agent of the B Bank. The parties to the transaction are the B bank and the card-holder.

The Act draws a distinction between a 'credit token' and a 'credit token agreement'. Under section 14(2) a credit token agreement is a regulated agreement for the provision of credit in connection with the use of a credit token. Thus, even if a card is a credit token within the meaning of the Act, there is no 'credit token agreement' unless the card is issued under a regulated agreement for the provision of credit in connection with the credit token involved.[49] If the credit token agreement only permits the card-holder

[44] The Consumer Credit (Exempt Agreements) (No. 2) Order 1985, SI 753, art. 3(1)(a)(ii). And note definition of 'consumer credit business' in the Consumer Credit Act 1974, s. 189(1).
[45] P. 63–65 above.
[46] See Consumer Credit Act 1974, Sched. 2, Pt. 2, example 21.
[47] Guest and Lloyd, *Encyclopaedia of Consumer Credit Law*, para. 2–015 (p. 2020).
[48] And see s. 14(4), under which the use of an object to operate a machine provided by the issuer or a third party is deemed the production of the object to such a person. Clearly, cashpoint cards are within the contemplation of s. 14!
[49] See Guest and Lloyd, *Encyclopaedia of Consumer Credit Law*, para. 2–015 (p. 2020/1). For the meaning of 'regulated agreement' see the Consumer Credit Act 1974, s. 8(3), and pp. 63–65 above.

to overdraw his current account, it remains exempt from the formalities pre-scribed in Part V of the Act.[50] At present, most cashpoint cards are confined to such arrangements. If in the future the issuing of such cards were to involve an agreement to provide to the holder other forms of credit, such as loans, then the exemption from Part V would probably be inapplicable.[51] Section 14(3) of the Act clarifies the nature of tripartite credit tokens. The issuer of such a token is deemed to provide the holder 'with credit drawn on whenever a third party [viz. dealer] supplies him with cash, goods or ser-vices'. Such an agreement is, therefore, a credit token agreement, unless it is an exempt agreement under section 16.[52]

The agreement leading to the issuing of a token may be within the ambit of the Act even if the token itself is outside it. Thus, example 21[53] suggests that the contract under which a bank supplies a cheque card to its customer is a credit agreement because the holder can draw cheques which the bank is bound to honour at the payee's demand even if the holder's account is over-drawn. The agreement is therefore said to be an unrestricted-use debtor–creditor agreement within the meaning of section 13(*c*) of the Act.

It has been objected that this analysis overlooks the fact that most cheque card agreements include a clause precluding the use of the card when the account does not have an adequate balance for meeting the cheques. It is said that the customer, therefore, is not 'entitled' to obtain credit under the card, and that his drawings in disregard of the arrangement ought not to form the basis of the definition of the agreement.[54] Example 21 is, thus, des-cribed as conflicting with section 8(1) of the Act, which regards an agree-ment as a binding arrangement.[55] The objection is questionable because, despite formal clauses drawn to the customer's attention, the bank meets his cheques without demur as long as the ensuing overdraft is within reason. The arrangement for an overdraft is, therefore, well understood.

It follows that, unless an agreement between the issuer and holder for the provision of a credit card or of a cheque card is an exempt agreement, it constitutes a regulated consumer credit agreement. Generally, such agree-ments fall into the category of 'unrestricted-use running account' agree-ments. The same applies to agreements leading to the issuing of a cashpoint card, provided the holder is allowed to acquire cash on credit. In all these arrangements, the issuer owes certain duties under the Act to the holder.

---

[50]   Consumer Credit Act 1974, s. 74(1)(*b*); p. 485–8 below.

[51]   See Guest and Lloyd, *Encyclopaedia of Consumer Credit Law*, para. 2–015.

[52]   In which case it is excluded from the definition of a regulated agreement under s. 8(3); and note credit limits regarding regulated agreements: p. 65 above (upper limit being £15,000).

[53]   Consumer Credit Act 1974, Sched. 2, Pt. 2, example 21.

[54]   A. P. Dobson, 'The Cheque Card as a Consumer Credit Agreement', [1977] JBL 126.

[55]   See Consumer Credit Act 1974, s. 188(2), which renders the examples subordinate to other provisions of the Act.

Moreover, in a credit card arrangement, the holder has to obtain the services or goods from dealers appointed, and hence designated, by the issuer. It will be shown that this imposes additional duties on the issuer of a credit card. It is uncertain if the contract between the holder and the issuer of a T & E card is also a regulated agreement. Naturally, if the card itself is a credit token,[56] the agreement falls within the definition of section 14(2). But if the card itself is not a credit token with section 14, the point is dubious. On the one hand, the agreement for the provision of the card may still constitute a regulated credit agreement, as the holder obtains credit until the date on which the periodic account is presented to him. On the other hand, the payment made by the issuer to the dealer or supplier frequently takes place after the date on which the card-holder has settled his account. It is forcefully arguable that, accordingly, the card-holder does not acquire credit facilities.

(ii) Misuse of token

The general rule is stated in section 83(1) of the Act. The debtor under a regulated consumer credit agreement is not liable to the creditor for any loss arising from the use of the 'credit facility' by an unauthorized person. The provision is wide enough to cover facilities other than credit tokens as defined, although cases concerning the misuse of cheques and other instruments covered under section 4 of the Cheques Act 1957 are expressly excluded.[57]

Section 84 makes an exception to the general rule by allowing the issuer to include in the credit token agreement a clause which makes the cardholder liable for loss to a certain extent. Its provisions may be summarized as follows. First, the holder may be made liable for the first £50 of any transaction made when the card was not in his possession.[58] Secondly, the holder may be made liable for any loss accrued from the misuse of the card by a person who acquires possession of it with his consent.[59] Thirdly, the holder cannot be rendered liable unless the credit token agreement sets out details of a person or body to be contacted in the case of the loss or theft of the card.[60] Fourthly, the holder's liability terminates (even for the first £50) when he gives notice of the loss to the issuer.[61] The notice may be given orally or in writing and takes effect when received; but the agreement may

---

[56] See p. 102 below.
[57] Consumer Credit Act 1974, s. 83(2); and see, as regards s. 4 pp. 421 et seq. below.
[58] Consumer Credit Act 1974, s. 84(1), as modified by the Consumer Credit (Increase of Monetary Limits) Order 1983, SI 1571.
[59] Ibid., s. 84(2); for the definition of an authorized person, see s. 84(7).
[60] Ibid., s. 84(3)–(4); and see for the relevant details the Consumer Credit (Credit-Token Agreements) Regulations 1983, SI 1555.
[61] Ibid., s. 84(3).

require an oral notice to be confirmed in writing. In such a case the holder has to write within seven days.[62] Fifthly, any sum paid by the holder for the issuing of the card is to be treated as paid towards his liability for loss, unless it has previously been set off against amounts due for the use of the token.[63] Where more than one token is issued under one agreement, the applicable provisions apply to each token separately.[64]

The holder's liability under section 84 is confined to cases in which the agreement between the parties includes appropriate clauses. If the agreement is silent, the position is governed by the general principle of section 83, which frees the holder from liability for loss in cases of misuse. But section 83 is subject to one important limitation. It applies only to the unauthorized use of the 'credit facility'. It has, accordingly, been argued that if 'the debtor maintains an account with the creditor and there is a credit balance on the account in favour of the debtor, nothing in section 83 would prevent the debtor being made liable to the creditor for any loss arising from unauthorized withdrawals of that credit balance'.[65] The words 'credit facility', however, are not defined. It is arguable that an account that may be overdrawn by the use of a credit token constitutes a credit facility even where, at a given moment, it is in funds. It seems disturbing that a 'facility' may be governed by the Act at one time but outside its operation a few minutes thereafter. Indeed, occasionally, it may be difficult to determine with certainty whether, at a given moment, an account is overdrawn or in credit.[66] The theoretical importance of this problem in respect of cashpoint cards issued by banks is obvious. In practice, though, the standard form agreements of banks are not onerous.

There is one further limitation to the liability of the holder of a credit token governed by the Act. Under section 66, the holder can be made liable for loss resulting from the use of the token only where he has previously accepted it. Acceptance takes place when the token or a receipt for it is signed by the holder, or by a person authorized by him, or when the token is validly used for the first time.[67] The onus of proving both the receipt and the acceptance of the card rests on the creditor.[68] Where the creditor does not have a receipt signed by the holder in person, it is of course difficult for him to prove delivery. But it is thought that even a valid receipt, given for a

---

[62] Ibid., s. 84(5).

[63] Ibid., s. 84(6).

[64] Ibid., s. 84(8). Note that under the Consumer Credit (Agreements) Regulations 1983, SI 1553, Sched. 2, Pt. 1, Form 15, the consumer has to be advised of the position in cases of loss or misuse.

[65] Guest and Lloyd, *Encyclopaedia of Consumer Credit Law*, para. 2–084; Goode, *Consumer Credit Legislation*, para. 828 does not discuss the point.

[66] As cheques may have been in the clearing process at the relevant time.

[67] Consumer Credit Act 1974, s. 66(2).

[68] Ibid., s. 177(4)(a).

parcel containing the card, is inadequate, as it fails to signify the acceptance of the card itself.[69]

Where the Act is inapplicable, the holder's liability for loss occasioned by the misuse of the card is governed by the terms of his agreement with the issuer and by the common law principles discussed earlier on. In practice, credit token agreements are not onerous. The standard provision frees the holder from liability (except for the first £30 or £50) as soon as he gives notice of the loss or theft of the card.

(iii) Unsolicited tokens

The Act forbids the supply of unsolicited tokens falling within its definition. The dispatch or delivery of such a token constitutes an offence.[70] The object of the prohibition is to avoid situations in which consumers are tempted to exceed their advisable credit limits by the provision of easily available finance.

The holder's request for a token must usually be expressed in a document signed by him.[71] But the prohibition of the supply of unsolicited tokens does not apply in two cases. First, the issuer may send an unsolicited token under an agreement already made. Secondly, the provision is inapplicable in respect of replacement tokens, even if the agreement under which they are sent is varied in any material detail.[72]

It is noteworthy that the Act does not free the holder from the duty to reimburse where he has accepted an unsolicited token.[73] This is surprising, as such a provision would have been the most effective deterrent of attempts to circumvent the provision.

(iv) The credit token agreement

The credit token agreement, made between the issuer and the holder, is usually a regulated consumer credit agreement.[74] Ordinarily, a copy of such an agreement must be sent by the creditor to the debtor within seven days

[69] Goode, *Consumer Credit Legislation*, para. 825.
[70] Consumer Credit Act 1974, s. 51(1); the section prohibits the 'giving' of an unsolicited token. Note that this provision applies even to a provisional token: *Elliott* v. *Director General of Fair Trading* [1980] 1 WLR 977. But see the definition of 'give' in s. 189(1).
[71] Ibid., s. 51(2). But note that exceptions apply where the credit token agreement is a small debtor–creditor–supplier agreement.
[72] Ibid., s. 51(3).
[73] And see s. 170(1), under which a failure to comply with prescribed requirements does not have any civil or criminal consequences except those expressly specified.
[74] See p. 404 above.

following its execution.[75] In credit token agreements this requirement is varied: a copy may be given to the consumer either before or at the time the credit token is supplied.[76] This may, of course, be at a date later than seven days following the making of the credit agreement itself. If the issuer fails to comply with this requirement, the agreement is not properly executed.[77]

The issuer must, further, supply a copy of the credit agreement and of documents mentioned in it when he furnishes to the issuer a replacement credit token.[78] If the issuer fails to comply with this requirement he is not entitled, during the period of default, to enforce the agreement, and if he does not remedy the breach within one month, he becomes guilty of an offence.[79]

Another document which has to be supplied by the issuer to the holder is a notice which sets out the holder's right to cancel the agreement.[80] This document must be supplied within the time limit applicable for the dispatch of the copy of the agreement and, in practice, is furnished together with it.[81] Naturally, the requirement applies only when the agreement is subject to cancellation.[82]

A credit token agreement may be cancelled in the same circumstances as any other regulated agreement.[83] On cancellation the holder is entitled to recover amounts paid to the issuer either from the issuer himself or from the supplier, whose bills have been charged by the issuer to the holder's account.[84] These rules are subject to an important saving. Repayments can be claimed by the holder only when he has returned the token to the issuer or surrendered it to the supplier.[85]

(v) Nexus with underlying transaction

In credit card transactions there is a connection between the agreement of the issuer and holder and the acquisition of the goods or services from the dealer or supplier. It stems from the fact that the issuer is able to use his cards only when he enters into contracts with the 'appointed dealers', who display the issuer's insignia. The transaction is therefore a 'debtor–creditor–

---

[75] Consumer Credit Act 1974, s. 63(2).
[76] Ibid., s. 63(4).
[77] Ibid., s. 63(5).
[78] Ibid., s. 85(1).
[79] Ibid., s. 85(2).
[80] Ibid., s. 64(1).
[81] Ibid., s. 64(2).
[82] P. 66 above.
[83] Pp. 66–67 above.
[84] Consumer Credit Act 1974, s. 70(3).
[85] Ibid., s. 70(5).

supplier' agreement.[86] Consequently, if the holder (debtor) has a claim based on a misrepresentation or on breach of contract against the dealer (supplier), he has an 'alike claim' against the issuer (creditor).[87] These two parties may be sued by the issuer jointly and severally, although the dealer will have to indemnify the issuer.[88] The holder has his claim even if, in entering into the agreement with the dealer, he has exceeded a credit limit set by the issuer.[89] It has been suggested that, as the holder has an 'alike claim' against the dealer, he is able to rely on the misrepresentation or breach of contract by the dealer to rescind his contact with the issuer.[90]

The provisions in point apply only to 'regulated agreements'. It will be recalled that certain transactions involving T & E tokens are encompassed. By way of contrast, transactions involving cheque cards are not debtor–creditor–supplier agreements, as the bank's offer in the card is directed to the world at large. The holder, thus, is not bound to seek out an 'appointed dealer'. In the case of cashpoint cards, the provisions presently discussed are clearly inapplicable, provided the holder can use the card only for obtaining cash from the issuer: there is then no third party. It is believed that the provisions in question are likewise inapplicable even if the card can be used at the automatic teller machines of another bank. In the first place, it is arguable that that other bank furnishes cash to the holder as the issuer's agent. Secondly, the provisions in question apply only 'in relation to a transaction financed by the agreement'. In the case of cashpoint cards, the holder does not incur a debt or a liability to the third party bank whose terminal he uses.[91] There is simply no transaction between them.

Even in the case of some credit cards, the position has become uncertain owing to novel schemes. The agreement for the furnishing of the token may, for instance, be concluded between the holder and his bank. Payments, however, are to be made by the holder to a separate company owned by a number of issuers. That joint company makes the contracts with the suppliers: it appoints them and pays their accounts. Is the transaction for the supply of goods or of services to a card-holder nevertheless a debtor–creditor–supplier agreement? On the one hand, it is clear that the card-holder's creditor—the issuer—has no privity with the supplier. On the other hand, section 12(c), which defines the type of debtor–creditor–agreement

---

[86] Ibid., s. 12(b)–(c). And see Goode, *Consumer Credit Legislation*, paras. 280–6, 683.2, 824.4. But note that agreements for the acquisition of items for a price of less than £100 or of more than £10,000 are excluded, as, indeed, are 'non-commercial agreements' (which, under s. 189(1), are made by the non-consumer party outside the scope of his business): s. 75(3) and see Guest and Lloyd, *Encyclopaedia of Consumer Credit Law*, para. 2–076.

[87] Consumer Credit Act 1974, s. 75.

[88] Ibid., s. 75(2).

[89] Ibid., s. 75(3).

[90] Guest and Lloyd, *Encyclopaedia of Consumer Credit Law*, para. 2–207 (p. 2074/1).

[91] This conclusion is based on reading s. 75(1) together with s. 14(3). Section 12(b)–(c) does not appear to alter the position.

created in the case of credit cards, refers to 'arrangements'. It is arguable that the entire transaction is based on an arrangement under which the supply of the goods or services is to be financed by the joint company.

The close connection between the two contracts in a credit card transaction leads to a further result. The supply of the goods or services is a transaction 'linked' with the regulated credit agreement.[92] It is therefore 'automatically rescinded if the debtor [holder] exercises a right to withdraw from or cancel the credit card agreement, and may be affected by various other events vitiating that agreement'.[93]

7. CRIMINAL PROCEEDINGS FOR MISUSE OF TOKEN BY HOLDER

When the holder of a token violates the terms on which it is provided to him, the issuer is inclined to demand its return. If the holder ignores the request and continues to utilize the card, the issuer may bring charges against him. It may be asked whether such a course is advisable. Undoubtedly, in the case of credit cards and T & E cards, the issuer has the more effective remedy of placing the card on a stop list. The appointed retailers will then refuse to deal with the holder on the basis of the card. In the case of cashpoint cards, the remedy is even more effective. The computer centre programmes the terminals to refuse requests for cash. Cheque cards, however, present a problem. It will be recalled that the bank's promise is directed to the world at large. It is difficult to find a way to recall such a promise effectively.

Moreover, even in the case of credit and T & E cards there is a practical limit to the number of tokens that can be realistically included in the stop list. In extreme cases, the customer's failure to heed a warning about his use of the card leads to the simultaneous placing of the card on this list and to the complaint. The criminal proceedings instituted when a bank charges a recalcitrant customer are supposed to act as a deterrent to others.

The provision invoked in cases of this type is section 16 of the Theft Act 1968, which makes it an offence to obtain a pecuniary advantage by deception. In *Metropolitan Police Commissioner* v. *Charles*,[94] which is the leading case in point, the customer used his cheque card in order to exceed substantially an overdraft limit granted to him by the bank. Despite this, the branch manager provided him with another cheque-book but insisted that

---

[92] Within the meaning of s. 19(1)(*b*) of the Consumer Credit Act 1974.

[93] Goode, *Consumer Credit Legislation*, para. 828.4; and see ibid., para. 860 as regards such vitiating events. The provisions in the Act concerning 'linked transactions' are ss. 57(1) and 69(1).

[94] [1977] AC 177.

he use only one cheque a day. In blatant disregard of this request, the customer drew twenty-five cheques forthwith in favour of a gambling club. Upholding his conviction under section 16, the House of Lords decided that, when the customer used the cheque card, he represented to the payee that he had the required funds with the bank for meeting the cheques. He further represented that he had the bank's authority to make a direct contract between it and the payee by the use of the cheque card. Lords Diplock and Edmund-Davies emphasized that the representation was not just to the effect that the cheques would be paid by the bank.[95]

Charles's case was followed by the House of Lords in *R. v. Lambie*,[96] which concerned a credit card. The holder exceeded her credit limit on a number of occasions and so the bank demanded the return of the token. Instead of keeping her promise to do so, the holder went on a shopping spree, resulting in her overdrawing the prescribed limit by more than £1,000. Her conviction by the Crown Court was quashed by the Court of Appeal but restored by the House of Lords.

The Court of Appeal distinguished *Charles*'s case in view of the difference between the practice pertaining to cheque cards and to credit cards. In the case of cheque cards, where there was no master agreement between the bank and the payee, reliance had to be placed on the holder's representation of his right to utilize the card. In the case of a credit card, an appointed dealer relied on his standing arrangement with the issuer and not on the holder's representation. In the House of Lords, Lord Roskill pointed out that a merchant would not accept a credit card if he knew that the holder was utilizing it in breach of his contract with the issuer. The holder therefore obtained credit by tacitly representing that he was using the token in compliance with this contract.

It has been suggested that, in cases of the misuse of a credit card, the bank's correct course is to put it on the stop list rather than to press charges.[97] There is, however, no doubt that, when the holder presents his card to a merchant or to a bank, he effectively warrants his right to utilize it.[98] It is believed that the issuer is within his rights and that he does not infringe the commands of sound business practice by pressing charges where the holder misuses his credit card in the blatant manner encountered in *Charles*'s case and in *Lambie*'s case.

[95] Ibid., 182 (Lord Diplock) and 191 (Lord Edmund-Davies). See also *R v. Kovacs* [1974] 1 WLR 370, 373 (per Lawton LJ). A similar rule applies where the customer draws a cheque which he knows to be uncovered and which he has no reason to believe would be met: *R v. Page* [1971] 2 QB 330; and see *R v. Gilmartin* [1983] 1 All ER 829 (post-dated cheque). And note that a prosecution can be brought in the United Kingdom even in respect of an abuse of the card overseas: *R v. Bevan*, *The Times*, 24 Oct. 1986. As regards an electronic fraud involving money transfers executed overseas, see *R v. Thompson* [1984] 3 All ER 565.
[96] [1982] AC 449, esp. 460.
[97] A. T. H. Smith, 'Criminal Misuse of Cheque Cards and Credit Cards', [1978] JBL 129.
[98] A. Kewley, 'The Dishonest Cheque and Credit Card User', (1983) 127 Sol. Jo. 719.

CHAPTER 14

The Bank's Role in Collecting Cheques

1. THE BANK'S ROLE IN THE TRANSACTION

A bank that is asked by a customer to present a cheque for payment to the drawee bank assumes either the role of a collecting bank or that of a discounting bank. In both types of transaction, this bank may be sued by the true owner of the cheque if the customer's title to the instrument is defective. The causes of action available to the true owner, which are identical regardless of whether the bank has collected or discounted the cheque, are discussed in section 2 of this chapter. There is, however, a difference between the defences available to the collecting bank and those of a discounting bank. For this reason, the distinction between the role of a collecting bank and of a discounting bank is of considerable importance. This question is discussed in section 3.

Sections 4 and 5 of this chapter deal, respectively, with the defences available to the collecting bank and those available to a discounting bank. Section 6 considers the plea of contributory negligence, and section 7 deals with a relatively recent problem which has arisen as a result of developments in banking practice in the wake of the 1967 agreement between the clearing banks.[1] Under this arrangement, a holder need not remit a cheque to the bank which maintains the account to be credited with the proceeds. The holder may request any bank which has subscribed to the agreement to arrange for the collection of the cheque for the credit of any account maintained with any bank within the system. The position of a bank which receives the cheque for such processing—the 'processing bank'—in situations in which the payee does not have a good title to the cheque is uncertain, and requires separate analysis.

2. THE TRUE OWNER'S CAUSE OF ACTION

A bank that collects a cheque for a person who has no title to it, or whose title is defective, faces the hazard of an action by the true owner of the instrument. Two causes of action are available to substantiate such an action. The first is an action in conversion, for the purposes of which the

[1] Discussed in detail on pp. 233 et seq. above.

cheque is treated as a chattel. The bank converts it by receiving if for the collection and by presenting it for payment.[2] The second cause of action is based on the waiver of the tort involved. In *Morison* v. *London County and Westminster Bank Ltd.*, in which an agent misused his authority by drawing on his principal's account cheques payable to his own order and by arranging for their collection for the credit of his personal account, Reading CJ explained the basis of this second cause of action as follows:[3]

The plaintiff is entitled to waive the tort and sue for the same amount as money had and received to his use.

From a practical point of view, the cause of action in conversion is to be preferred to the quasi-contractual action based on waiver of tort. The reason for this is that the collecting bank receives the funds as its customer's agent. It is established that an agent who in good faith has paid over to his principal money to which it is subsequently discovered that the principal has no right cannot be required to return the money to the payor.[4] This doctrine applies to a collecting bank that has received the proceeds of cheques collected by it on behalf of a customer. Once the money is paid to the customer, the bank has changed its position and, being a mere agent, is no longer answerable in an action in money had and received.[5] However, the doctrine in question applies only where the action is brought under this heading and is thus based on the wrongful receipt of the funds. The defence cannot be raised in the context of an action in trover, which is based on the misappropriation of a chattel.

For the purposes of the action in conversion, the cheque is deemed to have a value equal to the amount for which it is drawn.[6] This principle is based on equating the chose in action, or the debt, incurred when the cheque

---

[2] *Morison* v. *London County and Westminster Bank Ltd.* [1914] 3 KB 356. See also *A. L. Underwood Ltd.* v. *Bank of Liverpool* [1924] 1 KB 775; *Lloyds Bank Ltd.* v. *Savory & Co.* [1933] AC 201; *Bute (Marquess of)* v. *Barclays Bank Ltd.* [1955] 1 KB 202. The history of the action is traced in *Arrow Transfer Co. Ltd.* v. *Royal Bank of Canada* [1971] 3 WWR 241 affd. [1972] SCR 845 and [1972] 4 WWR 60.

[3] [1914] 3 KB 356, 365. See also *Bavins Jnr. and Sims* v. *London and South-Western Bank* [1900] 1 QB 270, 277–8 per Vaughan Williams LJ; *United Australia Ltd.* v. *Barclays Bank Ltd.* [1941] AC 1, 19.

[4] *Admiralty Commissioners* v. *National Provincial and Union Bank of England Ltd.* (1922) 127 LT 452; *Gowers* v. *Lloyds and National Provincial Bank Ltd.* [1937] 3 All ER 55; *Koster's Premier Pottery Pty. Ltd.* v. *Bank of Adelaide* (1981) 28 SASR 335 (Aust.), and see pp. 329–33 above.

[5] As to when the money is so paid over, see pp. 332–3 above.

[6] *Bobbett* v. *Pinkett* (1876) 1 Ex. D 368; *Fine Art Society Ltd.* v. *Union Bank of London Ltd.* (1866) 17 QBD 705; *Macbeth* v. *North and South Wales Bank* [1908] 1 KB 13, affd. [1908] AC 137; *Orbit Mining and Trading Co. Ltd.* v. *Westminster Bank Ltd.* [1963] 1 QB 794; *Stoney Stanton Supplies (Coventry) Ltd.* v. *Midland Bank Ltd.* [1966] 2 Lloyd's Rep. 373, 385. Note that the principle holds even if the instrument is not negotiable: *Morison* v. *London County and Westminster Bank Ltd.* [1914] 3 KB 356; *Lloyds Bank Ltd.* v. *Chartered Bank of India, Australia and China* [1929] 1 KB 40.

is issued with the value of the instrument itself. In *International Factors Ltd. v. Rodriguez*,[7] a company assigned all its book debts to a firm of factors. This meant that any debts paid to the company by its clients had to be remitted to the factors. In breach of this agreement, a director of the company arranged for the collection of cheques, sent to the company in discharge of book debts due to it, for the credit of the company's current account. The factors sued the director in conversion. Two defences were pleaded. The first was that the factors did not have a property in the instruments but merely a right in contract to the proceeds. The second was that, even if the factors had an action in conversion, they could recover nominal damages only. The Court of Appeal held that the factors had an equitable interest in the cheques which conferred on them the right to sue in conversion. As regards the measure of damages, Sir David Cairns observed:[8]

the general position in relation to the conversion of a cheque is that the conversion gives the person entitled to the cheque a right to damages measured by the face value of the cheque. That . . . has been established by a whole series of cases in some of which the defendants were banks. The damages may, of course, be mitigated by special circumstances; for example . . . if the cheque were stopped before payment into his bank by the wrongdoer and a fresh cheque in substitution for it which was duly met.

His Lordship added that such special circumstances had to be established by the defendant to the action in conversion. In the instant case, it was argued that the factors had not suffered any loss because they still had a right of action against the debtors, who had drawn the cheques. This, however, was irrelevant as the factors, who might have had a cause of action against more than one party, were entitled to make their election.

It is clear that the Court of Appeal equated the value of the cheques in question with the amounts for which they were drawn. On this basis, a countermanded cheque ought to retain its face value even if a substituted instrument is issued by the drawer. The reason for this is that the stop order does not vitiate the cheque. The drawer remains liable to an action brought by a holder in due course.[9]

The true object of treating a converted cheque as having its face value is to enable the 'true owner' to sue for the proceeds under the guise of an action brought in tort. The fictive element in the conclusive presumption that a cheque has a value equal to the amount for which it is drawn becomes apparent when one reflects on the true value of a cheque issued by an impecunious customer whose account is heavily overdrawn. The instrument is bound to be dishonoured by the drawee bank, and an action against the

---

[7] [1979] QB 351.
[8] Ibid., 358.
[9] Pp. 227–8 above.

penniless customer is hopeless. The real value of the cheque involved is, therefore, nil. Why, then, should it be regarded at law as having its face value?

The same question can be raised in respect of a cheque bearing a forged signature of the drawer or a cheque which has been materially altered by an unauthorized person.[10] Such an instrument is a nullity. It is therefore unrealistic to plead that it has a value based on the amount for which it is drawn. This inconsistency was recognized in *Mathew and Cousins* v. *Sherwell*[11] by Sir James Mansfield, who observed that, even if an action for a forged cheque was successful, the most that the true owner could recover would be the value of the piece of paper on which the instrument was written. A similar reasoning has been adopted in recent Canadian authorities.[12] However, English authorities cast doubts on this line of argumentation. Thus, in *Orbit Mining and Trading Co. Ltd.* v. *Westminster Bank Ltd.*[13] it was held that cheques drawn by a company's director in excess of his authority, and by means of the forgery of the signature of one of his co-directors, had a value equal to the total amount for which they were drawn. The Court of Appeal permitted the company to allege, at one and the same time, that the cheques were nullities but that they did not constitute worthless pieces of paper.

The collecting bank's liability in conversion and under the related action based on the waiver of this tort is founded on its having handled the cheque on behalf of the tortfeasor—its customer—who has misappropriated the instrument. The true owner of such a cheque is able to recover the amount of the instrument from the collecting bank. The action involved has to be based on the cheque and not on the proceeds thereof, as the law does not recognize an action in conversion for the misappropriation of money or of a mere chose in action. This point is demonstrated by the decision in *Bavins Jnr. and Sims* v. *London and South Western Bank.*[14] An instrument which was in the form of a cheque, but payment of which was conditional on the execution of a receipt, was converted after reaching the payee's hands. It was collected on behalf of the rogue by his bank. Before the proceeds were paid out to the rogue, the true payee informed the collecting bank that the instrument had been issued to him. His action against the collecting bank was successful under the heading of money had and received, but the Court

[10] See, respectively, the Bills of Exchange Act 1882 ('BEA') ss. 24 and 64.
[11] (1810) 2 Taunt. 439.
[12] *Arrow Transfer Ltd.* v. *Royal Bank of Canada* [1971] 3 WWR 241, 256–7, affd. [1972] 4 WWR 70, (1972) 27 DLR (3rd) 81; *Number 10 Management Ltd.* v. *Royal Bank of Canada* (1977) 69 DLR (3rd) 99, 105, where it was also held that an action would not lie in money had and received. And see also *Koster's Premier Pottery Pty. Ltd.* v. *Bank of Alediade* (1981) 28 SASR 355 (Aust).
[13] [1963] 1 QB 794; *Building and Civil Engineering Holidays Scheme Management Ltd.* v. *Post Office* [1964] 2 QB 430, 444–7; *Stoney Stanton Supplies (Coventry) Ltd.* v. *Midland Bank Ltd.* [1966] 2 Lloyd's Rep. 373, 385.
[14] [1900] 1 QB 270.

of Appeal was divided in respect of the action in conversion. A. L. Smith LJ thought that both causes of action ought to succeed. The action in money had and received was to be allowed, as the collecting bank had been informed before it changed its position that the proceeds of the instrument were in reality for the initial payee's use. His Lordship would have further allowed the action in trover, as the collecting bank had converted a document belonging to the payee. He attached no importance to the non-negotiable character of the document. Collins LJ preferred not to resolve the question of the availability of an action in conversion. His Lordship observed:[15]

the money . . . received by [the collecting bank] by reason of [the] wrongful user of the [payee's] document can be treated as money received by them to the use of the true owners of the document.

Vaughan Williams LJ was likewise inclined to base his action on the count of money had and received:[16]

Having received the money by presenting the document which belonged to the [payees] [the collecting bank] cannot . . . if the [payees] choose to waive the tort, say that they did not receive the money on account of the [payees].

They certainly could not say so after they obtained knowledge of the payee's title.

The reasoning in *Bavins*'s case is perplexing. Why should a person recover in waiver of tort an amount exceeding that recoverable in respect of the tort which he waived? The case, however, clarifies the policy involved in treating cheques as items of property for the purposes of the tort of conversion. The object is to enable the true owner of a cheque to recover the amount which he loses when the instrument is paid through the clearing house to the wrong party.

Under both causes of action—conversion and waiver of tort—the plaintiff has to establish that he is the true owner of the cheque. The phrase 'true owner' is mentioned[17] but is not defined in the Bills of Exchange Act 1882. It follows that whether or not a person is the true owner of a cheque is determined by common law principles, which in turn take into account the special features of negotiable instruments.

Fundamentally, the true owner is the person entitled to the immediate possession of the instrument. In *Bute (Marquess of) v. Barclays Bank Ltd.*,[18] warrants, akin to cheques, were drawn as payable to M but the words 'for the Marquess of Bute' were inserted in a box opposite the payee's name. The

---

[15] Ibid., 277.
[16] Ibid., 278.
[17] BEA, ss. 79(2), 80.
[18] [1955] 1 QB 202, followed in *International Factors Ltd. v. Rodriguez* [1979] KB 351.

instruments were collected for M's personal account. McNair J held that, in order to bring an action in conversion, all the plaintiff had to establish was his entitlement to the immediate possession of the instrument at the time the tort took place. He did not have to show that he had the property in the converted chattel.

Where an instrument had been forged, the true owner is the proprietor of the cheque-book from which the form had been extracted by the rogue.[19] Where a cheque payable to the order of a specific person is removed from that person's custody before he has negotiated the instrument, the title to it cannot pass to a third party; the ostensible payee remains the true owner.[20] The position differs if such a cheque is abstracted by the rogue after the ostensible payee has indorsed it in blank. The cheque thereupon becomes a bearer instrument which is transferable by mere delivery. A person who takes such a cheque for value and in good faith becomes a holder in due course, provided the cheque is complete and regular on its face at the time of its negotiation to the person concerned. A holder in due course acquires a good title to the instrument and hence becomes its true owner.[21] As a general principle, the true owner of the cheque is the last person to whom the instrument has been validly transferred. If the instrument has not been validly issued or negotiated, or if the issuing of the instrument is vitiated by forgery, then the original owner of the piece of paper remains the owner of the cheque.[22]

In certain cases the true ownership of a cheque may be determined only by reference to agency principles. In *Channon* v. *English Scottish and Australian Bank*,[23] a cheque posted by a debtor to his creditor was stolen from the mail by a thief, who successfully presented it for payment to the drawee bank. The Supreme Court of New South Wales held that the drawer's right to sue his own bankers in conversion[24] depended on his being the true owner of the instrument. If the drawer, the debtor, was asked by the creditor to post the cheque, then the Post Office was the creditor's agent for delivery and the creditor would therefore become the cheque's true owner as soon as it was put in transmission. The converse would be the case if the

---

[19] *Morison* v. *London County and Westminster Bank* [1914] 3 KB 356; *Bute (Marquess of)* v. *Barclays Bank Ltd.*, above.

[20] *Lacave & Co.* v. *Crédit Lyonnais* [1897] 1 QB 148, which shows that a person who holds a cheque payable to order under a forged indorsement is not a holder and has no title to it.

[21] *Smith* v. *Union Bank of London* (1875) 1 QBD 31. And see generally Chorley, *Gilbart Lectures* (1953).

[22] *Ladbroke & Co.* v. *Todd* (1914) 30 TLR 433. And see *Commercial Banking Co. of Sydney Ltd.* v. *Mann* [1961] AC 1.

[23] (1918) 18 SR (NSW) 30. See also *London Bank of Australia Ltd.* v. *Kendall* (1920) 28 CLR 401, 409.

[24] The action could, of course, have been brought in breach of mandate, in which case the question of the true ownership would not have arisen.

debtor mailed the cheque on his own initiative. In the absence of direct evidence in point, a new trial was ordered.

3. COLLECTION AND DISCOUNT DISTINGUISHED

The distinction between a collecting bank and a discounting bank is fundamental. A bank that presents a cheque for payment on its customer's behalf acts as an agent. It is a collecting bank which does not purport to acquire the property in the cheque and does not become its holder. The position differs where the bank discounts the cheque. In such a case the bank furnishes consideration to the customer by permitting him to draw against the proceeds of the cheque before its clearance. When the cheque is paid, the discounting bank receives payment of the amount involved for itself.[25]

Whether in a specific case the bank acts as a discounting bank or as a collecting bank depends on the facts. At one time it was thought that the bank became a discounting bank whenever it credited its customer's account with the amount of the cheque before clearance.[26] But on this view every collection of a cheque would have involved a discount because the amount of cheques remitted to a bank for collection has always been credited to the customer's account before clearance. This procedure is utilized as a matter of accounting practice with the aim of obviating the need for short entries of items pending clearance. It is traditionally employed even where the customer is not allowed to draw against the amount so credited until the cheque is cleared. It is now well established that a cheque is discounted only if, apart from crediting its amount to the customer's account before clearance, the bank agrees to grant the customer an overdraft against the proceeds or actually permits him to draw against them.[27]

Thus, in *Re Farrow's Bank Ltd.*[28] a customer's account with the F Bank was credited forthwith with the amount of a cheque payable to him. The pay-in slip, however, contained a note to the effect that the bank reserved to itself the right 'to defer payment of cheques drawn against uncleared effects which may have been credited to the account'. As the F Bank was not a member of a clearing house, it remitted the cheque to the B Bank, where the cheque was forthwith credited to the F bank's account subject to recourse. The cheque was duly honoured upon its presentment by the B Bank to the drawee bank, but the F Bank suspended payment before it received advice

---

[25] *Capital and Counties Bank Ltd.* v. *Gordon* [1903] AC 240, which, on this point, remains good law.
[26] Ibid.
[27] This was specifically clarified by the Bills of Exchange (Crossed Cheques) Act 1906, now replaced by s. 4(1)(*b*) of the Cheques Act 1957.
[28] [1923] 1 Ch. 41.

thereof, and before the proceeds were actually credited to the B Bank's account with the drawee bank. Two issues arose in the case. The first was whether the F Bank had acted as a discounting bank or as a collecting bank. The second was whether, in so far as the F bank had acted as a collecting bank, it had received the proceeds solely as its customer's agent or in the context of the banker and customer relationship between them, in which case the amount would become a debt due to the customer from his bank. In this latter case, the customer would have had to prove in the F bank's liquidation as a general creditor. This would also have been the position if the F Bank had assumed the role of a discounting banker. But if the amount involved had been received by the F bank as a mere agent, the customer would be entitled to have the amount remitted to him in specie.

Astbury J held that the mere crediting of the customer's account did not involve the furnishing of a consideration by the F. Bank.[29] This conclusion was supported by the language of the pay-in slip. To assume the role of a discounting bank, the F Bank would have had to permit its customer to draw against the proceeds. It was further held that the amount of the cheque was received by the F Bank as its customer's agent, and not in circumstances where these proceeds would be credited to his account as a debt owed to him by the F Bank. This regular relationship of debtor and creditor, prevailing between banker and customer under ordinary circumstances, was suspended when the F Bank closed its doors. Amounts received by that bank after that date were received purely on the customer's behalf.[30]

Re Farrow's Bank Ltd. establishes that a cheque is discounted where the bank agrees to grant its customer an overdraft against the proceeds, or actually allows the customer to draw against them before the instrument is cleared. Another instance in which the bank assumes the role of a discounter is where it reduces the customer's existing overdraft by the amount of a cheque before its clearance, with the effect that the proceeds are taken into account in the calculation of the balance, or ceiling, available for drawings.[31]

It follows that there is a clear conceptual demarcation between the collection and the discount of a cheque. In practice, though, the specific role assumed by a bank in a given transaction is not necessarily based on a conscious decision as to whether the cheque is to be collected or discounted. By way of illustration, take a customer's account which has a credit balance adequate for meeting all outstanding cheques drawn by him as they are

---

[29] See also *A. L. Underwood Ltd.* v. *Bank of Liverpool* [1924] 1 KB 775. *Westminster Bank Ltd.* v. *Zang* [1966] AC 182; *Barclays Bank Ltd.* v. *Astley Industrial Trust Ltd.* [1970] 2 QB 527, 539.

[30] The case suggests that the ordinary relationship of banker and customer is determined by the bank's insolvency. See pp. 112–3 above, regarding the bank's insolvency.

[31] *M'Lean* v. *Clydesdale Banking Corporation* (1883) 9 App. Cas. 95.

presented for payment. The question of the discount of any of the cheques paid in by this customer, with a view to granting him an overdraft against their uncleared proceeds, does not even arise. The absence of such a need may, however, be due to a coincidence rather than to a restraint by the customer as regards the drawing of cheques against uncleared effects, as the speed at which the cheques drawn by the customer are presented is out of his control. Indeed, although the customer may have arranged for an overdraft against uncleared proceeds, a delay in the presentment of cheques drawn by him may result in a situation where his bank collects rather than discounts effects payable to him!

Where the customer's balance is inadequate for meeting cheques drawn by him, the bank's decision to allow him to draw against uncleared effects payable to him may again be a matter of chance. If the customer is of good standing, then the bank will permit him to draw against uncleared proceeds within a given ceiling and usually without prior approval. But here, too, the extent of the required overdraft depends on the speed of the presentment for payment of cheques drawn by him. Moreover, if the customer has paid to the credit of his account cheques totalling more than the amount of the required overdraft, the bank will not resolve which of these uncleared items is to be regarded as the one against which a new cheque of the customer is to be debited.[32]

In the case of some banks, the position has been further complicated by the computer programmes currently employed by them in respect of the collection and the payment of cheques. Where a customer's balance, based on cleared effects, is marginally short of the amount required for meeting cheques drawn by him, the bank's computer automatically sanctions the payment of the cheques drawn. The computer does so quite regardless of whether or not there are any uncleared effects deposited for the credit of the customer's account.[33] In reality, the bank is prepared to grant its customer an unsecured overdraft within a given limit and, to this effect, a certain tolerance as regards 'cover' is programmed by the computer. The effect in law is, however, very different. When the bank grants in this manner an overdraft to its customer, if acquires a lien, which is a form of security, over all uncleared effects deposited to the credit of his account.[34] In this way the bank, unwittingly, becomes the holder for value of such effects to the extent of the overdraft or advance involved.[35] As the bank becomes the 'holder' of the uncleared effects, it cannot possibly be regarded a mere

[32] The answer probably depends on the 'rule of appropriation of payments', discussed below, pp. 482–5.
[33] A well-programmed computer can distinguish between the accrued balance and an amount available against uncleared effects.
[34] BEA, s. 27(3), and pp. 576–9 below.
[35] Ibid.

collecting agent. It receives payment of the uncleared effects in part for itself and in part for the customer.

This analysis suggests that, from a practical point of view, it is not easy to draw a clear-cut distinction between a collecting bank and a discounting bank. In effect, the two roles are not mutually exclusive of one another. A bank may be acting at one and the same time as its customer's collecting agent and as a discounting bank. This point has been recognized in *Barclays Bank Ltd.* v. *Astley Industrial Trust Ltd.*,[36] where it was observed that a bank that grants its customer an overdraft of £5 against an uncleared cheque for £100 has given value for it; but it cannot be said that—as a result—the bank ceases to be the customer's agent for collection.

4. THE COLLECTING BANK'S PROTECTION

(i) Background: section 82 and section 4

Conversion is a strict tort.[37] The tortfeasor's good faith is not a valid defence.[38] Banks, however, are not in a position to verify that each of their customers has a good title to every cheque paid to the credit of his account. To save banks from having to collect cheques at their peril, it was felt necessary to introduce a statutory defence.

The original provision in point, in the Crossed Cheques Act 1876,[39] was reproduced without substantial alterations in section 82 of the Bills of Exchange Act 1882. Under this provision, a bank was not liable to the true owner of the cheque where it received payment of the instrument for a customer, and provided the bank was able to establish that it had acted in good faith and without negligence. The two main limitations of this provision were that it applied, first, only to crossed cheques[40] and, secondly, only where the payment involved was received for the customer. The first limitation was introduced by inadvertence: the draftsman of the Act, who was guided by the provision taken from the 1876 Act, did not consider the need to protect banks in respect of the collection of uncrossed cheques. The significance of the second limitation became apparent in the wake of the House of Lords' decision in *Capital and Counties Bank Ltd.* v. *Gordon*.[41] It was there held that section 82 did not protect a bank that had credited the customer's account before the clearance of the cheque because, in such a case,

---

[36] [1970] 2 QB 527, 538.
[37] See, generally, J. G. Fleming, *Law of Torts*, 6th edn., Sydney, 1983, pp. 50 et seq.
[38] See, e.g., *Hollins* v. *Fowler* (1875) LR 7 HL 757.
[39] S. 12, proviso. Interpreted in *Matthiessen* v. *London and County Bank* (1879) 5 CPD 7.
[40] As to which see pp. 252 et seq. above.
[41] [1903] AC 240.

the bank received payment for itself. This decision would have destroyed the effect of section 82 as, under prevailing banking practice, cheques have invariably been credited to the customer's account when deposited by him and not after their clearance.[42] An amendment was, accordingly, passed in 1906,[43] under which a bank was deemed to have received payment of a cheque for a customer notwithstanding that the amount had been credited to his account before clearance.

Section 82 was repealed and replaced by section 4(1) of the Cheques Act 1957,[44] which reads:

> (1) Where a banker, in good faith and without negligence,—
>> (a) receives payment for a customer of an instrument to which this section applies; or
>> (b) having credited a customer's account with the amount of such an instrument, receives payment thereof for himself;
>
> and the customer has no title, or a defective title, to the instrument, the banker does not incur any liability to the true owner of the instrument by reason only of having received payment thereof.

This provision, which is still in force, is wider than section 82. In the first place, section 4 confers the defence involved not only on a collecting bank but also on a discounting bank. This aspect of section 4 is discussed subsequently. Secondly, section 4 is not confined to crossed cheques. Under subsection (2) it applies to all cheques, and is further extended to cover three types of instrument which, though not cheques within the orthodox definition of the term, serve a similar function. The first type comprises documents which though not bills of exchange (and hence not cheques) are issued by a bank's customer in order to enable a person to obtain payment from that bank of the amount of the instrument. The draftsman's object was to extend the protection of section 4 to instruments payable to 'cash or order', which do not constitute bills of exchange within the definition of section 3 of the Bills of Exchange Act 1882.[45] The second type of instrument to which section 4 is made applicable comprises documents issued by public officers with the intention of enabling a person to obtain payment of the sum involved from the Postmaster-General or from the Queen's or Lord Treasurer's Remembrancer. The documents involved are usually outside the definition of a bill, as they are specifically made payable to the designated person subject to his identifying himself and, furthermore, are issued as non-transferable. The third type of instrument comprises drafts payable on demand drawn by a banker on himself, whether payable at the head office

---

[42] Pp. 232–3 above.
[43] Bills of Exchange (Crossed Cheques) Act 1906.
[44] As regards the background of this Act, see pp. 308–9 above.
[45] *Orbit Mining and Trading Co. Ltd.* v. *Westminster Bank Ltd.* [1963] 1 QB 794.

or at some other branch. Such bankers' drafts fall outside the definition of a bill of exchange, as they are not drawn by one person on another.[46]

(ii) Analysis of section 4(1)

Section 4(1) applies a well defined test for the collecting bank's protection. To invoke it successfully the bank has to satisfy four requisites. First, it must establish that it has acted for a customer. Secondly, it must have 'received payment' either for that customer or, if it has credited the customer's account forthwith, for itself. Thirdly, the bank must act in good faith; and, finally, it must act without negligence.

The first requisite has not led to litigation in modern times. Indeed, the fact that section 4(1) applies only where the bank has acted for a customer gives effect to modern banking practice which discourages banks from acting for strangers. However, the construction of the word 'customer' in modern case law has given rise to an element of circularity in the test laid down in section 4(1). It has been shown that 'customer' means a person in whose name the bank has either opened or has agreed to open some type of an account.[47] It follows that, in so far as the other three requisites of section 4(1) are established, the provision applies whenever the bank has credited the amount of the cheque to the account of any person who maintains an account with that bank. The section does not require that the proceeds of the cheque be credited to an account maintained by the payee or by the holder. Section 4(1) would have achieved the same object by requiring that the proceeds be credited to an account other than one maintained in the bank's own name for internal accounting purposes, such as a hold or a suspense account. The reference in section 4(1) to the word 'customer' in addition to the word 'account' is, in effect, redundant. The use of the word 'customer' in the section is based on historical reasons. During the nineteenth century it was thought that a person became a customer, not upon the opening of his account, but after the lapse of some time whereupon the relationship became one of 'habit'.[48] The test aimed at by the draftsman of the 1876 Act was, thus, considerably narrower than that prevailing at present. His object was to confine the application of the protection conferred by the Act to cases in which the bank collected a cheque for an established customer.

The second requisite of section 4(1), to the effect that the proceeds must

---

[46] *Commercial Banking Co. of Sydney Ltd.* v. *Mann* [1961] AC 1, 7.

[47] Pp. 76–80 above.

[48] *Mathews* v. *Brown & Co.* (1894) 63 LJQB 494, which is still echoed in *Great Western Railway Co.* v. *London and County Banking Co. Ltd.* [1901] AC 414. The view was exploded in *Commissioners of Taxation* v. *English, Scottish and Australian Bank Ltd.* [1920] AC 683.

have been 'received', caused some apprehension when the original provision, section 82, was introduced in the Bills of Exchange Act 1882. It was
argued that the section applied only as from the time at which the proceeds
were properly *received* by the collecting bank. It was, indeed, arguable that
the receipt of the funds took place when the amount was credited to the collecting bank's account, i.e. when settlement took place at the Bank of England.[49] This settlement was, of course, preceded by certain steps, taken by
the collecting bank in respect of the cheque, which could in themselves
amount to conversion. As these steps took place before the time at which the
bank acquired its protection under section 4(1), the provision was at one
time described as a trap.[50] The apprehensions in point were, however,
allayed in *Lloyds Bank Ltd.* v. *Savory & Co.*,[51] in which the defence of section 82—the predecessor of section 4—was described as accruing as from
the time at which the cheque was handed to the collecting bank.

There is dearth of authority as regards the third requisite of section 4(1),
concerning the collecting bank's good faith. This is not surprising, as the
bank's good faith is readily established by a denial of actual knowledge and
of any suspicion of the existence of a defect in the customer's title. There is
only one reported case in which the collecting bank's good faith was questioned, and even in this instance the bank was successful.[52]

(iii) Negligence: general stand

Most of the actions against collecting banks concern the fourth requisite of
section 4(1), which is that the collecting bank must have acted without negligence. Section 4(1) does not establish a direct duty of care owed by the
bank to the true owner. Instead, it prescribes a standard with which the
bank has to comply in order to be able to invoke the defence conferred on it.
The distinction between a duty of care and a general observable standard is
of practical importance: the bank loses the protection of section 4(1) whenever it fails to act 'without negligence', and there is no need to establish that
the departure from the standard involved had any direct bearing on the true
owner's position or, indeed, that it was the cause of the loss involved.[53] This
is so although the standard of 'reasonable care' is prescribed in the interests
of the true owner.[54]

---

[49] For the procedure involved, see pp. 233–4 above.
[50] *Capital and Counties Bank Ltd.* v. *Gordon* [1903] AC 240, 244. And see *Morison* v.
London County and Westminster Bank Ltd. [1914] 3 KB 356, per Lord Reading.
[51] [1933] AC 201.
[52] *Lawrie* v. *Commonwealth Trading Bank of Australia* [1970] Qd. R 373.
[53] *Savory & Co* v. *Lloyds Bank Ltd.* [1932] 2 KB 122, 148, per Greer LJ, affd. [1933] AC
201, where the point is considered by Lord Buckmaster at p. 216. And see *Bissell & Co.* v. *Fox
Bros & Co.* (1884) 51 LT 663, varied on a different point: (1885) 53 LT 193.
[54] *Hannan's Lake View Central Ltd.* v. *Armstrong* (1900) 5 Com. Cas. 188, 191.

The standard of care imposed under section 4(1) depends, fundamentally, on what is considered expedient and reasonable in terms of general banking practice.[55] As this practice is subject to change, the standard prescribed by section 4(1) is equally subject to periodic variations. The point is illustrated by two cases.

In the first case, *Lloyds Bank Ltd.* v. *Savory & Co.*,[56] two stockbrokers' clerks misappropriated crossed bearer cheques of their employers. The clerks paid the cheques in at the head office of the defendant bank for the credit of two accounts maintained with branches. One account was maintained in the name of the first clerk and the other account in the name of the second clerk's wife. When opening these accounts, the bank had not asked for the name of the employers of the first clerk nor, in the case of the wife, for the name of her husband's employers. It was established that these oversights were contrary to the practice prescribed in the defendant bank's own manual.

It was held that the bank had failed to discharge its duty to act without negligence. Lord Warrington of Clyffe observed that the standard by which the absence or presence of negligence is to be determined must be ascertained by reference to the practice of reasonable men carrying on the business of bankers and endeavouring to do so in such a manner as may be calculated to protect themselves and others against fraud.[57] To this end, the defendant bank should have ascertained the identity of the employers of the male customer when it agreed to open his account and, in the case of the married woman, the relevant details about her husband's occupation.

In the second and more recent case of *Marfani & Co. Ltd.* v. *Midland Bank Ltd.*,[58] the plaintiffs, a firm of importers, had a substantial client called Eliaszade. A clerk of the plaintiffs, K, introduced himself as 'Eliaszade' to A, a respectable customer of the defendant bank. A in turn introduced K as 'Eliaszade' to this bank, and furnished in good faith a favourable reference. Initially, K paid a small amount in cash to the credit of his new account. He then stole a cheque, drawn by his employers in favour of the true Eliaszade, and arranged for its collection by the defendant bank for the credit of his 'Eliaszade' account. K then withdrew the proceeds.

The Court of Appeal held that the defendant bank had acted without negligence. Diplock LJ observed that the standard of care imposed on a collecting bank has to be interpreted with regard to current banking practice. The

---

[55] *Ross* v. *London County Westminster and Parr's Bank Ltd.* [1919] 1 KB 678, 685; *Commissioners of Taxation* v. *English, Scottish and Australian Bank Ltd.* [1920] AC 683, 689; *A. L. Underwood Ltd.* v. *Bank of Liverpool* [1924] KB 775; *Lloyds Bank Ltd.* v. *Savory & Co.* [1933] AC 201, 221; *Orbit Mining and Trading Co. Ltd.* v. *Westminster Bank Ltd.* [1963] 1 QB 794; *Marfani & Co. Ltd* v. *Midland Bank Ltd.* [1968] 1 WLR 956, 973.
[56] [1933] AC 201.
[57] Ibid., 221.
[58] [1968] 1 WLR 956.

fact that a bank's mode of conduct might be regarded as negligent under authorities decided in a previous era was not conclusive. Banking facilities were considerably less widespread in the past than in recent years, and the required standard of care had changed accordingly. His Lordship thought that whether or not a banker acted 'without negligence' depended on the following test:[59]

> [W]ere those circumstances such as would cause a reasonable banker possessed of such information about his customer as a reasonable banker would possess, to suspect that his customer was not the true owner of the cheque?

If the answer was negative, the banker had acted in accordance with existing banking practice. A court ought in such a case to be hesitant before it condemned as negligent a practice generally adopted by the banking world. One important rider was added to this observation in the concurring judgment of Cairns J. His Lordship warned bankers against an attempt to rely on this decision in order to relax the practice applying to the collection of cheques. Whilst 'the defendant bank here exercised sufficient care, it was . . . only just sufficient'.[60]

Savory & Co.'s case and *Marfani*'s case demonstrate the importance of banking practice for the determination of the bank's standard of care under section 4(1). In the former case the bank was held liable because it had departed from the very stringent practice prescribed in its own manual. In the latter case the bank succeeded because it had adhered to the standard practice of the day. That this new practice would have been regarded as negligent in 1933, when *Savory & Co.*'s case was decided, was considered inconclusive in 1968 when *Marfani & Co.*'s case came before the Court of Appeal. The lesson to be derived from the two cases is that older authorities concerning the collecting bank's standard of care have to be constantly reviewed in the light of changing circumstances. The validity of modern banking practice is, however, subject to the warning in Cairns J's judgment. A dramatic relaxation of the standard of care may induce a court to conclude that banks have manifested an intention to bear the risk of losses resulting from frauds related to cheques. Such a stand would be explainable either by the banking world's realization that it was better equipped to absorb such losses than individual firms or by its tendency to yield to expediencies motivated by the ever-increasing competition for custom.[61]

Although the standard of care expected from a collecting bank is subject to change, there are some well-defined situations in which negligence may

---

[59] Ibid., 973.

[60] Ibid., 982. And see *Crumplin* v. *London Joint Stock Bank Ltd.* (1913) 19 Com. Cas. 69, 109 LT 856, where Pickford J observed that pressure of business does not excuse the bank's carelessness.

[61] On the dangers of such a course, see also *A. L. Underwood Ltd.* v. *Bank of Liverpool* [1924] 1 KB 775, 793, per Scrutton LJ.

take place. Basically, these can be divided into cases in which the bank is careless at the time it opens the customer's account and cases in which the carelessness is directly connected with the cheque received for collection.

(iv) Negligence in opening an account

The notion that the collecting bank's negligence may occur at the time of the opening of the customer's account has its background in the banking practice of the nineteenth centry. Banking facilities were at that period extended primarily to the business community, to members of the professions, and to the landed classes. Banks were particular as regards the acceptance of customers. To date, it has remained customary for banks to demand a reference from a person who wishes to open an account, although in practice applications for the opening of an account with a bank are rarely rejected.[62]

It may be asked whether the bank's duty to make enquiries about new customers has any bearing on the type of case that gives rise to litigation involving the defence conferred under section 4(1). In many of the cases in point the fraud and conversion perpetrated by the collecting bank's customer takes place well after the opening of the account involved. But even in these cases the account is frequently opened by the customer to facilitate the fraud. In theory at least, the bank has the chance of obtaining by means of proper enquiries the type of information that may put it on its guard.

The connection between the bank's carelessness in making due enquiries concerning a new customer and frauds related to cheques collected on his behalf was discussed for the first time at the turn of the century in *Turner* v. *London and Provincial Bank Ltd.*,[63] but the point was left open. The bank's duty to make enquiries was established in *Ladbroke* v. *Todd*.[64] A letter containing a cheque payable to one R. H. Jobson, an undergraduate at Oxford University, was abstracted by a rogue who forged the payee's indorsement on the cheque, and then took it to the defendant, a London banker, asking to open an account for the credit of which he proposed to remit the cheque. The rogue, who pretended to be the true payee, explained that he wished to open this new account as the cheque was in payment of a gambling debt due to him from a bookmaker, and that, if he arranged for its clearing through his usual banking account at Oxford, the college authorities might come to know of his involvement in betting activities. The rogue gave the master of the college as referee, but in view of his story, the bank opened the account

---

[62] As regards current practice, see *Lumsden & Co.* v. *London Trustee Savings Bank* [1971] 1 Lloyd's Rep. 114, referring to the instructions in point to be found in a modern banking manual.
[63] (1903) 2 LDAB 33. Note that Paget, in 24 JIB 220, thought that the failure to make an enquiry was too remote to have a bearing on the fraud.
[64] (1914) 30 TLR 433.

and collected the cheque without making enquiries. The bank was held liable to the drawer of the cheque, who sued as the true owner. It was held that the bank's failure to take up the reference constituted negligence.

In this specific instance, an enquiry by the bank would have been effective, as the rogue was not familiar with the correct proper names of the payee, 'R. H. Jobson', and hence opened the account in the name of 'Richard Henry Jobson' instead of 'Robert Howard Jobson'. An enquiry would have revealed that the man who opened the account was not the person he purported to be. There is, however, authority for the view that the failure to make an enquiry is not excused even if it is unlikely to elucidate the truth.[65] Furthermore, the enquiry made by the bank has to solicit specific details about its propective new customer. In theory, the object of the enquiry is to satisfy the bank that it does not undertake an unusual risk when it opens the new account. The reply should provide the necessary information about the customer. For this reason, a referee's report is considered preferable to an identification, which is not a proper substitute for an introduction or a reference.[66] The only instance in which an identification may suffice is where a new customer, who wishes to open an account shortly after his arrival in the United Kingdom, is unable to furnish a suitable local referee.[67]

The referee's report has to supply certain minimal details. To start with, the referee has to be asked about the customer's character and creditworthiness and, generally, about his circumstances in life. The customer's employment and occupation are also relevant details, as they may alert the banker's attention if at some future time the customer attempts to convert cheques of his employer.[68] At one time, when employment used to be steady, this type of enquiry was of paramount importance. It will be recalled that in *Lloyds Bank Ltd.* v. *Savory & Co.*[69] it was held that the bank had to go so far as to make an enquiry about the employment of the customer's husband. In the present era, when changes in employment have become both common and acceptable, this point is likely to be given less emphasis by the courts. Thus, in *Orbit Mining and Trading Co. Ltd.* v. *Westminster Bank Ltd.*[70] it was held that the bank was not under a duty to keep an eye on changes in its customers' employment.

The ruling in *Orbit* is to be explained by the phenomenal increase in the

---

[65] A. L. Underwood Ltd. v. Bank of Liverpool [1924] 1 KB 775. As regards the need for references, see also *Hampstead Guardians* v. *Barclays Bank Ltd.* (1923) 39 TLR 229. Cf. *Commissioners of Taxation* v. *English, Scottish and Australian Bank Ltd.* [1920] AC 683.

[66] *Marfani & Co. Ltd.* v. *Midland Bank Ltd.* [1968] 1 WLR 956; *Lumsden & Co.* v. *London Trustee Savings Bank* [1971] 1 Lloyd's Rep. 114.

[67] *Lumsden & Co.* v. *London Trustee Savings Bank*, above.

[68] *Lloyds Bank Ltd* v. *Savory & Co.* [1933] AC 201.

[69] Above.

[70] [1963] 1 QB 794, 825.

number of persons who utilize banking facilities. At present, it has become impossible for banks to be familiar with the position of each of their customers. The courts have taken notice of this change of circumstances. Thus, in 1929 it was suggested in *Lloyds Bank Ltd.* v. *Chartered Bank of India, Australia and China*[71] that, in addition to the enquiries made when the customer's account is opened, the bank is under a duty to scrutinize the account from time to time so as to assure itself that everything appears regular. *Orbit*'s case shows that this suggestion is no longer in accord with modern banking practice.

In point of fact, there is good reason for doubting the entire usefulness of the request for a reference in the present era. Fundamentally, the prospective customer's referee may be either a person who is well known to the bank, such as an existing customer, or a stranger. In the former case, the bank is deemed to be entitled to rely on the referee's judgment. In the latter case, the manuals of most banks prescribe that a referee who is unknown to the bank be asked to give the name of his own bankers when he replies to the enquiry. *Marfani*'s case, discussed earlier on, shows the ease with which even a respectable customer of a bank can be misled by an imaginative rogue who wishes to use him as a referee. In the case of a referee who is a stranger, the hazard of a misleading reference is demonstrated by *Lumsden & Co.* v. *London Trustee Savings Bank.*[72]

In this case, a firm of accountants used to make cheques payable to their clients in an abbreviated manner. Thus, cheques payable to a firm by the name of Brown & Co. were made payable to 'Brown'. A clerk used this procedure to his own advantage. He opened an account with the defendant bank in the name of 'Brown' and gave himself as referee. Unsurprisingly, he wrote a glowing reference about 'Brown' but failed to comply with the defendant bank's request to mention the name of his own bankers. He then converted cheques drawn by his employers to the order of 'Brown', added his assumed initials, and paid the cheques into his 'Brown' account. The bank was held to have acted with negligence as it had not followed up the referee's reply by further enquiries as to his bankers. In failing to do so, the bank had deviated from the procedure laid down in its own manual. On this basis the decision is unexceptional: an enquiry as to the rogue's bankers would have disclosed that the 'referee' was employed by the very firm whose cheques were being paid into the bogus account!

In reality, though, a determined rogue usually finds means for defeating a system based on communications such as references. In a society in which a large segment of the population has free access to banking facilities, the

---

[71] [1929] 1 KB 40, 70.
[72] [1971] 1 Lloyd's Rep.114. And see *Nu-Stilo Footwear Ltd.* v. *Lloyds Bank Ltd.* (1956) 7 LDAB 121, 77 *JIB* 239.

reference of a customer loses a great deal of its significance. It is no longer what it used to be in the period of *Savory & Co.*'s case,[73] namely a document issued by a person whose status as the customer of a bank evidenced his standing and reputation. It is thus not surprising that some banks have effectively discontinued the practice of demanding references as a prerequisite to the opening of a new account.

(v) Negligence in collection: frauds by employees, trustees, and agents

The conversion by employees of cheques owned by their employers is a common source of litigation. In some cases the employee pays to the credit of his personal account a cheque payable to the employer. A forged indorsement of the employer's name is usually executed in such cases. In other cases the employee either abuses his authority to draw cheques on the employer's account or resorts to forgery of the employer's signature or to the making of material alterations in cheques handed to him by the employer in a semi-complete state.[74] Here again, the employee arranges for the collection of the cheques for his own credit. The same practices are occasionally employed by agents who abuse their principals' trust[75] and by directors or other officers of a company.

The basic rule is that whenever a bank is aware that an employer or a principal has an interest in a cheque paid to the credit of the account of an employee, an agent or a director, the bank is put on enquiry.[76] But this is only a general rule. There are circumstances in which the bank has no reason to become suspicious. Thus, the monthly wage cheque drawn by a firm's treasurer or secretary for his salary can be collected for the credit of his personal account without the need for an enquiry. The same applies to cheques for small amounts which can be taken to involve the reimbursement of expenses. But the fact that cheques payable to the employers are paid regularly into the employee's account, bearing a 'per pro' indorsement, does not exonerate the bank if it had failed to make an enquiry at the initial stages. The words 'per pro' may, in effect, constitute a red flag, as they indicate to the bank that the employee acts by procuration and that there is, therefore, a possibility of an abuse of authority.[77]

---

[73] [1933] AC 201, discussed above.

[74] *London Joint Stock Bank Ltd.* v. *Macmillan and Arthur* [1918] AC 777, discussed above, p. 293, is an illustration in point.

[75] As in *Slingsby* v. *District Bank Ltd.* [1932] 1 KB 544, discussed above, p. 294.

[76] *Souchette* v. *London County Westminster and Parr's Bank Ltd.* (1920) 36 TLR 195; *Lloyds Bank Ltd.* v. *Savory & Co.* [1933] AC 201; *Bute (Marquess of)* v. *Barclays Bank Ltd.* [1955] 1 QB 202. And see *A. L. Underwood Ltd.* v. *Bank of Liverpool* [1924] 1 KB 775; Cf. *Moser* v. *Commercial Banking Co. of Sydney Ltd.* (1974) 22 FLR 123 (Aust.).

[77] *Morison* v. *London County and Westminster Bank Ltd.* [1914] 3 KB 356, which on this point is actually supported by *Midland Bank Ltd.* v. *Reckitt* [1933] AC 1.

Two cases illustrates the ramifications of the bank's duty of care in cases of this type. In *Lloyds Bank Ltd* v. *Chartered Bank of India, Australia and China*,[78] the chief accountant of the plaintiff bank had the authority to draw cheques on an account which his principals had with another bank. In abuse of this authority, he drew cheques on this account, made them payable to yet a third bank, and had them collected for a personal account which he kept without his principal's knowledge with that third bank. The cheques were collected without enquiries although the collecting bank was aware of the accountant's employment. It was assumed that the drawings and the collection of the cheques in question had some taxation purposes. The collecting bank was held liable in conversion, as the defence of section 82 (now section 4(1)) failed. The bank was negligent in collecting without enquiries for the accountant's personal account cheques drawn on his principals. The bank's suspicions should have been aroused by a set of circumstances. First the cheques were drawn, without any discernible reason, by the accountant—an employee or agent—on the account maintained by his employers with another bank. Secondly, the amounts involved were substantial. Thirdly, as soon as the cheques were cleared, the accountant drew large sums against the proceeds in favour of persons who, to the collecting bank's knowledge, were his stockbrokers. Foul play should therefore have been suspected. An enquiry would have readily disclosed the truth.

In *Australia and New Zealand Bank Ltd.* v. *Ateliers de Constructions Electriques de Charleroi*,[79] the collecting bank was in a position that lulled it into safety. A foreign company carried on business in Australia through an agent. Amounts due to the firm were usually settled by cheques made payable to it. These cheques were sent to the agent, who indorsed them and arranged for their collection for the credit of his personal account. Amounts received were regularly remitted by the agent to the foreign principals but, in the end, he became heavily indebted to them, as he had used susbtantial sums for his own purposes.

The foreign firm's action in conversion against the collecting bank was unsuccessful. It was established that the cheques in question had been payable in Australian currency and that it would have been unreasonable to dispatch them overseas for the principals' indorsement. It was further proved that the agent had the authority to receive payments made to the principals in cash, and that the principals had never raised any objection to the clearance of cheques payable to themselves through the agent's account. The principals, thus, had been content to leave the settlement of all Australian accounts in the agent's hands. On these facts it was held that the course of business so established conferred on the agent an authority to indorse the

---

[78] [1929] 1 KB 40. And see *United Australia Ltd.* v. *Barclays Bank Ltd.* [1941] AC 1, 23–4; *Bute (Marquess) of* v. *Barclays Bank Ltd.* [1955] 1 QB 202.
[79] [1967] AC 86.

cheques, and that the collecting bank was therefore not negligent in crediting them to his personal account. The bank, furthermore, was under no duty to supervise the drawing of amounts received by the agent. Unlike the bank in the previously discussed case, the bank in the present case was not expected to keep a watchful eye. It may be that, to a certain extent, the apparent difference in standard is explainable on the basis of the change in banking practice that took place during the thirty-six years that had elapsed between the two decisions.

Employers and corporations are not the only targets of frauds committed by persons in positions of trust. Public authorities are occasionally defrauded by high-ranking officials, such as rate-collectors or officers employed in a paymaster's office. Banks have to exercise caution where cheques drawn on such bodies are paid into an officer's personal account.[80] The same applies where a cheque, collected for the credit of the personal account of a trustee, is drawn on a trust account.[81] Obviously, it is important for the bank to exercise common sense.[82] A trustee will, undoubtedly, be entitled to periodic payments for services rendered to the trust, just as a civil servant is entitled to his salary. But when the cheque, paid into a personal account out of a trust or a public fund, is of a particularly large amount, the bank ought to make an enquiry.[83]

(vi) Negligence related to crossings

Negligence on the collecting bank's part may take place at the time at which the cheque is handed to it. This occurs where the bank pays inadequate attention to specific details of the cheque such as a crossing and indorsements, or ignores specific aspects which question the regularity of the instrument.

It will be recalled that crossings can be divided into special and general crossings.[84] The former type is now obsolete and it is, in any event, unlikely

---

[80] *Ross v. London County Westminster and Parr's Bank Ltd.* [1919] 1 KB 678.

[81] *House Property Co. of London Ltd. v. London County and Westminster Bank Ltd.* (1915) 31 TLR 479.

[82] Thus, the bank need not scrutinize every cheque paid into a stockbroker's account although it is known that, in practice, he deals in trust money: *Thomson v. Clydesdale Bank* [1893] AC 282. See also *London and Montrose Shipbuilding and Repairing Co. Ltd. v. Barclays Bank Ltd.* (1925) 31 Com. Cas. 67, where Mackinnon J refused to accept that the bank was automatically put on enquiry where a cheque payable to a company was collected for an indorsee's account; this finding appears unaffected by the decision of the Court of Appeal, ibid., 182, which reversed the decision on the facts.

[83] *Lloyds Bank Ltd. v. Chartered Bank of India, Australia and China* [1929] 1 KB 40; *Motor Traders Guarantee Corporation Ltd. v. Midland Bank Ltd.* [1937] 4 All ER 90; *Baker v. Barclays Bank Ltd.* [1955] 1 WLR 822; *Day v. Bank of New South Wales* (1978) 19 ALR 32 (Aust.).

[84] Pp. 253–4 above.

that a bank will collect a cheque which is specially crossed to some other bank. An ordinary or general crossing does not impose any particular duty to take care on the bank to whom a cheque is remitted for collection. At one time, it was thought that the collecting bank had to exercise extra care when a crossing was accompanied by the words 'not negotiable', as these words could possibly hint at a defect in the payee's title.[85] But this view is no longer supported.[86] The words 'not negotiable' have the object of precluding a transferee of a cheque from becoming a holder in due course. They do not suggest that a cheque has to be collected for the account of the ostensible payee.[87] Such a cheque remains transferable[88] and may, therefore, be collected for an account other than the ostensible payee's.[89] However, it will be shown that if a cheque is collected for an account other than that of the ostensible payee, the bank needs to satisfy itself that it bears an indorsement appearing to be in that payee's name.

Extreme caution is needed where cheques are crossed and marked 'account payee only'. Some South African authorities suggest that the words in question restrict the transferability of a cheque so that it may under no circumstances be collected for an account other than the ostensible payee's.[90] But this view has been questioned in the latest authority in point,[91] and runs counter to the prevailing view in the United Kingdom and in Australia. The better view is that the words in question constitute a warning to the collecting bank that the cheque may be collected for an account other than the ostensible payee's only subject to an acceptable explanation.[92] This applies even if the words 'a/c payee only' are added to a cheque payable to X or bearer.[93] The words 'or bearer' are in such a case treated as superseded by the fact that the cheque is marked as payable to the account of a specifically designated payee.[94]

[85] *Great Western Railway Co.* v. *London and County Banking Co. Ltd.* [1901] AC 414, 422, echoed in *Morison* v. *London County and Westminster Bank Ltd.* [1914] 3 KB 356, 373. And see *Turner* v. *London and Provincial Bank Ltd.* (1903) 2 LADB 33.

[86] Paget, *Law of Banking*, 9th edn., pp. 347–8.

[87] Pp. 255–6 above.

[88] Pp. 246–7 above.

[89] *Crumplin* v. *London Joint Stock Bank Ltd.* (1913) 19 Com. Cas. 69, 109 LT 856. This applies also where the crossing is opened by the use of the words 'pay cash': *Smith and Baldwin* v. *Barclays Bank Ltd.* (1944) 5 LDAB 370, 375, 65 JIB 171.

[90] *Dungarvin Trust (Pty.) Ltd.* v. *Import Refrigeration Co. (Pty.) Ltd.* [1971] 4 SALR 300; *Rhostar (Pvt.) Ltd.* v. *Netherlands Bank of Rhodesia Ltd.* [1972] 2 SALR 703, 705.

[91] *Standard Bank of South Africa Ltd.* v. *Sham Magazine Centre* [1977] 1 SALR 48 (App. Div).

[92] *Bevan* v. *National Bank Ltd.* (1906) 23 TLR 65; *Morison* v. *London County and Westminster Bank Ltd.* [1914] 3 KB 356, 373–4 (obiter dictum); *Ross* v. *London County Westminster and Parr's Bank Ltd.* [1919] 1 KB 678, 687; *Rhostar (Pvt.) Ltd.* v. *Netherlands Bank of Rhodesia Ltd.*, above.

[93] *House Property Co. of London Ltd.* v. *London County and Westminster Bank Ltd.* (1915) 31 TLR 479.

[94] And see pp. 256–7 above.

The collecting bank's duty to make enquiries in respect of a cheque bearing the words 'account payee only' arises mainly in cases in which a cheque is remitted for collection by an individual or by an inland firm. In *Importers Co. Ltd.* v. *Westminster Bank Ltd.*,[95] a cheque bearing the words in question was remitted by a foreign bank to an English bank for collection for the credit of a person other than the ostensible payee. It was held that the English bank was not negligent, although it had failed to make enquiries as regards the identity of the person for whom the cheque was collected. The same reasoning ought to be applicable whenever a clearing bank is engaged to collect a cheque remitted to it by any other, non-clearing, bank.

Even where the bank is put on guard by the words in question, it is not obligated to refuse to collect the cheque. The collecting bank's duty is restricted to the making of due enquiries. It would be absurd to regard the bank as negligent if, at the request of the person for whose 'account only' the cheque was payable, it collected the instrument for the credit of some other account.[96] Such cases are common if the ostensible payee does not have a banking account of his own, or if some business consideration induces him to arrange that the cheque be credited to the account of some other person, such as his spouse or son.

(vii) Negligence related to indorsements

Until 1957 one of the traps encountered by collecting banks concerned the regularity of the payee's indorsement. There was authority for the view that, if the bank collected a cheque on which the payee's indorsement was absent or irregular, the bank forfeited its defence under section 82, the predecessor of section 4.[97] The seriousness of the problem is readily appreciated when one reflects on the general unfamiliarity of members of the public with the exact initials of individuals to whom they send cheques in payment of accounts, and with the exact style of the names of commercial firms. Misnomers of the payee are common. Up to 1957, bankers asked to collect cheques for their customers were therefore in a precarious position. To start with, it was cumbersome and time-consuming to verify the material correspondence of each indorsement of the payee of a cheque with the name by which he was described by the drawer. In addition, it would have brought the entire clearing system to a standstill if, on perusal, banks had to return to their customers every cheque which was irregularly indorsed.

[95] [1927] 2 KB 297.
[96] *Souhrada* v. *Bank of New South Wales* [1976] 2 Lloyd's Rep. 444, 452 (where the payee requested that the cheque be collected for the account of another person).
[97] *Bevins Junr. & Sims* v. *London and South Western Bank Ltd.* [1900] 1 QB 270. And see *Bissell & Co.* v. *Fox Bros. & Co.* (1884) 51 LT 663 varied, on a different point, (1885) 53 LT 193.

In some Commonwealth jurisdictions, the banking community solved its problem by supplying customers with cheque books including forms reading 'pay _____ or bearer'. As such an instrument, when completed, constitutes a bearer cheque,[98] an indorsement is not needed for its transfer and the collecting bank is, thus, not negligent by collecting it for any customer or 'bearer'. In the United Kingdom, in which cheque forms traditionally assumed the style of 'pay _____ or order',[99] there was a need for reform. The problem was considered by the Mocatta Committee,[100] which concluded that, in view of the volume of banking business, the need to verify the regularity of indorsements ought to be abolished.

This recommendation was given effect by the enactment of section 4(3) of the Cheques Act 1957, which provides that a banker is not negligent *by reason only* of his failure to concern himself with the absence of or the irregularity in an indorsement.[101] This provision was, however, considered too sweeping by the CLCB, which thought that it was in the interest of the public that, in certain cases, collecting banks should continue to require regular indorsements of cheques. A circular in point, issued on 23 September 1957, prescribed that indorsements continue to be required in three cases. The first was where a cheque was tendered for an account other than that of the ostensible payee. In such cases the bank had to verify the regularity of the indorsements of the original payee and of any subsequent party to whom the cheque had been specially indorsed, except the customer for whose account the instrument was collected. The second type of case was where the payee's name was misspelt on the cheque, or where he was incorrectly designated and the surrounding circumstances were suspicious. Thirdly, the indorsement of each payee continued to be needed where the cheque was payable jointly to more than one person but was collected for an account to which not all payees were parties.[102]

Although the circular in question did not have the force of law, the practice established by it has remained in effect. A bank that ignores it does so at its peril. This is due to the wording of section 4(3), under which a bank is not to be considered negligent 'by reason only' of the defect related to the indorsement. If the bank disregards the procedures consecrated by the

---

[98] See pp. 243–4 above.

[99] Oddly enough, bearer forms were common during the second half of the nineteenth century, but order forms have taken precedence from the beginning of this century.

[100] See pp. 308–9 above.

[101] The bank is therefore discharged from liability: *Westminster Bank* v. *Zang* [1966] AC 182, 218.

[102] Indorsements also remained necessary under the circular in the case of the collection of the following documents: bills of exchange other than cheques; promissory notes; drafts and other instruments drawn on the General Post Office; internal revenue warrants; drafts drawn on the Paymaster-General or the Queen's and Lord Treasurer's Remembrancer; drafts drawn on the Crown Agents and other specified agents; travellers' cheques and instruments payable by banks abroad.

circular, it is negligent not by reason of the irregular or absent indorsement but because it has departed from the guidelines concerning indorsements formulated by the CLCB, which can currently be taken to represent prevailing banking practice. It can, further, be assumed that where the circular requires the collecting bank to demand an indorsement, it is essential that this indorsement be regular.[103]

(viii) Negligence: summary

The instances outlined above are by no means an exhaustive list of the situations in which a bank may be held to have acted negligently within the meaning of section 4(1). The constant changes in banking practice may lead to the development of new case law in point. Thus, the practice under which cheques can be paid in at any clearing bank for the credit of an account with any branch of that very bank, or of any other bank, is likely to lead to litigation. It is equally possible that procedures which were considered to involve negligence in days gone by may currently be sanctioned by modern practice.[104]

It is further believed that one factor which has not been given adequate emphasis to date is the amount of the cheque.[105] It is arguable that, where an oddity or red flag appears in a cheque for a relatively small amount, the collecting bank is entitled to be satisfied on the basis of a cursory enquiry that may not suffice where the amount of the cheque is out of proportion to the known position in life of the customer.

In all cases of conversion, the bank's duty to act without negligence is given a reasonable construction. The bank is not expected to assume the role of an amateur detective, and need not be unduly suspicious.[106] Thus, in *Orbit Mining and Trading Co. Ltd. v. Westminster Bank Ltd.*[107] a rogue perpetrated a series of frauds by utilizing a cheque-book of the company left in his sole custody by a fellow director. In some instances, cheques had been signed by the fellow director in blank so that the rogue was able to complete them by adding his signature. In other cases he forged his fellow director's

---

[103] Paget, *Law of Banking*, 9th edn., p. 335.

[104] E.g., the failure to enquire at the time of the opening of the account about the occupation of the customer's spouse, which was held to involve negligence in *Lloyds Bank Ltd.* v. *Savory & Co.* [1933] AC 201.

[105] Although the collection without enquiry of a cheque the sum of which is out of proportion to the customer's station in life has been held to involve negligence: *Lloyds Bank Ltd.* v. *Chartered Bank of India, Australia and China Ltd.* [1929] 1 KB 40; *Motor Traders Guarantee Corporation Ltd.* v. *Midland Bank Ltd.* [1937] 4 All ER 90; *Nu-Stilo Footwear* v. *Lloyds Bank Ltd.* (1956) 7 LDAB 121, 77 JIB 239; *Day* v. *Bank of New South Wales* (1978) 19 ALR 32 (Aust.).

[106] *Penmount Estates Ltd.* v. *National Provincial Bank Ltd.* (1945) 173 LT 344, 346. See also *Smith and Baldwin* v. *Barclays Bank Ltd.* (1944) 65 JIB 171; 5 LDAB 370.

[107] [1963] 1 QB 794.

signature and added his own. He made all these cheques out either to 'cash or order' or to himself, and paid them for the credit of his personal account with the defendant bank. To camouflage his dual role as signatory and payee, he used for his indorsement a signature differing from that executed by him on the front of the cheque. The bank was unaware of the roque's current occupation because he had changed his post and entered the service of the company after the opening of his account. The bank, therefore, collected the cheques without making enquiries. The company's action in conversion failed as the bank was held entitled to the protection of section 4. The bank had not acted negligently by failing to compare the signature with the indorsement although, consequently, it did not discover that the customer was both the payee and the actual drawer of the cheque. The fact that some of the cheques were payable to 'cash or order' was likewise no cause for extra concern.

5. THE DEFENCE OF CONTRIBUTORY NEGLIGENCE

In certain situations the conversion of a cheque is facilitated by the true owner's carelessness. This is the case where a cheque is handed to an employee in an incomplete form, or where an employee is left in charge of the affairs of his employers without any attempt at supervision. In *Morison* v. *London County and Westminster Bank Ltd.*,[108] it was suggested that, on common law principles, the true owner of a series of cheques converted by his employee and collected by the latter's bank, ought not to succeed if his actions had lulled the bank into safety or alleviated its suspicions. The weakness in this argument is that, if the bank's own negligence had facilitated the conversion of the initial instrument, the bank should not be heard to argue that it was misled by the true owner's lack of vigilance on later occasions.

An alternative defence, which has been mooted for some time, is the plea of contributory negligence, under which the loss is to be apportioned between the bank and the true owner on the basis of their respective negligent acts. At one stage the availability of this defence was doubted because the true owner's action against the bank was brought in conversion or based on waiver of tort. It was, thus, not an action in negligence. It was thought that, as the true owner was not attempting to recover damages for a loss resulting from the bank's breach of a duty of care owed to him, he could equally not be regarded as being in breach of a duty of care owed by him to the bank.[109]

---

[108] [1914] 3 KB 356.
[109] This view is echoed in *Savory & Co.* v. *Lloyds Bank Ltd.* [1932] 2 KB 122 137 per Lawrence LJ, affd. [1933] AC 201.

The thrust of this analysis was to assert that contributory negligence could not be maintained as a defence in an action brought for a tort other than negligence. This view was refuted in 1950 by the New Zealand Court of Appeal in *Helson* v. *McKenzies (Cuba Street) Ltd.*[110] A handbag which a customer had forgotten at a counter of a department store was innocently delivered by a shop assistant to an impostor. A plea of contributory negligence raised as a partial defence to the customer's action in conversion was allowed on the basis of a local provision *in pari materia* with section 1 of the Law Reform (Contributory Negligence) Act 1945. The Court held that it was not necessary to establish that the customer—the plaintiff—had committed a breach of duty of care owed by her to the store-owners. Contributory negligence was established once it was shown that the plaintiff had acted in a careless manner that facilitated the conversion of the chattel.

The reasoning in *Helson's* case was adopted by Donaldson J in *Lumsden & Co.* v. *London Trustee Savings Bank,*[111] in which an employer's lack of vigilance and careless mode of drawing cheques enabled an employee to appropriate them to his own use. It was held that the employers' carelessness, which had facilitated the fraud, involved contributory negligence on their part, and could be raised as a partial defence to the employers' action in conversion against the collecting bank.

A series of Australian decisions[112] has questioned the correctness of this decision on the ground that, under section 1, the defence of contributory negligence is available only in situations in which it could have been pleaded as an absolute defence at common law. At common law, it is asserted, the plea was available only in respect of actions in negligence. The point is debatable from an historical point of view. In the United Kingdom it has been settled by section 47 of the Banking Act 1979, under which the defence is available to a banker 'in any circumstances in which proof of absence of negligence on the part of the banker would be a defence in proceedings by reason of section 4 of the Cheques Act 1957'.[113]

It is believed that the plea of contributory negligence provides an equitable solution. There is no justification for forcing banks to carry the full losses incurred in a fraud facilitated by the carelessness of the drawer of a cheque. The argument that, commercially, losses of this type can be more readily absorbed by banks than by individual firms is without merit. In the first place, a means test constitutes an arbitrary method for the distribution

---

[110] [1950] NZLR 878.

[111] [1971] 1 Lloyd's Rep. 114; facts discussed in full above, p. 429.

[112] *Wilton* v. *Commonwealth Trading Bank of Australia* [1973] 2 NSWLR 644; *Tina Motors Pty. Ltd.* v. *Australian and New Zealand Banking Group Ltd.* [1977] VR 205, 208–9; *Day* v. *Bank of New South Wales* (1978) 19 ALR 32, 42 et seq. Cf. *Varker* v. *Commercial Banking Co. of Sydney Ltd.* [1972] 2 NSWLR 967.

[113] The object of this provision was to resolve any doubts that could have arisen on this point under s. 11(1) of the Torts (Interference with Goods) Act 1977.

of losses. Secondly, if such losses have to be absorbed by the banks they are bound to be passed on to the general body of customers by means of eventual increases in bank charges. There is no reason for apportioning losses incurred due to the carelessness of specific individuals or firms among the general body of the collecting bank's customers.

6. THE DISCOUNTING BANK'S PROTECTION

On occasions a discounting bank is entitled to plead two defences against an action for the conversion of a cheque. The first is the defence based on section 4 of the Cheques Act 1957. The second defence is that, by discounting the cheque, the bank became its holder in due course and consequently acquired an indefeasible title to the instrument. Each defence has advantages as well as pitfalls.

For a considerable period of time some authorities continued to maintain that, even after the enactment of the Cheques Act in 1957, the defence of section 4 was not available to a discounting bank.[114] Support for this view was found in the marginal note of the section, which reads: 'Protection of bankers collecting payment of cheques etc.'. A discounting bank was, accordingly, alleged to be outside the ambit of this provision. However, the language of the section itself supports the very opposite view, as the provision explicitly protects a banker, who 'having credited a customer's account with the amount of such an instrument receives payment thereof for himself'.

The view that section 4 is wide enough to protect a discounting bank is further supported by a consideration of the historical background of this provision. It will be recalled that, originally, section 82 of the 1882 Act applied only where a bank 'received payment for a customer'. This phraseology induced the House of Lords to conclude, in *Capital and Counties Bank Ltd.* v. *Gordon*,[115] that the section was inapplicable where the bank credited the customer's account before clearance as, in such a case, the bank received payment for itself. Under the ensuing amending Act of 1906,[116] a bank was deemed to have received payment for a customer notwithstanding that it credited his account before receiving payment of the cheque. Obviously, this specific amendment did not purport to extend the protection of section 82 to a banker who, in addition to the crediting of the customer's account before clearance, agreed to grant him overdraft facilities against the cheque. In such a situation, the crediting of the customer's account was not

---

[114] See, e.g., Paget, *Law of Banking*, 7th edn., London, 1966; but see now ibid., 9th edn., p. 335. See also Chalmers, *Bills of Exchange*, 13th edn., p. 311.

[115] [1903] AC 240.

[116] The Bills of Exchange (Crossed Cheques Act) 1906, s. 1.

a mere matter of accounting procedure, and the bank became a holder of the cheque.[117] It followed that, in such cases, the bank received payment of the instrument for itself. Thus, between 1906 and 1957 the defence of section 82 remained available only to a collecting bank. It could not be pleaded by a discounting bank.

The position has been altered by section 4 of the 1957 Act, as its language is patently wider than that of the 1906 amendment. As pointed out above, subsection 1(*b*) extends the defence to a bank which, having credited the customer's account, receives payment for itself. This formula encompasses the discounting bank's activity. Obviously, to succeed under section 4 the discounting bank has to satisfy the requirements prescribed in this provision. The bank must have acted in good faith and without negligence for a customer. Furthermore, the discounting bank can invoke the defence of section 4 only if the amount of the cheque has been credited to the customer's account. If the discount was arranged by means of payment of cash against the instrument or by the crediting of some third party's account, the section is inapplicable.[118]

Where a discounting bank is unable to invoke the defence of section 4, it may still resist a claim by establishing that it received payment as the holder in due course of the instrument. The holder in due course of a negotiable instrument becomes its true owner and cannot be sued in conversion.[119] To be considered the holder in due course of a cheque, the bank has to prove that it took it in good faith and for value, and that the cheque was, at that time, complete and regular on its face.[120]

The last requirement can frequently constitute a pitfall. A cheque is considered incomplete if any material detail, such as the name of the payee or the amount payable, is missing. A cheque is considered irregular whenever anything in it ought to give rise to doubts or suspicion, as is the case where the words denoting the amount differ from the figures, or where the cheque is pasted together after having been torn.[121] Moreover, the word 'face' in section 29 of the Bills of Exchange Act 1882 includes the back of the cheque. Under this section a cheque payable to order is, therefore, considered irregular if it is unindorsed or if it is irregularly indorsed by the payee.[122] But the requisite concerning the indorsements has been mitigated

---

[117] *Re Farrow's Bank Ltd.* [1923] 1 Ch. 41; *A. L. Underwood Ltd.* v. *Bank of Liverpool* [1924] 1 KB 775.

[118] In this regard the position has remained the same as under section 82, which was discussed in this regard in *Capital and Counties Bank Ltd.* v. *Gordon* [1903] AC 240. And see *Great Western Railways* v. *London and County Banking Co Ltd.* [1903] AC 414; *Commissioners of Taxation* v. *English, Scottish and Australian Bank Ltd.* [1920] AC 683.

[119] Pp. 287–8 above.

[120] BEA, s. 29, discussed above, pp. 505–6.

[121] p. 505 below.

[122] *Arab Bank Ltd.* v. *Ross* [1952] 2 QB 216.

by the Cheques Act 1957. Section 2 confers on a bank which gives value for a cheque payable to order, which the holder delivers to it for collection without indorsing it, such rights as the bank would have had if the cheque had been indorsed in blank.

Two cases show that a discounting bank may rely on section 2 in order to establish that it is a holder in due course of an unindorsed cheque. In *Midland Bank Ltd.* v. *R. V. Harris Ltd.*,[123] a customer paid into his personal account with the plaintiff bank two cheques drawn by the defendant on Lloyds Bank and payable to the customer's firm. The cheques were dishonoured by Lloyds Bank, and the plaintiff bank brought an action claiming to be a holder in due course of the cheques. It was proved that the customer was allowed to draw against the cheques before their clearance. Although the cheques did not bear an indorsement, it was held that, under section 2, the plaintiff bank was to be treated as a holder in due course of the cheques despite the absence of an indorsement.[124]

In *Westminster Bank* v. *Zang*,[125] a customer of the plaintiff bank paid into the account of a company of which he was a director, and which maintained its account with the same bank, an unindorsed cheque, drawn by the defendant and payable to the customer's order. The defendant stopped the cheque, which was accordingly dishonoured by the drawee bank. The plaintiff bank brought an action to enforce payment, claiming to be a holder in due course. As it was proved that the plaintiff bank had not given value for the cheque, it was held that it was not a holder in due course or for value, and could not enforce payment. The House of Lords held, however, that if the plaintiff bank had given value for the cheque, it would have been a holder in due course despite the missing indorsement. It was further held that the fact that the cheque was not collected for the original payee's account was irrelevant.

These two cases demonstrate that a bank may be considered a holder in due course in circumstances in which an ordinary member of the public—who is less familiar with negotiable instruments than a bank—would not be so regarded. It should be noted that a person may be a holder in due course although he has acted with negligence.[126] Accordingly, a discounting bank may find it useful to rely on its being a holder in due course of a cheque if it is unable to prove that it had acted without negligence. If the bank cannot show that it is a holder in due course, for example, where it has discounted an order cheque bearing a forged indorsement,[127] it may still escape liability

[123] [1963] 1 WLR 1021.
[124] The circular of 11 Sept., 1957, mentioned above, was not discussed. Probably no reliance was put on it, as the plaintiff bank had discounted rather than collected the cheques.
[125] [1966] AC 182.
[126] P. 505 below.
[127] P. 504 below.

for conversion by relying on section 4, provided the cheque has been credited to the account of a customer.

7. THE PROCESSING BANK'S POSITION

In certain cases the holder of a cheque delivers it to a branch other than that with which he maintains his account. This appears to have been possible as from the turn of the century if both branches were of the same bank. The Golden Memorandum[128] of 1967 went further than that. It enabled a person to remit a cheque to any branch of one of the participating banks for the credit of any account maintained with one of the banks within the system. Although the memorandum is no longer in effect, there are specific arrangements—known as agency agreements—between the clearing banks which give effect to the system on a bank to bank basis.

Where a customer remits a cheque to his bank account through any branch of his own bank, the position is simple. As a bank constitutes one single legal entity regardless of the number of its branches, the branch to which the holder remits his cheque and the branch of the same bank at which he maintains the account credited with the proceeds constitute two arms of the collecting bank. The fact that the cheque is collected through a branch other than that with which the account is maintained does not in itself involve negligence, and does not deprive the collecting bank of the defence of section 4. The bank would, however, be considered negligent if knowledge possessed by the branch at which the account was maintained would have put that branch on enquiry.[129]

The position differs altogether where the cheque is remitted by the holder to one bank with a request that its proceeds be credited to an account which he maintains with a different bank. By way of illustration, take a cheque drawn on the West End Branch of Lloyds Bank, which the payee remits to the Piccadilly Branch of Barclays Bank with a request that the proceeds be credited to his account with the Holborn Branch of the Midland Bank. What is the position of Barclays Bank and of Midland Bank if it turns out that the cheque has been converted by the payee? For the sake of convenience the Midland Bank will be called the collecting bank and Lloyds Bank the processing bank.

It would appear that both the collecting bank and the processing bank can be sued in conversion. This analysis is based on the fact that in a

---

[128] P. 231 above.

[129] *Ross* v. *London County Westminster and Parr's Bank Ltd.* [1919] 1 KB 678; *Lloyds Bank Ltd.* v. *Savory & Co.* [1933] AC 201, 235 (note that in the Court of Appeal it was thought that the collection through another branch involved negligence: [1932] 2 KB 122, 141); *Orbit Mining and Trading Co. Ltd.* v. *Westminster Bank Ltd.* [1963] 1 QB 794, 814.

transaction of this sort the processing bank acts as the collecting bank's agent. As the payee of the cheque does not maintain an account with the processing bank and has no other relationship of contract with it, it is inconceivable that that bank agrees to act on his behalf without obtaining any direct or indirect remuneration. As the processing bank arranges for the presentation of the cheque to the drawee bank, it performs a proprietary act affecting the instrument. The fact that it performs this act on behalf of the collecting bank does not exonerate the processing bank from liability in conversion any more than the collecting bank, in an ordinary transaction, can be heard to say that it is discharged from liability as it acts as the customer's agent. The collecting bank, in the type of transaction here analysed, it also liable. It is answerable to the true owner as it is vicariously liable for the conversion of the cheque by its agent, the processing bank. If the collecting bank has not paid out the proceeds to the customer, it can, further, be sued in an action in quasi-contract based on the true owner's waiver of the tort.[130]

When an action is brought by the true owner, are the processing bank and the collecting bank entitled to plead the defence of section 4? This question gives rise to two problems. The first is whether either one of the two banks, or perhaps both of them, are encompassed by the language of section 4 in a transaction of the type here described. The second problem involves the consideration of the ability of each of the two banks to satisfy the most difficult requirement of the section, namely the absence of negligence. It will be convenient to discuss the position of the two banks separately.

The processing bank appears to be altogether outside the scope of section 4. It collects the cheque for the credit of an account maintained by the payee with another bank. The payee, therefore, is usually not a customer of the processing bank. Undoubtedly, there are cases in which the payee may be a customer of both the processing bank and the collecting bank, and may request for reasons of his own that the account to be credited be that of the collecting bank.[131] But even in such a case the processing bank does not receive the proceeds for the payee's account with itself. It arranges for the clearance of the cheque for the payee's account with the collecting bank and hence, in the specific transaction involved, is not acting for the payee qua customer. It may be asked whether the difficulty is to be overcome by treating the collecting bank as the processing bank's customer. The argument, however, is futile, as the processing bank does not receive the proceeds and does not itself credit the collecting bank's account. It simply remits the cheque to the drawee bank through the clearing house, and transmits an advice of the receipt of the cheque to the collecting bank. It is submitted that

---

[130] Pp. 412–3 above.
[131] E.g., if he has drawn cheques on his account with the collecting bank.

444   *Monetary Agency in Domestic Transaction*

the better view is that the processing bank cannot claim the defence of section 4. Moreover, even if it were able to rely on it, the processing bank would in all probability be unable to establish that it had acted without negligence: in practice a processing bank accepts such cheques without making any enquiries.

The position of the collecting bank is less hazardous. When the customer's account is credited by the clearing department and the customer is not permitted to withdraw the funds before the cheque is cleared, the collecting bank receives payment on the customer's behalf. The collecting bank then falls within the ambit of section 4(1) of the Cheques Act 1957. If the customer is granted an overdraft before clearance, his bank assumes the role of a discounting bank.[132] It is therefore engaged in a transaction covered by section 4(1)(b). The difficulty that is likely to arise relates, however, to the question of negligence. In the type of case here discussed, the collecting bank does not make a conscious decision to accept the cheque for collection. It usually receives the proceeds without demur. How, then, can it be heard to claim that it has acted without negligence?

The collecting bank's main hope in such cases is to establish that under current banking practice it is not obliged to exercise any discretion where a cheque is being collected through a processing bank. The importance of banking practice in determining the scope of the bank's duty to exercise care in the collection of cheques is, of course, well established.[133] But it would be an error to ignore the warning in *Marfani*'s case, where Cairns J indicated that the courts may decide to condemn as negligent a general banking practice which is found to be too lax or too risky as regards the public interest.[134] It is believed that the practice originally introduced by the 1967 memorandum, and currently consecrated in specific agreements between different clearing banks, may become a source of litigation.

8. THE COLLECTING BANK WHICH IS ALSO THE PAYING BANK

Up to now the discussion has related to situations in which two or more banks participate in clearing a cheque. In some cases, though, only one bank is involved in the process. This occurs in two types of situation. The first is where one branch of a given bank acts as the collecting agent of the payee and the cheque is drawn on another branch of the same bank. The second case is where both the drawer and the payee maintain their accounts with one and the same branch. Cases of the latter type are uncommon.

[132] Pp. 418–21 above.
[133] Pp. 425–6 above.
[134] P. 426 above.

Cases of the former type are numerous, as each of the four big trading banks has a substantial share of current accounts opened in England and Wales. Two branches of one of these giant chains often act respectively for the payee and for the drawer.

From a legal point of view, both types of case lead to complex problems. A bank has a single legal personality, which encompasses all its branches.[135] It is true that the owner of an account has to demand payment at the branch at which an account is kept.[136] But this rule is based on a term of the contract of banker and customer, and does not imply that, for the purpose of the clearance of cheques, each branch is to be treated as if it had a separate legal personality.[137] It follows that where two branches of the same bank act, respectively, as collecting agent and as the paying station, the bank itself performs both the function of a collecting bank and of a paying bank. What is such a bank's position? The specific protections which are given to banks under the Bills of Exchange Act 1882 and the Cheques Act 1957 confer separate defences on the bank as payor of cheques drawn on it and as collector of cheques remitted by customers. This clear-cut separation is based on historical reasons. In the nineteenth century the English banking world comprised a network of small and independent banks, many of which had one office only. It comes, therefore, as no surprise that the 1882 Act and the 1957 Act, which amended it, fail to deal with the type of situation discussed presently. Sections 60 and 80 of the 1882 Act, as augmented by section 1 of the 1957 Act, deal exclusively with the protection of a bank that wrongfully honours a cheque drawn on it; section 4 of the 1957 Act (which has replaced section 82 of the original Act) confers a protection on a bank that collects a cheque for a customer. Which defence is available to a bank that acts for both the drawer and the payees.

'Three basic solutions to the problem are possible. The first is to confer a right of election on the bank that acts, at one and the same time, as paying and as collecting bank. Under this solution, a bank that was sued for the wrongful payment of a cheque could still plead the defence of section 4, provided it had also acted as a collecting bank, and provided further that it was able to establish the absence of negligence in its having done so. The second approach is to expect the bank to carry out all duties imposed on it as regards both the collection and the payment of cheques.

The third possibility is to expect the bank to meet the standard prescribed in respect of the function or functions consciously performed by it in respect of a given cheque. Thus, if a cheque is collected and paid through two

---

[135] But not subsidiary companies, such as an affiliated merchant bank.

[136] P. 129 above.

[137] The same applies to cases in which the branches are situated in different countries. For a recent example, see *Power Curber International Ltd.* v. *National Bank of Kuwait* [1981] 1 WLR 1233.

separate branches, the bank consciously performs the roles of both a collecting and a paying bank. The bank may therefore be expected to act with the degree of care required by a bank in both capacities. Accordingly, it could plead the defences available to it in both roles. If a cheque is paid to the credit of a customer whose account is maintained with the branch on which it is drawn, the cheque is, in effect, paid rather than collected. The bank is, therefore, to be regarded as a paying bank rather than as a collecting bank. Its liability should not exceed that to which it is subjected when a cheque is presented for payment over the counter.

The courts appear to favour the third, functional, solution. Thus, in *Bissell & Co.* v. *Fox Bros. & Co.*,[138] a mercantile firm had a travelling salesman, whose personal account was maintained with the same single office bank as his employers'. This salesman indorsed a number of cheques payable to the firm by executing a 'per pro' indorsement, and arranged for their payment to the credit of his personal account. One of the cheques in question was actually drawn by the client on the bank with which the travelling salesman and the firm kept their respective accounts. At the trial, Denman J held that the bank was liable in conversion as a collecting bank in respect of the cheques drawn on other banks, but that it was protected in the case of the cheque drawn on itself under section 60 of the 1882 Act. The Court of Appeal affirmed this decision, treating the bank as having paid rather than collected the cheque drawn on itself. The Court reached this decision notwithstanding that the cheque in question was credited by the bank to the travelling salesman's account and not paid to him over the counter. A similar approach was adopted by the Court of Appeal in *Gordon* v. *London, City and Midland Bank Ltd.*[139] Collins MR held that, where the bank was able to satisfy the requirements set out in section 60, it was not liable as a collecting bank. In this case the cheque was collected by a branch other than that on which it was drawn; but the court regarded itself as bound by its previous decision. On the facts, however, the bank was held not to have been negligent. It is noteworthy that the exact role of a bank that assumes the dual capacity of paying and of collecting a cheque was not discussed by the House of Lords.[140]

A different view was taken by the Court of Appeal in *Carpenters' Co.* v. *British Mutual Banking Co. Ltd.*[141] In this case both the plaintiff company and one of its clerks maintained accounts with the defendant bank, which had only one office. By means of different types of frauds the clerk obtained

---

[138] (1885) 53 LT 193; 1 TLR 452.
[139] [1902] 1 KB 242, 274–5.
[140] [1903] AC 240 sub nom. *Capital and Counties Bank Ltd.* v. *Gordon*, affirming the decision of the Court of Appeal; the ratio related to the fact that the amount had been received before clearance and hence not for a customer.
[141] [1938] 1 KB 511.

cheques drawn by the company in favour of tradesmen and, having forged the required indorsements, paid these cheques for the credit of his personal account with the defendant bank. When the frauds were discovered, the company sought to recover its losses from the bank in an action based alternatively on the wrongful payment of the cheques and on their conversion. The bank relied on the defences available to it both as paying bank and as collecting bank. Branson J followed the decision of the Court of Appeal in the *Gordon* case but was reversed by the Court of Appeal. Greer LJ, who delivered one of the majority judgments, thought that section 60 'only protects a bank when that bank is merely a paying bank, and is not a bank which receives the cheque for collection'.[142] He thought that the trial judge had erred in treating the defendant bank as if it had merely paid the cheque. On the facts, the case involved an action in conversion and the only defence available to the defendant bank, qua collecting bank, was that of section 82 of the 1882 Act (now section 4 of the 1957 Act). Greer LJ was not convinced by the argument that the defendant bank should not be in a position more onerous than if it had paid the cheques over the counter. His Lordship observed:[143]

[The defendant bank] did not in this case cash the cheques over the counter, and it is unnecessary to consider what would have been the result if instead of passing them to [the clerk's] credit the bank had paid him the cash over the counter. In my opinion, though it is unnecessary to decide this in the present case, it would still as receiving bank be liable for conversion. Be this as it may, on the facts proved in the present case . . . when the bank received the cheques and passed them to the credit of [the clerk's] private account it converted the cheques by dealing with them as if they were [the clerk's] property and immediately crediting him with the amount thereof.

Greer LJ disagreed with the view expressed in *Gordon*'s case, in which the cheques were drawn on one branch and collected for the credit of an account maintained with another branch. He thought that in such a case, even more forcefully than in the case before him, the bank 'was no less a collecting bank because it was collecting from one of its branches for the customer and paying the money so collected'.[144] His Lordship thought that, in situations of the type considered in *Gordon*'s case, the bank would have to claim the defence of section 60 if sued as paying bank and the defence of section 82 if sued as collecting bank. Obviously, if the bank was sued in both capacities it would have to succeed under both sections to escape liability. Slesser LJ agreed with Greer LJ on the points under consideration. MacKinnon LJ, in a dissenting judgment, thought that, under *Gordon*'s case, he was bound to hold that the bank discharged its liability by successfully pleading

[142] Ibid., 529.
[143] Ibid., 531.
[144] Ibid., 532. See also *Woodland* v. *Fear* (1857) 7 E & B 519, discussed above, p. 270.

the defence of section 60, although he thought that the decision reached by Greer and Slesser LJJ was preferable.

It is clear that, of the three possible solutions discussed earlier on, the courts have favoured the last two. It is believed that the view of the majority of the Court of Appeal in *Carpenters' Co.*'s case is to be preferred to the solution propounded in *Bissell & Co.*'s case. In the first place, the effect of the *Carpenter's Co.* solution is to avoid a situation in which a bank which acts both as the collecting agency and as the payor of a cheque is absolved from liability although it has failed to exercise the duties expected of it in the performance of one of its two roles. Secondly, the solution of *Bissell & Co.*'s case, which would exonerate a bank that can plead the defence of section 60 from liability for neglect in collection, overlooks the historical background of this section. Undoubtedly, if the plaintiff is the drawer of the cheque, he can sue the bank both in conversion for the wrongful collection of the instrument and for breach of mandate based on its wrongful payment.[145] But if the plaintiff is a person other than the drawer, such as the ostensible payee of the instrument from whose possession it has been stolen, the action has to be based on conversion.[146] In such a case the bank is primarily sued as a collecting bank and not as a paying bank.[147] Section 60 was not meant to protect the bank against actions of this type. This much is clear from the history of the provision, derived, it will be recalled, from section 19 of the Stamp Act 1853 which aimed at protecting the bank in its role as payor of its customers' cheques.[148] It would be fortuitous to extend this defence to a bank which opened itself to an action in conversion based on the wrongful collection of the cheque, simply because that bank happened to have acted for both the drawer and the drawee of the instrument. The solution based on *Carpenters' Co.*'s case is, thus, preferable analytically and also on grounds of policy. It expects the bank to exercise the standard of professional skill imposed on it in respect of each of its roles.

It may be claimed that this argument is more appropriate where the cheque is collected by a branch other than that on which it is drawn than in situations in which the cheque is drawn on the very branch with which the payee maintains his account. In practice, though, the point is doubtful. If a cheque is processed in a single branch, the bank is still in a position to evaluate both the request for the collection of the cheque and the question of paying it. The only difference between this type of case, and that in which two separate branches of the bank are involved, is that the decisions concerning the collection and the payment of the cheque are made by one employee of the bank, and not by two separate tellers or branch managers.

---

[145] Pp. 286–7 above.
[146] Or on the complementary action in quasi-contract.
[147] Although the 'true owner' can sue also the paying bank in conversion; pp. 286–7 above.
[148] Pp. 303–5 above.

9. THE COLLECTING BANK'S DUTY TO ITS OWN CUSTOMER

(i) *The nature of problems arising*

The majority of the decided cases defining the position of a collecting bank concerned litigation in conversion instituted by the true owner of the instrument. It is important to bear in mind that, in usual circumstances in which a validly acquired cheque is remitted to a bank for collection, the bank's main duty is owed to its own customer. The bank's obligations are to process the cheque speedily, to take the necessary steps for crediting the customer's account, and to notify the customer, without delay, if the cheque is dishonoured by the drawee bank. The collecting bank's duties arise in part as a result of the provisions of the Bills of Exchange Act 1882 and in part under its contract of agency with the customer.

(ii) *The collecting bank's duty to effect presentment*

Under section 45(2) of the Bills of Exchange Act 1882, a bill has to be presented within a reasonable time after its issue in order to charge the drawer and within a reasonable time after its transfer to charge the indorser. This section, however, defines the duties which the holder has to discharge if he wishes to recover the amount of the instrument from the drawer or from the indorser. As the relationship of the collecting bank with its customer is based on the contract between them rather than on the bill, section 45(2) provides, at best, a guideline indicating that presentment needs usually to be effected within a reasonable time. The nature of the 'reasonable time' involved depends, under sections 45 and 74, on the practice of bankers which at present is contained in the Clearing House Rules. These, however, tend to give effect to established case law, which in turn supports the need for speedy presentment and has defined the available 'reasonable time'. If the cheque is collected by a branch operating at the same place as the branch on which the cheque is drawn, the collecting bank has to present the cheque, at the latest, on the day following its receipt.[149] If the cheque is drawn on a branch in another place, be it a branch of the same bank or of another bank, the bank may either present the cheque or forward it for clearing on the next day.[150] The Clearing House Rules are to the same effect.

As presentment needs to be effected through the clearing house, it is

---

[149] *Forman* v. *Bank of England* (1902) 18 TLR 339; *Hamilton Finance Co. Ltd.* v. *Coverley, Westray, Walbaum and Tosetti Ltd.* [1969] 1 Lloyd's Rep. 53 (the case law in point can be traced back to the beginning of the nineteenth century: *Rickford* v. *Ridge* (1810) 2 Camp. 537).

[150] *Prideaux* v. *Criddle* (1869) LR 4 QB 455; *Heywood* v. *Pickering* (1874) LR 9 QB 428. And see further, pp. 260–1 above.

customary for non-clearing banks, such as foreign banks who are not members of a clearing house, to remit their cheques to a clearing bank.[151] Such a remittance, which may involve extra time in the process of presentment, is sanctioned by the usages of merchants,[152] which also approve, where convenient, the remittance of cheques for presentment by one branch of a collecting bank to another branch of the same bank.[153]

A special type of case arises where the drawer of the cheque and the payee maintain their accounts with the same bank. Naturally, if the two parties bank, respectively, with different branches, then the payee's branch receives the cheque on a collection basis and sets it into motion in about the same way as if the cheque were drawn on a branch of some other bank.[154] But if the two parties bank with the same branch of a chain bank, or maintain their accounts with the same single-office bank, it is a question of fact whether the cheque is presented by the payee for payment or handed to the relevant branch or bank on a collection basis.[155] In the former case, the question of the bank's duty as a collecting bank does not arise. In the latter case the bank has the usual time for returning the cheque to the payee if, in its capacity as the drawer's bank, it resolves to dishonour it.[156] Basically, this means that the bank has one extra day for making its decision concerning the fate of the cheque. Presentment of the cheque to itself through the clearing house would be an absurdity!

It may be justifiably pointed out that in cases of this type the bank does not take a conscious decision whether to handle the cheque on a collection basis or as an instrument presented for payment. In some cases, the decision is made by the payee. If he presents the cheque over the counter for payment in cash, then it is clear that the bank is requested to pay the instrument; the question of collection does not arise. If the cheque is handed to the teller, accompanied by a deposit slip, the payee requests the bank to collect the cheque for the credit of his account. By accepting the two documents as presented by the payee, the bank in reality agrees to collect the instrument and, in this type of case, to act in the dual role of payor and of collecting agent. In other cases, though, the fate of the cheque and the role of the bank in regard to it is determined by the drawer! Where the cheque is a crossed cheque, the

---

[151] Presentment through the Post Office as between banks was at one time permissible: *Prideaux* v. *Criddle*, above.

[152] Ibid.

[153] Ibid. But note that currently they will be forwarded to the bank's clearing department in London.

[154] But it will not of course be exchanged at the clearing house.

[155] This point did arise directly in *Carpenters' Co.* v. *British Mutual Banking Co. Ltd.* [1938] 1 KB 511, discussed above, but the treatment of one branch bank as a distinct entity for collection and for payment suggests that it is entitled not only to the duties but also to the rights of a collecting bank.

[156] This point emerges from an early nineteenth century case: *Boyd* v. *Emmerson* (1834) 2 Ad. & El. 184.

bank is not allowed to pay it over the counter.[157] This means that the payee, or transferee, has to remit the cheque for collection. If he banks with the very branch, or single-office bank, on which the instrument is drawn, he is practically bound to ask this bank to act as his collecting agent.

Where the collecting bank fails to present a cheque speedily, it is liable to its customer for the loss sustained as a result of the delay. This liability is based on the contract of banker and customer. By presenting the cheque after an undue delay, the bank fails to comply with the instructions given to it by its principal, the customer.[158] The loss that may be incurred by the customer arises in three types of case. First, the drawer of the cheque may have either closed his account or become insolvent during the period of the delay. The effect of the delay is that the cheque will, thereupon, be dishonoured by the drawee bank. Secondly, the delay in presentment discharges any indorser. The collecting bank's client thus loses his action on the bill against the indorser. This is particularly significant where the drawer is insolvent. Thirdly, if the cheque is not duly presented and the drawee bank becomes insolvent in the meantime, the drawer suffers loss, as he is no longer able to dispose over the funds. In effect, the delay results in the non-payment of the cheque by the drawee bank. Under section 74(1) of the 1882 Act, the holder loses his right of action against the drawer if a delay in presentment has led to such a loss. If the holder has employed a collecting bank for presenting the cheque, this bank has to compensate the holder for the loss sustained by him due to its failure to present the cheque in time.

The collecting bank's liability to its customer is, however, incurred only if the customer is able to establish that the cheque would have been paid if presented on time. Thus, the collecting bank does not have to compensate the customer if the cheque was drawn against inadequate funds and did not bear the signature of an indorser. In such a case, the delay does not result in a loss. Where a loss is incurred, and the collecting bank compensates its customer, it is subrogated to the rights which he has as holder of the cheque.[159]

In the majority of cases, the customer's loss will be restricted to the amount of the cheque dishonoured by the drawee bank as a result of the delay in its presentment by the collecting bank. In some cases, though, there is room for additional loss incurred where the customer's balance with the collecting bank is inadequate, owing to that bank's failure duly to clear the cheque in question, for meeting the customer's own cheques. In such a case the bank is liable to its customer for the damage done to his

[157] Pp. 254–5 above.
[158] *Lubbock* v. *Tribe* (1838) 3 M & W 607; *Yeoman Credit Ltd.* v. *Gregory* [1963] 1 WLR 343.
[159] See, generally, p. 526 below.

creditworthiness.[160] Its liability is, then, that of a paying bank that has wrongfully dishonoured its customer's cheques.[161]

(iii) Notice of dishonour

When the drawee bank dishonours a cheque, it returns it to the collecting bank.[162] Under section 48 of the 1882 Act, notice of dishonour has to be given to the drawer and indorsers. Failure to do so discharges their liability on the instrument. However, the giving of such notice is excused in certain situations.[163] One of them is where the drawee is not bound, as between the drawer and himself, to honour the instrument. In such cases, which cover situations in which a cheque is drawn against an inadequate balance or on an account which has been closed,[164] it would be futile to make notice to the drawer a condition precedent to his liability on the instrument.

The rules as to the method of giving notice of dishonour are set out in detail in section 49 of the Act. From the collecting bank's point of view, the only relevant provision is subsection (13), under which an agent may either himself give notice to the parties liable on the instrument or may give notice to his principal. The standard banking practice is to return a dishonoured cheque to the customer with a note indicating that it has not been paid. It is believed that this practice is adequate under the Act, and, equally, all that can be expected from the bank as an agent.

[160] *Kilsby* v. *Williams* (1822) 5 B & Ald. 815.
[161] Pp. 310 et seq. above.
[162] This is the practice prescribed by the Clearing House Rules. The cheque is returned to the branch which received it from the payee or holder.
[163] BEA, s. 50(2).
[164] The rule is based on an eighteenth-century authority, *Bickerdike* v. *Bollman* (1786) 1 TR 405. Note, though, that if the balance is fluctuating the drawer may be unaware of the inadequacy of funds and hence may be entitled to notice: *Orr* v. *Maginnis* (1806) 7 East. 359; *Blackhan* v. *Doren* (1810) 2 Camp. 503.

CHAPTER 15

Incidental Services Performed by Banks

1. THE COMMON THREAD

The closeness of the relationship of the bank and its customer is best appreciated in the context of the incidental banking service. Three of the most common ones are the furnishing of references, the giving of advice on financial matters, and the provision of safe custody facilities.

Bankers' references have been furnished from at least the middle of the nineteenth century. Here, two banks are involved in rendering the relevant service. Suppose that X, a customer of Bank A, wishes to enter into business with Y, the customer of Bank B. To satisfy himself of the advisability of granting trade credit to Y (the 'person investigated'), X (the 'enquirer') needs a confidential financial report. X's ususal course is to ask Bank A (the 'reference-seeking bank') to obtain the necessary information from Bank B (the 'referee bank'). In modern practice, the procedure is occasionally varied, mainly where the parties involved are substantial business firms. If Y refers to the B Bank's name in correspondence or during the negotiations, X may approach the B Bank directly with a request that it furnish its report to the A Bank. Quite regardless of the procedure used, the report is invariably furnished without a charge. The referee bank renders it 'in confidence' and 'without responsibility on our part'.

The giving of advice on financial affairs is a relatively new service as regards the clearing banks. It was outside their accepted type of business activities at the beginning of this century,[1] and remained exceptional until the end of the Second World War.[2] But it was provided during the last three decades of the nineteenth century by the accepting houses.[3]

The furnishing of financial advice is currently carried on in a number of ways. In ordinary cases, banks advise a customer on an informal basis about an investment considered by him. The transaction may involve an acquisition of shares, the purchase of a business enterprise, or the export of goods on a deferred payment basis to a firm in a given foreign country. In cases of greater complexity the customer may request the bank to investigate the feasibility of a venture, and may authorize it to commission the required

---

[1] *Banbury* v. *Bank of Montreal* [1918] AC 626.
[2] See the argument and evidence in *Woods* v. *Martins Bank Ltd.* [1959] 1 QB 55.
[3] Information based on independent survey.

expert reports and studies. Yet another type of case in which the bank effectively gives financial advice is where it invests an amount of money on behalf of a customer. Usually the bank purchases marketable securities for the customer and keeps his 'portfolio' of commercial paper.

Whilst the bank does not charge a fee for informal advice given to the customer, it is natural for it to expect to make a profit in the other two instances. The method of charging varies to a considerable extent. Where the bank arranges for a complete feasibility study, it may charge a direct fee. In the case of portfolio investments, it gains a commission.

The banks function as bailees in two ways. First, they accept from their clients documents and valuable items, such as jewellery, for safe custody. In such a case the items are retained in the bank's own safety room, and the service is rendered on a gratuitous basis. In point of fact, some banks will accept sealed envelopes or locked small boxes from the public generally and not only from customers. The second method is the provision of 'safes' or safety lockers, which are situated in the bank's strongroom. The customer is given one key to his safe whilst another key is retained by the bank. The safe can be opened only by the use of both keys. Banks charge a rental for their safes. It is a fine question whether this arrangement involves hire or bailment.'[4]

It is clear that the common thread in the incidental services provided by the banks is not that they are furnished free of charge. Indeed, in some cases the bank makes a profit. It would, further, be wrong to say that the services are provided solely in the interest of the public. In the first place, banks render them in order to encourage the public to use their general banking facilities. Secondly, some other services provided by the banks, such as the clearing system, are furnished in the interest of customers and are not, in effect, a major source of profit. The common thread of the services described is in two other aspects. To start with, they are largely incidental to the bank's other, main, business. In addition, they are utilized by the public on the basis of its implicit trust in the bank's integrity, judgment, and skill. These expectations are emphasized by the courts in cases concerning the services involved.

2. BANKERS' REFERENCES

(i) *The rights of the person investigated*

The person who is the subject of the enquiry (the 'person investigated') may sustain loss either because of the inaccuracy of the information supplied or

---

[4] The problem is of major importance in tax cases.

if his bank fails to furnish a reference. Moreover, his loss may be induced either by his bank—the 'referee bank'—or by the reference-seeking bank. His rights against the two institutions are based on different causes of action.

The right of the person investigated against the referee bank are predominantly contractual. If his bank gives an unfavourable reference, he may consider three alternative actions. The first is based on the bank's duty of confidentiality, owed to him as a customer. The second, which is applicable only where the reference is incorrect, is for the bank's failure to exercise care and skill. In effect, the action is then one for a breach of a duty of care anchored in contract.[5]

The third possiblity is to institute an action in defamation. The main problem in such a case is that the information given by the bank is, arguably, privileged. Undoubtedly, this defence is available only if the bank has acted without malice. In the vast majority of cases this is so. An extreme case in point was *Robshaw* v. *Smith*.[6] The enquirer and the person investigated were customers of the same bank. That bank showed the enquirer an unfavourable anonymous letter received about the person investigated. Grove J concluded that the communication was privileged, as the bank had acted in reply to a request for information.

Some support for this view is to be found in *London Association for Protection of Trade* v. *Greenland Ltd.*,[7] which suggests that the giving of information is privileged whenever an organization has a contractual or business duty to provide it. An argument to the contrary is that the bank's information is not privileged, as it is not supplied in pursuance of a duty.[8] Although this assertion is formally true, it must not be overlooked that, in practice, banks are expected to answer enquiries coming from other banks. They may therefore be regarded as supplying references in conformity with a duty recognized by the business world.

A customer's action for breach of a duty of secrecy has not been attempted in the context of bank references. It will be recalled[9] that one of the exceptions to the bank's duty of secrecy is disclosure with the customer's implied or express consent. The view taken by banks is that, under a general usage, customers are deemed to give them the authority to reply to requests for references channelled through the banking network. There can be no doubt that this view is shared by other business enterprises in the City.

Moreover, it stands to reason that when any person supplies the name of

---

[5] It seems futile to investigate the feasibility of an action based on the breach of a fiduciary duty; see pp. 84–86 and 161–3 above.
[6] (1878) 38 LT 423.
[7] [1916] 2 AC 15.
[8] *Gatley on Libel and Slander*, 8th edn., London, 1981, para. 472.
[9] P. 104 above.

his bank in the context of some business dealings, he appreciates that a request for a reference is likely to follow. By way of illustration, take the case of an application for a credit card, such as Access or American Express, in which the customer is asked to quote the name of personal referees and also that of his bank. The object of the question must be apparent.

A more difficult question is whether the bank has a general authority to reply to requests for references. Whilst textbooks lend some support to the existence of such a usage-based authority,[10] there is no direct case in point.[11] The view taken by the Younger Committee on Privacy[12] is significant. It recognizes that banks and large business firms are keenly aware of the bankers' references system. Private customers, though, appeared unfamiliar with the practice. The Committee took the view that a customer should be asked whether or not he wished enquiries to be answered. The practice employed by some German banks provides a suitable model. The customer is asked, at the time his account is opened, whether answers to enquiries should be given as a matter of course or only after the matter is cleared with him.

A bank has to employ care and skill when it answers an enquiry. Although there is no direct authority in point, the position appears clear. The bank's duty in this regard can be put on the same basis as its duty to exercise care and skill in the provision of financial advice to a customer.[13] In both cases the bank is keenly aware that a negligently given reply, be it to an enquiry made by the customer himself or to one made by the reference-seeking bank, can cause the customer substantial loss.

The customer may sustain loss not only where the bank gives inaccurate information, but also where it fails to supply a reference. Naturally, this type of problem can arise only where the bank has been authorized to answer enquiries. The customer's only chance in such a case is to sue for a breach of an implied contractual duty, based on the mandate given by him to the bank. To date, there is no case in point, and the existence of such a duty is dubious.

In practice, such a case is unlikely to arise. If the referee bank fails to respond to the other bank's enquiry, it will be pressed for an answer. If it then advises that it is unable to comply, the innuendo is clear. Furthermore,

---

[10] Paget, *Law of Banking*, 9th edn., p. 158; Weaver and Craigie, *Banker and Customer in Australia*, pp. 171–2.

[11] But see *Tournier* v. *National Provincial and Union Bank of England* [1924] 1 KB 461, 473, per Bankes LJ; Atkin LJ *dubitante*, 483; and see the fine distinction of views in *Hedley Byrne & Co. Ltd.* v. *Heller & Partners Ltd.* [1964] AC 465, where Lords Morris of Borth-Y-Gest (503) and Pearce (540) echoed the existence of the practice, whilst Lord Reid (489) seems to have retained doubts.

[12] Cmnd. 5012 of 1972; and see White Paper on 'Computer and Privacy', Cmnd. 6353 and supp. 6354.

[13] Discussed below, pp. 463 et seq.

the reply is understood to be a warning. The customer's ensuing action may thus be founded in the same way as one brought where the bank is negligent in formulating its answer.

Another interesting question that has not been the subject of litigation concerns the rights of the referee bank's customer—the person investigated—against the reference-seeking bank. A case of this type may arise where the latter bank is careless in conveying the information obtained by it to the enquirer. Thus, the reference-seeking bank may advise that the person investigated trades 'unprofitably' on his capital, whilst the true message has been to the contrary. Obviously, the information may lead to a break in negotiations, resulting in loss to the person investigated. It is believed that this person's rights against the reference-seeking bank depend on his being able to establish a relationship of proximity between them. The question is similar to that arising as regards the duty owed by the referee bank to the enquirer. In both types of relationship there is no contract between the respective persons, and the action must therefore be brought in tort. Its feasibility is examined forthwith.

(ii) Position of the enquirer

There are rare instances in which the enquirer may wish to sue his own bank, the reference-seeking bank. This occurs where the information obtained from the referee bank is inaccurately conveyed to him. Thus, in the example given above, the enquirer may abandon the negotiations for a lucrative contract if he believes the person investigated trades unprofitably. Equally, an incorrectly transmitted opinion may lull the enquirer into a false sense of safety.

There is no doubt that, in cases of this type, the enquirer has an effective cause of action against the reference-seeking bank. It is established that, where information is requested by the customer, his bank has to convey to him the available details accurately and in full.[14] At the same time, the reference-seeking bank need not institute an independent enquiry of its own.[15]

The question of the enquirer's rights against the referee bank is more difficult. There is no contractual relationship between these parties. The only possible causes of action are, therefore, an action based on fraudulent statements and an action for a breach of a duty of care imposed at law.

The enquirer's right to bring an action based on the referee bank's dishonesty is affected by the Statute of Frauds Amendment Act 1828 ('Lord

[14] *Midland Bank Ltd.* v. *Seymour* [1955] 2 Lloyd's Rep. 147, 157–8; *Commercial Banking Co. of Sydney Ltd* v. *R. H. Brown & Co.* [1972] 2 Lloyd's Rep. 360 (High Ct. Aust.).
[15] *Commercial Banking Co. of Sydney Ltd* v. *R. H. Brown & Co.*, above.

Tenterden's Act'). Under section 6 of this statute, an action for any representation or assurance concerning the credit, character, ability or trade conduct of another person, made with the intent that the person concerned may obtain money, credit, or goods, lies only if the statement involved is made in writing and signed by the 'party charged therewith'.

The object of this provision was to put an end to the contemporary practice of instituting actions in misrepresentation for the purpose of indirectly enforcing guarantees which did not comply with the written form required under the Statute of Frauds.[16] A careful reading of the section suggests that its application is not confined to fraudulent misrepresentations. Its language is wide enough to encompass actions brought for misrepresentations of any kind, be they honest, fraudulent, or 'honest but negligent'. Historically, though, the aim was to curb actions for fraudulent statements. Actions in damages for negligent misrepresentations were unknown in 1828. It has been held in *Banbury* v. *Bank of Montreal*[17] that the defence of Lord Tenterden's Act could be pleaded only in the context of fraudulent statements.

Another prerequisite to the application of Lord Tenterden's Act is that the statement has to be signed personally by the party against whom it is asserted. In *Swift* v. *Jewsbury*,[18] the manager of one of the branches of the R Bank gave a favourable reference on the standing of one of his customers, knowing it to be false. The furnishing of the reference was within the manager's authority: but the R Bank had no knowledge of his dishonest behaviour. The Court of Exchequer Chamber affirmed the decision of the Court of Queen's Bench which held the branch manager personally liable to the enquirer, but which exonerated the R Bank. Both Lord Coleridge CJ and Bramwell B thought that Lord Tenterden's Act protected a person sued for issuing a fraudulent representation, unless he signed individually. The signature of an agent was inadequate for the purposes of section 6. To bring fraud home to a person, it was necessary to establish that the representation complained of was his own writing.[19]

Section 6 of Lord Tenterden's Act can be pleaded by individuals and by bodies corporate.[20] Furthermore, it applies even if the representation is partly in writing and partly made orally. Thus, the person who has signed it may be sued although some of the words complained of were uttered by word of mouth.[21] The scope of the section is, however, limited from a sub-

---

[16] *Williams* v. *Mason* (1873) 28 LT 232.

[17] [1918] AC 626, 693, per Lord Atkinson; 707–8 per Lord Parker; 713 per Lord Wrenbury. See also *Swift* v. *Jewsbury* (1874) LR 9 QB 301, 316, per Bramwell B; *W. B. Anderson & Sons Ltd.* v. *Rhodes (Liverpool) Ltd.* [1967] 2 All ER 850, 856.

[18] (1874) LR 9 QB 301.

[19] See also *Hirst* v. *West Riding Union Banking Co. Ltd.* [1901] 2 KB 560; *Banbury* v. *Bank of Montreal* [1918] AC 626, 693, 713.

[20] *Hirst* v. *West Riding Union Banking Co. Ltd.* above.

[21] *Tatton* v. *Wade* (1856) CB 371.

stantive point of view. In *Diamond* v. *Bank of London and Montreal Ltd.*,[22] a firm of brokers assured another that a given supplier was of good standing, and that a consignment of sugar which he purported to sell was in existence. Both points were alleged to have been untrue to the first firm's knowledge. In the context of the consideration of a preliminary point, Lord Denning MR observed that Lord Tenterden's Act might furnish a defence in respect of the representation concerning the supplier's standing but had no application in respect of the statement concerning the existence of the goods.

Lord Tenterden's Act leads to a strange result. A person can escape the consequences of a fraudulent misrepresentation unless it is established that he has made it in writing and signed it in his own hand. It will be shown that no formality of this type is applicable where the action is brought in negligence. It may, thus, be advisable for a plaintiff to sue in negligence even where he is able to establish the referee's fraud.

Another problem arises in respect of statements issued by bodies corporate. It is obvious that a misrepresentation cannot be signed by such a body 'individually': it has to be executed by an employee or agent. Presumably, the corporation is liable if an agent, acting within his authority, signs the relevant statement as 'X Ltd. per A, director'; but it can possibly escape liability on the technicality of section 6 if the statement is signed as 'A, director of X'. The former is to be regarded as a signature of the company executed by the agent; the latter is the agent's signature, executed in a representative capacity. Although this subtle distinction is of significance in another field,[23] it appears ill suited in the context of Lord Tenterden's Act.

The enquirer's right to recover damages from the referee bank by suing in negligence is governed by the leading decision of the House of Lords in *Hedley, Byrne & Co. Ltd.* v. *Heller & Partners Ltd.*[24] An advertising agency was asked by an industrial firm, which was one of its clients, to place advertisements for a substantial amount. As the agency had to undertake personal liability in respect of the contracts concerned, it arranged for its own bank to obtain a reference from the industrial firm's bank. That bank supplied a reference, given in confidence and without responsibility, for the sole use of the reference-seeking bank. The referee bank stated that the amounts mentioned in the request for information were higher than those

---

[22] [1979] QB 333.
[23] It is relevant under s. 26 of the Bills of Exchange Act 1882, in determining whether an agent signs an instrument personally or in a representative capacity: *Chitty on Contracts*, 25th edn., para. 2483.
[24] [1964] AC 465. The House of Lords relied on the judgments of Lord Haldane in *Nocton* v. *Ashburton* [1914] AC 932, and *Robinson* v. *National Bank of Scotland*, 1916 SC (HL) 154, 157. Cf. A. M. Honoré (1965) 8 *J. Soc. Pub. Teach. of Law* 284. The case has been discussed widely; for a detailed analysis of its implications to questions other than banking, see *Chitty on Contracts*, 25th edn., paras. 425 et seq.

for which the industrial firm usually traded, but at the same time described the firm as responsibly managed and as standing by its commitments. It failed to disclose that the firm was heavily indebted to itself in a manner that was causing the bank concern.

The House of Lords held that, in view of the disclaimer of responsibility, the referee bank was not liable. But their Lordships were unanimous in holding that, on the facts, the referee bank had committed a breach of a duty of care owed by it to the enquirer, the advertising agency. Despite some differences in the reasoning, it is clear that all judgments in the case are based on the fact that, by agreeing to supply the reference, the bank assumed a duty of care. Lord Reid described the scope of the duty as follows:[25]

> I can see no logical stopping place short of all those relationships where it is plain that the party seeking information or advice was trusting the other party to exercise such a degree of care as the circumstances required, where it was reasonable for him to do that, and where the other gave the information or advice when he knew or ought to have known that the inquirer was relying on him.

The duty was owed to the advertising agency (the enquirer), although the reference was supplied to its bank for that bank's own use. The reason for this was that the referee bank was aware that the information was needed for a person other than the reference-seeking bank. This knowledge established a relationship of proximity between the referee bank and the advertising agency.[26]

An important aspect of this duty of care is that it is not imposed automatically at law. In the words of Lord Devlin:[27]

> I do not understand any of your Lordships to hold that it is a responsibility imposed by law upon certain types of persons or in certain sorts of situations. It is a responsibility that is voluntarily accepted or undertaken, either generally where a general relationship, such as that of solicitor and client or banker and customer, is created, or specifically in relation to a particular transaction.

This view has been adopted in later cases.[28] It is thus clear that the enquirer's rights are based both on the referee bank's assumption of liability and on his own reliance on its judgment.[29]

---

[25] [1964] AC 465, 486. And see Lord Morris of Borth-Y-Gest, at 503; Lord Hodson, at 511.

[26] Ibid., per Lord Reid, at 486–7; Lord Morris of Borth-Y-Gest, at 502; Lord Hodson, at 511; Lord Devlin, at 529–30; Lord Pearce, at 539.

[27] Ibid., at 529. As to whether the duty may be owed to one who obtains the information from the original enquirer, see *Yianni* v. *Edwin Evans & Sons* [1982] QB 438.

[28] *Mutual Life and Citizens' Assurance Co. Ltd.* v. *Evatt* [1971] AC 793; *Commercial Banking Co. of Sydney Ltd.* v. *R. H. Brown & Co.* [1972] 2 Lloyd's Rep. 360 (High Ct. Aust.).

[29] *Commercial Banking Co. of Sydney Ltd.* v. *R. H. Brown & Co.*, above, 364, 367; and see *Esso Petroleum Co. Ltd.* v. *Mardon* [1976] QB 801.

The referee bank's duty of care is restricted to its giving a fair report based on such knowledge as it possesses. It need not institute an investigation of its own before it supplies the required information.[30] Moreover, the advice must be given in a proper business context. Advice given on a social occasion does not invoke liability.[31] It has to be given in respect of the type of business in which the referee has adequate expertise to justify a reliance on his judgment by the enquirer.[32]

Thus, where an insurance company gave advice to a policy-holder on the standing of one of its subsidiaries, it was held, by a majority of the Judicial Committee, not to be liable. The giving of financial advice was not within the province of an insurance company's business, and in the instant case there were no facts suggesting that the company had assumed liability.[33] The Judicial Committee concluded, therefore, that the company had not held itself out as having any expertise in the giving of financial advice. The fact that the enquirer is himself an experienced businessman does not, in itself, absolve the referee from liability.[34] At the same time, if the statement, or reference, is ambiguous, the enquirer has to ask for better particulars before he can rely on it with impunity.[35]

It is clear that a bank that supplies a reference on one of its customers does so in a business context and with the knowledge that it will be relied upon by a customer of the bank that makes the approach. To avoid the hazards of legal actions, banks invariably disclaim responsibility when they give their references. In the *Hedley Byrne* case, such a clause was held effective.

Another case in point is *Commercial Banking Co. of Sydney Ltd. v. R. H. Brown & Co.*[36] A firm of wool wholesalers was advised by its own bank that one of its purchasers was rumoured to be facing financial difficulties. To resolve their doubts, the wholesalers asked their bank to obtain a reference from the purchaser's bank. That bank supplied a favourable reference without believing in its truth. The Australian High Court held the referee bank liable, although it had disclaimed liability. By giving its reference without caring whether it was true or false, it committed a fraud as defined in

---

[30] *Parsons v. Barclay & Co. Ltd.* (1910) 103 LT 196; *Mutual Life and Citizens' Assurance Co. Ltd. v. Evatt*, above.

[31] *Hedley Byrne & Co. Ltd. v. Heller & Partners Ltd.*, above.

[32] This may be so even if the referee does not purport to act in a business capacity: *W. B. Anderson & Sons Ltd. v. Rhodes (Liverpool) Ltd.* [1967] 2 All ER 850.

[33] *Mutual Life and Citizens' Assurance Co. Ltd. v. Evatt*, above. Contrast *L. Shaddock & Associates Pty. Ltd. v. Council of the City of Parramatta* (1981) 150 CLR 225 where the Australian High Court, by a majority decision, refused to follow *Evatt*'s case, adopting the reasoning of its own majority in the judgment there reversed by the Judicial Committee: (1968) 122 CLR 556.

[34] *Rust v. Abbey Life Insurance Co. Ltd.* [1978] 2 Lloyd's Rep. 386.

[35] *McInerny v. Lloyds Bank Ltd.* [1974] 1 Lloyd's Rep. 246.

[36] [1972] 2 Lloyd's Rep. 360 (High Ct. Aust.).

Derry v. *Peek*.[37] Both Menzies and Gibbs JJ agreed that, in cases of this type, there could be no liability in negligence if the referee bank made it clear that it refused to assume a duty of care. Such a duty could, therefore, be disclaimed. But the referee bank could not avoid liability for fraud by relying on the clause in question.

A question of some difficulty is whether, even in respect of actions in negligence, the disclaimer is at present vitiated by the Unfair Contract Terms Act 1977.[38] Under section 2(2), a person cannot exclude loss or restrict his liability for negligence, except in so far as the term or notice satisfies the requirement of reasonableness imposed by the Act. Whether or not a term is reasonable depends on the facts of the case.[39] The problem as regards the application of this section to the type of case under consideration is that the bank's duty of care is a self-imposed one. It is not a duty of care imposed by law in the light of a general relationship of proximity which exists between parties, such as neighbours, or which is imposed on a class of person, such as the drivers of motor vehicles. As the referee bank's duty in the type of case encountered in *Hedley Byrne* or in *Brown* is assumed by it voluntarily, it is probably inaccurate to describe the disclaimer in question as an 'exclusion of liability' within the meaning of the 1977 Act.

It is, therefore, believed that the formula used in *Hedley Byrne* and in *Brown* constitutes an effective disclaimer of responsibility by the referee bank. In modern practice, the formula is in constant use. This means that an enquirer who wishes to sue a referee bank for providing a false report faces two hurdles. If he considers instituting proceedings based on a fraudulent misrepresentation, he has to reckon with Lord Tenterden's Act. If he wishes to proceed in negligence, he is faced with the usual disclaimer. His best course, in all probability, is to sue the branch manager who supplied the reference in fraud and in negligence. If the report is signed by him, Lord Tenterden's Act does not provide a procedural defence. There is, further, room for the argument that the disclaimer does not protect the person who signed the report. Whether or not this person owes the enquirer a duty of care remains to be seen. It will be recalled that he owes a duty of common honesty.

Where the enquirer suceeds in negligence or in fraud, the referee bank may raise questions concerning the quantum of damages. In *Commercial Banking Co. of Sydney Ltd.* v. *R. H. Brown & Co.*,[40] discussed above, the referee bank argued that the enquirer had not suffered any loss as a result of its misrepresentation, as he had concluded his contract with the person

[37] (1889) 14 App. Cas. 337.

[38] See also p. 468 below.

[39] S. 11. Note that s. 3 of the Act, which applies to exclusion of liability in consumer transactions, has no application, as there is no contract between the referee bank and the enquirer.

[40] [1972] 2 Lloyd's Rep. 360,

investigated before requesting the reference. The enquirer—the wool whole-salers—argued that if they had known the true facts they would have refrained from performing their contract with the purchaser. The enquirer was allowed to recover the full loss, as the High Court held that, if they had been forewarned and thereupon rescinded the sale of the wool, their liability to the purchaser would have been restricted to nominal damages.

A problem that awaits decision is the position of a bank which acts, at one and the same time, as both the referee and the reference-seeking bank. Whilst it may be rare to find cases in which the enquirer and the person investigated maintain their accounts with the one branch of the same bank,[41] there are bound to be numerous cases in which they are customers of different branches of one of the main clearing banks. It is understood that, in practice, the manager of the referee bank formulates his reply in exactly the same manner as when the request for information comes from a branch of another bank. Thus, it is possible that this type of case is one where, just as in respect of the collection of cheques,[42] the courts might decide to treat separate branches as if they were distinct banks. The bank itself, though, would appear to owe a contractual duty of care to both par-ties under its respective agreements with them.

3. GIVING ADVICE ON FINANCIAL INVESTMENTS

Where a bank gives advice to a customer or to a potential customer on a financial matter, it has to exercise reasonable care and skill. In *Woods* v. *Martins Bank Ltd.*,[43] it was held that the giving of such advice forms bank-ing business. The bank, therefore, cannot escape the consequences of care-lessly given advice by pleading that its personnel has acted outside the scope of its authority or employment by transacting an unacceptable type of busi-ness. It is noteworthy that even Canadian courts, which for a long period of time continued to regard the giving of financial advice as outside the scope of a bank's business,[44] have reversed their view on this point.[45]

At the same time, it is important not to assume that every financial advice given by a bank invokes liability. It should always be possible to establish by evidence that a certain type of advice is outside the scope of the bank's busi-ness, or is of a type on which the customer cannot expect to rely.[46] *Evatt*'s

---

[41] But see *Robshaw* v. *Smith* (1878) 38 LT 423 in which the two parties used the same branch. The matter did not there give rise to specific issues.

[42] Pp. 444–8 above.

[43] [1959] 1 QB 55, discussed in detail above, p. 85.

[44] *Banbury* v. *Bank of Montreal* [1918] AC 626; *Royal Bank* v. *Mack* [1932] 1 DLR 753; *Bank of Montreal* v. *Young* (1966) 60 DLR (2d) 220.

[45] *Royal Bank of Canada* v. *Nowosad* [1972] 6 WWR 705 (Manit. QB).

[46] *Thornett* v. *Barclays Bank (France) Ltd.* [1939] 1 KB 675, 684.

case, discussed earlier, shows that a body like an insurance company is not liable for advice given on corporate finance. The same ought to be applicable where a branch manager gives advice on a type of business which is known to the customer to be outside the bank's expertise.

Australian courts reached their conclusion on this aspect of banking law two decades before *Woods* v. *Martins Bank Ltd.* In *Barrow* v. *Bank of New South Wales*,[47] a branch manager induced customer A to invest funds in the firm of customer B, whose account was also maintained with the same branch. McArthur J held that, on these facts, the jury could validly return a verdict of fraud. He further held that the giving of advice had been within the scope of the branch manager's authority. However, in a later Australian authority, it was held that the bank discharged its duty by conveying to the customer the information available to it. It was not required to evaluate it for him.[48]

The bank's duty of care in giving financial advice is not confined to its dealings with customers. Even before the decision in *Hedley Byrne*, courts searched for means to establish contractual liability to enable a person to recover losses incurred by him as a result of his reliance on a bank's advice.[49] Thus, it will be recalled that, in *Woods* v. *Martins Bank Ltd.*, Salmon J based his decision alternatively in contract and on a duty of care arising out of a fiduciary relationship between the bank and the plaintiff, who had relied on its advice. Whilst a breach of a fiduciary duty may still be pleaded as the cause of an action to recover losses incurred due to a bank's negligent advice,[50] the plaintiff now has the alternative of suing in tort.[51] A recent Canadian authority supports the view that the relationship between the bank and a person whom it chooses to advise on financial transactions is proximate enough to give rise to a duty of care.[52]

It is clear from *Evatt*'s case that the circumstances of the enquiry must be such as to entitle the person who consults the bank to rely on its advice. Naturally, the bank, or an employee who acts on its behalf, is not expected to guarantee the investment. It is sufficient if such a person shows that he had reasonable grounds for his belief.[53]

Particular care needs to be taken if there is any possibility of a clash of interests between the bank and the person consulting it. Thus, in *Esso*

[47] [1931] VLR 323. And see also *Holmes* v. *Walton* [1961] WAR 96.

[48] *Byrne* v. *Nickel* [1950] QSR 57, esp. 71. Weaver and Craigie, *Banker and Customer in Australia*, pp. 180–1, point out that the bank had not been joined. It can hardly be doubted, though, that it would have paid damages awarded.

[49] For an extreme case, see *De la Bere* v. *Pearson Ltd.* [1907] 1 KB 483.

[50] Pp. 84 et seq. above.

[51] The point was made by Lord Morris of Borth-Y-Gest in *Hedley, Byrne & Co. Ltd.* v. *Heller & Partners Ltd.* [1964] AC 465, 495.

[52] *Federal Savings Credit Union Ltd* v. *Hessian* (1979) 98 DLR (3d) 488.

[53] *Howard Marine and Dredging Co. Ltd.* v. *A. Ogden & Son (Excavations) Ltd.* [1978] QB 574.

Petroleum Co. Ltd. v. *Mardon*,[54] a petrol company was held liable for a misrepresentation concerning the likely profits from a station it was negotiating to let to a prospective franchise-holder. The company was, primarily, held liable, as it ought to have known that the statement made by it was bound to influence the other party's decision. It is believed that the duty of care imposed on the company by the court was influenced by the fact that the representation was made in the company's own interest.

In cases of this type, the bank's best course is to give to the other party full details concerning the transaction. Thus, in *Rust* v. *Abbey Life Assurance Co.*,[55] an insurance company made a representation to a potential customer about the advantages of its property bonds but failed to mention that they constituted long-term investments and were not readily redeemable or transferable. It was held that the company's representative had disclosed all the required facts. There was, however, no doubt that anything short of this would have been inadequate. The fact that the customer was an experienced businesswoman who was capable of looking after her affairs was regarded as irrelevant.

It is clear that, on occasions, the law in point places an onerous duty on banks. Thus, in *Box* v. *Midland Bank Ltd.*,[56] a branch manager gave a customer the impression that the approval of a loan for which he had applied to the bank was a mere formality. In reliance on this advice, the customer concluded a transaction and, when the loan was refused, sustained a loss. It was held that, as the branch manager had chosen to express an opinion on the customer's chances, the bank was liable.

The amount of damages recoverable by the customer depends on the loss sustained by him. He could, undoubtedly, claim damages based on loss directly flowing or reasonably foreseeable. In the majority of cases, though, he would be inclined to claim the actual amount lost as a result of the bank's inapt advice. This, indeed, was recovered by the plaintiff in *Woods* v. *Martins Bank Ltd.* An Australian authority, *Holmes* v. *Walton*,[57] suggests that the plaintiff may, in addition, be awarded interest on this amount. This decision is supportable in principle as the bank's careless advice deprives the person consulting it of both his capital and a reasonable profit. Thus, in *Woods* v. *Martins Bank Ltd.*, the plaintiff lost an amount of approximately £5,000, which he could have invested in a bank's interest-bearing account.

The existing case law is primarily based on situations in which a representation made by a bank's employee in the course of his occupation causes the customer, or other person advised, a financial loss. By the same token, the bank is liable if its negligent management of a fund entrusted to it by the

---

[54] [1976] QB 801.
[55] [1978] 2 Lloyd's Rep. 386.
[56] [1979] 2 Lloyd's Rep. 391.
[57] [1961] WAR 96.

customer results in losses. Thus, in *Wilson* v. *United Counties Bank Ltd.*,[58] a bank was held to be in breach of a duty of care where it showed negligence in carrying on the business of a customer who entrusted it to the bank when he joined the army. Similarly, a bank would be liable if it mismanaged the portfolio investments of one of its customers.

In all these cases, the customer is best advised to sue in negligence. An action in fraud is fraught with hazards. First, fraud is hard to establish. If the bank, or one of its employees, has not derived a pecuniary interest from the transaction, the court is reluctant to find fraud. *Woods* v. *Martins Bank Ltd.* demonstrates this point. Secondly, if the action is based on a representation made to the customer, he has to reckon with Lord Tenterden's Act. It is true that in an action in negligence the bank may be able to establish a disclaimer of liability. In practice, though, such clauses are not usually used in the context of business counselling. Such a transaction is conducted in a manner less formal than the supply of bank references and, frequently, without any writing whatsoever.

4. THE BANKER AS BAILEE AND CUSTODIAN

(i) Safe deposit services

The most common incidental service rendered by banks to their customers, and frequently to the public in general, is the acceptance of small locked boxes or sealed envelopes for safe custody. As pointed out earlier, the item is then placed in the bank's own safe or strongroom, and is returned to the owner against the production of a receipt or an identification. In practice, the owner may authorize another person to collect the relevant item for him.

What is the extent of the bank's liability for items which it has in safe custody? Usually, the bank does not receive any payment for its service. On this basis, it was suggested in *Giblin* v. *McMullen*[59] that in such cases the bank is to be treated as a gratuitous bailee. In the majority of cases, though, the items are received for safe custody from a customer with whom the bank has a relationship of contract. It is therefore arguable that, although the bank is not paid a specific fee for the safe custody of an item, it obtains consideration under its general contract with the customer.[60]

Moreover, even in the case of a member of the public who is not a customer, it is arguable that the bank renders him its services as a bailee without obtaining a remuneration in the hope of inducing him to utilize the

[58] [1920] AC 102.
[59] (1868) LR 2 PC 317. See also *Kahler* v. *Midland Bank Ltd.* [1948] 1 All ER 819–20, affd. [1950] AC 24.
[60] *Port Swettenham Authority* v. *T. W. Wu & Co. (M.) Sdn. Bhd.* [1979] AC 580, 589.

bank's other services. The type of benefit derived in this way, which is best described as part of the general drive for the custom of the public, has been regarded as consideration in another context.[61] The view that, in the light of this principle, the bank can hardly be regarded as a gratuitous bailee, is supported by *Re United Service Co.*[62] A customer gave his bank shares for safe deposit, but also instructed it to collect the dividends payable thereon, and for this purpose the bank was given conditional access to the documents. In an action based on the conversion of the shares by an absconding employee, it was held that the bank was to be treated as a bailee for reward. *Giblin v. McMullen* was distinguished as, in the instant case, the bank had some access to the documents involved. The court further emphasized that, in the instant case, the bank had received consideration, as its banker's lien attached to the documents. This reasoning may have a wide scope of application, as the banker's lien would appear to attach to any items held in safe deposit for a customer.[63]

It may be asked whether these considerations have remained significant in view of the decision of the Court of Appeal in *Houghland v. R. R. Low (Luxury Coaches) Ltd.*[64] It was there held that it was unnecessary to put different types of bailment into watertight compartments, such as gratuitous bailments on the one hand and bailments for reward on the other. A bailee is under a duty to exercise in each case a degree of care warranted by the circumstances. But in *Morris v. C. W. Martin & Sons Ltd.*,[65] Lord Denning expressed the view that a more stringent duty of care will usually be expected from a bailee for reward than from a gratuitous bailee. As, in the hope of attracting custom, bankers usually advertise that they offer safe custody facilities, it stands to reason that they derive a general pecuniary benefit from furnishing these. It is, therefore, reasonable to assume that a high degree of care is expected of them. It is noteworthy that one of the leading texts of the first part of this century took the view that a high duty of care was expected from the bank even where it received goods as a gratuitous bailee.[66]

The bank's duty of care as a bailee can be defined as covering both the exercise of skill in the custody of the items and in the appointment of the persons charged by it therewith.[67] There are, furthermore, some forms of loss for which the bank is liable even in the absence of negligence. Thus, where the bank agrees to store an item at a specific place and yet stores it

---

[61] *De la Bere v. Pearson Ltd.* [1907] 1 KB 483.
[62] (1871) LR 6 Ch. App. 212.
[63] Pp. 576–9 below.
[64] [1962] 1 QB 694, 698.
[65] [1966] 1 QB 716, 725–6.
[66] Grant, *Law Relating to Bankers*, 7th edn., London, 1924, pp. 282–3.
[67] *Williams v. Curzon Syndicate Ltd.* (1919) 35 TLR 475, where a club was held liable for carelessness in the appointment of a night porter.

elsewhere, it is liable for any loss unless it can be shown that such loss would have been inevitably occasioned even if the terms of the contract had been strictly observed.[68]

Strict liability is also borne by the bank in cases of misdelivery. The reason for this is that the surrender of goods to a person who is not entitled to them is tantamount to conversion.[69] Any doubts that could have existed on this point have been removed by section 2(1) of the Torts (Interference with Goods) Act 1977.[70] Under section 11(2) of the same Act, the bank cannot raise a plea of contributory negligence where it has misdelivered the items.[71] Under the 1977 Act, the action in conversion is available also where the goods are destroyed or damaged.[72]

Exclusion of liability presents problems. The bank's duty of care in cases involving the deposit of documents or valuables is based on the law of bailment. It, thus, arises in law. Under section 2(2) of the Unfair Contract Terms Act 1977, liability can be restricted only if the exclusion clause meets the test of reasonableness introduced by section 11 of the Act. It remains to be seen whether the usual disclaimer, in which a bank notifies a customer that a sealed envelope or locked box is held at his risk, meets the requirements of this provision. It is believed that, to the extent that the notice purports to exempt the bank from liability for wrongs committed by its own servants, the exclusion would be considered extravagant.

There are, of course, cases in which a bank is placed in a quandary when it receives a request to return documents or valuables deposited with it. Thus, it may have doubts about the genuineness of a letter asking it to deliver the items to the 'holder', or it may simply have doubts as to the identity of the person who makes the request. The bank should in such cases follow two guidelines. First, it need not make a prompt decision. The bank is entitled to retain the items for a reasonable time to enable it to make the necessary enquiries. Thus, in *Clayton* v. *Le Roy*,[73] an antique watch stolen from the plaintiff was sold to an innocent bidder. The latter asked the very shop from which the plaintiff had purchased the watch originally to assess its authenticity. Having been informed of the theft, and recognizing the watch, the shop-owners advised the plaintiff. When they refused to deliver

[68] *Lilly* v. *Doubleday* (1881) 7 QBD 510.
[69] *Stephenson* v. *Hart* (1828) 4 Bing. 476, 482–3; *Hiort* v. *London and North Western Railway Co.* (1879) 4 Ex. D. 188, 194; *Glyn, Mills, Currie & Co* v. *East and West India Dock Co.* (1880) 6 QBD 475, 493, affd. (1882) 7 App. Cas. 591.
[70] Before the passing of the Act, it was uncertain whether misdelivery constituted detinue or conversion. Note that under the Act conversion has remained a strict tort.
[71] Note that s. 47 of the Banking Act 1979, which enables a collecting bank to plead contributory negligence as a defence for the conversion of a cheque handled for a rogue, does not apply in the context of bailment.
[72] S. 2(2).
[73] [1911] 2 KB 1031.

the watch, without enquiry, to a solicitor charged with its collection, a writ was issued forthwith. Delivering one of the majority judgments, Fletcher-Moulton LJ observed that a man did not act unlawfully in refusing to deliver up property upon a demand made to him. He was entitled to take adequate time to enquire into the claimant's rights. If, despite its precautions, the bank misdelivers the items, it is of course liable in damages. A judgment given against it transfers to it the bailor's title to the items.[74]

The second guideline to be observed by banks in cases of this sort is where there remain substantial doubts about the rights of the person claiming the goods. Cases of this type can arise in the context of inheritance or where two spouses claim a given item. The bank should then interplead, which means that, effectively, it asks the court to determine the course to be adopted by it.[75] In reality, such proceedings involve a settlement of the dispute between the contesting parties.[76]

A problem that has not arisen in this country is the bank's liability for cash or documents placed by a customer in one of its night safes. Again, one may see in this a service rendered by banks to attract custom. An American authority suggests that, despite its unawareness of the deposit when made, the bank is to be treated as a bailee for reward.[77] In the case in question, the principle was applied to cash deposited in the night safe, although the court observed that the usual relationship of banker and customer would supersede that of bailment when the funds had been credited to the customer's account. There is no doubt that in English law, an amount of money placed in a 'bag', and thus treated as a 'specie', can be the subject of a bailment agreement.[78]

(ii) Items deposited by foreign banks

Modern problems have arisen from attempts by political refugees to recover securities which have been deposited with English banks by their overseas correspondents. In such cases there is usually no privity of contract between the English bank and the refugee. Proof of ownership does not, in itself, justify the surrender of the items involved by the English bank unless it obtains the appropriate instruction from the foreign bank. In the absence of such an instruction, the English bank cannot act unless the refugee establishes that

---

[74] *United States of America and Republic of France* v. *Dollfuss Mieg et Cie SA and Bank of England* [1952] AC 582.

[75] Under RSC, O. 17.

[76] See, generally, *Halsbury's Laws of England*, 4th edn., vol. 25, para. 1039.

[77] *Bernstein* v. *Northwestern National Bank of Philadelphia* 41 A 2d 440 (1945).

[78] See the analysis of nature of notes by F. A. Mann, *Legal Aspects of Money*, 4th edn., Oxford, 1982, pp. 8–9.

he is beneficially entitled both to the securities and to their immediate possession.[79]

The problems that arise in cases of this type are demonstrated by *Kahler* v. *Midland Bank Ltd.*[80] Shares owned by the plaintiff were, at his request, deposited by his own bank in Prague, the Z Bank, with the M Bank in the Z Bank's name. During the German occupation, the plaintiff was forced to order that the shares be transferred into the ownership of the Czech B Bank in London. Notice thereof was given to the M Bank, which accordingly attorned to the B Bank. At the end of the war, the ownership of the shares was restored to the plaintiff. But under Czech exchange control regulations, the B Bank, which was subject to Czech law, could not release the shares to the plaintiff, who was at that time resident in the United Kingdom, without an approval of the Czech authorities.

The plaintiff's action for the possession of the shares was unsuccessful. In the Court of Appeal, Lord Evershed MR thought that the plaintiff had failed to establish his right to immediate possession.[81] In the House of Lords, Lords Normand and MacDermott emphasized that the position was governed by Czech law.[82] Undoubtedly the outcome would have been different if the shares had been kept by the M Bank in the plaintiff's own name. The M Bank would then have been his bailee. It would, then, have been arguable that, where a foreign national arranged for the deposit of items in his own name with an English bank, the proper law of the contract was the *lex loci contractus*. In the instant case, regard was had to the proper law of the contract relating to the original bailment of the securities. It stands to reason that other considerations would have applied if that initial contract had been made as a result of duress.

(iii) Safe deposit boxes

There is no English authority in point, but the bank's position as owner of 'safes' or safety lockers was considered by the Australian High Court in *Commissioner of Taxation* v. *Australia and New Zealand Banking Group Ltd.*[83] The case concerned the interpretation of a provision which entitled the Commissioner to require any 'person' to produce 'all goods, documents and other papers whatever in his custody or under his control' and relating

---

[79] *Gorden* v. *Harper* (1976) 7 Term Rep. 9; 101 ER 828; *Bradley* v. *Copley* (1845) 1 CB 685; 135 ER 711.

[80] [1948] 1 All ER 811, affd. [1950] AC 24. See also *Zivnostenska Banka National Corporation* v. *Frankman* [1950] AC 57; cf. *Isaacs* v. *Barclays Bank Ltd.* [1943] 2 All ER 682.

[81] [1948] 1 All ER 811, 818.

[82] [1950] AC 24, 33, and 37.

[83] (1979) 53 ALJR 336. And see *Smorgon* v. *Australia and New Zealand Banking Group Ltd.* (1976) 134 CLR 475, 478, which concerned the issues arising in the same case between the customer and his bank (including the question of confidentiality).

to tax investigations.[84] In the instant case, the Commissioner requested the bank to produce documents retained in a safe of one of its customers. It was established that the safe could be opened only by the use of two keys, one of which was retained by the bank and the other by the customer. However, the bank retained in a sealed envelope a duplicate of the customer's key, which was to be used in emergencies such as the loss by the customer of his own key.

It was argued that the bank did not have the control or custody of the contents of the safe, as it undertook in its contract to refrain from opening it. Rejecting this argument, Gibbs ACJ observed:[85]

the physical retention of the two keys by the Bank gives it control of the documents contained in the locker to which the keys give access, and that any agreement or arrangement made by the Bank with the depositor does not affect the question whether the Bank has the documents in its control and is able to produce them. The Bank has actual custody or physical control of the contents of the locker, even if it has bound itself by contract to refrain from exercising the power which it has in fact.

It is clear that, in the instant case, the court was not considering the law of bailment. The decision, though, is significant. One of the main requisites of a bailment contract is that the bailee be given the exclusive possession or custody of the subject matter of the contract.[86] This resembles the concepts of 'custody' and of 'control' considered by the High Court.

It may, accordingly, be concluded that if the bank makes a safe available to one of its customers but retains a duplicate of the key delivered to him, the bank has the custody of the contents. It is, therefore, a bailee. A charge being usually made for the hiring of a safe, the bank would appear to bear the full responsibility of a bailee for reward. It is probably in the same position even if it does not have a duplicate of the customer's key but has a master key which enables it to have access to all the safes.

Where no such access is retained by the bank, the contract concerning the safe constitutes the hiring out of the facility. In such a case the bank does not bear the responsibility of a bailee.

[84] Income Tax Assessment Act 1936, s. 264.
[85] (1979) 53 ALJR 336, 339.
[86] *Fairline Shipping Corporation* v. *Adamson* [1975] QB 180, 189–90; and see *Chitty on Contracts*, 25th edn., para. 2341.

PART III

THE BANK AS FINANCIER AND LENDER IN DOMESTIC TRANSACTIONS

CHAPTER 16

Current Account Financing and Loans

1. OVERDRAFTS AND LOANS COMPARED

Conceptually, an overdraft involves the extension of credit to a customer for a relatively short period of time. The customer is given a ceiling, which defines the maximum amount he is allowed to overdraw on his account at any given time. Interest is calculated on the daily balance but is debited to the account periodically. The customer's best course is to have a respectable margin available for drawings. Further, he should attempt to keep the amount utilized by him to a minimum. It is obvious that, in this way, he saves interest. However, he may have to pay a commitment fee if the bank grants him an overdraft which he does not use.

In a loan, the customer is granted a given amount which is credited forthwith to his current account and stands at his disposal at any time. The amount so lent is debited to a loan account opened in the customer's name. Interest is charged on the debit balance entered in the loan account regardless of whether or not the customer makes use of the proceeds. Repayments have to be made on a regular basis; a right to make early repayments is usually available to the customer. The loan may be granted for a short or a medium period, and, in some cases, even for a long period of time.

The rate of interest charged on a loan is higher than the rate of an overdraft. However, even in the case of loans, interest is frequently charged on a variable basis. It is then quoted as 'X per cent above base rate'. Usually, it is at least $\frac{1}{2}$ per cent higher than the comparable rate charged for overdrafts.

In terms of cost, an overdraft is thus more attractive than a loan. But a loan has at least one advantage as compared with an overdraft. Conceptually, an overdraft is repayable at call or on demand. A loan is granted for a fixed period of time. Moreover, where the customer takes a loan from his bank he is more likely to be granted an occasional overdraft than if his current account is already in debit.

Apart from these practical considerations, there is a conceptual distinction between an overdraft and a loan. An overdraft constitutes current account financing. It is a flexible means for financial accommodation, and is frequently granted for a general object or for multiple purposes. Its main aim is to enable the customer to continue his running account operations. A loan is to be regarded as the converse of an interest-bearing account. The bank extends it so as to invest the funds available to it. The customer applies for it in order to achieve some financial object, such as the raising of money for a project.

In modern banking, the practical distinction between the purpose of an overdraft and of a loan is being eroded. But the law continues to treat bank loans and overdrafts on a different basis. This is most clearly manifested in respect of the consumer credit legislation. It will be shown that overdrafts are less affected by the Consumer Credit Act 1974 and by regulations made thereunder than bank loans, which are fully within the ambit of the Act.

2. OVERDRAFTS

(i) Prevailing practice

Where a customer who maintains a current account with his bank requires financial accommodation, the branch manager considers the possibility of granting him an overdraft. In such a facility, the bank authorizes the customer to draw cheques on his account up to a ceiling which may not be exceeded at any one time. As amounts are paid to the credit of the account, the available balance of the overdraft increases. As cheques are drawn by the customer and paid by the bank, the balance decreases. An overdraft may be either secured over assets of the customer or unsecured.[1]

As a matter of practice, the letter in which the bank advises the granting of the overdraft to the customer specifies not only the ceiling but also the period for which the overdraft is available. To protect its interest, the bank usually adds a specific proviso to the effect that the overdraft is repayable at call. Whilst the customer can expect to utilize the overdraft for the nominated period, the bank can, under the standard formulation, demand immediate repayment if there are any unfavourable developments.[2]

The method of charging interest on an overdraft has been explained above. When the accrued interest is debited to the customer's account, it is capitalized. It becomes part of the outstanding balance for future calculations. The bank thus earns compound interest on the amount overdrawn, although this aspect is eliminated if the customer, forthwith, pays to the credit of his account an amount equal to the interest charged.[3]

The rate of interest charged on overdrafts varies from customer to customer, and from transaction to transaction. The lowest rate at which accommodation is granted to particularly sound customers in respect of low risk ventures, is known as the prime rate. A customer is usually notified whether he is charged on this basis or at a higher rate, for example, 2 per

[1] See generally, Chap. 18 below.
[2] For an analysis of the legal aspects of the question, see pp. 478–9 below.
[3] The legality of this method of charging interest is discussed below, pp. 479–81.

cent above prime rate. As the prime rate is subject to variations depending, inter alia, on the base, or minimum, rate quoted by the Bank of England, the interest rate charged on bank overdrafts is reviewed from time to time. Lending at a fixed rate is not a practice used widely by banks in the United Kingdom.[4]

(ii) The legal nature of an overdraft

It is well established that, from a legal point of view, an overdraft is a loan granted by the bank to the customer.[5] Where the customer draws a cheque without having the balance required for meeting it, his act is construed as a request for an overdraft.[6] An undertaking by the bank to grant an overdraft is binding on it. Thus, where the customer gave his bank a document of title as a security for an advance he was promised, the bank was held bound to stand by its commitment. The giving of the security was adequate consideration for the bank's undertaking.[7]

When the bank honours a customer's cheque which is drawn under an overdraft, it acts as his agent. Thus, in *Re Hone, ex p. The Trustee* v. *Kensington Borough Council*,[8] a customer sent a cheque to the Council in payment of rates. The bank honoured the cheque, although by doing so it permitted the customer to exceed an agreed overdraft ceiling. Shortly thereafter the customer was adjudicated a bankrupt. The cheque in question was credited to the Council's account before this, but the actual decision by the paying bank to honour the instrument took place thereafter. The Trustee in Bankruptcy claimed the amount of the cheque back from the Council under section 45 of the Bankruptcy Act 1914, on the basis that it had been paid without his approval after the commencement of the bankruptcy.[9]

Giving judgment for the Trustee, Harman J held that the moment of payment was that on which the drawee bank resolved to pay the cheque. Up to that moment, any credit entry in the Council's account was reversible and hence constituted conditional payment. The amount was recoverable by the Trustee, as the money paid was, in his Lordship's opinion, that of the customer. Harman J observed:[10]

a payment by a bank, under an arrangement by which the customer has an overdraft, is a lending by the bank to the customer of the money. It is the customer who

---

[4] Banks in other countries appear to grant financial accommodation to a customer at a fixed rate of interest. The German practice is to this effect.

[5] The point can be made by saying that when an account is overdrawn, the customer becomes the debtor and the banker the creditor. See p. 84 above.

[6] *Cuthbert* v. *Robarts Lubbock & Co.* [1909] 2 Ch. 226, 233, per Cozens-Hardy MR.

[7] *Fleming* v. *Bank of New Zealand* [1900] AC 577.

[8] [1951] Ch. 85.

[9] As regards the position under the Insolvency Act 1986, see pp. 281–2 above.

[10] Ibid., 89.

pays the money and not the bank. Otherwise, the bank might be able to sue the payees of the cheque for the money, which they clearly cannot do. They have only paid it as agent for the customer just as if [he] had money there.

It seems clear that the money in question had been paid by the bank on behalf of the customer,[11] and that payment took place when the drawee bank resolved to effect it.[12] There is, however, a conceptual difficulty in regarding the amount involved as the customer's money. It was, undoubtedly, paid in pursuance of a credit facility granted to him by the bank; but, until the moment of payment, the money remained co-mingled with the bank's remaining funds.[13] Conceptually, therefore, it remained the bank's money, though placed at the customer's disposal. This clarification does not affect the actual conclusion in the case.

The fact that an overdraft is considered a loan gives rise to a problem concerning repayment. Can the bank demand repayment at any time, without regard to the customer's interests? In *Rouse* v. *Bradford Banking Co.*,[14] a partnership was reorganized. The new partnership was allowed to increase an existing overdraft granted to the original firm. The question was whether a surety was thereupon discharged on the ground that the bank had given time to the partnership—the debtor—without his consent. The argument was that the increase of the overdraft ceiling, coupled with the mention of a new date, effectively gave the partnership the right to expect to have the overdraft available for the period involved. The House of Lords rejected this argument. Lord Herschell LC said:[15]

It may be that an overdraft does not prevent the bank who have agreed to give it from at any time giving notice that it is no longer to continue, and that they must be paid their money. This I think at least it does; if they have agreed to give an overdraft they cannot refuse to honour cheques or drafts, within the limit of that overdraft, which have been drawn and put into circulation before any notice to the person to whom they have agreed to give the overdraft that the limit is to be withdrawn.

His Lordship added that, although an overdraft arrangement may not in itself grant the customer a period in which he would be able to utilize the facility, neither of the parties would contemplate a withdrawal of the overdraft without notice shortly after the time of its extension. This view is echoed in *Cripps (R. A.) & Son Ltd.* v. *Wickenden*,[16] where Goff J observed that, although an overdraft was repayable on demand, the customer had to be given reasonable notice before it was withdrawn.

---

[11] See pp. 228–9 above.
[12] See pp. 234–5 above describing the clearing process.
[13] See pp. 81–84 above.
[14] [1894] AC 586.
[15] Ibid., 596.
[16] [1973] 1 WLR 944, esp. 954–5. And see *Buckingham & Co.* v. *London and Midland Bank Ltd.* (1895) 12 TLR 70.

The bank's right to reclaim payment of the overdraft at its pleasure may be abrogated by an agreement, express or implied. In *Williams and Glyn's Bank* v. *Barnes*,[17] the bank granted its customer an overdraft in order to enable him to finance some transactions of a company which he controlled and which was facing solvency problems. When that company's affairs deteriorated further, the bank demanded the repayment of the amount outstanding under the overdraft. It was argued that the bank had abrogated its right to demand payment at call, as it was clear from the circumstances of the transaction that the advance was made for the purposes of a given scheme. The calling up of the balance was contrary to the object of the agreement between the bank and its customer.

Gibson J rejected this defence on the facts, as the documentation established that the bank had expressly retained the right to withdraw the overdraft at any time. He was further of the view that a mere knowledge on the part of the bank of the nature of the transaction to be financed would not in itself suggest that the overdraft was available for a fixed time. In the instant case, the bank had had more than a mere knowledge of the object of the transaction. It had granted the overdraft for a specific purpose which entailed its being available for a suitable period of time. Had the bank not expressly retained its right of withdrawal, his Lordship would have treated it as abrogated by the implied terms of the arrangement between the parties.

This view was followed recently in an unreported decision. In *Titford Property Co. Ltd.* v. *Cannon Street Acceptances Ltd.*,[18] a document in which the customer was granted an overdraft described it as available for twelve months, but included a printed clause providing for repayment at call. Goff J held that the overdraft was not repayable at call, as such an interpretation would have frustrated the object of the transaction, and as, otherwise, the borrower could be led into a disastrous position. His Lordship cited *Photo Production Ltd.* v. *Securicor Transport Ltd.*,[19] in which the House of Lords held that, if one party to a contract proffered one of its standard forms for signature to the other, then any printed clause would be construed as subordinate to the main object of the transaction.

(iii) The right to charge interest

The interest charged by a bank on an overdraft is based on the variation of the rate in the financial market. Surprisingly, the only authority which expressly recognizes a bank's right to charge such a variable rate is a

[17] [1980] Com. LR 205.
[18] [1975] cited in Cresswell et al., *Encyclopedia of Banking Law*, vol. 1, para. c/183.
[19] [1980] AC 827.

decision of the Victorian Supreme Court of 1895.[20] It is believed that if the right were ever seriously disputed, banks would be able to establish a suitable trade usage.

There have been attempts to question the banks' right to add the half-yearly interest to the outstanding balance, and to charge interest for the next six months on a balance comprising the capitalized interest. The validity of the practice was recognized by the Judicial Committee,[21] and affirmed by the House of Lords in *Yourell* v. *Hibernian Bank Ltd.*[22] It was there held that the method of charging involved was legitimate as between banker and customer despite the compound interest involved.[23]

What is the effect of the debiting of the accrued interest to the customer's account? Is his liability for interest discharged thereby, or is the nature of the debt merely converted? Basically, the question is one of fact. Thus, if the customer's account has a credit balance at the relevant time, and this balance is reduced by the amount debited, the interest is paid. It has been shown elsewhere that a debit entry can constitute payment.[24] If the customer's account is in debit, the increase of the amount of the overdraft by the interest charged does not, in reality, discharge a liability.

The bulk of the case law in point recognizes this fact. Although the decision of the Court of Session in *Reddie* v. *Williamson*[25] suggests that the debiting of the interest to the balance of the overdrawn account constitutes payment of the amount so due, later cases take the opposite view.[26] They suggest that even for tax purposes, the periodic debiting of interest does not constitute payment.

The bank's right to charge interest on a periodic basis is related to the nature of its continuing contractual relationship with the customer. When this relationship is abrogated, the position changes. In *Deutsche Bank und Disconto Gesellschaft* v. *Banque des Marchands de Moscou,*[27] the account of the Russian M Bank with the German D Bank became inactive during the First World War. At the end of this period, the M Bank was nationalized in the wake of the revolution. The question was whether the D Bank was entitled to charge interest on the usual basis for the entire period involved.

[20] *Re City and County Property Bank* (1895) 21 VLR 405, 410–1.
[21] *National Bank of Australasia* v. *United Hand-in-Hand and Band of Hope Co.* (1879) 4 App. Cas. 391, 409.
[22] [1918] AC 372.
[23] Ibid., 385, per Lord Atkinson, and 393, per Lord Parker. Their Lordships regarded the debt accrued on the basis of the interest charge as accrued on the day it was debited to the account.
[24] See pp. 384–7 above.
[25] (1863) 1 Macph. 228 (Ct. of Sess.), per Lord Cowan. But note the differing view on this point of Inglis LJC, at 237, as explained by Lord Atkin in *Paton* v. *IRC* [1938] AC 341, 349–51.
[26] *Re Jauncey, Bird* v. *Arnold* [1926] Ch. 471, 476; *Paton* v. *IRC*, above.
[27] (1931) 4 LDAB 293.

Giving judgment against the D Bank, the Court of Appeal held that the right to charge compound interest was abrogated by the war. During this period, in which Russia and Germany were on opposite sides, the parties could not trade with each other. Greer LJ explained the position as follows:[28]

First, there can be no title to compound interest without a contract express or implied between the debtor and the creditor; and, secondly, that it is never implied except as to mercantile accounts current for mutual transactions.

Their Lordships relied on *Fergusson* v. *Fyffe*,[29] in which it was held that the abrogation of the relationship by the customer's death would have a similar effect. It is, perhaps, arguable that the outbreak of war suspends rather than modifies the nature of the relationship of a bank and a customer from an alien country. Under the special circumstances of the case, and taking into account the nationalization of the M Bank and the ensuing question of succession, the conclusion is acceptable.

(iv) The bank's duty of care

Usually the bank does not owe its customer a duty of care to advise on the soundness of the transaction for which he requires the overdraft. Undoubtedly, the bank frequently studies the nature of the transaction which it is asked to finance. If it finds it unsound, it may decline the customer's application. The perusal, though, is in the bank's interest and not made by it as the customer's financial adviser.

The point arose in *Williams & Glyn's Bank* v. *Barnes*,[30] discussed earlier. It was there argued that the bank should have warned its customer that the transaction involved was unsound. Rejecting this argument, Gibson J said:[31]

no duty in law arises upon the bank either to consider the prudence of the lending from the customer's point of view, or to advise with reference to it. Such a duty could arise only by contract, express or implied, or upon the principle of the assumption of responsibility and reliance stated in *Hedley Byrne*[32] or in cases of fiduciary duty. The same answer is to be given to the question even if the bank knows that the borrowing and application of the loan, as intended by the customer, are imprudent.

It is obvious that the cases defining the bank's duty as a fiduciary agent or as

[28] Ibid., 296.
[29] (1840) 8 Cl. & F 121.
[30] [1980] Com. LR 205.
[31] Ibid., 207.
[32] Discussed above, pp. 459–60.

an adviser on financial transactions[33] would not be applied lightly where the customer seeks to avoid repayment of an overdraft.

(v) Appropriation of payments

A feature of overdrawn accounts is that the debit balance keeps changing from day to day. These fluctuations occur because of the current nature of the account and the mutual dealings transacted through it. For most purposes it is adequate to determine the net credit or debit balance as standing at the end of each trading day.[34] In certain cases, though, it is important to consider which of the debit items in the account are to be regarded as discharged by the incoming credit entries. Principally, the problem is relevant in two types of case: in transactions in which a bank seeks to enforce a security covering a revolving amount; and in respect of the account of a partnership following the firm's dissolution.

A guarantee given to secure an overdraft extended to a customer illustrates the first type of case. Suppose that the guarantor is liable for debts incurred up to a specified date. The bank decides not to freeze the debtor's account on that date, and allows him to continue operating it in the ordinary manner. Accordingly, further cheques are drawn by the customer and met by the bank, whilst the proceeds of effects payable to him continue to be credited. If, subsequently, the bank seeks to enforce the guarantee,[35] a dispute is bound to arise as regards the amount covered. It is in the bank's interest to claim that the guarantee covers the balance shown on its final validity day. The guarantor's natural argument is that the amount for which he is liable ought to be reduced by any sums paid to the credit of the account involved after that date.

The same problem arises in a partnership. Basically, each partner is answerable for the debts of the firm.[36] His liability terminates when the partnership is dissolved and notice thereof is publicized.[37] Thus, if an account of a partnership continues to be operated upon despite its dissolution, or despite the withdrawal of the partner sought to be charged, the question that arises is the extent of his liability.

The principle used by the courts to solve problems of this type is known as 'the rule of appropriation of payments'. It treats each item paid to the

---

[33] Discussed above pp. 84–89 (fiduciary relationship aspect) and pp. 463–6 (bank's duty as financial adviser).
[34] The problem can be relevant in other cases too; see below.
[35] Assuming that, under the surety agreement, the guarantor's liability is not discharged on that day.
[36] Partnership Act 1890, s. 5; and see Lindley, *On Partnership*, 15th edn., London, 1984, ch. 12.
[37] Partnership Act 1890, s. 37; and as regards a partner's death, s. 36(3). And see Lindley, *On Partnership*, 15th edn., pp. 378 et seq.

credit of the account as discharging the earliest debit items entered in it. Where applicable, this principle works against the interests of the creditor.

It is clear that the principle, which may be described as 'first incurred first discharged', constitutes a rule of convenience.[38] It was established at the beginning of the nineteenth century in *Devaynes* v. *Noble; Clayton's Case*.[39] One of the partners in a bank died. Although the partnership was thereupon dissolved, the remaining partners continued to carry on its business as a going concern. Eventually the bank became insolvent. A customer thereupon sought to recover the balance due to him from the estate of the deceased partner. The customer had had a substantial credit balance at the time of the partner's death. During the period following it he drew cheques for an amount exceeding it; but he also paid in numerous items during this period, so that the balance due to him when the bank became insolvent was actually higher than the original one.

The partner's estate argued that its liability was discharged when the bank met the cheques drawn by the customer during the relevant period. Giving judgment for the estate, Sir William Grant MR emphasized that in practice neither the customer nor the bank contemplated that any specific debit item would be set off against a given credit entered in the account. All that the parties were concerned with was the existence of an adequate fund, or balance, for meeting cheques drawn on the account. His Lordship explained:[40]

In such a case, there is no room for any other appropriation than that which arises from the order in which the receipts and payments take place, and are carried into the account. Presumably, it is the first sum paid in, that is first drawn out. It is the first item on the debit side of the account, that is discharged, or reduced, by the first item on the credit side. The appropriation is made by the very act of setting the two items against each other. Upon that principle, all accounts current are settled, and particularly cash accounts.

If the creditor wished to depart from this arrangement, he had to make his intention clear to the debtor. In the instant case, there was no evidence to this effect. The amounts paid out by the bank had, therefore, discharged the initial balance due to the customer at the day of the relevant partner's death. The estate was not liable for debts incurred by the bank in respect of money deposited with it thereafter.

Although the rule in *Clayton's Case* is based on a presumption as to the probable intention of the parties, it is not easily displaced. In *Deeley* v. *Lloyds Bank Ltd.*,[41] the bank obtained from its customer a first mortgage to

[38] So described in *Re Diplock* [1948] Ch. 465, 554.
[39] (1816) 1 Mer. 572.
[40] Ibid., 608.
[41] [1912] AC 756, esp. 783, reversing [1910] 1 Ch. 648.

secure an overdraft. When the bank received notice that the customer had granted a second mortgage over the property to another house, it failed to freeze the balance as it stood, allowing the customer to continue operating the account in the ordinary manner. The amounts paid in by him were higher than the balance of the overdraft at the date of the notification, although the fresh drawings of the customer had left the account in debit. The second mortgagee argued that his title had become superior to that of the bank, as under the rule in question the credits made by the customer had discharged the earlier indebtedness.

The Court of Appeal took the view that the rule in *Clayton's Case* had been displaced by the intention of the parties. It was absurd to assume that the bank had intended to appropriate the payments made by the customer against the earliest debit items. It was in the bank's interest that the relevant credits cancel the later, unsecured entries, rather than the secured ones. The House of Lords reversed. It held that primarily the right to appropriate a payment made to the credit of a current account rested with the debtor. If he did not evince an intention, the creditor had the opportunity to do so. In the absence of a specific appropriation the position was governed by the rule in *Clayton's Case*. If the bank, or creditor, had intended to appropriate the payments made to it after it received the second mortgagee's notification, it could resort to the simple device of striking a balance in the account and of then opening a fresh account in the customer's name.[42]

It is clear that the opening of a fresh account displaces the rule of appropriation of payments.[43] The viability of this advice was recently reiterated by Slade J in *Siebe Gorman & Co. Ltd. v. Barclays Bank Ltd.*[44] His Lordship further pointed out that the rule in *Clayton's Case* was subject to two exceptions. First, it would not apply in respect of secured transactions where the second mortgagee agreed to the making of fresh advances by the first mortgagee. Secondly, the rule would be equally displaced where the fresh advances were made in pursuance of the terms of the initial agreement between the debtor and the first mortgagee. It is believed that, in addition, the rule would be inapplicable if a clause respecting further advances to be made by the first mortgagee was brought to the second mortgagee's attention.[45]

[42] See *Royal Bank of Canada* v. *Bank of Montreal* (1976) 67 DLR (3d) 755. For an interesting modification of the rule, see the Consumer Credit Act 1974, s. 81. Where the debtor has incurred a number of debts, he is entitled to appropriate a payment made by him to any one of them; if he fails to do so, the amount paid in is to be credited to the different outstanding debts on a pro rata basis.

[43] *Re Sherry; London and County Banking Co.* v. *Terry* (1883) 25 Ch. D 692. (Note that, at 706, Cotton LJ expressed the view that the guarantee covered the balance standing to the credit of the account from time to time.)

[44] [1979] 2 Lloyd's Rep. 142, 164.

[45] As to whether the inclusion of a clause in a charge, registered under s. 395 of the Companies Act 1985, is adequate for this purpose, see pp. 556–61 below.

In modern practice, banks include clauses in their contracts with customers which have the object of excluding the rule in *Clayton's Case*. One such clause provides that the security furnished by the customer is to apply in respect of his indebtedness as standing from time to time.[46] A complementary clause prohibits the granting of any fresh security by the customer without the bank's consent, and provides that an arrangement made in violation of this term is to be void against it.[47]

Banks exercise their right to appropriate payments by making their own decision, in the absence of the customer's instruction, as to the account to be debited with the credit made.[48] Furthermore, the rule is displaced if the bank makes it clear that, although it does not seek to exercise its right immediately, it reserves the right to do so in due course.[49]

The rule in *Clayton's Case* applies only to current accounts. In '*The Mecca*',[50] the House of Lords held it inapplicable to accounts which were not of a running nature. It was further held that, even in a current account, the rule did not apply in respect of a number of payments made on a single day, as the order in which these were settled was fortuitous. In addition, the rule is inapplicable where its effect is contrary to the interests of a beneficiary of a trust.[51]

(vi) Consumer credit aspects

It will be recalled that the Consumer Credit Act 1974 applies certain protective measures to regulated credit agreements.[52] Basically, the relevant provisions apply if the credit extended is for an amount not exceeding £15,000, and provided the customer is an 'individual'.[53] A bank overdraft falls within the definition of a regulated consumer credit agreement for unrestricted-use running account credit,[54] even if it is extended by the bank without prior arrangements with the customer.[55]

The Act seems to apply where the bank has agreed to grant the customer an overdraft but has not finalized details of the arrangement. A case in point

---

[46] As to when further advances may be made without losing the protection of the security, see pp. 544, 562 below.

[47] As to the viability of such a clause, see pp. 562–3 below.

[48] That they need to do so, see *Simson* v. *Ingham* (1823) 2 B & C 65; *London and Westminster Bank* v. *Button* (1907) 51 Sol. J 466.

[49] '*The Mecca*' [1897] AC 286, 294; *Seymour* v. *Pickett* [1905] 1 KB 715.

[50] Above.

[51] *Re Hallett's Estate* (1880) 13 Ch. D 696; and see the Australian authority of *Lofts* v. *MacDonald* (1974) 3 ALR 404.

[52] See, generally, Ch. 3 above.

[53] Consumer Credit Act 1974, s. 8; as regards current limit, see p. 65 above.

[54] Ibid., s. 10(1); and see s. 9, under which credit includes a loan and any other form of financial accommodation.

[55] Ibid., Sched. 2, example 17.

is where the bank advises the customer that no bank charges are incurred when the account is in credit, but that such charges will be levied if the account is overdrawn. Often a minimum limit for an available overdraft is set at this time. It has been pointed out that such an arrangement involves multiple agreements within the meaning of section 18(1)(*g*), and that, under section 18(2), each part is treated as a separate agreement for the purposes of the Act.[56] Naturally, any agreements falling within its ambit (such as overdrafts) are covered.

But although overdrafts extended to individuals for amounts not exceeding £15,000[57] fall within the ambit of the Act, its stringent requirements are relaxed in respect of them. The most important instance concerns Part V, which makes provisions applicable to the entering into a credit agreement, to its form and contents, and to its cancellation.[58] The Director of Fair Trading has made a determination under section 74(3)[59] exempting bank overdrafts from the provisions of this Part of the Act,[60] subject to certain conditions as to notification.

Finance rate computation is another area in which there are special provisions pertaining to overdrafts. Regulations made under the Act in respect of advertisements and quotations[61] define the 'total cost of credit' which is to be disclosed in certain instances. Its computation takes into account not only the interest but also other charges made for the extension of the credit.[62] In the case of overdrafts, all that needs to be disclosed is the interest rate alone; other charges, such as a commitment fee, are to be shown separately.[63]

This exemption is of considerable importance to banks. The disclosure provisions of the Act have been brought into effect in respect of quotations[64] and advertisement,[65] and, as from May 1985, apply at the time the

[56] Goode, *Consumer Credit Legislation*, vol. 1, para. 297.

[57] Under s. 10(2), which overrides s. 82(2), an approval for occasional overdrawings beyond the £15,000 limit are to be disregarded; and see Goode, *Consumer Credit Legislation*, vol. 1, para. 264.

[58] Pp. 66–68 above.

[59] As amended by s. 74(3A), inserted by the Banking Act 1979, s. 38(1); and see Determination under s. 74(1)(*b*) made on 3 Nov. 1983; Guest and Lloyd, *Encyclopaedia of Consumer Credit Law*, para. 4-4801.

[60] Except s. 56, relating to antecedent negotiations. A clause is void if it deems a negotiator to be the debtor's agent or if it frees the creditor from liability.

[61] S. 20 of the Act and the Consumer Credit (Total Charge for Credit) Regulations 1980, SI 51, made by the Secretary of State thereunder.

[62] Ibid., regs. 3–7.

[63] The Consumer Credit (Advertisements) Regulations 1980, SI 54, Sched. 2, para. 7(3).

[64] The Consumer Credit (Quotations) Regulations 1980, SI 55, made under s. 52. Note that in respect of overdrafts the same provision applies as in respect of advertisements: Sched. 1, para. 2(6).

[65] See, generally, the Consumer Credit (Advertisements) Regulations 1980, SI 54, Sched. 2, paras. 3(1)(*a*) and 3(7) and the Act, s. 43; Goode, *Consumer Credit Legislation*, vol. 1, para 541; Guest and Lloyd, *Encyclopaedia of Consumer Credit Law*, para. 3–142.

contract is made.[66] But from the banks' point of view, the only practical effect of the disclosure provisions is to require them to advertise their rates when these are changed from time to time,[67] and to set them out in a specific quotation given to a customer. However, the provisions do not apply to the making of an overdraft agreement.

Another important modification of the general provisions of the Consumer Credit Act 1974 in respect of overdrafts concerns canvassing, which means the soliciting of business off trade premises.[68] Generally, the Act prohibits the canvassing of persons to enter into debtor–creditor agreements.[69] But section 49(3) exempts the canvassing of entry into overdraft agreements where two conditions are fulfilled. First, the exemption applies only to accounts covered by a determination of the Director of Fair Trading. Current accounts operable by cheques have been the subject of such a determination.[70] Secondly, the person canvassed has to be the holder of an account. It is irrelevant whether his account is of the current type or an interest-bearing account.

The Act preserves the bank's right to demand repayment of an overdraft without notice. It is true that section 76(1) provides that seven days notice must normally be given by a creditor. But under subsection (2), this provision applies only if the loan is extended for a given period. As overdrafts are conceptually repayable on demand, the bank need not give such notice where it considers it advisable to demand immediate repayment,[71] unless the overdraft has been granted for a particular time and is called up within that time. If repayment is demanded because of default, then a default notice under section 87 is also needed.

The last relevant provision concerns the giving by the bank of information regarding the state of an existing account. The bank is obliged to give its customer information on the state of his account, and, further, is required to send him periodic statements.[72] Notably, in a joint overdrawn current account, all but one of the owners can dispense with such notice.[73]

---

[66] See s. 60 of the Act which, being in Part V, does not apply to bank overdrafts. And see the Consumer Credit (Agreements) Regulations 1983, SI 1553, which came into effect on 19 May 1985. In the case of running account agreements, credit limits and some other details have to be disclosed: Sched. 1, para. 8. But these regulations, as a whole being made under Part V, do not apply to overdrafts over running accounts of banks.

[67] Consumer Credit (Advertisements) Regulations 1980, SI 54, Sched. 2, paras. 3(7) and 4(1). And see the Consumer Credit (Agreements) Regulations 1983, SI 1553, Sched. 1, para. 8.

[68] P. 70 above.

[69] As regards the prohibition of canvassing, see s. 49 of the Act; and see Guest and Lloyd, *Encyclopaedia of Consumer Credit Law*, paras. 2–049 et seq., and pp. 70–1 above, as regards the meaning of canvassing.

[70] Determination of 1 June 1977; Goode, *Consumer Credit Legislation*, Pt. 4, para. 200; Guest and Lloyd, *Encyclopaedia of Consumer Credit Law*, para. 4–4800.

[71] Goode, *Consumer Credit Legislation*, vol. 1, para. 891.

[72] Required under s. 78(4) of the 1974 Act and the Consumer Credit (Running-Account Credit Information) Regulations 1983, SI 1570.

[73] Ibid., s. 185(2).

The Banking Act 1979[74] makes it clear that this dispensation remains effective even if the 'running account' is modified, as is the case where the agreed ceiling is increased.

It should be obvious that the Consumer Credit Act 1974 has not introduced cumbersome provisions affecting overdrafts. As pointed out above, the main practical effect of its provisions is to induce banks to advertise their prime lending rates. The computation of the relevant figure has not required any significant alteration. The provisions concerning disclosure in quotations are, from a practical point of view, irrelevant. The bank's right to demand immediate repayment of an overdraft has remained effective in practice. In point of fact, the Act has consolidated the banks' position as issuers of overdrafts, as advertisements may not refer to such a facility unless it is of the traditional type.[75]

3. BANK LOANS

(i) Scope

Bank loans are granted to customers for a variety of purposes. Some are business loans made either to a company or to an unincorporated borrower, such as a partnership. Other transactions are of the consumer type.

The Consumer Credit Act 1974 requires that commercial and consumer loans be treated separately. At the same time, the basic concepts of a loan apply in both types of transaction. Initially, the bank has to satisfy itself of the viability of the proposition made to it. The agreement itself tends to follow a given pattern, except that in consumer transactions it has to be adapted so as to meet the requirements of the Act and the regulations made thereunder.

A detailed discussion of all doctrines applying to loans is outside the scope of this work. They fall within the domain of the general law of contract. It is, however, necessary to review the banks' approach to loans. Their policies are, basically, the same in both commercial and consumer transactions. One aspect of lending that is of particular importance in banking transactions is the provision for security. Chapters 18–21 deal with this subject.

(ii) Review of the transaction by the bank

Where a bank reviews an application for a loan, it considers both the soundness of the venture and of the borrower. Points which the bank has to bear

---

[74] S. 38(3).
[75] See, for example, the Consumer Credit (Advertisements) Regulations 1980, SI 54, reg. 12(*a*).

in mind are the profitability of the transaction, its legality, and its regularity. Thus, the bank will not extend a loan if it has any doubt about the mandate or the bona fides of the officers of a company who apply on its behalf for a loan.

In perusing a loan application, the bank attempts to avoid speculative transactions. It also attempts to avoid 'accommodation banking'.[76] This phrase denotes transactions in which a party guarantees or grants accommodation without a financial interest in the business venture, be it direct or indirect.

One of the main concerns of a bank, particularly in the case of business loans, is the borrower's cash-flow and source of repayments. In many cases it is appreciated that, where a loan is needed for setting-up purposes, the borrower may not be able to repay capital at the initial stages. In such a case the bank may agree to charge him interest only for a given period of time. Generally, the bank attempts to identify the fund which will enable the borrower to make repayments although there is no provision in the contract that these are to come exclusively from that fund.[77]

The conditions in the loan agreement concerning security, interest and repayments vary a great deal. The arrangement for security depends on whether the borrower is a public corporation, a private company, an unincorporated trader, or a person borrowing for private purposes. A great deal depends on the object of the loan. In many cases the loan is, in any event, unsecured. This is particularly so where it is extended to an individual.

The interest rate charged depends largely on the bank's assessment of the risk, on the period for which the loan is extended, and on the security furnished. The rate is usually variable, being quoted at a given percentage above the bank's prime lending rate.

It is clear that the object of a loan may vary from that of a personal loan for such purposes as travelling, to a syndicated loan extended to enable a corporation to finance a capital project. One province in which the banks have not been traditionally active is that of loans for the purchase of private dwellings.

Virtually all lending agreements include a clause under which the entire amount advanced becomes repayable if some given event takes place. A typical event is the borrower's default or bankruptcy; or, in the case of a corporate borrower, its being taken over by a receiver or being wound up. Where the Consumer Credit Act 1974 is inapplicable, the clause is valid. However, a bank that attempts to call up a loan in the case of a minute delay

---

[76] See, further, pp. 523–5 below.
[77] Although it may obtain an assignment by way of security or charge for security purposes; see Chap. 21.

in the payment of a single instalment, stands to lose a customer.[78] To date, there is no case law in point.[79]

(iii) Consumer credit implications

There is one fundamental distinction between overdrafts and bank loans in so far as the application of the Consumer Credit Act 1974 is concerned. Part V of the Act, which concerns the making of the agreement and which has been excluded in respect of overdrafts, applies to bank loans. Naturally, the transaction has to be of one of the types covered by the Act, such as a loan for not more than £15,000.[80] In practice, many loans extended to individual customers fall within this group.

Part V of the Act introduces some far-reaching measures for the protection of consumers. Agreements are subject to cancellation by the consumer within a prescribed period if, in the course of the antecedent negotiations, some representations were made to him by or on behalf of the other party. But this provision does not apply in the following cases: (*a*) if the loan is secured over land or has been given for its acquisition; or (*b*) if the agreement is signed at the premises of the creditor, of a 'negotiator', or of a 'linked party'.[81] Problems are, however, presented by section 58(1), which requires the bank to follow a stringent procedure where a loan is secured by a mortgage over land. The problem is discussed in Chapter 19.

In practice, very few loans are cancelled by a borrower against the bank's will. In the first place, banks are prepared to accept at any time the repayment of money lent by them. Secondly, bank loans are usually made on terms more favourable than those available to the borrower from other sources. It is far more common for a borrower to ask for an extension of the time of repayment than to offer to discharge the debt prematurely.

A more onerous provision of the Act affecting bank loans is section 60, which empowers the Secretary of State to make regulations prescribing, inter alia, the form of regulated consumer credit agreements. The highly technical Consumer Credit (Agreements) Regulations 1983,[82] made in pursuance of this provision, must be strictly complied with; otherwise the loan is unenforceable by the bank without an order of the court.

The regulations require certain information to be contained in the agree-

---

[78] Note that the Unfair Contract Terms Act 1977 has no application, as there is here no attempt by the bank to rely on an exemption clause.

[79] It is, further, unlikely that the general doctrine of unconscionability, which may be developing at present, would apply in a case of this type. See *Chitty on Contracts*, 25th edn., paras. 516–18; the following cases concern the doctrine: *Shiloh Spinners* v. *Harding* [1973] AC 697, 726; *Schroeder (A.) Music Publishing Co. Ltd.* v. *Macaulay* [1974] 1 WLR 1308, 1315.

[80] See p. 65 above.

[81] S. 67; and see pp. 72–73 above.

[82] SI 1553 of 1983; as regards exempt agreements see p. 64 above.

ment. They also prescribe that the agreement bear a heading stating that it is an agreement regulated by the Consumer Credit Act 1974, that it contain a statutory notice advising the debtor of his rights under the Act, and that the signature of the debtor be executed in a signature 'box' in a prescribed form. Traditionally, loan agreements by banks have often been constituted by an informal 'letter of offer' setting out the basic terms of the arrangement, which is signed and returned by the customer. Such informal agreements will now disappear and be replaced by formal agreements complying with the Act. Particular difficulties arise for banks with respect to the 'financial and related particulars' which the Regulations require to be inserted, setting out, for example, the amounts of repayments and the dates on which these are to be made. Computer systems set up by the banks contain variations, e.g. where payments fall due on a non-banking day, and these may entail lengthy explanations in the statutory particulars. The Act itself also requires all the terms of the agreement (other than implied terms) to be embodied in the document,[83] and certain terms are 'prescribed terms', the absence of which makes the agreement wholly unenforceable.[84]

The Regulations[85] make elaborate provisions concerning cost of credit and rate of credit disclosure. Where the agreement involves fixed sum credit, the contract has to disclose the total charge of credit and the rate thereof.[86] In the case of a running credit account, the contract has to show the available ceiling and the manner in which it may be determined from time to time.[87] Both in this case, and where the contract is for a fixed amount but at a variable interest rate, the initial rate has to be shown as well as the total amount of additional charges.[88] It is further necessary, in the case of a variable rate, to disclose the base rate and the mode to be used for its periodic review.[89] A statement that the rate is to be kept at a given figure above 'prime rate' should be acceptable. Special provisions apply where the rate is quoted as an annual percentage rate (APR) taking into account the available tax relief.[90] It is clear that these regulations are onerous. To prevent hardship, a certain tolerance in calculations is permitted.[91]

Further difficulties arise under the Act and Regulations where the

---

[83] Consumer Credit Act 1974, s. 61(*b*).

[84] Ibid., s. 127(3).

[85] The Consumer Credit (Agreements) Regulations 1983, SI 1553, Sched. 1, esp. paras. 11–12.

[86] Ibid., para. 9 and reg. 2(6) as augmented by Sched. 1, paras. 15–17; and note that a restricted-use fixed sum credit agreement has to disclose details of the venture in respect of which it is granted.

[87] Sched. 1, para. 8.

[88] Ibid., para. 10.

[89] Idem, and see paras. 18–19 as to when no variation has taken place.

[90] Ibid., para. 17 (under s. 19 of the Income and Corporation Taxes Act 1970 and Sched. 4 of the Finance Act 1976).

[91] Consumer Credit (Agreements) Regulations 1983, SI 1553, reg. 2(2).

agreement is varied by an additional agreement between the bank and the customer.[92] For example, a further advance may be made under an existing agreement, or the security for the loan may be varied (as is the case where a customer sells a home charged to the bank and buys a new one, or where stock and shares lodged as security are sold and replaced by others). In such cases a modifying agreement will arise, and the Regulations applicable to such an agreement are of even greater complexity. Questions may arise as to whether there is a modifying agreement when the bank grants indulgence to the customer by allowing him to defer payment of one or more instalments or reduces the amount of the instalment and extends his time to pay. Such acts of indulgence probably do not constitute modifying agreements. But they do so, for example, where the customer furnishes consideration by agreeing to pay a higher rate of interest on the overdue amount.

Where the loan agreement is secured on land (other than s. 58(2) cases) the Act contains special provisions which require the bank to send the customer an advance copy of the agreement and legal charge. The bank must then allow him at least seven days to consider whether he wishes to withdraw from the transaction. At the end of this period (if he has not withdrawn), the bank must send him the agreement and legal charge for signature. There then must follow a further seven-day 'consideration period', during which the bank must not approach the customer in any way except at the customer's own request. The object of these elaborate provisions is to ensure that the customer has a chance to peruse the agreement and make up his mind without any pressure from the bank. But they also have the effect of preventing the customer from getting the loan quickly, especially since the charge document has to be complete in all respects before the advance copy is sent.[93]

Where the bank has pre-signed the loan agreement, or it is signed by the bank and the customer at the same time, only one copy of the executed agreement has to be given to the customer.[94] Otherwise, two copies must be provided. The first copy (of the unexecuted agreement) must be supplied when the agreement is delivered or sent to him for signature. The second copy, of the executed agreement, has to be given to him within seven days following the making of the agreement. If there are joint borrowers, each of them has to receive these copies.[95] As a result, where there are joint borrowers and the agreement is secured on land, up to fourteen copies of the agreement may be required.

The creditor's duties of disclosure under the Act do not end when the contract is executed. Under section 77, which applies in the case of a fixed

---

[92] Consumer Credit Act 1974, s. 82(2).
[93] And see, further, pp. 536–40 below.
[94] Cf. Consumer Credit Act 1974, s. 64(1)(*b*), concerning notice of cancellation rights.
[95] Ibid., ss. 62–3.

sum credit agreement, the creditor must provide the debtor, at his request, with a copy of the agreement and with details about the financial state of the transaction. The creditor's duties in the case of running account credit agreements have been discussed in respect of overdrafts.[96]

The Act regulates certain aspects of the transaction during its currency. Whilst a detailed analysis is outside the scope of this work, it is important to mention that, if the customer defaults in payment, the bank must give him at least seven days' notice before it calls in the loan or enforces any security (including any guarantee). The notice must be in a statutory form which advises the customer that, if he pays off the arrears, no further action will be taken against him or any surety.[97] It also informs him that if he has difficulties in making the payments he can apply to the court, which may make an order giving him time to pay. Similar (but different) notices have to be served in non-default cases where the bank wishes to call in a loan[98] or terminate the agreement, for example, on bankruptcy.[99]

[96] Pp. 485–8 above.
[97] Consumer Credit Act 1974, ss. 87–8.
[98] Ibid., s. 76(1); and see the Consumer Credit (Cancellation Notices and Copies of Documents) Regulations 1983, SI 1557.
[99] Consumer Credit Act 1974, s. 98.

CHAPTER 17

Acceptance Credits and Bills of Exchange

1. THE NATURE OF ACCEPTANCE CREDITS

In some cases a bank may not be prepared to grant its customer an advance or to extend him a loan but may be willing to back his arrangements with another credit provider. One way to achieve this purpose is for the bank to guarantee a loan obtained by the customer from some financial institution. Another method is to provide him with a line of credit or an acceptance credit.

In the letter of facility issued in respect of an acceptance credit, the customer is authorized to draw bills of exchange on the bank for an amount not exceeding a given ceiling at any one time. The bank's signature as acceptor enables the customer, who figures as drawer, to discount the instruments in the commercial bills market.[1] When any bill is due, the discounter, who acquires the bill through a bill broker, presents it for payment to the bank that issued the acceptance credit (the issuing bank). The customer may place the issuing bank in funds for meeting the acceptance, or may require that the bill be 'rolled over'. Under the latter arrangement, the customer draws a fresh bill for the amount required to discharge (viz. 'retire') the original bill. In many cases the roll-over is sanctioned by the acceptance credit. Thus, if the ceiling has not been reached at the time the initial instrument is due, the customer is entitled under the facility to draw a new bill. If the ceiling has been reached, or if the acceptance credit has expired, a new arrangement must be made between the customer and the issuing bank.

The bank's remuneration is a fee charged for the granting of the facility plus an acceptance fee for each bill drawn on it. In addition, the customer has to bear in mind that the amount paid to him when the bill is negotiated is its face value less the discount charge. Accordingly, he has to draw a bill for a gross amount that would assure him of obtaining the required net. It further follows that, whenever a roll-over is required, the new instrument is for an amount higher than that of the retired bill.

The effect of an acceptance credit is to enable the customer to raise funds on the issuing bank's credit. In this respect, the arrangement is similar to one in which the customer obtains a loan granted by a financial institution in

---

[1] For an excellent description, see Gillett Bros., *The Bill on London*, London, 1964.

reliance on the bank's guarantee.[2] But there is a substantive distinction between the two arrangements. Where the bank guarantees a loan granted to its customer, it assumes secondary or ancillary liability.[3] The customer is the main debtor although, on his default, the creditor is usually entitled to enforce the guarantee forthwith.[4] The acceptance credit involves a more sophisticated arrangement. As against its customer, the bank functions as a surety. It has the right to obtain reimbursement from him for any amount paid out on bills drawn under the facility. As against the discounters of the customer's bills, the bank, which figures as an acceptor, assumes primary liability.[5]

One of the main advantages of an acceptance credit is that it leaves the customer considerable freedom as regards the sources from which he obtains each advance when needed. He can discount the bills accepted by the bank with the credit provider who offers the most favourable terms.

For most purposes, the customer's rights and liabilities depend on the terms of the acceptance credit and on the law of bills of exchange. A general discussion of the law of bills of exchange, to be followed by a discussion of the special problems pertaining to bills drawn under acceptance credits, is required.

2. BASIC PRINCIPLES OF BILLS OF EXCHANGE

(i) Nature of the bill and its practical use

The law of bills of exchange is technical and complex. The case law is substantial, and is reviewed in works of considerable length.[6] For the purposes of this book it is adequate to provide a general discussion of bills and their function; of the role of the parties to the instruments; of the rights of the holder; and of the main principles governing negotiation, discharge, and the procedure applicable upon the dishonour of a bill. A form of a bill of exchange is reproduced in the Appendix.

---

[2] In the United States, acceptance credits issued by banks are valid under the Federal Reserve Act, 12 USC, para. 24, 7th power, as they are not considered to be guarantees. See generally, *Benjamin's Sale of Goods*, 2nd edn., para. 2257.

[3] See, generally, *Chitty on Contracts*, 25th edn., vol. 2, paras. 4434 et seq.

[4] *Belfast Banking Co.* v. *Stanley* (1867) 15 WR 989; but note that a demand by the debtor may be made a condition precedent to the creditor's right to sue the guarantor: *Re Brown, Brown* v. *Brown* [1893] 2 Ch. 300.

[5] Bills of Exchange Act 1882 (BEA), s. 54.

[6] Byles, *Bills of Exchange*, 25th edn., London, 1983; Chalmers, *Bills of Exchange*, 13th edn.; *Chitty on Contracts*, 25th edn., vol. 2, ch. 3.

The Bills of Exchange Act 1882, which is the cardinal statute in point, defines a bill as an unconditional order in writing, addressed by one person to another, signed by the person giving it, requiring the person to whom it is addressed to pay on demand or at a fixed or determinable future time, a sum certain in money to or to the order of a specified person, or to bearer.[7] Thus, a bill has to be drawn by one person on another; an instrument drawn by a person on himself is not a bill.[8] By way of contrast, the bill may be made payable to the drawer's own order.[9]

The order given by the drawer to the drawee has to be unconditional. This point has been discussed in respect of cheques.[10] Of importance is the fact that an order requiring the drawee to pay the bill out of a specific fund is deemed conditional.[11] However, an order which is in itself unqualified is not rendered conditional because it is coupled with an indication of a particular fund out of which the drawee is to reimburse himself (or an account to be debited) or a statement of the transaction which gives rise to the bill.[12] Consequently, a bill remains unconditional although it includes a statement that it is drawn under a given contract of sale or letter of credit.[13]

A bill may be payable in one of three ways: on demand (which means on its presentment to the drawee); at a fixed future time, such as 4 August 1986; or at a determinable future time, such as ninety days after 'sight' (meaning, after the date of its presentment to the payee for acceptance). The determinable date on which it is to fall due has to be definite. The better view is that an instrument payable *before* or *not later than* a given day is not a bill.[14] Furthermore, the 'determinable' future time must be related to an event which is certain to happen though the time of its occurrence may be uncertain.[15] It has been held that a bill payable at a given time after the arrival of a specified ship in a named port is valid;[16] though it is arguable, of course, that the arrival of a ship at a port is subject to its remaining in

---

[7] BEA, s. 3(1).

[8] But note that under BEA, s. 5, the holder may treat such an instrument either as a bill or as a note. Under s. 6(2), a bill may be addressed jointly to a number of drawees; but it may not be addressed to them in the alternative or in succession.

[9] Under s. 7(2), it may be payable to joint payees or in the alternative to two payees or more. As regards the vexed question of the fictitious payee, see, pp. 244–6 above.

[10] Pp. 240–2 above.

[11] BEA, s. 3(2).

[12] Ibid., s. 3(3).

[13] *Guaranty Trust Co. of New York* v. *Hannay & Co.* [1918] 2 KB 623, 656. And see generally, as regards the problems of a claused bill, *Benjamin's Sale of Goods*, 2nd edn., para. 2023.

[14] *Williamson* v. *Rider* [1963] 1 QB 89; *Salot* v. *Naidoo* [1981] 3 SA 959. Contrast *John Burrows Ltd.* v. *Subsurface Surveys Ltd.* [1968] SCR 607 (Canada); *Creative Press Ltd.* v. *Harman* [1973] IR 313. Cf. *Korea Exchange Bank* v. *Debenhams (Central Buying) Ltd.* [1979] 1 Lloyd's Rep. 100, noted by Hudson, [1981] JBL 101.

[15] BEA, s. 11(2).

[16] *Palmer* v. *Pratt* (1824) 2 Bing. 185; and see *Chitty on Contracts*, 25th edn., para. 2462.

operation. The Act gives a clue to what is meant by a 'certainty', as it provides that an instrument expressed to be payable on a contingency is not a bill.[17] Presumably, the distinction is between an event which is on its face contingent and one which is usually treated as a certainty.

Finally, the bill must be for a sum certain in money. A sum is certain although it is payable with interest,[18] by stated instalments (even if coupled by a provision that the total balance falls due upon default in one of them) or at a specified rate of exchange.[19] However, the nature of the obligation has to be set out clearly. Thus, a statement that a bill is payable with 'lawful interest'[20] or at the rate applied to advances made to 'most credit worthy customers'[21] introduces uncertainty and invalidates the instrument. But a bill payable at a rate which is determinable by reference to everyday practice, such as 'with interest at 4 per cent above base rate at date of discharge', ought to be valid as the rate in question is readily ascertainable. A bill for a given amount plus 'bank charges' has been held to be for an uncertain amount.[22]

Whilst the Act prescribes the requisites of a bill, it does not purport to define the main characteristics that distinguish a bill from a simple contract. These may be summarized as follows. First, an action on a simple contract may be brought either by the initial parties to it or, in certain cases, by assignees.[23] An action on a bill can be instituted by any 'holder'. Under section 2 of the Act, 'holder' means the payee or indorsee of the instrument who is in possession of it or the bearer.[24] There is thus a fundamental difference in the concept of privity. In a simple contract, a party is a person who enters into the contract initially or an assignee. In the case of a bill, any holder becomes a party. Secondly, although most contracts may be assigned, an assignor has to follow a certain procedure, and, in particular, notice must be given to the debtor.[25] By way of contrast, a bill may be transferred by the payee or by any subsequent holder to a third party. If the bill is

---

[17] S. 11, proviso.

[18] But not if the interest is to commence running from a date which is not certain on the face of the instrument, such as the date of the making of an advance: *Macleod Savings and Credit Union Ltd.* v. *Perrett* [1978] 6 WWR 178.

[19] The rate, though, must clearly relate to the obligation to pay: *Tropic Plastic and Packaging Industry* v. *Standard Bank of South Africa Ltd.* [1969] 4 SA 108.

[20] *Smith* v. *Nightingale* (1818) 2 Stark. 375; *Bolton* v. *Dugdale* (1833) 4 B & Ad. 619. That the statement need be certain, see *Temple Terrace Assets Co. Inc.* v. *Whynot* [1934] 1 DLR 124. Cf. *Rosenhain* v. *Commonwealth Bank of Australia* (1922) 31 CLR 46, where a bill payable with 8% p.a. 'until arrival of payment in London for cover' was held uncertain. As interest would have continued to run until the very arrival of the cover, the decision is questionable.

[21] *Bank of Montreal* v. *Dezcam Industries Ltd.* (1983) 5 WWR 83 (Can.).

[22] *Dalgety Ltd.* v. *John J. Hilton Pty. Ltd.* [1981] 2 NSWLR 169 (Aust.).

[23] Except where there is an equitable assignment of a legal chose in action. See, generally, *Chitty on Contracts*, 25th edn., vol. 1, paras. 1273, 1280–90.

[24] P. 504 below.

[25] *Chitty on Contracts*, 25th edn., paras. 1272–3, 1278, 1289–90.

payable to order, it is transferable by indorsement (which means, the holder's signature on its back) and delivery; if it is a bearer bill, it is transferable by delivery alone.[26] No notice of the transfer need be given. Thirdly, when a simple contract is assigned, the assignee's rights are usually subject to the equities between the debtor and the assignor.[27] In the case of a bill, a transferee obtains the right to enforce payment of the instrument, despite any defects in the title of or equities available to the parties sued, provided the transferee is a 'holder in due course'. A 'holder in due course' is a person who takes an instrument which is (a) complete and regular on its face, (b) for value (i.e. consideration), and (c) in good faith.[28] Thus, the rule *nemo dat quod non habet* applies to a bill of exchange subject to considerable modifications.

There is a further fundamental distinction between simple contracts and negotiable instruments. The formation of a contract confers upon the parties thereto certain rights. These rights are not dependent upon the physical possession of the instrument in which the terms of the contract are recorded. They arise from the creation of the contract itself and are enforceable by action. Bills of exchange, likewise, confer rights on the payee and the transferees, namely, the procedural right to sue on the instrument and, in certain cases, the right to enforce payment. To this extent, bills of exchange resemble contracts.[29] But the possession of a bill of exchange is also of considerable importance. Usually a person who acquires the possession of a bill becomes its holder and thereupon obtains the right to enforce it. Moreover, a person can have a title to a negotiable instrument.[30] The concept of ownership is, thus, applicable. Bills of exchange may, therefore, be regarded as a special type of personal property. They differ from most types of chattel in that their possession confers on the holder certain contractual rights. But they differ from contracts by reason of the existence of proprietary terms. The same analysis applies to all other types of negotiable instruments, such as promissory notes and cheques.[31]

The definition set out in section 3 of the 1882 Act throws no light on the mercantile function of bills of exchange. Originally, they were used to effect transfers of money and to assist travellers to raise funds without their having to

[26] P. 512 below.
[27] *Chitty on Contracts*, 25th edn., para. 1308.
[28] Pp. 505–7 below.
[29] Cf. *R. v. Duru* [1974] 1 WLR 2, 8; *Pollway Ltd. v. Abdullah* [1974] 1 WLR 493, 496. Bills thus constitute book debts which may be the subject of a charge registrable under s. 395 of the Companies Act 1985; *Siebe Gorman & Co. Ltd. v. Barclays Bank Ltd.* [1979] 2 Lloyd's Rep. 142.
[30] See, e.g., BEA, s. 80, which refers to the 'true owner' of a cheque. Note that a cheque is a variety of a bill.
[31] See *R. v. Kohn* [1979] Crim. LR 675.

carry cash with them. This last function is currently performed by travellers' cheques and by cheques backed by credit cards, whilst the transfer of funds is predominantly effected by electronic means.[32] Bankers' drafts remain the only negotiable instrument which is currently utilized to effect the transfer of money overseas.[33]

In modern trade, bills of exchange serve two functions. The first—which is that of bills drawn under acceptance credits—is to raise credit for the drawer's business operations. The projects backed by such a facility vary a great deal in their nature. They encompass major international projects, such as the financing of an oil rig, as well as the financing of considerably smaller operations, and also purely domestic transactions.[34] A related type of transaction is one in which a company or other enterprise allows another to draw on it in order to facilitate the discount of the bills involved. In such a case, the drawee 'accommodates' the drawer. Unlike a bank, which accepts bills in pursuance of its acceptance credit, an accommodation party does not stand to make a direct profit from his acceptance of the bills. Bills drawn for accommodation are governed by some specific provisions of the Act. As it is not altogether certain that bills drawn under acceptance credits are outside the scope of these provisions, it will be necessary to discuss these in some detail.[35]

The second major function of bills of exchange is in the field of international transactions. Where goods are sold and transported by sea, land, air, or by means of combined transport, the seller frequently draws a bill for the price on the buyer. The bill can be discounted by the seller's own bank, or through it on the bills market. The seller thus obtains the required funds before the delivery of the goods at their destination. The importance of the bill—the subject of the discount—is even greater where the seller grants the buyer trade credit for a period such as ninety, or 180 days. The bill, drawn at the relevant 'usance' (viz. so as to fall due at the end of the period of credit) is in practice the subject of immediate discount. Bills are used for these purposes in the context of f.o.b., c.i.f, and similar contracts.

The provisions of the Bills of Exchange Act 1882 do not demarcate between bills drawn under acceptance credits and bills drawn in respect of international sales. As the latter type of bill is an instrument of international trade, it is proposed to concentrate in illustrations on bill of the former type.

---

[32] See above, pp. 262–3 (travellers' cheques); Ch. 12 (money transfers), and Ch. 13 (credit and cheque cards).

[33] Pp. 358–9 above.

[34] But not in respect of consumer transactions covered by the Consumer Credit Act 1974; pp. 527–8 below.

[35] Pp. 522–6 below.

(ii) The parties to a bill

There are at least two parties to every bill: the drawer and the drawee. The payee may be either a third party or the drawer himself. When a bill is nego-tiated, which means that it is transferred by the payee or by a subsequent 'holder', the transferor frequently adds currency to the bill by adding his sig-nature on the back. He thereupon becomes an 'indorser', whose position is similar to the drawer's.

The drawer of the bill performs a dual function. In the first place, he instructs the drawee to honour the bill. Secondly, he undertakes that, on due presentment of the bill to the drawee, it will be duly 'accepted' (where acceptance is needed) and paid.[36] The drawer thus warrants that the bill will be honoured by the drawee. His undertaking is similar to that of a surety, who guarantees the payment of a loan extended to the debtor.[37] This explains the principle under which the drawer's liability is discharged if the payee or holder does not follow the procedures prescribed where a bill is dishonoured.

The drawee of the bill, who is the person charged with payment, does not incur liability on the bill by reason only of its being drawn on him. Under section 53 of the Act, a bill, 'of itself, does not operate as an assignment of funds in the hands of the drawee available for the payment thereof, and the drawee of a bill who does not accept [it] as required by [the] Act is not liable on the instrument'.[38] The drawee's refusal to accept the bill may, however, involve a breach of his contract with the drawer. Thus, a bank which dis-honours by non-acceptance a bill drawn in conformity with the provisions of an acceptance credit issued by it commits a breach of its contract with the drawer.

The drawee incurs liability on the bill if he accepts it. 'Acceptance' is defined as the 'signification by the drawee of his assent to the order of the drawer'.[39] To be valid, the acceptance has to be written on the bill and be signed by the drawee. His mere signature is adequate,[40] although the com-mon practice is to add the word 'accepted' and the date of its execution. A bill may be accepted before it has been signed by the drawer or whilst it is

[36] BEA, s. 55(1)(a).
[37] Thus, the drawer as well as an indorser are entitled to the equities of a surety if they have to pay the bill: *Duncan, Fox & Co.* v. *North and South Wales Bank* (1880) 6 App. Cas. 1, 19–20; see also *Rouquette* v. *Overmann* (1875) LR 10 QB 525, 537; *Scholefield Goodman & Co. Ltd.* v. *Zyngier* [1985] 3 All ER 105, noted in [1986] JBL 399.
[38] BEA, s. 53(1).
[39] Ibid., s. 17(1). Note that a simple assent constitutes a general acceptance; the Act recog-nizes the existence of a qualified acceptance, such as a conditional or partial one: s. 19. The holder is entitled to refuse to take any qualified acceptance and, if he chooses to take it, the drawer and indorsers are usually discharged: s. 44.
[40] BEA, s. 17(2)(a).

otherwise incomplete.[41] This principle is of importance in respect of acceptance credits, as in some cases the bills are accepted by the issuing bank before their execution by the drawer.[42] A bill may also be accepted when it is overdue, or after an initial dishonour of it by the drawee.[43]

When the drawee accepts a bill, he becomes its acceptor and engages that he will pay it according to the tenor of his acceptance.[44] He becomes liable as primary obligor or debtor. Defences available to him against the drawer cannot usually be raised against subsequent parties.[45] A person other than the drawee of the instrument cannot accept it. If he purports to do so, he probably incurs the liability of an indorser.[46]

In practice, not all bills are presented to the drawee separately for acceptance and for payment. Thus, a bill payable on demand is ordinarily presented simultaneously for acceptance and for payment or simply for payment. Similarly, if a bill is payable at a fixed date, or at a given time after its date of issue, presentment for acceptance is not necessary to determine the tenor of the instrument.[47] The drawer or holder may, however, wish to present the bill for acceptance in order to charge the acceptor and, thus, to increase the currency of the instrument. Presentment for acceptance is required, and constitutes a duty imposed by the Act on the holder, where a bill is payable at a fixed time after sight. It is clear that, unless such a bill is presented for acceptance, its date of maturity remains undetermined.[48] Further, a bill has to be presented for acceptance if this requirement is spelt out in it or if it is drawn as payable at a place other than the drawee's place of business.[49]

As bills of exchange are meant to be discounted, they do not usually remain in the hands of the ostensible payee until their date of maturity. When the payee transfers or 'negotiates' a bill,[50] he is generally asked to indorse it. He thereupon engages that the bill will be duly accepted and paid, and that 'if it be dishonoured he will compensate the holder or a subsequent indorser who is compelled to pay it'.[51] The liability of an indorser is, therefore, incurred towards every party who acquires the bill after him and who is compelled to pay it. The indorser is precluded from denying to any such party (a 'subsequent indorsee') that the bill was, at the time of his

[41] Ibid., s. 18(1).
[42] This can be the case where the issuing bank furnishes instruments of given amounts to be completed by the drawer.
[43] BEA, s. 18(2).
[44] Ibid., s. 54(1).
[45] Pp. 506–8 below.
[46] BEA, s. 56, discussed below, p. 502.
[47] BEA, s. 39(3).
[48] Ibid., s. 39(1).
[49] Ibid., s. 39(2).
[50] As to how a bill is negotiated, see below, pp. 511 et seq.
[51] BEA, s. 55(2).

indorsement, a valid and subsisting instrument and that he had then a good title to it.[52]

In the majority of cases, the indorsement serves two purposes. First, it is executed to transfer the bill.[53] Secondly, it gives extra currency to the bill, as it binds the indorser to pay it if it is dishonoured by the drawee. The indorser's liability is, thus, similar to the drawer's. He, too, is in the position of a surety.

In some cases a party may be asked to indorse a bill even if he is neither the ostensible payee nor a subsequent transferee. Occasionally, the indorser's signature appears on the back of the bill above that of the ostensible payee. If the placing of the indorsement in what would appear to be the wrong position is due to inadvertence, the order of the signatures is to be ignored.[54] Moreover, the fact that the indorsement is placed on the bill before its execution by the drawer is irrelevant as, under section 20, the drawer is entitled to complete such a bill by using the signature on the back as that of an indorser.[55]

However, in no case of this type can it be assumed as a matter of course that the indorser is liable on the bill to the drawer.[56] To treat the indorser as undertaking such liability, it is necessary to investigate the facts of the case and the intention of the parties.[57] Thus, the indorser will be liable to the drawer if it is established that he has intended to be so bound when he signed the instrument.[58] His liability is based on the bill and not on an ancillary surety contract which arguably could require a separate written memorandum.[59]

An indorsement is to be regarded as a sui generis type of signature. Under section 56, where 'a person signs a bill otherwise than as drawer or acceptor, he thereby incurs the liabilities of an indorser to a holder in due course'.[60] In the majority of cases, a party's intention to act as indorser is manifested by the placing of his signature on the back of the bill. But a sig-

---

[52] Ibid., s. 52(2)(c).

[53] It is not required for this purpose where the bill is payable to bearer (p. 512 below); but most bills currently issued in the United Kingdom are payable to the order of a designated payee, whose indorsement is, accordingly, required.

[54] *National Sales Corporation Ltd.* v. *Bernardi* [1931] 2 KB 188; *Lombard Banking Ltd.* v. *Central Garage & Engineering Co. Ltd.* [1963] 1 QB 220.

[55] *McDonald (Gerald) & Co.* v. *Nash & Co.* [1924] AC 625; *National Sales Corporation Ltd.* v. *Bernardi*, above; *Yeoman Credit Ltd.* v. *Gregory* [1963] 1 WLR 343.

[56] *Steele* v. *M'Kinlay* (1880) 5 App. Cas. 754; *Jenkins & Sons* v. *Coomber* [1898] 2 QB 168 (doubted on some points in *McDonald (Gerald) & Co.* v. *Nash & Co.*, above; cf. *Mander* v. *Evans & Rose* (1888) 5 TLR 75.

[57] *Glenie* v. *Smith* [1908] 1 KB 263; *Re Gooch* [1921] 2 KB 593; *National Sales Corporation Ltd.* v. *Bernardi* [1931] 2 KB 188.

[58] *McCall Bros. Ltd.* v. *Hargreaves* [1932] 2 KB 423.

[59] Under the Statute of Frauds: *Steele* v. *M'Kinlay*, above; *Jenkins & Sons* v. *Coomber*, above.

[60] As to the meaning of a 'holder in due course', see pp. 505–6 below.

nature placed by a person other than the drawee on the front of the instrument is also treated as an indorsement.[61] It cannot be treated as an acceptance of the bill, as a stranger cannot assent to an order which is specifically directed to the drawee.

English law does not recognize an 'aval' or guarantee written on the bill itself. In this regard it differs from the Uniform Law of the Geneva Convention, which applies in most European countries,[62] and from the Uniform Commercial Code of the United States.[63] An 'aval' binds the guarantor as joint obligator with the drawee; he is liable for the payment of the bill to all parties to it, regardless of whether they become parties to it before or after the execution of his undertaking. In English law an 'aval' is treated as an indorsement, and the party executing it assumes liability to subsequent parties only and on the same footing as the drawer.[64]

The drawer, the acceptor and the indorsers are the parties against whom the bill is enforceable. Primarily, they incur liability to the 'holder'. It will be recalled that, under section 2, the holder is the payee, the indorsee or the bearer of an instrument who has possession thereof. Ordinarily, the holder seeks to enforce the bill against prior parties. But there is authority for the view that, if an instrument is acquired back by the drawer from a subsequent transferee or holder, the drawer obtains that party's rights against all intermediary parties.[65] On another view, the drawer reverts to his original position because, on the face of the bill, he has initially warranted the payment of the instrument and this undertaking accrues in favour of all subsequent parties.[66]

Payment of the bill is to be arranged by the acceptor. Where this role is assumed by a bank—as is the case in bills drawn under an acceptance credit—the instrument is made payable at the premises of that very bank or a designated branch of it. Where a bill is drawn on a body other than a bank—as is the case where a bill is drawn by a seller on a buyer under a contract c.i.f.—the drawee normally accepts the bill as payable at his own bank. Such an acceptance is considered a general one,[67] although the holder is then obliged to present it at the designated 'domicile'.[68] The bank at whose

---

[61] *Young* v. *Glover* (1857) 3 Jur. (NS) 637; *Ex p. Yates* (1857) 2 De G & J 191.

[62] The Uniform Law on Bills of Exchange and Promissory Notes, promulgated by the Geneva Convention of 7 June 1930, League of Nations Treaty Series, vol. 143, p. 259, No. 3313. The relevant provisions are arts. 30–32.

[63] S. 3-416.

[64] *Jackson* v. *Hudson* (1810) 2 Camp. 447, 448; *Steele* v. *M'Kinlay* (1880) 5 App. Cas. 754, 772.

[65] *Jade International Steel Stahl und Eisen GmbH & Co. KG.* v. *Robert Nicholas (Steels) Ltd.* [1978] QB 917.

[66] BEA, s. 37, on its plain construction, lends support to this view.

[67] Ibid., s. 19(2)(c). The acceptance is 'local' and hence 'qualified' if the bill is made payable solely at the particular place specified.

[68] BEA, s. 45(4)(a).

premises the bill is domiciled does not become a party to the instrument. In effect, its position is similar to that of a bank on which a customer draws a cheque. When the acceptor designates the bank as the domicile of the bill, he instructs it to effect payment.[69] The bank's duty to obey this order is owed to the customer alone.

(iii) Position of the holder

It has been pointed out that 'holder' means the payee or indorsee of the bill, who has possession thereof, or the bearer.[70] An indorsee is a person who has acquired the bill under an indorsement. As a forged indorsement is a nullity, a person who claims to hold a bill thereunder is not a holder.[71] The problem does not arise in the case of a bearer, as his rights are incurred by mere delivery and are not based on the indorsement to him of the bill.[72]

The rights of the holder depend on whether he is a 'mere holder', a 'holder for value', or a 'holder in due course'. In certain cases, it is also relevant whether a dispute is between 'immediate parties' or 'remote parties'. Immediate parties are those who, in addition to the privity created by the bill, have a direct legal relationship with each other. The drawer and the acceptor, the drawer and the initial payee, and an indorser and his indorsee are usually parties who have entered into a contract with one another, such as an agreement to extend credit, a sale of goods, or an arrangement for the discount of a bill of exchange; they are therefore predominantly immediate parties. But in some cases even these may be remote parties. Thus, the drawer may make a bill payable to the order of the payee at a third party's request. Similarly, the drawee of a bill may agree to accept it on the basis of his contract with a stranger to the bill.

Some writers maintain that, generally, the defences which can be pleaded against a remote party are more restricted than those available against an immediate party.[73] It will be shown, however, that the distinction between remote and immediate parties is relevant mainly in respect of actions brought on a bill by a holder for value. The superior rights of a holder in due course are defined in section 38 of the Act, which does not draw a distinc-

---

[69] *Bank of England* v. *Vagliano Bros.* [1891] AC 107.
[70] BEA, s. 2. As regards the meaning of 'bearer', see p. 511 below.
[71] *Lacave & Co.* v. *Crédit Lyonnais* [1897] 1 QB 148.
[72] P. 513 below.
[73] Chalmers, *Bills of Exchange*, 13th edn., pp. 101 et seq.; Byles, *Bills of Exchange*, 25th edn., pp. 214–16; Falconbridge, *Banking and Bills of Exchange*, 7th edn., pp. 665 et seq.; Cowen, *Law of Negotiable Instruments in South Africa*, 4th edn., pp. 226 et seq. The distinction is not fully worked out in decided cases, but see *Watson* v. *Russell* (1864) 5 B & S 968; 34 LJQB 93 (suggesting that the drawer and the drawee of a bill are not always immediate parties).

tion between remote and immediate parties.[74] At the other end of the scale, a mere holder who does not furnish value appears to hold the bill subject to virtually all equities available against prior parties, including immediate ones.[75]

The most clearly defined rights are those conferred on a 'holder in due course'. This phrase needs to be clarified. Under section 29, four requirements must be fulfilled before a person is considered a holder in due course. First, he must take the bill when it is complete and regular on its face. Basically, this means that the bill must not include on its front or back any detail that is out of the ordinary. Examples are where there is a discrepancy between the words and the figures denoting the amount,[76] or where the name by which the bill appears to be indorsed by the payee differs materially from the name inserted by the drawer in the front of the bill. Thus, an indorsement by 'John Williams' of a bill drawn payable to 'J. Williams' is regular; but an indorsement in such a case by the payee as 'Walter Williams' would be irregular.[77] So is the indorsement of a firm described by the drawer as a company if the word 'Ltd.' or 'plc' is missing.[78]

The second requirement laid down by section 29 is that a person is a holder in due course only if he has taken the bill before it is overdue[79] and without notice of any act of dishonour that might have taken place. The third requirement is that the holder has to take the bill in good faith and without having any notice of a defect in the transferor's title.[80] Under section 90, a thing is deemed to be done in good faith where it is in fact done honestly and regardless of negligence. It has been held that the holder does not act in good faith where he takes a bill despite his suspicion that something is wrong, although he may not have notice of the exact nature of the defect.[81] A recent authority suggests that the defect of which the holder has notice vitiates his rights only where it is in the nature of a common law type

[74] Note that only a transferee can be a holder in due course (p. 506 below) and that only his transferor can be regarded an immediate party. From a practical point of view, the circumstances under which a transferee has to take a bill in order to attain the status of a holder in due course are such as to rule out the need to distinguish in his case between an action against an immediate and a remote party.
[75] Cf. Chalmers, *Bills of Exchange*, 13th edn., p. 101, suggesting that privity is in all cases created by want of consideration.
[76] For an extreme case, see *Banco di Roma SpA* v. *Orru* [1973] 2 Lloyd's Rep. 505.
[77] *Arab Bank Ltd.* v. *Ross* [1952] 2 QB 216, although, if genuine, the indorsement is effective to transfer title.
[78] Ibid.
[79] A bill payable on demand is deemed overdue where it has been in circulation for an unreasonable time: BEA, s. 36(3).
[80] A list of events deemed to constitute 'defects of title' is set out in s. 29(2); it includes duress, fraud, and illegal means utilized by the transferor to obtain the acceptance of the bill.
[81] *Jones* v. *Gordon* (1877) 2 App. Cas. 616, 628; *Baker* v. *Barclays Bank Ltd.* [1955] 1 WLR 822; *Bank of Cyprus (London) Ltd.* v. *Jones* (1984) 134 NLJ 522. And note that under s. 30(2) a party is presumed to be a holder in due course and thus to have acted in good faith; but the burden of proof is shifted where there has been fraud or illegality in the transaction.

of fraud.[82] Canadian authorities have taken a broader view. They suggest that a firm, such as a finance company, cannot claim to be the holder in due course of bills transferred to it by another firm, such as that of a car dealer, with which the first firm has a very close business relationship.[83] However, it is difficult to agree that if the first firm does not have notice, within the meaning of section 29, of any irregularity or suspicious circumstances concerning the transaction financed by means of the bill, it loses its status as a holder in due course by reason only of its general business relationship with the second firm.

The last requirement set out in section 29 is that, to be a holder in due course, a party has to take the bill for 'value', which means for a 'consideration'.[84] Apart from the stipulated four requirements, it is clear from the language of section 29 that a holder in due course is only one who has 'taken the bill'. It has been held that these words refer to a holder to whom the bill has been negotiated, and that the original payee of a bill cannot, therefore, be a holder in due course.[85]

Under section 38(2), a holder in due course holds the bill free from any defects in the title of previous parties as well as from any equities available to prior parties among themselves, and may enforce payment against all parties liable on the bill. In effect, this means that such a holder can enforce payment notwithstanding defences available to prior parties among themselves, and despite defects in the title of any prior party.[86] In this way, section 38(2) enables bankers and other financial institutions to discount bills of exchange without getting embroiled in disputes concerning the underlying business contracts. Thus, where the discounter is a holder in due course, he can enforce the bill of exchange against a drawee who has accepted it in the mistaken belief that a forged bill of lading, attached to it, was genuine.[87] The position of a holder in due course is further safeguarded by the

---

[82] *Österreichische Länderbank* v. *S'Elite Ltd.* [1980] 2 All ER 651 overruling *Banca Popolare di Novara* v. *John Livanos & Sons Ltd.* [1965] 2 Lloyd's Rep. 149. Note that a transferee's knowledge that an indorsement has been effected for a restrictive purpose precludes him from being a holder in due course: *Williams & Glyn's Bank Ltd.* v. *Belckin Packaging Ltd.* (1981) 123 DLR (3rd) 612.

[83] *Rand Investments Ltd.* v. *Bertrand* (1966) 58 DLR (2d) 372; *Keelan* v. *Norray Distributing Ltd.* (1967) 62 DLR (2d) 466. See also *Stenning* v. *Radio and Domestic Finance Ltd.* [1961] NZLR 7. Contrast *Automobile Finance of Australia Ltd.* v. *Henderson* (1928) 23 Tas. LR 9; *Scottish Loan and Finance Co. Ltd.* v. *Payne* (1935) 52 WN (NSW) 175.

[84] As to what is adequate value, see below, p. 508. Note that a holder may be constituted a holder in due course by reason of his having a lien over the instrument: *Barclays Bank Ltd.* v. *Astley Industrial Trust Ltd.* [1970] 2 QB 527, 539. Under s. 30(1), a party is presumed to have acquired a bill for value. But note the displacement of the presumption in the cases set out in s. 30(2): see note 81 to this chapter.

[85] *R. E. Jones Ltd.* v. *Waring & Gillow Ltd.* [1926] AC 670. See also *Williams* v. *Williams* 1980 SLT (Sh. Ct.) 25.

[86] See further, *Chitty on Contracts*, 25th edn., vol. 2, para. 2502.

[87] *Guaranty Trust Co. of New York* v. *Hannay & Co.* [1918] 2 KB 623, 652.

following sections of the Act: 12, 20(2) (inchoate instruments); 21(2) (conclusive presumption of the delivery of the bill); 54 (2), 55(2) (precluding the acceptor, the drawer, and the indorsers from raising certain defences invalidating the bill); and 64(2) (precluding the assertion of alterations to the bill in certain cases). To defeat an action by a holder in due course it is necessary to establish a defect in his title, in which case he is not really a holder in due course.[88]

The rights of a holder in due course accrue also to any holder (whether for value or not) who derives his title from a holder in due course.[89] Naturally, these rights cannot be pleaded by a transferee who is a party to any fraud affecting the bill. But mere knowledge of fraud or illegality does not deprive such a transferee of his rights.[90] It has been held that, if the bill returns to the hands of the drawer who takes it for value, he may assume the status of a holder in due course.[91] But this proposition is questionable.

The rights of a mere holder, who is a holder other than a holder in due course or a holder for value, contrast sharply with those of a holder in due course. Under section 38(1), a mere holder has the right to bring an action on the bill in his own name. Such an action is usually brought in summary procedure;[92] judgment is entered for the plaintiff unless the defendant is granted leave to defend by the court.[93] The Act does not indicate what type of defences have to be alleged in order to induce the court to make such an order.[94] A comparison of the language of this subsection with section 38(2) suggests that, as against a mere holder, a defendant is entitled to raise defences stemming from a defect in the title of prior parties and at least some personal defences available to them. Old authorities, which remain good law due to the absence of express provision in point, support this view. Thus, the absence of consideration[95] and the total failure of consideration[96] are valid defences against a mere holder. Partial failure of consideration is a

---

[88] This can, for example, be done by showing that he holds the bill under a forged indorsement. He is then not a holder, let alone a holder in due course: p. 504 above.

[89] BEA, s. 29(3).

[90] *May* v. *Chapman* (1834) 16 M & W 355.

[91] *Jade International Steel Stahl und Eisen GmbH & Co. KG.* v. *Robert Nicholas (Steels) Ltd.* [1978] QB 917; see further pp. 516–7 below.

[92] Under RSC, ord. 14, r. 1.

[93] See, generally, *The Supreme Court Practice*, para. 14/3-4/15.

[94] *James Lamont & Co. Ltd.* v. *Hyland Ltd.* [1950] 1 KB 585; *Brown, Shipley & Co. Ltd.* v. *Alicia Hosiery Ltd.* [1966] 1 Lloyd's Rep. 668; *Barclays Bank Ltd.* v. *Aschaffenburger Zellstoffwerke AG* [1967] 1 Lloyd's Rep. 387; *All Trades Distributors Ltd.* v. *Agencies Kaufman Ltd.* (1969) 113 SJ 995; *Saga of Bond Street Ltd.* v. *Avalon Promotions Ltd.* [1972] 2 QB 325; *Cebora SNC* v. *SIP (Industrial Products) Ltd.* [1976] 1 Lloyd's Rep. 271. As regards the general rule as to when leave would be granted, see *S. L. Sethia Liners Ltd.* v. *State Trading Corporation of India Ltd.* [1985] 1 WLR 1398; *Forestal Mimosa Ltd.* v. *Oriental Credit Ltd.* [1986] 1 WLR 631. Basically, the defendant has to establish that he has a prima-facie defence, which—if proved—is arguably good in law.

[95] *Forman* v. *Wright* (1851) 11 CB 481, 492–4; cf. *Milnes* v. *Dawson* (1850) 5 Exch. 948, 950–1.

[96] See note 110 to this chapter.

valid defence where a liquidated amount is involved;[97] but it cannot be raised where the amount involved is unascertained or unliquidated.[98] Thus, a claim for damages due under an underlying contract c.i.f. cannot form the basis of a defence to an action on a bill drawn for the price. Neither can the claim involved be raised by way of a set-off or a counterclaim.[99]

The position of a holder for value who is not a holder in due course is not expressly defined in the Act. Conceptually, such a holder is one who cannot, for some technical reason, be considered a holder in due course. By way of illustration, take a transferee who takes a bill which is irregularly indorsed. Similarly, the ostensible payee of the bill, who cannot be a holder in due course, may nevertheless be a holder for value.

Value or consideration for a bill is defined in section 27(1). It encompasses any consideration sufficient to support a simple contract, and also an antecedent debt or liability. Past consideration is, thus, good consideration for a bill. Accordingly, if a customer negotiates to his bank a cheque payable to his order, so as to reduce an existing overdraft, the bank becomes a holder for value of the instrument. The pre-existing debt or overdraft is sufficient consideration for the transfer of the cheque to the bank.[100] But although section 27(1) abrogates the rule against past consideration, it does not modify the principle that consideration has to move from the promisee. The better view is that an antecedent debt or liability of a third party does not constitute value for the negotiation of a bill of exchange.[101] The only modification of the principle in question is to be found in section 27(2), which provides that if value has at any time been given for the bill, the holder is deemed to be a holder for value as regards the acceptor and all persons who have become parties to the bill prior to such time.[102] However, the holder who eventually furnishes consideration may be regarded as a promisee of all prior parties. He is within their contemplation when they assume liability on the bill.

The principle that past consideration is adequate value for a bill of

<hr/>

[97] *Forman* v. *Wright*, above; *Agra and Masterman's Bank Ltd.* v. *Leighton* (1866) LR 2 Ex. 56, 64, 65; *Thoni GmbH & Co. KG* v. *RTP Equipment Ltd.* [1979] 2 Lloyd's Rep. 282.
[98] *Sully* v. *Frean* (1854) 10 Exch. 535; *Warwick* v. *Nairn* (1855) 10 Exch. 762.
[99] *Nova (Jersey) Knit Ltd.* v. *Kammgarn Spinnerei GmbH* [1977] 1 WLR 713. For some exceptions, see *Chitty on Contracts*, 25th edn., vol. 2, para. 2503.
[100] *M'Lean* v. *Clydesdale Banking Co.* (1883) 9 App. Cas. 95. See also *Ex p. Richdale* (1882) 19 Ch. D 409; *Royal Bank of Scotland* v. *Tottenham* [1894] 2 QB 715; *Barclays Bank Ltd.* v. *Astley Industrial Trust Ltd.* [1970] 2 QB 527, 539. As regards a consideration which fails in toto, see *Miller Associates (Australia) Pty. Ltd.* v. *Bennington Pty. Ltd.* (1975) 7 ALR 144, noted in (1981) 55 ALJ 135. As regards the effect of the furnishing of an illegal consideration, see *Ladup* v. *Shaik* [1983] QB 225.
[101] *Crears* v. *Hunter* (1887) 19 QBD 341; *Pollway Ltd.* v. *Abdullah* [1974] 1 WLR 493, 497; *Hasan* v. *Willson* [1977] 1 Lloyd's Rep. 431. Cf. *Oliver* v. *Davis* [1949] 2 KB 727. For a detailed discussion see *Chitty on Contracts*, 25th edn., vol. 2, paras. 2485–6.
[102] For illustrations, see *Scott* v. *Lifford* (1808) 1 Camp. 246; *Diamond* v. *Graham* [1968] 1 WLR 1061, 1064.

exchange is closely related to an additional rule. Where the holder of a bill has a lien on it arising either from contract or by implication of law, he is deemed to be a holder for value to the extent of the sum for which he has the lien.[103] In the majority of the cases, such a lien is based on a contract or implied at law in respect of a debt incurred before the issuing of the bill of exchange in question.

The Act does not define the rights of a holder for value. For most practical purposes, he is in the same position as a mere holder.[104] Thus, his rights are defeated if the bill was obtained by means of fraud or duress, or if there were any other defects of the type specified in section 29(2). This proposition is based on the language of the Act. Section 38(2) renders the rights of a holder in due course effective, notwithstanding the defects in question; but the Act fails to confer similar rights on a person who, though not a holder in due course, is a holder for value. The latter's rights are, therefore, principally governed by section 38(1), which is applicable to those who are not holders in due course.

At the same time, some defences cannot be raised against a holder for value because he has furnished consideration for the bill. Thus, the absence of consideration between prior parties does not constitute a valid defence against him.[105] In respect of partial failure of consideration, it is necessary to recall the distinction between immediate parties and remote parties. An immediate party is entitled to plead partial failure of consideration as a defence to an action by a holder for value, provided the 'partial failure' involves an ascertained and liquidated amount. For instance, if a seller supplies only one half of the goods, he cannot recover more than one half of the amount of the bill drawn for the price and accepted by the buyer.[106] The same applies if the drawer's breach entitles the acceptor to a quantified or liquidated amount by way of compensation or damages.[107] But if goods turn out to be of an inferior quality, whereupon the buyer becomes entitled to recover an amount of damages to be determined by the court, this claim cannot be raised as a defence to the seller's action on the bill.[108]

Partial failure of consideration does not appear to afford a defence against a remote party who is a holder for value, even if the deficiency or loss is liquidated.[109] One authority suggests that total failure of

---

[103] BEA, s. 27(3).
[104] *Whistler* v. *Forster* (1863) 14 CB (NS) 248, 258.
[105] This follows from s. 27(2). And see *Mills* v. *Barber* (1836) 1 M & W 425, 430–1; *Barber* v. *Richards* (1851) 6 Ex. 63; cf. *Forman* v. *Wright* (1851) 11 CB 481, 492–4.
[106] *Agra and Masterman's Bank* v. *Leighton* (1866) LR 2 Ex. 56, 65, 66.
[107] *Thoni GmbH* v. *RTP Equipment Ltd.* [1979] 2 Lloyd's Rep. 282.
[108] *Fielding and Platt Ltd.* v. *Majjar* [1969] 1 WLR 357; *All Trades Distributors Ltd.* v. *Agencies Kaufman* (1969) 113 SJ 995; *Montecchi* v. *Shimco (UK) Ltd.* [1979] 1 WLR 1180; *Montebianco Industrie Tessili SpA* v. *Carlyle Mills (London) Ltd.* [1981] 1 Lloyd's Rep. 509.
[109] *Archer* v. *Bamford* (1822) 3 Stark 175; cf. *Harris (Oscar) Son & Co.* v. *Vallerman & Co.* [1940] 1 All ER 185 (which regards the rule as insufficiently settled to justify the striking out of an action).

consideration does not constitute a defence to an action brought by a holder for value who is a remote party.[110] This view deserves support. As a remote party who is a holder for value has furnished consideration for the bill, it seems irrelevant that a consideration furnished by prior parties has failed.

Usually the holder of a bill of exchange is entitled to judgment for its full amount. But when he sues as agent or as trustee for another person, or when he sues wholly or in part for another person, any defence or set-off available against that person may be raised, pro tanto, against the holder.[111] A stay of execution may then be ordered in respect of that part of the amount of the bill which the holder seeks to recover on behalf, or for the benefit, of the third party.[112] The judgment itself will be for the full amount of the bill.

The enforcement by the holder of the right of action conferred on him by the bill depends on his performing certain duties imposed on him by the Act. Some, which arise only if the bill is dishonoured by the drawee, are discussed subsequently. But there are two basic duties with which the holder has to comply whilst the bill is current. The first is to effect presentment for acceptance where the bill is of the type that needs to be so presented.[113] The rules as to what constitutes valid presentment for acceptance are technical.[114] Basically, presentment for acceptance has to be made to the drawee personally or to his authorized agent at a reasonable hour on a business day and before the bill is overdue. If the bill is payable at a fixed time after sight, the holder has to present it for acceptance or to negotiate it within a reasonable time.[115] Presentment for acceptance is excused in certain cases, including that in which it cannot be effected despite the exercise of due diligence by the holder.[116]

Secondly, every bill must be presented by the holder for payment. Basically, the bill must be presented when it is due, at a reasonable business hour, and at the proper place for payment. This place is usually either the drawee's place of business or an address specified for presentment in the bill. The bill may, for example, be made payable by the acceptor at the premises of a given bank.[117] Unlike presentment for acceptance, presentment for payment is a localized rather than a personalized exercise. Delays in presentment for

---

[110] *Watson v. Russell* (1864) 5 B & S 968; and see *Misa v. Currie* (1876) 1 App. Cas. 554, 566.

[111] *De La Chaumette v. Bank of England* (1829) 9 B & C 208 (as explained in *Currie v. Misa* (1875) LR 10 Ex. 153, 164; (1876) 1 App. Cas. 554, 570); *Thornton v. Maynard* (1875) LR 10 CP 695.

[112] *Barclays Bank Ltd. v. Aschaffenburger Zellstoffwerke AG* [1967] 1 Lloyd's Rep. 387. See also *Re Bunyard, ex p. Newton* (1880) 16 Ch. D 330, 336. Cf. *Nova (Jersey) Knit Ltd. v. Kammgarn Spinnerei GmbH* [1977] 1 WLR 713.

[113] BEA, s. 39; and see above, p. 501 as to which bills require presentment.

[114] BEA, ss. 40–1.

[115] Ibid., s. 40(1).

[116] Ibid., s. 41(2).

[117] Ibid., s. 45, which makes detailed provisions.

payment, or non-presentment of the bill, are excused, inter alia, where presentment cannot be effected despite the exercise of reasonable diligence.[118] A case in point is that in which the premises of the domiciled bank are closed on the date of the bill's maturity. In addition, a party cannot complain of the holder's failure to present the bill for payment if, as between himself and the drawee, the party involved was not entitled to expect the discharge of the instrument.[119] Presentment for payment may also be waived by a party to the bill.[120]

If a bill is dishonoured by the drawee by non-acceptance or by non-payment, the holder acquires an immediate right of recourse against the drawer and the indorsers.[121] However, he has to comply with certain formalities before he is entitled to enforce this right.[122] Even then, his right is exercisable only against parties who have signed the bill without excluding a right of recourse.[123] If the holder fails to present a bill for payment, the drawer and indorsers are discharged.[124] They are equally discharged if a bill payable after sight is not presented for acceptance or negotiated by the holder within a reasonable time.[125] However, the drawer and any indorser may waive, as regard himself, some or all of the holder's duties.[126] The drawer and indorser may, thus, agree to remain bound even if the holder fails to present the bill.

(iv) Negotiation of a bill

A bill is negotiated when it is transferred from one person to another in such a manner as to constitute the transferee the holder of the bill.[127] It follows that not every delivery of a bill has the object of negotiating it. For instance, an indorsement followed by delivery may be effected to facilitate the collection of the instruments. In such a case, the indorser usually adds words clarifying his intention, such as 'pay Bank X for collection'.[128] In other cases, the same intention may be inferred from the circumstances. Thus, it was held by an Australian authority that the payee's signature on a cheque payable to himself 'or bearer' was not to be regarded as an indorsement because the bill

---

[118] Ibid., ss. 46(1) and 46(2)(*a*).
[119] Ibid., s. 46(2)(*c*)–(*d*).
[120] Ibid., s. 46(2)(*e*).
[121] Ibid., ss. 43(2) (non-acceptance); 47(2) (non-payment).
[122] Pp. 518–20 below.
[123] Under BEA, s. 16(1).
[124] Ibid., s. 45.
[125] Ibid., s. 40(2). In the case of other bills, the failure to present the bill for acceptance postpones the holder's right to present it for payment: BEA, s. 39(2).
[126] Ibid., s. 16(2).
[127] Ibid., s. 31(1).
[128] See, e.g., *McDonald (Gerald) & Co. v. Nash & Co.* [1924] AC 625, 634.

was transferable by mere delivery.[129] But this decision can be questioned. The payee may have been asked to indorse the bill by his immediate transferee with the object of rendering the payee liable on the instrument. It is arguable that, in the absence of clear evidence to the contrary, a party's signature on the bill is to be regarded as an indorsement for negotiation purposes.

An indorsement is not always required to negotiate a bill. The procedure for transfer depends on whether the bill is payable to the order of a specified payee or to bearer. A bill is payable to bearer either if it is expressed to be so payable or if the only or last indorsement executed on it is in blank.[130] An indorsement in blank is one in which the indorser does not designate a specific person as the one to whom the bill is to be payable.[131] It is known as a 'blank' indorsement as the indorser executes his signature without adding the name of an indorsee. An indorsement in which the indorser specifies the name of the indorsee or transferee is known as a 'special indorsement'.[132] Where a bill is either drawn as payable to a designated payee or to such payee's order, it is an order bill.[133] It remains an order bill as long as the transferees execute special indorsements on it.[134]

It is thus clear that an order bill can be converted into a bearer bill. The Act does not state expressly whether a bearer bill can be converted into an order bill by the execution on it of a special indorsement. According to an Australian authority, a special indorsement does not have the effect of so converting a bearer bill.[135] But it has been shown that this view is questionable.[136]

Transfer or negotiation is easiest where the bill is payable to bearer. It can be effected by the mere delivery of the bill by the transferor to the transferee.[137] An order bill is negotiated by the indorsement of the payee, or the indorsee to whom it has been specially indorsed, and by the delivery of the

---

[129]   *Miller Associates (Australia) Pty. Ltd.* v. *Bennington Pty. Ltd.* (1975) 7 ALR 144.

[130]   BEA, s. 8(3).

[131]   Ibid., s. 34(1).

[132]   Ibid., s. 34(2).

[133]   Ibid., s. 8(4), (5).

[134]   A bill is payable to bearer if the payee is a fictitious or non-existing person: BEA, s. 7(3); and see *Bank of England* v. *Vagliano Bros.* [1891] A.C. 107; *Vinden* v. *Hughes* [1905] KB 795; *North and South Wales Bank Ltd.* v. *Macbeth* [1908] AC 137; *Fok Cheong Shing Investment Co. Ltd.* v. *Bank of Nova Scotia* (1981) 32 OR (2d) 705 (Can.); cf. *Paul* v. *Western Canada Lottery Foundation* (1981) 127 DLR (3rd) 502. As regards the position where the payee is known to have died before the drawing of the bill, see *Canada Trust Co.* v. *The Queen* [1982] 2 FC 722 (Can.). It is doubtful if the section applies where the words 'or bearer' have been struck out and a crossing with the words 'a/c payee only' added to the instrument: *Rohstar (Pvt.) Ltd.* v. *Netherlands Bank of Rhodesia Ltd.* [1972] 2 SA 703, 709–11.

[135]   *Miller Associates (Australia) Pty. Ltd.* v. *Bennington Pty. Ltd.* (1957) 7 ALR 144; W. J. Chappenden, 'Liability of Signatories and Indorsers', (1981) 55 ALJ 135.

[136]   Above, pp. 243–4.

[137]   BEA, s. 31(2). As regards delivery, see s. 21.

instrument.[138] If the holder of a bill payable to his order transfers it without executing an indorsement, the transferee acquires such title as the transferor had in the bill. In addition, the transferee acquires the right to have the transferor's indorsement.[139] However, unless such an indorsement is obtained, the transferee remains a mere assignee of the chose in action based on the bill, and cannot acquire rights superior to the transferor.[140]

In practice, the transferor of a bill is asked to indorse it even where the instrument is payable to bearer. The reason for this is that the transferee wishes to ensure that the transferor is liable on the bill as indorser. If a bearer bill is transferred without being indorsed, the transferor is known as a 'transferor by delivery'.[141] Such a party is not liable on the bill.[142] But by negotiating the bill, the transferor by delivery warrants to his immediate transferee that the bill is what it purports to be, that he has the right to transfer it, and that he is not aware of any fact that renders it valueless. This warranty, which is given only to an immediate transferee who is a holder for value, enables the transferee to bring an action on the bill against the transferor.[143] If the bill is worthless, the transferee may seek reimbursement of the amount paid by suing the transferor in quasi-contract.[144] The transferee's position must not be confused with the drawee's. A holder who presents a bill for acceptance or for payment does not seek to transfer it, and does not warrant the authenticity or validity of the instrument to the drawee.[145]

The requisites of a valid indorsement are spelt out in section 32. Basically, the indorsement has to be executed on the bill, and has to transfer it in its entirety. If a bill gives a wrong designation of the payee or an indorsee to whom it is payable, the person concerned may indorse it in the way he is described and may, further, add his ordinary signature. Moreover, a genuine indorsement of the correct payee is valid even if executed in a name differing from that by which he is described on the front of the bill.[146] Where there are two or more indorsements on a bill, they are deemed to have been made in the order in which they appear on the bill.[147]

Not every bill can be negotiated. In the first place, the drawer may insert

---

[138] Ibid., s. 31(3).

[139] Ibid., s. 31(4); and see *Walters* v. *Neary* (1904) 21 TLR 146.

[140] *Whistler* v. *Forster* (1863) 14 CB (NS) 248. And see *Geo. Thompson (Aust.) Pty. Ltd.* v. *Vittadello* [1978] VR 199, 208–12.

[141] BEA, s. 58(1).

[142] Ibid., s. 58(2).

[143] Ibid., s. 58(3); the liability is not incurred *vis-à-vis* subsequent parties: *Miller Associates (Australia) Pty. Ltd.* v. *Bennington Pty. Ltd.* (1975) 7 ALR 144.

[144] *Gurney* v. *Womersley* (1854) 4 E & B 133.

[145] *Guaranty Trust Co. of New York* v. *Hannay & Co.* [1918] 2 KB 623, 631–2.

[146] *Bird & Co. (London) Ltd.* v. *Thos. Cook & Son Ltd.* [1937] 2 All ER 227. But the transferee will not be a holder in due course if there is a material difference between the payee's true name and the misnomer: *Arab Bank Ltd.* v. *Ross* [1952] 2 QB 216.

[147] BEA, s. 32(5).

in the bill words prohibiting transfer or evincing an intention that the bill be non-transferable. Such a bill remains valid as between the immediate parties to it but cannot be negotiated.[148] Thus, where a bill is made payable to 'Mr X only', a purported transferee cannot become its holder, let alone a holder in due course, entitled to sue on it.[149] The intention to prohibit negotiation must, however, appear clearly on the face of the bill. If the drawer makes a bill payable to a particular person, without adding the words 'or order', but fails to add words prohibiting transfer, the bill is treated as payable to that person's order.[150] Similarly, the mere cancellation of the printed words 'or bearer' or 'or order' in a bill does not in itself restrict its negotiability.[151] Such a bill is payable to the payee's order.

The second method that can be used to restrict the negotiability of a bill is the execution of a restrictive indorsement. An indorsement is restrictive if it either prohibits further transfer or states that it is not executed to effect transfer but constitutes a mere authority to the indorsee to deal with the bill as thereby directed. Examples are indorsements accompanied by the words 'pay D only', or 'Pay D for the Account of X' or 'Pay D for collection'.[152] A statement to the effect that consideration has been furnished by a third party does not render restrictive the indorsement to which it is added.[153] An indorsement of a bill to a specified person without the addition of the words 'or order' is not restrictive. The bill remains negotiable and is to be treated as if the words in question were included.[154]

A restrictive indorsement denies the indorsee the power to transfer the bill unless it expressly authorizes him to do so.[155] But the indorsee who takes the bill under the restrictive indorsement retains the right to receive payment of the instrument, and is entitled to sue any party that is liable to his transferor.[156] Where a restrictive indorsement authorizes further transfer, all subsequent indorsees take the bill with the same rights and subject to the same liabilities as the 'restricted indorsee'.[157] It follows that an indorsee who takes a bill under a restrictive indorsement, and who is accordingly aware of the limitation of the title of the transferor, cannot be a holder in due course. At the same time, the restrictive indorsement does not

---

[148] Ibid., s. 8(1).

[149] *Hibernian Bank Ltd.* v. *Gysin and Hanson* [1939] 1 KB 483. As regards restrictions of negotiability imposed by the acceptor, see *Meyer & Co.* v. *Decroix, Verley et Cie* [1891] AC 520.

[150] BEA, s. 8(4).

[151] For a full analysis, see *Chitty on Contracts*, 25th edn., vol. 2, para. 2467.

[152] BEA, s. 35(1).

[153] *Buckley* v. *Jackson* (1868) LR 3 Ex. 135.

[154] BEA, s. 8(4) read in conjunction with s. 34(3).

[155] A restrictive indorsement that enables the indorsee to effect transfer is: 'Pay X or order for collection'.

[156] BEA, s. 35(2).

[157] Ibid., s. 35(3).

put the drawee or acceptor on enquiry. Further, he is not liable to the indorser who restricted transfer, if the indorsee misappropriates the amount paid to him against the bill.[158]

In the ordinary course of business, a bill of exchange is negotiated a number of times following its discount. In this regard, a bill of exchange differs from a cheque, which in the vast majority of cases is paid by the payee to the credit of his own account or presented for payment over the counter. In some cases, a bill may be transferred back to a party already liable on it, such as the drawer or an indorser. Under section 37, such a party may reissue the bill and negotiate it over again.[159] But he is not entitled to enforce the bill against a party to whom he has previously been liable, such as an indorser who became a party to the bill in the meantime. Section 37 applies, further, to the relationship between the party who regains its possession and the acceptor. It has been held that, on this basis, the drawer or indorser is to be treated as a holder in due course as against the acceptor, provided this status was enjoyed by the party from whom he acquired the bill back.[160] But this reasoning is questionable, as section 37 does not purport to confer any right on the party who regains the bills except his power to reissue it. Usually, the party who regains the bill strikes out all the indorsements executed by intermediary parties. This act does not discharge parties who were liable to him initially.

Whilst primarily an indorsement is regarded as a means for the negotiation of a bill, it is wrong to regard this as its only function. Frequently, an indorsement is executed by a party for the sole purpose of assuming liability on the bill. The indorser here acts as a surety,[161] whose signature gives extra currency to the bill. In such a case, and as against a party other than a holder in due course, it can be shown that when the surety executed his indorsement and delivered the bill back to the drawer, he did so for a restrictive purpose.[162] But as against a holder in due course, delivery per se by the indorser is conclusively presumed.[163] This last point is of general importance as usually any contract on the bill, be it the drawer's, the acceptor's or an indorser's, is incomplete and revocable until the delivery of the instrument.[164] However, where a bill is no longer in the possession of the party involved, a valid and unconditional delivery by him is presumed until the contrary is proved.[165]

---

[158] *Williams Deacon & Co. v. Shadbolt* (1885) 1 Cab. & E 529; (1885) 1 TLR 417.
[159] The section is subject to ss. 59–64 concerning discharge.
[160] *Jade International Steel Stahl und Eisen GmbH & Co. KG. v. Robert Nicholas (Steels) Ltd.* [1978] QB 917.
[161] Pp. 501–3 above.
[162] BEA, s. 21(2).
[163] Idem, proviso.
[164] Ibid., s. 21(1).
[165] Ibid., s. 21(3).

(v) Discharge of a bill

A bill is discharged in any of the five following ways: by payment in due course (section 59); when the acceptor becomes its holder after its maturity (section 61); by express waiver or renunciation (section 62); by cancellation (section 63); and, in certain cases, by a material alteration executed without the assent of the parties liable on the instrument (section 64). When a bill is discharged, it ceases to be a negotiable instrument and all rights based on it are extinguished.[166] But what is the position of a person who, in good faith and for value, takes a bill that does not show on its face that it has been discharged? It has been suggested that where such a person is able to establish that he is a holder in due course, he is entitled to enforce the bill.[167] A person, though, can be a holder in due course only if he takes a bill before it is overdue. It follows that the problem could arise only in the case of bills payable on demand, or where a bill payable at another 'usance' is discharged before its maturity. In such cases it is, perhaps, arguable that an acceptor who fails to indicate that the bill has been discharged is estopped from asserting this fact.

According to section 59(1), a bill is discharged by payment in due course when the drawee pays it at or after maturity to a holder, provided the drawee effects payment in good faith and without notice of any defect in the holder's title. The word 'holder' retains its technical meaning in the context of this section. It encompasses the payee, the indorsee and the bearer of a bill. A transferee of an order bill who holds the instrument under a forged indorsement is, of course, not a holder.[168] Payment to such a transferee is, therefore, not payment in due course and does not discharge the bill.[169] But payment of a stolen bearer bill to a thief constitutes payment in due course, as the thief or his transferee does not hold the bill under an indorsement.[170] Payment in good faith by the drawee to an indorsee who has obtained the bill by fraud constitutes a discharge.[171]

The payment of a bill by the drawer does not constitute a discharge.[172] If the bill is payable not to the drawer's own order but to that of a third party, the drawer who pays it is entitled to enforce it against the acceptor, but may not re-issue it. If the bill is payable to the drawer's own order and is paid by him after he has negotiated it to a third party, the drawer is restored to his

---

[166] *Harmer* v. *Steele* (1849) 4 Exch. 1, 13; *Burchfield* v. *Moore* (1854) 23 LJQB 261.

[167] *Glasscock* v. *Balls* (1889) 24 QBD 13, 15; Kadrigamar, (1959) 22 MLR 146; Chalmers, *Bills of Exchange*, 13th edn., p. 198.

[168] P. 504 above.

[169] Except in the case of cheques: pp. 303 et seq. above.

[170] As the bill is transferable by mere delivery: p. 512 above; and see *Chitty on Contracts*, 25th edn., vol. 2, para. 2527.

[171] *Robarts* v. *Tucker* (1851) 16 QB 560, 576–7, 579.

[172] Except where the instrument is an accommodation bill.

former rights against the acceptor and any antecedent parties;[173] he is entitled to strike out his own indorsement and to negotiate the bill over again. This is also the position of an indorser who pays the bill.[174] When a drawer pays a bill to the holder, he becomes entitled to the benefit of securities given to the holder by the acceptor. The reason for this is that the holder and the indorsers are sureties of the acceptor's debt to the holder. They are, accordingly, subrogated to the rights which the holder, as creditor, has against the acceptor—the debtor.[175]

A bill is discharged if its acceptor becomes its holder at or after maturity. The principle, however, applies only if the acceptor acquires the bill in his own right.[176] Thus, if the acceptor becomes the executor of the holder's estate, the bill is discharged.[177] However, this would probably not be the case if the acceptor became an administrator, as he would then not hold the bill 'in his own right'.[178] If a bill, accepted jointly by a number of drawees, is indorsed at its maturity to one of them, it is discharged; the remaining acceptors cannot be sued on the bill although they may be liable to contribute as joint debtors.[179]

A bill is discharged if, at or after its maturity, the holder expressly and absolutely renounces his rights against the acceptor either in writing or by delivering the bill to him.[180] A bill is likewise discharged if it is delivered to the acceptor's executors or administrators with the intention that it be discharged.[181] An acceptance by the holder of the acceptor's offer to pay a composition is not a renunciation of the holder's rights.[182] Other parties to the bill may also be released from their liability by the holder's renunciation of his rights. But the rights of a holder in due course are not affected by the holder's waiver.[183]

A bill is discharged by an apparent cancellation, intentionally executed by the holder or his agent.[184] The holder or agent may also discharge any party liable on the bill by cancelling his signature. In such a case, any indorser who had initially enjoyed a right of recourse against the party concerned would also be discharged.[185] A cancellation is effective only if it is

---

[173] Such as an indorser who signed as surety before the bill was issued.
[174] BEA, s. 59(2).
[175] *Duncan, Fox & Co.* v. *North and South Wales Bank* (1880) 6 App. Cas. 1.
[176] BEA, s. 61.
[177] *Jenkins* v. *Jenkins* [1928] 2 KB 501.
[178] Chalmers, *Bills of Exchange*, 13th edn., p. 213.
[179] *Harmer* v. *Steele* (1849) 4 Exch. 1; cf. *Forster, Hight & Co.* v. *Ward* (1883) 1 Cab. & E 168.
[180] BEA, s. 61(1).
[181] *Edwards* v. *Walters* [1896] 2 Ch. 157.
[182] *Rimalt* v. *Wartwright* (1924) 40 TLR 803.
[183] BEA, s. 62(2).
[184] Ibid., s. 63(1).
[185] Ibid., s. 63(2).

obvious.[186] A holder is entitled to prove that a cancellation was effected unintentionally, under a mistake of fact or without his authority. The cancellation is, then, inoperative.[187]

A bill is avoided if the instrument itself, or an acceptance executed on it, is materially altered without the assent of all the parties to it. The only party who remains bound by it is the one who made the alteration,[188] and presumably all those who took the bill subsequently.[189] It is provided that where a bill has been materially altered, but the alteration is not apparent, it may be enforced by a holder in due course 'according to its original tenor'. Consequently, if the amount of a bill has been fraudulently altered from £500 to £5,000, the holder in due course would be able to enforce payment of £500![190] An alteration on a bill is considered apparent if it would be observed by a person who intends to acquire it and scrutinizes it with reasonable care.[191]

The Act treats certain alterations as material. These are: alterations of the date,[192] of the sum payable, of the time of payment, of the place of payment and, where the bill has been accepted generally, the addition of a place of payment without the acceptor's assent.[193] The specified list, though, is not exhaustive. Whether any other alteration is material or not is a question of fact. An alteration which is not deliberately executed by any person but is caused by an accident does not invalidate the bill.[194] An alteration made before a bill is completely issued, such as the alteration by the drawer of a purported place of issue inserted by an acceptor who has accepted the bill in blank, is not a material alteration,[195] although the very same alteration would be material if made after the bill had been issued.[196]

(vi) Procedure on dishonour

When a bill is dishonoured by non-acceptance or by non-payment, the holder has to take certain prescribed steps. If he fails to do so, the drawer

---

[186] *Bank of Scotland* v. *Dominion Bank* [1891] AC 592. There is authority for the view that a bill, which has been pasted together after being torn into two pieces, is valid in the hands of a holder in due course: *Ingham* v. *Primrose* (1859) 7 CB (NS) 82. But the practice of dividing a bill into two parts which, for security reasons, are sent by separate mailings is now obsolete. It is, therefore, to be doubted if the case in point would be followed today.

[187] BEA, s. 63(3).

[188] Ibid., s. 64(1).

[189] They would be able to rely on the estoppels discussed above, pp. 501–2.

[190] *Scholfield* v. *Londesborough* [1896] AC 514.

[191] *Woollatt* v. *Stanley* (1928) 138 LT 620; Hudson [1975] JBL 108.

[192] For a recent authority comparing the materiality of the date on which the bill is made with the date on which it falls due, see *Heller Factors Pty. Ltd.* v. *Toy Corporation Pty. Ltd.* [1984] 1 NSWLR 121 (Aust.).

[193] BEA, s. 64(2).

[194] *Hong Kong and Shanghai Banking Corporation* v. *Lo* [1928] AC 181.

[195] *Foster* v. *Driscoll* [1929] 1 KB 470, 494.

[196] *Koch* v. *Dicks* [1933] 1 KB 307.

and the indorsers are discharged.[197] The acceptor, however, remains bound.[198] The reason for this is obvious: as the acceptor has assumed the primary obligation to pay the bill, it would be unreasonable to render his liability subject to the performance of formal duties imposed on the holder. For the same reason, the acceptor is not discharged if the holder fails to present the bill for payment.[199] The only duty which the holder owes to the acceptor or drawee is to exhibit the bill when he demands payment and to deliver it up when honoured.[200] At the same time, the holder cannot bring an action on the bill unless it has been dishonoured when presented for acceptance or for payment.

The basic procedure with which the holder has to comply if he wishes to recover payment from the drawer and the indorsers is to send notice of dishonour.[201] The object of this notice is to advise the drawer and the indorsers that the bill has been dishonoured by the acceptor or drawee. The rules prescribing the requisites of a valid notice are set out in section 49. Basically, the notice has to be given promptly,[202] either in writing or by personal communication.[203] The return of the dishonoured bill to the drawer or the indorser constitutes adequate notice.[204] It is clear that a party to a bill may be unable to extend notice to anyone except his immediate transferor, as the addresses of prior indorsers may be unknown to him. It is, therefore, provided that, where a party receives due notice of dishonour, he has thereafter a period of time for giving notice to antecedent parties identical with the time available to the holder.[205]

The stringency of the procedure prescribed for the giving of notice is mitigated by the provisions of section 50. Basically, delay in giving notice is excused where it is due to circumstances beyond the control of the party charged with it. Notice is altogether dispensed with in circumstances similar to those leading to the dispensation of presentment for payment.

The need to dispatch notice of dishonour applies in the case of all bills of exchange. A further requisite, which is known as protesting or noting, applies to 'foreign bills'. The key definition is that of an 'inland bill', which is a bill that purports on its face either to be drawn and payable in the

[197] BEA, s. 48.
[198] Ibid., s. 52(3).
[199] BEA, s. 52(1), (2); this is so even in the case of a qualified acceptance, unless it expressly renders the acceptor's duty subject to due presentment.
[200] Ibid., s. 52(4).
[201] Ibid., s. 48.
[202] Ibid., s. 49(12); if the sender and the recipient reside in the same place, it has to be given so as to reach the recipient on the day following the dishonour; in other cases, it has to be dispatched not later than on that day, provided there is a post at a convenient hour.
[203] Ibid., s. 49(5); the notice has to identify the bill.
[204] Ibid., s. 49(6).
[205] Ibid., s. 49(14).

British Islands or to be drawn within the British Islands on a person resident therein. Thus, a bill drawn in London on a merchant in Birmingham but payable in Paris is an inland bill.

Under section 51(2) noting is mandatory where the dishonoured instrument is a foreign bill or purports to be such a bill. Under section 51(1), noting is discretionary in the case of an inland bill. A protest is carried out by the presentment of the bill for acceptance or for payment by a notary public following its initial dishonour upon its presentment by the holder. If the bill is dishonoured again, the notary public makes a copy of the instrument in his register and 'notes' on the bill the date of its presentment by him, the answer given, and the amount of his fee. After this noting, a copy of the 'protest' has to be sent to each indorser and to the drawer. If this is not duly done, these parties are discharged.[206] The correct procedure for a protest is set out in section 51(3)–(8).[207] The provisions concerning both excuses for the delay in noting and the dispensation of noting are similar to those prevailing in the case of notice of dishonour.[208] Where the services of a notary public cannot be obtained, a householder or substantial resident of the relevant place, acting in the presence of two witnesses, may give a certificate attesting the dishonour of the bill.[209]

(vii) Promissory notes

The bill of exchange is the main negotiable instrument used in business transactions. The other instrument figuring in them is the promissory note. The cardinal distinction between the two instruments is that, whilst a bill is an order given by the drawer to the drawee, a note embodies a promise to pay a certain amount of money to the order of a specified payee or to bearer. The maker, in effect, combines the role of the drawer and the acceptor. Like the former, he issues the instrument. Like the latter, he assumes the primary obligation to pay it. A note payable to the maker's own order does not become an effective instrument until it has been indorsed by him. In all other regards, the requisites of a note are the same as those of a bill. The promise has to be in writing and unconditional; the sum involved has to be certain; and the time of maturity can be any of the 'usances' which are valid in the case of a bill.[210] A note which is payable 'on or before' a given date

---

[206] Ibid., s. 51(2).
[207] Under s. 93, it is adequate if the noting of the bill is carried out within the specified period of time. The formal protest may be extended subsequently.
[208] BEA, s. 51(9).
[209] Ibid., s. 94.
[210] Ibid., s. 83. For a form of promissory note, see Appendix.

has been held to be invalid as it is not payable at a fixed or determinable future time.[211]

Promissory notes are frequently made payable in instalments, and subject to the condition that the total balance is to fall due in the case of a single default. In *Kirkwood* v. *Carroll*,[212] a note of this type, which was signed jointly by two makers and which provided that the giving of time to either of them would not prejudice the holder's right to proceed against the other, was held to be a valid note. In *Mason* v. *Lack*,[213] an instrument in the form of a bill, signed by a person as drawer and, though not addressed to anyone, accepted by another person, was treated as a note and not as a bill. But in *Haseldine* v. *Winstanley*,[214] a similar instrument, which had been completed by the holder with the drawer's consent by adding the acceptor's name as addressee, was held to be good as a bill if the alteration was justifiable, or good as a note if it was not. An IOU embodying a promise to pay, which meets the requisites spelt out for notes in the Act, constitutes a promissory note.[215]

Under section 89(1) of the Act, the provisions governing bills of exchange apply with the necessary modifications to promissory notes. The maker of the note is deemed to correspond with the acceptor of a bill, and the first indorser with the drawer of an accepted bill payable to his order.[216] The provisions concerning acceptance and presentment for acceptance are altogether excluded.[217] Presentment for payment is, however, required to charge the indorsers.[218] It is a condition precedent to the maker's liability only if the bill is made payable at a particular place.[219] Protest is not required where a promissory note is dishonoured, even if it is a foreign note.[220] A note is inchoate and incomplete until its delivery.[221]

A promissory note may be executed by two or more makers. If such parties are jointly liable, a judgment against one of them is a bar to proceedings against the others even whilst it is unsatisfied. But this principle is inapplicable where the parties assume several or 'joint and several' liability.[222] The

---

[211] *Williamson* v. *Rider* [1963] 1 QB 89, 97–8, adopting the reasoning in *Crouch* v. *Crédit Foncier of England Ltd.* (1873) LR 8 QB 374 and in *Dagger* v. *Shepherd* [1946] 1 All ER 133 and followed in *Salot* v. *Naidoo* [1981] 3 SA 959. But contrast *John Burrows Ltd.* v. *Subsurface Surveys Ltd.* [1968] SCR 607 (Canada), which followed Ormerod LJ's dissenting judgment in *Williamson* v. *Rider*.

[212] [1903] 1 KB 531.

[213] (1929) 45 TLR 363.

[214] [1936] 2 KB 101.

[215] *Muir* v. *Muir*, 1912, 1 SLT 304.

[216] BEA, s. 89(2).

[217] Ibid., s. 89(3).

[218] Ibid., s. 87(2). If the note is payable on demand, presentment must be effected within a reasonable time after its indorsement: BEA, s. 86.

[219] Ibid., s. 87(1).

[220] Ibid., s. 89(4).

[221] Ibid., s. 84.

[222] *Kendall* v. *Hamilton* (1879) 4 App. Cas. 504.

fact that one of the joint makers of a note is not liable does not release the other. Thus, in *Wauthier* v. *Wilson*[223] a father and his minor son made a joint and several note to secure a loan given to the son. The son was not liable, but the father was bound.

Although promissory notes conceptually resemble bills of exchange, they serve an entirely different function. Promissory notes are principally issued to secure the payment of instalments due under lending agreements and other types of commercial transaction. The note which is issued to cover a given instalment can be discounted by the payee or kept in portfolio. In the latter case, it provides an effective means for instituting an action to recover the amount for which the note is issued. Its advantages in this respect are that the action can be instituted in summary procedure, and that not all defences based on the underlying transaction can be raised against the action on the note, even where the plaintiff is the immediate payee.[224]

A novel version of the promissory notes is the sterling commercial paper. The instrument in question, issued by financial institutions other than banks, assumes the form of a promissory note payable to bearer. It may be for a usance as short as seven days or as long as one year.[225] Sterling commercial paper serves the same function as bankers' certificates of deposit, which, however, do not include the type of formal undertaking that would render them promissory notes within the definition of the 1882 Act. It has been argued that they constitute a novel form of negotiable instrument binding under a mercantile usage.[226]

3. SPECIAL PROBLEMS OF BILLS DRAWN UNDER ACCEPTANCE CREDITS

(i) The problems defined

Bills of exchange drawn under acceptance credits give rise to special problems. These stem principally from the fact that, as between the bank, which assumes the role of the acceptor of the bills, and the customer, who figures as drawer, the bank in reality acts in a role similar to that of surety. It accepts the bills in order to facilitate their discount. The object of the transaction is to enable the customer to obtain funds on the bank's credit. Two

---

[223] (1912) 28 TLR 239.

[224] See pp. 506 et seq. above.

[225] R. MacVicar, 'Sterling Commercial Paper', (1986) 2 Butterworth Journal of Int. Banking and Financial Law 40.

[226] *Encyclopaedia of Banking Law*, vol. 1, para. F/112–13; relying on *Customs and Excise Commissioners* v. *Guy Butler (International) Ltd.* [1977] QB 377, 382, which , however, raises the point in passing.

major problems arise as a result. The first is that the bills appear to be accepted by the bank for the customer's accommodation. If, as a result, they are 'accommodation bills', within the technical meaning of the phrase in the Bills of Exchange Act, they are governed by some special provisions which distinguish them from ordinary bills. Secondly, problems arise if the bank is unable to meet its acceptances. Usually the bank obtains securities from the customer when it agrees to open the acceptance credit. What is the fate of these where the bills have to be met by the drawer or, if he too is insolvent, by one of the indorsers?

The two problems require separate analysis.

(ii) Are bills drawn under acceptance credits accommodation bills?

The phrase 'accommodation bill' is not defined in the Act. Instead, section 28(1) states that 'an accommodation party to a bill is a person who has signed a bill as drawer, acceptor, or indorser, without receiving value therefor, and for the purpose of lending his name to some other person'. In practice, a bill is called an 'accommodation bill' where it is accepted, drawn, or indorsed for the accommodation of a party who furnishes no consideration for it.

Three special principles apply to such a bill. First, an accommodation party is liable on the bill to a holder for value even if, at the time the holder took the bill, he knew that the party involved signed it for accommodation purposes.[227] This principle may be seen as an extension of the rule that absence of consideration, or its failure, cannot be pleaded as a defence to an action instituted by a holder for value.[228] However, the accommodation party can plead, as a defence to the holder's action, any specific defect in the transferor's title of which the holder was aware when he took the bill.[229] Secondly, the party accommodated is not always discharged from his liability if the holder fails to comply with one of the procedural steps prescribed by the Act. Thus, presentment for payment is dispensed as against an indorser, for whose accommodation the bill has been drawn, if he has no reason to expect that payment would be made if presented.[230] Notice of dishonour and protest are dispensed with in similar circumstances.[231]

The third and most important principle is that where 'an accommodation

---

[227] BEA, s. 28(2).

[228] Pp. 509–10 above.

[229] *Hornby* v. *McLaren* (1908) 24 TLR 494.

[230] BEA, s. 46(2)(*d*). It is equally dispensed with against a drawer, even where he is not an accommodated party, if he has no reason to expect that the bill would be met: s. 46(2)(*c*).

[231] Ibid., s. 51(2)(*d*) (notice re an indorser; there is no need to establish that he was not entitled to have the bill paid); the drawer's position is governed by s. 51(2)(*c*)); and see s. 51(9) (protest; applying the principles pertaining to notice).

bill is paid in due course by the party accommodated, the bill is discharged'.[232] The bill thereupon ceases to be a negotiable instrument and the
accommodated party, be he the drawer or an indorser, cannot enforce it
against the acceptor.[233] It further follows that he cannot re-issue it.[234]

It is, thus, clear that an accommodation bill is governed by the general
principles of the law of negotiable instruments, subject to well-defined
modifications. It is, therefore, of practical importance to consider whether a
bill, drawn under an acceptance credit, is an accommodation bill. The
answer, unfortunately, is not clear. A person is an accommodation party if
he draws, accepts, or indorses the bill for another person's accommodation,
and provided he acts 'without receiving value therefor'. It is clear that a
bank that accepts a bill drawn under an acceptance credit does so for the
drawer's accommodation. But the bank invariably receives a fee. Can it,
therefore, be said that it receives no consideration for its acceptance?

Cases decided both before and after the passing of the Bills of Exchange
Act 1882 are divided. In *Oriental Financial Corporation* v. *Overend,
Gurney & Co.*,[235] Malins VC thought that bills drawn under an acceptance
credit were not accommodation bills, as the acceptor had received a fee. The
point was left open on appeal, although Lord Hatherley LC's[236] reference to
the fee as 'some commission' may indicate that he did not regard it as being
directly related to the bank's acceptance of the bills. On this very basis,
James LJ expressed the view in a later case that the commission received by
the issuer of an acceptance credit did not preclude the bills drawn thereunder from being accommodation bills.[237]

Modern authorities are equally inconclusive. In *Re Securitibank Ltd.*,
Barker J,[238] in the New Zealand Supreme Court, thought that bills drawn
under an acceptance credit were not accommodation bills. But his Honour
relied on the fact that, in the case before him, the fee paid by the customer
was not a mere acceptance fee. The transaction was in the nature of a 'clear
mercantile arrangement', and the fee was to escalate sharply if the customer
failed to remit to the bank on time the amounts required for meeting the
acceptances. The bank, accordingly, received a valuable consideration
beyond a mere acceptance fee. It is uncertain whether Barker J would have
reached the same conclusion if the bank's remuneration had been confined
to an acceptance fee, which might have been treated as a consideration for
the issuing of the acceptance credit rather than for the acceptance of the
bills. It is noteworthy that in a recent Australian decision, *K. D. Morris &*

[232] Ibid., s. 59(3).
[233] *Lazarus* v. *Cowie* (1842) 3 QB 459; *Solomon* v. *Davis* (1883) 1 Cab. & E 83.
[234] But see pp. 506–7 above as regards the rights of a holder in due course.
[235] (1871) LR 7 Ch. App. 142.
[236] Ibid., 151.
[237] *Re Yglesias, ex p. Gomez* (1875) LR 10 Ch. App. 639.
[238] [1978] 1 NZLR 97, 154.

Sons Pty. Ltd. (in Liqu.) v. *Bank of Queensland Ltd.*,[239] bills issued under such a facility were referred to as accommodation bills although all the issuing bank had received was such an acceptance fee. The point, though, was not an issue in the case.

It is arguable that none of the authorities involved gives full effect to the words of section 28(1). The question is whether a consideration, received by the accommodation party, is furnished for his becoming a party to the bill. In the case of an acceptance credit, the question is whether the fee is received by the bank for its acceptance of the bill or for the issuing of the facility. It is believed that, in terms of mercantile reality, the fee is received by the bank for the promise made to the customer in the acceptance credit. This view derives support from the fact that the fee is not refundable if the customer fails to utilize the facility. It is, therefore, not a fee received for the signing of the bills. On this basis, the fee is not related directly to the instruments, and these are to be considered bills accepted by the bank for the accommodation of the customer without its receiving any direct remuneration therefor. The bills are, accordingly, accommodation bills.

This conclusion is desirable in the light of the true nature of the transaction. The bills here discussed are accepted by the bank to enable the customer to discount them on the bills market. The customer undertakes to remit to the bank funds required for the meeting of the bills. It would be monstrous if, having paid such a bill by direct payment instead of by the remission of funds to the bank (the acceptor), the customer could bring an action to enforce the bills against the bank. It would be equally startling if the customer, who is in reality the principal debtor as between the bank and himself, could defeat an action brought against him on the bills by a third party on the basis of procedural technicalities, such as the failure to give him due notice of dishonour.

(iii) Bankruptcy problems

In many transactions involving acceptance credits, the issuing bank requires the customer to furnish security. Thus, the customer may be asked to deposit commercial paper with the bank, or may be asked to give a charge over assets. Problems arise where the bank fails after receiving these securities but before it meets bills drawn under the acceptance credit.

The first question is whether, in such a case, the customer is bound to pay the bills himself. The law of negotiable instruments is clear. The customer, acting as drawer and possibly as first indorser, is liable jointly and severally with the bank.[240] If the bills are dishonoured by the bank, the customer is obliged to pay them. Moreover, the law of contract does not provide an

---

[239] [1980] 54 ALJR 424, 425, 429–30, 436.
[240] And see p. 503 above.

escape route. Even if the discounter of the bills drawn under the acceptance credit knows of the arrangement between the bank and its customer, he is still to be regarded as relying on the credit of both the bank and the customer. When he discounts the bills he therefore expects them to be paid. If they are not paid, he can sue the customer on the bills, as well as under any underlying agreement between them.[241]

It follows that a customer who has remitted the funds needed for meeting the bills to the issuing bank before its collapse has no option but to pay the amount involved over again to the holder. His only remedy against the bank is to prove for the debt as a general creditor. The customer is in a better position if the bank fails before he has remitted the funds to it. In such a case, the customer should use the funds in order to pay the bills to the holder. The bank's inability to meet the bills constitutes a total failure of the consideration furnished by it, and the customer's duty to remit funds to it (assumed in the acceptance credit) is discharged.[242] The advice to be given to the customer is, therefore, to refrain from remitting the required funds to the bank if there are any doubts concerning its solvency. In the majority of cases, though, the dealings between the customer and the bank are conducted on the basis of a current account, in which case the customer is a general creditor of the bank for any amount standing to his credit.[243]

When the customer pays the bills drawn under the acceptance credit, he is entitled to reclaim any securities deposited with the bank. Moreover, if a bill is paid neither by the bank nor by the customer, then an indorser who has met it becomes subrogated to the holder's rights. He is, accordingly, entitled to claim any securities held by the holder.[244] Furthermore, he should have the right to claim any securities furnished by the customer (the drawer) to the bank (the acceptor). The reason for this is that, as between these two parties, the customer is the main debtor. By discharging the bill, the indorser settles the very debt for which the securities were furnished by the customer to the bank.[245]

---

[241]   See, by way of analogy, cases involving documentary credits which are not honoured by an insolvent issuing bank: *Saffron* v. *Société Minière Cafrika* (1958) 100 CLR 231, 244–5; *Sale Continuation Ltd.* v. *Austin Taylor & Co. Ltd.* [1968] 2 QB 849; *W. J. Alan & Co. Ltd.* v. *El Nasr Export & Import Co.* [1972] 2 QB 189; *Maran Road Saw Mill* v. *Austin Taylor & Co. Ltd.* [1975] 1 Lloyd's Rep. 156, 159; *E. D. & F. Man Ltd.* v. *Nigerian Sweets and Confectionery Co. Ltd.* [1977] 2 Lloyd's Rep. 50.

[242]   *Sale Continuation Ltd.* v. *Austin Taylor & Co. Ltd.*, above. The case has been criticized by H. C. Gutteridge and M. C. Megrah, *Law of Bankers' Commercial Credits*, 7th edn., London, 1984, pp. 43–44; contrast *Benjamin's Sale of Goods*, 2nd edn., paras. 2179–80.

[243]   Pp. 76 et seq. above.

[244]   *Duncan, Fox & Co.* v. *North and South Wales Bank* (1880) 6 App. Cas. 1. See also *Scholefield Goodman & Co. Ltd.* v. *Zynqier* [1985] 3 All ER 105, noted in [1986] JBL 399.

[245]   For the complex problems arising in the case of the double bankruptcy of the issuing bank and its customer, see E. P. Ellinger, 'Securitibank's Collapse', (1978) 20 Malaya L Rev. 84 et seq.; *Re Securitibank Ltd.* [1978] 1 NZLR 97; *Re Standard Insurance Co. Ltd.* [1970] 1 NSWLR 392.

4. NEGOTIABLE INSTRUMENTS AND THE CONSUMER CREDIT ACT 1974

Traditionally, negotiable instruments were used both in commercial transactions and in consumer transactions. The bill of exchange has been associated with commercial transactions such as international sales and acceptance credits, but occasionally was used to accommodate private individuals. The promissory note is also used in some commercial transactions, notably in the context of export credit guarantees, but was prevalent in consumer transactions such as hire purchase agreements. In such transactions, the notes were frequently instrumental in assisting the finance company to enforce its rights regardless of justifiable claims raised by the hirer against the dealer in respect of the goods covered.[246]

Abuses of this type induced the legislature to intervene. Section 123 of the Consumer Credit Act 1974 restricts the use of negotiable instruments in 'regulated' consumer credit agreements and in consumer hire agreements.[247] Subsection (1) prohibits the taking of negotiable instruments other than cheques in discharge of amounts payable by the debtor or hirer or by a surety. Subsection (3) prohibits the taking of any negotiable instrument (including a cheque) as a security for an amount payable under such an agreement.[248] A person who takes an instrument in contravention of these provisions is unable to enforce it.[249]

Although the owner or creditor may take a cheque in payment of an amount due to him under a regulated agreement, he is not allowed to negotiate it except to a banker.[250] This provision seeks to preclude the negotiation of a cheque to an assignee of a regulated agreement, or to the finance company's nominee, who may purport to enforce the cheque notwithstanding disputes related to the underlying contract. The object of the saving is to enable the finance company to remit the cheque for collection to a bank. In effect, the use of the word 'negotiation' in this context is puzzling. It will be recalled that an instrument is negotiated when it is transferred to a holder, who becomes its new owner and acquires the right to enforce it.[251] This is not the object of the remittance of a cheque to a bank for collection. It would have been more consistent with the policy of the 1974 Act to prohibit negotiation altogether, but to sanction the transfer of a cheque to a bank for collection.

---

[246] The company usually relied on its position as holder in due course of the notes made by the hirer.

[247] Pp. 63–65 above. But note s. 123(5), making an exception in respect of 'non-commercial' agreements.

[248] As to when an instrument is considered to be taken as a security, see s. 123(4).

[249] S. 125(1).

[250] S. 123(2).

[251] P. 511 above.

In effect, the Consumer Credit Act 1974 has abolished the use of bills of exchange (other than cheques) and of promissory notes in regulated agreements.[252] Cheques may be used for the purpose of effecting payment, but not in lieu of bills or notes. Thus, the Act prohibits the use of post-dated cheques appearing to be issued on the dates on which instalments fall due and serving the purpose of securing payment thereof. The Act further protects consumers by prohibiting the transfer of cheques drawn by them except to a collecting bank.

---

[252] But note exemption respecting certain consumer hire agreements which have a connection with external trade: Consumer credit (Negotiable Instruments) (Exemption) Order 1984, SI 435.

CHAPTER 18

Securities for Bankers' Advances: The General Part

1. THE OBJECT SERVED BY AND THE CLASSIFICATION OF SECURITIES

(i) The object of securities

The granting of loans and the making of advances covered by a security over some of the debtor's assets is not an exclusive type of banking business. Building societies, finance houses and insurance companies are also engaged in it. The word 'security' itself is used in more than one sense. Thus, shares or debentures, which are often furnished by a borrower to a lender to secure a loan or an advance, are loosely called 'securities'. The word is even used to describe negotiable instruments issued to secure instalments due under a credit facility. In the strict sense, though, a 'security' is an interest which the debtor confers on the creditor in an item of property owned by himself or, by arrangement, in the property of some third party such as a surety. To be effective, the interest acquired by the creditor must confer on him a right to satisfy the debt out of the proceeds of the property in question. Guarantees and indemnities, which are also described as securities, are distinct arrangements under which a third party—the surety—agrees to assume liability if the debtor defaults or causes loss to the creditor. The former arrangement is a guarantee; the latter involves an indemnity.

The object of the security is, thus, to provide a source for the satisfaction of the debt covered by it. Usually, the terms of the agreement provide that the security may be realized whenever the debtor is in default.[1] Primarily, though, it is utilized when he is insolvent. Accordingly, the main object of a security is to protect the creditor against the debtor's bankruptcy or, where the debtor is a body corporate, in the event of its liquidation. Whilst a security becomes particularly attractive if it further protects the creditor against the debtor's fraud, this does not form a major object of the arrangement.[2]

---

[1] But see below, pp. 534–6, as regards the equity of redemption and pp. 536 et seq. as regards the effect of the Consumer Credit Act 1974.
[2] Cf. *Sanders Bros.* v. *Maclean & Co.* (1883) 11 QBD 327, 343 per Bowen LJ.

(ii) Classification of securities

Securities can be classified in two ways. One is based on the rights which the arrangement confers on the creditor. The other looks at the manner in which the security attaches itself to the designated property.

The first classification divides securities into proprietary securities and possessory securities. The former type encompasses all arrangements that confer on the creditor an ownership right in the relevant property. Such a right, which is also known as a special property or as a title to the goods, vests in the creditor the right to seize the goods if the debtor defaults or becomes insolvent, and to satisfy the debt from the proceeds of their sale. But during the currency of the arrangement—whilst the debtor pays the instalments due from him—the property is left in his possession. He is, therefore, able to utilize it. The mortgage, both over chattels and over real property, as well as a fixed and a floating charge granted by a corporation, falls into this group. It may be asked whether hire purchase agreements and long-term leases are, likewise, arrangements involving proprietary securities. Conceptually such arrangements differ from securities because the finance company, which lets the goods, has the general property (viz. the full ownership) of the chattels involved and not a mere security title or specific property.[3] Economically, though, the finance company obtains the title to the chattels in order to retain a security over them. When all the rentals or instalments are paid, the lessor acquires the title to them. This is expressly provided in a hire purchase agreement[4] and, in practice, is contemplated in some leases. The lessor is simply given the opportunity of acquiring the chattel concerned for its residual value.

Possessory securities, as indicated by their name, are based on the acquisition by the creditor of the possession of the chattel which serves as security. The classic example is the pledge, in which the creditor is given the custody of a chattel until the discharge of the debt by the debtor. Stocks and other marketable securities and documents of title, such as bills of lading, can also be the subject of a pledge. The pledge confers on the creditor a right to sell the chattel involved and to satisfy the debt from the proceeds.[5] The creditor's rights are therefore identical with those acquired by him under a proprietary security. In effect, the custody of the chattel gives him extra protection, as the debtor is unable to whisk the chattels away in breach of the arrangement. Another possessory security is the lien, which is of particular

---

[3] See the basic analysis in *Helby* v. *Matthews* [1895] AC 471.

[4] This is so regardless of whether the agreement is a genuine hire purchase agreement, in which the hirer is given an option to purchase the goods for an amount to be determined in accordance with a given formula, or a conditional sales agreement, in which the property passes to him automatically when all instalments have been paid.

[5] See pp. 570–1 below.

importance to bankers.[6] From the debtor's point of view, a possessory security carries a patent disadvantage. He does not enjoy the exclusive possession and, hence, the unrestricted right to use the chattel. However, it will be shown that, to a point, this difficulty is avoided by the release of the item covered by the possessory security to a third party or custodian, who holds it on behalf of the creditor but has the power to grant access to the debtor.[7]

In the case both of a proprietary and of a possessory security, the debtor has certain defences which save him from the effect of the harsh contractual terms pertaining to default in payment. First, he has the equity or redemption, which enables him to reinstate the contract and to regain the possession of the property, the subject of the security, if he pays arrears and interest before the items are disposed of by the creditor.[8] Secondly, the Consumer Credit Act 1974 protects the debtor or purchaser where the contract is a regulated agreement.[9]

The division of security devices into proprietary and possessory securities is not suitable in the case of securities over money or choses in action, such as contractual rights. The very concept of possession is inapplicable, and that of property is subject to substantial variations. There is thus no room for a pledge or a lien over a contractual right. A security over such an item is usually effected by means of an assignment, which may be an absolute one or by way of charge.[10] The assignment of an amount standing to the credit of a customer's bank account and the assignment of an insurance policy are examples in point.

The second classification of securities divides them into open-ended and closed-ended securities. An open-ended security is one that covers all or some of the property of the debtor for the time being. The classic example is the floating charge. It hovers over the corporate debtor's property without precluding the disposal of that property in the ordinary course of trade. Items so disposed of cease to be covered, but the charge hovers over property acquired after its creation. When the charge 'attaches'—upon the debtor's default—it becomes, in effect, a fixed charge covering the debtor's property as at that time. A banker's lien is similar in nature. It attaches to items, such as shares acquired by the customer, whilst they are in the bank's custody. Such securities are open ended, as the chattels or assets covered by them continue to change and, basically, are unaffected by the security unless the debtor is in default.

A closed-ended security is attached to a given chattel or item of real prop-

---

[6] See Pp. 576–9 below.
[7] Pp. 573–4 below.
[8] Pp. 534–6 below.
[9] Pp. 536–40 below.
[10] Note that an absolute assignment may be either equitable or statutory; an assignment by way of charge is an equitable assignment: pp. 582–3 below.

erty. A mortgage over land, a fixed charge given by a body corporate over a specific piece of machinery, and a pledge of given documents of title are illustrations in point. An assignment of a specific chose in action, such as a life policy, is also a closed-ended security. But an assignment by way of charge of a company's book debts resembles an open-ended security over chattels if it covers the debts outstanding from time to time. An absolute assignment of book debts, stipulating for their discharge to the assignee, is of course a close-ended security.

Of the two classifications of securities, their division into proprietary and possessory securities is more closely related to the legal nature of the arrangement involved. The classification of securities into the open-ended and the closed-ended types is based on economic factors. It is, therefore, preferable to adopt the former classification in a work like this. Accordingly, Chapter 19 deals with proprietary securities and Chapter 20 with possessory securities. Securities over choses in action are discussed in Chapter 21. There are, however, four problems which are of importance in respect of all security arrangements. The first is the effect of a valid security in the debtor's insolvency; the second concerns the creditor's protection against bona fide purchasers of the chattels, the subject of the security; the third is the effect of the equity of redemption; and the fourth concerns the relevant provisions of the Consumer Credit Act 1974.

2. THE EFFECT OF VALID SECURITY IN INSOLVENCY

When a private individual or an unincorporated business, such as a partnership, becomes insolvent, the position is governed by the Insolvency Act 1986.[11] The bankrupt's estate, or property, is vested in the trustee in bankruptcy,[12] who realizes it for the purpose of dividing the proceeds among the creditors. The bankrupt's debts are, for this purpose, divided into three groups: preferential claims, claims of the general creditors, and deferred claims. The preferential claims, which include debts due to the Inland Revenue department, debts respecting rates, and wages payable to employees for the four months immediately preceding the receiving order, are paid in priority to all other claims.[13] The balance of the amount recovered by the trustee from the realization of the bankrupt's assets is

[11] Until recently the position was governed by the Bankruptcy Act 1914. This Act was repealed and replaced by the Insolvency Act 1985 which, in turn was repealed and replaced by the 1986 Act. For the sake of clarity, and to assist readers familiar with the old system, it has been thought advisable to refer in some cases not only to the current provision but also to the section of the 1914 Act replaced in 1986.

[12] Insolvency Act 1986, s. 306, derived from the Bankruptcy Act 1914, s. 18.

[13] Insolvency Act 1986, ss. 328, 386, and Sched. 6 (and see the Bankruptcy Act 1914, s. 33). As regards corporations, see the 1986 Act, s. 175.

divided on a pro rata basis among his general creditors.[14] Obviously, not all the assets are necessarily utilized at one and the same time. Once the preferential claims have been settled, a dividend payable to the general creditors is declared whenever the trustee acquires sufficient funds for making meaningful payments.[15] Any balance left after the general creditors have been satisfied is used to satisfy certain deferred claims.

Most trade creditors are general creditors. So are an insolvent bank's customers, in respect of money standing to the credit of their accounts.[16] Similarly, a bank is a general creditor in respect of any unsecured overdraft or loan granted to a defaulting customer. It is obvious that any creditor who falls within the group of a bankrupt's general creditors stands to incur a substantial loss. If the debtor were able to discharge his running debts, he would not be forced into bankruptcy!

The object of a security is to enable the creditor to recover the debt due to him in priority to the general creditors. The security cannot constitute his claim a preferential one, as the list of such claims is exhaustively set out in the Act. The object of the security is to arrange that some property—be it real property, chattels, or choses in action—be utilized in the debtor's insolvency to satisfy the secured creditor's claim in priority to those of the general creditors. If the proceeds of the security exceed the amount of the debt, the balance is paid over to the trustee in bankruptcy, and forms part of the general assets or 'the estate' of the bankrupt. If the proceeds are less than the amount due, the secured creditor can prove for the deficiency as a general creditor.[17] The secured creditor's position depends, therefore, both on the validity of his security and on the adequacy of the value of the property covered by it. Frequently, the validity of a security is subject to the observance of certain formalities. Thus, certain charges granted by a company are invalid against the liquidator unless registered.[18]

The principles of the law of bankruptcy concerning the rights of creditors, which have just been discussed, apply with certain modifications to the winding-up of companies.[19] However, it will be shown that in some regards securities furnished by bodies corporate are governed by principles

---

[14] Insolvency Act 1986, s. 328(3) (and see the Bankruptcy Act 1914, s. 62(1)).

[15] Insolvency Act 1986, s. 324; and see as regards winding-up, ibid., s. 168(4).

[16] The point has been clear since the decision of the House of Lords in *Foley* v. *Hill* (1848) 2 HLC 28, in which the relationship of banker and customer was defined as one of creditor and debtor.

[17] Insolvency Act 1986, s. 269 (cf. Bankruptcy Act 1914, s. 7(2), Sched. 2, r. 10).

[18] Pp. 559–61.

[19] Under the earlier regime, the relevant provisions of the Bankruptcy Act 1914 were applied to the winding-up of corporations by s. 317 of the Companies Act 1948 (which was replaced by s. 612 of the Companies Act 1985). The Insolvency Act 1986 repealed this provision; at present the similarity in the provisions of the winding-up of companies and the bankruptcy of individuals is a direct outcome of the fact that the two procedures have been brought under the umbrella of one codification, viz. the Insolvency Act 1986.

differing to a certain extent from those applicable to securities provided by individuals and by unincorporated business firms. Thus, a body corporate can grant a security over after-acquired property, whilst other debtors' securities attach only to property which is in existence at the time of the arrangement.[20]

Both proprietary securities and possessory securities give an adequate protection to the creditor against the debtor's insolvency. Possessory securities, though, have the added advantage of protecting the creditor against any unauthorized dispositions by the debtor. This result is due to practical rather than conceptual reasons. Thus, if the creditor acquires a security by way of pledge, the debtor is no longer able to dispose of the property, as it is no longer in his possession. The debtor regains the ability to make dispositions of the pledged property if the creditor relinquishes his possession. But in such a case the pledge is usually destroyed.[21]

The position is less certain in the case of proprietary securities. Some of them do not aim at protecting the creditor against dispositions of the debtor's property to third parties. Thus, the floating charge, which hovers over all the company's assets, envisages that dealings in the company's ordinary trade will continue as before. Accordingly, the company may sell property owned by it, and the purchaser acquires a good title although he is aware of the existence of the charge.[22] The assumption is that the charge will hover over the proceeds. The question is discussed separately in respect of the various proprietary securities covered.

3. THE RIGHT OF REDEMPTION

The right of redemption is a principle developed in regard to mortgages over land. Its basic tenet is simple. The debtor (mortgagor) is entitled to redeem or free his property from the mortgage by repaying the amount due at the time of discharge.[23] The right remains in effect throughout the currency of the agreement and is available even where the date of an instalment has passed[24] and despite the fact that valid steps have been taken to put the mortgaged property up for sale.[25] The right of redemption cannot be excluded by agreement. A clause to this effect is considered a clog on the

[20] Pp. 551–2 below.
[21] Pp. 568–9 below.
[22] P. 558 below.
[23] *Fairclough* v. *Swan Brewery Co. Ltd.* [1912] AC 565; *Krelinger* v. *New Patagonia Meat and Cold Storage Co. Ltd.* [1914] AC 25, 48.
[24] *Re Moss; Levy* v. *Sewill* (1887) 31 Ch. D 90; *Cromwell Property Investment Co. Ltd.* v. *Western & Toovey* [1934] Ch. 322.
[25] See, for a general analysis, *Duke* v. *Robson* [1973] 1 WLR 267.

equity of redemption and is void.[26] The parties may, however, agree that the right should not be exercisable for a given period during the currency of the agreement. [27] The right is effectively lost only when the mortgaged property has been sold by the mortgagee upon the debtor's default.[28]

The person primarily entitled to exercise the right of redemption is the debtor (mortgagor). But other parties who have an interest in the property mortgaged are also entitled to exercise it. Persons encompassed in this group are a second mortgagee[29] who, on exercising the right, steps into the first mortgagee's shoes, a surety or guarantor of the debt,[30] or even the mortgagor's tenant who wishes to remain in occupation.[31] Any attempt to restrict the right of redemption to the mortgagor or other given parties is treated as a clog on the equity.[32] A party that exercises the right must, however, redeem the property in full.[33]

Redemption is effected by means of a notice served on the mortgagee. Where the mortgage is for a fixed term, the mortgagee must, if the contract so provides, be given adequate time to make alternative arrangements for the investment of his money.[34] If the mortgagee is not given adequate notice, the debtor may have to pay interest for the period involved. Notice is not required where the mortgagee has taken possession of the property, has made a demand for payment in full, or has instituted proceedings to realize the security.[35] Similarly, the debtor can of course repay without notice any debt payable on demand—such as an overdraft—and thereupon redeem any security.[36]

Traditionally, the right of redemption has been applicable in the case of mortgages and charges over property. It is equally available in respect of other types of proprietary securities.[37] It has also been applied in the case of

---

[26] *Noakes & Co. Ltd.* v. *Rice* [1902] AC 24, 30. And see *Samuel* v. *Jarrah Timber and Wood Paving Corporation* [1904] AC 323 (reservation by mortgagee of right to purchase held a clog); except in the case of a debenture issued by a company: Companies Act 1985, s. 193. But note that the mortgagor can sell his equity of redemption to the mortgagee in a transaction subsequent to the arrangement of the loan: *Reeve* v. *Lisle* [1902] AC 461.

[27] *Teevan* v. *Smith* (1882) 20 Ch. D 724, 729; *Williams* v. *Morgan* [1906] 1 Ch. 804 (postponement for 14 years held valid); *Knightsbridge Estates Trust Ltd.* v. *Byrne* [1939] Ch. 441. But in certain cases, a postponement for a long time, such as 28 years, may be regarded unreasonable: *Morgan* v. *Jeffreys* [1910] 1 Ch. 620.

[28] See, generally, *Halsbury's Laws of England*, 4th edn., vol. 32, paras. 407, 603–4.

[29] *Smith* v. *Green* (1844) 1 Coll. 555, 563; *Pearce* v. *Morris* (1869) LR 5 Ch. App. 227.

[30] By operation of the doctrine of subrogation; p. 526 above.

[31] *Tarn* v. *Turner* (1888) 39 Ch. D 456.

[32] *Salt* v. *Marquess of Northampton* [1892] AC 1.

[33] *Hall* v. *Heward* (1886) 32 Ch. D 430.

[34] *Cromwell Property Investment Co. Ltd.* v. *Western & Toovey* [1934] Ch. 322 (six months usually).

[35] *Bovill* v. *Endle* [1896] 1 Ch. 648.

[36] See, as regards a temporary loan, *Fitzgerald's Trustee* v. *Mellersh* [1892] 1 Ch. 385.

[37] See, e.g., *Salt* v. *Marquess of Northampton* [1829] 1 AC 1, where an assured was allowed to redeem a life policy assigned by him for security.

some possessory securities, such as the classic pledge.[38] In the case of other security arrangements, such as regulated hire agreement, similar rights are conferred by statute.[39] These rights are of major importance, as they mitigate the harshness that can otherwise manifest itself in agreements providing for security.

4. EFFECT OF THE CONSUMER CREDIT ACT 1974

(i)　*Basic terms and structure of part of the Act*

Part 8 of the Consumer Credit Act 1974 (ss. 105–126) makes provisions concerning securities. The relevant sections are not drafted specifically with a view to affecting the relationship of banker and customer, but they have a considerable impact on securities taken by banks with respect to regulated consumer credit agreements.[40] The main object of the Act is to confer certain protections on a surety. It is necessary to review the relevant basic definitions of the Act and the provisions in point, and to consider the impact of Part 8 on banking practice.

The fundamental term—'security'—is broadly defined, encompassing a mortgage, a charge, a pledge, a bond, a debenture, an indemnity and a guarantee, a bill or note, and any other right provided by the debtor, or at his express or implied request by another person, to secure the performance of the agreement involved.[41] The Act therefore applies both to securities furnished by the debtor and to those provided at his request by a surety. It thus affects the traditional forms of proprietary securities taken by banks such as charges over land, shares, insurance policies, and bank balances and also extends to guarantees and indemnities.

The provisions of the Act apply not only to securities given in respect of concluded agreements but also to securities meant to cover prospective agreements of the type covered.[42] But in the latter case, the security becomes subject to the main provisions of Part 8[43] at the time the agreement is concluded. Up to then, the security is unenforceable.[44] Furthermore, up to that time the person who furnishes the security may, by serving notice on the creditor, invalidate the security under section 106. In practice, these provisions do not pose serious problems to banks. If the main agreement, such

---

[38] See p. 570 below.
[39] Pp. 68–69 above.
[40] For the definition of which, see pp. 63–65 above.
[41] S. 189(1).
[42] Idem.
[43] Except s. 113(6).
[44] Idem.

as the contract for a loan, is not executed, the bank does not require the security. If the surety exercises his right of withdrawal before the conclusion of the underlying contract, the bank in turn is entitled to refuse to extend the credit involved.

The Act defines two other basic terms. First, under section 105(2) a 'security instrument' is defined as a document made in writing in conformity with the provisions of section 105(1). As the latter provision is excluded in respect of securities furnished by the debtor,[45] it would appear that a document executed by him is not a 'security instrument'. In this way, the Act distinguishes between a security granted by the debtor and a security effected by a third party. It will be shown that, in some respects, the Act applies different regimes to the two types of arrangement. Banks, of course, take securities of both types.

The second central definition is that of a surety. He is defined so as to include the debtor if he furnishes a security, any third party who provides it, and any 'person to whom [the maker's] rights and duties in relation to the security have passed by operation of law'.[46] The last branch of the definition is of importance where a third party is subrogated to the original surety's rights. A bank that pays a customer's debts may occasionally be in such a position.

The Act introduces four measures aimed at regulating the taking of securities issued in respect of regulated agreements. First, it makes provisions concerning the form and contents of securities (s. 105). A security which is not properly executed is enforceable only on a court order.[47] If such an order is not granted, the security is avoided by section 106, and the surety is entitled to be repaid any amount advanced by him. It will be shown that these provisions have an impact on banking practice. Secondly, it is provided that specified information be furnished to sureties (ss. 107–11). These provisions impose certain cumbersome duties on banks but, in reality, do not pose serious obstacles to the ordinary functioning of the banking world. Thirdly, regulations could be made under section 112 of the Act for the purpose of governing the realization of securities. But no such regulations have been made to date, and it is questionable if any action would be taken.[48] The possibility, though, ought to be borne in mind. Fourthly, section 113(1) precludes the use of a security for the purpose of evading any provisions of the Act applicable to regulated agreements. To this end, a security may not be enforced so as to benefit the creditor to an extent greater

---

[45] S. 105(6).
[46] S. 189(1).
[47] S. 105(7).
[48] On 20 July 1982, the Minister for Consumer Credit announced that he had decided for the present not to make regulations under this section; Guest and Lloyd, *Encylopaedia of Consumer Credit Law*, para. 2–113.

than would be the case if the security were not provided. Furthermore, if the agreement itself is enforceable only on the order of a court or of the Director, the security is also subject thereto.[49] This provision has a considerable impact on certain types of guarantees and indemnities furnished to banks, which include clauses to the effect that the security remains valid even it the main agreement is avoided.

All the provisions which have just been mentioned, and which are applicable to all securities, are discussed in the following section. Special provisions applicable to pledges and replacing the Pawnbrokers Acts 1872–1960 are discussed in Chapter 20.

(ii) Form of the security instrument

Under section 105(2)–(3), regulations may be made in order to prescribe the form and content of security instruments. In particular, the regulations may prescribe the information to be included in the documents and the manner in which it is to be set out. But the only regulations made so far under this provision affect guarantees and indemnities,[50] and it is unlikely that any further regulations will be made. There is certainly no need for such regulations in so far as securities effected by the debtor are concerned. The terms of such securities have to be included in the document setting out the terms of the regulated agreement,[51] and are accordingly governed by regulations pertaining to the latter document.[52]

Section 105(4) lays down a number of requisites concerning the 'proper execution' of a security instrument. To start with, the document, which needs to embody[53] all the express terms of the security, has to be signed by or on behalf of the surety. When presented for signature, the document must be in 'in such a state that its terms are readily legible'. Obviously, a document with print that is too small to be read comfortably militates against this provision. Furthermore, when the document is presented to the surety for execution, or sent to him for this purpose, he must be furnished with a copy.[54] These provisions have an undesirable effect on banking practice.

---

[49] S. 113(2). The cancellation or termination of the main agreement usually renders the security ineffective: s. 113(2). But note exceptions in subss. (4)–(5) and extension of provision to indemnities: sub s. (7). And note that, undersub s. (3), a security is avoided under s. 106 if it is declared unenforceable by the court.

[50] Consumer Credit (Guarantees and Indemnities) Regulations 1983, SI 1556.

[51] Consumer Credit Act 1974, s. 105(9).

[52] The Consumer Credit (Agreements) Regulations 1983, SI 1553, discussed above, pp. 66–68 and Chap. 16.

[53] And see comparable provisions where the security instrument is executed either before or after the execution of the regulated agreement: s. 105(5).

[54] But note that under s. 189(4) a document 'embodies' a provision either if this provision is set out in it, or if it is set out in a document referred to in the main documents.

They militate against some of the informal arrangements developed by banks, such as securities affected by means of the mere deposit of title deeds or of commercial paper.

A security agreement that does not comply with the provisions of section 105 is treated as having never been effected.[55] Property lodged with the creditor has, thereupon, to be returned by him forthwith. He is, further, required to repay any amounts received in the realisation of the security.[56]

(iii) Information to be supplied by the creditor

As in the case of other types of agreement covered by the 1974 Act,[57] a creditor is required to supply information on request. The Act draws a distinction in this regard between securities provided for the different types of credit agreements—namely, agreements for fixed-sum credit (section 107)—agreements for running account credit (s. 108), and consumer hire agreements (s. 109). Basically, the creditor is required to supply to the surety a copy of the regulated agreement and the security instrument, and a financial statement which, inter alia, has to disclose the amounts payable under the regulated agreement.[58] If the creditor fails to comply with a request for information, he is unable to enforce the security during the period of his default.[59] The information required by the surety has to be supplied by the creditor within twelve working days.[60] The creditor is, further, under a duty to supply on request a copy of the security instrument to the debtor.[61]

The creditor is also under a duty to serve on the surety a copy of any default notice served on the debtor.[62] If the creditor fails to comply with this requirement, the security is enforceable on a court order only.[63] However, no time is prescribed for the services of such a document on the surety. In

---

[55] Consumer Credit Act 1974, s. 106. But a court may order that the security be enforceable against the surety: s. 105(7). And see the savings in s. 177 for registered charges over land; p. 550 below.

[56] He is also required to remove or cancel from the relevant register any entries of the charges or mortgage created by the security.

[57] Pp. 67–68 above.

[58] Consumer Credit Act 1974, ss. 107(1)(*c*); 108(1)(*c*); 109(1)(*c*). For forms used, see Guest and Lloyd, *Encyclopaedia of Consumer Credit Law*, paras 8-267–8-269.

[59] Ibid., ss. 107(4), 108(4), 109(4).

[60] Consumer Credit (Prescribed Periods for Giving Information) Regulations 1983, SI 1569, reg. 2 and Sched. And see some special provisions applicable in the case of a variation of a security: Consumer Credit (Cancellation Notices and Copies of Documents) Regulations 1983, SI 1557, reg. 7.

[61] Consumer Credit Act 1974, s. 110. The period within which this request has to be met and the consequences of failure to comply with it are the same as in the case of the other provisions.

[62] Consumer Credit Act 1974, s. 111(1); as regards default notices served under ss. 76(1) and 98(1), see pp. 68–69 above.

[63] Ibid., s. 111(2).

particular, it is not expressly stated that the creditor has to dispatch the copy at the time the original is served on the debtor, although the section is generally construed in this way.

The requirements of providing information related to securities and of providing copies and of serving default notices generate a great deal of work for the banks. But the provisions in point would not appear to have made a major impact on any substantive aspect of banking practice.

(iv) Realization of security

As no regulations have been made under section 112,[64] the position is governed by the Bills of Sale (1878) Amendment Act 1882, as amended by the Consumer Credit Act 1974.[65] Banks, however, are strongly disinclined to take securities by way of bills of sale. The problems concerning the realization of the typical securities used by banks, such as charges or mortgages over land, are discussed where relevant.

(v) Anti-evasion provision

Section 113 of the 1974 Act seeks to combat the evasion of the provisions of the Act by the use of security devices. The basic rule is that 'the security shall not be enforced so as to benefit the creditor . . . directly or indirectly, to an extent greater (whether as respects of the amount of any payment or the time or manner of its being made) than would be the case if the security were not provided'.[66] Specific applications of this principle are that, where the regulated agreement is improperly executed, the security is enforceable on a court order only[67] and that, where the contract itself is cancelled, the security is rendered ineffective.[68] It is clear that banks have to be wary of this provision: obviously security arrangements cannot readily be utilized to escape the mandatory provisions of the Act, seeking to protect the debtor and his backers.

---

[64] See note 48 to this chapter.
[65] Consumer Credit Act, Sched. 4, Pt. 1 para. 1, which inserts a new section 7A in the 1882 Act.
[66] Consumer Credit Act 1974, s. 113(1).
[67] Ibid. s. 113(2); and see s. 113(3)(c).
[68] Ibid., s. 113(3).

CHAPTER 19

Proprietary Securities

1. SCOPE

The general principles common to all security arrangements were discussed in the previous chapter. The present chapter deals with proprietary securities over both land and other corporeal property. Banks, of course, make use of all security devices available to financiers generally. Thus, the mortgage over land is used by banks just as it is employed by building societies and by other financiers. Similarly, the floating charge and fixed charges over chattels are in general use by financial institutions. The object of the discussion of these arrangements in this book is to review their salient points and to highlight elements relevant to banking law. Naturally, a detailed review of the mortgage over land or of corporate securities is outside the scope of this book.

A specific problem that arises from the classification of securities in this book is that different arrangements concerning a given type of property occasionally have to be covered in separate chapters. Thus, the hypothecation of goods and the chattel mortgage, which are proprietary securities, are discussed in this chapter. The pledge over goods and over documents of title falls within the scope of Chapter 20, devoted to possessory securities. Security arrangements over choses in action, such as bank balances and life policies, fall into yet a different class, and are discussed in Chapter 21.

It will be recalled that, in practical terms, the common thread of proprietary securities is that the debtor or surety retains the possession and use of the subject matter. Conceptually, all securities of this class are arranged on the basis of conferring on the creditor some specific rights in the land or the goods. Although the exact nature of the rights so acquired by him may differ from arrangement to arrangement, in all cases the creditor will be able to satisfy the debt from the proceeds of the sale of the property in priority to other creditors.

The security arrangements covered in this chapter are the mortgage over land, chattel mortgages, hypothecation of goods, and fixed and floating charges granted by corporate borrowers.

2. MORTGAGES OVER LAND

(i) Freehold and leasehold: unregistered and registered land

In its technical sense, the word 'land' means the ground itself, any buildings erected on it, and any chattels affixed to it. A mortgage over land attaches to everything that forms part of the property in this sense. The mortgagor may have a freehold or a leasehold in the land. This distinction can be traced back to the land tenure system of feudal times. Today, the holder of a freehold has a perpetual interest in the land, while the holder of a leasehold has rights which technically are for a period of time, though that time may be very long, for instance 999 years. From a practical point of view the difference may not be very great. Thus a leaseholder can assign his interest and grant a sub-lease over it, and in this way a mortgage can be granted over a leasehold as well as over a freehold, although some technical distinctions have to be noted.

Rights in freehold and in leasehold may exist in law and in equity. A legal estate in fee simple gives the owner full rights to deal with the property. An equitable interest will give lesser rights, for instance for life only. In some cases the equitable interest may be created by a contract in which the owner undertakes to convey his title or to mortgage it. An equitable interest is generally as enforceable as a legal estate, though compliance with some statutory requirements for protection may be necessary.

The division into legal estates and equitable interests is based on the Law of Property Act 1925. As a result of section 1, only two estates may exist at law, the fee simple and a lease. But some other rights may also exist at law. The one here relevant is the charge over land by way of legal mortgage. In commercial transactions the practice is to mortgage the legal estate, if available. A deed is then needed.

When a bank is prepared to grant a secured loan to a customer, it has to satisfy itself that he is legally in a position to grant a mortgage over the relevant property. To this end, the bank conducts a search into the title. The procedure depends on whether the land involved is in an area covered by the land registration system or by the older system, based on deeds.

In the case of unregistered land, the bank first arranges for a search of the deeds concerning the property. These are usually held by the freeholder or leaseholder, except that, if the land is already subject to a mortgage, the deeds may be in the mortgagee's custody. In addition to the deeds, the bank has to arrange for a search of the register kept under the Land Charges Act 1972, which will bring to light details about interests and rights adverse to those of the owner and not disclosed by the deeds. In this way question marks may be raised for the bank. If the debtor is a body corporate, the bank will further search in the register kept under the Companies Act 1985.[1] It is also important to search the register of local land charges, kept under the Land Charges Act 1925, in which councils record certain liabilities, for instance in respect of road charges.

To simplify conveyancing, a system of registered land was promoted under the Land Registration Act 1925. It will in due course replace the protection of title through deeds by the making of entries in official registers of titles to land. These entries obviate the need of tracing the history of the title, but the existence of ordinary rights means that it is still sometimes necessary to look beyond the register itself. This new system presently covers the main urban areas in England and Wales, but will be extended to the rest of these countries by the end of the century.

(ii) Legal and equitable mortgages and equitable charges

Legal and equitable mortgages can be granted over legal estates. Only equitable mortgages can be granted over equitable interests. A lender requiring security may in addition be satisfied in certain circumstances, such as in relation to a bridging loan or a short-term loan, with an equitable charge, which provides him with some but not all the protections furnished by a mortgage.[2]

The form of a legal mortgage may be either the creation in the mortgagee of a lease for a term of years or the creation of a mortgage by way of legal charge.[3] The mortgage by way of legal charge is an innovation of the Property Law Act 1925.[4] It confers on the mortgagee the same rights, protection and remedies as a mortgage by way of lease. Thus, there are two ways of achieving the same object. Where, however, the mortgage is over leasehold property, the mortgage by lease cannot be granted if the mortgagor's leasehold includes a covenant prohibiting any sub-leases.[5] A mortgage by way of legal charge, which does not expressly grant the mortgagee such an interest, is unaffected by such a covenant or by a covenant prohibiting assignments.[6]

In the case of leasehold the mortgage assumes the form of a sub-lease, granted for a period shorter by at least one day than the period of the mortgagor's lease.[7] Usually, the term is a few days shorter than that; the object is

[1] See pp. 559–60 below.
[2] R. E. Megarry and H. W. R. Wade, *Law of Real Property*, 5th edn., London, 1984, pp. 929, 953.
[3] Law of Property Act 1925, s. 87(1); Land Registration Act 1925, ss. 25(1), 27(1).
[4] Megarry and Wade, *Law of Real Property*, 5th edn., pp. 915–25.
[5] Although the landlord's consent may not be unreasonably withheld: Law of Property Act 1925, s. 86(1); Landlord and Tenant Act 1927, s. 19.
[6] *Grand Junction Canal Co.* v. *Bates* [1954] 2 QB 160. But note that the creation of a mortgage may be precluded if the restrictive covenant forbids the creation of 'charges'.
[7] Law of Property Act 1925, s. 86(1).

to make room for subsequent mortgages which, in practice, are made for a term slightly longer than the first mortgage so as to facilitate realization if required.

An equitable mortgage operates not by way of the grant of a lease but by an assignment by the mortgagee of his equitable interest therein, subject to a provision for reassignment on redemption. Very frequently, however, an equitable mortgage will arise in relation to a legal estate through an agreement for the grant of a legal mortgage. This is available both in the case of registered and unregistered land.

In practical terms, this form of an equitable mortgage over a legal estate may well be as effective as a legal one. This is so because a court of equity will compel the mortgagor to execute the legal mortgage provided the loan secured by it has been advanced.[8] The equitable mortgage can also be made secure against third parties. A third party who has obtained the land gratuitously is in no better position than the mortgagor. As against a third party who has given value, the equitable mortgagee can protect himself by registration.[9]

Unlike a legal mortgage, which needs to be created by deed, an equitable mortgage of this variety can be made by a contract in writing.[10] In practice, equitable mortgages obtained by banks are executed on a standard form. Such mortgages are used mainly to secure short term loans.

Mortgagees may take possession of title deeds or of the certificate of title under the land registration system. But mortgagees may also protect their position by causing an entry to be made in the appropriate register. Retaining the mortgagor's title deeds is, however, an effective protection in many cases, for without inspecting these a later mortgagee cannot obtain priority. The two methods of protection are equally applicable to equitable mortgages.

(iii) Remedies[11]

A distinction exists between a legal and an equitable mortgage in relation to the mortgagee's remedies. Upon the mortgagor's default, a legal mortgagee has five effective remedies. First, he may bring an action to enforce the debt and, thereupon, acquires all the rights of a judgment creditor. Secondly, as mortgagee under a deed, he has the right to sell the property either by public auction or under a private contract.[12] An order of a court is not a prerequi-

[8] Fry, *Specific Performance*, 6th edn., pp. 24–5; Megarry and Wade, *Law of Real Property*, 5th edn., pp. 926–9.
[9] Megarry and Wade, *Law of Real Property*, 5th edn., p. 175.
[10] Law of Property Act 1925, s. 40(1).
[11] See, generally, Megarry and Wade, *Law of Real Property*, 5th edn., pp. 931 et seq.
[12] Law of Property Act 1925, s. 101(1), (4).

site. In practice, the bank demands immediate repayment and warns the mortgagor that, if he fails to comply, the property will be put up for sale.[13] Thirdly, the mortgagee has the power to appoint a receiver of the property.[14] This remedy is available in the same circumstances as the power to sell. The appointment of a receiver is useful where a property is subject to a lease, so that a purchaser cannot take vacant possession. The receiver is entitled to claim the income derived from the property,[15] and is also in a position to lease the property and to obtain the surrender of a lease.[16] Fourthly, the mortgagee may ask for foreclosure,[17] which has the effect of vesting in him the mortgagor's title regardless of any difference between the balance of the debt and the value of the property. Foreclosure, though, is available only by a court order, and is rarely granted. Where the value of the property materially exceeds the amount due, the court usually exercises its power to direct a sale in lieu of foreclosure.[18] Finally, the mortgagee is in theory entitled to take possession of the land. But this right is rarely exercised.[19]

The position of an equitable mortgagee depends on whether his mortgage is created by deed or otherwise. In the latter case, he has the right to sue for the debt and the right to seek foreclosure. But the right to sell the property or to appoint a receiver are not exercisable by him. This problem is overcome if the equitable mortgage is created by deed.[20] Thus, to acquire these remedies an equitable mortgagee has to demand that the mortgagor honour his contract to execute a legal mortgage. If the mortgagor refuses to comply, the equitable mortgagee has to apply to the court for an order vesting in him a title equal to that of a legal mortgagee.[21] The mortgagee's rights are, then, the same as those of a legal mortgagee. The only remaining difficulty is that an equitable mortgagee is unable to convey a legal estate to a purchaser. Banks surmount this difficulty by including in their standard forms an irrevocable power of attorney, which gives them the right to convey the land regardless of the mortgagor's death or bankruptcy or, in the case of a body corporate, its winding-up.[22]

---

[13] Usually by auction: *Cuckmere Brick Co. Ltd.* v. *Mutual Finance Ltd.* [1971] Ch. 949.

[14] Law of Property Act 1925, ss. 101(1), 109(1).

[15] Ibid., s. 109(3).

[16] Ibid., s. 99(19).

[17] Ibid., ss. 88(2), 89(1).

[18] Ibid., s. 91(2).

[19] For the reason see *White* v. *City of London Brewery Co.* (1889) 42 Ch. D 237.

[20] But no equitable mortgagee is entitled to take possession without a court order: *Barclays Bank Ltd.* v. *Bird* [1954] Ch. 274, 280. Contrast H. W. R. Wade, 'An Equitable Mortgagee's Right to Possession', (1955) 71 LQR 204.

[21] Law of Property Act 1925, s. 90(1).

[22] For the validity of the undertaking, see Power of Attorney Act 1971, s. 4(1).

(iv) Second mortgages

A second mortgage is an additional encumbrance on the mortgagor's title, effected in order to secure an additional advance on the security of the property. The second mortgagee acquires a title that takes priority after the first mortgagee's. For this reason, banks prefer to lend on first mortgage. Sometimes, however, they take a second mortgage, provided it is clear that the value of the land substantially exceeds the amount covered by the first mortgage.

The form of a second mortgage is similar to that of a first mortgage. It will, however, be for a period longer by one day than the period of the first mortgage. Banks that take out a second mortgage tend to insist that it be a legal one. As the second mortgagee is frequently unable to obtain the deeds, which will probably be held by the first mortgagee, it is essential that he register his interest.[23]

When the second mortgage is created, the second mortgagee should notify the first mortgagee. The first mortgagee is then under an obligation to hand the title deeds over to the second mortgagee when the first mortgage is discharged. The second mortgagee should also ask the first mortgagee to state the amount due to him, and to confirm that he is not under a duty to make further advances to the mortgagor. If such further advances are called for under the first mortgage, they will rank in priority to the second mortgage. If it is confirmed that no such obligation is imposed on the first mortgagee, then the debt covered by the second mortgage ranks above advances made by the first mortgagee after he receives the second mortgagee's notification.[24]

The remedies of the second mortgagee are similar to those of the first mortgagee. In particular, he is entitled to arrange for the sale of the property upon the mortgagor's default.[25] He can resort to this remedy without obtaining the consent of the first mortgagee. However, the property is then sold subject to the first mortgage. Usually, therefore, the second mortgagee persuades the first mortgagee to obtain repayment on the same occasion. If the first mortgagee withholds his consent, he may be compelled to join in.[26] In effect, the second mortgagee has the power to redeem the property from the first mortgage.

A second mortgage has to be distinguished from a sub-mortgage.[27] In a sub-mortgage the mortgagee passes rights to a third party in respect of those

---

[23] Megarry and Wade, *Law of Real Property*, 5th edn., p. 920; Land Charges Act 1972, s. 2(4); Land Registration Act 1925, ss. 48–9.

[24] Law of Property Act 1925, s. 94(1).

[25] Law of Property Act 1925, s. 101(1),(4).

[26] Ibid., s. 50.

[27] Megarry and Wade, *Law of Real Property*, 5th edn., p. 984.

contained in the main mortgage. The sub-mortgage is, therefore, similar to a transfer of the mortgagee's rights. Usually, the sub-mortgage assumes the form of an equitable assignment by way of charge of the mortgagee's rights to another financier. There are also cases in which a company, engaged in lending on mortgages, gives a bank a floating charge over its assets. If this charge crystallizes, it attaches also to the mortgages held by the company.

(v) Priorities

The problem of priorities arises where a number of mortgagees who have extended to the mortgagor loans totalling more than the present value of the property, and who have not made an agreement as to the ranking of their claims, seek to satisfy their demands from the proceeds of the land. Priority is determined by a variety of factors, principally involving the possession of the deeds pertaining to the property and by the chronological order of the registration of the charges.[28]

Many land mortgages granted by customers to their banks cover overdrafts, and in this context a particular problem of priorities arises. The revolving nature of the overdraft, which provides for advances to be made from time to time up to a given ceiling, means that some of the advances may be extended to the customer after he has executed an additional security over his land. Under the general principle, embodied in section 198(1) of the Law of Property Act 1925, the bank would be deemed to have notice of such a mortgage upon its registration. But this rule, by virtue of section 94(2), does not apply in respect of mortgages securing a current account or providing for 'further advances'. In such cases the mortgagee is not deemed to have knowledge of a competing mortgage by reasons only of its registration, even though the further advance has taken place after the time of the creation of his own mortgage or of his last search. His position is further protected by the third branch of section 94(1), under which the advances made under the mortgage securing the current account attain priority if made without knowledge of the existence of the second mortgage.

Ordinarily in cases of this type the second mortgagee attempts to secure his own position by giving notice of his security to the bank. There are two methods, based on section 94(1), in which the first mortgagee, or bank, can safeguard his interests in such a case. First, his further advances rank in priority if he enters into a suitable agreement with the competing mortgagees. In practice, this agreement is not as hard to obtain as may be imagined at first glance. By refusing to make further advances, or to allow further drawings under the facility, the bank can bring the customer's

---

[28] See, generally, ibid., pp. 986 et seq.

enterprise to a standstill. The second mortgagee, whose position is then subordinate to the bank's, is likely to sustain a substantial loss; his only option
is to yield to the bank's demands. The second situation in which the bank's
priority would be unaffected by its notice of the second mortgage is where
the agreement with the customer obliged it to make the further advances.
Usually, however, banks refrain from giving express promises to this effect.
Where there is no such undertaking, the bank's reference in the overdraft
agreement to the making of advances from time to time does not give it a
priority over second mortgages of which it is given notice.[29]

When notice of a second mortgage is received, the bank faces the hazard
based on the rule in *Clayton's Case*.[30] Any amounts paid by the customer to
the credit of the current account reduces the portion of the balance which
ranks above a second mortgage of which the bank has notice. In this way,
any credit entry made thereafter in the current account dissipates the value
of the bank's security. The best advice that can be given to the bank is to
'rule off' the mortgagor's account and open a new account for his current
operations.

The problem of priorities as between the bank and a second mortgagee
does not usually arise where the security is granted to the bank in respect of
a loan extended to the customer. In the ordinary course such an arrangement does not contemplate the making of future advances. But is the bank
entitled to refuse to honour cheques drawn on the customer's current
account, which has an adequate credit balance, if, without the bank's consent, he has granted a second mortgage over the land securing his borrowings from the bank? Most loan and mortgage agreements, executed on
standard forms current in banking, prohibit the execution of a second mortgage without the bank's consent. It has been argued that a breach of this
condition entitles the bank to combine the loan account with the credit
balance of the current account.[31] But if the value of the mortgaged property
is adequate to cover the debt due to the bank, it is unlikely that such a
course will be adopted.

(vi) Common clauses

To give themselves maximum protection, banks include a number of provisions in their standard forms for land mortgages. The ones concerning
priorities have already been mentioned. Other terms attempt to safeguard

---

[29] Law of Property Act 1925, s. 49(3), which refers to the making of further advances as
'tacking' (the traditional expression).
[30] *Devaynes* v. *Noble, Clayton's Case* (1816) 1 Mer. 572 as applied to mortgages in *Deeley*
v. *Lloyds Bank Ltd.* [1912] AC 756.
[31] J. M. Holden, *Securities for Bankers' Advances*, 6th edn., London, 1980, pp. 65–6.

the bank's interest during the currency of the mortgage. Foremost among these is a term which requires the mortgagor to keep the property in good repair.

Another term requires him to keep the property fully insured against fire and other natural disasters. The mortgagor is further required to pay the premium regularly and, on his failure to do so, the bank is given the power to pay the premium at his expense. To protect itself fully, the bank further notifies the insurance company of its interest in the property. If the property is subsequently destroyed by fire, the company will not pay the amount insured to the owner without consulting the bank.

Another clause common in bank mortgages prohibits the leasing of the property during the currency of the mortgage.[32] The object of this clause is to ensure that the bank is able to obtain vacant possession of the property on the mortgagor's default.[33] A lease made in contravention of such a clause is invalid as against the mortgagee.[34]

(vii) Effect of Consumer Credit Act 1974

The provisions of the Act governing securities, discussed in Chapter 18, apply to regulated agreements secured by mortgages over land. However, section 16 exempts such agreements from the provisions of the Act if the creditor falls within a defined class of lender. Included are local authorities, building societies and other bodies specified by the Secretary of State from among insurance companies, friendly societies and other listed types of organization.[35] Banks do not fall within the scope of this provision and, accordingly, mortgages extended to them are subject to all the relevant provisions of the Act.[36] The only relevance of section 16 from a bank's point of view is that, where it becomes the assignee of an exempt agreement, it need not concern itself with the 1974 Act.

The Act, further, makes two special provisions concerning regulated agreements secured by land mortgages. One is that section 67, which confers on the debtor a right of cancellation in certain circumstances,[37] does not apply to a regulated agreement secured over land, to a restricted-use credit agreement to finance the purchase of land, or to a bridging loan granted for

---

[32] In the absence of such a clause, the mortgagor is entitled to lease the property for a term not exceeding 50 years under s. 99 of the Law of Property Act 1925.

[33] The clause is valid under s. 99(13) of the Law of Property Act 1925.

[34] *Dudley and District Benefit Building Society* v. *Emerson* [1949] 1 Ch. 707. Cf. *Universal Permanent Building Society* v. *Cooke* [1952] Ch. 95, where the lease was granted fractionally before the creation of the mortgage.

[35] See, generally, the Consumer Credit (Exempt Agreements) Order 1980, SI 52.

[36] But banks could be so exempted if the Banking Bill is enacted (cl. 84).

[37] Pp. 66–68 and, as regards specific exemptions of individual bank's, p. 64 above.

such a purchase.[38] A different withdrawal procedure is provided for contracts secured by land mortgages under section 58. Before sending the mortgage documents to the debtor for execution, the creditor is required to send him a copy of the unexecuted agreement 'which contains a notice in the prescribed form indicating the right of the debtor or hirer to withdraw from the prospective agreement'. This provision replaces the right of cancellation with a procedure that has the effect of giving the mortgagor a cooling-off period before he concludes the contract. The procedure is not compulsory where the contract is a restricted-use credit agreement[39] to finance the purchase of the mortgaged land, or where it is for a bridging loan to finance such a purchase. In reality, it is doubtful if section 58 serves any useful purpose. In an economy in which credit is scarce and banks lend at a competitive rate of interest, it is unlikely that a lender would wish to withdraw from his agreement or that, if he were so inclined, the bank would raise any objection.

The other special provision applicable to land mortgages securing a regulated agreement concerns the question of enforcement. Under section 126, such a mortgage is enforceable (so far as provided in relation to the agreement) on the order of a court only. A shortcoming of this section is its failure to confer on the mortgagor any remedy for the breach of this provision. A mortgagee who, in violation of this provision, takes possession of the land or puts it up for sale, is not subject to any civil remedy.[40] Moreover, the purchaser of the mortgaged land is expressly protected.[41] The best advice that can be given to a mortgagor who finds that the mortgagee fails to observe section 126 is to apply for an injunction.[42] There are, of course, cases in which the mortgagor is prepared to allow the mortgagee, or bank, to realize the security. The expense of obtaining a court order under section 126 may, then, be avoided by securing the mortgagor's express consent.[43]

3. PROPRIETARY SECURITIES OVER GOODS

(i) General considerations

The making of banks' advances against chattels or goods is best known in international transactions involving the financing of exports and imports.

[38] Consumer Credit Act 1974, s. 67(*a*). Note that s. 57, governing the effect of the withdrawal from a prospective agreement (pp. 73 above) is applicable to regulated agreements secured over land: s. 57(4).
[39] As to meaning of the phrase, see pp. 64–65 above.
[40] Consumer Credit Act 1974, s. 170(1).
[41] Ibid., s. 177(2).
[42] Available under ibid., s. 170(3).
[43] Ibid., s. 173(2).

The security used in such transactions is mainly the pledge, which is discussed in the next chapter. Such a pledge is effected by means of the transfer of the possession of the document of title to goods which are on board a ship. In domestic transactions, banks provide finance for the acquisition of goods mainly in respect of plant and equipment required by major firms, although banks also finance the operations of finance companies active in the consumer market. In this last type of financial operation, the banks normally acquire a security over the finance companies' book debts or obtain a security by way of a floating charge.[44] The financing of transactions involving specific chattels is usually effected by means of letters of hypothecation; chattel mortgages or bills of sale are not ordinarily used by banks.[45]

From an economic point of view a security over chattels or goods is less satisfactory than a land mortgage. Experience has shown that the price of land tends to rise steadily. As long as a bank ensures that its lending against land is within safe margins, and that the borrower has an equity in the property which encourages him to maintain it properly, the bank holds a sound security. Moreover, registration of the mortgage, or the retention of the deeds, gives the bank an excellent protection against sharp practices.

By way of contrast, the value of goods or chattels is subject to substantial fluctuations, depending on the supply and demand in the market, which may be dictated by seasonal factors. Furthermore, some goods depreciate quickly or, in modern technology, are rendered obsolete within a short period of time. Another hurdle is that goods are not easily traceable if spirited away by an unscrupulous debtor. At the same time, transactions involving the acquisition of goods have the advantage of being usually for a shorter term than transactions involving the acquisition of land.

(ii) Chattel mortgages

A chattel mortgage is a security based on the transfer to the mortgagee of the legal or equitable property in the goods. Such an instrument falls within the definition of a bill of sale which has to be registered within seven days of its execution.[46] Furthermore, if the bill is given by way of security,[47] it is void unless issued in a prescribed form.[48] Yet a further hurdle is that a bill of

---

[44] As regards the transfer of book debts, see pp. 582–4 below; as regards floating charges, see pp. 562 et seq below.

[45] Leverage leasing, which is one of the methods for arranging transactions of this sort, is also not widely used by banks.

[46] Bills of Sale Act 1878, ss. 8, 10; Bills of Sale Act (1878) Amendment Act 1882, s. 8. An unregistered bill is invalid against the trustee in the debtor's bankruptcy.

[47] Since the Amendment Act of 1882, there are certain distinctions between the law applicable to absolute bills of sale and to those given by way of charge or as security. Naturally, a bank seeks to obtain a security by way of charge.

[48] Bills of Sale Act (1878) Amendment Act 1882, s. 9.

sale cannot attach to chattels acquired by the mortgagee after the execution of the instrument.[49] This provision renders a chattel mortgage an unsuitable security where the goods may be replaced from time to time.[50]

The cumbersome provisions for registration and the need to follow the prescribed form render the bill of sale an unattractive security. Furthermore, for historical reasons the granting of a bill of sale tends to cast doubts on the standing of the merchant who effects it. The tendency in modern trade is to avoid it whenever possible. Thus, a merchant who wishes to raise credit against a security over his plant or equipment is frequently asked to incorporate his business, whereupon the bank is able to provide the required finance against a debenture secured by a floating charge.

The only lending in which an unincorporated business is frequently asked by its bank to provide a security by way of a mortgage attached to chattels occurs in transactions concerning farming stock and agricultural assets generally. Such mortgages can be given under the Agricultural Credits Act 1928, and do not require registration as bills of sale.[51]

(ii) Hypothecation

When a customer hypothecates goods to his bank, he purports to create a security which constitutes neither a legal charge nor a pledge. The goods are made available to the bank as a security without the bank obtaining either the possession of the goods or a legal title to them.[52] Instead, the debtor agrees to hold the goods in trust for the creditor. It has been held that such an arrangement confers on the creditor an equitable charge or interest in the goods.[53] This arrangement is distinguishable from the *hypothec* of Roman Law and of modern civil law, which is comparable to a mortgage.

British banks use the hypothecation of goods where the customer is unable or unwilling to give the bank the actual or the constructive possession of the goods by way of pledge and, as is common, the parties wish to avoid the use of a bill of sale. It is true that the word 'hypothecation' is used loosely in practice. Thus, when a bank acquires a pledge over documents of title, it may require the customer to execute a 'letter of hypothecation'.[54]

---

[49] Ibid., s. 5. But note the different position in the case of companies: p. 557 below.

[50] E.g. a dealer's stock in trade.

[51] They are mortgages within the meaning of s. 205(1)(xvi) of the Law of Property Act 1925. As to a bank's power to provide such finance, see p. 59 above.

[52] Holden, *Securities for Bankers' Advances*, 6th edn., p. 311.

[53] *Re Slee, ex p. North Western Bank* (1872) LR 5 Eq. 69; *Re Hamilton Young & Co.*, [1905] 2 KB 722; *Official Assignee of Madras* v. *Mercantile Bank of India Ltd.* [1935] AC 53, per Lord Wright at 64.

[54] The term is used in this way by Gutteridge and Megrah, *Law of Bankers' Commercial Credits*, 7th edn., p. 214.

The use of the phrase in this context, however, is a misnomer. A genuine hypothecation is effected where the goods are not in the debtor's immediate possession or control. An example is where they are in a warehouse together with other of the customer's goods. A pledge is then feasible only if it is practical to separate the goods in question from the rest.[55] If such a separation of the goods which are to serve as a security from the bulk is impractical, the debtor's best course is to grant the bank a hypothecation over them. Hypothecation is also used in respect of goods which are not in existence at the time the security is given, or goods which are in the manufacturing process.[56]

Although the hypothecation of goods is a valid transaction,[57] it constitutes a poor security. As the creditor acquires no control over the goods, the debtor has no difficulty in dealing with them in disregard of the hypothecation. The creditor is unable to contest such dispositions, as he has no title. Thus, an innocent purchaser[58] and a pledgee who obtains possession in good faith[59] are unaffected by the hypothecation. By the same token, a mortgagee of the goods who registers his bill of sale or, where the debtor is a company, his charge, is bound to defeat the claim of the creditor to whom the goods are hypothecated. This is so as the mortgagee acquires a title or special property in the goods whilst the hypothecation creditor acquires a non-proprietary right, or right *in personam*, which crystallizes only upon the debtor's default.[60]

Another weakness inherent in the hypothecation of goods arises from the provisions of the Bills of Sale Acts. The essence of the letter of hypothecation is the debtor's undertaking to hold the goods for the account or as a trustee of the creditor. The document constitutes, therefore, a declaration of trust over the goods without effecting a transfer. As such it falls within the definition of a bill of sale in section 4 of the 1878 Act. Under section 8 of the same Act, a bill of sale is void against the debtor's trustee in bankruptcy unless registered. Thus, in *National Provincial Bank and Union Bank of England* v. *Lindsell*,[61] a letter in which a car-owner instructed a repairer to hold the car and the proceeds thereof on behalf of a bank was held void for want of registration. This decision can be contrasted with *Re Slee, ex p.*

---

[55] For the need of to identify goods to execute a pledge by means of constructive possession, see pp. 568–9 below.

[56] See, e.g., *Re Hamilton Young & Co.* [1905] 2 KB 772.

[57] *Re Slee, ex p. North Western Bank Ltd.* (1872) LR 15 Eq. 69; *Re Hamilton, Young & Co.* [1905] 2 KB 772; *Re David Allester Ltd.* [1922] 2 Ch. 211.

[58] *Re Slee, ex p. North Western Bank Ltd.*, above.

[59] *Lloyds Bank Ltd.* v. *Bank of America National Trust and Savings Association* [1938] 2 KB 147, 165; *Mercantile Bank of India Ltd.* v. *Central Bank of India Ltd.* [1938] AC 287. Both cases concerned letters of trust. The basis of letters of trust and of letters of hypothecation is conceptually the same.

[60] p. 551 above.

[61] [1922] 1 KB 21.

North Western Bank,[62] where it was held that a letter of hypothecation concerning wool in the debtor's own warehouse was not registrable, as such a mercantile facility was altogether distinguishable from a bill of sale.

The position is further complicated by the fact that the 1878 Act excludes from the definition of a bill of sale any document used in the ordinary course of business as proof of the possession or control of goods.[63] The relevance of this saving to letters of hypothecation was considered in *Re Hamilton, Young & Co.,*[64] which concerned a security by way of a 'letter of lien' over wool which was being processed into cloth. The document in question, which had all the attributes of an hypothecation, was held to confer on the creditor a valid equitable charge. However, as the document was of a type used in the ordinary course of business as proof of the possession or control of goods, it did not require registration as a bill of sale.

But the case law is not uniform, and a conclusion to the contrary was reached in *R. v. Townshend.*[65] It was there held that a letter of hypothecation, in terms similar to those used in the previous case, constituted a declaration of trust without transfer, and there was no finding to the effect that it was made in the ordinary course of business. The transaction would have been avoided for want of registration, except that it fell within the scope of another exception applicable to goods on board a ship.

It is believed that the decision in *Re Hamilton, Young & Co.* cannot stand the test of analysis. It is unrealistic to regard a letter of hypothecation as constituting proof of the possession of goods by the creditor. In reality, its words import a message to the contrary. The person who has possession and control declares that he holds the goods for the account of another person. But there is no attempt to confer the actual possession or control on that beneficiary.

Furthermore, it is wrong to regard an hypothecation as anything but a declaration of trust without transfer and hence as a bill of sale. It is typical that, in *Ladenburg v. Goodwin Ferreira & Co. Ltd.,*[66] a letter of hypothecation, which attached to the proceeds of goods which had been sold at the time of its execution, was held registrable as a charge over a company's book debts. The case suggests that the true object of a letter of hypothecation is to create a charge or chattel mortgage, and not to constitute proof of the possession of goods. This, too, supports the view that an hypothecation granted by an unincorporated trader constitutes a bill of sale.

A letter of hypothecation is thus a questionable security. This applies not

---

[62] (1872) LR 15 Eq. 69. The case was decided under the Bills of Sale Act 1854, which was *in pari materia* with the later Act of 1878.
[63] Bills of Sale Act 1878, s. 4.
[64] [1905] 2 KB 772.
[65] (1884) 15 Cox CC 466
[66] [1912] 3 KB 275.

only to hypothecations effected by individuals but also to those effected by companies. The reason for this is that any charge which would require registration as a bill of sale if effected by an individual has to be registered as a charge under the Companies Act 1985 if effected by a company.[67]

An important exception is made in respect of letters of hypothecation made over imported goods prior to their being warehoused, stored, reshipped for export, or delivered to a person other than the debtor who executes the document. In the interest of commercial practice, such letters have been expressly excluded from the scope of the Bills of Sale Acts.[68]

(iv) Consumer credit considerations

Both a chattel mortgage and a letter of hypothecation issued in the context of a regulated agreement fall within the definition of a security for the purposes of the Consumer Credit Act 1974.[69]

4. SECURITIES GRANTED BY COMPANIES[70]

(i) Nature and flexibility of companies' charges[71]

The security used most widely to secure advances made to a company is the charge. It will be recalled that such a security differs from both a mortgage, which gives the creditor an estate in the property, and a pledge, which confers on him the actual or constructive possession. Basically, a charge gives the creditor the right to realize the security upon the debtor's default, and to recover his debt from the proceeds in priority to other claims. Conceptually, therefore, a charge may be identified with an hypothecation.

Although a charge would have been regarded as a mere agreement to confer some security title, equity treated the security as being effected at the time of the execution of the agreement.[72] Three conditions had to be fulfilled for equity to intervene. First, it had to be shown that the advance had been made.[73] Secondly, it had to be established that the parties intended to confer on the creditor an equitable interest in the property and not a mere

[67] s. 396(1)(c); and see *Dublin City Distillery Ltd.* v. *Doherty* [1914] AC 823.
[68] The Bills of Sale Amendment Act 1891, s. 1.
[69] P. 536 above.
[70] I should like to acknowledge my debt to the contributions on the subject by W. J. Gough, *Company Charges*, London, 1978, and R. M. Goode, *Legal Problems of Credit and Security*, London, 1982.
[71] For an analysis of the meaning of 'charge', see Gough, *Company Charges*, pp. 3 et seq.
[72] See generally Gough, *Company Charges*, pp. 216 et seq.; Goode, *Legal Problems of Credit and Security*, p. 5.
[73] *Rogers* v. *Challis* (1859) 27 Beav. 175.

contractual right.[74] Thirdly, the parties had to manifest an intention that the interest attach immediately or, if the property was to be acquired by the debtor at a later date, as soon as he acquired the title thereto. A charge which is to attach on a contingency constitutes a mere contract to furnish security and is ineffective.[75] In *Holroyd* v. *Marshall*,[76] Lord Westbury proposed, as a general rule, that a charge was effective if the agreement under which it was created would be specifically enforced in equity.[77]

The charge is not commonly used by banks for the financing of individual merchants and of unincorporated business firms. The two main reasons for this are to be found in the Bills of Sale Acts. First, a charge, like an hypothecation, falls within the definition of section 4 of the Bills of Sale Act 1878[78] and, accordingly, requires registration as a bill of sale. Being in the nature of a security, it also has to be in the form prescribed by section 9 of the 1882 amendment.[79] These factors render it an unattractive security. Secondly, a bill of sale is ineffective to cover property acquired by the debtor after its execution.[80] A charge granted by an individual or by an unincorporated business firm is, therefore, unsuitable for financing the acquisition of plant that may have to be changed from time to time, or of stock in trade.

These considerations are inapplicable in the case of charges granted by companies. Such charges are outside the ambit of Bills of Sale Acts, being registrable under section 395 of the Companies Act 1985.[81] Consequently, the onerous requisites of form and the restriction on covering after-acquired property are inapplicable.

It may be asked whether, quite regardless of the Bills of Sale Acts, equity recognizes the validity of a clause applying a charge to after-acquired property. To grant a valid security, the debtor must have some existing interest in the property to be charged.[82] The answer is that the interest need not be a legal title. Thus, in the landmark case of *Holroyd* v. *Marshall*,[83] the owner of a mill granted a financier a mortgage covering the existing plant of his enterprise and any machinery acquired by way of replacement. It was held

---

[74] *Tailby* v. *Official Receiver* (1888) 13 App. Cas. 523, 547.

[75] *Re Jackson & Bassford Ltd.* [1906] 2 Ch. 467; *Re Gregory Love & Co. Ltd.* [1916] 1 Ch. 203; *Williams* v. *Burlington Investments Ltd.* (1977) 12 SJ 424. And see Goode, *Legal Problems of Credit and Security*, p. 28. But a charge on an interest which is bound to materialize at a future date, such as an expectancy, is valid: *Re Lind* [1915] 2 Ch. 345.

[76] (1862) 10 HLC 191.

[77] Cf. Goode, *Legal Problems of Credit and Security*, p. 5.

[78] Pp. 551–2 above; most charges, given in lieu of mortgages, would not fall within any of the exceptions.

[79] P. 551 above.

[80] P. 552 above.

[81] *Re Standard Manufacturing Co.* [1891] 1 Ch. 627; *Richards* v. *Kidderminster Overseers* [1896] 2 Ch. 212; and see Gough, *Company Charges*, pp. 380–2, analysing s. 17 of the Bills of Sale (1878) Amendment Act 1882.

[82] For a detailed analysis, see Gough, *Company Charges*, pp. 16 et seq.

[83] (1862) 10 HLC 191.

that the mortgage attached to the after-acquired property from the date of its acquisition by the mill-owner, notwithstanding that his interest in it was acquired at a date later than the execution of the mortgage. It was adequate that the parties to the transaction contemplated the substitution of the existing plant during the currency of the mortgage. Moreover, the charge retains its priority even if competing charges are given in the period preceding the acquisition of the property by the debtor, and although the debtor becomes insolvent in the meantime.[84] In effect, the newly acquired asset is treated as having been charged for fresh consideration.[85]

The resulting flexibility of charges created by companies render them attractive to banks that finance the running commercial activities of their customers. Frequently, individual traders and partnerships are asked to incorporate their business so that they may secure an overdraft obtained from the bank by a floating charge or by a fixed charge attaching to after-acquired property.

(ii) Fixed and floating charges

The availability of companies' charges covering after-acquired property has facilitated the development of two separate categories of charge: the fixed charge and the floating charge. A fixed charge is attached from its inception to a specific chattel or asset; a floating charge hovers over the company's property for the time being and attaches to it only when the charge crystallizes upon the company's default.

The floating charge is unique to English law, which has recognized its validity for over one hundred years,[86] and to systems derived from it. American law has refused to recognize the validity of such a security, as it fails to give the creditor adequate control over assets covered by the charge.[87]

The conceptual distinction between a floating charge and a fixed charge is complicated by the fact that a fixed charge may cover future assets. It

---

[84] *Re Reis* [1904] 2 KB 769; *Re Lind* [1915] 2 Ch. 345 discussed in detail by Goode, *Legal Problems of Credit and Security*, p. 8. For a forceful criticism of the case law, see P. Matthews, 'Effect of Bankruptcy on Mortgages of Future Property', [1981] LMCLQ 40. And note that, under s. 127 of the Insolvency Act 1986, a disposition is void only if made after the commencement of the winding-up; the charge, though, is notionally regarded as attached when the agreement is made.

[85] *Re Collins* [1925] Ch. 556.

[86] *Re Panama, New Zealand and Australia Royal Mail Co.* (1870) LR 5 Ch. App. 318; followed by the House of Lords in *Illingworth v. Houldsworth* [1904] AC 355 affg. *Re Yorkshire Woolcombers Association Ltd.* [1903] 2 Ch. 284.

[87] Grant Gilmore, *Security Interests in Personal Property*, Boston and Toronto, 1965, para. 11.7. See also P. F. Coogan and J. Bak, 'The Import of Article 9 of the UCC and the Corporate Indenture', (1959) 69 Yale LJ 203, 251 et seq.; R. Pennington, 'The Genesis of the Floating Charge', (1960) 23 MLR 630.

follows that not every charge which attaches to a class of assets is floating. The classic definition of a floating charge is to be found in Romer LJ's judgment in *Re Yorkshire Woolcombers Association Ltd.*,[88] which stresses three requisites. First, the charge must cover a class of assets of a company. Secondly, the assets involved must be of a type that, in the ordinary course of the business of the company, would change from time to time. Thirdly, until some future step is taken by or on behalf of the creditor, the company must be permitted to carry on its dealings in this class of assets in its ordinary course of business. It has been pointed out by Buckley LJ in a later case, that such a floating charge is not a specific mortgage of the assets involved, coupled with a licence to the mortgagor to continue trading in them; it is a 'floating mortgage applying to every item comprised in the security, but not specifically affecting any item until some event occurs or some act on the part of the mortgagee is done which causes it to crystallize into a fixed security'.[89]

The mere fact that a charge is granted over a class of assets does not necessarily establish that it is a floating charge. By way of illustration, take a charge over all existing and future book debts of a company coupled with a stipulation that the amounts covered by it be paid directly into the account maintained by the company with the bank that acquires the security. It has been held that such an arrangement involves the creation of a fixed charge, because the company is deprived of the freedom to deal with its book debts in the ordinary course of business.[90] By the same token, an arrangement between a bank and a customer for the financing of stock-in-trade, stored in the bank's name and replaced from time to time with its consent, has all the ingredients of a fixed rather than a floating charge. From a practical point of view, though, it is often more convenient to leave the management of the stock-in-trade in the company's hands, which means that the charge will be floating.

What, then, is the main practical distinction between a floating charge and a fixed charge? There is no doubt that the fixed charge gives the creditor better protection than the floating charge against third parties' interests. This point is discussed in the context of priorities. Furthermore, a floating charge given within twelve months preceding the company's liquidation may in certain cases be defeated unless it has been given for fresh consideration.[91] There is no similar danger in the case of a fixed charge. However, it is important to bear in mind that the floating charge gives the company

---

[88] Above, at 295; and see Goode, *Legal Problems of Credit and Security*, p. 12, who compares a floating charge to a river which is in existence although the water in it changes constantly.

[89] *Evans* v. *Rival Granite Quarries Ltd.* [1901] 2 KB 979, 999.

[90] *Siebe Gorman & Co. Ltd.* v. *Barclays Bank Ltd.* [1979] 2 Lloyd's Rep. 142. And see, further, pp. 582–3 below.

[91] Insolvency Act 1986, s. 245.

greater freedom in its operations than does a fixed charge. It will further be seen that it is an acceptable security in liquidation. Where a bank has confidence in its corporate customer's standing and creditworthiness, the floating charge is considered an adequate protection.

(iii) Registration of companies' charges

Certain charges granted by companies require registration under sections 395 and 396 of the Companies Act 1985.[92] The list, set out in section 396(1) is comprehensive. It includes a charge given to secure an issue of debentures, a charge on the uncalled share capital of the company, a charge on calls made but not paid, and any floating charge on the undertaking or property of the company. Specific charges require registration in the following cases: a charge over book debts, a charge over a ship or aircraft or any share therein, a charge on goodwill, on a trademark or patent or on a copyright or a licence made thereunder, and, most importantly, 'any charge created or evidenced by an instrument which, if executed by an individual, would require registration as a bill of sale'. The last type of charge encompasses a wide variety of charges although, occasionally, there is room for uncertainty. Thus, a chattel mortgage granted by an individual by word of mouth may be effective even if a complimentary document has been avoided for want of registration as a bill of sale. It has been suggested that a similar principle applies in the case of a security granted by a company.[93]

Charges encompassed by section 396(1) are registered at the Companies Registration Office.[94] Special provisions apply to land mortgages granted by a company. Such a mortgage requires to be registered as a charge under section 396(1)(d) and, further, unless comprised in a floating charge, requires to be registered as a charge over land.[95] Failure to register such a charge under the Companies Act renders it void against the liquidator and any creditor. Failure to register it as a land charge renders it void against a bona fide purchaser[96] and a subsequent mortgagee who is unaware of the earlier encumbrance.[97] The deposit of the title deeds with a bank obviates the need to register the charge under the 1972 Act, but not under the Companies Act.

Registration of companies charges encompassed by section 396(1) has to be effected within twenty-one days of their creation. When a certificate of

---

[92] Certain charges are expressly exempted: s. 396(2).

[93] See generally Gough, *Company Charges*, pp. 279 et seq.

[94] This applies even to charges created by a foreign company over property situated in England, if the company has established an office in the United Kingdom: *W. V. Slavenburg's Bank* v. *Intercontinental Natural Resources Ltd.* [1980] 1 WLR 1076; A. J. Boyle, (1981) 2 Company Law 218.

[95] Land Charges Act 1972, s. 3(7)–(8).

[96] Pp. 544–6 above.

[97] Under the Land Charges Act 1972, s. 17(1), which treats a mortgagee as a purchaser.

registration is issued by the Registrar of Companies, it constitutes conclusive evidence that all requirements of the Act have been complied with.[98] It has been pointed out that registration is not a prerequisite to the creation of the charge but a means of its perfection.[99] If the charge is not registered within the prescribed period of twenty-one days, it is void against the liquidator; but it remains valid against the company itself as long as the company is solvent.

Registration of a charge gives notice of its existence to those who can be reasonably expected to search the register. This includes prospective lenders who seek to obtain a security of their own, and any person[100] who wishes to acquire the entire enterprise of the company.[101] But it does not normally include a person who purchases goods from the company in the ordinary course of business, because such a person cannot be expected to search the register before he enters into an ordinary contract of sale with the company.[102] Registration gives notice of the charge and of the details filed with the Registrar. These usually include the identity of the bank or creditor, the amount covered, the date of the creation of the charge and particulars of the property attached.[103]

Registration does not give notice of the full contents of a charge.[104] This is understandable, because a person who searches the register cannot acquire, in addition to the particulars disclosed in it, access to the full documentation. It has been argued that registration should, in addition, give notice of provisions which are commonly found in company charges, such as restrictions on the giving of further security.[105] But this view is contrary to authority.[106] Furthermore, it conflicts with the notion that constructive notice is based on a person's ability to familiarize himself with the facts of which he is deemed to have knowledge.[107] There appears to be but one exception. If a charge attaches to a main asset, such as land, and to property affixed or attached to it, notice of these details is given even if the incidental

[98] Companies Act 1985, s. 401(2); and see *Re C. L. Nye Ltd.* [1971] Ch. 442.

[99] Goode, *Legal Problems of Credit and Security*, p. 23.

[100] For the leading case, see *Re Monolithic Building Co., Tacon v. Monolithic Building Co.* [1915] 1 Ch. 463, and the analysis of Gough, *Company Charges*, pp. 335–6.

[101] For a thorough analysis of the doctrine and its origin, see Gough, *Company Charges*, pp. 355 et seq.

[102] *Feuer Leather Corporation v. Frank Johnstone & Sons* [1981] Com. LR 251, and [1983] Com. LR 12; cf. *Manchester Trust v. Furness* [1895] 2 QB 539.

[103] Companies Act 1985, s. 401(1).

[104] *English and Scottish Mercantile Investment Co. Ltd. v. Brunton* [1892] 2 QB 700; *Wilson v. Kelland* [1910] 2 Ch. 306; *Siebe Gorman & Co. Ltd. v. Barclays Bank Ltd.* [1979] 2 Lloyd's Rep. 142.

[105] J. H. Farrar, 'Floating Charges and Priorities' (1974) 38 *Conv. & Prop. Law* (NS) 315, 318; J. R. Lingard, *Bank Security Documents*, London 1985, p. 107.

[106] *Siebe Gorman & Co. Ltd. v. Barclays Bank Ltd.* [1979] 2 Lloyd's Rep. 142, 160 and authorities there cited.

[107] Goode, *Legal Problems of Credit and Security*, p. 26.

property covered is omitted by error from the details set out in the register.[108] Whether or not notice is given of details which are not required to be registered, but which are entered voluntarily, is an open question. It is arguable that such details are discoverable by a search. Against this view, it is asserted that, as these details are not within the requirements of registration, they should not be the subject of constructive notice, which is based on deeming persons to know that which ought to be disclosed in a public record.[109]

(iv) Priorities

It has been seen that both a fixed and a floating charge confer on the creditor, or bank, a security interest in the assets involved. Whilst the registration of such a charge under section 395 confers on the bank priority over (or protection against) the claims of the general creditors in the company's liquidation, it does not affect disputes between the bank and an innocent purchaser of a chattel covered by a charge granted by the company. In the case of a floating charge, the proposition is self-evident, because the agreement envisages that the company, the 'chargor', will continue to trade freely.[110] In the case of a fixed charge, the same conclusion is reached on the basis that a person who enters into an ordinary trading transaction with a company is not expected to satisfy himself that the subject matter is unencumbered.

The rule that a legal title prevails over an equitable one is of importance where there are competing claims between the holders of different securities effected by the company. If Bank A obtains and registers a land mortgage during the twenty-one days following the execution of a charge granted by the company to Bank B, Bank A acquires priority, although Bank B is not in breach of section 395 by postponing registration to the last day available to it. The position would be unaffected if Bank A came to know of Bank B's charge before the registration of the land mortgage, provided Bank A did not have any knowledge when it made its advance to the company.[111] It is, thus, adequate if the bank made the advance secured by the legal mortgage before it came to know of a competing equitable interest. Bank A could equally obtain priority under the same circumstances by acquiring some other legal title. Naturally, if Bank A made its advance with the knowledge

---

[108] *National Provincial and Union Bank of England* v. *Charnley* [1924] 1 KB 431; *Re Eric Holmes (Property) Ltd.* [1965] Ch. 1052; *Re Mechanisations (Eaglescliffe) Ltd.* [1966] Ch. 20.

[109] Goode, *Legal Problems of Credit and Security*, p.25.

[110] The position differs where the acquisition of the goods takes place outside the ordinary course of business; see generally Gower, *Modern Company Law*, 4th edn., et seq.

[111] *Taylor* v. *Russell* [1892] AC 244; *Bailey* v. *Barnes* [1894] 1 Ch. 25.

of the existence of Bank B's equitable interest, its claim would be subordinate.[112]

As between competing charges, the general rules are simple. The charges take priority in the order of their creation.[113] But this rule applies only if the charges are duly registered. If the charge created first in order of time is not registered, a subsequently effected charge takes priority,[114] arguably even if the second creditor is aware of the unregistered charge at the time he takes his security.[115] Further exceptions apply as regards the ranking of a floating charge against a fixed charge. These will be discussed subsequently.

One problem that arises in respect of all charges concern the amount for which a given charge attains priority. Does it cover any amount outstanding at the time of the dispute, or only the amount that was due under the first ranking charge when the subordinate charge was registered or communicated to the superior chargee? The problem, thus, is whether 'future advances' made under the preferred charge are entitled to priority. The solution, which is of major importance in the case of bankers' running accounts, is in all probability the same as that discussed in respect of land mortgages.[116]

(v) Special rules governing floating charges

The effect of a floating charge during the period in which it hovers over the company's assets differs considerably from its effect at any time following crystallization. Prior to its crystallization, the floating charge ranks as subordinate to a later fixed charge. The reason for this is that the fixed charge is regarded as created under the implied consent or licence of the creditor secured by the floating charge.[117] The registration of the floating charge and the knowledge of its existence by the creditor with the fixed charge make no difference. To avoid this result, it is common to include in a floating charge a clause prohibiting the creation of charges ranking in priority to, or *in pari passu* with, the floating charge. As neither the registration of the floating

---

[112] For a succinct analysis of the rules of priorities, see Gough, *Company Charges*, pp. 399 et seq.

[113] See Gough, *Company Charges*, pp. 401–2, but note exception concerning book debts: pp. 588–90 below.

[114] *Re Monolithic Building Co.; Tacon* v. *Monolithic Building Co.* [1915] 1 Ch. 643 (decided under a section *in pari materia* in the Companies Act 1908). Note, though, that the 21-day period provided for registration can be extended by a court order.

[115] Ibid., but cf. *Watson* v. *Duff Morgan & Vermont (Holdings) Ltd.* [1974] 1 WLR 450.

[116] P. 546 above; Gough, *Company Charges*, pp. 403–4.

[117] *Re Hamilton's Windsor Ironworks, ex p. Pitman and Edwards* (1879) 12 Ch. D 707; *English and Scottish Mercantile Investment Co. Ltd.* v. *Brunton* [1892] 2 QB 700; *Governments Stock and Other Securities Investment Co.* v. *Manila Ry. Co. Ltd.* [1897] AC 81; *Re Castell and Brown Ltd., Roper* v. *Castell and Brown Ltd.* [1898] 1 Ch. 315. And see Gough, *Company Charges*, pp. 149 et seq.

charge[118] nor the inclusion of the restrictive covenant in the particulars filed[119] has the effect of conferring notice of the clause on subsequent creditors, it is common to require the company to pass a special resolution approving the floating charge and incorporating the restrictive covenant. Such a resolution has to be registered,[120] whereupon it is believed by some authors that it becomes the subject of constructive notice.[121]

A floating charge is subject to some additional disadvantages before its crystallization. First, a floating charge, unlike a fixed charge, is subordinate to the claims of the preferential creditors[122] accrued up to the date the company is put into receivership or into winding-up.[123] Secondly, a charge created within twelve months prior to the onset of the company's insolvency is invalid except to the extent of cash paid, or some other value provided, to the company at the time of or subsequent to the creation of the charge.[124] However, even if such a consideration has not been furnished, the charge is valid if, at the time of the creation of the charge, the company was solvent.[125] This fact is established by showing that the company was at that time able to discharge its debts.[126] Thirdly, a floating charge enables the company to deplete its assets.

The floating charge becomes a far more effective security when it crystallizes or attaches to the company's assets upon the occurrence of a given event.[127] At that stage, as has been shown, the floating charge is effectively transformed into a fixed charge.[128] When that takes place, the company ceases to have the power to carry on business transactions affecting the property covered. In terms of agency law, the company loses its creditor's, or bank's, mandate to make dispositions over the property the subject of the charge.[129] The crystallization, though, is an undesirable event, taking place when the company is either insolvent or in breach of its obligations under the charge.

[118] P. 560 above.
[119] Ibid.
[120] Companies Act 1985, s. 380.
[121] Holden, *Securities for Bankers' Advances*, 6th edn., p. 375.
[122] As to which creditors fall within this group, see p. 532 above.
[123] Insolvency Act 1986, s. 40 (receivership); s. 175(2) (winding-up).
[124] Ibid., s. 245; but note that where the chargee is connected with the company, the period is two years. A payment made a short period before the execution of the charge and in anticipation of the conclusion of the transaction is valid: *Re Columbian Fireproofing Co. Ltd.* [1910] 2 Ch. 120; *Re F. & D. Stanton Ltd.* [1929] 1 Ch. 180.
[125] Insolvency Act 1986, s. 245(4).
[126] Within the meaning of ibid., s. 123; and see *Re Patrick and Lyon Ltd.* [1933] Ch. 786.
[127] *Governments Stock and Other Securities Investment Co. Ltd.* v. *Manila Ry. Co. Ltd.* [1897] AC 81, 86.
[128] Gough, *Company Charges*, pp. 84 et seq.; Goode, *Legal Problems of Credit and Security*, p. 33; and p. 557 above.
[129] *Re Florence Land and Rubber Works Co., ex p. Moor* (1878) 10 Ch. D 530, 541 per Jessell MR; *N. W. Robbie & Co. Ltd.* v. *Witney Warehouses Co. Ltd.* [1963] 3 All ER 613.

Thus, a floating charge crystallizes upon the appointment of a receiver[130] or the commencement of its winding-up,[131] and where the company ceases its business operations[132] or the creditor seeks to enforce his security by taking possession of the goods or by other means, such as asking the court to appoint a receiver.[133]

When a floating charge crystallizes, its ranking changes. Primarily, it gives the creditor priority over all charges created after crystallization.[134] It has been argued that one exception to this rule is that the subsequent mortgagee's position is unaffected if, at the time he took his fixed charge, he had neither knowledge nor the means of knowing of the crystallization.[135] Such a creditor is entitled to rely on the company's undisturbed apparent authority to deal with its assets. Naturally, this type of case cannot arise when the crystallization takes place upon the appointment of a receiver or the company's winding-up. The crystallization of the charge also affects its ranking as against preferential claims. In such a case the charge has metamorphosed into a fixed charge at the relevant time and the preferential claims will not defer it.[136]

Crystallization, though, tends to take place too late. If it eventuates upon the appointment of a receiver or the commencement of the winding-up, the preferential claims 'attach' before the floating charge becomes fixed. The bank's claim is then subordinate. Similarly, if the bank appoints a receiver or takes possession after the company has created a fixed charge in defiance of the terms of the floating charge, the gates are shut after the horses have bolted. The contravening charge retains its priority.

To provide against such events, banks have introduced into debentures

---

[130] *Evans* v. *Rival Granite Quarries Ltd.* [1910] 2 KB 979, esp. 986. Crystallization takes place when the receiver accepts his appointment: *Windsor Refrigerator Co. Ltd* v. *Branch Nominees Ltd.* [1961] Ch. 375; *Cripps (Pharmaceuticals) Ltd.* v. *Wickenden* [1973] 2 All ER 606. Gough, *Company Charges*, p. 87 argues that crystallization takes place when the receiver takes possession of the assets; but the cases are inconclusive. As the management of a company by a receiver is conducted for the benefit of the creditors and not merely the shareholders, the company can no longer be seen as operating independently in its own interest.

[131] *Re Colonial Trusts Corporation* (1879) 15 Ch. D 465; *Re Panama, New Zealand & Australian Royal Mail Co.* (1870) LR 5 Ch. App. 318; *Edward Nelson & Co. Ltd.* v. *Faber & Co.* [1903] 2 KB 367, 376; *Evans* v. *Rival Granite Quarries Ltd.*, above. Where the winding-up is compulsory, crystallization takes place upon the presentation of the petition; *Stein* v *Saywell* [1969] ALR 481; otherwise it occurs at the time the court order is made: *Re Victoria Steamboats Ltd.* [1897] 1 Ch. 158.

[132] *Edward Nelson & Co. Ltd.* v. *Faber & Co.* [1903] 2 KB 367, 376.

[133] *Evans* v. *Rival Granite Quarries Ltd.* [1910] 2 KB 979.

[134] *Business Computers Ltd.* v. *Anglo-African Leasing Ltd.* [1977] 2 All ER 741 and cases there cited.

[135] Goode, *Legal Problems of Credit and Security*, p. 45; Gough, *Company Charges*, pp. 104–7, who also discusses exceptions.

[136] *Re Christonette International Ltd.* [1982] 1 WLR 1245, based on the fact that the assets covered by the crystallized charge do not constitute 'assets' available in a winding-up commencing subsequently. The position appears to be unaffected by ss. 40 and 175 of the Insolvency Act 1986.

obtained from their customers the 'automatic crystallization clause'. This clause usually specifies that a charge is to crystallize automatically if any one of a number of given events takes place. Included are usually the grant of a security to another creditor; the levy of distress or execution against the debtor's assets; the failure of the company to meet any of its debts; and the failure to keep a stated minimal ratio of assets *vis-à-vis* liabilities.

It is not altogether certain that such a clause is valid in English law. Moreover, the word 'valid' needs to be clarified in this context. Does it refer to validity as between the creditor secured by the charge and the company, or does it refer to validity as against third parties, such as bona fide purchasers and competing secured creditors? Naturally, the effect of the clause on the position of a liquidator of the company (which effect determines its validity against the general creditors) depends on the validity of the clause between the parties to it.[137] As between these parties, the automatic crystallization clause has the effect of terminating the company's actual authority to deal in its assets. As against third parties, the clause is relevant only if it terminates the company's apparent authority to trade. It is obvious that different considerations apply.

As between the parties, there is good reason to uphold the clause. There appears to be no contractual principle which militates against it.[138] Equally, the clause ought to be valid as against unsecured creditors levying execution after crystallization. Such creditors have no cause for complaining about the effect of the clause.

The position differs in the case of third parties such as bona fide purchasers or subsequent mortgagees. Their complaint is bound to be that they have no means of ascertaining that the automatic crystallization clause has come into effect. A modern New Zealand authority, *Re Manurewa Transport Ltd.*,[139] illustrates the point. A debenture included a clause under which the floating charge was to crystallize automatically if the company gave, or attempted to create, a fixed charge without the debenture holder's prior consent. In breach of this clause, the company executed a chattel mortgage to a garage-owner over a truck . Speight J held, inter alia, that under section 4 of the Chattels Transfer Act 1924 the garage owner had constructive notice of the restrictive covenant of the floating charge. The mortgage

---

[137] For a full analysis, see Gough, *Company Charges*, pp. 96 et seq.; Goode, *Legal Problems of Credit and Security*, p. 36. And see Speight J's analysis in *Re Manurewa Transport Ltd.* [1971] NZLR 909.

[138] Dicta in some cases disclose a tendency in the opposite direction: *Re Horne & Hellard* (1885) 29 Ch. D 736; *Davey & Co. v. Williamson & Sons Ltd.* [1898] 2 QB 194; *Governments Stock and Other Securities Investment Co. Ltd. v. Manila Ry. Co. Ltd.* [1897] AC 81; *Illingworth v. Houldsworth* [1904] AC 355. But see the explanation of the cases by A. J. Boyle, 'Validity of Automatic Crystallization Clauses', [1979] JBL 231.

[139] [1971] NZLR 909. See also *Stein v. Saywell* [1969] ALR 481 (Aust.). Cf. *R v. Consolidated Churchill Copper Corporation Ltd.* [1978] 5 WWR 652.

was, therefore, subordinate to the charge. His Honour further held that the automatic crystallization clause was valid, and that it had the effect of deferring the mortgage to the crystallized charge.

The conclusion is that, if a third party has notice of the crystallization of the floating charge, it is effective against him. If he has no such notice, he is in all probability unaffected by it. As English law does not have a provision similar to section 4 of the New Zealand Act of 1924, it is questionable if, on the facts of *Re Manurewa*, the decision would have been similar in this country. The mortgagee would not have been deemed to have constructive notice of the terms of the charge unless details of it were the subject of a special resolution. A bona fide purchaser of any chattel would, undoubtedly, be unaffected by the clause, as he is not expected to search the register and is not deemed to have notice of charges.[140]

The automatic crystallization clause has an effect on the ranking of the secured creditor against preferential claims. Such claims take priority if the charge is 'floating' at the time of the appointment of a receiver or of the commencement of the winding-up.[141] Naturally, if crystallization takes effect before that time the charge, which becomes a fixed one, ranks in priority to these claims.[142]

(vi) Assessment

The floating charge is the security favoured by the banks. The explanation is to be found in economic rather than in legal factors. Such a charge leaves the customer the desired freedom of action. It enables him to carry on his business without the need constantly to seek the bank's consent to dispositions over property covered by the security. If the customer's credit is good and his trading methods fair, the bank need have no worries. It can acquire additional protection, which overcomes some of the inherent weaknesses of the floating charge, by obtaining a fixed charge over the customer's permanent assets, such as land or plant.

The floating charge has one further conceptual attraction from a bank's point of view. In its monetary dealings with the customer, the bank operates on the basis of a current account which has been shown to resemble a reservoir of money available to the customer. The same type of flexibility is attained in respect of security by means of the floating charge. Naturally, the floating charge does not mirror the movement of funds through the customer's account. The company's assets may actually increase and the security replenish itself quite regardless of the balance of the customer's account.

---

[140] So argued by Goode, *Legal Problems of Credit and Security*, p. 39.
[141] P. 564 above.
[142] For details, see Goode, *Legal Problems of Credit and Security*, pp. 46 et seq.

Notionally, though, the revolving nature of a current account and of a floating charge is in harmony with a bank's way of transacting business. It is believed that this element explains the banks' preference for a floating charge over more effective securities.

The utilization of company charges as a whole is further explainable by one important consideration. Historically, charges are outside the ambit of the onerous bills of sale legislation. Since 1974, they have the added convenience of being outside the scope of the consumer credit legislation. It is believed that company charges will remain the security most favoured by banks.

CHAPTER 20

Possessory Securities

1. THE PLEDGE

(i) Utilization of pledges by banks

A pledge is created when the creditor is given the possession of some items belonging to the debtor as a security for the amount advanced. The pledge is by its nature a contract of bailment for security purposes. The pledgee acquires both the possession of the items covered and some special right or interest in them. It is common to describe this right as a special property,[1] although in 'The Odessa'[2] the Judicial Committee of the Privy Council pointed out that the pledgee's only power was to sell the goods upon the pledgor's default and concluded that, analytically, this was not a right of property at all. The point is well taken, as the pledgee does not have the power to acquire the full ownership of the subject matter by means of foreclosure.[3] One thing is clear: the general property or ownership in the items pledged remains vested in the pledgor.[4] It has been said that the pledge ranks between a mortgage, which confers on the mortgagee a definite property right, and a lien, which is purely possessory in nature.[5] On the view taken by the Judicial Committee, the pledge is of course much closer to the latter than to the former. The main distinction between a pledge and a lien is that a lienee's only right is to detain the subject matter pending satisfaction of the debt. He does not have a right of sale.[6]

Ordinarily, the pledge is effective only whilst the pledgee retains possession.[7] There is, however, authority for the view that the release of the goods to the pledgor, or to a nominee, for a restricted purpose, such as the

---

[1] *Donald v. Suckling* (1866) LR 1 QB 585; *Burdick v. Sewell* (1883) 10 QBD 363, 376, affd. (1884) 10 App. Cas. 74.

[2] [1916] 1 AC 154, 158–9.

[3] *Carter v. Wake* (1877) 4 Ch. D 605, 606.

[4] *Re Morritt, ex p. Official Receiver* (1886) 18 QBD 222; *Attenborough v. Solomon* [1913] AC 76, 84.

[5] *Halliday v. Holgate* (1868) LR 3 Ex. 299, 302.

[6] P. 576 below.

[7] *Singer Manufacturing Co. v. Clark* (1879) 5 Ex. D 37; *Babcock v. Lawson* (1880) 5 QBD 284.

making of arrangements for their storage, does not destroy the pledge.[8] From a bank's point of view the general principle, under which possession is essential,[9] is cumbersome. Banks do not wish to keep in custody goods, plant or machinery belonging to a customer. In the first place, they do not have the necessary facilities. Secondly, such a genuinely possessory transaction, which is best known as a 'pawn' is not banking business. Thirdly, such an arrangement defeats the object of the typical transaction financed by a bank. Quite regardless of whether credit is extended to the customer to finance the acquisition of plant, of equipment or of stock-in-trade, he requires the custody or use of the items involved. The giving of actual possession thereof to the bank is thus out of the question.

The solution in the case of a transaction involving goods is to confer on the bank the constructive instead of the actual possession of goods.[10] This object can be achieved in two ways. One method is to deliver to the bank the possession of documents of title which constitute the symbol of the goods. Such a transaction is effective where the goods are on board a ship, when the bill of lading confers property in the goods,[11] or when they are stored in a warehouse pending their resale.[12] A sophisticated system involving the use of 'trust receipts' has developed for the release of such goods to the customer to enable him to continue dealing in them. The other method involves the storing of the goods in a warehouse in the bank's name or in a part of the pledgor's own warehouse, the key of which is then given to the bank.[13] Both types of constructive possession are effective to create a pledge.

Although the first method is utilized mainly in respect of overseas trans-

---

[8] *North Western Bank Ltd.* v. *John, Poynter, Son and Macdonalds* [1895] AC 56, 64–8; *Official Assignee of Madras* v. *Mercantile Bank of India Ltd.* [1935] AC 53; *Lloyds Bank Ltd.* v. *Bank of America National Trust and Savings Association* [1938] 2 KB 147. And see *Re David Allester Ltd.* [1922] 2 Ch. 211, in which the practice of releasing pledged goods to the pledgor to facilitate a sale was not regarded as defeating the pledge. But both *David Allester* and the *Bank of America* case clarify that the pledgor can, in such cases, confer a good title on an innocent purchaser or mortgagee.

[9] *Martin* v. *Reid* (1862) 11 CB (NS) 730, 734; *Ayers* v. *South Australian Banking Co.* (1871) LR 3 PC 548, 554.

[10] The basic principle can be traced back to *Reeves* v. *Capper* (1838) 5 Bing NC 136. And see analysis in *Young* v. *Lambert* (1870) LR 3 PC 142; *Hilton* v. *Tucker* (1888) 39 Ch. D 669; *Wrightson* v. *McArthur and Hutchinsons (1919) Ltd.* [1921] 2 KB 807.

[11] *Sewell* v. *Burdick* (1884) 10 App. Cas. 74; *Bristol and West of England Bank* v. *Midland Ry. Co.* [1891] 2 QB 653.

[12] Provided it has the power to issue warehouse receipts of a negotiable character. Such a power is conferred on given warehouses by personal Acts: *Benjamin's Sale of Goods*, 2nd edn., para. 1498. Otherwise, the same object is achieved by requiring the warehouseman to attorn to (i.e. to declare that he holds the goods for) the bank. See, generally, *Official Assignee of Madras* v. *Mercantile Bank of India Ltd.* [1935] AC 53; *Alicia Hosiery Ltd.* v. *Brown, Shipley & Co. Ltd.* [1970] 1 QB 195.

[13] *Young* v. *Lambert* (1870) LR 3 PC 142; *Hilton* v. *Tucker* (1888) 39 Ch. D. 669; *Wrightson* v. *McArthur and Hutchinsons (1919) Ltd.* [1921] 2 KB 807.

actions, it constitutes an important facet of banking business, and hence requires discussion. The second method, often described as 'field warehousing', is used to finance a dealer's stock-in-trade. There are no other methods used by banks in order to obtain a pledge over goods. A traditional 'pawn', in which the bank retains the possession of the security, can however be utilized in the case of other items that are capable of being pledged. These include negotiable instruments[14] and all types of marketable securities.[15] In all three types of pledge, banks use certain general terms which will now be reviewed.

(ii) Standard conditions in pledges, and rights conferred on banks

When a customer pledges goods to his bank, he is usually required to sign a document described as a 'letter of pledge' or 'letter of lien'. Some banks prefer to execute such a document in respect of every transaction, whilst others request the customer to sign a general document in the nature of a master agreement. Quite regardless of the form, the tendency is to stipulate that the pledge be extended to all of the customer's property which is given into the bank's possession or custody. This provision is of specific importance in the case of a pledge to the bank of marketable securities which the customer purchases and delivers to the bank from time to time. Another important provision is that the pledge is to secure all amounts advanced by the bank to the customer.

Where the pledge covers goods, the customer undertakes to keep them fully insured, and promises to pay all charges due for their storage. Usually, it is provided that if he fails to comply with this condition, the bank can make suitable arrangements and demand reimbursement of the expenses incurred. The document further confers on the bank the right to dispose of the goods in a public or private sale if the customer fails to comply with the provisions of the underlying credit transaction.

The last provision does not, in effect, confer on the bank any powers beyond its common law rights. The power of sale is inherent in the security arrangement created by the pledge.[16] The pledgor, however, has a right to redeem the pledge, notwithstanding his default and quite regardless of the terms of the contract, at any time preceding the sale of the property pledged.[17] Where the pledgee sells the goods, he does so for

---

[14] As these constitute choses in possession; p. 498 above.

[15] *Donald* v. *Suckling* (1866) LR 1 QB 585 (debentures); *Langton* v. *Waite* (1868) LR 6 Eq. 165 (railway stock); *Halliday* v. *Holgate* (1869) LR 3 Ex. 299 (scrip).

[16] *Martin* v. *Reid* (1862) 11 CB (NS) 730; *Pigot* v. *Cubley* (1864) 15 CB (NS) 701; *France* v. *Clark* (1883) 22 Ch. D 830; *Re Morritt, ex p. Official Receiver* (1886) 18 QBD 222, 235.

[17] *France* v. *Clark*, above; *Re Morritt, ex p. Official Receiver*, above; '*The Ningchow*' [1916] P 221, 224.

the benefit of both the pledgor and himself. Accordingly, the pledgee has to account to the pledgor for any surplus. He has also to arrange for a prudent sale.[18]

The pledgee ranks as secured creditor in respect of all items pledged before the commencement of the pledgor's bankruptcy or winding-up. If the proceeds of the sale of the pledge are insufficient to settle the debt, the pledgee can prove for the balance, but ranks in this respect as a general creditor.[19] However, such a claim is unavailable if the goods perished or were destroyed due to the pledgee's fault.[20]

These general principles apply to all pledges. Special problems arise in respect of the three special arrangements, mentioned earlier, which are the pledge of documents of title, 'field warehousing', and the pledge of negotiable instruments and marketable securities.

(iii) Pledge by means of documents of title

Lickbarrow v. *Mason*[21] established that a document of title has the effect of conferring on its holder the constructive possession and the right to the delivery of the goods. An indorsee of the documents of title obtains a special property in the goods, regardless of whether the transfer is effected by way of sale or of pledge.[22] The pledge of the bill of lading accordingly constitutes a pledge of the goods,[23] and gives the bank, or pledgee, a power of sale. The bank's right has been described as 'a right of property . . . to secure the amount . . . advanced.'[24]

The only document of title recognized at common law is the bill of lading. Special or personal Acts confer a similar status on warehouse receipts issued by designated bodies.[25] Although the Factors Act 1889 recognizes other documents as falling within its own definition of a 'document of title',[26] such documents do not acquire the common law attribute of becoming

---

[18] '*The Odessa*' [1916] 1 AC 145, 159.

[19] P. 533 above.

[20] *Polak* v. *Everett* (1876) 1 QBD 669; *Ellis & Co.'s Trustees* v. *Dixon-Johnson* [1925] AC 489, 493.

[21] (1787) 2 TR 63; revd. (1790) 1 H Bl. 357 but restored (1793) 2 H, Bl. 211. And see *Sanders Bros.* v. *Maclean & Co.* (1883) 11 QBD 327, 341.

[22] *Sewell* v. *Burdick* (1884) 10 App. Cas. 74, 86; *Brandt* v. *Liverpool, Brazil and River Plate Steam Navigation Co. Ltd.* [1924] 1 KB 575.

[23] *Official Assignee of Madras* v. *Mercantile Bank of India Ltd.* [1935] AC 53, 60.

[24] *Rosenberg* v. *International Banking Corporation* (1923) 14 Ll. LR 344, 347.

[25] Such as a dock warrant covered by the Port of London Act 1968, s. 164. And see *Benjamin's Sale of Goods*, 2nd edn., para. 1498.

[26] S. 1(4), applied by reference to the Sale of Goods Act 1979 by its s. 61(1). Included are, inter alia, delivery orders.

symbols of the goods covered by them.[27] New forms of documents of title may, of course, be recognized by reason of a mercantile usage.[28]

When the bill of lading, or some other effective document of title, is transferred to the bank by way of pledge, the bank acquires the necessary control over or special right in the goods.[29] If the carriers deliver the goods to some other person, without demanding the production of the bill of lading, they are liable to compensate the bank in an action in conversion.[30]

Whilst the bank retains the bill of lading it has an effective security. It could, further, arrange for the delivery of the goods, and for their storage, by using an agent. In practice, though, banks release the documents to the customer for this purpose under a 'trust receipt' or 'letter of trust'. Such a document usually stipulates that the customer will hold the documents and the goods as the bank's trustee or agent. He is authorized to sell the goods, but the proceeds are impounded with a trust in the bank's favour and usually are to be paid into the customer's account with it. It is clear that in his handling of the documents and the goods the customer acts as the bank's agent. In *Re David Allester Ltd.*[31] his position was described as that of a 'trust agent'.

The trust receipt enables the bank to retain an adequate security against the customer's insolvency. The release of the bill of lading to him for the special purpose of storing the goods does not destroy the pledge.[32] If the customer fails before he has disposed of the goods, the bank is therefore able to claim the documents and the goods as its own property.[33] Moreover, even before 1986 the customer was not normally considered the 'reputed owner' of the goods under section 38(c) of the Bankruptcy Act 1914.[34] This was important because if the customer had been so considered, the documents and goods would have been deemed to form part of his estate for bankruptcy purposes. The Insolvency Act 1986 has, of course, repealed the doctrine of reputed ownership. It can be safely concluded that the trust

---

[27] It may be operative merely for the purposes of certain provisions in the Act concerning mercantile agents. See, generally, *Benjamin's Sale of Goods*, 2nd edn., para. 1463.

[28] *Merchant Banking Co. of London* v. *Phoenix Bessemer Steel Co.* (1877) 5 Ch. D 205 (warrants used in iron trade); *Kum* v. *Wah Tat Bank Ltd.* [1971] 1 Lloyd's Rep. 439 (mate's receipt in trade between Singapore and Sarawak).

[29] *Sewell* v. *Burdick* (1884) 10 App. Cas. 74; *Guaranty Trust Co. of New York* v. *Hannay & Co.* [1918] 2 KB 623, 651, 653.

[30] *Bristol and West of England Bank* v. *Midland Ry. Co.* [1891] 2 QB 653; *Sze Hai Tong Bank Ltd.* v. *Rambler Cycle Co. Ltd.* [1959] AC 576. That the carrier's duty to deliver is subject to his being tendered the bill of lading, see *Barclays Bank Ltd.* v. *Commissioners of Customs and Excise* [1963] 1 Lloyd's Rep. 81, 89.

[31] [1922] 2 Ch. 211, 219.

[32] *North Western Bank Ltd.* v. *John Poynter, Son, and Macdonalds* [1895] AC 56, 68.

[33] *Idem.*

[34] *Re, Hamilton, Young & Co.* [1905] 2 KB 381, 389–90; affd. ibid., 772. And note that the reputed ownership doctrine was in any event inapplicable in the liquidation of companies: Bankruptcy Act 1914, s. 126.

receipt furnishes an effective security over the goods. The bank is, further, protected in respect of the proceeds. If the customer fails after the sale of the goods, the bank has priority over the amount realized.[35]

The trust receipt is a far less effective security against sharp practices perpetrated by the customer. The customer is considered the bank's mercantile agent within the meaning of section 2 of the Factors Act 1889. A sale or pledge of the goods to an innocent third party is accordingly valid against the bank.[36] To protect itself against such abuses, the bank should require the customer to store the goods in its name. If they have been stored in the customer's name, the warehouseman should be required to attorn to the bank. This means that he is to be required to confirm to the bank that he is holding the goods on its behalf. Thereafter any release of the goods from the warehouse requires the bank's authority, and an attempt to create a pledge ranking in priority will be abortive.[37]

The trust receipt does not appear to require registration as a bill of sale. In *Re Hamilton, Young & Co.*[38] a trust receipt was held to be exempt therefrom by reason of its being a document used in the ordinary course of business as proof of the possession or the control of goods. It is further arguable that the trust receipt does not create a charge but simply broadens the bank's existing rights over the documents and the goods. On this basis it is altogether outside the scope of the relevant definition of the Bills of Sale Act 1878.[39] On the same basis, the trust receipt does not require registration as a charge under section 395 of the Companies Act 1985.[40]

(iv) Field warehousing

Trust receipts and the hypothecation of goods are used mainly when the bank finances an import of goods right from the early stages of the transaction. In some cases a bank is asked for accommodation at a later stage, when the goods have arrived and been stored, either at an independent warehouse or at the customer's own premises. In both cases, a pledge of the

[35] *North Western Bank Ltd.* v. *John Poynter, Son, and Macdonalds,* above; *Re David Allester Ltd.* [1922] 2 Ch. 211.
[36] *Lloyds Bank Ltd.* v. *Bank of America National Trust and Savings Association* [1938] 2 KB 147. Cf. *Mercantile Bank of India Ltd.* v. *Central Bank of India Ltd.* [1938] AC 287, which is distinguishable in that the question of the bank's position under the Factors Act 1889 was not raised on the facts.
[37] See, generally, *Chitty on Contracts,* 25th edn., vol. 2, para. 2353A.
[38] [1905] 2 KB 772.
[39] *Re David Allester Ltd.* [1922] 2 Ch. 211.
[40] Idem. But note that if the goods have been sold before the execution of the trust receipt, in which case the security is to attach to the proceeds, the instrument may constitute a charge over book debts, which is registrable: *Ladenburg & Co.* v. *Goodwin, Ferreira & Co. Ltd.* [1912] 3 KB 375.

goods can be used as a security by conferring on the bank the constructive possession of the goods.

Where the goods are in an independent warehouse, the constructive possession is given to the bank by means of appropriate documentation. If the warehouse has the power of issuing negotiable warehouse receipts or warrants,[41] which are documents of title, the delivery of the document to the bank has the same effect as the delivery of a bill of lading. If the document is not of this type, it is necessary to ensure that the warehouseman will not deliver the goods without the bank's authority. To this end, the warehouse is notified of the bank's interest and is requested to attorn to the bank.[42] The warehouseman then enters the bank's name as the party entitled to the delivery of the goods, and issues a new receipt or warrant in its name. The goods are thus held at the bank's disposal.[43]

One risk borne by the bank in such an arrangement is that the goods are subject to the warehouseman's lien for the storage charges. To safeguard the bank's position, the customer is required to execute a letter of pledge, which includes the usual conditions rendering him liable for all expenses.

Where the goods are stored on the customer's own premises or in a warehouse owned by him, the constructive possession is conferred on the bank by means of the key to the warehouse or to the room in which the goods are stored.[44] The pledge is not destroyed if the customer, or pledgor, is given the key to enable him to have access to the goods for limited purposes, such as their maintenance, or in order to enable potential purchasers to inspect them.[45] To avoid any suggestion that the customer has been given general access to the goods and in this way has relinquished the pledge, it is preferable to appoint one of his employees as a 'custodian', who is empowered to give the customer occasional access to the goods when required.

Due to the artificiality involved in the arrangement, banks tend to avoid field warehousing. It is utilized mainly by finance companies and by some merchant banks. The clearers and most merchant banks prefer to secure their advances by floating charges.

(v) Pledge of marketable securities and negotiable instruments

Negotiable instruments and marketable securities can be the subject of a pledge.[46] They qualify because they are not only choses in action, in that

---

[41] P. 571 above.

[42] As to the meaning of the phrase, see p. 573 above.

[43] *Official Assignee of Madras* v. *Mercantile Bank of India Ltd.* [1935] AC 53; cf. *Alicia Hosiery Ltd.* v. *Brown, Shipley & Co. Ltd.* [1970] 1 QB 195.

[44] The method is not new: *Young* v. *Lambert* (1870) LR 3 PC 142; *Hilton* v. *Tucker* (1888) 39 Ch. D 669.

[45] *Wrightson* v. *McArthur and Hutchinsons (1919) Ltd.* [1921] 2 KB 807. For the position in the USA, see Gilmore, *Security Interests in Personal Property*, ch. 6.

[46] P. 530 above.

they confer a right to their proceeds on the holder, but also choses in possession, and hence a special category of property.[47] A pledge over negotiable instruments is effected by means of a written document in which the instruments are constituted a continuing security granted in respect of all advances made by the bank to the customer.[48] For all practical purposes, the effect of such a pledge is similar to that of a pledge of goods.

A pledge is unsuitable in the case of documents, such as share certificates, which are issued in a given person's name and are not negotiable in character.[49] Such documents are not choses in possession or items of property, and their retention does not in itself create a possessory security. Thus, in *Harrold* v. *Plenty*,[50] Cozens-Hardy MR held that the deposit of share certificates involved the creation of an equitable charge or an agreement to execute a transfer of the shares by way of mortgage.

(vi) Consumer credit implications

Sections 114–22 of the Consumer Credit Act 1974[51] make provisions governing 'pawns' or pledges taken under a regulated agreement.[52] Pledges of documents of title and of bearer bonds are excluded.[53] Many of the pledges obtained by banks fall within the ambit of these exclusions. This is so despite the fact that the exclusions involved are narrower than may appear at first glance. To start with, as 'document of title' is not defined, the phrase is confined to documents of title in the strict (or common law) sense of the word. Accordingly, whilst a pledge of a bill of lading is unaffected by the 1974 Act, a pledge of documents such as delivery orders and non-negotiable warehouse receipts is regulated by the Act. Similarly, whilst a pledge of bearer bonds is excluded, a pledge of share warrants is a 'pawn'. A pawn is also created by a field warehousing agreement, made to secure a regulated agreement. Banks have to be wary of the Consumer Credit Act whenever they take a pledge which secures a regulated agreement and which is not within the exclusion.

Fortunately for the banks, the provisions of the Act are not cumbersome. First and foremost there is a procedural requisite. When the pledge is

[47] P. 498 above. The discussion of negotiable instruments there undertaken applies also to marketable securities, such as stock, share warrants, and bonds which are transferable.
[48] *Carter* v. *Blake* (1877) 4 Ch. D 605; *Harrold* v. *Plenty* [1901] 2 Ch. 314 (latter case may have been a mortgage).
[49] *Longman* v. *Bath Electric Tramway Ltd.* [1905] 1 Ch. 646, 665.
[50] [1901] 2 Ch. 314, 316.
[51] For the repeal of the Pawnbrokers Act 1872, see the Consumer Credit Act 1974, s. 193(2) and Sched. 5, and the Consumer Credit Act 1974 (Commencement no. 8) Order 1983,, SI 1551, paras. 5, 6.
[52] Pp. 63–65 above.
[53] Consumer Credit Act 1974, s. 114(3)(*a*) as amended by s. 38(2) of the Banking Act 1979.

effected, the pledgee must give the pledgor a 'pawn receipt'.[54] Secondly, the pledged property remains effectively redeemable until the very time it is realized by the pledgee.[55] An unreasonable refusal by the pledgee to consent to the redemption of the property constitutes an offence.[56]

If the property has not been redeemed by the end of the prescribed redemption period (which is usually six months), the pledgee is entitled to realize the security.[57] The Act prescribes a procedure,[58] based on giving the pledgor a last notice to enable him to make a final effort to redeem. Naturally, where the proceeds of the sale exceed the debt, the pledgee has to account to the pledgor for the balance.[59] The pledgee must use reasonable care to ensure that the sale realizes the true market value. If the pledgor disputes that this has been done, the onus of proof rests on the pledgee.[60]

It is believed that the provisions in point are not so onerous as to dissuade banks form using the pledge. It is worthwhile recalling that where the amount of the agreement involved exceeds £15,000, or where the pledgee is a company, the transaction is not a regulated agreement.

2. THE BANKER'S LIEN

By mercantile usage, a bank has a lien over commercial paper deposited by the customer in the ordinary course of business. Accordingly, there is no need for an express agreement between the parties to bring the lien into existence. It attaches in the absence of an express agreement or of circumstances evincing an intention to the contrary.[61] A special feature is that, unlike other types of lien, a banker's lien carries with it the right to sell the security.[62] In this respect, the banker's lien resembles a pledge. The instruments, the subject of the lien, are delivered to the bank for collection, or for retention until maturity, which means that realization is contemplated by the parties.

Usually the lien attaches to secure the customer's total indebtedness to the

---

[54] Consumer Credit Act 1974, s. 114(1); as regards the form of such a receipt, see the Consumer Credit (Agreements) Regulations 1983, SI 1553, reg. 4; the Consumer Credit (Pawn-Receipts) Regulations 1983, SI 1566, reg. 2.

[55] This is the outcome of reading together ss. 116(1)–(3) of the Act. As to the redemption procedure, based on the surrender of the pawn receipt, see s. 117.

[56] Consumer Credit Act 1974, s. 119(1).

[57] Ibid., s. 120.

[58] Ibid., s. 121. As regards the length of the period of notice, see Guest and Lloyd, *Encyclopaedia of Consumer Credit Law*, para. 2–122.

[59] Consumer Credit Act 1974, s. 121(3).

[60] Ibid., s. 121(6).

[61] *Brandao* v. *Barnett* (1846) 12 Cl. & F 787, 806. And see *Jones* v. *Peppercorne* (1858) John. 430; *Re London and Globe Finance Corporation* [1902] 2 Ch. 416; *General Produce Co.* v. *United Bank Ltd.* [1979] 2 Lloyd's Rep. 255 (suggesting that the terms of an express letter of lien displaces the bankers' common law lien).

[62] *Rosenberg* v. *International Banking Corporation* (1923) 14 Ll. LR 344, 347.

bank at any one time.[63] But the effect of the lien can be abrogated by an agreement, express or implied. Thus, in *Re Bowes*[64] a policy of insurance was deposited with the bank, accompanied by a memorandum to the effect that it was to constitute a security for all sums up to £4,000. North J held that the lien did not secure any amounts exceeding the agreed overdraft. The generality of the lien may also be abrogated by the circumstances of the transaction. The most common example is a deposit made to cover an advance arranged for a specific purpose.[65] But the customer's conduct in such a situation may, in the end, result in the creation of a general lien. A case in point is where the customer permits the bank to retain the securities after the discharge of the debt. The securities then become the subject of a general lien securing all future advances.[66]

The banker's lien extends to all classes of negotiable and semi-negotiable instruments deposited by the customer and belonging to him.[67] Included are the traditional bills of exchange, cheques, promissory notes, bonds, and share warrants,[68] as well as share certificates,[69] money transfer orders,[70] and deposit receipts.[71] The lien, accordingly, has a wider scope of application than a pledge of securities which, it will be recalled, attaches to negotiable securities alone.[72] As both the pledge and the lien are possessory securities, this distinction is fortuitous. However, even a lien is not all-embracing in its application. It does not attach to documents that are mere choses in action. Thus, in *Wylde* v. *Radford*,[73] it was held that a deed respecting the conveyance of land was not covered by the banker's lien. But this rule is not conclusive. In *Re Bowes*,[74] for instance, an insurance policy was assumed to be subject to the lien. It has been suggested that where title deeds to land are deposited with a bank, the effect is to create a special type of charge akin to a lien, though not to be confused with the bank's general lien.[75] In practice, the deposit of the deeds is normally made in the context

---

[63] *Re London and Globe Finance Corporation* [1902] 2 Ch. 416, 420; *Re Keever* [1967] Ch. 182, 189; *Bank of New South Wales* v. *Ross, Stuckley and Morawa* [1974] 2 Lloyd's Rep. 110, 112.

[64] (1886) 33 Ch. D 586.

[65] *Wilkinson* v. *London and County Banking Co.* (1884) 1 TLR 63.

[66] *Re London and Globe Finance Corporation* [1902] 2 Ch. 416.

[67] Instruments belonging to a third party are probably not covered: *Cuthbert* v. *Robarts, Lubbock & Co.* [1909] 2 Ch. 226, 233. But see *Siebe Gorman & Co. Ltd.* v. *Barclays Bank Ltd.* [1979] 2 Lloyd's Rep. 142, 166 suggesting that this rule applies only where the bank was aware that the securities were not the customer's property at the time it granted the advance.

[68] *Wylde* v. *Radford* (1863) 33 LJ Ch. 51, 53.

[69] *Re United Service Co., Johnston's Claim* (1870) LR 6 Ch. App. 212.

[70] *Misa* v. *Currie* (1876) 1 App. Cas. 554.

[71] Pp. 221–2 above.

[72] *Jeffreyes* v. *Agra and Masterman's Bank* (1866) LR 2 Eq. 674.

[73] (1863) 33 LJ Ch. 51. Cf. the explanation of the case in *Re London and Globe Finance Corporation* [1902] 2 Ch. 416, 420.

[74] (1886) 33 Ch. D 586.

[75] Paget, *Law of Banking*, 9th edn., p. 407.

of a mortgage and hence is the subject of an express contractual arrangement.[76]

The lien attaches to all securities remitted by the customer to the bank for collection, although these are delivered to the bank for a specific purpose.[77] This is so because the transaction as a whole involves the delivery of the documents to the bank in the ordinary course of its business.[78] Moreover, a bank that receives negotiable instruments for collection from a correspondent retains a lien over them to secure the correspondent's indebtedness.[79] The lien is not defeated by the bank's knowledge that the instruments are the property of the correspondent's customer. It attaches to all cheques paid to the credit of his account, and to any bill of exchange or promissory note remitted by him to his bank. When the instruments have been paid by the drawee, the bank is entitled to apply the proceeds in reduction of the customer's overdraft or other debit balance, unless the amount received has been earmarked for a different purpose.[80]

The lien does not attach to securities remitted to the bank for safe custody. In such a case the securities are retained by the bank as a bailee, and not in the ordinary course of its banking business. Occasionally, it is not easy to determine in what capacity the bank has received some instrument. Thus, bonds may be deposited with the instruction that the bank cut off the coupons and use them to collect interest payments. It has been suggested that, in such a case, the bonds and coupons are subject to the bank's lien.[81] If the customer requires the bank to keep the securities but retrieves them periodically in order to collect the interest due, the arrangement is said to involve safe custody. In terms of commercial reality, the principle is questionable. A customer may deposit his securities with a bank purely for safe custody, but may instruct the bank to collect the interest as his agent. In other instances, he may intend to deposit the instruments for security purposes but, for reasons of his own, may wish to collect the interest due by presenting the coupons on his own. It is believed that the lien attaches whenever the bank and its customer regard the instruments as a security. The matter thus depends on their intention.

A lien does not attach to the balance standing to the credit of the customer's account with his bank. The reason is clear: the funds in question

---

[76] P. 544 above.

[77] *Akrokerri (Atlantic) Mines Ltd.* v. *Economic Bank* [1904] 2 KB 465. And see *Sutters* v. *Briggs* [1922] 1 AC 1, 18 where doubts were expressed as to the application of s. 27(3) of the Bills of Exchange Act 1882 to a collecting bank on the ground of its probably not being a holder in its own right. But the case does not cast any doubt on the existence of the lien.

[78] *Misa* v. *Currie* (1876) 1 App. Cas. 554, 565, 569, 573.

[79] *Johnson* v. *Roberts* (1875) LR 10 Ch. App. 505; cf. *Re Dilworth, ex p. Armistead* (1828) 2 Gl. & J 371.

[80] *Re Keever* [1967] Ch. 182.

[81] *Re United Service Co., Johnston's Claim* (1870) LR 6 Ch. App. 212; Paget, *Law of Banking*, 9th edn., pp. 410–11.

represent a debt due from the bank to the customer, and not 'money' or cash owned by him. The bank's right in such a case is to effect a set-off against the credit balance involved in respect of debts due to it from the customer.[82]

It is more difficult to define the rights that the bank has in a balance in foreign currency maintained at the customer's request. Such a balance may be credited to an account opened in the customer's name by his bank's overseas correspondents. In such a case the contract is between the foreign bank and the customer, and his local bank cannot have any lien or right of set-off against the funds involved. But in many cases the amount involved is remitted to the credit of the local bank's own account with its correspondent, and the balance is shown as standing to the credit of the customer's account with his local bank. It is then a debt in foreign currency due to the customer from his own bank, and payable either in specie in the foreign country concerned or in local currency at the rate of exchange prevailing at the time of payment. Until payment, though, it remains a debt. In *Choice Investments Ltd.* v. *Jeromnimon (Midland Bank, Garnishee)*,[83] it was held that such a balance was a debt attachable by means of a garnishee order. By the same token, it should be a valid subject of a set-off and, being a mere chose in action, unaffected by the bank's lien.

The bank's lien gives it an effective security against the interests of competing creditors. There are, however, some restrictions on its effect. First, the lien is ineffective in respect of property which is not owned by the customer,[84] although this point may be doubted in respect of negotiable instruments.[85] In this last case, the bank has the benefit of the lien if it obtained the instruments in good faith and for valuable consideration. The second limitation to the effect of the lien is that it fails to protect the bank in respect of advances made after notice that the instruments have been mortgaged or assigned in equity to a third party.[86]

---

[82] Pp. 139 et seq. above.
[83] [1981] 1 All ER 225, 228.
[84] *Cuthbert* v. *Robarts, Lubbock & Co.* [1909] 2 Ch. 226, 233.
[85] *Brandao* v. *Barnett* (1846) 12 Cl. & F 787, 805–6.
[86] *Jeffreyes* v. *Agra and Masterman's Bank* (1866) LR 2 Eq. 674; *Siebe Gorman & Co. Ltd.* v. *Barclays Bank Ltd.* [1979] 2 Lloyd's Rep. 142.

CHAPTER 21

Choses in Action as Securities

1. BASIC PROBLEMS AND SCOPE OF SECURITY

Choses in action differ from choses in possession in that they are mere rights, usually for the receipt of an amount of money. A balance standing to the credit of a customer's bank account, an amount owed to a supplier by a tradesman for goods delivered on credit, and a debt due to a finance company under a hire purchase agreement are all examples in point. From a legal point of view, the amounts involved constitute debts enforceable at their maturity.[1] Economically, they will be shown as assets in the creditor's balance sheet. Accordingly, they can be utilized for the creditor's business transactions. In the first place, they can be converted into cash by sale or transfer. The drawing of a cheque on a bank is but one illustration. Similarly, a supplier may 'sell' all the amounts receivable from his customers. In such a 'factoring' transaction the purchaser acquires the right to be paid by the tradesmen. In the second place, choses in action can be utilized to secure the 'owner's' transactions with third parties. Thus, a finance company may grant its bank a charge over amounts due under all its hire purchase agreements.

The value of a chose in action as a security depends on two factors. One is the debtor's creditworthiness: obviously, an amount due from an insolvent tradesman is worthless. The other is the nature of the debt in question. Thus, amounts due under a long-term transaction, such as the financing of a capital project, may be less attractive than debts due within a short term. At the same time, choses in action have generally one attractive feature. Unlike land and goods, which would have to be sold in the process of realization and the value of which may fluctuate considerably, choses in action have a fixed value, and realization is relatively simple. Choses in action are therefore considered good security. In view of their liquidity, they are particularly appropriate in the context of a transaction involving bank finance.

A security over choses in action has to be effected in a form recognized as valid at law or in equity. Naturally, a pledge over a chose in action is ruled

---

[1] He will usually be able to obtain summary judgment under O. 14, r. 1 of the Rules of the Supreme Court.

out by the fact that the concept of possession is inapplicable to mere rights.[2] In the ordinary course, transactions over choses in action are effected by means of a statutory or an equitable assignment. A statutory assignment, which has to be effected in the manner prescribed by section 136 of the Law of Property Act 1925, involves an outright sale or transfer of the debts to the assignee. Such an assignment is complete when notice thereof is given to the debtor. An absolute sale or transfer may, likewise, be effected by an equitable assignment, in which case notice to the debtor is advisable but not a requisite. An equitable assignment can also be used for an assignment by way of charge, effected to create a security.

It may be asked whether, from an economic point of view, there is any practical distinction between an outright assignment and an assignment by way of charge. Goode[3] has pin-pointed three important differences. First, the sale of a chose in action is usually not registrable, whilst the converse is true in the case of a charge;[4] secondly, there is a difference as regards the applicable stamp duty;[5] and thirdly, the transactions are treated in a different manner for tax purposes.[6] In addition, there is a fundamental distinction as regards the relationship of the assignor and the assignee. Where the transaction is a charge, the assignee (or secured party) retains the right to recover the amount due to him from the assignor. He has to account to the assignor for any surplus left after realization, but is entitled to claim any deficiency left after the discharge of the debts assigned. In an outright sale, the assignee acquires the debts transferred to him for better or for worse. He is entitled to retain a windfall, such as may accrue in cases where the assigned debt is in a foreign currency which increases in value, but has to sustain a loss resulting from an adverse fluctuation.[7]

[2] A pledge of negotiable instruments and marketable securities is valid as these instruments constitute both choses in action and choses in possession; p. 498 above. For the same reason they are subject to a lien.

[3] *Legal Problems of Credit and Security*, p. 82. And see Gough, *Company Charges*, ch. 19; (and *Australian Supplement* thereto, 1983, pp. 24–5).

[4] P. 586 below.

[5] *Ad valorem* on sales; duty has been abolished on mortgages or charges: Finance Act 1971, ss. 64, 69.

[6] When a debt is sold, the proceeds may show a profit obtained by the assignor, which is taxable. The asset itself is no longer the property of the assignor. In a mortgage, the asset remains the property of the assignor, and the amount advanced to him is treated as a loan. In certain situations, the interest paid on this loan is tax deductible.

[7] But note that the fact that the assignor guarantees the payment of the debt assigned, or that the assignment is subject to recourse, does not necessarily convert it into a security transaction: *Olds Discount Ltd.* v. *John Playfair Ltd.* [1938] 3 All ER 275; *Chow Yoong Hong* v. *Choong Fah Rubber Manufactory* [1962] AC 209. The fact that the language used in the documents may suggest a charge is not always relevant, provided it is clear that the parties intended to effect an outright sale: *Lloyds & Scottish Finance Ltd.* v. *Cyril Lord Carpet Sales Ltd.* (1979) 129 NLJ 366, discussed by A. D. C. Giddins, 'Block Discounting—Sale or Charge', (1980) 130 NLJ 207.

2. SECURITY OVER BOOK DEBTS

(i) Nature of security

A book debt is an amount of money due to a company or to an unincorporated firm in the course of its business.[8] It has been described as a debt that would ordinarily be entered in a trader's books regardless of whether or not it is so entered in a given case.[9] The price of goods sold on credit, rentals due under a hire purchase agreement or a lease, and amounts due from clients for services rendered by tradesmen or by professional men such as accountants are all covered by the definition. A balance standing to the credit of an account with a bank is not encompassed.[10] Although the amount involved constitutes a debt due from the bank, it is not one due to the customer in the course of his trading operations or ordinary course of business.[11] It is a deposit made by him for investment purposes, or to maintain a balance for regular drawings.

The value of a book debt as a security is based on the debtor's payment obligation. Although every business acquires some bad debts, a global security over all its 'receivables' is bound to provide a safe yield if realization becomes necessary. Banks take such a security where they finance either the entire business operations of the customer or some well-defined facet thereof. Frequently, the security is additional to a charge over some goods. Thus, the bank may demand a fixed charge over goods acquired by means of the credit extended to the customer and over the proceeds of their sale. Such an arrangement is preferable to a floating charge, available in the case of a corporate customer, for reasons discussed earlier.[12]

That a charge over present and future book debts may in certain cases constitute a fixed and not a floating charge has been established in *Siebe Gorman & Co. Ltd. v. Barclays Bank Ltd.*,[13] A company gave its bank a fixed charge over existing and future book debts. Under the charge, the company was required to pay all proceeds of its transactions into its account with the bank. The charge included a clause prohibiting the creation of any subsequent charge and the making of any assignment without the bank's

[8] *Shipley* v. *Marshall* (1863) 14 CB (NS) 566, 571; *Dawson* v. *Isle* [1906] 1 Ch. 633.
[9] *Independent Automatic Sales Ltd.* v. *Knowles & Foster* [1962] 1 WLR 974.
[10] *Re Stevens, Stevens* v. *Keily* [1888] WN 110; *Watson* v. *Parapara Coal Co. Ltd.* (1951) 17 GLR 791 (NZ); Gough, *Company Charges*, p. 290.
[11] But it is important to bear in mind that some institutions specialize in placing on the money market amounts borrowed by them. The balances accrued by the placings may possibly constitute book debts, as the institutions involved are in the business of borrowing for relending to the banks participating in the money market.
[12] Pp. 558–9 above.
[13] [1979] 2 Lloyd's Rep. 142, 159; see also *Evans, Coleman & Evans Ltd.* v. *R. A. Nelson Construction Ltd.* (1958) 16 DLR 123. Contrast *Re Keenan Bros. Ltd. (in Liq.)* [1958] ILRM 254.

prior consent. In breach of this undertaking the company executed an absolute assignment to another creditor of amounts represented by certain bills of exchange. To determine the question of priorities, it was necessary to decide whether the charge granted to the bank was a floating charge that would have been subordinate to the competing absolute assignment or a fixed charge that would rank above it. Although the bank lost on the basis of another issue, Slade J upheld its argument that the charge was a fixed one. His Lordship held that the company was able to create an equitable charge that attached to future book debts as soon as they were paid. In the instant case the charge was fixed rather than floating because the requirement that the amounts received be paid into a designated account precluded the customer from disposing of the debts at will.

Siebe Gorman was distinguished in *Re Armagh Shoes Ltd.*,[14] in which the facts were basically similar except that the charge did not require that the amounts involved be paid into a designated account. The charge was, therefore, held to be of the floating variety. Some Australian cases[15] go in the same direction. The conclusion in *Re Armagh* is sound because in effect the debtor retained the right to dispose over the book debts.

A security over book debts is effected by means of an assignment by way of charge or of mortgage. Naturally, some banks attempt to obtain a statutory assignment as defined in section 136 of the Law of Property Act 1925. But such an assignment has to be absolute and not by way of charge[16] and, further, is complete only when notice has been given to the debtor.[17] This last requirement causes problems, as a firm that assigns its receivables in order to raise credit does not usually wish its customers to be aware of the fact. Furthermore, the only practical advantage of a legal assignment is that, where enforcement is necessary, the assignee can sue in his own name;[18] in the case of an equitable assignment of a book debt (which constitutes a legal chose in action), he has to join the assignor as a party.[19] This procedural point is of little practical significance. The assignment by way of charge, which is of the equitable type, is therefore generally used.

---

[14] [1982] NI 59, reproduced in [1984] BCLC 405.
[15] *Hart* v. *Barnes* (1982) 13 ATR 694; *Re Wallyn Industries Pty. Ltd.* (1983) 7 ACLR 661; *Waters* v. *Widdows* [1984] VR 503.
[16] This is clear from the language of s. 136. And see *Jones* v. *Humphreys* [1902] 1 KB 10. Cf. *Tancred* v. *Delagoa Bay & East Africa Ry. Co.* (1889) 23 QBD 239, which suggests that an assignment by way of mortgage is within the contemplation of the section. The reasoning is irreconcilable with the plain language of the provision. And note that a statutory assignment has to apply to the entire debt: *Durham Bros.* v. *Robertson* [1898] 1 QB 765, 774; *Forster* v. *Baker* [1910] 2 KB 636; *Re Steel Wing Co. Ltd.* [1921] 1 Ch. 349; *Williams* v. *Atlantic Assurance Co. Ltd.* [1933] 1 KB 81.
[17] Section 136, and see *Holt* v. *Heatherfield Trust Co. Ltd.* [1942] 2 KB 1.
[18] 136(a).
[19] *Durham Bros.* v. *Robertson*, above; *Performing Right Society Ltd.* v. *London Theatre of Varieties Ltd.* [1924] AC 1.

(ii) Choses covered

An assignment of book debts may cover three types of choses in action: those which are both in existence and due at the time of the assignment; those which are in existence at that time but are yet to mature;[20] and those to be accrued by the assignor in his future dealings. The last type encompasses future book debts in the widest sense of the word. It may be asked whether the value of such assets is predictable. If it is not, then these future book debts constitute a poor security. In practice, though, a business firm's dealings over a number of years give a good indication of book debts bound to stand to its credit from time to time. Commercially, it is therefore possible to assess the value of the security. Moreover, a global assignment of future book debts is valid in equity[21] regardless of whether it is effected by an incorporated or unincorporated assignor.[22] An assignment covering both existing and future book debts is equally unexceptional.

At the same time, an assignment is ruled out in the case of two types of book debts: book debts which are rendered unassignable in the contract made between the assignor and the debtor, and debts, such as bank balances, owed by the assignee to the assignor. In the first case, the impediment is contractual; in the second, the problem is posed by substantive law.

There can be good reasons for rendering a book debt non-assignable. The debtor may wish to avoid the risk of making the error of paying twice owing to an oversight of a notice of assignment.[23] In addition, he may wish to retain up to the very date of the discharge of the debt his right of set-off and the right of raising counterclaims based on different liabilities. It would appear that a covenant prohibiting assignments is valid as between the debtor and the assignee of the book debt. In *Helstan Securities Ltd.* v. *Hertfordshire County Council*,[24] in which a contractor assigned an amount due to him from the Council in breach of a clause prohibiting the assignment of the contract or of any benefit arising thereunder, Croom-Johnson J held that the prohibitive covenant was an equity as between the debtor and the assignor, and hence effective against the assignee. As the clause in question is part and parcel of the debt, it is difficult to quarrel with this decision. His

---

[20] Such a 'growing debt' is considered an existing chose in action: *G. & T. Earle (1925) Ltd.* v. *Hemsworth RDC* (1928) 140 LT 69.

[21] *Tailby* v. *Official Receiver* (1888) 13 App. Cas. 523 (but note that it must be for valid consideration); *Norman* v. *Federal Commissioner of Taxation* (1963) 109 CLR 9; *Independent Automatic Sales Ltd.* v. *Knowles & Foster* [1962] 1 WLR 974, explained in *Paul and Frank Ltd.* v. *Discount Bank (Overseas) Ltd.* [1967] 1 Ch. 348. Conceptually, it is regarded an agreement to assign, which equity will enforce: *Anson's Law of Contract*, 26th edn., p. 385.

[22] The problems arising as regards registration are discussed below p. 586–7.

[23] Goode, *Legal Problems of Credit and Security*, pp. 85–6.

[24] [1978] 3 All ER 262. See also *Re Turcan* (1889) 40 Ch. D 5; *Tom Shaw & Co.* v. *Moss Empires Ltd. and Bastow* (1908) 25 TLR 190; *Spellman* v. *Spellman* [1961] 2 All ER 498.

Lordship, however, further implied that the clause in question avoided the assignment even as between the assignor and the assignee. This aspect of the decision has been rightly criticized on the basis that the debtor cannot have any legitimate objection to the fate of the amount paid once it has reached the hands of his creditor, viz. the assignor.[25] The point is of importance, as an assignment which is valid between assignor and assignee gives the assignee a priority over the sum involved in the assignor's bankruptcy.

A charge granted to a bank over a credit balance standing in its own books to the customer's credit is ineffective, for the very reason that precludes it from being subject to the bank's lien.[26] It is true that a lien is a possessory security whilst a charge and mortgage constitute proprietary securities. The balance, though, is a mere chose in action due from the bank to the customer. How, then, can the bank have a charge or mortgage over its own indebtedness?[27] Goode points out that the essence of an assignment is to enable the assignee to recover the debt. It would be absurd to argue that, in the type of case here discussed, the bank, which is both the debtor and the assignee, ought to sue itself.[28]

(iii) The assignee's position

It is a well-known principle that an assignee's title is subject to the equities (or defences) available to the debtor against the assignor.[29] Included are claims for damages available to the debtor against the assignor for the breach of the underlying contract[30] and a right of set-off. The assignee can, however, improve his position by giving notice of the assignment to the debtor. Any right of set-off or equity arising from transactions undertaken between the debtor and the assignor after this date cannot be pleaded against the assignee.[31]

The notice to the debtor confers additional benefits on the assignee. First, the debtor is unable 'to take away or diminish the rights of the assignee as they stood at the time of the notice'.[32] Thus, if, after having received notice, he makes payment to the assignor, he can be compelled to pay the amount

---

[25] Goode, *Legal Problems of Credit and Security*, p. 86; and, by the same author, 'Inalienable Rights', (1979) 42 MLR 553; and note reference to s. 9–318(4) of the Uniform Commercial Code, which avoids such a prohibitive covenant.

[26] P. 142 above.

[27] See, further, as regards a contractual right of set-off, p. 597 below.

[28] Goode, *Legal Problems of Credit and Security*, p. 86.

[29] *Anson's Law of Contract*, 26th edn, p. 401.

[30] *Young* v. *Kitchin* (1878) 3 Ex. D 127; *Government of Newfoundland* v. *Newfoundland Ry. Co.* (1888) 13 App. Cas. 199.

[31] *Roxburgh & Co.* v. *Cox* (1881) 17 Ch. D 520; *Re Pinto Leite and Nephews* [1929] 1 Ch. 221; *N. W. Robbie & Co. Ltd.* v. *Witney Warehouse Co. Ltd.* [1963] All ER 613; *Business Computers Ltd.* v. *Anglo-African Leasing Ltd.* [1977] 2 All ER 741.

[32] *Roxburgh & Co.* v. *Cox*, above, 526.

over again to the assignee.[33] Secondly, the agreement between the debtor
and the assignor cannot be modified without the assignee's consent in any
manner that affects the amount due.[34] Thirdly, it will be shown that notice
plays a role in determining priorities.

(iv) Registration, and the effect of failure to do so

Registration is required in the case of charges over the book debts both of an
incorporated and of an unincorporated business. Although the provisions
for registration and the machinery provided therefor differ as between the
two types of enterprise, the failure to comply with the applicable procedure
has one and the same effect in both cases. It renders the charge ineffective in
the assignor's insolvency. In neither case does registration determine priorities between competing assignees.

A charge or mortgage[35] over the book debts of a company requires registration under section 396(1)(e) of the Companies Act 1985. This provision
applies to charges over future book debts[36] and to any instrument which
effectively creates a charge, even if it fails to describe the transaction as such.
Thus, in *Re Kent and Sussex Sawmills Ltd.*[37] a supplier (the assignor)
ordered his purchaser (the debtor) to remit all amounts due under the contract to a designated bank (the assignee) and stipulated that the instruction
could be revoked only with the bank's written consent. It was held that the
arrangement constituted a registrable charge over book debts. But section
396(1)(e) applies only to charges created by agreement; it has no application
to encumbrances created by operation of law.[38] It is also inapplicable to
charges effected over book debts by the pledge of negotiable instruments
representing them.[39]

The registration of a company's charge over book debts has the same
effect as the registration of other corporate charges. Whilst registration does
not determine priorities, it affects them by giving constructive notice to
those who can be expected to search the register.[40] The effect of non-regis-

---

[33] *Brice v. Bannister* (1878) 3 QBD 569; the information, if definite, is equally effective
where it is obtained by the debtor from another source: *Lloyd v. Banks* (1868) LR 3 Ch.
App. 488. But payment made to the assignor before the debtor was given notice discharges the
debt: *Stocks v. Dobson* (1853) 4 De G M & G 11; *Warner Bros. Records Inc. v. Rollgreen Ltd.*
[1976] QB 430, 442.
[34] *Brice v. Bannister*, above, esp. per Bramwell LJ at 581.
[35] Charge includes mortgage: Companies Act 1985, s. 396(4).
[36] *Independent Automatic Sales Ltd. v. Knowles & Foster* [1962] 1 WLR 974, decided
under s. 95(1)(e) of the Companies Act 1948 which was identical.
[37] [1947] 1 Ch. 177.
[38] *Capital Finance Co. Ltd. v. Stokes* [1969] 1 Ch. 261.
[39] Companies Act 1985, s. 396(2). And see *Dawson v. Isle* [1906] 1 Ch. 633, illustrating
when a negotiable instrument falls within the definition of a book debt.
[40] P. 560 above.

tration is to avoid the charge against the liquidator and creditors in the company's winding-up.[41] But this is not the case as regards any book debts which are paid over to the assignee, or become the subject of a set-off between the assignor and the assignee, before the commencement of the winding-up.[42]

The registration of the assignment of the book debts of an unincorporated firm, which is outside the immediate scope of the Bills of Sale Acts,[43] is governed by section 344 of the Insolvency Act 1986, which has replaced section 43(1) of the Bankruptcy Act 1914. Under section 344(1), a general assignment by a trader of his existing or future book debts or any class thereof is void against his trustee in bankruptcy unless it has been registered under the 1878 Act. Under subsection (4) such an assignment is treated as if it were a bill of sale given otherwise than by way of security. 'Assignment', in this context, includes any assignment by way of security and other charges over book debts.[44] The use of the word 'includes' suggests that other assignments, such as outright assignments or sales, may also be included.

Under section 344(4), the provisions of the 1878 Act are applied to a registrable assignment with the necessary modifications. Significantly, the section makes no reference to the 1882 Act, which means that the restriction on charges covering future property are inapplicable. Section 344(3)(*b*) excludes four types of assignment of book debts from the registration requirement. The first is an assignment of the debts due from persons specified in the instrument. Such an assignment is usually made for collection purposes and not to effect a charge. The second is an assignment of debts 'becoming due under specified contracts'. This exclusion is probably motivated by the fact that this type of assignment serves the same purpose as a surety agreement. The third is any assignment made in the course of the bona fide transfer of a business, and the fourth is any assignment of assets for the benefit of the general creditors. These four types of transaction do not constitute 'general assignments' within the meaning of section 344.

Section 43(1) of the 1914 Act, which preceded the current section 344, has not been the subject of a great deal of litigation in the United Kingdom.[45] It is clear from the phraseology and context of both the old and the new provision that they do not purport to settle questions of priorities. Canadian authorities suggest that registration under such a provision does not have the effect of conferring constructive notice on third parties.[46]

---

[41] P. 559 above.
[42] *Re Row Dal Construction Pty. Ltd.* [1966] VR 249.
[43] Being excluded from the definition of a chattel in s. 4 of the Bills of Sale Act 1878.
[44] Insolvency Act 1986, s. 344(3)(*b*).
[45] For a discussion of its background, see *Re Lovegrove* [1953] Ch. 464.
[46] *Snyder's Ltd.* v. *Furniture Finance Corporation Ltd.* [1931] 1 DLR 398; *Re Royal Bank of Canada* (1979) 94 DLR (3d) 692, the importance of which is pointed out by Goode, *Legal Problems of Credit and Security*, p. 98.

(v) Priorities

The problem of ranking competing claims to book debts is complicated by the fact that the adverse rights often accrue under different types of contract. Undoubtedly, there are cases in which the owner of the book debts, the assignor, creates two conflicting assignments over them. In some cases his motives are fraudulent; in others he may not be fully aware of the terms of each security furnished by him. In certain instances, though, the competing claims arise from entirely separate arrangements. Two types of situation are common. One involves a conflict between the claims of a trade creditor, who has a security over goods supplied to the assignor and their proceeds, and of a bank, which has a charge over existing and future book debts to secure a general overdraft. The other case involves competing types of security, such as a charge over book debts granted to one merchant bank and a debenture secured by a floating charge granted to another. In addition, there may be a clash between the holder of a charge over the assignor's book debts and an absolute assignment thereof to a factor.

The basic principle for determining priorities of competing assignments is known as the rule in *Dearle* v. *Hall.*[47] The assignee who is the first to give notice of the assignment to the debtor takes precedence. If neither of the competing assignees gives notice, the assignments take priority in the order of their execution.

The rule in *Dearle* v. *Hall* is not easily supportable by policy arguments. Notably, it was established before the introduction of provisions for the registration of securities. Although it also preceded the earliest provision for a statutory form of assignment,[48] it has been held to apply even as between competing absolute assignments and assignments by way of charge.[49] The rule is therefore applicable in cases involving a conflict between the claims of a bank, which is an assignee by way of charge of a firm's book debts, and a factor who has purchased them. The rule is equally applicable where the competing assignments cover future book debts.

The priority conferred on an assignee by the rule in *Dearle* v. *Hall* would be defeated if he knew or ought to have known, at the time he took the assignment, of the existence of an earlier one.[50] But the question of constructive notice, based on the registration of the charge, appears not to arise in the case of charges over the book debts of an unincorporated trader.[51] The converse applies in the case of companies' charges. An assignee cannot claim priority

---

[47] (1828) 3 Russ. 1.
[48] In the Judicature Act 1873, s. 25(6).
[49] *Harding Carpets Ltd.* v. *Royal Bank of Canada* [1980] 4 WWR 149, cited by Goode, *Legal Problems of Credit and Security*, p. 99.
[50] The previous assignment would be an equity.
[51] P. 587 above.

over a charge which was registered at the time he took his security. If the charge was unregistered at that time, priority is governed by the rule in *Dearle* v. *Hall*.

Registration under section 396(1)(*e*) does not solve the inherent problems of the ranking of a fixed charge over book debts as against a pre-existing floating charge on all the assets of the company. *Siebe Gorman & Co. Ltd.* v. *Barclays Bank Ltd.*,[52] discussed earlier, supports the view that, even where a floating charge covers book debts, its registration does not confer on subsequent creditors of the company knowledge of the contents of the registered charge. Thus, registration does not confer constructive notice of a clause in a floating charge which precludes subsequent assignments of the book debts.

The most difficult problem arises where there is competition between the claims of a trade creditor and of a bank that is an assignee by way of charge of a customer's book debts. By way of illustration, take the case of a supplier who obtains a reservation of title over both the goods delivered by him on credit and the proceeds accrued from their sale (the famous *Romalpa* clause).[53] If the purchaser resells the goods involved on credit terms, the supplier is bound to regard the debt as accrued subject to his security. A competing right will be asserted by a bank that has granted the supplier a general overdraft, or credit facility, secured by an assignment of all existing and future book debts. Which claim takes precedence in the purchaser's insolvency?

The rule in *Dearle* v. *Hall* is inapplicable, as the supplier is not an assignee of a debt accrued to the purchaser. His claim is based on the purchaser's duty to hold the proceeds of the goods as trustee or fiduciary.[54] Registration is equally irrelevant. Where the supplier is an unincorporated body, registration, it will be recalled, does not give constructive notice of the assignment of the book debts. The supplier is therefore unaffected by it. Equally, where the purchaser is a company, the supplier has no reason to search the register. Far from seeking to acquire a charge over goods and proceeds, his only object is to reserve (or 'retain') his pre-existing rights in the goods and in the proceeds. Goode suggests that the supplier acquires

---

[52] [1979] 2 Lloyd's Rep. 142; see, for facts, p. 582 above.

[53] First recognized in *Aluminium Industrie Vaassen BV* v. *Romalpa Aluminium Ltd.* [1976] 1 WLR 676. See generally R. M. Goode, 'The Right to Trace and its Impact in Commercial Transactions', (1976) 92 LQR 360, 528; A. G. Guest, 'Romalpa Clauses', (1979) 95 LQR 477 and [1980] CLJ 48; G. A. Muir, 'Recent Developments in Reservation of Property Clauses' (1985) 13 ABLR 3; *Benjamin's Sale of Goods*, 2nd edn., paras. 392–6. As regards the attachment of the clause of proceeds, see in particular *Re Bond Worth Ltd.* [1980] Ch. 228.

[54] D. W. McLauchlan, 'Priorities—Equitable Tracing Rights and Assignment of Book Debts', (1980) 96 LQR 90. Contrast Goode, *Legal Problems of Credit and Security*, p. 95, who believes that the rule in *Dearle* v. *Hall*, above, applies even where one of the competing claims is derived not from an assignment but from an equitable tracing right. There is no direct authority in point.

priority, as the bank's rights are subject to the equities prevailing between the purchaser and the supplier.[55] But the point is uncertain. The answer may depend on whether the supplier's equitable rights over the proceeds attach before they become subject to the bank's charge. If the supplier's rights attached thereafter, the bank would take priority.[56]

3. BANK BALANCES AS SECURITY

(i) Basic problems

A balance standing to the credit of a customer's account constitutes a debt owed to him by the bank.[57] This is the position regardless of whether the balance is accrued on a current account, a savings account, a fixed deposit, or any other interest-bearing account. From the customer's point of view, such a debt is an asset.[58] He may, therefore, wish to utilize it as a security either in respect of a transaction financed by the bank itself or in respect of one backed by another financial institution. By way of illustration, take a case in which the customer requests the bank to issue a guarantee or a letter of credit to back his purchase of goods. His deposits with the bank, which may be earmarked for some other specific purpose, are a good security for the bank's promise to the supplier. The customer's credit balance may also be utilized as a security where the letter of credit, guarantee, or some other facility is issued by a third party, such as a merchant bank or a confirming house.

Quite regardless of whether the balance is used to back a transaction with the bank or with a third party, the creation of a security is fraught with practical difficulties. First, the balance or deposit may be depleted by the customer by withdrawals. Although this hurdle can be overcome by the arrangement of a suitable date of maturity, the solution is unattractive. The customer's object in depositing funds with his bank is to maintain his liquidity. Even in the case of a fixed deposit, it is understood that the agreed date of maturity can normally be altered to accommodate the customer, provided he is prepared to countenance a loss of interest. To render a deposit unclaimable until the winding-up of the transaction secured by it may induce the customer simply to make immediate payment to the secured party.

Secondly, a bank balance standing to the credit of a current or interest-

[55] Relying on *Harding Carpets Ltd.* v. *Royal Bank of Canada* [1980] 4 WWR 149.
[56] Note that under s. 9–312 of the Uniform Commercial Code, the trade creditor, who has a purchase money security, would take priority.
[57] Pp. 81–84 above.
[58] That it is not a book debt, see p. 582 above.

bearing account is subject to garnishee proceedings by a judgment creditor.[59] Naturally, this hazard undermines the value of a security over a bank balance. The techniques used to overcome it will be shown to place impediments on the customer's freedom of action. Thirdly, the security is valueless unless it affords protection in the depositor's bankruptcy. It will be shown that this outcome is not always attainable. Finally, in the case of a depositor, who is a natural person, the security has to be phrased so as to be effective against his estate in the event of his demise.

Different techniques are used for the granting of a security over a bank balance. Basically, the form used depends on whether it is to be given to the bank with which the funds are deposited or to a third party.

(ii) Security to a bank with whom funds are deposited: set-off in equity and insolvency

The right of a bank to effect a set-off by combining a customer's different accounts has been discussed in Chapter 6.[60] The right is based on the principle of equity which allows a debtor to reduce the amount claimed by his creditor by any liquidated sum due from the creditor to himself. It is, accordingly, a procedural right, and does not confer on the party entitled to exercise it a property right.[61] The subject of the set-off need not be an amount standing to the customer's credit in a specific bank account. It is sufficient if it is a definite and liquidated claim.[62] A contingent claim and, possibly, one maturing at a future date cannot, in equity, be set off against an immediate right.[63] An important requisite of an equitable set-off is that the claims must be mutual, in the sense of arising between the same parties and in their own respective rights.[64] If the set-off involves a liquidated demand, that demand need not be based on the same transaction as the right in respect of which it is exercised or a transaction closely linked with it. If the claim arises from such a transaction, it may be set off even if it is unliquidated.[65]

It is clear that the equitable set-off is of considerable assistance to banks. Thus, a bank that is required to make payment under a bank guarantee issued by it can reimburse itself by exercising a set-off against credit

[59] Pp. 271–5 above.
[60] Pp. 139 et seq. above.
[61] Goode, *Legal Problems of Credit and Security*, p. 102.
[62] *Hanak v. Green* [1958] 2 QB 9, 17.
[63] *Jeffryes* v. *Agra and Masterman's Bank* (1866) LR 2 Eq. 674; *Bower* v. *Foreign and Colonial Gas Co. Ltd.*, *Metroplitan Bank (Garnishees)* (1874) 22 WR 740; cf. *Business Computers Ltd.* v. *Anglo-African Leasing Co. Ltd.* [1977] 1 WLR 578.
[64] *Middleton v. Pollock* (1875) LR 20 Eq. 515; *Re Pennington and Owen Ltd.* [1925] Ch. 825; *N. V. Robbie & Co. Ltd.* v. *Witney Warehouse Co. Ltd.* [1963] 3 All ER 613; *Re Whitehouse & Co.* (1878) 9 Ch. D 595.
[65] *Aries Tanker Corporation* v. *Total Transport Ltd.* [1977] 1 All ER 398, 406–7; Goode *Legal Problems of Credit and Security*, p. 104.

balances standing to the credit of the customer's accounts. But two limitations of this right of set-off pose problems. First, up to the time its own claim is due, the bank cannot effect a set-off in order to preclude the customer from drawing on the balances in question. Secondly, its right is subordinate to those of a judgment creditor who has served a garnishee order nisi before the exercise of the set-off, except in respect of a claim of the bank that is due at the very time the order nisi is served on it.[66]

When an unincorporated customer is adjudicated a bankrupt, the bank's right of set-off is no longer governed by the equitable principles in point, but by section 323 of the Insolvency Act 1986, which applies also in the winding-up of companies.[67] This provision has been discussed earlier on,[68] but it will be convenient to mention here its salient features. First, the application of the section cannot be excluded by agreement.[69] Secondly, the claims which are the subject of the set-off must be based on mutual dealings, a phrase that has the same meaning as in respect of the equitable set-off. Claims arising in the course of transactions involving the financing of a customer by his bank are within the ambit of the definition.[70] Thirdly, it is doubtful if a contingent claim can be the subject of such a set-off,[71] although it is, of course, provable.[72] It follows that, if the customer becomes insolvent, the bank cannot exercise in his bankruptcy a set-off based on the customer's duty to reimburse the bank for payments that it may be forced to make under a performance bond granted at his instruction.

The fourth and most complicated requirement is that debts can be the subject of a set-off under section 323 only if they have been in existence at the time of the commencement of the bankruptcy.[73] This restriction handicaps the creditor, or bank, where it wishes to set off against the customer's balance a claim that came into existence at a date later that the adjudication, such as a claim for reimbursement arising out of the payment of a letter of

---

[66] *Tapp* v. *Jones* (1875) LR 10 QB 591, 593; and see p. 274 above.

[67] The predecessor of s. 323, which was s. 31 of the Bankruptcy Act 1914, applied to the winding-up of companies under s. 317 of the Companies Act 1948. This provision was replaced by s. 612 of the Companies Act 1985, which was, in turn, repealed by s. 438 of the Insolvency Act 1986. It is expected that regulations made under s. 411 and Sched. 8, paras. 12 and 14 will ensure that s. 323 will apply in the same way as the old s. 31.

[68] Pp. 155–8 above.

[69] *National Westminster Bank Ltd.* v. *Halesowen Presswork and Assemblies Ltd.* [1972] AC 785.

[70] Idem.

[71] *Re Fenton, ex p. Fenton Textile Association Ltd.* [1956] 1 Ch. 85; *Re a Debtor* [1956] 1 WLR 1226.

[72] Insolvency Act 1986, s. 322(3), replacing s. 30(3) of the Bankruptcy Act 1914. It has accordingly been argued that such a claim may be set off under s. 323: Cresswell et al., *Encyclopedia of Banking Law*, vol. 1, para. E2474, referring to *Day and Dent Constructions Pty. Ltd.* v. *North Australian Properties Pty. Ltd.* (1981) 34 ALR 595, affd. (1982) 40 ALR 399. But note that the Australian provision in point is differently worded.

[73] *Re Daintrey* [1900] 1 QB 546. As to when a bankruptcy commences, see Insolvency Act 1986, s. 278 (individuals), and ss. 86, 129 (winding-up).

credit that matured after the relevant date.[74] The disadvantage to the bank is clear, as in all cases of this sort it has to prove its debt instead of being able to resort to the more attractive set-off. The restriction, though, is not as wide as it may appear at first glance. A debt which is in existence at the relevant time can be the subject of a set-off although its date of maturity is yet to arrive.[75] Thus, where a bank had undertaken to pay on its customer's behalf instalments due to a supplier for goods delivered on credit, the bank can exercise a set-off covering future payments.

It may appear perplexing that instalments to be paid in respect of a contract for the supply of goods on credit may be the subject of a set-off, whilst claims for the reimbursement of amounts paid by the bank under a letter of credit maturing after the relevant date are excluded. The rationale is that the payments made in respect of the sale are due unconditionally at a future date. The debt is therefore in existence at the time of the customer's adjudication. By way of contrast, the bank's right to claim reimbursement in the context of the documentary credit transaction arises only if it is required to discharge its own duty to make payment to the beneficiary. This claim would not arise unless the beneficiary tendered a set of documents strictly conforming with the requirements of the letter of credit. The bank's right of reimbursement is therefore contingent. From a practical point of view, though, the distinction seems arbitrary, as both debts are incurred in respect of commercial liabilities undertaken by the bank in the course of the extension of credit to its customer.

(iii) Security to bank with whom funds are deposited: contractual set-off

In view of the restricted scope of application of the equitable right of set-off and the set-off applicable on insolvency, it has become a practice to confer on a bank that finances its customer a contractual right of set-off. The right may be the subject of a special agreement, known as a letter of set-off, or may be created by means of specific clauses incorporated in the underlying financial agreement between the bank and its customer. The object of the clause is to confer on the bank a right to set-off against balances maintained with it by the customer any claim that it has against him, be it contingent, unconditional, liquidated, unliquidated, future, or existing.

It has been pointed out that, in practical terms, the clause aims to confer two rights on the bank. The first is to suspend the customer's right to make withdrawals as long as he is subject to any liability to the bank. The second is to enable the bank to debit against the balance accrued any amount due to

---

[74] *Kitchen Trustee* v. *Madders* [1949] 2 All ER 54; *Re a Debtor* [1956] 1 WLR 1226. Contrast *Re Charge Cards Services Ltd.*, [1986] 3 All ER 289, Millett J.

[75] *Rolls Razor Ltd.* v. *Cox* [1967] 1 QB 552.

itself. By way of illustration, take the case in which the customer is under an obligation to reimburse to the bank any amount that may be demanded by the beneficiary of a performance bond. The set-off clause precludes the withdrawals of amounts standing to the customer's credit as long as this liability is contingent. It further entitles the bank to debit against the balance any amount falling due once this liability crystallises.[76] It is clear that, in the majority of cases, the bank is loath to shackle its customer's business operations. The clause may therefore be so drafted as to preclude withdrawals only if their affect is to reduce the balance beneath an agreed figure.

A variant of the set-off agreement is the fashionable 'flawed asset arrangement'.[77] As indicated by its title, the arrangement imposes a 'flaw' on the customer's 'asset' or, in plain language, restricts his rights to utilize his balance with the bank. The arrangement is, thus, based on the first element found in the classic set-off agreement. The right to exercise the set-off is not conferred on the bank. It is believed that, as a result, the agreement does not require to be registered as a charge.[78] In practical terms the flawed asset arrangement has practically the same effect as a contractual set-off. Under both types of agreement the bank is entitled to freeze the bank balance until such time as the customer's liability to it is discharged. Four legal problems arise in respect of a set-off agreement, and some apply equally to a flawed asset arrangement. They concern the validity of the agreement in the customer's insolvency and the question of priorities.

The first problem concerns conflicts between the right of the bank to effect its set-off and the rights of an assignee of the bank balance. Being a chose in action, a bank balance may be assigned under section 136 or in equity.[79] But regardless of its form, the assignee's rights are subject to the equities available to the bank (the 'debtor') against the assignor (the 'customer'). To this rule there is one important limitation. An equity could be so set up only if it was accrued before the debtor was given notice of the assignment.[80] The set-off agreement between the bank ('debtor') and the customer ('assignor') constitutes an equity which is accordingly available against the assignee if it has 'accrued' before the serving of notice on the bank. 'Accrued' in this context probably means 'effected' under the set-off agreement. It would appear to follow that a set-off agreement takes priority over an assignment notified to the bank after the execution of the agreement.[81]

Does the flawed asset arrangement constitute a similar equity, which can

[76] Goode, *Legal Problems of Credit and Security*, p. 112.
[77] F. W. Neate, 'set-off', (1981) 9 *Int. Business Lawyer* 247.
[78] P. 598 below.
[79] Pp. 583–4 above.
[80] P. 585 above.
[81] For the same view, see Cresswell *et al.*, *Encyclopedia of Banking Law*, vol. 1, para. E2466. And see *Business Computers Ltd.* v. *Anglo-African Leasing Ltd.* [1977] 1 WLR 578, 585.

be pleaded against an assignee of the bank balance? On the one hand, it is arguable that the restriction on the customer's right to draw on the funds is a restrictive covenant which constitutes an equity.[82] On the other hand, the arrangement does not confer rights on the bank but simply restricts the customer's freedom to dispose of his assets. It may be that the answer is to be found in a consideration of the fundamental effect of the arrangement, which is to postpone the bank's duty to repay the debt represented by the bank balance in question. It seems clear that the assignee of the balance cannot enforce its repayment where the assignor (customer) is unable to do so. Nevertheless, the assignee can enforce payment if the terms of the deposit are varied by means of the flawed asset arrangement after the serving of notice of assignment on the bank.

The second problem respecting a contractual set-off arises where a judgment creditor serves on the bank a garnishee order nisi. Is the bank entitled to reap the benefit of the set-off or is the entire balance to be garnished? Two principles are here in conflict. One is that contingent liabilities cannot be set-off against the claim of a garnishee creditor.[83] The other is that the judgment creditor cannot obtain by means of the garnishee order rights superior to those held by the debtor.[84] It is believed that, again, the correct answer is to be found in a basic principle. A garnishee order does not attach to a debt unless it is due at the time the order is served.[85] It is true that this principle has been abrogated in respect of balances standing to the credit of a deposit account.[86] But where the debt is suspended indefinitely, as is the case in a set-off agreement, it is realistic to regard it as not having accrued at the time the garnishee order is served. The order therefore ought not to attach to it. The same solution applies in cases where garnishee proceedings are instituted in respect of a customer who has effected a flawed asset arrangement in favour of his bank.

The third problem is whether the set-off agreement requires registration as a charge or, if effected by an individual, as a bill of sale. It has been shown that a bank balance is usually not a book debt.[87] Ordinarily the question should therefore not arise.[88] In the case of an unincorporated customer, the answer would remain the same even if the balance constituted a book debt, as registration is not required where the debtor is specified in the instrument creating the assignment.[89] The position differs in the case of an incorpor-

---

[82] P. 584 above.
[83] P. 274 above and *Tapp* v. *Jones* (1875) LR 10 QB 591, 593.
[84] *Re General Horticultural Co., ex p. Whitehouse* (1886) 32 Ch. D 512, 516.
[85] P. 271 above.
[86] Ibid. For an interesting analysis, see *Evans Coleman & Evans* v. *R. A. Nelson Construction Ltd.* (1958) 16 DLR 123.
[87] P. 000 above.
[88] Goode, *Legal Problems of Credit and Security*, pp. 103 et seq.
[89] Insolvency Act 1986, s. 344(3)(*b*); and see p. 587 above.

ated customer, as any charge on book debts requires registration under section 396(1)(e). But is a set-off agreement a charge? Its effect is to postpone payment and to enable the bank to strike a balance when the debt matures. It is therefore incorrect to regard the balance as an asset set aside to enable the bank to recover its claim from its proceeds.[90] The same argument applies, a fortiori, to the flawed asset arrangement.

The fourth problem arises only where an incorporated customer, who has entered into a set-off agreement with his bank, is being wound up. The basic principle, originally propounded in section 302 of the Companies Act 1948, which has now been effectively replaced by sections 107 and 143 of the Insolvency Act 1986,[91] is that all claims which are not given a special status (such as preferential claims or claims of secured creditors) are to rank pari passu. In *British Eagle International Air Lines Ltd.* v. *Compagnie Nationale Air France*,[92] the House of Lords held invalid an agreement which gave to a party a position similar to that of a secured creditor but in a manner that avoided the need of registering a charge. It was held that the agreement was contary to public policy, in that it defeated the principle enshrined in section 302. The fact that the offending agreement was not made with a view to defeating the provision in point, but constituted an acceptable commercial arrangement, was held irrelevant.

It is significant that the agreement used in the *British Eagle* case achieved its object by arranging for a set-off. It has been argued that, on the same reasoning, the courts would invalidate a contractual set-off and a flawed asset arrangement.[93] It is, however, possible to distinguish the agreement in *British Eagles* from the type of agreement used by banks. In the former, the set-off was to be executed by a third party, with whom both the creditor and the insolvent debtor maintained their accounts. In the latter types of agreements, the set-off is to be effected directly in respect of cross-claims of the creditor and the debtor. It is, accordingly, unrealistic to regard these agreements as seeking merely to create priorities in winding-up. Both the contractual set-off and the flawed asset arrangement provide an effective machinery for treating a number of transactions between the same two parties as comprising one basic relationship. Moreover, both the set-off agreement and the flawed asset arrangement postpone the bank's duty to repay the debt owed by it to the customer up to the time the latter has discharged his liability to the bank. The clause ought to be effective up to the time the condition is met.[94]

---

[90] Contrast Cresswell et al., *Encyclopedia of Banking Law*, vol. 1, para. E2477, relying on *Swiss Bank Corporation* v. *Lloyds Bank Ltd.* [1982] AC 584.
[91] Initially, s. 302 of the Companies Act 1948 was replaced by s. 597 of the Companies Act 1985, which in turn was repealed by s. 438 of the Insolvency Act 1986.
[92] [1975] 1 WLR 758.
[93] Cresswell et al., *Encyclopedia of Banking Law.*, vol. 1, para. E2478.
[94] Note that, if the agreements were considered invalid, the bank would still have its right of set-off under s. 323.

(iv) Charges over bank balances

A balance standing to the credit of a customer's bank account is a chose in action. It can accordingly be the subject of a charge or mortgage, effected by means of an assignment. Some firms tend to utilize section 136 of the Law of Property Act 1925, in order to effect an absolute assignment of a bank balance,[95] coupled with a right of redemption.[96] Whilst the existence of this equity does not in itself convert the absolute assignment into a charge,[97] care need be taken so as to avoid the use of language suggesting that the assignment is made solely for the purpose of providing a secure source of payment for the assignee. Thus, in *Durham Bros. v. Robertson*,[98] an assignment to a financier of the proceeds of a building contract was held to be outside the scope of section 136, as it was expressly stated to lapse upon the repayment of the amounts advanced to the builder.[99]

In practice, an assignment by way of charge, which is of course an equitable assignment, is an adequate security.[100] Where such a security is given to a third party, such as a financier or a supplier of goods on credit, it is essential to include provisions precluding the depletion of the security by drawings. This is easily achieved in the case of a balance standing to the credit of a fixed deposit or other interest-bearing account. It is more difficult to achieve this result in the case of a current account, as any attempt to freeze it is bound to interfere with the customer's ability to carry on his ordinary trading transactions.

Can a security over a bank balance be given to the very bank with which it is maintained? Opinion is divided. Those who argue against the validity of such a charge rely on the reasons given for questioning that a balance is subject to the bank's lien.[101] It is not overlooked that a lien is a possessory security, whilst a charge and mortgage constitute proprietary securities. The bank balance, though, is a chose in action due from the bank to the customer.[102] How, then, can the bank have a charge or mortgage over its own indebtedness? Goode points out that the essence of an assignment is to

---

[95] Cresswell *et al.*, *Encyclopedia of Banking Law.*, vol. 1, para. E2487.

[96] *Tancred* v. *Delagoa Bay and East Africa Ry. Co.* (1889) 23 QBD 239; *Durham Bros.* v. *Robertson* [1898] 765; *Hughes* v. *Pump House Hotel Co. Ltd.* [1902] 2 KB 190.

[97] *Tancred* v. *Delagoa Bay and East Africa Ry. Co.*, above.

[98] Above; and see *Jones* v. *Humphreys* [1902] 1 KB 10.

[99] But note that the assignment could still be valid in equity: *Palmer* v. *Carey* [1926] AC 703; *Rother Iron Works Ltd.* v. *Canterbury Precision Engineers Ltd.* [1974] QB 1; *Swiss Bank Corporation* v. *Lloyds Bank Ltd.* [1982] AC 584.

[100] As regards its purported disadvantages, see p. 581 above.

[101] P. 143 above.

[102] Cf. *Alcom Ltd.* v. *Republic of Columbia* [1984] AC 580 in which a bank balance was considered 'property' within the meaning of s. 13(2)(*b*) of the State Immunity Act 1978. But the construction of this provision cannot be regarded as modifying the common law classification of bank balances as choses in action.

enable the assignee to recover the debt. It would be absurd to argue that, in the type of case here discussed, the bank, which is both the debtor and the assignee, ought to sue itself.[103]

The argument to the contrary is based on considering the nature of the bank balance from the customer's viewpoint.[104] It is undeniable that, for the purposes of his dealings and his balance sheet, a bank balance constitutes an asset. As its date of maturity is in the future, it is suggested that the bank can discount it and perhaps even acquire a lien over it.[105] In effect, this argument purports to treat the balance as an item of property by reason of its being one of the customer's assets.[106]

It is submitted that the correct answer is that a purported charge granted to a bank over a balance standing to the customer's credit with itself operates as a contractual set-off agreement. The covenants included in the standard forms used for the creation of a charge are, indeed, similar to those to be found in a contractual set-off. That the purported security agreement does not create a charge or a mortgage is supported by two Australian authorities.[107] It is believed that the bank's interests are adequately served by the recognition of the agreement as a valid contractual set-off.

It remains to be considered whether the arrangements in question requires registration. Naturally, it does not require registration if it is a set-off agreement.[108] This would be so regardless of whether the customer is incorporated or unincorporated. It is believed that the same is true if the agreement creates a charge or a mortgage. Where the customer is unincorporated, registration is not required under section 344 of the Insolvency Act 1986, as long as the assignment covers a book debt due from a designated party. A bank balance at a designated bank would therefore be outside this registration provision even if it constituted a book debt. But, in any event, it has been shown that the prevailing view is that, usually, a bank balance does not constitute a book debt.[109] For this reason, a charge created over a bank balance, or an assignment thereof, does not fall within the scope of one of

---

[103] Goode, *Legal Problems of Credit and Security* p. 86. See also Weaver and Craigie, *Banker and Customer in Australia*, p. 614. And see *Re Charge Card Services Ltd.* [1986] 3 All ER 289, Millett J.

[104] W. J. L. Blair, 'Charges over Cash Deposits', *Int. Financial Rev.*, Nov. 1983, 14; Hapgood, ibid., 34.

[105] See also p. 590 above.

[106] And see *Alcom Ltd. v. Republic of Columbia*, [1984] 2 All ER 6.

[107] *Broad* v. *Commissioner of Stamp Duties* [1980] 2 NSWLR 40; *Estate Planning Associates (Australia) Pty. Ltd* v. *Commissioner of Stamp Duties* (1984) 16 ATR 862. Cf. *Re Hart, ex p. Caldicott* (1884) 25 Ch. D 716, cited by Hapgood, loc. cit., which suggests that the arrangement confers some security on the bank. But the case does not suggest that the security constitutes a mortgage or a charge. Note also *Swiss Bank Corporation* v. *Lloyds Bank Ltd.* [1982] AC 589, in which it was assumed that a bank could have a charge over proceeds of shares deposited with it. The point, though, was not fully argued.

[108] To date, it has not been argued that a set-off constitutes a charge.

[109] P. 582 above.

the other types of charge requiring registration under section 396 of the Companies Act 1985.

4. LIFE POLICIES AS SECURITIES

Life assurance policies can provide security against two events: loss that the creditor may incur upon the debtor's demise, and loss from his insolvency or default. As against the former risk, the policy is a good security for the amount insured. As against the latter, the policy is a security only for the amount that it yields at the time of the default or insolvency. For this purpose it is necessary to distinguish between two arrangements that may take place if a policy is relinquished before its maturity. One involves the immediate conversion of the insurer's payment obligation into cash. The assured is then paid the 'surrendered value' of the policy, which is calculated by an actuary on the basis of the amounts paid to date. By and large, the surrendered value of a policy is negligible during its first three years and increases proportionately thereafter.

The other arrangement for the discontinuation of a policy involves its conversion into a 'paid-up policy'. The amount accrued at the relevant time from the premiums paid by the assured (plus a bonus) is retained by the company as a fund payable at the original maturity date. Naturally, the paid-up value of a relinquished policy is considerably higher than its surrendered value. In the context of commercial transactions banks are disinclined to treat a policy as a security for an amount considerably higher than its surrendered value at the time the loan is extended to the customer.

From a bank's point of view, life policies can broadly be divided into two types: 'whole of life' policies and 'endowment' policies. In a 'whole of life' policy, the assured's main object is to protect his family against his own death. The amount of the policy is therefore payable on his death. In an endowment policy, the amount involved plus profits is payable either on the assured's death or when he reaches an agreed age. The policy therefore provides protection for his old age. By and large, the amount yielded by an endowment policy is smaller than the amount for which the policy would give cover, on payment of the same premiums, in a whole of life policy. But the surrendered value of a whole of life policy is usually lower than that of an endowment policy for a similar amount. An endowment policy is therefore a superior security in the hands of a bank.

An insurance policy is a chose in action.[110] A security over it may be effected by means either of an equitable charge or of a legal charge. An equitable charge is created by the deposit of the insurance policy with the

[110] *Torkington* v. *Magee* [1902] 2 KB 427, 430.

bank followed by the serving of notice of the bank's interest on the insurance company. The deposit of the policy does not in itself create a security valid against other interests. But where the assured attempts to give a security over the same policy to another financier, the latter is probably put on notice by the assured's inability to produce the document.[111] He may therefore not be able to claim the priority normally attained by a legal mortgagee. The serving of notice on the insurance company is important in this regard, as any financier, approached subsequently, is able to ascertain the true position by making an enquiry.

A legal mortgage has to be effected by means of an assignment executed under the Policies of Assurance Act 1867. Such an assignment may be excuted either by means of an indorsement on the policy or in a separate document.[112] The assignee is given the right to recover the amount of the policy by instituting proceedings in his own name.[113] The assignment itself will usually confer on him the right to surrender the policy on behalf of the assured.[114] Notice of the assignment has to be served on the insurance company; until this is done the assignment is ineffective against it. As from the date of the notice, any payment by the company to the assured is made at its peril. The date of the notice is also used for determining the ranking of competing assignments.[115] ∕

Although an insurance policy is an effective security, the bank has to be aware of a number of risks. First, an insurance policy is an *uberrimae fidei* contract. This means that the assured owes a duty of absolute honesty and of full disclosure to the company. If he fails to disclose any material fact, or gives any inaccurate answer to the questions put to him in the 'proposal form' (completed when he applies for cover), the policy is void.[116] Although many policies include a clause waiving the insurance company's right of cancellation if the policy has been in operation for three years, the policy can still be avoided if the assured has fraudulently given an untruthful answer. Insurance companies are usually unwilling to avoid a policy which has been assigned by way of security. They do, however, have the right to do so as the bank—the assignee—takes subject to the equities.[117]

Secondly, the amount of a life policy is not recoverable by the assured's estate if he commits suicide whilst in sound mind.[118] It is not certain that an

---

[111] *Spencer v. Clarke* (1878) 9 Ch. D 137; *Re Weniger's Policy* [1910] 2 Ch. 291.
[112] Policies of Assurance Act 1867, s. 5.
[113] Ibid., s 1.
[114] Most assignments exclude the operation of s. 103 of the Law of Property Act 1925, so as to exclude any restrictions on the bank's power to realize the security.
[115] Policies of Assurance Act 1867, s. 3. As to what constitutes proof of notice, see ibid., s. 6.
[116] See, generally, *Chitty on Contracts*, 25th edn., vol. 2, paras. 3684 et seq.
[117] And see the Policies of Assurance Act 1867, s. 2.
[118] *Beresford v. Royal Insurance Co. Ltd.* [1938] AC 586.

assignee, too, is unable to recover in such a case.[119] On general principles, though, it is believed that his position cannot be superior to the estate's. A bank that takes a life policy as a security does therefore take subject to this risk. It is true that suicide is no longer a crime in English law.[120] But the assured's estate should not be allowed to recover from the insurance company a loss occasioned intentionally by the assured's own hand.

Thirdly, if a bank is asked to take a security over a policy taken out by its holder on the life of another person, the bank has to satisfy itself that the holder has an 'insurable interest' in the 'life assured'. Under the Life Assurance Act 1774,[121] a policy is void where the policy-holder does not have such an interest. A person is deemed to have an insurable interest in his own life and in that of his spouse.[122] Common law further recognizes that a person has an insurable interest in the life of another by reason of a valid pecuniary interest.[123]

Finally, the bank obtains a good security against the assured's bankruptcy or demise. On his demise the bank can give a good discharge to the insurance company for the amount of the policy.[124] Undoubtedly, if the amount received exceeds the debt due from the assured, the bank holds the surplus as trustee of the estate. Where the bank has a legal charge it is, of course, able to enforce its assignment against the trustee in bankruptcy. Moreover, it has been held that even an equitable charge, which has not been perfected by notice, is valid against the trustee.[125] But such a charge would be ineffective against subsequent equitable mortgagees who gave notice to the company and, of course, against legal mortgages.

---

[119] Ibid.
[120] The Suicide Act 1961, s. 1.
[121] S. 1.
[122] Ibid.
[123] Such as debtors or partners—to the extent of their financial interest; see, generally, *Chitty on Contracts*, 25th edn., vol. 2, para. 3665.
[124] Law of Property Act 1925, s. 107.
[125] *Re Wallis, ex p. Jenks* [1902] 1 KB 719.

Appendix of Forms

Published by kind permission of
the Royal Bank of Scotland plc

PROMISSORY NOTE

26 THE BOULEVARD
HIGH STREET
ANYTOWN
ENGLAND

ANYTOWN   1 JUNE 1987

THREE MONTHS AFTER DATE I PROMISE TO PAY TO ANDREW SMITH OR ORDER THE
SUM OF ONE HUNDRED POUNDS FOR VALUE RECEIVED.

(Signed) _____

(JAMES BROWN)

Promissory Note

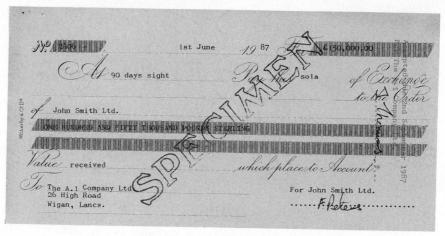

Bill of Exchange (Fine Trade Bill)
Payable at a usance of 90 days after sight.

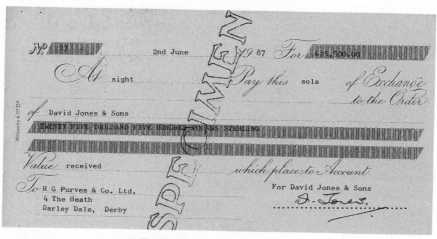

Bill of Exchange (payable at sight)
(*Above*) front of bill. (*Below*) back of bill.
(Special indorsement of payee and general indorsement of indorsee)

Bank Giro Credit
Details of Jack Smith's cheque are set out on the back of the form

The Royal Bank of Scotland plc
To be written by party making the credit
Date 14.6.87
Bank The Royal Bank of Scotland
Branch Oxford
Credit Dr. A. Healer

Teller's stamp and initials £ 150 —

Paid in by Jack Smith
Subject to verification of items other than cash

02743 (3/85)

The Royal Bank of Scotland plc
Date 14.6.87
Teller's stamp and initials
Items Fee Deferment

bank giro credit

Code No 83 89 98

Bank The Royal Bank of Scotland
Branch Oxford
Paid in by Jack Smith
Credit Name Dr. A. Healer
Account No 00123456
Please do not write or mark below this line

Notes over £20		
£20 Notes		
£10 Notes		
£5 Notes		
£1 Notes/Coin		
Silver		
Bronze		
Total Cash		
Cheques etc (See over)	150	—
Total £	150	—

⊪ ?0

Crossed cheque

The Royal Bank of Scotland plc

14 June 1987

83-04-20

SPECIMEN

24 Lombard Street London EC3V 9BA   a/c payee only

or order

Pay Jack Smith

Two thousand five hundred
and sixty pounds only

£2,560.00

CLIVE & MRS R A THORBURN

Premium Account

Clive Thorburn

⊪103444⊪ 83⊪0420: 0027041 6⊪

Bankers' Payment

Receive from
The Royal Bank of Scotland plc

Branch Oxford

Manager R. Wood
For Account of Jack Smith
01582600

To Midland Bank plc
27 High Street
TAUNTON

The Royal Bank of Scotland plc
Payments Control Centre
5-10 Great Tower Street
London

Bankers Payment   15-00-00T

Date 14.6.87

Pay Selves One hundred pounds   £SPECIMEN

SPECIMEN

⊪570249⊪ 16⊪5900: 99999524⊪ 12

The Royal Bank of Scotland plc

15-00-00T

Date 14 . 6 . 87

On demand pay to Jack Smith

The sum of One thousand pounds

or order

£1000

SPECIMEN

To The Royal Bank of Scotland plc
Payments Control Centre
5-10 Great Tower Street
London

Manager M. Jones.

⑈141581⑈ 16⑈5900⑈ 999997451⑈

Bankers' Draft

19

SANDERSON CHASE LTD

Date 14 - 6 19 87

Warehousemen
25-29 Blackfriars Street Lane Kelso

83-23-18

The Royal Bank of Scotland plc
6 The Square Kelso TD5 7HG

Pay Jack Smith

or order

Fifty Two Pounds only

SPECIMEN

£52

For and on behalf of Sanderson Chase Ltd

£

John Brown (Secretary)
Designation (as required)

Jim Brown (Treasurer)
Designation (as required)

123456

⑈123456⑈ 83⑈2318⑈ 00123456⑈

Crossed cheque
(on form used by companies)

Index

Acceptance credit
  bills drawn under, 523–8
  described, 494–5
  distinguished from guarantee, 495
  origin, 15
  subrogation in insolvency, 525–6
Accepting Houses
  business, 15
  characteristics, 15–16
  history, 15
  position, 4
Accommodation bills
  acceptance credit, whether bill drawn
    thereunder is, 524–5
  discharge of, 523, 524
  dispensation of formalities, 523–4
Advice on Financial Investments
  bank's duty of care, 463–4, 466
  damages available, 465
  strangers, to, 464–5
Agency element in bank's contracts
  agent, where is, 80, 84
  ambiguous instructions, customer's, 84,
    299–300
  current account, in, 128
  duty to adhere to mandate, 84, 285–6
Appropriation of payments
  basic rule, 482–5
    when displaced, 482–4
    when inapplicable, 485
  Consumer Credit Act, under, 68
  mortgages, operation in, 548
Assignment
  absolute, 581
  bank balances, of, see Bank balances
  charge, by way of, 581
  equitable, 367
  equities, subject to, 227–8, 497–8,
    584
  giro operation, whether is, 366–8
  statutory, 366

Bailment, see Safe custody
Bank as bailee, see Safe custody
Bank balance
  assignment, clash with garnishee, 274
  bank's money, is, 82, 121, 127
  charges over, 597–9
  lien over, see Bankers' lien
  set-off, see Set-off

Bank defined
  Banking Act, under, 36–7
  common law, at, 51–5
  reputation as ingredient, 54–5
  when not defined in Act, 61–2, see
    Privileges of banks
Bank loans, see loans
Bank of England
  annual reports of, 35
  central bank, as, 28, 29, 30, 47–50
  exchange control, function in, 30
  history, 27–8
  issuing bank, as, 28, 29
  monetary control, by, 47–50
  organization, 30
  settlement bank, 30
  supervisory power, 31, and see Banking
    Act, 1979
  Treasury, relation to, 30
Bank secrecy
  agent's duty of secrecy, 96
  computer centres, duty of, 387–8
  disclosure, generally when, 98
    bank's own interest, 103–4
    compulsion at law, 99
    implied consent, 104–5
    public interest, 102–3
  extraterritoriality, 105–13
  general principle, 98
  letters rogatory, 105–7
  references, bankers', 104, 455–7
  solicitors', compared with, 96–7
  subpoena duces tecum, 107–8
Bankers' Automated Clearing Services
    (BACS)
  controlled by CLSB, 7
  process, 345, 354–6
  secrecy, duty of, 387–8
Bankers' Books Evidence Act 1879
  application, 60, 101, 102
  copies, production of entries, 99
  documents covered, 101–2
  inspection order, 99
  third-party, against, 101
Bankers' draft
  banks' position, 243
  nature, 243, 358
  crossing of, 258
  collection of, 422
  risks, 358–9

Bankers' draft—*cont.*
  use, 358–9
Bankers' lien
  covers total indebtedness, 577
    special abrogation, 577
  effect, 579
  items attached, 576–9
    collection items, 578
    not items in safe custody, 578
  nature, 576
  not over deposits with itself, 142, 578–9
    foreign balance, 579
Bankers' payments
  nature, 354
  town clearing, 236
  use of, 345
Bankers' references
  banks' right to furnish, 104, 455–6
  charge, none made, 453–4
  enquirer's right against referee, 457–63
    against own bank, 457
  fraudulent statements, 458–9
  negligent statements, 459–63
  person investigated's right against his
      bank, 455
    against enquiring bank, 457
  writing, when needed, 458–9
Banking Act 1979
  advertisements, 42
  appeals, 40–41
  application procedures, 38
  background, 31–2
  "bank", use in name, 42
  Bank of England, powers under, 32, 42–3
  banking services, 36
  basic structure, 31–2
  cancellation of licence or authorization 38,
      39–40
  deposit protection fund, 43
  deposit taking business, 33
  deposits, acceptance of, 32, 41–2
    defined, 33–4
  foreign institutions, 37
  information to be provided by banks, 43
  licensed deposit takers and licensing, 34–6
  recognised banks and recognition, 36
  Schedule 1 bodies, 44–5, *see* Banking Bill
      1986
Banking Bill 1986
  proposals, 46–7
  White paper, 45
Banking business
  Banking Act, under, 33–6
  common law, at, 52–5
  economic function, 117–19
  reservoir of money, 119–20
Banking in United Kingdom

banks' standing, 121
classification, 24
economic function, 117–19
effect of statutory control, 75–6
structure, 3
Bills of exchange
  acceptance, meaning of, 501
  acceptor, 501
    absolute liability, 519
    holder at maturity, 517
  accommodation bills, *see* Accommodation
      bills
  bearer bill, conversion to order, 512
  cancellation, discharges, 517
  commercial function, 498–9
  consideration for bill, 508–9
  consumer credit aspects, 527–8
  defined, 496
  determinable time defined, 496–7
  discharge of bill, 516–18
  distinguished from contract, 497–8
  domicile, of bill, 503
  drawee, position of, 500–1
    as acceptor, 501
  drawer, position of, 500
    when acquiring bill, 503, 515
    when discharged, 519
  holder, position of, 503, 504–11
    rights of, 507–8
  holder for value, defined, 508
    rights of, 509–10
  holder in due course, defined, 505–6
    rights of, 506–7
  holder taking from a holder in due course,
      507
  immediate and remote parties, 504–5
  indorsee, meaning of, 501
  indorsement, effect of, 502, 515
    in blank, 512
    on front of bill, 503
    restrictive, 514–5
    special, 512
    when valid, 513
  indorser, liability of, 501, 502
    discharge, 519
  material alterations, 518
  negotiation, meaning of, 501
    by indorsement, 511–12
    of bearer bill, 512–13
  negotiability, restriction of, 514
  notice of dishonour, 519–20
  noting, 520
  payment, in the course of, 516
    by drawer is not, 516
    of accommodation bill, 524
  presentation for acceptance, 510
  presentment for payment, 510–11

protest, 520
sum certain, 497
transfer by delivery, 513
unconditional order, 240–2, 496
value, *see* consideration for bill
Book debts
assignment, 583
assignee's position, 584–5
charge over, 582
choses covered, 584–5
defined, 582
notice, effect of, 585–6
priorities, 588–90
registration, 586–7
security, value as, 582
British Bankers' Association
function, 5, 21
membership, 4–5, 21
British Overseas and Commonwealth Banks
    Association (BOCBA)
business of, 19
function, 4
membership, 4, 19
Building societies
Banking Act, application to, 22, 44
business of, 22
cheques, issue by, 22–3
   defences in respect of, 23
comparison with banks, 21–3
structure, 22

Cashpoint card, *see* Credit token
Certificates of deposit
nature, 522
Charges, *see* Company charges
Chattel mortgages
bill of sale, is, 552
consumer credit, 555
nature, 551–2
why not used, 552
Cheque card, *see* Credit token
Cheques, *see* Bills of exchange
account, only for itemized, 209
"account payee only", *see* crossing of
   cheque
alterations on, 240
assignment, drawing of cheques is not,
   229, 265
bearer, payable to, 229
   when is, 243
clearing of, *see* Clearing process
companies', 193–7
countermand, 229, 286, 299–300
crossing of cheques, 225–6
   background, 252–4
   effect, 254–5
   other instruments, 258

with "a/c payee only", 256–8
with "not negotiable", 255–6
date is material, 240
definition, 239
donatio mortis causa, is not, 279
drawee, not enforceable against, 265
drawn by one person on another, 242–3
fictitious payee, 134, 244–7, 512
form, 265
functions, 226
history, 227
holder, utilization of cheque, 229
   in due course, 229, 440–2
instruction, as, 229
itemized, to given account, 265–6
marking of cheque, 250–2
negotiability, restrictions on, 247–8
noting, *see* protest
order cheques, 244
payee, 244
payment in due course, 288, 302–3, 516
payment in ordinary course, 303–6
payment without negligence, 306–7
payment when fault in indorsement,
   307–10
post-dated cheques, 176, 177, 248–50
presentment for payment through clearing,
   237–8
   holder's duty, 259–60, 449–50
protest and noting, 261–2, 452, 520
signature, 242
simultaneous presentment of, 269
stolen, 129, 240
unconditional order, 240–2
undated, 129
writing, 242
Choses in action
assignment, outright, 581
   as charge, 581
bank balances, *see* Bank balances
book debts, *see* Book debts
defined, 580
negotiable instruments, as, 227–8, 497–8
security, as, 580–1
Clayton's Case, Rule of, *see* Appropriation of
   payments
Clearing banks
amalgamations, 6
current position, 4
development of, 5–6
functions, 10
functional clearers, 7, 11–14
importance in payment settlements, 8
Scottish and North Irish clearers, 10–11
Clearing house
general clearing, *see* Clearing process
history, 7, 230

Clearing house—*cont.*
  membership, requisites for, 8
  town clearing, *see* Clearing process
Clearing House Automated Payment System
    (CHAPS)
  controlled by CLSB, 7
  procedure, 345, 356–7
  secrecy, duty of, 387–8
Clearing house rules
  classified, 237
  development, 237
  inadvertence rule, 234
  legal effect of, 237–8
Clearing process (cheques)
  agency banks, 9, 235–6
  comparison with giro operations,
    350–1
  computerization of, 231
  general clearing, 7, 232–5
    same branch clearance, 236
    where cheque paid in a third party bank,
      235
  Golden memorandum, *see* Golden
    memorandum
  history, 230, 231
  inadvertence rule, 234
  non-clearing banks, process used, 235–6
  "out of order" list, 233, 234
  settlement, 234, 236
  simultaneous presentment, 268–9
  structure, 7
  systems described, 7–8
  town clearing, 7, 236
  walks, 9
Clearing process (giro), *see* Giro operations
Collecting bank's position
  causes of action against, 413–18
    conversion, 413–18
    waiver of tort, 413, 415, 416
  contributory negligence, 437–9
  crediting of account as ingredient of
    defence, 423
  defence of, under s. 4, 421–37
  discounting bank, distinguished from,
    418–21
    protection of, 422, 439–42
    when is holder in due course, 440–42
  duties owed to customer, 449–52
  negligence of, general, 421–3, 424–7,
    436–7
    in collection process, 430–2
    in opening account, 427–30
    respecting crossings, 432–4
    respecting indorsements, 434–6
  paying bank, when same, 444–9, 450–1
  processing bank, protection, 442–4
    should not act for stranger, 347

  receipt of proceeds, ingredient of defence,
    424
  true owner, who is, 416–18
  value of cheque, 414–15
Combination of accounts
  abrogation by appropriation, 150–1
  advantage to bank, 140
  agreement not to combine, 147–9
  banker-customer, as part of contract only,
    145
  branches, accounts at different, 146
  contractual set-off, *see* Set-off
  customer's interest, duty to effect in,
    159–60
  exceptions, generally, 145
  insolvency, special problems in, 156–9
    mutual dealings, 156
    preference, 158–9
    s. 323, contracting out, 157
    third parties, to protect, 160–1
  joint account, as subject of, 152–3
  legal nature, 141
  lien, is not, 142
  loan account with current, 149, 150
  notice, need for, 154–5
  partnership account with personal, 179
  problem defined, 139
  set-off is, 143–4
  trust account, of, 151–2
Committee of London and Scottish Banks
    (CLSB)
  functions, 7
  membership of, 3
Committee of London Clearing Banks
    (CLCB)
  function, 4
  superseded by CLSB, 4
Companies' accounts
  borrowing, 192
  cheques drawn by, 193–7
  negotiable instruments of, 193–6
  non-trading company, cheques of,
    196–7
  ultra vires, relevance, 191–2
Company charges
  after acquired property, 556–7
  assessment, 566–7
  bills of sale, are not, 556
  charge explained, 555–6
  fixed compared with floating, 557–9
  floating, *see* Floating charge
  notice, 560–1
  priorities, 561–2
    future advances, 562
  registration, 559–60
    as bills of sale, *see* Hypothecation
Confidentiality, *see* Bank secrecy

Consortium banks
  business of, 20
  function and nature, 4, 19
  membership, 4, 20
  organization, 4, 19
Constructive trustee, bank as
  customer's suit, *see* Fiduciary duties
  elements, 163–4
  knowledge, 93–5
  stranger's suit against bank, 163–4
Consumer credit
  advertisements, 69–70
  APR, 65
  appropriation of payments, 69
  background, 62–3
  cancellation, right of, 66
  canvassing, 70–1, 487
  connected transactions, 72–3, 409–10
  contractual disclosure, 66–8
  credit brokerage, 71–2
  credit reference agencies, 72
  credit tokens, 401–10
  debt counselling, 72
  default provisions, 68
  disclosure, in case of overdraft, 67, 486–7
    in case of loans, 491–2
  exempt agreements, 64
  fixed credit agreements, 65
  implications of, to banks, 73–4
  land, contracts respecting, 67, 492–3, 549–50
  licensing, 65–6
  linked transactions, 73, 410
  loans, 490–3
  monetary limit, 62, 485
  negotiable instruments, 527–8
  overdrafts, 65, 67, 70, 485–8
  partially regulated agreement, 64
  pledge, 575–6
  quotations, 71–2
  rate of total cost of credit, *see* APR
  regulated agreement, 62–3
  regulated credit agreement, 64
  regulated hire agreement, 64
  running account credit, 65
  securities, 536–40
    anti-evasion provision, 540
    form, 538–9
    information, 539–40
    measures applicable, 537–8
    realisation, 540
    security instrument, 537
  termination, by creditor, 68–9
    by debtor, 68
  unenforceable agreement, when, 66
Contract of banker and customer
  agency element, 80, 84, 285

bailment, distinguished from, 81
constructive trusts, *see* Constructive trustee, bank
as creditor-debtor relationship, 81–3, 127
current account, in, *see* Current account
demand, when needed, 83
duty of care, bank's, 87, 90–3
  in lending, 481–2
duty of strict adherence to mandate, 285–6
duty as collecting agent, 449–52
fiduciary duties, *see* Fiduciary duties of banks
mental incapacity, effect on, 205–7
one contract only, 141, 270
termination, by bank, 112–13
  by customer, 112
trust, distinguished from, 81
Control of banking activities
  alternative approaches, 26–7
  "bank", use in name, 42
  deposit, soliciting of, *see* Banking Act 1979
  licensing, *see* Banking Act 1979
  monetary controls, 47–50
  need for, 25–6
  reform, *see* Banking Bill 1986
Conversion, action in
  collecting bank, against, 413–18
  contributory negligence, as defence, 437–9
  paying bank, against, 286
  true owner defined, 416–18
  value of cheque, 414–15
Co-operative Bank
  described, 13
Countermand
  cheque of, 229, 286, 299–300
  money transfer order, 377–84
Credit tokens
  cashpoint card, basic, 390
    misuse, 400–1
    systems, 399–400
  cheque card, basic, 389
    analysed, 395–6
    compared with letter of credit, 396–7
    Consumer Credit Act, not governed by, 397
    misuse of, 397–9
  classified, 389–90
  Consumer Credit Act, 401–10
    credit token agreement, 403–4, 407–8
    misuse of token, 405–7
    nexus with underlying contract, 408–10
    tokens covered, 397, 401–3
    unsolicited token, 407
  credit card, 391–3
    countermand, 392
    issuer's liability for dealer, 393
    legal nature, 391–2

612 *Index*

Credit tokens—*cont.*
  criminal cases, 410–11
  T & E card, basic, 389
    countermand, 394–5
    issuer's liability for dealer, 394–5
    loss, risk of, 393–4
    reimbursement, dealer's right of, 395
Current account
  adequacy of funds, 128, 129, 266–9
  agency element, 128
  bank's duty to pay, 128–9, 266
  branch, demand to be at, 129, 270–1
  cheque, demand by, 128
  combining accounts, *see* Combination of
    accounts
  demand, withdrawals by, 128, 129
  insolvency, effect of, 83
  interest on, 130
  interest bearing account, compared, 208–9
  limitation period, 83
  office hours, demand during, 129
  one contract only, 141, 270
  regularity of cash flow, 122
  stale cheque, 129
  undated cheque, 129
Customer
  ambiguous instructions of, 84
  corporate customers, *see* Companies'
    accounts
  defined, 78–9
  habitual relationship not needed, 78
  insolvency, position of in bank's, 120
  intention, 79
  position of, 80
  where no express consent, 80

Defamation
  action for wrongful dishonour, 313–14
Deposit receipt, *see* Interest bearing accounts
Discount Houses
  business of, 4, 17
  origin, 17
Discounting bank, *see* Collecting bank
Documents of title, *see* Pledge

Electronic fund tranfers, *see* Giro operations
Equitable doctrine (Liggett)
  described, 285–6
  effect and application, 300–1
  joint account, relevance to, 170
Estate agents' accounts
  nature, 188–9
Exchange control
  abolition of, 30, 75 n. 133, 357
  Bank of England, 30
Executor's accounts

distinguished from partnership account,
    179
  executor's power, to borrow, 180
    to draw, 180
  personal assurance, executor's, 180
  pledge by executor, 181

Fiduciary duties of banks
  benefit to bank element, 87, 88
  conflict of interests, 95–6
  duty of care, in context, 87, 90–3, 95
    in lending, 481–2
  knowledge, 93
  reliance, 86
  undue influence, 88, 89
  unfair advantage, 88, 94
  when arising, 85
Field warehousing, *see* Pledge
Fixed deposits, *see* Interest bearing accounts
Floating charge
  assessment, 566–7
  crystallization, 563–4
    automatic, 564–6
  described, 562–3
  disadvantages of, 563
  notice, 563
    of negative pledge, 563
  ranking, 563–4
Foreign Banks Association and foreign banks
  American banks, 4, 20
  business of, 18
  Japanese banks, 4, 20
  nature, 4, 18

Garnishee orders
  assignment, clash with, 274
  availability, 271
  effect, 272–3
  interest bearing accounts, in respect of,
    218, 272
  objections to, 274–5
  owing and accruing, 271–2
  solicitors' accounts, 187–8
  sum paid in after order, 273
Giro operations
  agency, as governing, 345, 346, 363, 368
  assignment, whether applicable, 366–8
  bank and national giro, 343
  bank giro credits, 347–8
  basic nature, 344
  compared with cheques, 350–1
  correspondent bank, position of, 371–2
  direct debits, 349–50
  eft-pos, 123
  negotiable instruments, compared with,
    364–6
  payment out of time cases, 384–7

recipient bank, position of, 373–5
secrecy, *see* Bank secrecy
standing order, 348–9
time of payment, problem, 375–7
  principle, 379, 380, 382, 387
traders' credits, 349
transferring bank, 368–71
  duty of care, 369–71
Golden memorandum
  agency arrangement, as, 346
  clearing process, classified, 345
    BACS, 354–6
    CHAPS, 356–7
    manual, 352–4
  effect, 231
  replaced by individual agreements, 231,
    346
Guarantee
  described, 529
  distinguished from acceptance credit, 485

Holder and holder in due course, *see* Bills of
  exchange and cheques
Hypothecation of goods
  assessment, 553
  bill of sale, whether is, 553–4
  consumer credit, 555
  given by companies, 555
  inherent problems, 553
  nature, 552–3

Insolvency
  bank's, customer's position in, 120, 127,
    533
  commencement of bankruptcy, 281
  customer's insolvency, effect on bank,
    281–4
  constructive trust, significance in, 162
  general creditors, 533
  preferential claims, 532–3
  secured creditor, bank as, 533
  set-off, effect on, *see* Combination of
    accounts
Interest bearing accounts
  assignment of balance, 215
  at branch, 211
  cheques, not used for, 208
  creditor-debtor relationship, 210
  current account, differences, 208–9
  deposit receipt, use discontinued, 211,
    224–5
    as security, 221
    delivery, effect of, 215–16, 221–2
    donatio mortis causa, as, 223–4
    loss of, 219, 222
    negotiable instrument, whether is, 211,
      220–1

term set out in, 213
garnishee order, *see* Garnishee order
joint deposits, 213–14
limitation period, 218–19
one contract only, 210
overdraft, not available, 209
passbook, *see* deposit receipt and Periodic
  statement
payment to wrong party, 212
set-off, against, 216–17
International transfers
  legal nature, *see* Giro operations
  mail and telegraphic transfers, 359–61
  SWIFT. *see* SWIFT
Issuing Houses
  business of, 15
  position, 4

Joint accounts
  combination of accounts, 152–3
  equitable doctrine, effect of, 170
  fraud, bank's duty where, 171
  insolvency of one owner, 282–3
  joint deposits, 213–14
  moiety, recovery of, 170
  nature of, 168
  right to draw, 168–70
  survivorship, 171–5

Land mortgages
  common clauses, 548–9
  consumer credit, 549–50
  deed, when required, 544
  equitable mortgage defined, 594
  legal and equitable estates, 542–3
  legal and equitable mortgages
    distinguished, 543–4
  legal mortgage defined, 543
  priorities, 547–8
    appropriation of payments, 548
    future advances, 547–8
  registered and unregistered land, 542–3
  remedies, 544–5
    foreclosure, 545
    receiver, appointment of, 545
    right of sale, 545
    taking possession, 545
  second mortgages, 546
  sub mortgage, 546
  tacking, 547–8
Lending agreements, *see* Loans
Letters rogatory, *see* Bank secrecy
Lien, *see* Banker's lien
Life policies
  assessed as securities, 599–600
  chose in action, is, 599
  mortgages over, 600–1

Liggett doctrine, *see* Equitable doctrine
(Liggett)
Loans
assessment of transaction, 488–9
compared with overdrafts, 475–6
consumer credit, 490–3
default, 489
Local authorities' accounts
bank's duty, 190–1
borrowings, 189–90

Mareva injunction
effect, 276–7, 278
origin, 276
third-parties, rights of, 277
Married women's accounts
borrowings, 199, 200
drawings, 199
joint property, 200
wife's guarantee, 200
Mentally incapacitated persons' accounts
bank's position, 206–7
general principles, 205
notice of customer's insanity, effect of,
278–80
Merchant banks, *see* Accepting houses;
Issuing houses
Banking Act, position under, 16
business of, 14
comparison with clearers, 14
Minors' accounts
borrowings, 203
contractual liability, 200
current accounts and drawings, 201–3
guarantee by adult, 203–5
set-off against, 200
Money transfer system, *see* Giro operations
and International money transfers
Mortgages over land, *see* Land mortgages

National Girobank
business of, 13
legal position of, 13
linking of its giro with bank-giro, 343
structure, 13
Negotiable instruments
action, right of, 227–8
compared with contracts, 227–8, 497–8
consumer credit aspects, 527–8
giro operations, compared with, 364–6
holder's superior title, 228
item of property, 228, 498
tranferability, 228
Noting, *See* Cheques and Bills of exchange

Overdrafts
appropriation of payments, 482–5

bank's duty of care, 481–2
compared with loans, 475–6
consumer credit, 65, 67, 70, 485–8
demand, whether payable on, 84, 129,
478–9, 487
described, 476–7
interest, how charged, 479–81
interest bearing account, not to be, 209
legal nature, 477–8
limitation period, 84

Partnership accounts
borrowing, 177
combination with partner's personal
account, 179
drawing rights, 176, 177
dissolution, effect of, 177–8
insolvency, effect of, 179
nature, 175–6
surviving partner's rights, 178
Passbook, *See* Periodic statement and Interest
bearing accounts
Paying bank's position
ambiguity of instruction, bank's defence,
299–300
availability of funds, 128, 266–8
uncleared effects, as funds, 128, 129,
268
branch, payment at only, 270–1
cheque, bank not liable on, 265
collecting bank, when also, 444–9
conversion, action against, 286–7
countermand, 286, 299–301
customer's carelessness, as defence, 291–6
customer's death, effect of, 278–80
customer's insanity, effect of, 278–80
customer's insolvency, effect of, 281–4
defence of, outline, 285–6, 290
duty to obey mandate, 285–6
equitable doctrine, *See* Equitable doctrine
estoppel, as defence of paying bank,
291–6
payment, in due course as defence, 288,
302–3
in ordinary course, 303–6
without negligence, 306–7
payment when fault in indorsement,
307–10
ratification, as defence to action, 297–8
not of forgery, 298–9
simultaneous presentment, 268–9
terms of, not in folder, 265
true owner, action by, 287–9
uncleared effects, drawings against, 268
wrongful dishonour, defence in cases,
310–13
defamation, 313–14

Periodic statement
  account stated, entries as, 136–8
  bank's right to rectify, 131–2
  change in customer's position, 131–2
  customer's right to object, 132–4
  estoppel, by customer's silence, 138–9
  reasonable time, 132
  verification clauses, 134–6
Pledge
  common clauses, 570–1
  consumer credit, 575–6
  documents of title, of, 571–2
  executor, if given by, 181
  field warehousing, 573–4
  legal nature, 568
  marketable securities, of, 574–5
  possession, constructive, 569–70, 573–4
    essential, 568–9
  redemption, 535–6, 570
  trust receipts, *see* Trust receipts
Privileges of banks
  agricultural credits, 59
  Bills of Exchange Act, under, 51–2
  deposits, of insurance brokers, 59
    of solicitors' funds, 58
  home purchase credits, 60
  trust funds, 59
Promissory notes
  application of law affecting bills, 521
  defined, 520–1
  distinguished from bills, 520
  function, 522
  joint, 521–2
  novel forms, 522
  payable in instalments, 521
Protest, *see* Cheques and Bills of exchange

Recovery of money paid by mistake, *see*
  Restitution
Redemption, right of
  application, 535–6
  general principle, 534–5
  how exercised, 535
  persons entitled to exercise, 535
  pledges, application to, 535
Relationship of banker and customer, *see*
  Contract of banker and customer
Restitution
  bank's action against payee, nature, 315–6
  classification, 316
  basic principles, 319–21
  between payer and payee, mistake need not
    be, 321–3
  cases involving negotiable instruments,
    334–41
    operative mistake in, 334–7
    payee's change of position, in, 338–41

change of position, as defence to action,
    325–8
collecting bank, suit against, 329–32
  appropriation, 332–3
consideration, effect of giving, 328–9
customer, action not available to, 128
mistake known to payee, where 317–19
operative mistake, nature of, 323–5
tracing order, in cases of, 341–2
true owner's against paying bank, 288–9
  waiver of tort, 289

Safe custody of valuables
  bailment, nature of, 83, 466–7
  bank's duty of care, 467–8
  contributory negligence, not available, 468
  deposits by foreign banks, 469–70
  exemption clauses, 468
  misdelivery, action for, 468
  night safes, 469
  safe deposit boxes, 470–1
Savings account, *see* Interest bearing accounts
Secondary bank crisis
  nature, 25, 26
Secrecy, *see* Bank secrecy
Security, generally
  consumer credit, *see* Consumer credit
  effect in insolvency, 532–4
  land compared with chattels, 551
  object, 529
  open-ended and closed-ended, 531–2
  possessory and proprietary, 530–1
    in respect of chattels, 551–2
Set-off
  assignment, clash with, 216–17, 594–5
  charges over, 597–9
  combination of accounts, *see* Combination
    of accounts
  contingent claims, 591–2
  contractual, 593–6
  garnishee as against, 591, 595–6
  insolvency, in, 592–3
  minor, against, 200
  public policy, 596
  registration, 595–6
  set-off in law and equity, *see* Combination
    of accounts
Sight
  meaning of, 496
Solicitors' accounts
  bank's duty, 186–7
  duty to maintain, 186
  garnishee order, *see* Garnishee orders
  object and nature, 186
Statement of account, *see* Periodic statement
Sterling commercial paper
  use of, 522

Subpoena duces tecum, *see* Bank secrecy
Subrogation to securities
  in drawer's insolvency, 525–6
Society for World Wide International
    Financial Communications (SWIFT)
  centres, 361–2
  operations generally, 345
  process, 362–3
  secrecy, duty of, 387–8

T & E card, *see* Credit token
Tacking, *see* Land mortgages
Tracing order
  effect, 164
  elements, 163
  in lieu of restitution, 341–2
  third parties, when exercisable against,
      165–6
  when available, 165, 166
Travellers' cheques
  nature, 262–3
  use, 358
Trust accounts
  bank's liability to cestui, 183
  borrowings, 182
  combination with personal, 151–2
  constructive, *see* Constructive trust
  death of trustee, 182
  delegation of authority, 181
  drawing rights, 181

fiduciary, *see* Fiduciary duties
knowledge, 183, 184, 185
red flag, duty to note, 184, 185
trustee, function of, 181
Trust receipts
  effect, 572
  problems, 573
Trustee Savings Banks
  Banking Act, position under, 12, 44
  business, 12
  clearing, involvement with, 11
  functions and history, 11–12
  investment of funds, 12
  nominations, 12
  structure, 12–13

Undue influence, *see* Fiduciary duties of
  banks
Unincorporated associations' accounts
  borrowings, 197–8
  liability, 197

Verification clauses
  effect of, 138–9

Winding up, *see* insolvency
  commencement, 283
  customer's, effect on bank, 281–4
  similarity to bankruptcy, 533–4